Legal Communication
and Research

Legal Communication and Research

Lawyering Skills for the Twenty-First Century

Ian Gallacher

CAROLINA ACADEMIC PRESS
Durham, North Carolina

Library of Congress Cataloging-in-Publication Data

Gallacher, Ian, 1956- author.
  Legal communication and research : lawyering skills for the twenty-first century /
Ian Gallacher.
      pages cm
  Includes bibliographical references and index.
  ISBN 978-1-61163-610-9 (alk. paper)
  1. Legal research--United States. 2. Legal composition. 3. Communication in law-
-United States. I. Title.

  KF240.G35 2015
  340'.14--dc23

                        2015012809

Carolina Academic Press
700 Kent Street
Durham, NC 27701
Telephone (919) 489-7486
Fax (919) 493-5668
www.cap-press.com

Printed in the United States of America
2017 Printing

For Julie, who glitters.

Contents

THE WRITING PROCESS

ANALYSIS

Foreword

It probably seems ominous for a book about writing to need a foreword to explain what it contains and how it works. You, as the book's reader, might legitimately ask what a book about writing can offer if it needs its own explanation.

Don't worry. Or, at least, don't worry for that reason. This foreword is here to make things easier, but I hope and think the book isn't too difficult to understand without any introduction. But having said I would try to make this even easier, let me try.

The book is organized into five principal sections: Writing in Theory, The Writing Process, Analysis, Persuasion, and Legal Research. There are four appendices as well: a checklist to help you with editing and proofreading, a quick overview of judicial structure, a very short review of the litigation process, and a reminder about the three branches of the federal government. Each of the chapters in the five principal sections consists of three parts: an introductory section that describes what the chapter's about and what you should know once you've read the chapter, the chapter itself, and a series of focus questions you might want to use to help you as you work through the material in the chapter.

The focus questions are designed to mirror the active reading process I hope you'll use throughout your reading of this book and, in fact, your reading of all material while you're in law school and in law practice. Some of these questions are provocative and appear to question the material in the chapter, but that's an intentional strategy; I want you to question the text aggressively in order to be sure that you're getting the most out of it. If you end up disagreeing with the text as a result, that's fine as long as you are confident in your position and can back it up in the face of questioning as aggressive as yours has been.

Some chapters also have exercises accompanying them. These are designed to help to reinforce some of the material in the chapter, not to give you extra work to do or to add to your general stress level. So please feel free to ignore them unless your legal writing professor says otherwise.

What you won't find in here are extended examples of the writing styles and the types of documents the book discusses. This is a considered choice, not just an accidental omission.

Examples can be very helpful in providing clarification to a discussion. After you've read about how to write and structure an analysis memo, it would probably be reassuring to see a complete memo written in the style you've learned: a validation, in a way, that what you'd learned is in fact what's expected.

But examples can also have a more powerful negative effect. Some students believe that they needn't learn so much about the "why" of doing something a particular way because the example gives them the "how" and that, they think, is all they'll need. They don't believe they need to understand the reasons behind the way a document is written or structured as long as they understand the superficialities.

And they might be right. That probably will get them through the course, and might even get them a good grade. But that isn't the purpose of this book and it shouldn't be your purpose either: good grades are important, of course, but they're a by-product of learning rather than its ultimate goal. What I'm going for with this book, and what you should be aiming for in your law school education, is a solid and secure foundation for a writing style that will see you through law school and on into practice. You'll improve on it all the time, I hope, but your own fundamental writing style should be in place by the end of your legal writing course. And the only way to make sure you've really assimilated the suggestions of this book is to work through writing assignments on your own and have that work commented on by a skilled legal writing professor who's working towards the same goal as you. Writing, with helpful critiquing of your work, is the only way to learn how to write, so I've stayed away from extended examples to remove the temptation of trying to learn by emulation.

The book is written in a voice that is assuredly not one you should use in your formal legal writing. I'll make this point several times because it's very important: the texts you read in law school—especially in your first year—aren't intended to be models for your legal writing, whether it be the predictive style you might learn first or the persuasive style of writing you learn later in your first year. Most law school textbooks are written in a lofty, impersonal style and the court decisions they excerpt are written to reflect the court's decisions, not to persuade a court of the correctness of a particular position, as lawyers must do in litigation. This book uses a different strategy, and is intentionally written in a chatty, relaxed voice that is just as inappropriate for formal attorney writing as the impersonal style of most textbooks or the detached style of court opinions. I'm much more interested in persuading you of the things I'm saying than in imposing them on you, so I tried to adopt a voice that would reflect that intent. Please don't copy this style for your memos, briefs, exam answers, papers, or law review comments and notes.

Writing is an inherently personal activity. No one can tell you how you should write and what your writing process should be; only you can decide that for yourself. But writing is an intentional, not reflexive, activity, so the process by which you produce a piece of writing, and the writing itself, should be subjected to careful and thoughtful scrutiny. That's the purpose of this book: to give you the tools necessary to help you decide how best to express your legal analysis in writing and what process will best accomplish that ideal expression.

Legal research—the other main subject of this book—is the most challenging area you will study in law school. That's a bold claim, but I stand by it. The technological developments of the past twenty years mean that hardly anything about legal research has gone unchanged and the pace of that change is increasingly dramatically. No area you study in law school is changing as rapidly as legal research. And no static book can hope to stay current with all the developments in the legal research world, which is why this book doesn't even try. Rather, it discusses the world of legal information as it is at the time of writing and uses that baseline as a place from which to discuss the research process. That process has remained unchanged since the advent of computer-assisted legal research and the possibilities for self-indexed, as opposed to the more traditional pre-indexed, research offered by computers. If you concentrate on how to research rather than where you're going to research, the superficial changes in the various media available to the legal researcher won't affect you nearly as much as you might think.

For many of you, the prospect of studying writing and research intensely will seem like an unchallenging way to spend your time. Those who believe this will doubtless be experienced writers and researchers, and will assume that those strategies that have served you well in the past will be easily adapted to the law. For others, the thought of having your writing and research skills subjected to the detailed scrutiny that is certainly coming will seem like a daunting prospect. Those who believe this might have succeeded in their academic careers up until now without having to write much and you are now concerned that the learning curve will be too steep for your comfort.

The news—bad or good, depending on your perspective—is that you're both wrong. Legal writing is a very different skill from anything you might have learned before, and that means you are all—experienced and inexperienced writers alike—starting more or less from the same place. For much of the time during your introduction to legal writing, the more experienced writers might feel unduly constrained by the new technical requirements being imposed on you, and that—ironically enough—might make legal writing harder than it is for those with little writing experience: you have habits to unlearn, while they are starting from the beginning. But if you work at it, you'll all improve.

The best thing to do, whatever your belief about the state of your writing skills, is to set aside any preconceived notions about legal writing and come to the subject as fresh and willing to learn as possible. If you do that, and take what you learn as the sincere attempt of your writing professor, and me, to help you develop your own voice as a legal writer, you'll get as much out your legal writing studies as possible.

So. Thank you for reading this book, and thank you for (I hope) approaching it in the spirit it was written. And relax. Really: studying the law can be difficult and confusing at times, but you'll only get as much out of it as you can if you don't tense up against it. Try to enjoy yourself and look forward to improving your writing skills, regardless of how advanced they were when you came to law school.

Okay. Let's get started.

Acknowledgments

Writing a book is a solitary business but anyone who tries to write anything without help is unwise in the extreme, and anyone who pretends they got no help is probably self-delusional. I've been indescribably fortunate to have met, and to have learned from, some wonderful people in my life. Some of them helped directly in the preparation of this book, some helped indirectly, and some would find it astonishing that I'm writing a book like this and mentioning them in it: I fear I've forgotten more people than I've remembered, and I owe a debt of gratitude to everyone who has helped me that a simple listing of their name in this acknowledgements section can't come close to repaying. But it's a start.

So. Thank you to:

Those who gave me permission to reprint material, Ruth McKinney, Thomson Reuters, Kendall Svengalis, the Professional Education Group, and the various law reviews and journals mentioned in the text;

My Legal Communications and Research colleagues at Syracuse University College of Law: Elizabeth August, Andrew Greenberg, Lynn Levey, Aliza Milner, Kathleen O'Connor, Lucille Rignanese, Richard Risman, and Shannon Ryan, as well as to Sonya Bonneau, Kate Dole, Elton Fukumoto, Susan James, Tomas Gonzalez, Lynn Oatman, Deborah O'Malley, Jill Paquette, Kim Wolf Price, and Christy Ramsdell. Thank you also to my other wonderful colleagues at Syracuse, especially Antonio Gidi, who was kind to read an earlier draft of this and to Dean Hannah Arterian for all her support throughout the years. Thanks also to the Legal Rhetoric faculty at the Washington College of Law, American University, with whom I was fortunate enough to spend three amazing years: Amy Dillard, Nancy Modesitt, Jeremy Mullem, Susan Thrower, Becky Troth, and the astounding Penny Pether, without whom I wouldn't be doing what I'm doing;

My colleagues teaching legal research and writing across the country, especially: Mary Algero, Christine Bartholomew, Mary Beth Beazley, Sara Benson, Linda Berger, David Caudill, Ken Chestek, Jessica Clark, Jason Cohen, Melody Dailey, Kirsten Davis, Diana Donahoe, James Dimitri, Eric Easton, Diane Edelman, Linda Edwards, Lyn Entrikin, Kristin Gerdy, Melissa Greipp, Jeffrey Jackson, Steve Johansen, Robin Leisure, Elizabeth Lenhart, Sue Liemer, Heather McCabe, Hether Macfarlane, Debby McGregor, Ruth McKinney, Joan Magat, Richard Neumann, Anthony Niedwiecki, Ann Nowak, Stephen Paskey, Terrill Pollman, Anne Ralph, Ruth Anne Robbins, Jennifer Romig, Judith Rosenbaum, Terry Seligmann, Lou Sirico, Amy Sloan, Craig Smith, Amy Stein, David Thomson, Kristen Tiscione, Carol Wallinger, Marilyn Walter, Melissa Weresh;

My students over the years have been the best writing teachers anyone could have, and thanks especially to: Amy Stover (the only person to sit through three consecutive years of my teaching anything), Jessica Caterina, Juliana Chan, Jesse Endler, Stefanie Gruber, Katherine Laubach, Thuy Le, Jeff Morland, Rachel Ostrowski, Michelle Parker, Ed Thater, and all the students in LCR sections 1 and 2 over the years, especially those who were (mostly) willing test subjects for this book: Anna Castillo, Riley Christian, Robert Clark, Alex Cortland, Christina Farrell, Jesse Feitel, Tesla Goodrich, William Graves, John Hartoonian, David Huber, Lyndsey Kelly, Bourke Krauss, Jeanette Luna, Jordan Meeks, Arya Oskui, Anne Rackoczy-Kostrycky-Zwil, and Jessica Yanette;

My practice colleagues who taught me everything I know about how lawyers write, especially: David Allen, Kamil Ismail, Richard Barnes, James Comodeca, Donald De-Vries, Scott Fisher, Charles Goodell, Andrew Graham, Nancy Gregor, Amy Heinrich, Kelly Iverson, Bethany Jackson, Bruce Parker, Susan Preston, Gina Saelinger, Thomas Waxter, and Robert Wilczek, who taught me more about legal writing in one intense afternoon in Baltimore than any single person before or since;

My friends and teachers over the years, especially: Harold Farberman, Larry Goldberg, Shannon Thee Hanson, Istvan Jaray, Linda Lacy, Keith Lockhart, Michele Pilecki, the Honorable Theodore McKee, Robert Page, Donald Portnoy, Roger Quick, Roger Raphael, Jean Redman, Martin Rutherford, Mel Shapiro, Scott Sipe, and the Honorable Frederic Smalkin;

My parents, Joan Upton Holder and Henry Gallacher, my step-father Roy Upton Holder, and my grandparents, Henry and Barbara Gallacher and Jack and Elsie Olley, taught me many things and gave me the happiest and most secure base a child ever had on which to build.

As ever and always, this is for Julie McKinstry, without whom everything I've done would have been impossible and would have had no point.

Legal Communication
and Research

Introduction

What You Should Learn from This Chapter

This chapter was written to introduce you to the challenges and opportunities offered by legal research and writing.

After reading this chapter, you should have:

- formed an impression as to the ease or difficulty of writing as a lawyer;
- considered the challenges associated with the constantly changing world of legal research;
- considered how you will react to having your writing scrutinized and possibly criticized; and
- decided that good, competent, legal writing is a skill that can be learned and improved upon and one that can even be enjoyable for the writer as well as the reader.

Writing is easy. We know how to form words and we know how to put words together to form sentences, paragraphs, and larger structural units; those are skills we learned without even thinking back when we were children. We learned to write when we were children as well, and we were taught the rules of composition as we got older. The law might be hard, but writing about it will be the easiest thing about law school. Learning the doctrine in our other first year classes will be much more difficult because it will involve concepts and ways of thinking we haven't been exposed to yet. But legal writing is just writing in a legal context. Once you know what to say, you just put it into the word processor and either print out the finished product, attach it to an email, or upload it to a server. There's nothing too complicated about that. Writing is easy.

Writing is difficult. What we've learned about writing prior to coming to law school is similar to learning the rules of a game. Now we're being asked to play the game at a very high level and there's a lot of pressure to get things right. We've forgotten most of anything we knew about formal English composition and the papers we wrote as undergraduates were not held to the same level of scrutiny as will be our written work as lawyers. We won't just be able to write a first draft of something and hand it in as a finished product anymore. We can't know what we think about something until we've written it down first and had a chance to think about it, and the deadlines we'll be facing are so extreme that we're not going to have much time for thoughtful reflection. Writing is difficult.

Both of these are reasonable positions to take and both have elements of truth in them. It's true that you know how to write—you couldn't possibly have made it to law school if you didn't. But it's also true that law school will test your writing in ways that it hasn't been tested before, and that your writing will likely be subjected to a higher level of scrutiny—in terms of technical perfection, method of expression, and quality of thinking—than your writing has faced before. Even seasoned writers are surprised by the degree to which every punctuation mark, word, phrase, sentence, and paragraph are examined and critiqued in law school, and the experience is no less intense once one gets out into practice. Law is hard, but so is legal writing. And legal research is like nothing you've done before.

1. Legal Research

Information is all around us. We are bombarded by a ceaseless flow of information from mass-media outlets like television, radio, newspapers, and magazines; from advertising placed almost everywhere our eyes can fall; from our friends, teachers, and conversations between complete strangers that we might overhear; and, most significantly, from the internet and social media. Gaining access to information is not difficult for us. The hard part is to avoid drowning in it.

As in normal life, so also in the law. We have to take a little more trouble to gain access to legal information, but only a little. Law libraries are stacked with books full of legal information, the specialist legal information databases are only a few clicks (and, for those in practice, many dollars) away, and, of course, there is the ubiquitous internet, now also a source of vast amounts of legal information. As with life away from law school, the problem is not finding legal information, it's knowing what you have and what to do with it once you have it.

This book will help you figure out how to find the information that will help you to answer legal questions you might ask yourself or might be asked by others. The research techniques you've learned in life and in your previous academic careers will be helpful to you, but you'll also need to refine them for legal work. Everything you learn here and in your research classes this year is only a beginning—a foundation upon which your own personal research technique can be constructed. But be prepared for that construction process to take time; more than anything else you'll learn in law school—more than your doctrinal knowledge, and more than even your writing skills— a solid, effective research technique takes years of thought and practice.

The legal research world is changing rapidly at the moment—more rapidly than textbooks can keep up. Recently, two new legal information sites—Google, which provides free information, and Bloomberg, which charges for its use—have arisen to challenge LexisNexis and Westlaw, the two market leaders in legal information for the past thirty years. And there are many other legal information sites that offer a variety of services, some of them free and some of them for-profit sites charging substantially less than the two major sites. Westlaw and LexisNexis have responded to these challenges with new search engines that are vastly different in appearance, theory, and practice from the engines that powered those databases in the past.

All these changes have profound implications for the ways in which law firms conduct research, and that in turn means that they have profound implications for you in law school as well; there's no point in our teaching you practical skills that you won't be able to use in practice. Experienced legal researchers are concerned about these developments and the loss of control over the ways a search is conducted. We do not know how much these changes will affect the quality and depth of legal research, but there is concern that the new search engines will make research less nuanced and individualized.

This book will focus as much as possible on things that aren't going to change with the changing fashions of research outlets. So we'll concentrate here on the strengths and weaknesses of various methods of legal information retrieval, on ways to formulate searches, and on ways of thinking about the results of research after one has conducted a search. We'll talk about the various search engines, of course, but we'll try to steer clear of information that might become outdated too quickly. Rather, it's this book's goal to give you the tools you need to conduct efficient and effective research regardless of the medium in which you conduct that research.

So while we'll spend some time talking about the mechanics of finding legal information, we'll spend much more time considering what to think about before you start looking for that information and what to think about once you've found it. It's not difficult to find legal information, but understanding what you've found—and perhaps even more importantly, knowing what you haven't found—is a much more complicated business. This book will get you going on the process of conducting research, thinking about what you've found and what you haven't found, and integrating those research results into your writing.

2. Legal Writing

And as for writing, there's some good news that doesn't, at first hearing, sound all that much like good news. Everyone expects you to write badly. They don't want you to write badly, of course, but the general perception—among members of the public, lawyers, and judges—is that lawyers are bad writers. Not just bad, in fact: the general perception is that we're dreadful writers. That's the good news: when expectations are high it's almost impossible to exceed them, but when expectations are low it's almost impossible to fail to meet them.

Most people who deal with practicing lawyers assume that lawyer writing will be lousy. And when they encounter your writing they'll be more than pleasantly surprised because you will not just exceed their expectations, you'll clear them with ease. Or, at least, you will if you put in just a normal amount of work in your legal writing classes and do a couple of other things as well.

First, you'll have to try hard to take your ego out of the process. This isn't easy. Law school has a wonderful way of making us doubt ourselves: your torts, contracts, and other "doctrinal" teachers will ask you many questions in every class and will rarely answer any of them. And they'll be asking you questions about things you didn't get from your reading for that day's class. Soon the questions will start compounding and you'll be left wondering if you have a brain in your body. This will probably be a new and dis-

orienting experience for you. You've done well in school for as long as you can remember and you've probably never been made to feel that you don't, and can't, understand what's going on in your classes. You realize that you'll get through it, but it's
not going to be pleasant for the first couple of months at least.

But writing is something you've done before. You know how to write—you've been
doing it since pre-school! So when your legal writing professor starts to tell you about
the problems in your writing, or suggests ways in which your writing could improve,
the natural response is to shut down and say that at least as far as writing, you know
what you're doing and no legal writing professor can tell you otherwise.

This is perfectly understandable, but it's a mistake. Your legal writing professor has
no incentive to be other than completely honest with you, and if your professor is telling
you that your work would improve if you do something or don't do something, the
logical response would be to give the benefit of the doubt and give what your professor is suggesting a try. Once you have more experience, you might decide that you really don't agree with the advice you were given and that you want to write in a different
way, and that will be fine. Legal writing classes are all about helping you to develop
your writing technique. Once your technique is solidly in place, you might decide to change
parts of it. That should be easy for you to do then, but you need to have your technique in place first. That's what the classes are for so please: take your ego out of the
process, give your teacher the benefit of the doubt, and accept what he or she has to say.

The other thing you need to do is hinted at in the previous paragraph. If you need to
wait until your writing technique is solidly established before discarding something your
legal writing professor asked you to do, you need to accept that you'll be working on
your writing for a long time—much longer than the first semester, or even the first year,
of law school. It might be a cliché, but it's also true to say that we never stop working on
our writing and that there are always things we can do to improve our writing skills.

And this is different from many other things we study in law school. Someone who
becomes a criminal prosecutor, and later a criminal defense lawyer, for example, might
have no need to have anything but a rudimentary understanding of tort law or civil
procedure. That lawyer might study torts in the first semester of law school, study it again,
in accelerated form, for the bar exam in the summer after graduation, and then never
think again about torts or civil procedure as a practicing lawyer. The same is true for
a lawyer who specializes in tort litigation and doesn't give much consideration to criminal law and criminal procedure law outside of law school and the bar exam.

This isn't to say that there aren't excellent reasons for you to be paying close attention to every doctrinal class you take in law school. Don't ever fall into the trap of thinking that you don't plan to practice in a certain area of law so you don't really need to
pay that much attention. For one thing, you might be completely wrong about your career path: the area of law you found so boring in law school might be the one in which
you spend your entire professional career. That happens to more lawyers than you might
expect. Moreover, the doctrinal classes you take are designed to give you a broad overview
of how law operates in society. That's an extraordinarily valuable thing to understand,
no matter in what areas of the law you end up working in practice, and you need to pay
attention to every insight in every class in order to get the most out of the experience.

But while you might not know in what area of the law you'll end up, the one thing
you can be sure about is that you'll be doing a lot of writing once you're there. Lawyers

write—it's the defining characteristic of our profession. It used to be true that lawyers spoke, and that's often still how we think of them and how the legal profession is often portrayed in popular culture. That's fine; watching someone sitting at a computer typing all day wouldn't make for compelling television. But the reality of a lawyer's professional life—at least a junior lawyer's life—is that much of it is taken up in writing or reviewing documents. Those documents might be memos, emails, briefs, motions, wills, contracts, discovery requests, letters (lots of letters), or any number of other documents, depending on the specifics of the lawyer's area of practice. But you will be writing a lot as a lawyer, and you'll be judged on the quality and reliability of your writing.

If you do these two things—take your ego out of the learning process and remember that the process of improving your writing skills is something that will take longer than just one semester or even three years—you'll be well on your way to becoming an effective and competent legal writer. And that's all you need to be. If you target effectiveness and competency as things to aim for, and you do the work, you stand a very good chance of impressing people with your writing and getting and retaining a job on the strength of your writing skills.

3. Goals of This Book

The ultimate goal of this book is to help you to serve your clients competently and effectively. If you can do that, you will also impress your employer with your writing and research skills. As an interim goal, of course, it's designed to help you do well in your legal research and writing classes, but while that's an important result, it's secondary to the ultimate goal of being an effective and competent writer in practice. This book talks about research as well as writing because, as you'll discover, you can't really consider one thing without the other. The writing process requires research to provide the information it needs in order to make and communicate predictions and to persuade others of a position, and research requires communication in order to be relevant; there's no value to conducting legal research without a communicated purpose in mind.

As we work through issues of writing and research technique, I'll try to use as few technical concepts as possible, but we will have to consider some issues of grammar, punctuation, and rhetoric and I'll have to use some terms that you were probably hoping to have left behind in middle school. I'll do my best to keep the jargon down to a minimum. When we talk about research, I'll spend very little time on research technique and a lot more time on research theory. That might sound deadly and uninteresting, whereas the technique of finding legal authority on a given topic might sound much more useful. But the theory is important because it gives you a solid basis to develop a research technique which you can use with any of the databases currently existing or that might come into being in the future.

Writing is a conversation between at least two people, albeit a very strange form of conversation in which one participant says everything he or she has to say at one time rather than engaging in the usual statement/response form of oral conversation, and then the other party receives everything the first participant has said. This type of conversation means that writers must try to predict the questions their conversational partners, also called readers, will have about what they're saying and try to answer them at the time—often far in the future—that our readers will have them.

A final introductory thought, one that often gets lost in law school and the practice of law. Try to have fun as you're doing your writing and research. Both are difficult activities, often conducted under tight deadlines. And both have a lot riding on the result: good grades, if you're in law school, and your client's success and your professional advancement if you're in practice. But as lawyers, everything we do is important and few of our activities give us as much opportunity for pure enjoyment as do writing and research. The joy of finding the perfect theory to explain your client's position; of finding the support necessary to advance that theory; and in selecting the right words, sentences, and paragraphs to make those theories persuasive, is something that should never be denied. So even though writing and researching can be difficult and frustrating activities, they can also be tremendously rewarding. Don't deny yourself the good part.

Focus Questions

1. What challenges have you found in conducting research for your previous academic studies or in general life? How do you expect those challenges to manifest themselves when you conduct legal research?
2. Are you surprised that the legal research world is moving as quickly as it is?
3. What search engine do you usually use when conducting online research? Are you generally satisfied with the results you get from that search engine?
4. Have you ever used a commercial (fee-based) database in research before? If so, what differences did you find between it and the free search engines you're used to using?
5. Without knowing any more about legal research, how would you rate your research abilities? Do you think legal research will be a difficult or an easy skill to master?
6. How comfortable are you in your writing skills? Do you think of yourself as a strong, medium, or weak writer?
7. If your grammar and punctuation knowledge was tested right now, what's your best evaluation of how you would do?
8. Do you find writing easy or difficult? Of the two opening paragraphs in this chapter, which one do you think is closer to being correct? Why?
9. Before you came to law school, did you have a sense of whether lawyers are good writers or bad writers? Why did you think that? Now that you're in law school, has that sense changed?
10. Do you agree it's a good thing that the expectations bar for legal writing is set so low?
11. Will you be able to take your ego out of the process of learning how to write like a lawyer? What do you think that will involve?
12. Do you accept that you'll be working on your writing skills for the rest of your career as a lawyer? Does this seem like an exciting or a depressing prospect to you?
13. How do you respond to the assertion that writing is like a conversation? Have you considered that idea before? Do you think the insight is a useful one? Do you think this insight will change the way you think about writing or reading?

WRITING IN THEORY

Chapter 1

Reading in Law School

What You Should Learn from This Chapter

This chapter is about reading, and in particular, the role of reading in law school. The texts you are, and will be, reading in law school are likely different from anything you have read before. Extracting all the necessary information from them will probably require you to change the reading strategies you've employed in your previous academic career. This chapter is designed to help you make the transition from novice to skilled reader of legal texts, and to help you to think about the role of the reader in the writing process—something that will become relevant to you when you begin to write the documents that others will read.

After reading this chapter, you should:

- understand that the legal texts you're reading for law school are not a good guide to how to write like a lawyer;
- understand that legal writing, like other styles of writing, has various genres, and that you're going to be called on to write like a lawyer, not a judge;
- be wary of claims that you can multi-task effectively;
- understand that reading slowly will be an effective approach for you in law school;
- appreciate the value of reading on paper, as opposed to on a computer screen; and
- appreciate the importance of active reading, of engaging in a conversation with a text's writer, and of asking questions of a text as you read it.

Here's an odd question. Trust me, this will link up with the topic of reading in law school eventually.

Imagine you work at a publishing house and you've just been given permission to commission two books, one a horror novel and one a how-to book on home entertainment. And imagine that you've been given permission to hire two writers—Martha Stewart and Stephen King. The question is, which writer do you match with which project?

This isn't a trick question. And while Mr. King might be a dab hand at home entertainment, and while Ms. Stewart might have a flair for the macabre that is as yet untapped in her extensive output, my guess is that you'll pick King for the horror novel and Stewart for the home entertainment book. Or, at least, you will if you want to keep your job.

This is a heavy-handed way of making an obvious point: genre writers write in particular genres, and you don't read them expecting cross-genre writing. You would be disturbed to buy a Stephen King novel only to find it packed with recipes and ways to fold napkins, and you would be equally disturbed if you bought a Martha Stewart book that turned into a horror novel. Rather, you understand that each writer serves a particular and self-selecting audience and you wouldn't expect anything else.

But we make the mistake of forgetting this when we come to law school and read the court opinions that form the core of our course textbooks. We read the heavily edited opinions in our torts, civil procedure, contracts, and other books, and we think they're legal writing manuals, crammed with examples of how we should write as lawyers, all the while forgetting that court opinions are written by judges to tell lawyers about a result and that lawyers write briefs and other documents seeking to persuade judges to reach a particular decision. These are very different types of writing, and the documents are written for very different audiences. Judges and lawyers use words in their documents, of course, just as Mr. King and Ms. Stewart use words in theirs, but opinions and briefs are genres as unlike and separate as horror and home entertainment.

This isn't going to be easy for you. The cases in your course books are the first examples of "legal" writing you're exposed to, and they likely confirm everything you thought about legal writing: in all probability they're densely written, use difficult-to-understand language (perhaps even some Latin or Old French phrases that are completely incomprehensible without a legal dictionary), and have lots of passive voice and string citations in them. They yield their secrets, if at all, only after slow, careful, patient reading and re-reading, and once you penetrate their hidden meanings, and your interpretation is confirmed in class by your professors, you feel as if you've been initiated into the lawyers' guild.

These opinions were likely written some time ago. Most of them were written last century, some of them were probably written in the nineteenth century, and some of them were maybe even written in England or another common law country. So not only were these opinions written by someone who was writing for a different audience than you'll be writing for, they were written for a different time as well. In fact many (not all, but many) of these opinions would be viewed by today's judges as being poorly written for the purposes for which they were intended. There might be worse things to model your legal writing after, but not many.

This isn't to criticize the opinions. They were never intended to be models for twenty-first century lawyer writing, and they were perfectly fine examples of judicial writing for the times in which they were written. Nor is it to criticize the authors for selecting them to be included in your textbooks: the cases doubtless do the job they're being asked to do in articulating and explaining the doctrinal principles they contain, and that's all they're being used for.

No, the mistake is ours, in trying to make them models of something they were never intended to be. We need to do a better job of remembering that they're products of a genre we're not trying to copy—they're home entertainment books when we're trying to write horror novels, or two other equally ill-matched genres.

Try to keep this in mind as you read those cases, with their Latin and Old French and impenetrable English. Most contemporary lawyers don't write like that. Maybe they did once, when that was the understood mode of communication between lawyers and judges. But lawyers don't write like that now, and you're training to be a lawyer today, not in the late nineteenth century. Lawyers write documents to persuade or predict, not command, and they write them in a simple, plain, direct style that as much as possible uses simple words organized in the active voice. When transactional lawyers draft contracts or other agreements, they try to write them in such a way that everyone— lawyers, clients, and judges who might have to read the documents if things go wrong— can understand what the parties intended when they negotiated the agreement. Most contemporary lawyers would be horrified to find themselves writing in the style of many of those court opinions you're reading, and they don't want to hire someone who reproduces that style.

If you can remember this, then reading those old court opinions will do you no harm and you'll be able to extract their meaning without copying their style. If my home entertainment/horror novel analogy wasn't helpful, try this one: you'll be able to learn from those old opinions without dressing like the people who wrote them. Just as you would look odd walking around law school wearing the robes and clothes of judges from a different time, so your thoughts would look odd if they were clad in the language and writing style used by those same judges.

Rather, you want to sound like a competent, professional, contemporary lawyer. You want to be able to adopt the voice and rhetoric of the lawyer you want to be, not a judge who lived long ago. So when you read those opinions for your other classes, remember that your purpose in reading them is to extract the information about the law they contain, not to use them as models for your own writing, just as you shouldn't use the style of this book—it was written for the purpose of giving you information about legal writing and research, not to persuade you to rule in a particular way. My audience is law students, not judges.

But how should you read what those judges wrote? And, for that matter, how should you read anything now that you're in law school? Reading is crucial to the writing and research process, because once you've found information you need to assimilate it in order to understand it and include it in your written analysis, and the recent technological advances in information storage and retrieval raise reading issues that didn't exist before.

On the one hand, it's exciting to be involved and thinking about something that has literally been impossible to think about until just a couple of years ago; until the widespread acceptance of computers and other digital devices at home and in the office, the book was the only available technology for storing and retrieving large amounts of information. That is no longer true, and we are all contemplating the implications of that change. On the other hand, though, this is an unsettling time, when old and new ways of doing things are at odds in ways no one has experienced before. No one has definitive answers to the issues this new technology raises yet, and as we think about these issues, technology is changing again and again, constantly bringing up new possibilities and new problems for us to consider.

These issues are particularly important to lawyers because most of us practice in environments where time, literally, is money; the faster we can do our work, it seems, the more we can cram into a day and the more we'll be able to bill for our services. That perception might be partially accurate, but it's also misleading and can be harmful to you in the long run.

1. People Take a Long Time to Change

Whatever your views about how people came to exist, we can surely all agree on one thing: the process takes some time. Changes in basic human physiology and neurology don't happen overnight, nor do they happen in the span of the twenty or so years since the world wide web has been in existence.

This suggests that despite all claims to the contrary, the advent of the internet as a communications tool likely has not wrought substantial changes in the way your "millennial" or "Google" generation thinks, just as the advent of television did not give my "baby boom" or "television" generation (yes, that's what we were called—the first generation to grow up watching television) the square eyes our mothers warned us of if we spent too much time watching television and not enough time on our homework.

And that in turn means that most claims that your generation can multi-task effectively, whereas older generations cannot, are likely not correct. In fact, very few of us are good at doing more than one thing at a time, and hardly anyone can do more than two. Maybe in time the human brain will change to allow for greater skill in multi-tasking, but we're unlikely to be around to benefit from such a change.

That's an important concept because it informs much of what we know about reading. And that can all be distilled into one core idea: we learn less well if we're trying to do something else at the same time. So when you're reading the results of your research, try not to be doing anything else; don't listen to music, don't answer email or text messages, don't speak on the phone, and so on. You might believe that you can do some, or even all, of these things and still be able to read as carefully as if you were just concentrating on your reading. But that's a belief based on culture, not science. I can't say definitively that you're wrong, but I can say that the evidence is strongly against you.

2. Reading Should Be a Slow Process

If there's one general rule about reading, it should probably be this: we should do it more slowly than we do. This probably runs counter to everything you've been taught. Nonetheless, I believe it to be true; we read more quickly than is good for us.

Speed reading has been held up as a virtue in our educational system for as long as anyone can remember. All the reading comprehension tests you've taken—including the LSAT—emphasized the importance of reading texts carefully, but reading them quickly. It's a mistake.

This isn't to say that you don't read well. Of course you do—you're in law school! You've shown that you're highly skilled at extracting information from texts and at comprehending that information, and you can do it quickly. But now you're dealing with a new field, and one in which a lot of information can be coiled into sentences that can be written in English so dense and opaque that it can almost seem to be a foreign language. When we read, say, a court opinion, we're not just trying to extract the rules articulated by the court, we're trying to decide why the court reached the decision it reached, whether the case we're reading supports a position we'd like to take or whether it can be distinguished by the other side, why the court chose to support its decision with the authority it selected, and on and on. We're trying to understand the rhetorical choices the court made in the language it selected and what significance, if any, those choices might have for us, we're trying to understand the jurisprudential context of the case, and—as researchers and analysts—we're trying to fit all of this information into a decision matrix that locates the case in the context of the result we're trying to obtain. In short, we're trying to get a lot of information from the opinion.

The faster we try to do these things, the less well we're likely to do them. You probably won't miss the actual holding of the case or the rules the case articulates—although we've all had the experience of reading a case so quickly that we've skimmed over some crucial language, thereby creating a fundamental misunderstanding about the court's ruling—but it's very easy to gloss over the nuances of a piece of legal writing if you're not taking a great deal of care. One can always read cases more than once, of course, and often we'll read them many times in order to draw all the possible information out of them. But the best time to really come to grips with a case is the first time you read it. If you can learn as much as possible from the case when you first encounter it, you're in a much better position to read the next case, and the next one, more intelligently than you otherwise would be and that, ironically, suggests that the slower you read, the more time you'll save in the long run.

3. Reading on a Computer Is Not As Easy As Reading on Paper

Computers, of course, are the big game-changers in reading. They're the first fundamentally different method of storing and retrieving information since the development of paper, and we're right at the beginning of the computer reading era. Because it's such a new phenomenon, we don't know that much about reading on computer screens except this: it isn't as easy as reading information written on paper.

There are several reasons reading is harder on a computer than on paper, and at least a few of those reasons are relevant to us as lawyers. First, of course, is the simple reality that a computer's screen resolution isn't as high as a sheet of paper. The flickering that happens on a screen might be beyond our ability to register consciously, but our eyes are still aware of it and they tire more quickly reading text on a screen than they do when reading words on paper. This doesn't mean that reading on paper is easy; we all know that reading large amounts of text on paper will tire out the eyes as well. It just means that computer screens are worse.

Other ergonomic issues count against computer screens as well. Screens reflect glare, which can be a particular problem in places like law schools, where there's often a lot of fluorescent lighting. And we often read computer screens at odd angles, meaning that our backs and necks tense up and that can contribute to tiredness and headaches if we spend too much time in front of a computer.

Probably the worst feature of reading law on a computer, though, is the possibilities of distraction they offer. This doesn't just mean that you can check your email, or the sports scores, or the latest news, or any of the myriad of other things we can do on computers other than getting our work done; it also means that the principle legal databases, LexisNexis and Westlaw (and, to an extent, the other legal databases as well), are designed to support our worst computer reading habit.

When we read on the internet, most of us bounce constantly from one source of information to another, rarely spending more than a minute reading one document, and often much less time than that. We've all had the sensation of finding something online that looks to be helpful to our research, seeing a hyperlink to a supporting document and clicking on that, finding it helpful and then seeing another hyperlink, clicking on that, and so on. Sometimes we might reflexively hit the "print" button to preserve our trail of documents. More often, we just bounce around the virtual information world until we tire of the process.

That is not a reading strategy designed for success, at least not for legal researchers. Bouncing around between documents might be entertaining, and it might have a place in less important research tasks, but it's a really bad idea for lawyers to use this approach. For one thing, we're not following a coherent research path when we jump from document to document. For another, we might be incurring costs without realizing it, especially if we hit "print" all the time (LexisNexis and Westlaw both charge substantial amounts of money to print a document and while this isn't a concern for you while in law school, it might well be a significant issue once you're in practice and the bad habits learned in law school are hard to break). Most importantly, though, we're not engaged in deep reading when we bounce from document to document.

It might sound like a criticism of Westlaw and LexisNexis to say that their tools encourage this type of bounce reading (or whatever name you want to give to this practice), but that's not correct. These services are both designed to be as helpful as possible to us, and the addition of hyperlinks to move us as smoothly as possible from one document to another, and of focusing tools that allow us to zoom in to precisely the text in an opinion that corresponds to our search, are extraordinarily helpful features for experienced researchers. But they also allow us to fall victim to our worst instincts as readers: hyperlinking allows us to bounce read our way through databases, never spending long enough to really read anything carefully. Focusing tools allow us to selectively read only portions of a document, perhaps missing contextualizing language before or after the language that corresponds to our search, which changes entirely the nature of the passage we're interested in. Courts will often write that if the facts of a case were one way, the decision would be X, but since the facts are not that way, the decision is Y. If you only read the Y part of the decision, you might miss important language that would allow you to distinguish the holding, and the likelihood of this is much greater if you read the decision online.

4. Suggestions for Effective Reading

Of course, none of this will change your preferred reading strategy, which is likely to be researching and reading on your computer. And that's fine, as long as you use some caution while you read. These are some suggestions that might help you.[1]

---

1. For more on effective reading, you might consider Ruth Ann McKinney's book *Reading Like a Lawyer: Time-Saving Strategies for Reading Law Like an Expert*, 2005. This book is an excellent place

A. Don't Print Everything

This might seem to contradict everything I've just said, but don't print everything you find online. For one thing, it's an environmentally unsound practice to use that much ink and paper. For another, it doesn't solve the problem. Really, all you're doing if you print everything that looks as if it could be relevant to your research is deferring your reading, and your thinking, until a later point. If you do this, you're likely skimming documents—making a fast evaluation that a case might be helpful to your research and printing it so you can read the document more carefully later. Don't do that. Take the time to read the document carefully now. If it still looks interesting after that reading, print the document to disk—save it in a folder on your computer. This is a good habit to get into for practice purposes: Westlaw and LexisNexis might still charge you for a print event, but you'll have the electronic version of the document on your hard drive afterward and may print it, or share it, as often as you need to without incurring additional expenses.

B. Slow Down

This is obvious advice, based on everything I've said until now. But it bears repeating: don't read so quickly. Start from the beginning of a document and read it carefully. If it's a case, try to understand the facts before you move on to reading the legal analysis. Even if there seem to be some legal issues that aren't relevant to your case, read about them anyway; you never know what might stimulate your thinking. And try to take notes on the case as you read it. These will help to stimulate your memory when you start to write up the results of your research.

C. Ask Questions and Read for a Purpose

The best advice anyone can give you about reading is to engage the text. That means you have to ask the text questions and to read it for a purpose. I'll try to explain both of these concepts briefly here.

Imagine you've been called on in a law school class. Your professor asks you to give the facts of a case and to explain the holding. As you do, your professor asks you questions: What if this fact was different? What did the court mean when it said something? Was the court correct in its decision? How does this case relate to one you discussed in your previous class? And so on. We're all familiar with how that process works and what it looks like.

Now imagine that you're the professor and the text you're reading is like the student in class. Ask it questions, just as the teacher would ask questions of the student. That's the process of active reading in a nutshell. Reading is not, in fact, a passive process. We gain insight and acquire knowledge when we engage in the reading of a text, not when we sit and let words float past our eyes. It's easier to do face-to-face than it is when we're reading a text, but we are, in essence, engaged in a dialog with the text's writer whenever we read.

---

to go for a much more detailed discussion of reading techniques that will serve you well in law school and has inspired much of my thinking in this chapter.

And that's what it means to say that writing is engaging in a conversation with a reader. The writer anticipates that the reader is going to be asking these questions and tries to answer them at the moment the writer thinks the reader will be asking them. It's not a perfect process, of course, but the more both participants—writer and reader—try to engage the other, the better the results will be for both.

But this can only happen if we read for a purpose. That's something more than just reading a text because it's required of you or because it looked as if it might help you in your research; reading with a purpose means reading because the process will benefit you in some way and keeping that benefit in mind as you read. As legal researchers, that's easier for us than for most readers, because we're reading the fruits of our research to help us solve problems and answer questions. But it's important to not forget our purpose for reading a text while we're reading it because that purpose helps us to pose the questions we need to be asking the text.

So as you read something, ask yourself why you're reading it. Are you a lawyer, trying to help your client resolve an issue? Are you a judge, trying to pick between two competing answers to a problem? Are you a client, trying to understand the advice you're being given or a ruling that's being handed down in a case that involves you? Put yourself in the role that will best help you get the most out of whatever you're reading and then read the document with that role in mind. It'll make the questions easier to ask and will make the answers you're able to derive from the text more relevant to you.

Conclusion

A lot of this might seem like unnecessary information, personal bias, and conjecture. Well, perhaps. But I've tried to distill a lot of other people's research and a lot of experience into this chapter because the subject is crucial to your success in law school and as lawyers. And the bottom line is simple and uncontroversial: you can't do well in law school if you don't read effectively.

The reading strategies you've employed up until now have done well for you. But this isn't the time to rest on your laurels. If there's something—anything—you can do better, now's the time to improve, so you can give yourself as much of a competitive advantage as possible.

Focus Questions

1. Why is there a chapter on reading in a legal writing and research text?
2. Do you agree with the proposition that the claim your generation can multi-task effectively is overstated?
3. Do you think of yourself as a fast or slow reader? Do you find yourself having to read things more than once in order to fully understand them? If so, has this tendency improved, worsened, or stayed the same since coming to law school?
4. Do you usually read on paper or on a computer? Do you notice a difference when you read in one medium or the other? Do you agree that reading on a computer is more difficult than reading on paper?

5. Does the advice about reading surprise you? Do you usually read documents with a specific purpose in mind? Do you usually ask questions of a text while you read it? If so, what questions are you asking this text as you read it? Do you think you will adopt any of these reading strategies if you don't employ them at present?

6. Had you thought of legal writing as a type of genre writing? Does that insight help you when thinking about the different types of writing you're seeing in law school?

7. Did you think that the court opinions you've been reading in your doctrinal classes were good examples of legal writing? Had you considered that they were written for a different audience than the one for whom you'll be writing? Does that help you to think about whether or not to copy the writing style to be found in those opinions?

8. How much writing by lawyers had you read before coming to law school? If you had to evaluate the lawyer writing you've seen, what words would you use?

9. Have you devoted much time and thought to the skill of reading? Or has reading been something you've done reflexively since you learned to read? Has this chapter convinced you to spend more time thinking about reading in the future?

10. What types of writing do you read outside of law school? Do your reading habits change when you read that writing as opposed to when you read cases for law school? Should they? If you think you read differently when reading as a non-lawyer, what are the differences and do you think you could use some of those non-law-school reading techniques in law school?

Chapter 2

What Is Legal Writing?

What You Should Learn from This Chapter

This chapter takes the idea of legal writing as a genre, introduced in the previous chapter, and explores it in greater detail. It considers the idea that legal writing, like all forms of genre writing, sets up expectations in its readers, and discusses ways in which legal writers can be aware of, and use, those expectations.

After reading this chapter, you should:

- have a greater appreciation for legal writing as a genre;
- have considered the genre expectations in the types of writing you enjoy;
- have thought about the genre expectations that might have been made by those who write the legal texts you have read; and
- have thought about how you, as a legal writer, can use your readers' genre expectations to your clients' advantage.

Asking what legal writing is isn't as foolish a question as at first it might seem. If you asked a cross-section of legal writing professors across the country to define legal writing, you would likely get a host of different answers, all of them likely including concepts like "written by lawyers" and "written on behalf of a client" and "written to achieve a purpose related to the civil or criminal justice system or to secure an agreement between two or more parties," but there's no one standard, or even agreed-upon, definition.

In fact some people argue that there is no such thing as "legal" writing at all, and that instead there is only writing. Good writing, they maintain, is good writing regardless of the genre and the same goes for bad writing. Nothing helpful to the discussion of what makes for "good" or "bad" writing is added by qualifying the concept of "writing" with "legal."

On the one hand, it's hard to argue with the logic of that claim. Law has its own words and phrases, of course—it's unlikely that one would encounter a phrase like *res ipsa loquitur* anywhere outside of something written by and for lawyers, for example—but that's just an externality that doesn't define "legal" writing. Similarly, writing done by and for lawyers conforms to specific citation requirements and practices, but while those flag a piece of writing as something intended for a legal audience, they don't transform writing into "legal" writing, any more than writing that conforms to the

Chicago Manual can be called "academic" or "scholarly" writing. The core of "legal" writing—the majority of the words, and the grammar, punctuation, spelling, and so on—are the same as for any other piece of writing, and the stylistic preference for the active voice and for clear, plain English are no different whether one is writing about legal, historical, or journalistic writing.

1. Legal Writing as Genre Writing

But on the other hand, the concept of "legal" writing does seem to carry some value. For one thing, the qualification reminds us that we are engaged in genre composition that has its own set of conventions and forms, just as forms of genre fiction carry their own conventions and forms. When you pick up a cowboy novel, for example (and how often have you done that recently?), you know to expect that the book will be set in a relatively specific period of American history—post-Civil War but pre-1917,[1] in all probability—it will be located somewhere in the American West, it will involve people who mainly use horse transportation, and so on. There's a vocabulary you'll expect, a certain type of behavior from the characters, a demarcation between "good" and "bad" characters that is fairly easy to understand, doubtless at least one scene in a saloon with swinging doors, and so on.

Genre fiction relies on these stereotypes to stand-in for a lot of text. One needn't spend time describing the social structure inherent in a Western town, for example, or the importance of effective law enforcement and the fact that "effective" can sometimes mean "violent" in a way that would be entirely inappropriate and unrealistic in, for example, a contemporary crime novel; someone writing about contemporary life would have to have a very good reason for describing a gun fight on Main Street, where the two participants stood a distance apart and then tried to draw a six-shooter from a holster and shoot it faster than their opponent. And if the writer put a scene like that into a book, the writer would doubtless be relying on the images to evoke genre expectations for cowboy novels in the reader.

Stereotypical genre expectations do that work for the writer, freeing the writer to proceed without narrative interruption in a way that a non-genre writer can't do. If Victor Hugo had attempted to write a cowboy novel, the book would doubtless have contained many chapters explaining every nuance of social and cultural relationships between the characters. By contrast, if Zane Grey had written *Les Misérables*, the book would have been much shorter than it is, and would likely have had few, if any, references to the specifics of the Parisian sewer system.

Although lawyers aren't writing fiction, this notion of genre writing is quite important for them. When a lawyer writes a brief to be filed in court, for example, the lawyer knows pretty well who the audience for the document will be, even if the lawyer doesn't know the specific judge who will be deciding the issues raised,[2] and the lawyer knows

---

1. This year was chosen because it marks the start of America's involvement in the First Word War, the next major conflict this country fought.

2. Sometimes, in fact, the lawyer might know precisely which judge will read the brief. In courts with differentiated dockets, a case is assigned to one judge who retains authority over that case throughout its stay in the court. Sometimes the judge will refer the case to a magistrate or other judge for

that the reader will have some expectations of the document. The judge will expect technical perfection and will likely note any spelling mistakes, grammatical errors, and so on, and might—depending on the judge—think less of the lawyer's argument if any of these technical problems are found in the document. The judge will expect the brief to be laid out in a particular way, with a statement of the relevant facts preceding the analysis, and each issue raised in the analysis placed in its own section. And the judge will expect that all legal rules proposed by the brief will be supported by authority and applied to the facts of the case under consideration.

All of these are genre expectations. In some courts there are specific rules for what a legal brief must contain, but most of what the judge will expect from a piece of legal writing is more cultural than regulatory. The same is true of interoffice memos—documents for which there are no "rules" but often seemingly rigid expectations—contracts, correspondence, and, in fact, any other document a lawyer writes.

These genre expectations do a lot of work for the writer. Just as with the cowboy novel, the writer can rely on those expectations to be uniform and to prime the reader to expect certain information to be presented in a certain way. And if the writer knows what expectations the reader has, and is feeling confident enough, the writer can play with those expectations and even, on occasion, go against them. This practice—the fancy term is "subverting" the reader's genre expectations—can be remarkably effective when handled carefully. Let's consider one devastating example.

2. Subverting Genre Expectations in Legal Writing

Petitions for writs of certiorari—known as "cert. petitions" because the proper name is so long and presents so many possibilities for mispronunciation and misspelling that lawyers try to avoid using those words whenever possible—are standard genre documents filed with the Supreme Court whenever a party wants the Court to hear a case. Only a tiny fraction of these petitions are granted each year. In the case we are considering, the Court of Appeals for the Fifth Circuit had decided an issue and the losing party had petitioned the Supreme Court to hear the case. The Court, however, had decided a case in the interim that the Justices thought might resolve the issue between the parties, and so they remanded the case to the Fifth Circuit with an instruction to reconsider its ruling in light of this recent opinion.

When the Fifth Circuit reconsidered, though, it decided the case in the same way as before, and it released its decision in a short *per curiam* decision. This type of decision is unusual because it is not signed by the judge who wrote it, but rather is issued as the decision of the court as a whole (the phrase *per curiam* means "by the court"). In this case, the shortness of the opinion, its *per curiam* nature, and the wording the Fifth Cir-

---

pre-trial issues, but even then, the attorneys will be notified of this and likely will have some familiarity with the other judge as well. So in those cases, it is possible to write something that's tailored to a very narrow audience indeed.

cuit used all made clear that that court thought it had decided the issue correctly before and wasn't too thrilled about having to consider the case again.

Unsurprisingly, the party who had petitioned the Supreme Court to hear the case filed another cert. opinion. One of the elements required of these petitions is a section called the "Statement of the Case" in which the party asking the Supreme Court to hear the case must file a short statement of the material facts that led to its decision to ask the Court to rule and, because this was a case coming from a federal appellate court, a brief statement of how the federal courts had jurisdiction to decide the case. This is a standard part of any appellate brief, and it usually begins with a very bland statement like "This case comes before this Court because of the following facts." Actually, that's a terrible sentence that would be edited out of any brief filed by any self-respecting lawyer, and I use it here not to suggest that this is what a lawyer might actually write in this situation but to point out that this opening sentence is not something that typically is used to convey an argument or to actually say anything at all. It's typically a throat-clearing sentence; something that doesn't actually say anything but prepares the reader for something that will be said soon.

Not the cert. petition in this case, though. The first sentence of the Statement of the Case in that petition was "Some people just can't take a hint."[3] Now, this is pretty aggressive writing. It refers to the United States Circuit Court of Appeals for the Fifth Circuit—a serious group of judges—as "some people," it describes the Supreme Court's initial remand of the case as "a hint," and it uses a contraction, something which certainly gets a reader's attention in a piece of genre writing as conservative as a cert. petition. In seven words it conveys the writer's disdain for the Fifth Circuit's decision, it suggests that the writer's client has a very strong argument in support of overturning that decision (if you aren't extraordinarily confident that you're going to win, or, at least, don't want to suggest that you're not that confident, it would be better to not be this aggressive in your writing style), and it suggests that the writer is a very senior lawyer who can speak in this manner to the Supreme Court without fear.[4]

For our purposes, though, the sentence is especially interesting because it subverts the reader's genre expectations. Instead of just starting a snowball rolling down a mountain in hopes of creating an impressive effect later on, the writer has started with a full-blown avalanche. The sentence grabs the reader's attention and sets up expectations for the rest of the brief. And, in fact, the rest of this brief was relatively straightforward and uncontroversial; it laid out its argument that the Court should grant the petition and hear the case, but not in the same aggressive style as this opening. That wasn't necessary; the writer had done almost all the work in the first seven words, and everything else in the brief just needed to support the impression created in this first sentence. The Court granted the petition and, after full briefing and oral argument, overturned the Fifth Circuit's decision, just as the petitioner had been asking it to do.

I don't offer this example as an example of the type of writing you'll be asked to do in law school, but to show how an experienced legal writer can play with the reader's

---

3. Petition for Writ of Certiorari at 1, *Ortiz v. Fibreboard Corp.*, 527 U.S. 815 (1999), (No. 97-1704), 1998 WL 34081053, at *1.

4. The lawyer who signed this brief was, in fact, Laurence Tribe, a highly respected and well-known professor of constitutional law at Harvard and someone who regularly argues cases before the Supreme Court.

genre expectations and, on occasion, go against them to create an effect. The important thing for now is to recognize that legal readers have those genre expectations. Once you know what a reader expects of you, it's easier to understand how you can meet or, in the rare case, intentionally avoid those expectations.

So, is there such a thing as legal writing? With apologies to those who disagree, I think there is, and it can be defined as "the genre writing that professional readers expect lawyers to produce on behalf of their clients." That's a very broad definition, of course, and some might argue that it's too broad to be helpful. It certainly does have a disturbingly industrial image; do we really want writing to be "produced"? But "produce" serves to remind us that lawyers, unlike some other professional writers, write on demand, not for aesthetic satisfaction. "On behalf of their clients" reminds us that in their professional lives, lawyers write to further the interests of their clients, not themselves; by defining the type of writing lawyers do in terms of our readers, I'm hoping to get across the idea that legal writers must think carefully about who they're writing for and how to best serve their clients' interests by focusing on how their writing will affect their readers.

And by defining legal writing in terms of a genre, I'm hoping that you'll remember that your readers will have definite and particularized expectations of your writing. How you should go about meeting, or subverting, those expectations is the subject of the rest of this book.

Focus Questions

1. What do you think legal writing is? Do you agree with the definition supplied at the end of this chapter or would you prefer a different definition? If so, how would you define legal writing? Why?

2. Other than what's discussed in this chapter, are there other genre expectations a legal reader would have for a piece of legal writing? How might those expectations make your life as a legal writer more difficult? How might they make your life easier?

3. Does it surprise you to think of legal writing defined in terms of the client and the reader? Does this make the legal writer appear too subservient in the process? What is the lawyer's proper position in the legal hierarchy?

4. Does the notion of subverting the reader's genre expectations make sense to you? What do you think of the example of expectation subversion supplied in this chapter? If you read genre fiction, can you think of an example of expectation subversion in something you have read? Did you find it to be effective? Do you see why this is a technique that must be handled carefully?

5. Do you read genre fiction? What types of information are understood as a result of the genre in which the writer is writing and what types of information can the writer of such genre fiction assume the reader will understand?

6. Do you understand why the text talks about the assumptions a reader of genre writing can make about the writing?

Chapter 3

Legal Rhetoric

What You Should Learn from This Chapter

This chapter introduces rhetoric in the context of legal writing. This is only a very brief introduction to a subject that could, on its own, be the basis of an entire degree program, but it explores the idea of language and communication as tools of persuasion, something that lies at the heart of much legal writing. The chapter introduces this concept by the study of a television commercial, and discusses the way language is used to create impressions that might or might not be completely accurate.

After reading this chapter, you should:

- be relieved that you will not have to learn more about rhetorical figures;
- have considered the ways in which the careful use of language can create impressions in the mind of the listener or reader;
- have considered how the roles of advertiser and lawyer have points of intersection;
- have considered the meanings of *logos*, *ethos*, and *pathos* and contemplated the ways in which lawyers use all three to enhance the arguments they make; and
- have considered the coded rhetorical messages we send out each day by our appearance and what the process tells us about how we already employ rhetoric to persuade others to do or think something.

"Rhetoric" can be a tricky concept. For some, the word carries associations of stuffiness, academia, and impracticality. Rhetoric, to them, is the study of the techniques long-dead Romans and Greeks used when orating speeches to the public, and has no place in contemporary law schools. Rhetoric is a discipline that studies strict, and strangely named, figures of speech like *zeugma*, where a word links two parts of a sentence, even though it only logically applies to one part,[1] *tmesis*, the separation of parts of a word,[2] or *metaplasmus*, the intentional misspelling of a word.[3] To those people, rhetoric is as dead as the languages the Romans and Greeks used when they practiced those techniques.

---

1. "After tripping over the curb in a futile attempt to stop his girlfriend from leaving him, Fred's leg and heart were broken."

2. "That meal was in-I-can't-believe-it-was-that-bad-edible."

3. "When cows look for entertainment, do they go to the *moovies*?" (Thanks to Tasha Clark for this suggestion.)

In fact, though, rhetoric is a vibrant and living discipline. It's true that ancient Romans and Greeks first wrote about rhetorical technique, but they frequently did so in practical terms that still have relevance to us all today, and especially to lawyers. Cicero and Quintilian—two Romans who are among the most famous of classical rhetoricians—were both, among other things, highly skilled and practical lawyers who used rhetoric to structure the arguments they made on behalf of their clients. And just because they lived a long time ago is no reason to not learn from what they taught, if it can help us do our jobs better.

But don't worry. You don't have to read Latin, you don't have to learn rhetoric from someone who was used to wearing togas when making legal arguments and is only familiar to us from marble busts that probably look little like the person anyway, and you certainly don't have to learn anything about rhetorical figures. Understanding the figures and the techniques they describe can certainly be helpful to you as a contemporary writer, but it's much more important that you learn how to use language to communicate and persuade than it is that you learn the terms for the techniques you're using. You won't see the word *zeugma* again in this book.

One important thing that rhetoric teaches us is that there's more going on with language than just words. A crucial feature of rhetoric is its ability to describe and analyze some of these important, but difficult to perceive, effects of language. In fact, we're all aware of the way words and images are used to persuade us every day. Let's look more closely at one very small example of this, from a hypothetical television commercial.

1. Rhetoric Used As a Tool to Communicate

The commercial opens with a caption—"Strong Wood for a Strong America"—and the first pictures we see are of a forest of trees spreading as far as we can see into the horizon. The camera pans down until we can see a white man standing in a clearing of trees. He's wearing a battered hard-hat, a red tartan shirt, faded jeans, and work boots, and he's carrying a well-used chain saw over one shoulder. He looks at the camera, which is now at eye height, and says, "America's strength has always come from its bountiful supply of natural resources: its land, its water, and its trees."

Another white man walks towards the camera. He's dressed similarly to the first man. He says, "Today, we use our trees for many things, but most importantly, we use the lumber from the trees we harvest to make the homes that keep us safe and secure." They both smile at the camera as it pans back up to show us the forest vista again. As it does so, a voice-over says, "At American Tree Constructors, Inc., we only use 100% North American Lumber from trees grown in America and all our wood is American processed. We don't ship wood from overseas to build our homes. And for every tree we harvest, we plant ten so that our supply will never run out. Because we all live here."

The shot dissolves to a picture of a young African-American couple, in military fatigues, being handed the keys to a new house from a smiling female realtor, wearing a striped, red, white, and blue jacket with stars on the lapel. The jacket resembles the Stars and Stripes. The house, surrounded by a white picket fence, and with two rocking chairs on the porch, stands in the background. The young lady says, "We're glad our house was built using American lumber" and the young man nods in agreement, saying, "It's good to know that we're all working to keep our homes, and our country, strong."

As the camera pulls back and up, showing many similar houses, all with couples standing in their yards and children playing in the gardens, the voice-over says, "American Tree Constructors. 100% North American Lumber for American homes. Keeping our country strong and safe." Patriotic music swells in the background and the company logo—a shield with stars on the right-hand side and stripes, in the form of tree outlines, on the left—swoops in to take up the screen with the words "American Tree Constructors, Inc." below it.

Well. I obviously have no future as a screenwriter for commercials. Still, there's a lot to talk about here, even though this commercial is relatively simple in its message, making it a useful tool to discuss the use of visual and spoken rhetoric to send messages to the viewer. To start with, we should consider one important way in which the commercial uses language. In written and spoken language, the commercial sends two crucial messages—that its products are made from "100% North American Lumber" and that its wood comes from trees that are "grown in America." These claims are supported by the unsubtle double allusion to this country: the realtor's Stars and Stripes jacket and the corporate logo with trees taking the form of the stripes. So the claims and the visual support might appear to be saying the same thing—the lumber is processed in this country from trees that were cut down here. In fact, though, that's not at all what the words mean.

The United States of America is only one of over forty countries on the North American continent and not even the largest one in terms of size; that honor goes to Canada. In addition to Canada, "North America" includes Greenland, which is politically part of Denmark, the United States, Mexico, the Central American countries of Guatemala, Costa Rica, Panama, El Salvador, Honduras, Bermuda, and most of the Caribbean countries, including Anguilla, Antigua and Barbuda, the Bahamas, and Barbados.

To claim that one's product is "100% North American Lumber," then, means that it could come from any of the countries that fall under the geographical designation of North America. And to claim that one's wood is "grown in America" is to be even broader, because that could also include all the countries in South America as well; the countries of the North and South American continents together make up the "American" countries on the planet.

Even American Tree Constructor's claim that it doesn't ship wood from overseas doesn't necessarily mean what one might think, since wood could come from the southernmost tip of Chile or the northernmost part of Greenland and not come from "overseas" in any meaningful sense of the word or require a ship to transport it.[4]

So we can already see that the commercial is a carefully constructed piece of work, persuading us that its words mean one thing by use of an image that makes it appear that "American" just means "United States of America," while at the same time never actually limiting the words to that meaning. This language would certainly be carefully

4. If something came from Greenland it is possible that it would, technically, cross the sea, but the sea in those parts has been frozen for a while. Whether it remains frozen, of course, is a topic of much interest these days, but that is a topic for another time and place. This is, of course, a theoretical point since there is insufficient wood in Greenland to make it commercially viable for anyone to cut it down and send it anywhere.

vetted by lawyers to make sure that no claims were being made that could not be defended in court, if necessary, should it some day be true that the company's wood did not come from the United States of America.

The images used in the commercial are similarly created with great care. There is racial diversity, as shown by the white lumberjacks and the African-American couple who are buying the home. And there is gender balance, with two women and three men featured in the commercial. The house-buying couple are also members of the military, reinforcing the patriotic theme of the commercial. The pictures we see suggest to us that all members of this culturally diverse country are behind the simple goal of keeping the country strong by using American lumber in our homes.

So there's a lot going on in this short commercial, some of it very obvious and some of it quite subtle. But hardly any of what we are supposed to learn from the commercial comes from the language of the commercial itself. Instead, we have been sent visual and cultural clues that send powerful messages of inclusiveness and single-minded purpose, and that cover over a potentially tricky issue if the "100% North American Lumber" is not, in fact, all from the United States of America.

2. Metaphors and the Way They Work

Metaphors are a crucial part of communication. They work by restating a concept in terms of a different concept, thereby adding meaning to the original concept. Calling someone a "pillar of the community" doesn't mean that you actually think someone is a structural feature, usually made of stone, who is holding up a community, but that someone is an important member of the community whose work and presence "supports" the community. It's a familiar and well-understood rhetorical device.

As with all things to do with legal writing, it's important that we consider carefully the meaning and significance of every word we use, even if we're using that word in a metaphorical sense. To aid us in considering how we might do that, and to consider some of the benefits and dangers associated with metaphor, let's think about the idea of using counter-analysis to inoculate the reader in order to make the reader resistant to the influence of an opponent's argument.

"Inoculate," of course, is a metaphor. In its standard and direct use, the word means to inject a quantity of an active biological substance in order to encourage the body to develop resistance to that substance when encountered in its full strength. Although not exactly synonymous with "vaccination," the two words are used interchangeably in general, even if not scientific, use and it's in that more general sense we'll be using it here.

The beauty of this metaphor is in the many ways it functions. First, and most simply, the word is sufficiently exotic to make the reader stop momentarily to think about its meaning in the context in which it's being used. Rather than writing "the idea of using counter-analysis to prepare the reader ..." or "the idea of using counter-analysis to influence the reader ..." in the second paragraph, I used the less-standard and metaphorical "inoculate." It works in that context, but you probably had to think a little to confirm that; any reader would. And after you confirmed that it was a valid use, you had slightly more faith in what I was telling you than you might have had before because you had tested my writing and found that my word choice was appropriate.

Using effective metaphors enhances our credibility with our readers.

Metaphors, though, do more than enhance credibility. This simple word actually does a lot of work for the writer because it imports from its more scientific use a lot of information with it. Because it's a scientific/medical word, it has the aura of accuracy, precision, and well-being that another word like "prepare" or "influence" wouldn't have; "inoculate" makes the practice of counter-analysis seem more valuable, helpful, and healthy because inoculation is a scientific practice used to ward-off illness.

And because we understand the concept of inoculation and how it's supposed to work, we already know how the process of counter-analysis is supposed to help a legal writer: just as with medical inoculation, analytical inoculation must involve, as it does, the practice of introducing the reader to a weakened version of an opponent's argument in order to make that argument ineffective when the reader encounters it in the opponent's document. Just by its use, the word tells the reader a lot; a simple eleven-letter word has done its work neatly and efficiently within the context of a sentence.

But there's a problem. Recently, the practice of inoculation has come under criticism from those who argue that by injecting a patient with a weakened strain of a disease, one can actually cause the very problems one is seeking to avoid and give the patient the illness you're seeking to prevent. For this reason, many parents have avoided giving their children vaccinations, or inoculations, for common childhood diseases. For those to whom inoculation is a bad thing, using the word as a metaphor as part of an introduction to a positive subject like counter-analysis might have precisely the contrary effect to that intended, and "inoculate" might, to that audience, suggest a negative effect—something to be avoided at all costs.

This is why we have to think carefully about each word before we use it. In the end, I used "inoculate" in the context of counter-analysis because I decided, on balance, that its positive effects outweighed its negative effects. That doesn't suggest my personal opinion on the value of inoculation in the medical area, because writing is not about the writer but is rather about the reader. What it does suggest, then, is that even though I don't know you and how you feel about the idea of medical inoculation, I believe you're sufficiently familiar with how the concept is supposed to work that you understand its metaphorical use in this context. It's reasonable for a writer to believe that a reader will come some way towards the acceptance of a metaphor, despite the reader's personal beliefs, if the metaphor effectively translates a concept from one context to another. But think carefully about your reader, and how you think your reader will respond, before deciding to use any metaphor.

3. *Logos, Ethos,* and *Pathos*

In addition to metaphor, we need to look for the *logos*, the *ethos*, and the *pathos* in the messages we send to, and receive from, one another. I promise, these are the last Greek terms you'll have to read in this chapter. And what's more, few practicing lawyers would understand what you were talking about if you used these words; they're terms that are beloved of legal writing professors and rhetoricians, but they're not part of the general vocabulary, in the law or anywhere else. But the concepts represented by these words are very well understood by all lawyers and, in fact, by everyone. If we look at what the words stand for, you'll understand what I mean.

Arguments relying on *logos* are, as you might expect, arguments that rely on logic. By contrast, arguments based on *pathos* are arguments that have a strong emotional appeal. And arguments based on *ethos* rely on the credibility of the person making the argument. Those are the three central pillars of all forms of argumentation, and lawyers use a combination of them every day to make arguments on behalf of their clients, even though they don't use the words and might not even think consciously about what they're doing. So important are these concepts that they pervade every part of an argument, and arguments carry both overt and coded messages based on them.

The idea of an overt message based on logic, emotion, or the credibility of the speaker is easy to understand, but what are these coded messages I spoke of? How does that happen? Actually, that's very easy to understand. To see what I'm talking about, all you have to do is look in the mirror.

4. Coded Rhetorical Messages

No, seriously. Go and look in the mirror. What do you see? I don't know, of course because I can't see you. But you'll see the person you set out to be this morning. The way you appear—hair probably combed or brushed, jewelry, if any, in place, clothing appropriate for law school, or home, or wherever you are at the moment—is all the result of careful thought at some point in the past. Perhaps not this morning, when you might have left fairly quickly in order to get to school, but at some time in the past you decided how you wanted your hair to look when you last had it cut, and you spent time deciding whether or not to buy the clothes you're wearing. And when you decided on your appearance, you made some decisions about the messages you wanted to send about who you are.

To test that idea, try this. Look at yourself in the mirror again, and now think if this is how you would like to be dressed for an interview for your dream job. How about going out on a date with someone you would very much like to impress? How about going to court as a lawyer? As a defendant in a speeding ticket case? You would probably say you would like to be dressed differently for all of those social situations, unless you're engaging in one at the same time you're reading this (and if you're on a date and reading this book, the date's not going as well as you would like). We all understand the idea that we dress appropriately for a specific occasion, and few people would try to wear the same clothes for a regular day at law school, a court hearing, a job interview, and a date. Some elements might be the same, but the total presentation would be different. And the reason, of course, is that we're sending out different messages about ourselves by the way we present ourselves.

These are clearly *ethos*-based messages; we seek to establish credibility in various social settings by trying to dress appropriately for those settings. When we succeed, we send out coded messages that we belong in the setting, and when we fail, we send out clear messages to that effect as well. And what is true in social settings, with clothing and appearance, is true with legal arguments as well.

If you make the simple translation of personal clothing to clothing for your legal analysis, you'll see what I mean. The argument itself is likely a logically based argument, relying on legal authorities carefully selected to fit neatly into the facts and theory of your case. Even though you can't make legal arguments overtly based on emotion, it's quite possible that if you have facts that have emotional appeal, you'll at least have taken those into account as you were structuring your theory of the case and writing your analysis. Credibility was partly taken care of by the simple fact that you're a lawyer, but you can solidify and enhance your credibility by respecting the genre requirements of the type of document you're writing, and by clothing your analysis in those requirements, and you can just as easily destroy your credibility by failing to respect those genre requirements.

A novice legal writer with experience in other areas, for instance, might misunderstand what is meant by the term "memorandum" in the legal context. In some areas—politics, for instance, and some businesses—a memorandum is a short document where the writer identifies a problem and supplies a quick answer to that problem. There is no protracted analysis, no citation to authorities, no (or, at least, very little) explanation of the reasons for the conclusion; there is just the issue and the solution to the problem posed by the issue. In law, by contrast, the cultural context in which we work has the expectation that you will show support for everything you say, and that you'll reach your conclusion only after a full working out of all the issues and—at least as important—a display of the ways in which those issues were worked out. In law, as in mathematics, the notion of "showing your work" is paramount.

Given the conflict between the two cultures, a novice legal writer who has extensive political experience might get into trouble if all the writer's memos were short and, from a legal perspective, insubstantial.[5] It might well be that the writer had done all the necessary research to reach a correct conclusion and that the answer described by the memo was, in fact, correct. But because the memo didn't conform to the genre requirements of law—because it was, in a sense, improperly "dressed" for the situation in which it found itself—it, and its writer, might be discounted. Once the same writer learned how to present legal information, the writer's memos might well be well-received and the writer's work praised. Without that understanding, though—without understanding how to encode the document with the rhetorical messages needed for the writer's work to be taken seriously—the writer might be dismissed or not offered a job.

So rhetoric is something you understand at an instinctive level, and its effects are, in part, built into the writing advice you've been given all your life. You have to spell words correctly, for example, not because the person with whom you're communicating won't understand what you're saying (the human brain has a remarkable capacity to understand words and to correct spelling errors or even to fill in gaps when letters in words are omitted), but because that person won't take anything you say seriously. The same holds true for correct grammar, careful attention to information organization, and even to the type and size of the font you use; it might not seem fair, but the cleverest thought will be ignored, misunderstood, or discounted if it is not properly expressed.

Rhetoric is much more than spelling, grammar, and typography, of course, and we'll encounter rhetorical issues throughout this book. But these things all carry rhetor-

---

5. My thanks to Kelly Iverson for suggesting this example.

ical implications and you will need to pay attention to all of them in order to make sure that your work carries the correctly encoded messages that support, not undermine, the analysis you're presenting. The rhetorical messages you send might not be as important as the quality of your thinking on a legal issue, but they come a close second.

Exercises

1. Pick a commercial you can find on television or the internet and identify the rhetorical messages encoded into it. Ideally, pick a commercial advertising a law firm or lawyer.
2. Find a dramatic television show or movie based on the practice of law, or in which some of the principal characters are lawyers, and analyze the rhetorical messages built into the show's costume and set design. How influential do you think shows and movies like this are in framing the public's sense of lawyers and law practice?
3. Analyze some of the reading you're doing for your other classes this week and identify rhetorical devices being used by the writer. How successful was the writer in using these devices to persuade you of the correctness of the result under discussion?

Focus Questions

1. Had you studied rhetoric before coming to law school? Were you expecting a discussion of rhetoric in a legal writing book?
2. Did anything surprise you in the discussion of the commercial? Do you agree that the commercial appears to be sending out messages that go further than, or are slightly different from, the textual message in the commercial?
3. Have you ever seen a lawyer being interviewed on television? Was the lawyer filmed in front of a bookcase full of law books? Do you think the lawyer uses those books for legal research? If not, why are those books still to be found in the law firm? What message are those books designed to send?
4. Do you think carefully about the metaphors you use in your everyday conversation? In your writing? Did you identify "inoculate" as a metaphor before the discussion of its metaphorical uses? Did that discussion make you more aware of the metaphors you use?
5. How do you use the concepts of *logos*, *ethos*, and *pathos* in your daily life? Have you consciously thought of the ways in which your appearance sends coded messages about who you are to those whom you meet during the day? Will you change the way you dress for class, for an interview, or for any other occasion, based on what you now know about visual rhetoric?
6. How does what you've learned about visual rhetoric affect the way you will write as a lawyer? Has this chapter suggested ways in which you might think about the written documents you produce? Is the notion of a document being "dressed" for a specific purpose helpful to you?

Chapter 4

The Reader As Client

What You Should Learn from This Chapter

This chapter introduces the client as the crucial figure in the lawyering process. And it discusses how the lawyer/client relationship acts as a helpful metaphor for the writing process.

After reading this chapter, you should:

- have considered the ways in which the writer/reader relationship mirror the lawyer/client relationship;
- have considered the crucial role that empathy plays in the act of communicating in writing;
- have considered the idea that law is about the client, not the lawyer; and
- have considered the dehumanizing nature of legal study and why this is destructive to the work lawyers undertake on behalf of clients once in practice.

One of the difficult things about the first year in law school is that hardly anything students do reminds them of what they imagined lawyers do. In particular, the idea of representing a client is almost completely missing from the process. Instead, students read cases before class, go to class, take notes, participate in class discussion, go home, read cases, and so on.

You get a sense of the lawyering process in your legal writing and research classes, where much of the work is centered on working on documents for hypothetical clients who have problems that lawyers can solve. But the writing act actually provides a more direct, and more specific, metaphor for lawyering that often goes unnoticed, yet is crucial to becoming an effective legal writer or, in fact, a writer of anything. Every writer serves the reader in the same way that a lawyer serves a client, and therefore the act of writing for a reader is directly related to the lawyer/client relationship.

That might seem like an odd claim, so let me explore it a little in order to explain it. At its core, the act of writing words intended to be read by someone else is an attempt to communicate over time. I am sitting at a desk on January 5, 2013, writing these words you are reading I don't know when, but certainly later in time than today. And since I'm trying to persuade you that my claim about the core of the writing act, I'm trying to communicate an idea to you using the time-shifting medium of recording my words in writing.

So far, so good. It's certainly not the way we usually think of writing, but I'm hoping that you're still with me. Less obvious, perhaps, is the concept that writers must expect the communication between writer and reader to be a conversation. In other words, the communication happens in both directions. But since you haven't yet read the words I'm writing, I have to anticipate your part of the conversation and write my response to it. It's a strange form of communication, but communication none the less. And if the writer is really attuned to the reader's needs, it can be a thrilling experience for both.

Writing makes the perfect place to practice your empathetic skills, because just as in the case of the lawyer trying to understand the true motivation of her client, the writer must try to understand how the reader is responding to the writer's work and must try to supply the information the reader requires precisely at the moment the reader requires it. Writing, then, is a quintessentially empathetic act.

And because writers should think at all times about the needs of their readers, and should be evaluating their writing to make sure that it best serves the needs of their readers, the writing process serves as a valuable metaphor for the attorney/client relationship. If you keep the notion of your reader as a client in mind constantly as you write, two things will happen. First, your writing will improve dramatically because you will be writing for someone, rather than to satisfy a course requirement, and because you will be asking yourself the right questions as you write ("Does this best deliver the information I'm trying to convey in a way that the reader will understand it?" "What might a reader who doesn't know anything about this subject need to know in order to understand the point I'm making here?" "Have I given the reader that information early enough so that this point will make sense?" and so on). And second, your lawyering skills will be much more developed at the time when you're called upon to use them. You will be better able to listen to what your client is really asking for when you're retained, and you'll be better able to listen to all the stated and implied messages inherent in all human communications— between you and the client, you and your partners, you and the lawyers on the other side, you and the judge, and so on. In short, you'll be a better lawyer.

Perhaps the most important thing you can gain from an empathetic approach to writing, though, is a sense of perspective. This is something that's very difficult to get at law school but it's very important to you as a legal writer. To understand what I mean, let's think about the explicit and implicit messages sent out about law school— all law schools—that can distort your perspective.

First, law school is relatively difficult to get into. We require you to have an impressive undergraduate GPA, we require you to score high on the LSAT, a special test designed just to test your ability to cope with the rigors of law school, and any number of books, TV shows, and movies have told you that law school is very hard even for those with the impressive credentials to get in. Those who survive law school, these messages tell you, are the intellectual elite.

Once in law school, we spend the first year teaching you about the law. This hardly seems surprising: why else did you come to law school? But think a little more about how we teach you. You learn from cases decided by state and federal appellate courts— very occasionally from the trial-level courts—and you learn from those cases the legal principles that they either developed or clarified. Rarely, though, do you learn anything about the people involved in the case, why they did what they did in order to be before the court or what happened to them as the result of the circumstances discussed in the case. We study the limited set of facts revealed to us by the court opinion (and often edited down even further by the casebook editors), but not to learn anything about the human circumstances of the case, but rather so that law school professors can change the facts subtly in order to see how well you understand the underlying doctrinal principles revealed by the case: "supposing the facts were this way instead of what happened in the case, would the court rule the same way? How about this way? And this?" It's a technique with which you're already doubtless familiar, and if you're not, you will be soon.[1]

In fact, we're so interested in the law of these cases, and so little interested in the people, that often they lose their names; they become "plaintiff" and "defendant," or sometimes even "p" and "d." This is, perhaps, the inevitable result of using real cases as educational tools; they became corpses laid out on an operating table in order for us to learn the anatomy of the law. Medical students don't learn the identity and life history of the bodies on which they work, why should law students care about such things when they learn about the law?

Well, there's a very good reason, one that you might have experienced if you've been to see a doctor. It can happen that doctors get so bound up in treating the diseases they see that they forget to treat the patient, and they start to make decisions about treatment that might conflict with what the patient wants—planning a regimen of aggressive chemotherapy, for example, in the case of a cancer patient who is more interested in improving the quality of the remainder of his or her life than in extending the length of that life by a few weeks. Just as with lawyers failing to understand the actual desires of their clients, situations like this are caused by a failure to empathize with the patient and to understand that it is the patient, not the doctor, who should make the final decision about treatment and it is the doctor's job to give the patient as much information as possible in order to allow that decision to be as fully informed as possible.

Never having been a medical student, I can't say this with any certainty, but I assume that one of the reasons for this type of breakdown of the doctor/patient relationship is the same as it is for some breakdowns of the lawyer/client relationship: both professional schools encourage their students to focus on their roles in the process at the expense of developing an understanding of the ways in which it's the person, not the professional, who deals with the consequences of the professional's actions. If a patient visits a doctor to discuss the amputation of a limb and the doctor talks about what "we" should do, the patient is entitled to remind the doctor that unless the doctor's limbs are also in jeopardy, the use of "we" is inappropriate. Similarly, lawyers who speak of "our" case or the strategy "we" will follow are inappropriately identifying with the client's case. Empathy does not mean substitution, and unless the lawyer pays the settlement or serves the prison sentence, it is the client's case, not the lawyer's.

---

1. Oddly, the lawyers involved in the cases we study also usually disappear completely. These lawyers, who often framed the issues discussed by the courts and who might have suggested the analysis adopted by the courts, are made to disappear by the judges who wrote the opinions and the casebook editors who included the cases in the books, even though the work the lawyers did is precisely what we're training you to do. My thanks to Professor Elizabeth Lenhart for this observation.

This kind of behavior is easy to understand when we consider how law schools go about teaching law students. When we take the people involved in cases almost completely out of the picture, treating them as ciphers necessary for the law to have a factual framework on which to hang, but irrelevant in any meaningful way to the development of the law, it is an easy next step to assume that the law is really all about lawyers, and that clients are an inconvenient necessity who bring us cases and who pay our bills but who should otherwise stay in the background while we practice the law for our own intellectual gratification and professional development.

As you might expect, though, that's not an attitude that goes down well with clients. And we need to think a little more about the term "client" before we fully understand the ramifications of this kind of behavior. The traditional view of "client" is the non-lawyer who comes to a lawyer's office seeking help because he or she has, or wants to have, an interaction with the legal system and needs a lawyer's help to navigate through that interaction. It might be that the person wants a will, or wants to buy a house, or wants to enter into a business contract, or the interaction might concern the civil or criminal justice system, but traditionally, a lawyer's "client" is thought of as a layperson who needs the lawyer's expertise and advice.

That definition is too limiting, though. If we think instead of a "client" as someone who comes to you as a lawyer for help answering a question, or solving a problem, the definition expands dramatically. We could now include judges, who need your help in answering the questions posed by litigation that is before them, or juries who need your help reaching their verdicts. The definition could include lawyers on the other side of a negotiation or a case, who need your help understanding your client's position so a successful compromise can be achieved. And the definition could include a partner or senior associate at your firm who gives you an assignment to work on. All these people, at one time or other, could be your "client," and practicing an empathetic response to understand what those clients need, and giving them the information they need, when they need it, to answer their questions or resolve their problems, is a vital part of being a lawyer.

And that gets us back to treating your reader as your client. In fact, all the various people who read your writing are your "clients" in a sense, and practicing good writing technique by thinking about how best to inform your reader about your analysis, or persuade your reader of your position—in essence, how you will serve your client's needs—is a very good way of working on your ability to empathize with your client, whichever form your "client" might take. And the good news is that you can start doing this now, in the first year of law school, when empathy might not appear to be as important as it assuredly will be later in your professional lives. To that end, let's think a little more closely about empathy in the next chapter.

Exercise

Consider some documents you have read recently in different contexts: a letter or other communication from your law school about your first year, a newspaper or magazine article, a work of fiction, a work of non-fiction, a law school casebook, and this book. In particular, think about whether the writer of those documents had you in mind when the document was written, and whether the writer attempted to engage you in the type of asynchronous conversation described in this chapter. How successful was the writer in predicting what information you might seek and providing that information at the right time? Do you feel as if you were that writer's client?

Focus Questions

1. Are you persuaded by the idea that the writer/reader relationship can serve as a metaphor for the attorney/client relationship? Had you considered the idea of a writer/reader relationship before?

2. Have you considered the idea that writing a document is a way of conducting an asynchronous conversation with a reader? Have you ever felt that you were a participant in such a conversation? Do you think that the ability to draw you into such a conversation is the mark of a good writer?

3. As you consider documents you've written before now, have you tried to imagine what questions readers might have as they read your writing? Do you think you will try place yourself more in the reader's place now when you write?

4. Have you considered a lawyer's perspective on the importance of our profession to the legal system might be artificially skewed? Are lawyers integral to the legal system?

5. Have you ever found yourself forgetting that the cases you've been studying happened to real people? Do you understand why the text refers to the law as reducing litigants to ciphers during our study of the law? Is this appropriate or should we be more concerned about those whose lives we study?

6. Have you ever been a lawyer's client? If so, did you experience the sense that the lawyer thought your case was more the lawyer's case than yours? How did that make you feel? If you have not been a client, how do you think this experience would make you feel?

7. Is the notion that the law is about and for lawyers something with which you agree or disagree? How will your answer be different from the way your client might answer that question? Does that difference matter? Why or why not?

Chapter 5

Empathy, Lawyering, and Writing

What You Should Learn from This Chapter

This chapter[1] explores the role of empathy in legal writing. It concludes that empathy is a core lawyering skill and supports that conclusion by considering three situations in which empathy, or its lack, had a role in the outcome of trials.

After reading this chapter, you should have considered:

- the idea that empathy is an important skill for lawyers;
- the idea that lawyers must be able to both think like lawyers and think like non-lawyers in order to communicate effectively with other lawyers, judges, and non-lawyers;
- how jurors construct their own narratives after listening to the narratives offered at trial by the lawyers on both sides, and how these juror narratives decide trial outcomes;
- the effects of applied empathy in the practice of law; and
- how a writer's empathy with you as a reader can enhance your reading experience, and considered how important it will be for you as a writer to maintain a sense of empathy for your readers.

"Empathy" is an often misused and misunderstood word in this country. It's a word that's been bounced around like a political basketball, with a president saying that empathy is "an essential ingredient for [a judge to arrive] at just decisions and outcomes"[2] and a senator saying, in reply, that "this view—that a judge should use his or her personal feelings about a particular group or issues to decide a case ... stands in stark contrast to the impartiality that we expect in the American courtroom."[3] Without trying to inject ourselves into the debate about whether or not empathy is essential for a

---

1. Much of this chapter is based in an article I wrote in 2011. Ian Gallacher, *Thinking Like Non-Lawyers: Why Empathy Is a Core Lawyering Skill and Why Legal Education Should Change to Reflect Its Importance*, 8 Leg. Comm. & Rhetoric: JALWD 109 (2011).
2. President Obama said this in his remarks about the process to replace Justice Souter on the Supreme Court bench.
3. Senator Jeff Sessions of Alabama said this in the Weekly Republican Address of June 6, 2009.

judge or not, let's try to demystify empathy and talk about why it's such an important concept. In particular, let's talk about why empathy is so important to lawyers and to writers.

At its simplest, "empathy" is the act of placing oneself in another person's position in order to understand what that person might be experiencing. It's not the easiest thing to do, and perhaps the idea that we can place ourselves sufficiently into someone else's situation to think and feel as they do is a little optimistic. But the essential idea of this definition—that empathy allows you to put yourself into the mind of someone else and see things from that person's perspective—is central to our understanding of what empathy should be. And when you understand this aspect of empathy, its importance for lawyers and writers can readily be seen. As lawyers, we seek to understand what our clients want and we try to accomplish those goals as effectively and efficiently as possible. And as writers, we try to understand what our readers need and expect from the documents we write and supply them with what they need at the moment they need it. Both of these tasks require an empathetic understanding of our audience. Viewed in this way, empathy is a crucially important lawyering skill.

1. Empathy and Logic

The idea of empathy as a skill all lawyers must have isn't what you might expect from your first year at law school. You're taught to think coolly, analytically, and dispassionately about the law. This is why we transform people into algebraic symbols when we talk about cases; instead of saying "Mr. Smith was driving his car," we say things like "X was driving a car" and we show little concern for the people whose lives we consider when we read the cases that describe likely some of the most important events of their lives: we usually show little concern for Mrs. Palsgraf when we consider whether she should have been able to recover against the Long Island Railroad Company, and we rarely ask why Mr. Tompkins was walking down the tracks of the Erie Railroad.

And maybe that's as it should be. It's important for you, as young lawyers, to be able to think carefully and analytically about the law and to be able to construct a theory of the case, based on the facts and the relevant law, which will withstand all logical challenges. There's nothing wrong, and almost everything right, in your being able to think like a lawyer.

But you need to be able to think like a non-lawyer as well as to think like a lawyer, because usually our clients, and almost always our jurors—if we have to litigate cases at trial—are not lawyers. And in order to be able to understand what our clients need, and what will persuade a juror, we need to remember what it means to think like non-lawyers as well. Good lawyering, then, combines logic with empathy; it combines the ability to think like lawyers when necessary and to think like non-lawyers as well.

For writers, though, empathy is always a crucial skill, regardless of whether they're legal writers or otherwise. All writers must consider their readers and write to serve those readers' needs. Lawyers, of course, are writing documents in order to serve their clients' needs, but if they're writing to persuade a reader of something then they can only do this by empathizing with their readers.

It's impossible to do this unless you can successfully imagine what your reader needs when reading a document. In part, this skill depends on an understanding of the cultural and genre requirements of the document you're writing. That's why we spend so much time talking about the structure and format of legal documents in legal writing classes: if you can't reproduce the look and structure of a particular type of legal document, you will find it difficult to persuade a legal reader that you have considered the reader's needs. In other words, in order to be accepted as a legal writer, you have to write things that look and are structured the way legal writers write documents.

So far, so good. If this were all that is required of a legal writer, we could teach you how to structure and format documents that look and feel like legal documents, and give you some instruction about the technical requirements expected of legal writers—accurately spelled, grammatically conservative, carefully punctuated documents, for example—and that would be that. But the idea of legal writers empathizing with their reader goes much deeper than this.

You're an adult, so you should be suspicious of any view of the world that is so monochromatic that only one viewpoint is allowed. By your age, you're doubtless aware that hardly anything is a binary proposition—on or off, right or wrong, black or white. Certainly you're learning in law school that almost everything can be argued in a number of different ways, depending on what facts you emphasize, how you interpret the law, and what cases are included in the analysis. If this weren't the case, lawyers would hardly have any work to do. If the world worked on a yes or no basis, clients wouldn't need lawyers to make arguments for them because there would be no ambiguities and the answers to questions would be, if not pre-determined, then at least readily apparent.

But life isn't like that. Ambiguities surround us every day and hardly anything is one way or the other, black or white, logic or empathy. In fact, lawyers need to be able to construct logical positions—whether in support of a litigation position or to support a contract negotiation, or to support a creative tax deduction—but must also be able to test those positions empathetically to see how effective they will be with their intended audience.

2. Empathy in Action

In litigation, lawyers develop case theories which allow them to fit the facts and law together into one coherent package. Because "case theory" sounds a little sterile and dry, more and more lawyers are using the term "story" to describe this process, although that word has some dangerous implications that suggest fiction and invented details that are, of course, out of place in the legal context. A compromise term is "narrative," which is a fancier and longer way of saying "story" but, because it carries less baggage with it, might be a better word to use.

A lawyer's narrative (and the concept can extend beyond litigation to cover all areas of practice) must encompass all the known facts and law concerning a client's situation and explain them all in a convincing manner. But your narrative is not alone in seeking to convince. Lawyers working for "the other side," whether in litigation or in a negotiation, or some other setting, will have constructed their own narrative, seeking to explain the same facts and law in a convincing manner that's most helpful to their client.

This plays out most obviously in a trial setting, where one side argues that the evidence suggests one interpretation and the other side suggests a contrary interpretation. In a criminal case, the prosecution calls witnesses and introduces evidence to support its narrative that the defendant is guilty, and the defense might offer its own counternarrative to suggest that the defendant isn't guilty.[4] In a civil case, the dueling narratives frequently concern the question of liability, although they can be about contract interpretation or any number of other things as well.

Both sides present their narratives to the jury, which then has to decide which narrative is the most convincing. But we sometimes forget that the jury reaches its decision by constructing its own narrative and then seeing which of the parties' narratives most closely match its own.[5] That's why empathy is such a crucial skill for lawyers: without it, a lawyer might believe that the most logical, lawyer-like, interpretation of the evidence is the most compelling narrative and that ignores the fact that the jury is almost certainly not comprised of lawyers. Thinking like a lawyer, in other words, won't help you to understand how nonlawyers think. Let's look at some examples to see how this might work in the real world.

A. Criminal Trials

Imagine a case involving a murdered woman. Her estranged husband is the immediate suspect but there are no eyewitnesses to the crime and she is not found at home. There is a strong amount of circumstantial evidence tying the husband to the case, and some direct evidence as well. But the prosecution feels that the strongest evidence is that of the frequent calls to the police from the couples' home in the months prior to the murder. The woman had called the police, alleging domestic abuse, and there was evidence of such abuse on a few occasions.

The prosecution's narrative in this case might be that the murder was an extension, an escalation, of the prior domestic abuse. What had been shouting, and then hitting, had now become murder. The prosecutor might therefore seek a jury that, the prosecutor believes, would be persuaded by such a narrative; a jury that would construct a narrative that would closely match the prosecution's narrative of domestic abuse turned deadly.

But if the prosecution misreads the cultural context of the jury, that theory might not be persuasive. If, for example, the jury was made up principally of members who would be disinclined to accept that theory, the jury's narrative would conflict so badly with the prosecution's narrative that it would be almost irrelevant what defense narrative was offered because the presumption of innocence would operate to acquit the defendant.

If this example appears to be far-fetched, it is—according to some accounts, at least—what happened in the criminal trial of O.J. Simpson. While the defense offered numerous possible theories to support its position that Mr. Simpson was not guilty, the posttrial comments of various jurors suggested that the jury simply did not accept the

---

4. Because of the presumption of innocence, a defendant is not required to produce any evidence to support a not-guilty narrative and if the defense lawyer believes that the prosecution has failed to overcome its heavy burden of overcoming that presumption by the "beyond a reasonable doubt" standard, the lawyer might simply rest the case without calling witnesses or introducing evidence.

5. We don't have time or space to explore this phenomenon in more detail, but it is one of the more fascinating and—for trial lawyers—one of the more frustrating aspects of practice that this third, jury, narrative typically controls the outcome of trials.

prosecution's theory, or narrative, that domestic abuse had escalated into murder in this case. And there was at least some reason for the prosecution to have known that this narrative was likely not going to gain much support with the jury early on in the case.[6]

B. Civil Litigation

Let's consider another example, this one from the civil litigation area. Imagine a company that makes a painkilling drug that proves particularly effective in the treatment of arthritis pain. Millions take the drug and it quickly becomes one of the bestselling painkillers in the market. Reports begin to surface, though, of complications associated with heart disease and the drug is withdrawn after studies reveal that the drug is associated with an increased risk of the formation of blood clots which can lead to sudden heart attacks and patient death. During its four years on the market, the drug raised $2.5 billion in sales for the manufacturer.

The widow of a former consumer sues the manufacturer after her husband dies of a heart attack caused, according to his autopsy, by an arrhythmia. The autopsy also revealed that the plaintiff's husband had suffered from hardening of the arteries. Neither of these conditions is associated with blood clots, something which both parties agree is the only risk posed by the drug. The plaintiff relies on the testimony of the doctor who performed the autopsy, who testifies that she found no blood clot but that a blood clot could have been dissolved during the CPR the patient received in an attempt to revive him.

The plaintiff's lawyer develops a narrative that shows the deceased husband as an active and fit man in the prime of life who took the drug to help manage the pain associated with his regular running, and that shows the defendant manufacturer as a large corporation more concerned with its profits than with the safety of those who took its drugs. The defendant, by contrast, proposes a narrative based on the logical position that since the plaintiff can show no evidence other than vague speculation that the drug caused the plaintiff's injuries, the defendant shouldn't be found liable. In other words, the plaintiff proposes a narrative designed to appeal to its belief that the jury will be suspicious of the motives of a large pharmaceutical manufacturer, and the defense proposes a logical narrative that should appeal to any lawyer: no causation means no liability.

This is a radically foreshortened description of *Merck & Co. v. Ernst*, 2008 WL 2201769 (Tex. App.—Houston 14th Dist. May 29, 2008), *rev'd*, 296 S.W. 3d 81 (Tex.App.—Houston 14th Dist. 2009). In that case, the jury returned a verdict in favor of the plaintiff and awarded $253 million in actual and punitive damages.[7] But when the case was appealed and considered by a panel of judges, the jury's verdict was overturned and a defense verdict was entered. The appellate court concluded that the testimony about the possibility of an unseen blood clot being broken up during CPR was "mere speculation" and that since the plaintiff had failed to prove causation, there could be no finding of liability.

It is as impossible to tell why the jury did what it did in this case as it is to know why the jury in the O.J. Simpson criminal trial ruled as it did. But the *Merck* case offers us

---

6. Gallacher, *Thinking Like Non-Lawyers*, 8 J ALWD at 125–30.

7. *Id.* at 130–133.

an interesting contrast in the way a jury, comprised of non-lawyers, and a panel of law-trained judges responded to the narratives offered by both parties. The different results suggest that the plaintiff's narrative was empathetically attuned to the jury's narrative, but that the defendant's logical and legalistic narrative was better suited to the judges' narrative. One possible lesson from this case, and from the Simpson trial as well, is that lawyers must be careful to develop case theories, or narratives, that are not just well suited to the facts and law of the case but that are also constructed in such a way that they will persuade the audience for which they are intended, and that the lawyers should try hard to put themselves into the minds of their audience in order to understand how the people comprising that audience think about the world. And that's why empathy is a very important skill for lawyers.

C. Applied Empathy

One last example, this one of a stunningly effective piece of trial advocacy and a powerful example of applied empathy. And while the facts of this case are disturbing, and the testimony you're about to read is graphic and describes a tragic incident in the country's history, they also show a skillful lawyer who reacted quickly, effectively, and empathetically to a difficult lawyering challenge.

The case followed the Triangle Shirtwaist Fire in New York City in March 1911. The fire, forgotten today by many, was New York's worst disaster until the terrorist attacks of September 11, 2001. The facts, briefly, were these.

The Triangle Waist Company was the largest manufacturer of women's blouses in New York City, occupying three floors of the Asch Building in Greenwich Village. On Saturday, March 25, 1911, close to the end of the work day, a fire broke out. It spread quickly and 146 people — 123 women and 43 men — were killed. An investigation into the fire revealed that the exit doors had been locked. The two owners of the Triangle Waist Company — Max Blanck and Isaac Harris — were prosecuted for manslaughter because they caused the doors to be locked. To defend them, Harris and Blank hired one of the most successful trial lawyers of his time, Max Steuer.

To convict Harris and Blank, the prosecution needed to identify at least one victim who died as a direct result of the door being locked and they needed a witness who could testify to the circumstances of the victim's death. Incredibly, they found such a victim in Margaret Schwartz, and a witness to her death in Kate Alterman, a woman about whom little is known except that she was working for the Triangle Waist Company on March 25, 1911 and was believed to have been a recent immigrant to the country. No one who heard her testimony doubted for a second that she had been in the building when it caught fire.

The easiest way to understand what Max Steuer was facing at trial is to reproduce the portion of Kate Alterman's testimony that concerned the fire.

Q. Margaret Swartz [sic] was with you at this time?

A. At this time, yes sir.

Q. Then where did you go?

A. Then I went to the toilet room, Margaret disappeared from me, and I wanted to go up Greene Street side, but the whole door was in flames, so

I went and hide [sic.] myself in the toilet rooms, and then I went out right away from the toilet rooms and bent my face over the sink, and then I ran to the Washington side elevator, but there was a big crowd and I couldn't pass through there. Then I noticed some one [sic.], a whole crowd, around the door, and I saw Bernstein, the manager's brother trying to open the door, and there was Margaret near him. Bernstein tried the door, he couldn't open it, and then Margaret began to open that door. I take her on one side—I pushed her on the side and I said, "Wait, I will open that door." I tried, I pulled the handle in and out, all ways, and I couldn't open it. She pushed me on the other side, got hold of the handle and then she tried. And then I saw her bending down on her knees, and her hair was loose, and the trail of her dress was a little far from her, and then a big smoke came, and I couldn't see, I just know it was Margaret, and I said "Margaret," and she didn't reply. I left Margaret, I turned my head on the side, and I noticed the trail of her dress and the ends of her hair begin to burn. Then I ran in, in a small dressing room that was on the Washington side, there was a big crowd and I went out from there, stood in the center of the room between the machines and between the examining tables. I noticed afterwards on the other side, near the Washington side windows, Bernstein, the manager's brother throwing around like a wild cat on the windows, and he was chasing his head out of the window, and pull himself back— he wanted to jump, I suppose, but he was afraid. And then I saw the flames cover him. I noticed on the Greene Street side some one else fall down on the floor and the flames cover him. And then I stood in the center of the room, and I just turned my coat on the left side with the fur to my face, the lining on the outside, got hold of a bunch of dresses that was lying on the examining table not burned yet, covered up my head and I tried to run through the flames to the Greene Street side. The whole door was a red curtain of flame, but a young lady came and she began to pull me in the back of my dress and she wouldn't let me in. I kicked her with my foot and I don't know what became of her, and I ran out through the Greene Street side door, right through the flames, on to the roof.

Q. When you were standing toward the middle of the floor had you your pocketbook with you?

A. Yes sir, my pocketbook began to burn already, but I pressed it to my heart to extinguish the fire.[8]

It's not difficult to imagine Max Steuer's problem. This is astonishingly powerful and vivid testimony now, read on paper over one hundred years after the events it describes. It must have been devastating to hear it delivered in the courtroom.

Compelling though it was, something about Ms. Alterman's testimony must have struck Steuer as odd. So after opening his cross-examination with some questions about with whom Ms. Alterman had spoken since the fire, Steuer took the illogical and po-

---

8. *Max Steuer's Cross Examination of Kate Alterman in* People v. Harris & Blank vol. 1, (*"Cross-Examination"*) 2–3 (Prof. Educ. Group 1987).

tentially disastrous—from a textbook perspective on how to try a case—step of asking her to repeat her story.[9] When she did, Ms. Alterman again used phrases like "I pressed it to my heart to extinguish the fire," and "a red curtain of fire."[10] After she was done, Steuer pointed out that Ms. Alterman hadn't said that Mr. Bernstein was jumping around "like a wildcat" and she confirmed that he was "like a wildcat."[11]

After a few more questions, Steuer asked Ms. Alterman to tell her story for a third time and when she did, she again used many of the same words and phrases to describe the events she had seen. After a lunch break, and after he had asked Ms. Alterman to confirm that she hadn't discussed her testimony with anyone, Steuer asked her to tell her story for a fourth time. And again, she used many of the same expressions, and though she then testified that she could tell her story using different words, she left the stand without doing so.[12]

At closing, Steuer was able to argue to the jury that Ms. Alterman must have prepared her testimony with someone in advance because the language she used, and re-used so precisely, could not have been her own. He argued further that her testimony was not her honest memory of what happened but that it was someone else's version which Ms. Alterman had memorized and had repeated, verbatim, several times to the jury.[13] This was probably further than the logical limit of what the jury heard; it was apparent that Ms. Alterman had rehearsed her testimony but that did not mean that her testimony did not describe what she saw during the fire. Nonetheless, the jury was apparently persuaded and acquitted both defendants.

Steuer's response to Ms. Alterman's testimony was doubly empathetic. First, he was able to listen to the words she used and while he was considering them for their legal and emotional impact on the jury, he was also realizing that her use of language suggested that her language had been rehearsed. That realization—which must have come simultaneously with Ms. Alterman's testimony—gave Steuer the chance to impeach testimony which seemed certain to convict his clients, but this left him with a difficult tactical problem.

A typical destructive cross-examination, in which the attorney accuses the witness of lying when she said she had not prepared her testimony with someone beforehand and further accuses the witness of testifying to things that didn't happen, would have been disastrous in this case; Ms. Alterman's testimony was so compelling that the jury would have been horrified if Steuer attacked her with accusations of lying and would have likely been protective of her and her testimony. So Steuer's second remarkable act of empathy was to place himself in the minds of the jurors, understand how they would likely respond to the standard lawyer's tactic of bullying the witness, and to come up with a strategy that might persuade them that Ms. Alterman's testimony had been coached without actually telling them as much.

Max Steuer was a remarkable trial attorney. Very few lawyers, then or now, would be so quick as to hear not just what was being said and understand the effect it would

---

9. You should never do this, most lawyers would agree, because you're giving the jury a second chance to hear this devastating story told by an extremely sympathetic witness.

10. *Cross-Examination*, at 8.

11. *Id.*

12. *Id.* at 13–15.

13. *Cross-Examination*, at 2.

have, but also to hear how it was being said, what that must mean, and to develop a strategy—in minutes—that would allow him to destroy the impact of the testimony without destroying the witness in public. And it was his advanced sense of empathy that allowed him to pull off one of the most unlikely results in American trial history.

But while Steuer's skills were remarkable, they point out the importance of empathy as something all lawyers should possess and exercise. All lawyers, no matter what their practice area, must be sensitive to what they are told, how they are being told it, and whether the information they are given makes not just logical but also emotional sense. And they must be able to construct theories—narratives, if you will—that make not just logical but also emotional sense. In order to do this they need to practice the logical skills acquired in law school through long hours of careful and methodical analysis of the Constitution, case law, statutes, regulations, and all the other sources of law they studied, but they also need to retain and enhance their empathetic skills, responding thoughtfully and carefully to not just the message but the medium in which it is conveyed, and they need to practice their communication skills so that they can send out messages that are carefully and empathetically calibrated to align logic and emotion in one persuasive package.

All of this takes time. Very few reach this level of communication skill without effort and practice. But we are all capable of decoding the multiple messages enclosed within all forms of communication and we are all capable of sending those complex messages ourselves. Indeed, we are incapable of communicating in any other way. All that's required for lawyers is that they not allow the empathetic sense that allows them to understand and send coded the messages contained in their communications to be trained out of them. And that's where writing and, especially, reading come in.

3. Empathy and Reading

We've already discussed the importance of empathy to writers. The ability to craft writing that meets the reader's needs and that anticipates, and answers, questions the reader might have at exactly the moment the reader asks them is central to skillful writing, whether it be legal writing, fiction, non-fiction, or any other style. But unless you have a strong background in writing before coming to law school, you're much more likely to be familiar with this concept from the reader's perspective. Have you read something that seemed to flow easily and quickly, drawing you through the document and making it easy to turn the pages? Did you find yourself asking questions of the document only to find them answered almost as soon as the question formed in your mind? If so, this was likely an enjoyable experience for you as a reader—the kind of experience you want your readers to have when they read what you've written.

By contrast, have you read some documents that were difficult, almost impossible, to read, documents where the writer seemed almost to be hiding information from you rather than revealing it, and where the writer seemed to be actively hostile towards you rather than welcoming and helpful? How did that make you feel towards the writer and the point the writer was trying to make, or the fictional world the writer was trying to create? Do you want your readers to feel that way towards you?

Once you understand the idea that a writer is, or should be, trying to engage you in a conversation, many things about the writing process become easier to understand. Once you realize that you have an active role to play in the process—that your questions, input, and engagement are vital to the act of communication between you and the writer and that the writer has anticipated, and relies upon, your engagement in order to fulfill the document's purpose—then the idea of writer's empathy becomes much easier to understand and the good habits you've appreciated in other writers can more readily become your good habits as a writer yourself.

And you can learn and reinforce these lessons from anything you read. In this sense, those who argue that there is no such thing as "legal writing," only good writing and bad writing, might have a point. Because at this fundamental level, the genre of writing, or the subject matter of the particular document, is unimportant: all good writers share the same desire to engage their readers in active communication, and are sensitive to their reader's responses to the word choices and organizational decisions they make. All good writers have a strong empathetic sense for the effect words will convey, and will select and organize those words so as to convey not just their direct surface meanings but also their deeper, emotional meanings that will, if the writer was sufficiently skillful, convey themselves just as directly to the reader as the dictionary meaning of each word.

Reading—and especially reading fiction—can help us develop and exercise our sense of empathy. Literature—and by that word I intend a very wide definition to include high-level works of literary art as well as genre fiction like detective, romance, or science fiction novels—allows us to experience what the writer wants us to believe is the experience of the characters, whether they be good or bad, male or female (or, I suppose in the case of science fiction, alien or robotic), young or old, or whatever else the character might be. We can experience the emotional highs and lows the characters experience, but at a safe distance that allows us to engage fully in the emotion for the duration of our reading session but allow us to disengage once we stop reading and reflect on what we have experienced.

That, in a nutshell, is the empathetic experience and its importance to lawyers: we place ourselves into the mind of the character in order to experience, in a way, what that character experiences, and then we separate ourselves from that experience to contemplate what we learned. Once we add the consideration of how the writer produced that experience for us, and how we might adapt those techniques in our own writing, we can understand how empathy can be of professional, as well as personal, benefit to us as lawyers.

Exercise

Read the facts carefully and then work on the four assignments that follow them.

Facts

Max Burns was a 22-year-old man living in Towson, Maryland, a town close to Baltimore. Max had no close friends growing up and was later described as a "loner" in school who was frequently bullied by other children. After leaving high school, he tried to enlist for the Marine Corps but failed the physical. He then attended community college for eight months and then dropped out, working in a convenience store and living in a small apartment in Towson.

Max spent a substantial amount of his free time playing video games, in particular a so-called "first-person shooter" game called "Mercenary War." The game comes in several versions, all of them involving the activities of a fictitious group of mercenary soldiers—all former Marines and Navy SEALS—who fight various enemies when paid to do so. One version of the game is set in Central Africa, where the group—which calls itself "Merc. Group Four"—fights Islamic rebels on behalf of the government. Another version has Merc. Group Four infiltrating Iran in an attempt to save a group of hostages.

One of the consistent features of the "Mercenary War" series of games is the Islamic identity of the group's opponents, and another is the group's habit of leaving a playing card next to each of its victims as a sign of its involvement. The game is popular in many non-Islamic countries and has brought its manufacturer, Dempellen Production, named after the company's two founders John Dempster and Mary Ellenberg, many millions of dollars in sales. Dempster and Ellenberg are still actively involved with the company and both have net worths in the hundreds of millions of dollars. Dempster programmed the original "Mercenary War" game but has handed over responsibility for subsequent versions of the game to company employees.

Max had all available versions of the game. In the online version of the game he named his character Chesty Puller after the famed Marine officer. At work, Max had taken to telling people to call him "Chesty."

Over the years, Max had bought many guns including several shotguns, four 9-mm handguns, and two assault rifles. These purchases were all legal and the guns were properly registered. Other than playing with video games, Max's principal form of recreation was taking the guns to a local firing range. He talked very little with the other users of the gun range, telling them that he had bought the guns for self-defense and hinting, without actually saying, that he wanted to join the Marines and wanted to have a strong firearms background.

The owners of the gun range, who had had a chance to observe Max's skill, especially with the handguns and assault rifle, rated him no better than "adequate" until March of this year. They noted that Max appeared to be too emotional to be an especially skilled shot, that he would talk to himself as he fired, and that he would sometimes drop his gun in frustration after a particularly poor performance. The owners had several times spoken to Max strictly about the importance of gun safety and told him that such displays would not be tolerated and that if he repeated them he would be banned from the range.

In March, though, the owners noticed a change in Max. He appeared calmer and more in control when he was firing and his accuracy improved noticeably. They also noticed that Max spent less and less time practicing with the assault rifles and more time with his handguns. When asked how they would rate his shooting after March, they said he was "excellent."

Max's improvement, and his emphasis on handguns, coincided with the release of a new version of "Mercenary War," this one called "Mercenary War: Homeland Security." In this version, Merc. Group Four was hired by a wealthy

American to identify, hunt down, and kill a group of Al Qaeda-backed terrorists who had infiltrated the Washington, D.C., area. Because of the nature of the assignment, the members of Merc. Group Four decided to avoid using their longer-range weapons and used handguns instead. The guns used by the characters in the game were identical to those bought by Max.

One of the features of this game is the premium placed on covert activity and accuracy. Players who kill innocent bystanders during their "missions," or who are identified or captured, lose the game and must begin again.

In the middle of May, the local Baltimore newspaper noted the unsolved murders of six local Muslims. Each man had been shot in the head, in a manner reminiscent of an execution. The men had been killed in one location and their bodies then moved to another. On each body, the article said, the police had found a playing card in the victim's pockets. The article noted the striking similarities between the video game and the real-life crimes.

By July 1, an additional three victims had been found—all in Baltimore and its suburbs and all found with a playing card in their pockets—and the Maryland Islamic community was in an uproar. Max had stopped going to the firing range in early June and was fired from his job on June 28. His former employer later told police that his behavior, which had been erratic for a few years, had become increasingly difficult. Max had become withdrawn, had only responded to being called "Chesty," and was sullen and irritable with the customers. On June 28, Max had refused to serve a Muslim customer and had called him several offensive names. The store owner fired Max on the spot and made him leave the store immediately. He did not see Max after the incident.

On July 4, Max appeared at the fireworks display in Baltimore's Inner Harbor. He started running through the crowd, firing a handgun indiscriminately at the people gathered to watch the fireworks and, with his other hand, throwing playing cards into the air. Onlookers reported that he was shouting something about "Muslims" and "9/11" but they could not understand him clearly. Max killed eight people and wounded another 15 before police shot and killed him. Five others were killed in the crush of people attempting to flee the shootings, and 53 people were injured.

When police went to Max's apartment they found cell phone pictures of the nine murder victims and other incriminating evidence that made clear that Max was the murderer. They also found, by checking his computer, that Max had been playing "Mercenary War: Homeland Security" for more than two days straight before going to the Inner Harbor. The police have found no evidence that Max was ever seen or treated for mental illness and, in fact, have discovered no signs that Max was seen by a doctor for any reason in over three years.

The families of the murder victims—those killed in the shooting spree, and those who were killed or injured as a direct or collateral result of Max's actions—are now suing all those they consider responsible. Max himself had no assets, but the manufacturers of the three different handguns Max used are all multi-million-dollar companies and the family has sued them as well as the gun dealers who sold Max the guns.

The families are also suing Dempellen Productions and John Dempster and Mary Ellenberg. Their theory is that the "Mercenary War" series, and "Mercenary War: Homeland Security" in particular, helped Max to prepare—both practically and emotionally—for his murderous activities. They contend that Max used the game to perfect his shooting technique, and that he learned the techniques he used to kill his victims from playing the game. They also contend that the game caused him to kill his victims, and that without his involvement in the game he would not have acted as he did.

Assignment One

After thinking about the facts of this case, write a short description of your personal feelings about the suit the victims' families are pursuing. Without considering the legal issues involved, and without doing any research to determine whether the families' suit is legally viable or not, describe whether you think they should be able to prevail or not and why you believe this.

Assignment Two

Writing as a lawyer for the victims' families, construct a narrative that supports the lawsuit against Dempellen Productions and its two founders.

Assignment Three

Writing as a lawyer for Dempellen Productions, construct a narrative that opposes the lawsuit against the company and its two founders.

Assignment Four

Test your two persuasive narratives against the facts of the case to make sure they account for all relevant facts, and make sure that both arguments are logically consistent. Which narrative do you find more compelling? Does your answer align with your personal feelings about whether the families should win? How can you strengthen the weaker of the two narratives in order to make it more compelling?

Focus Questions

1. Have you thought of empathy as an important lawyering skill before now? Does this chapter persuade you that empathy is a valuable skill for lawyers or are you still unconvinced?
2. As you've been reading cases for other classes, have you given any thought to the litigants in those cases and what those people actually experienced? Have your professors emphasized the experience of those whose lives created the facts that allowed us to study the law, or have they focused primarily on the legal principles to be derived from the cases?
3. Have you considered the importance of empathy to a writer before?

4. Is the idea that a jury might form its own narrative, based on the details of a case, surprising to you? Is this something courts should encourage or discourage, or is it something that happens naturally and about which a court can do nothing?

5. Consider the case of the murdered spouse who had previously been a victim of domestic abuse. Was the prosecution's case theory persuasive to you? Why or why not? What alternative case theories might have been more, or least equally, persuasive to you?

6. In the case of the painkilling drug, what alternative case theory might the defense have attempted that might have been more persuasive to a jury? Remember that you are constructing a case theory to persuade a jury that a multi-billion-dollar corporation should not be liable to the widow of someone who was in apparent good health before taking your client's product.

7. Did you notice something strange in Ms. Alterman's testimony as you were reading it? Or does the fact that the case is from more than 100 years ago make it impossible to "hear" the words as Max Steuer heard them? Even if the nuances of Ms. Alterman's testimony can't be recaptured by a contemporary audience, does the point about having to listen carefully and empathetically to not only what you are being told but also to how you are being told it, and the effect that the telling might have on others, make sense to you?

8. Have you considered that reading fiction might be a good way to develop and exercise your sense of empathy?

Chapter 6

The Ethics of Writing

What You Should Learn from This Chapter

This chapter is about some of the ethical challenges that face legal writers. It emphasizes the primary importance of the client in law practice and maintains that the client's interests and goals must always come before the lawyer's concerns. The chapter also delves into the issue of plagiarism, both in law school and in law practice, and discusses some of the reasons for, and consequences of, plagiarism.

After reading this chapter, you should:

- have considered the idea that law is a form of service industry in which the client's needs must be served;
- have considered how the client's primary role affects some of your writing decisions;
- understand what an *ad hominem* attack is and why you should never make one;
- understand why improper factual characterization is a problem for lawyers;
- have contemplated the meaning of "plagiarism" and identified specific characteristics of "plagiarism" in your law school;
- understand why the idea of a "technical" violation of a rule or standard is not a useful concept for lawyers;
- understand why plagiarism is bad lawyering;
- understand some of the reasons for plagiarism and why they are not good reasons; and
- understand why lawyers must disclose mandatory negative authority to courts to which they are making arguments.

All lawyers should be ethical all the time. This is hardly a controversial statement; we swear an oath to act as officers of the court, and that means we have to behave honestly and according to the rules of professional conduct that are applicable to the jurisdiction in which we find ourselves. When we call someone to testify, at deposition or at trial, we require them to take an oath to tell the truth, the whole truth, and nothing but the truth, and society has a right to expect no less of us.

And yet the number of lawyer jokes that rely on the notion of lawyers being unethical, lying, cheating, and generally bad people suggests that what ought to be an uncontroversial proposition would be laughed at if aired in public. Lawyers are not a popular group with the general public: some of that likely has to do with the fact that people typically encounter us only when they're unhappy—either they feel they've been wronged and are seeking redress, they're being sued by someone who's seeking redress, they're being accused of a crime, or they feel that they're paying us too much money to draft documents that ought to be cheaper and easier to read—and maybe some of it has to do with the way lawyers are portrayed on television and in the movies. But whatever the reasons, people often don't think fondly of lawyers. And almost the last word that would come to their minds when talking about us is "ethical."

Well, there's not much we can do to change public opinion at large, but the one thing we can do is behave in a scrupulously ethical way ourselves. That might not change the public's perception of our profession as a whole, but over time, if people meet enough ethical and honest lawyers, maybe public opinion will come around. And if that isn't enough motivation for you, there's a practical benefit to being ethical: you're much less likely to be censured, sanctioned, disbarred, or fired if you're consistently ethical in your professional life.

1. The Client Comes First

The thing about law school is that it gives you a distorted sense of the lawyer's importance to the legal system. As law students, we're taught how to find, analyze, and manipulate the law to predict legal outcomes and to persuade others to believe what we want them to believe. We're taught a special guild language with many phrases in foreign languages that are so old that no one speaks them anymore and other phrases that are in English but might as well be in a foreign language because they're so difficult to understand. We're given the keys to the very powerful engine that is the law and we spend all our time learning how to get the most out of that engine.

We often forget that the law is a service industry. And while there are notable differences between us and the person who stands behind a fast-food counter and asks us if we want fries with our order, there are also notable similarities. Principal among these is the reality that, just like in a restaurant or store, the customer is always right. Except in our case, the customer has the fancier name of "client" because we're lawyers and it helps us to have a fancy name for most things.

This is a little exaggerated of course but the principal point is valid: everything we do as lawyers, we do on behalf of someone else. We work so hard, and deal with such complicated issues most of the time, that it's easy to be fooled into thinking that everything's about us, but someone is relying on us to speak, write, or negotiate on their behalf and it's their interests, not ours, that should be served by what we do.

If you're ever in doubt of this, try this simple test. Imagine you're working as a criminal defense attorney and ask yourself who goes to jail if the jury comes back with a "guilty" verdict. Or imagine you're a civil litigator and ask who gets the jury award or has to pay that award? If it's you, then you get to make all the decisions. But if your liberty or bank balance isn't directly on the line, then your range of decision-making authority is a lot more limited than you might like to believe.

You do get to make some decisions, of course. If the lawyer on the other side calls to ask you for an extension of time within which to file responses to discovery because his wife is having a baby, or because her children have some nasty illness, you can make that decision without contacting your client. But if that same lawyer calls you with a settlement offer, or a plea deal, you have no authority to accept or reject the offer; that's your client's decision to make, and even if you disagree with your client's decision you can't veto it. The client controls the case, not you.

What does this have to do with writing? Well, it explains the important advice to not use personal pronouns signifying yourself when writing as a lawyer. While you are, in fact, the person who constructs and drafts the legal arguments in a case, using "I" improperly inserts you into the analysis. Nor is it correct to speak of "our" case, what "we" think about something, or to use "me" or "my" to describe the position you're taking in the case.

This might seem like odd advice in a book where the writer has, often, used "I" or "my" in addressing you. But remember: this isn't a piece of legal writing, it's a book about legal writing, and that's a crucial difference. This book is written in an intentionally informal voice, where I use "I," contractions, and colloquial language in a calculated attempt to communicate more directly with my reader than I would ever consider in a piece of legal advocacy.

2. Don't Plagiarize

Plagiarism is one of those subjects no one likes to talk about. It's much more enjoyable for everyone concerned to speak of the positive aspects of legal writing and it's hardly any fun to speak of the negative ones. And plagiarism is certainly a negative subject; in most law schools, a student who is proven to have plagiarized will receive, at a minimum, a significant sanction and a note in the student's permanent record. When a state bar contacts a law school about that student's character and fitness, it's likely to be informed about the plagiarism and that, on its own, might be enough for denial of bar membership.

And yet once a member of the bar, a law student might find that behavior that would have been punished in law school appears to go on every day in practice. If lawyers can copy the work of others, they might think, why can't law students? The issues are complicated and the answers might not seem adequate, but since plagiarism is always related to writing, it seems reasonable for us to have a conversation about those issues here.

3. Plagiarism in Law School

There's a simple, but unsatisfying, way of thinking about law school plagiarism: it's against the rules, so don't do it. This is like a child asking why something is forbidden and being told "because." It resolves the immediate question of whether you can or can't do something, but isn't very informative about the reasons. And while the dissatisfaction you might feel about that answer is actually a very important response that we'll come back to and discuss later in this book, let's stick to plagiarism and talk about why it's disfavored in law school in more detail.

4. A Definition of Plagiarism

To do that, we need to have a working definition of plagiarism. I say "working definition" because each law school has its own definition, usually found in its Code of Conduct or Student Handbook, and each definition is slightly different. For present purposes let's define plagiarism as "the intentional use of another's work as one's own without adequate acknowledgement of the work's source." This definition isn't perfect, as we'll discuss in a second, but it will serve us for the moment. But remember that the definition of plagiarism, and any related offenses, that applies specifically to you is the only important one. It's a good idea for all students, and especially law students, to learn precisely what is expected of them and what they can and can't do under their school's regulations. As you'll be reminded often enough in law school, ignorance of the law is no excuse.

Plagiarism has two key elements. A plagiarized piece of work must rely on the work of another that is used intentionally, and it must lack adequate acknowledgement of the work's source. If we knowingly use someone else's work—their words, or even their ideas—without giving that person credit, we've committed plagiarism.

I said the definition I provided wasn't perfect. One reason for that is that it assumes that one can't plagiarize from oneself; the definition specifically notes that it's only relevant to the use of the work of "another," meaning that one can't plagiarize oneself. It's likely that copying from oneself violates at least one, and perhaps several, other provisions of a school's Honor Code, but not all definitions of plagiarism include self-plagiarism and the simpler route was to omit it from this discussion.

Another problem with my definition is what "adequate" acknowledgement might be. Does this mean that you can have some acknowledgement of the source of work and still have plagiarized it? If there is some acknowledgement that some work comes from a source other than the writer of the document before the reader, isn't that acknowledgement—however slight—enough to render the work non-plagiarized? Well, perhaps and perhaps not. It might be possible to make a general acknowledgement that an idea originated with someone else while at the same time hiding the fact that the idea as expressed by the writer is taken word-for-word from another source.

So for me, inadequate acknowledgement is insufficient, and non-plagiarism requires a sufficiently complete citation to explain to the reader the origin of all non-original thoughts and the depth to which the writer is indebted to another. Some common sense is required, but it's not difficult to be sure of when we're using the thoughts or words of someone else verbatim. Citation manuals give us a handy starting place for thinking about what "adequate" attribution might be. But again, different definitions of plagiarism might deal differently with this issue, and not every interpretation of plagiarism requires full manual citations for every source, so be sure to check the definition of plagiarism that applies to you.

5. Is Plagiarism a Problem?

To most people, it might seem ridiculous to even pose the question of whether plagiarism is a problem. For those people, plagiarism is the theft of ideas, the pilfering of someone else's work and thought and the use of that work as one's own in order to persuade the reader that the work is one's own. But to others, plagiarism is a mark of respect, a sign that the original writer's work and thinking about an issue can't be improved upon. And to still others, plagiarism is like driving at 70 miles per hour when the speed limit is 65; a technical violation, but a mostly harmless one. And in any case, if you're keeping up with the flow of traffic, and everyone else is driving at 75 or 80 miles per hour, is driving at 70 so bad? If everyone's doing it, is it really even an issue?

Let's answer that last question first. Yes. Plagiarism is wrong every time it happens and just because someone else has also done a bad thing does not legitimate the bad act. In fact, it's more likely that most people—even the overwhelming majority—don't plagiarize and stick to the rules. So even attempting an "everyone does it" defense to plagiarism is likely to be unsuccessful.

It's also incorrect to assume that the violation is harmless. Without getting into a debate about the ethics of other schools or colleges within a university setting, there can be no doubt that law requires faithful adherence to the codes of conduct governing the profession. There's no such thing as a "harmless" violation of the rules governing our conduct as lawyers, because any such violation diminishes the trust everyone has a right to place on a lawyer's integrity. All the lawyer jokes aside, ours is an honorable and trustworthy profession, and any act that lessens that trustworthiness is a harm to us all.

The issue of plagiarism as a mark of respect, on the other hand, is much trickier and is freighted with all sorts of cultural issues. In some cultures, in fact, this notion of plagiarism is the operating one, and the idea that plagiarism is a bad thing can seem odd or even incomprehensible. This is an important reminder to us that just because we think one way does not mean that all people everywhere will see the matter in the same way as us. Just as our society changes over time, making some acts acceptable that were unacceptable in the past and rendering unacceptable today some things that were considered perfectly normal in previous years, so our view of plagiarism is not shared by everyone today.

But we view plagiarism as wrong, and that view is perfectly valid and appropriate from our cultural perspective. Anyone seeking to operate in the American legal educational system must accept our cultural reference point on an issue like plagiarism. So the cultural defense to plagiarism, while interesting, is unlikely to succeed or persuade.

6. Why Is Plagiarism a Problem?

Another question that can seem too obvious to answer is why plagiarism is a problem. Certainly in an evaluation-based system like that prevailing in American law schools, no one can be in any doubt that the work to be evaluated should be that of the student alone: allowing a student to submit plagiarized work for a grade would be no different to allowing a student to hire a test-taker to take exams. In both cases, the student would be submitting the work of another as the student's own and seeking a grade for something the student did not do. It simply is not the way the system works.

Beyond this simple answer, though, are at least two other concerns that support law schools in their prohibition of plagiarism, the first obvious and the second perhaps less so. In short, plagiarism is lying—something no lawyer should do—and plagiarism is bad lawyering because it deprives legal analysis of the support that can strengthen it.

7. Lawyers Tell the Truth

Lawyers are truthful. This is an article of faith in the profession and it is the only way the system can operate. If we were constantly forced to check the veracity of each thing every lawyer said, the civil and criminal justice system in this country would grind to a halt and nothing would get done. So lawyers are expected to be truthful at all times and in all ways.

Of course, to believe that all lawyers tell the truth all the time would be naïve. Many lawyers a year, in fact, are disbarred or sanctioned in lesser ways for acts that amount to untruthfulness in one way or another. Lawyers are like any other group in society and are subjected to the same set of temptations and pressures; it should come as no surprise that some succumb to them.

What might be surprising is that the percentages are as low as they are for a profession that has a less-than-stellar reputation with the general public. In fact most—it's probably not an exaggeration to say almost all—lawyers are truthful and honest at all times and in all ways related to their work. They are truthful because it is the right thing to do, because they took an oath to be truthful, and because as officers of the court, they have a role to play in the orderly activities of the law in society. And some, perhaps, are truthful because the punishments associated with a lack of candor are so severe—including the loss of the ability to make a living as lawyers—that the costs of being untruthful substantially outweigh the benefits.

What applies to lawyers applies, probably in about equal measure, to law students. Most—indeed, almost all—law students follow the rules and submit their own work at all times because it's the right thing to do, because they agreed to be bound by the law school's code of conduct when they enrolled, and because they're learning how to be officers of the court. And for law students, the potential punishments for plagiarism are as severe in their own way as those for lying are to lawyers: expulsion from law school, or even lesser sanctions, can make it difficult or even impossible for a law student to ever be admitted to the bar and to practice law. The costs of such sanctions—in terms of law school tuition that cannot be offset by law practice income, the lost opportunities to work in an important and meaningful profession, and the personal toll taken by such a public punishment—just as much as the costs associated with lawyer sanctions—substantially outweigh the benefits.

8. Plagiarism Is Bad Lawyering

But in addition to all these reasons to not plagiarize, there is a substantial disadvantage to the practice that is often overlooked. Law students who plagiarize can't support their work with the work, or works, from which they're plagiarizing and therefore their work is less credible and substantial than it would be if they had incorporated the thoughts and ideas from the plagiarized work into their own work and had correctly cited to that work for support. Of course, plagiarized work has the support of the authorities on which the original, unaccredited, work relied, but it cannot—almost by definition—rely on the work from which it is plagiarizing. This is often a substantial and helpful authority and its omission from the list of authorities relied on by the plagiarizing writer usually makes the student's work less effective than it might have been.

One of the bedrock principles of American law is that it builds on what came before. In conducting legal analysis we look to identify the rules that have been articulated in the past that apply to the present set of facts under consideration, and then we look for authorities that interpret and explain those rules. Once we have identified the rules that apply, and the authorities that allow us to analogize, or distinguish, those authorities from the facts we are analyzing, we can either predict an outcome or try to influence it. Without reference to those prior authorities, though, we are merely arguing that things should be the way we want or predict them to be because we say so. Relying on this approach is a sure way of turning in substandard work.

So there are sound practical and ethical reasons for not plagiarizing. Yet while most students do not plagiarize, each year some do. Why? That's a much harder question to answer, but it's also a very important one to address.

9. Why Do Law Students Plagiarize?

There are many reasons why law students might plagiarize, and perhaps each student—of the very few who do plagiarize—does so for a different reason. But trying to understand at least some of the motivations for this practice is important because it is easier to come up with solutions to a problem when you understand the reasons for it.

A simple reason to plagiarize is because it seems to be so easy to do, especially in the cut-and-paste world of the internet. So much information is available and moving it from the web to a document on one's own computer is a simple matter. A few formatting changes and the words on the page brought in from another source look indistinguishable from those typed by a writer.

Indeed, some writers accused of plagiarism have defended themselves by claiming that they had brought over language from the internet and, because of sloppy note-taking habits, had failed to bring over the source information at the same time. Then, the writers claimed, they had forgotten over time that the language in the document was not, in fact, their language and the document had been submitted under their name.

As reasons go, though, this is a fairly weak one. It is certainly a description of how plagiarism happened, but it can't be used to justify it. Just because a thing is possible, or even easy, does not mean that we are justified in doing it, and that is especially true when the act is prohibited in some way. The solution to the ease with which information can be taken from the internet is either to resist the temptation to take it or, if the practice is the best way to collect source material (and it rarely is), to take accurate and complete notes of the necessary bibliographical information and keep them in the same place as the source material so the source can be properly and fully cited to when the writer uses the material.

Another possible reason for law student plagiarism is fear. Put simply, law school places great pressure on students to do well: each semester students are expected to do a lot of work in all classes, and the legal writing class is no exception. Students want to do well but either are insecure about their writing skills or are concerned that the press of work will be too great for them to do adequate work. The fear of a low grade then motivates the students to find ways to have someone do their work for them—either directly, by paying someone to write an assignment for them, or indirectly, by plagiarizing the work of one or more other writers and claiming it as their own. These students recognize that they are wrong to do what they do, but are concerned that in no other way can they succeed in law school.

There are many responses to this. First, and most obviously, a student who plagiarizes for this reason has fundamentally misunderstood the purpose of law school assessment. Although students often believe that law school classes are simply preludes to an exam, and the purpose of the exam is to get a good grade that is placed on a transcript along with other sufficiently good grades to get a "good" job upon graduation, that is not, in fact, just what law school classes, exams, and assignments are for. Law school exists to teach students about the law: how the law works, how society has set up laws to govern the actions of its citizens, and how we analyze and communicate as lawyers. Exams, assignments, and other assessment tools allow law schools to determine which students are learning at the pace they determine is adequate in order to progress towards becoming practicing lawyers, but they also allow students to test themselves and to identify places where their understanding could be improved. When students view law school assessment in that light, and work towards improving their understanding or skills in places where they are weaker, they can better cope with the inevitable stress of the bar exam, which comes immediately after law school, and the rigors of practice.

Plagiarism is no help in this. A student who plagiarizes, and who isn't detected (and it is worth pointing out here that in addition to plagiarism-detection software, many times plagiarized work is written in a different style—often dramatically so—from the work into which it is placed. When a student's vocabulary, writing voice, and writing style changes from paragraph to paragraph, most law professors will notice and become suspicious), will likely have weak skills that have not been adequately tested. The student will not receive accurate information about the strength of the student's skills and will not learn how best to improve those skills. The student will move on to practice, where most weaknesses are ruthlessly exposed. The student, in short, has at best substituted an illusory short-term gain for a long-term deficit that can't be made up: if the student truly can't handle the pressure of drafting and submitting a legal writing assignment without plagiarizing, then that student would be better leaving law school quickly and saving both the tuition costs and the student's mental health, rather than taking a chance on escaping detection (and the ensuing consequences) for plagiarism and facing the pressures of practice without adequate resources to cope.

Fear, then, is not a reason to plagiarize; it's a reason to consider not being in law school. Rather than being a cure for fear, plagiarism is a valid diagnostic marker of the problem. If students can recognize it as such, and honestly examine the desire to plagiarize to identify its root causes, then the students might be able to resist the temptation to plagiarize and either submit their own work, even if less polished and well-written than a plagiarized piece of work would be, or else recognize that law school—and the practice of law—might not be the place for them.

10. Plagiarism in Law Practice

Ironically, though, it seems—at least at first glance—that once a student makes the transition to practice, there is no such notion as plagiarism. Lawyers often will go to work they, or other lawyers, have written, cut portions of that work, and paste it into a document they're currently drafting. What would have been plagiarism in law school, apparently, is common and accepted behavior in law practice.

What explains this seeming inconsistency? The differing natures of law school and law practice, in large part. Even though law school is not entirely about evaluation and grades, it is partially about those things. In order to be able to determine how a specific student is doing, a professor must be able to evaluate that student's work. The integrity of the grading process demands that no one else's work is being evaluated in place of the student's, and plagiarism makes that impossible. In practice, by contrast, the grading element is absent. In many cases, appellate briefs are corporate products, worked on by many people, only a few of whom will be credited on the signature block. Similarly, many documents that come from a law firm with one name—letters, discovery documents, even articles and speeches—were often ghost-written by other lawyers in the firm. The nature of law practice, where the signer takes responsibility for the work but need not actually have written the work, is sufficiently different from law school that the same definition of plagiarism cannot apply in both situations.

But it would be a mistake to think that there is no such thing as plagiarism in law practice, or that no rules apply to the documents lawyers write. The fact that practice runs on different rules from law school doesn't mean that it has no rules at all.

Lawyers must be careful, for example, not to bill clients for work they didn't perform. Suppose a lawyer wrote a brief last year and billed the client $10,000 for research and writing (that's quite a modest price for such a complex document). This year, the lawyer has to write a brief on a similar legal subject and discovers that 50% of the previous brief can be taken directly from one brief and pasted into the second one. If the two briefs are to be written for the same client, the situation is not too complicated; the lawyer can take 50% of the first brief for the second one, and can charge the client $5,000 for drafting the second brief. In that way, the client is only paying for the work the lawyer did for both briefs and the lawyer is not double-billing—seeking to be paid twice for the same work.

If the clients for the two briefs are different, however, the situation is more complicated. The lawyer certainly can't charge the second client $10,000 for doing work that should only cost $5,000, but if the lawyer takes 50% of the first brief and charges the second client $5,000, the first client has essentially paid for half of the second client's brief; the second client got the same brief but only paid half as much for it. The lawyer might claim the knowledge acquired in the drafting of the first brief as the lawyer's intellectual property, separate from the first client's work product, and might argue that the brief is the joint property of the client and the lawyer, and the lawyer can use it in any way the lawyer sees fit. The first client, by contrast, will likely claim that having paid for the brief, it owns the particular mode of expression used in that document; if the lawyer needs to argue the same issues again, then the lawyer should go about the process of researching and drafting that issue afresh.

The resolution of that issue is a topic best left for your Professional Responsibility class. For our purposes, we need only note that whatever the outcome, the lawyer can't profit twice from the same piece of work. Were the lawyer to double-bill, the lawyer would, essentially, be trying to receive credit for previously written work: while the offense might not be plagiarism, it would certainly belong in the same family.[1]

Beside this quasi-plagiarism, it is also possible to commit direct plagiarism in practice. If a lawyer finds a perfect articulation of an issue in a legal treatise, for example, and copies that language directly into a brief without attribution, that lawyer has committed plagiarism and if caught, will likely be sanctioned. At the very least, the lawyer will not be able to charge the client for writing the language of another.

So while a new lawyer might look at the practice world and feel that there is no such thing as plagiarism in the way lawyers actually work, that would be an incorrect and misleading assumption. Plagiarism, in short, is something to be avoided now and for the rest of your career.

Plagiarism is not a happy topic but the good news is that this should be the last time you have to consider it. Law students—and lawyers—who give credit to the sources of their work where appropriate will never have to worry about plagiarism. But you should be aware that law schools and lawyers take charges of plagiarism very seriously and you should never give in to whatever temptation you might face to engage in it. And always remember that not only is plagiarism affirmatively a bad thing, but that appropriate acknowledgement is affirmatively a good thing. It tells your reader that you are not alone in having the thought that you're expressing, and that other lawyers, judges, or legal scholars agree with the position you're taking. It's always good to have some support on your side when you make an argument.

11. Disclose Mandatory Negative Authority

The requirement that lawyers must disclose mandatory negative authority often causes junior lawyers some concern because it seems to fly in the face of the zealous advocacy they're supposed to be practicing on behalf of their clients. How can it be, they wonder, that they're supposed to be making an argument on behalf of their clients but then have to reveal to the court that there's an opinion that disagrees with the position they're taking? If they make that disclosure, are they not destroying any chances their clients have of prevailing on that issue?

Not really. This issue does point out the place where the zealous advocacy requirement joins up with the lawyer's obligations of honesty and candor as an officer of the court, but it should never pose an actual problem for a careful advocate. In fact, this

---

1. Another question best left for a Professional Responsibility discussion is how to account for the work the lawyer did with the time saved by not having to research and write the same issue twice. Perhaps the lawyer didn't bill the second client for that work, but with the time the lawyer saved by reusing 50% of the first brief, the lawyer was able to do additional work. Is that permissible? Has the lawyer's first client essentially underwritten the time the lawyer used to work for someone else? The law presents innumerable fascinating questions, all of which have very practical effects on those involved.

situation can be an opportunity to make a strong and effective argument on behalf of your client if it's handled correctly.

The first, and most obvious, thing to say about mandatory negative authority is that it must be both mandatory authority and negative to your position before the ethical requirement that it be disclosed is triggered. This doesn't mean that you should try to get tricky with the definition of "mandatory": if you're in, say, the Fourth Circuit and there's a previous Fourth Circuit decision that is directly contrary to a position you're seeking to assert, you might try to argue that since the previous decision is from a court at the same level, it doesn't constitute mandatory authority since one panel of the court can't bind another panel of the court.

That argument will fail. For purposes of determining when you have to disclose mandatory negative authority, it's simpler to assume that any decision from a court directly above the court where you are now or at the same level within the hierarchy of authority should be revealed if it's directly against a position you're asserting. That doesn't mean that you would be required to disclose any Third or Fifth Circuit decisions to the Fourth Circuit, nor does it mean you would be required to disclose any trial court opinions from courts that fall below the Fourth Circuit, but it does mean you should disclose opinions from the Fourth Circuit and, of course, from the Supreme Court.

But just because you're not required to disclose negative authority from other Circuit Courts of Appeals doesn't mean that you shouldn't disclose those opinions anyway. There's a mandatory component to disclosure, certainly, but there's also a practical component to it as well. You can be sure that if there's a negative opinion from another circuit, your opponent will find a way of letting your court know about it so from a practical perspective, it's as well to think about disclosing that opinion yourself. Doing so allows you to control the context in which your court learns of the opinion and allows you to draw some of the sting associated with an opinion that contradicts a position you're taking. Allowing your opponents to disclose a case that supports their position, or ignoring such a case if your opponents had a chance to write first to the court, puts you in a weak position. One way or the other, if there's a negative opinion out there, you're going to have to deal with it.

It would be simple and glib to say that the best way to deal with negative opinions is to change your theory. That way, the case is no longer contrary to a position you're asserting and you don't have to disclose anything. And when that's possible, it's good advice: the best theory is one that is entirely supported by mandatory authority and is, in essence, the same case that courts have decided favorably for your client's position in the past. And on the rare occasion you're working on such a case, you should by all means make the most of your argument, because what usually happens in such situations is that your opponent drops the case or agrees to settle. It's the rare occasion when you have a genuine "slam dunk" winner, in the sports jargon lawyers so often use to describe their cases, so enjoy it while you can.

The more common situation is that the negative authority you're facing is distinguishable in some way from the case on which you're working. And if you can distinguish the two cases, then the previous authority might not be considered sufficiently negative to be disclosed. But you should still think about revealing it in your argument and show the court why that case should not control your situation. This is often handled in counter-argument and it can be a highly effective tool, showing the present court how the previous court would have ruled in your favor if the facts of that case had been as they are in your case.

If the negative authority you're seeking to avoid can't be distinguished, and if you can't come up with a theory that provides you with a path around that authority, you have few options. Seeking to settle the case is one such option—you might be in the position of trying to oppose the other side's "slam dunk" case and settlement can be a more appealing option than trying to go forward with a case like that. Another choice is arguing that the previous decision should no longer stand and that the court should reverse itself.

This is a difficult argument, and should only be attempted by an experienced attorney, and it depends on what policy arguments you can marshal in favor of asking the court to reverse itself and how recently the court reached the previous decision—a court is unlikely to reverse a position from earlier in the same year, for example, and might be more inclined to reverse a decision that is more than a hundred years old. But "might" is the operative word; just because an opinion is old doesn't mean it's automatically invalid, so any attorney making this argument is well-advised to proceed with caution.

Negative authority is a fact of life for most attorneys who litigate cases on behalf of their clients, and the only way to deal with such cases is to face them head-on. Use them as a chance to modify and strengthen your case theory, or as a way to persuade your client that settlement is the best solution. But always reveal mandatory negative authority to the court. It's your obligation as an officer of that court, and it's also the right thing to do, both ethically and professionally.

12. Don't Engage in *Ad Hominem* Attacks

Lawyers sometimes get caught up in the passion of arguing cases and have difficulty distinguishing between legal opposition and personal aggression. The first is appropriate and, indeed, is required of a zealous advocate. The second is a logical and professional error and should be avoided at all costs.

Just because our client takes the opposite position from the person or entity on the other side of the "v." in a case caption, and just because we represent that client's position in opposition to an attorney who represents our client's adversary, doesn't mean that we should make personal attacks on that person or that person's attorney. Such attacks against the person are called "*ad hominem*" attacks and they are unethical.

They're also illogical, if you think about it: just because someone opposes your client's position, that doesn't make them a bad person nor does it make their attorney a bad attorney. In fact, *ad hominem* attacks have long been recognized as logical fallacies—arguments that have no basis in logic. Whether or not Mr. Smith is a good person (whatever that might mean) has no bearing on whether or not he drove through an intersection when the light was red. He might have intended to hit someone in the intersection, in which case his intent would be an issue, but characterizing that intent wouldn't be persuasive, nor would an argument that Mr. Smith was a "bad" man be effective.

So far, so good. But one can also make an indirect *ad hominem* argument that's just as illogical and unethical but which can be harder to spot. This can happen when you try to get a reader to draw some specific conclusion about a person from an assumption about a generalized attribute. If, for example, you argue that someone holds pro-life views because that person is a Republican, or holds pro-choice views because that person is a Democrat, you're making a veiled *ad hominem* argument because you're making an assertion about a person's specific beliefs based on that person's general beliefs. Not only is this sort of assertion ineffective because it mischaracterizes the relationship between general and specific belief—many Republicans are pro-choice and many Democrats hold anti-abortion views—it's also an improper line of argument, even if the question of the person's views on abortion was relevant to the case.

It's not difficult to avoid falling into the trap of making *ad hominem* arguments. One simply has to avoid making unsupported or irrelevant personal assertions, and avoid attacking the character of the opposing attorney or the trial judge when arguing to an appellate court. On the very rare occasion when you have to argue that a lawyer's or judge's actions were improper, it is the actions that should be the focus of your argument, not the person's character. These are difficult arguments to make, because the line between appropriate argument and *ad hominem* attack can sometimes be blurry, but you should always be sure that you can see it clearly before proceeding.

13. Don't Improperly Characterize Facts or the Law

Another ethical trap that is more common than you might expect is the improper characterization of facts or the law. Some lawyers believe that their obligation to argue zealously in favor of a client's position means that they should try to mischaracterize a fact or a court's opinion. As you can imagine, though, that's not an ethical thing to do.

Fact mischaracterization is relatively easy to avoid: don't characterize any facts. If you stay away from all characterization, you won't mischaracterize anything and since any characterization of facts is bad writing practice, this should be relatively simple for you to do. If you're writing about someone's cancerous tumor, don't call it a "large" or "massive" tumor, tell the reader that it was a tumor larger than 5 cm and allow the reader to characterize the fact without your help. And even though any tumor is large to the person suffering because of it, characterizing a 2 cm tumor, for example, as "massive" might be seen as mischaracterization, depending on the tumor's location.

Mischaracterizing a court's opinion is trickier for attorneys, because we spend a lot of time analogizing and distinguishing cases to show why they support, or don't support, various positions we and our opponents assert. Simply saying that a court ruled one way when in fact the court ruled another, of course, is easy to spot and is obviously unethical, but writing about the *dicta* in an opinion as if it's the holding, while equally wrong, is more difficult to spot without a careful review of the court's opinion.

Another way of mischaracterizing a court's opinion is the selective editing of what the court wrote, thereby changing the court's meaning. Here's a simple example to illustrate the point. For our purposes, it doesn't matter about which rule the court was writing. In *Schofield v. Merrill*, 386 Mass. 244, 435 N.E. 2d 339 (1982), the court wrote "[w]e are told that the rule is an old one with many exceptions, and therefore is obsolete. But the fact that a rule of law is old does not necessarily mean that it no longer serves a valid purpose." *Id.* at 252, 344.

This language could be selectively edited to suggest a very different conclusion. " … [T]he rule is an old one with many exceptions, and therefore is obsolete." *Id.*, at 252, 344. And we could be even more misleading if we omitted the three ellipses at the start of the sentence to show that language had been omitted: "[T]he rule is an old one with many exceptions, and therefore is obsolete." The court wrote exactly those words in exactly that order, but by quoting it in this way we've completely changed the meaning the court gave to these words when it wrote them.

This is an almost cartoonishly obvious example, but many lawyers—and law students—think that just because a court has written words in an opinion, those words can be used selectively to support a position, even if the context in which those words was written suggests an entirely different result. This belief is wrong, and any lawyer found to be chopping up a court opinion to make the language fit a position it wasn't intended to fit will be in trouble for engaging in unethical behavior.

14. Don't Make Things Up and Don't Lie

Perhaps the easiest of all examples of unethical behavior is simply making something up or lying. This doesn't happen often—certainly not as often as television dramas about lawyers might lead you to believe—because the consequences can be dire, up to and including disbarment.

There are complications, as with all things, but this is one place where the simple advice is the best: don't make things up and don't lie. And don't allow your client to make things up or lie either. Follow that rule and your life as a lawyer will be much simpler and your career will be longer than if you ignore it.

15. Remember at All Times That You're an Advocate and an Officer of the Court

When you become a lawyer you take an oath of honesty and candor towards the tribunal which makes you an officer of the court. This is an important obligation to understand, because not only do you have tremendous power as a lawyer, you also have significant responsibilities of which you can never lose sight. As you'll learn in some of your other classes, many of your communications are protected from scrutiny by the attorney-client privilege or the work product doctrine. These protections allow you to pursue your client's cases with energy and vigor.

But as you'll also learn, the rules of professional responsibility, whichever ones that apply to the jurisdiction in which you practice, place important limits on what you can do. To an extent, these rules are technical in nature, and as with all rules, they set boundaries against which lawyers are very good at placing their toes; not many lawyers ignore those boundaries but many come as close to the line as they can without stepping over.

Learning what those boundaries are, and how far you can, or should, push them, is something you'll learn over time. For now, the simplest moral compass to adopt is that of the officer of the court. If you ever wonder whether you should or shouldn't do or write something, think of your responsibility of honesty and candor to the tribunal in which you're practicing. If your considered action falls short of the highest standards of ethical behavior, then you have your answer.

Conclusion

Ethical behavior is not always convenient, and it has nothing to do with the chance of getting caught. Just as with the honor code under which you operate while a law student, an oath is broken at the time the offending action is taken, not when the action is discovered. The integrity of the entire legal system depends on us behaving ethically at all times. And while the rules of behavior might seem complicated, their essence is very simple: always do the right thing. It's hardly ever difficult to figure out what that is.

Focus Questions

1. Why do you think there are so many lawyer jokes, and why do you think people enjoy telling them so much?
2. Does the concept of the law as a service industry surprise you? Does it disturb you?
3. Had you considered the importance of the client to the lawyer before? Does the first year of law school emphasize or minimize the importance of clients? Do you talk about clients in your other classes at all?
4. Does the advice to omit references to yourself in your writing surprise you? Are there other reasons you might think to not insert yourself into the documents you write as a lawyer?
5. Have you experienced situations in which you felt someone might have been plagiarizing? Have you consulted your school's Honor Code to discover what the definition of plagiarism at your institution might be? Are there any features of that definition that might surprise you?
6. Do you agree that plagiarism is a problem when it occurs and that it should be punished?
7. Does the assertion that most lawyers are truthful and honest agree with your perception of most lawyers?
8. Had you considered the idea that plagiarism makes legal work less persuasive because it removes the support on which good legal work relies?
9. Do you understand how plagiarism can be detected even without the use of plagiarism detection software? Are you surprised that changes in writing "voice" can often reveal plagiarism?

10. Are you surprised that lawyers in practice might copy portions of one document into another? Would this practice disturb you if you experienced a lawyer in your firm copying your work? What about a lawyer outside of your firm?

11. Are you surprised by the requirement that lawyers must disclose all mandatory authority that is negative to the positions they assert?

12. Is the idea of drawing the sting of adverse authority by disclosing it yourself familiar to you? Have you ever pursued a similar strategy in your personal or professional life?

13. Do you see the danger of characterizing the facts or the law?

THE WRITING PROCESS

Chapter 7

The Writing Process

What You Should Learn from This Chapter

This chapter is an introduction to the writing process, the technical side of legal writing. Although you have written many documents before coming to law school, you should be willing now to reexamine the writing strategies you have used until now, abandon practices that will not help you, and adopt new strategies that are better designed to help you become an efficient and effective legal writer.

After reading this chapter, you should:

- have gained a sense of the unpredictable writing life of a lawyer;
- have considered where and how you write and considered whether you can identify a more effective writing process;
- have considered how long you can work on a document without taking a break; and
- have considered how a writing budget might be helpful to you and what such a budget might look like.

One of the striking things about reading how professional non-legal writers go about the process of writing is that they have many varied routines that help them get into the necessary frame of mind to write. Just like athletes with pre-game warm-ups, musicians with scales and exercises, or dancers with stretching, these writers have well-developed practices that get their minds attuned to the process of writing.

If legal writers had the luxury of time, many would likely develop similar rituals. Unfortunately—or fortunately, depending on your perspective—legal writing is almost always deadline writing. Lawyers spend a lot of their time writing, but it's by no means all they do during the course of a day and it's virtually impossible to block off sufficient time every day to develop a predictable writing routine.

You might decide, for example, that you're going to concentrate on the more complex documents you write—appellate briefs, trial memoranda, and so on if you're a litigation practitioner—from 4:00–6:00 pm every day; that's going to be your writing time. On Monday, though, there's an emergency call with a client that runs from 3:00–5:30, and you have to be on that call. And on the call you discover that the client needs your firm to file a temporary restraining order against a local company that's infringing on one of its trademarks. That's a time-intensive project that takes up the remainder of Monday, all of Tuesday (including your writing time), and some of Wednesday. You're done before 4:00 pm, though, so you close your office door and sit down ready to start on a brief. But then a partner knocks on your door, comes in, and starts to talk about a new case she's trying to bring into the firm. It sounds like a perfect opportunity for your skills and she wants you to review the file in anticipation of a meeting with the prospective client on Thursday morning.

And so on. You get the idea. Practice life for lawyers is rarely structured enough to allow them predictable blocks of time they can set aside to write, meaning that they have to write whenever they can. As you probably noticed, the lawyer in my example still had complex documents to write and three full weekdays had gone by without one word being added to those documents. That's why lawyers tend to stay at the office late into the evening and come in on weekends; those are often the only times they can get to the long-term projects they need to complete.

So lawyer writing, in practice if not in form or content, has much in common with other types of deadline writing like journalism. Just like journalists, lawyers have to be able to produce quality work quickly—often under grinding pressures—and in stress-laden environments; the morning ritual involving a soothing cup of tea and time for quiet reflection with our hand-written journal before we start to put words to paper is probably not for us.

Doesn't this description of how lawyers write run counter to the advice you will often hear (and read, in this book) that you should revise your work often and should never turn in your first draft of anything? In fact, doesn't this description of how lawyers write sound exactly like how you worked as an undergraduate, waiting until the last second before writing up your term papers, justifying the practice because you "write better under pressure"?

No. It might sound like that, but the similarities are only superficial. In fact, most good legal writers are able to find a state of writing concentration that is, if not identical to that of the professional writers with long preparatory writing process rituals, at least similar to it. The difference is that they're able to enter and exit that state very quickly, and their writing technique allows them to craft effective sentences quickly and effectively. They write well quickly, and that allows them to revise their work within their deadline, producing finished work that is highly polished and effective even though it was written quickly and often in piecemeal fashion in the odd moments when the lawyer had time away from other tasks to return to the document.

The skill to do this takes time to learn. In fact, as with sports, learning a musical instrument, and almost every other complex activity, you will have to start slowly and develop a technique that is consistent and reliable before you will be able to write quickly and well. So banish thoughts of speed writing from your head; you'll be working slowly and methodically for the first year of law school, and probably for the remainder of your time in law school as well. This is the time when you're working on your technique, honing and refining it until it's ready to withstand the rigors of practice. If you do that, you'll be better equipped to hold up when you're told that the fifteen-page memorandum you wrote for filing, and which was already reduced from the 30 pages you had originally planned, now has to be reduced to ten pages because the judge has a chambers rule that no one told you about. And it has to be done in the next hour, or your filing will be deemed late.

The first step you need to take is to find a place where you can write. Lawyers usually have offices, or at least cubicles, that are their spaces. When they go there they can create, and recreate, the ideal set of circumstances to help them focus on writing, whether that be hanging a sign outside a closed door asking for no interruptions, disconnecting the phone or turning off the cell phone (although that's usually a dangerous approach to take if the lawyer needs to be able to answer calls from clients and partners), or playing music (quietly; headphones might be necessary to avoid disturbing other lawyers, even if your doors are closed) to act as a distraction from outside stimuli.

For you, finding a place to write might not be so easy. Law school space is often limited and sometimes can't be reserved. You might find a perfect place to work, but when you go there the next day someone else might have taken that spot or the person working on the next cubicle over has a habit of humming along to something playing on his iPhone. And if space at home is limited, you might find yourself trying to write on the kitchen table or, if space is really limited, in the space that also functions as living room and bedroom.

If you can, though, find a place you can go back to, day after day, that might be your writing space. Ideally, it will be quiet, have enough table space for your computer (you need to become comfortable with composing directly onto your computer, even if you're not yet; there just isn't time for you to write things out longhand and then type them up later) and your notes, your printer, and perhaps some room for some books or other reference materials you find helpful when you're writing.

If you can't find such a place, and are destined to roam about, setting up your word processor wherever you can find space, try at least to find somewhere quiet where you won't be interrupted, or asked to move, for several hours. You might also want to invest in a pair of headphones that block out as much of the outside world as possible. Even if you don't listen to music through them, they can be a useful sign to others that you don't want to be disturbed, and they can also help to keep other outside distractions to a minimum.

Some will tell you that you should write in silence, and that listening to music is the last thing you should do because it can divide your concentration, making it too easy for you to pay attention to anything other than what you're writing. It's also possible that listening to music can make it harder—even impossible—for you to listen to the sound of the words you're writing; you're likely not sounding out words in your head as you type them but it can be important to stop sometimes and go back and listen to your writing in order to make sure you're hitting the right voice or tone.

Others will tell you, though, that silence can be oppressive, and that music can help to block out the outside world. Listening to music, they argue, can help anesthetize the part of your brain that gets in the way when you write—the part that makes you want to edit everything as you're writing—so that you can write without getting in your own way.

The bottom line, of course, is that this is a personal decision and that it's one you'll have to make for yourself. The one piece of advice I can offer is that however you usually write—in silence or with musical distraction—try it the other way for a week. That way, you can be sure that you're doing something because it actually helps you, not because it's a habit. And you need to give it a week because you need to commit to really experiencing the other approach. If, after the end of the week, you still find yourself missing the way you used to write, then go back to it, comfortable in the notion that you've found something that works for you and that helps you to be a better writer.

One thing all writers agree on, though, is that you shouldn't edit yourself as you write your first draft. The act of getting a first draft on paper (or on screen, these days) is the act that helps organize your thoughts in order to put them in a coherent order. You need to get through that process before you start to edit, or else you'll never get anything completely down on paper. The notion that you can edit as you go, so your first draft will also be a polished final draft, is immensely appealing but it's also an illusion. It never happens that way in real life, and all that happens is that you write slowly and incompletely.

You should also recognize that writing takes a tremendous amount of concentration and energy. If you do it right, you should come away from the keyboard feeling drained. That means you probably can't write at a high level for too long at a stretch; three or four hours in one session is probably the most you should shoot for, at least at first, and you might find you only last an hour or so when you start out. That doesn't mean an hour of checking emails, fiddling with your music player to find a sequence of songs you like, chatting with a friend who walks by, and sitting staring into space, waiting for the right word to strike you. It means putting your fingers on the keyboard to make words, sentences, and paragraphs, putting your thoughts down so you can refine and improve them later. If you do that for an hour at a stretch, and you don't feel tired, try it for two hours, and keep working up until you find your limit.

An essential part of the writing process is also the ability to stop writing and walk away from a document for a while. That's hard to do if you're on a deadline, of course, but remember that for the moment you're just working on developing your technique; in time, all of this will become more compressed and you'll be able to spend less time between drafting and editing. But just as muscles can get tired and you can actually harm them if you spend too much time exercising, your brain and eyes can get tired while writing. At that point, once you've stopped being productive, it's usually best to get away from your work for a while.

So once you decide to stop, stop. Don't go back over what you've just written; you don't have enough perspective yet to be able to make a reasonable decision about whether it's any good or not. Once you stop, get as far away from the document as possible; read your casebooks to prepare for tomorrow's class, go to the cafeteria and get a cup of coffee, do something completely unrelated to the law—exercise is often a good option. You need to clear your mind of what you were doing so you can come back to it fresh. This is one time when the diversity of a practicing lawyer's life can be an advantage; it's not hard to find other things to do that will clear your mind of the document you were working on.

One tip that might seem strange. Once you make the decision to stop writing, stop as soon as you can. Don't keep going to try and finish the thought you're working on. In fact, you'll be much better off stopping about a paragraph or two before you need to. This helps you the next time you start to write because when you open the document, you will know exactly what you want to write. You might only have a few minutes of words to get down before you're in new territory, but that can often be enough to get your mind and hands working so that you don't experience any form of block at the start of a writing session.

When you come back to a writing session after a break, I'd recommend reading over the last few pages of what you wrote, just to get you back to the frame of mind you were in before you stopped. As you become more experienced with legal writing, you should find that this gets easier and easier, but if you're having difficulty with it at first, you might want to leave yourself a short note at the point in the document where you ended up reminding you of the topics you planned to cover next.

The time you spend writing is, of course, a crucial part of the writing process but it's not the only—or, arguably, the most important—part of the process. That seems like an odd thing to say, but you did read it correctly.

Let's assume that you've already done the research you needed to in order to begin writing, so that time isn't included in this discussion of the writing process. But even if we can skip a discussion of initial research, continuing research is a crucial element of the writing process. Put simply, you hardly ever are finished with your research at the point when you start a document, and you almost always will identify areas that require additional research once you start writing. That's because you don't really understand the dimensions of the problem you're seeking to address until you've started writing them down. Writing is expressed analysis, and the act of writing is itself an analytical one. As you write, you understand the issues you're writing about at a deeper level than you did before, and that should also expose gaps in your thinking which need to be filled by additional research.

There is nothing unusual about this; it happens to every writer and rather than being concerned about it you should be delighted when it happens. Writing is a dynamic process and the need for additional research is a sign that you're engaging fully with the issues and you're thinking carefully about what you're writing. Your analysis will be richer and more complete as a result of the additional research you're about to do, and that means you'll be producing a better work product.

But the additional research will take some time to do, slowing down your completion time, and if things follow their usual course, you will need to conduct additional research at several points during the course of drafting a complex document. You have to build in enough time to do this research and not skimp on the drafting of the document itself; the most brilliant piece of legal analysis ever conceived will persuade no one if it isn't reduced to writing and submitted on time.

Another crucial part of the writing process is the editing and proofreading that must follow the conclusion of the drafting phase. If anything, these are even more important than the drafting itself, because this is the time when your rough first draft is transformed into a finished piece of analysis. This is when you take your basic work product and turn it into something that will educate and, perhaps, persuade a skeptical reader to rule in your client's favor. This polishing phase is crucial and can be time-consuming. As with the additional research you'll be doing, you'll need to budget time for this phase into your initial writing plan in order to be finished in time for the document to be submitted.

We'll talk about the specifics of the editing and proofreading phase of the writing process later. For now, just know that you can't avoid editing and proofreading and you can't skimp on them either. This is perhaps the part of the process that you avoided as undergraduates; it's hard to spend too much time on polishing your writing if you wait until the last second to start writing in the first place. That won't be adequate now, though, nor will it be adequate once you're in practice. The time in which you have to write documents—even lengthy, complex documents—is incredibly compressed when you're in practice, and you need to develop your technique now so you will be able to cope with the rapid turnaround time you'll be given to produce top-quality written work.

The best advice is to map out a writing budget and stick to it as closely as you can. Use the first few writing assignments in law school to give you a sense for how long it takes you to do certain things and then develop a budget that's specific to your writing style. Start from the end date—the day and time your document needs to be submitted in order to not be late—and (working backwards) include time for proofreading, editing, additional research, drafting, initial research, and planning, making sure that the earliest date in your plan doesn't predate the day on which you got the assignment, and remembering that you have many other things to do while you're in law school; you can't just stop preparing for your other classes, for example, just because you have an appellate brief to write for your writing course.

It might seem strange to think of having a writing process, especially if you haven't thought of yourself as being a writer before. But there's no question that you're a writer now; a typical lawyer writes every day in practice, and if the total number of words a lawyer writes professionally in a year were tabulated, it would likely come close to matching the output of most novelists, journalists, and others who make their livings by writing. So like it or not, you're a writer now and you need to have a process by which you produce all those words. The more consistent you're able to keep that process, the faster you'll be able to get yourself into the daily rhythm of writing you'll need in order to be productive and efficient. Unfortunately, there's no single way of getting into that rhythm; if there were, it would be simple to outline the steps and tell you to go away and practice them until they become second nature. But everyone is different, and their writing processes are different as well. So find a process that works for you and stick to it as closely as you can. In time, that process will be the trigger that puts you into the writing frame of mind, allowing you to write fluently and effectively every day.

Focus Questions

1. Do you have any rituals you follow when you're writing?
2. Have you ever worked in a situation where your time was predictable from day to day, or have you worked in a situation as fluid as the one described here for law practice? Do you think you will be comfortable working in an environment as changeable as the one described here?
3. Have you ever argued that you write better under pressure? Have you used that as an excuse to delay working on some writing until the last minute? Do you believe that you write better under pressure or do you think this is just a convenient excuse for not writing more than one draft of a piece of work?
4. Do you have a place where you can write without distractions?
5. Do you typically write in silence or do you listen to music or have some other form of distraction when you write? Do you isolate yourself from external distractions such as emails or text messages when you write, or do you pay attention to outside

distractions? Might your writing process be easier if your answer was different? Have you tried writing in a different way? Will you consider trying a different approach for a week before deciding on the best approach for you?

6. Do you find yourself editing your work as you write? Have you been told before that this is a bad idea?

7. Are you tired after you finish a writing session? Are you able to follow the text's advice to stop writing and not immediately go back over what you've written or do you feel the need to review your work right away?

8. Does the description of writing as a dynamic process surprise you or are you familiar with the process of research and writing proceeding at the same time?

9. Have you ever tried to prepare a writing budget before? Do you think this idea will be helpful?

10. Does the idea of a lawyer being a professional writer surprise you? Will that easily become part of your self-image as you proceed through law school and into law practice?

Chapter 8

Voice

What You Should Learn from This Chapter

This chapter deals with issues surrounding "voice," the metaphor we use to describe how your writing should "sound" to your reader. Voice is an important aspect of legal writing: you should be aware of the voice you intend to use for a particular document and the techniques available to you to produce that voice. It is important that the voice you use be a conscious, rather than reflexive, result of your writing, and this chapter introduces you to some of the ways you can manipulate your voice to control the tone of the documents you're writing.

After reading this chapter, you should:

- be sensitive to the voice used by the writers of the documents you read while in law school and elsewhere;
- be aware of the voice you wish to use in any document you write; and
- be aware of some of the techniques you can use to change the voice you use in the documents you write.

It's interesting that for something as visual as writing, in which we use visual symbols to stand-in for sounds during both the creation and reception of information, and which we use to convey information from writer to reader without any sound occurring, we use many aural metaphors to discuss it. "Discuss," for example, is a word that imports notions of conversations about a topic, which seems both entirely correct and strangely out-of-place when speaking about writing. And "speaking" is another, even clearer sound metaphor. In fact, we speak of the "sound" of someone's writing, we talk about "listening" to an argument, even when it's written down, and—perhaps most importantly—we speak of a writer's "voice."

We don't use these aural metaphors because we expect our readers actually to sound out the words we write, any more than we speak the things we write as we write them. Some might do this, perhaps, but usually only in private and only those writers and readers who are unsophisticated enough to be incapable of creating or reading a piece of writing in silence. But the idea of "listening" to writing is familiar to most, as should be the notion that we write in a "voice" that can change based on the context in which we're writing.

All well and good, you might say, but how much does this discussion help us become better legal writers? A lot, in fact. Once you become familiar with the neutral professional voice typically associated with predictive writing—a style that places distance between the writer and the reader, as if the writer was trying to hide behind the logical and balanced analysis and to not insert any personality into the writing—you need to become familiar with the more personal style, or voice, associated with persuasive writing. "Personal" doesn't mean that you get to refer to yourself; there should still be no "I," "me," "we," or "our" in your writing. But it does mean that your writing can take on some personality and the voice you use can become more individual.

Precision matters in all writing, so note that I didn't speak of "your" voice in that previous paragraph. In fact, one of the interesting aspects of developing a professional voice is that the voice you develop need not be yours, at least not for everything you write. You're free to use any voice that seems appropriate for the situation in which you're writing and you should be able to vary your voice as required. Once you become confident in your ability to put one word after another in a logical, coherent fashion, and the effect the words you write have on readers, you can begin to manipulate that effect by choosing different words and different punctuation to "sound" crisp, or relaxed, or happy, or friendly, or angry, or anything else you want to sound like.

You need not be any of the things you want to sound like, and it is almost always best to not write anything when you are experiencing particularly strong emotions: we might be lawyers but we are also human beings, not automatons, and strong emotions affect us after we get our law degrees in just the same way they affected us before. Among other things, strong emotions cloud our critical faculties and dull our sense of the effect our writing will have on others so that we lose the ability to censor our writing at the same time that we lose the ability to know whether we should be censoring it. That can lead to disastrous consequences, and is something best avoided.

The insight that we need not be the person our reader thinks we are can be a valuable one. Lawyers in court have relied on their ability to project an image of themselves to the jury that need not be, but might be, at odds with who they are, and they have to do much the same thing in writing. Changing your writing voice gives you that ability, and the metaphor helps to explain how that process works. Just as you can mask, or alter, your speaking voice to project a different image of yourself to a listener, so you can alter your written voice to create the same effect in a reader.

And it's important that you think of it that way, because your job as a legal writer is not to create a response in yourself, but rather to create a response in others. Like an actor, or a trial lawyer, you need to be able to evoke a response in your audience—your reader, in this case—without necessarily feeling that response yourself. Your technique should be sufficiently solid that you can change your voice at will (although usually not within a document) to convey information in the way that will evoke what you believe to be a favorable response in your reader.

This sounds fanciful, I realize. And, to be sure, the range of voices we use as professional legal writers is narrowly limited by the types of documents we write and the readers for whom we write them. Legal arguments, for example, are made to judges who are supposed to choose the argument that best fits the facts and the law relevant to an issue, not be swayed by an emotional reaction generated by an impassioned piece of writing. In this way our job as writers is much harder than, say, the trial lawyer, who can use a much broader emotional canvas on which to paint the picture of a case.

But there are ways in which we can reach out to our readers and engage them in a more directly emotional way than might be expected. By thinking carefully about word choice, word order, punctuation use, sentence length, and other technical elements, we can subtly use our selected voice to convey information in the way we believe it will be most readily accepted by our reader.

This book, for example, is written in a voice that's very different from the one I use when I write academic articles and both of those voices are different from the several voices I used when writing memos or briefs for courts when I was in practice. For internal memos to other lawyers in the firm where I worked, I tended to use different voices as well, based on the nature of the information I was trying to deliver and the audiences I thought might read the document.

What's the voice I use in this book? A relatively relaxed and informal one, I hope, in which I try not so much to tell you things as suggest ideas and hope that you'll engage in a (silent) conversation with me in order to test whether or not you agree with me. I intend this voice to be friendly and encouraging, not cold and distant. I do this by occasionally co-opting your voice to speak through my writing (the rhetorical questions like "What's the voice I use in this book?" from earlier in this paragraph), by using simple words that don't place distance between us instead of by using words with which you might not be familiar, by using relatively longer sentences and paragraphs than I would when I was writing appellate briefs, by using the active voice as much as possible to hold and keep your attention rather than letting it wander with the sentence, and by using contractions (something I'd never do in a piece of formal legal writing) and informal punctuation (like these parenthetical clauses set off by actual parentheses, something—like the dashes in this sentence—I would never do in formal writing either).

Am I successful? Does this more conversational style work to create the effect I want? Are you reading this more carefully than you would if I adapted the more common authoritative voice for academic writing? I don't know. I think you might be, but it's also possible that you find this voice annoying, or insufficiently authoritative to be appropriate in a law school textbook, or that it contains some other defect that causes it to fail to be as user-friendly as I want it to be.

And, of course, it's almost certain that having had this discussion of the voice I'm using here, you won't be able to hear that voice in the same way as you would if I hadn't said anything about it. If I understand anything about the Schrödinger's cat experiment, it's that observation changes the result and in this case, what is true in quantum mechanics is true in writing as well; knowing why I'm writing the way I'm writing completely changes your perspective. But that fact alone should convince you that voice has an effect on the way you read: if it didn't, then knowing how I was trying to manipulate you through the voice I'm using should have had no effect.

Well. Enough of theory. Let's talk of practice. How do you develop a voice, or voices, of your own and use those voices to create different responses in your reader? There are only a few technical means at your disposal, and I've already mentioned them: short words and short, active voiced sentences tend to make your writing sound brisk and clipped and speed the reader through a document. Depending on the vocabulary you use and the content of what you're writing, that might make you sound angry or efficient or any-thing else where such a voice might be appropriate. By contrast, longer, languorous, and lazy-sounding vocabulary, placed in passive-voiced and lengthy sentences with lots of breaths, and pauses imposed by punctuation, can slow the reader down and can sound, for example, calm, or sleepy, or downright soporific.

You get the idea. There are other tricks as well: the alliteration of "l" words in the previous paragraph worked to slow the sentence down even further while typograph-ical tricks like using **bold type** or *italics* can change your voice's volume. Typography, though, is something you should use rarely if at all because it is so overt a way of mod-ifying voice and in general, readers don't like to be so obviously dictated to. You might—might—get away with bolding or italicizing one word in an entire legal doc-ument, as long as that word is carefully chosen, but never more than one. My per-sonal advice would be to never use typography to make a point, and that instead you should use your vocabulary to show the reader when you want to place emphasis on a word. But I might be slightly too conservative when it comes to these things. You should make your own, thoughtful decision about your own writing style and then modify what you thought based on the input you get about how your writing was actually re-ceived by readers.

About one thing, though, we probably can all agree. Readers, in general, don't like to be told things, or made to feel foolish if they don't think something. Phrases like "it is obvious that" or "self-evidently" or even "it is clear that" are often perceived as chal-lenges to readers, who, having read them, will work hard to prove the writer wrong. It might be "clear" that something is the way you say it is, but your reader might well spend some time and thought to show it isn't clear at all. If that happens, you've lost your reader twice over; once when your reader disliked being told that they would be foolish not to see something as "clear," and a second time when the reader spent time trying to prove that the thing wasn't clear at all rather than focusing on the next part of the doc-ument you've written.

Readers also tend to be unpersuaded when they're told things. Rather, readers pre-fer to come to ideas themselves. In order to persuade your parents to let you use the fam-ily car, for instance, or to let you stay out past your curfew time when you were in high school, you probably didn't just tell them that they were going to allow these things. In fact, that was probably the best way to make sure you didn't get what you wanted. In-stead, you probably presented all the reasons you could think of that might persuade your parents to act in the way you wanted, and let them come to that decision as much as possible by themselves. The voice you adapted—not the physical voice in this case but the persona you used—was probably that of a rational, reasonable adult, rather than an emotional teenager. The more your parents could come to the decision as if it was their idea, and the more they could be led to that decision by a rational adult, the more likely you were to get your way.

In fact, the most persuasive voice you can adopt is almost always that of the guide who walks a reader through an analysis but doesn't tell the reader what to think about it. You're not really letting the reader form his or her own conclusions because you're only showing the reader what you want the reader to see so that the reader has to reach the conclusions you want the reader to reach, but in reaching them alone, rather being told what to think, the reader is more likely to accept those conclusions as correct. If you can persuade people that your idea is really their idea, they are much more likely to accept it. That might sound like the manipulative philosophy of an advertising executive, but advertisers—whatever else you might think of them—are highly effective persuaders. In that sense, they're valuable models for lawyers who are themselves also seeking to persuade.

One way to work on your own voice is to recognize the use of different writing voices in the work of others. So when you read anything, listen for the writer's voice and try to analyze whether the writer has control over the mode of expression. If not, what does that tell you about the writer? And if you can identify a voice in the writing, how effective is it? What does that voice tell you about the writer? What does it tell you about what the writer is saying? If this is something you'd read before, had you noticed the voice before? Now that you recognize it, does that change your perception of the written work?

Once you can identify voice in someone else's writing, listen for it in your own writing. You might not—or, at least, not at first—be able to control your voice while you're in the drafting stage of the writing process. But when you start to edit, you should be careful and unemotional about the way you correct the written voice you want to use. To do this, you have to ask yourself what voice you intend to use and you have to be able to explain why you want to use it. Do you want to be distant and reserved because you think that's the most effective voice to use? Or will the reader of this document respond to a more conversational and friendly style? Do you want to convey to the reader the sense that you're angry about something? If so, what response do you want that sense to evoke in the reader?

Knowing what voice you want to use, and what effect you want that voice to have on the reader, you should go back over your work and read it with those ideas firmly in mind. Test your document, at every stage, for its alignment with the voice goals you set for it. If it doesn't meet those goals, revise it—cutting words out, substituting one word for another, changing the voice from active to passive or passive to active, shortening or lengthening sentences, and so on—until you have a document that speaks to the reader in the voice you want it to have.

A word of caution. None of this is guaranteed to work. You can draft a perfect document, using exactly the right voice to evoke a response in the reader, and still lose an argument. You have no control over the facts in a case, or in the law that controls the case. You have some control over the way those facts are presented and you can select the legal precedent that you can shade in a way most favorably to your client, but if the facts, or the law, and sometimes both, are against you, you probably won't win. But you still need to try as hard as possible to give your client the best chance to win because that's what lawyers do. And that means paying close attention to the voice you use to deliver the client's position and aligning it as closely as possible with the result you want to achieve. It's one of the few things you do have control over, and you need to use everything at your disposal as effectively as possible in order to do as professional a job as you can.

Exercise

Consider the voice used by each of the following examples. Decide on the nature of the voice used and decide whether the voice is appropriate for the message contained in each of the examples and why.

1. Email

Professor,

I have received my grade for your course. I believe there is a mistake: you have given me a C+ when my evaluation of my work suggests a grade of no lower than A-. I am available on Monday after 3:00 pm and Tuesday at any time to discuss this matter. Please let me know at your earliest convenience when we should meet.

John Smith

2. Letter

Dear Mr. Habberly,

I have enclosed a copy of Plaintiff Stephen Hampson's Motion for Summary Judgment and Memorandum in Support thereof in the above-captioned matter which I will file with the court by next week's deadline. I would appreciate the chance to speak with you about the possibility of settlement in this matter in order to spare both sides additional litigation expense. Accordingly, please call me once you have had a chance to consider my client's position and have had a chance to speak with your client also. I will be out of the office all day on Monday but should be generally available for your call any other day next week.

Thank you for your consideration of this matter.

Very truly yours,

Jane Ray

3. Brief

The Plaintiff contends that he should recover damages as a result of the defendant's failure to provide medical care, but the Plaintiff is dead wrong. He not only got Constitutionally adequate medical care while incarcerated in the State Correctional Institute, the care he got was pretty good by any standards. In order to win a case like this, the Plaintiff had to show that his care constituted "deliberate indifference to a serious medical need" and that "the treatment [was] so grossly incompetent, inadequate, or excessive as to shock the conscience or to be intolerable to fundamental fairness." *Miltier v. Beorn*, 896 F.2d 848, 851 (4th Cir. 1990). Well, no one's conscience is going to be shocked by the facts of this case. The Plaintiff is unhappy because he complained of a sore head after bumping it on the wall of his cell while fighting with his cell mate. But he got immediate care, including a transfer to the local hospital, a head x-ray (which revealed no damage), and some Advil for a headache. What more did he want? Brain surgery? The Plaintiff got the same treatment anyone complaining of a similar problem would have received, and he has no reasonable expectation of anything different.

4. Court Opinion

The Plaintiff seeks the Court to enchant, in hopes the judge is a dilettante, but the facts he evades, the law is no aid, Defendant's motion therefore I grant.

Focus Questions

1. Have you considered how many aural metaphors we use when we write about writing? Other than the ones mentioned in the text, can you think of any additional aural metaphors frequently used when discussing writing?

2. Are you familiar with the idea of every writer assuming a "voice" when writing to an audience? Had you given any thought to the idea that lawyers would have an assumed voice when writing? Are you surprised by the idea that you can have multiple voices as a lawyer and that you should feel comfortable about speaking in all such voices?

3. Do you agree that it is generally a bad idea to write when under the influence of strong emotions? Have you ever found yourself writing something when you were happy or angry that you regretted later? How do you think your emotional state affected your writing style?

4. Are you surprised by the idea that your writing should not reflect your own emotional state but that your writing should evoke a response in your reader? Will that idea affect the way you write?

5. Do you agree with the text's description of the voice in which this book is written? If you disagree, how would you describe the voice used in this book? Looking at the cases you have been reading for your other classes this week, how would you characterize the voices those writers used when they wrote the opinions? How would you characterize the voice you plan to use for your next legal writing assignment? Why have you selected this particular voice? How would your writing be different if you had selected a different voice?

6. Have you considered ways in which to modulate the voice you use when you write? In addition to the techniques described here, what techniques have you used to change the tone of your written voice?

7. Do you agree that readers tend not to like to be told how to listen to a writer's voice by use of typographical tricks? Do you overuse typography in your writing? Underuse it? Get the balance about right?

Chapter 9

Words

What You Should Learn from This Chapter

This chapter is about words, the fundamental building blocks of writing. It explains the problems associated with working in a language as large as English and also takes a cursory look at the nature of words as signs, or metaphors, for the concepts they describe. After considering some of the problems associated with the translation from concept to word, and the impenetrable jargon that has formed around the law over the centuries, the chapter considers the notion of plain English and why, even though some criticisms of the practice of writing in plain English might be valid, it is the best approach for contemporary lawyers.

After reading this chapter, you should:

- have contemplated the differences between your active and passive vocabularies;
- have considered the metaphorical nature of language;
- have considered some of the magical properties of written communication;
- have considered how the history of the English language has allowed legalese to develop;
- have considered why plain English is a superior choice to legalese; and
- have considered some of the dangers associated with legalese.

Words come at the beginning. It's impossible to have a conversation about legal writing, or writing, or, in fact, anything, without thinking about words. Words are our tools, our building blocks of communication. Words are the embodiment of thought, and some people would go even further and say that without words there could be no thought, at least not thought as we understand it. Words, in short, are a big deal.

And that presents us with a problem, because there are a lot of words for us to deal with. English is a very big language. No one knows how big, because the language changes constantly. We have no official committee that decides what is or isn't an English word, so we have to wait until an unofficial body like the Oxford English Dictionary decides whether or not to include a new word into its ranks. But that doesn't mean that we can't use the word in the meantime. And just as new words are added to the language all the time, so words fall out of use or change their meaning. Do we include both the old and the new meaning as different words? Is "gay" one word or two?

So exactly how big English is, no one can say. But we know that it has a lot of words, most of which, frankly, we don't know. You might protest that notion and say that you know a lot of words, and I'm sure you do, but English is so vast that no one can know more than a small percentage of it. The problem—well, one of many problems, really—is that we don't all not know the same words. So we all know a small percentage of English words, but we all know an even smaller percentage of the same words. As we'll see, this has significant real-world implications for you as a legal writer.

We use an even smaller percentage of English words than the percentage of words we know. Take the word "battlement" for instance. I pulled that word out of my vocabulary at random when I was looking for a word I know but don't use on a regular basis. In fact, when I typed the word just now, that was probably the first time I've ever used "battlement" in an English sentence, spoken or written, since I first acquired language skills. It's just not a word that typically comes up in conversation. In fact, I would guess that you both know what the word means and have also never used it in a sentence.

The issue of inactive vocabulary will have significant real-world implications for you as a legal writer. Before we talk about those implications, though, let's spend a little time—only a little—thinking about the nature of words. For something that's so important to us, we don't usually spend much time thinking about words or their nature. In fact, words are fascinating, magical objects that offer many surprises.

For one thing, for something that has so much power over our lives that without it, we literally could not express our thoughts to others, a word is a startlingly ephemeral thing. The written word is, of course, a letter or collection of letters formed together to signify something, but the word itself has no substance. If you doubt that, try writing down the word "chair" and then sitting on what you've written.[1] In fact, the word "signify" was carefully chosen to describe this characteristic of words because that's what words are: not the thing they describe, but rather a sign of that thing. Words, in fact, are metaphors—translation devices that allow us to think of things without themselves being the thing we think of. This is true of physical objects such as chairs, and also of non-physical concepts, like "love."

"Love" is a useful example because it points out one of the problems we have with words. In order for a word to have its necessary effect—to translate the concept of love from one person to another—both people need to understand what the word means. And we do, in general, all understand what "love" is. But we use the word in a variety of ways, shading the meaning by context: saying you'd love to have a cup of coffee with a person, for instance, means something very different from saying that you love that person. In order to fully understand the meaning of the word, we have to understand the context in which it's used. Easy enough, perhaps, when the two options are an informal social meeting over coffee and an emotional attachment to another person, but more complicated when speaking of love as an act of friendship or a more specific emotional bond.

The significance of this to lawyers becomes perhaps more apparent when we consider other words. Let's think about one of the opposites of love—"war"—for instance. We all understand "war" in the context of a formal state of aggression that exists between two countries: between America and North Korea, for example, between 1950 and

---

1. My thanks to Professor Linda Berger for that example.

1953. But is that war over? Yes, of course, in one sense, but all that was signed in 1953 was an armistice. So do the countries continue to exist in a state of war? "War" might be a slipperier concept than first we thought.

To make the problem worse, was this country at "war" in Vietnam? Many men and women served in Vietnam, and many died there, but there was, in fact, no formal declaration of war between the two countries. Does that matter? To lawyers it should, because the word carries legal implications: How is war declared? Who gets to declare war? Is it possible for the executive branch of government to commit the country's military services to armed conflict or is that an action for the legislature? To the soldier being shot at in a distant country, these distinctions are doubtless irrelevant: "war," to that soldier, is a distinctly personal concept. But in deciding whether or not the soldier is technically, as opposed to practically, justified in shooting back, it might be necessary to parse the concept of "war" more formally, in order to determine the rules of engagement applicable in that soldier's situation. The context in which the interpretation of the word "war" is made, then, can have profound results.

The historical, as well as the factual, context is also crucial in understanding the meaning of a word. The word "gay," for example, has changed its meaning. The phrase "gay nineties" means one thing if you're speaking about the 1890s, and another thing if you're using the phrase to speak about the 1990s. The practical implications of this for lawyers become especially clear when discussing the textualist philosophy of judicial interpretation. For some judges—most famously, Justice Antonin Scalia—words should carry their intended meaning at the time they were used, and more contemporary interpretations of those words have no place in judicial interpretation. Others argue that this is an impossibly austere standard, and that judges should be free to interpret words more broadly—to incorporate the intent behind the words as well as historical dictionary meanings. And still others argue that words must be interpreted according to many possible meanings, including the meanings they carry today, and that judges should not be limited to a strictly historical interpretative role.

Interesting, perhaps, and maybe even fascinating. But "magical"? How can I defend the use of that word to describe words? Well, think of the last work of fiction you read. It described things the author made up—things that have never happened in real life—and yet the writer was able to communicate those events to you as clearly as if the writer was describing an actual event. You spent good money to buy something you knew was a complete lie—a fabrication from beginning to end—and you probably enjoyed being lied to, and maybe even found yourself drawn into a narrative that you knew to be false.

In fact, writing—all writing, not just fictional—allows you to engage in a conversation with a writer who you might never meet, and who might have been dead for years, decades, or even centuries, before you were born. Someone writing in a different place and time from where and when you were reading was able to place images, ideas, even conversations, in your mind without ever knowing of your existence. Written words allow us to travel in time and space, to change the way people think about things, and even to persuade them to act, or not act. If you doubt that words have magical properties, the idea of persuading a judge to rule in favor of your client just by taking words—things of no substance that are merely signs for other things—and stringing them together in combinations of phrases, sentences, paragraphs, and sections, will be a difficult one for you to accept.

Words, then, are both less and more than we might expect—less, in the sense that they themselves are not the thing they describe, and more, in that they can, taken alone or in combination, produce a remarkable effect on the future behavior of people we might not know. As we'll see, the nature of words can have important ramifications for lawyers.

For now, though, let's consider more closely the translation effect of words. It seems obvious to say, but translation is of little value if you don't speak the language into which a word is translated. Imagine, for instance, that you want to read Dostoyevsky's "Crime and Punishment," figuring that it might have some relevance to a lawyer. Unless you speak Russian, you'll need to find a translation of the book, but if the only translation you find renders the original Russian into German, and if you don't speak German either, the translation won't help. In order for translation to be useful then, the original concept must be translated into a language you understand: an entirely obvious conclusion.

But consider the phrase "well-regulated militia" from the Second Amendment. The words are in English, but do they translate eighteenth-century concepts effectively into the twenty-first century? Do the words mean something similar to the National Guard, which is, after all, a form of civil militia, or do they mean something more like the posse a law enforcement officer could summon into existence in order to cope with sudden, and transitory, threats to law and order? Or do they mean something else entirely? And how does the phrase "well-regulated" qualify the word "militia"? We need to understand much more about the context of "militia" in order both to understand its meaning and the meaning of its qualification.

This isn't the place, of course, to talk about what those words might actually mean, and they're used here not to ignite, or re-ignite, the debate about gun ownership in this country but rather to demonstrate how important words are to lawyers and how difficult their meanings can be to pin down. When the word we use doesn't translate seamlessly from writer to reader, we can be stuck with difficult and contentious debates about meaning and context that can rage bitterly and without ultimate resolution.

As you can imagine, it's desirable for contemporary lawyers to avoid causing such debates. The last thing a lawyer wants is to introduce any uncertainty into written work that means a reader is less than certain about its meaning. And that brings us back to the real-world implications of this brief discussion of the meaning of words.

Put simply, if words need to translate ideas as seamlessly and easily as possible from the writer to the reader, the writer needs to use words that are easily understood by both parties, with no controversy or difficulty. And because we share a small common active vocabulary, writers should be very careful about only using words that they are certain they have in common with their readers. But that's where things get complicated for us, because not only is English a very big language, but lawyers also have to contend with at least two other languages as well—Latin and Old French.

English is, in fact, a stew of many other languages: Latin (because the Romans invaded England), French (because the French did too, in 1066), Saxon (they invaded many times), Celtic (actually at least two distinct strains of Celtic, one from Scotland and Ireland, and the other from Wales), and so on. And that's just the direct assimilation into words that we now think of as "English." There's also the importation of foreign words that remain in their foreign form—"gestalt" and "schadenfreude" from German, for example, "savoir faire" and "je ne sais quoi" from French. We might think we know what these words and phrases mean, but we have to be careful because our understanding might not be exactly correct, and if we think the word means one thing and our reader thinks the word means something else, we're not communicating effectively.

But things get even more complicated when we start to think about the law. Law has its own foreign vocabulary that is alien even to English speakers with large vocabularies. "Res Judicata" (Latin) for example, and its related concept of Collateral "Estoppel" (French). We speak of the writs of "certiorari" and "habeas corpus" (Latin), and when we go into court to speak of those writs, the bailiff likely calls us to order by saying "Oyez, Oyez, Oyez" (French). A simple three-word phrase like "Action in replevin" is enough to confuse anyone and make it appear that lawyers use code to communicate with one another.

In fact, that's a possible explanation of why lawyers speak in the way we do. Words are powerful things, as we have seen, and as with all powerful things those with access to them tend to guard them carefully. Being able to understand legalese—that specific, impenetrable vocabulary peculiar to the law—can be seen as a form of guild membership, a secret language that only lawyers know and that keeps out non-lawyers. If everyone knew that "res judicata" could also be called "claim preclusion" and "collateral estoppel" could also be called "issue preclusion," it would be easier for non-lawyers to involve themselves in the law and maybe to learn that the law isn't as complicated as they think it is.

Or maybe not. In fact, lawyers tend to use the phrases "claim preclusion" and "issue preclusion" themselves these days, and just because the names are more understandable now than they used to be doesn't make the concepts themselves that much simpler to understand. You might imagine that "claim preclusion" means that someone can't bring a claim, and you'd be right, but that only gives you a little more information than you had before. When the principle of "claim preclusion" applies and when it doesn't, and the consequences of that result, are questions that take knowledge and experience to answer. Just because lawyers might use plain English to describe the concepts with which they work doesn't mean that society doesn't need lawyers.

But plain English gives everyone a fighting chance. And it allows us to spend our time and energy thinking about the concepts that are being discussed or analyzed, not the words that are being used in the analysis. So the legal community has begun to back away from legalese and is instead embracing plain English as its preferred vocabulary for expressing ideas, both to clients and to each other.

What is plain English? The answer isn't as simple as you might expect. It's English, certainly, meaning that words that are obviously taken directly from a non-English language like Latin or Old French don't qualify. Of course, there are some words and phrases for which we have no obvious English counterpart and which are therefore part of our legal vocabulary, plain English or not. Words like "certiorari," for example, or phrases like "habeas corpus" are clearly not English, but we have to use them because there isn't an equivalent English word or phrase that embodies the concepts of those two famous writs nearly as effectively as the foreign words. But there's no reason for me to write *expressio unius est exclusio alterius* ("the express mention of one thing excludes all others," i.e., when you list a series of things, anything not listed is presumed to be excluded), *ignorantia juris non excusat* ("ignorance of the law is no excuse"), or *nemo plus iuris ad alium transferre potest quam ipse habet*. I'll let you figure the last one out for yourself. Irritating, isn't it?

So Latin, and other foreign languages, aren't plain English, but how about English words, always assuming we can figure out what an "English" word is, given the astonishing number of languages from which English takes words. Well, no, not all English words can really be thought of as "plain" either. Words like "crepuscular," (relating to twilight, dim, indistinct), "epistemology," (the study of knowledge), or "sesquipedalian" (multi-syllabic or one who uses long words) are words that show that English can be just as impenetrable as a foreign language.

For a lawyer, the size and complexity of the English vocabulary presents some real problems. Lawyers want to be understood; the most brilliant thought ever conceived is meaningless if it can't be communicated, and the most brilliant argument in favor of a client's position is unpersuasive if it's written in a language the judge can't decipher. Judges, like any intelligent person, can come to understand almost anything written in technically correct English as long as they have enough time and access to a dictionary. But judges don't have enough time to work with a text written in inaccessible prose and neither do most lawyers. Instead, they'll likely dismiss the argument—and the lawyer making it—because as you learned with the untranslated Latin phrase above ("no one can transfer a greater right than the one that person possesses"; it means that a thief can't transfer title to a stolen object), we don't enjoy it when language makes us feel foolish.

That might seem like a negative reason for using plain English, but not making a judge or lawyer feel foolish is a perfectly valid reason for keeping to a simple and limited vocabulary. There are other reasons, however, one of which is maintaining a good writing flow. There are few things as disruptive to a fluid writing style than using words the reader doesn't understand. Even supposing the reader is willing to take the trouble to look the word up in a dictionary, you've lost the reader's attention for the time that process takes and it's very difficult to get the reader's attention back again once it's interrupted. Legal writing might never be as gripping as a good novel, but good legal writing can hold a legal reader's attention almost as tightly as well-written fiction and that's the ideal response to something a lawyer writes. Judges have to read many thousands of words a day. If a judge wants to keep reading your work, then you have that judge's attention and you stand a much better chance of persuading the judge that your analysis is the correct one if the judge is paying attention to what you write.

So plain English is not just a desirable approach to language, it's a valuable lawyering skill as well. But many law students have an understandable fear of using plain English because they fear they will seem, at best, semi-literate with limited vocabularies that don't display the years of high-level education they've had. They came to law school believing that this would be their chance to show off the many long and complex words they learned in high school and college, and they assumed that since lawyers write in legalese, a wordy dense writing style would be the expected approach.

But the goal of legal writing should be to impress your reader with the strength and depth of your analysis, not your vocabulary, and words that draw attention to themselves distract from the concept they're representing. Rather than trying to get your reader to spend time focusing on your writing, it's better to have your reader spending time on the analysis your writing discloses.

Another danger of non-plain English—one that's not often talked about but which should be of concern to you—is that it's possible to misuse words you're not entirely sure about. Put simply, it's possible for a writer who doesn't fully understand all possible meanings of a word to use it incorrectly, either because the word doesn't mean what the writer thinks it means or because the word has additional meanings of which the writer isn't aware. Where a word is used incorrectly, or suggests multiple possible meanings, the reader can be confused and led to believe that the writer is semi-literate, exactly the opposite impression you're trying to achieve. This leads to one simple rule—one of the few rules of writing you should believe and stick to at all times: know the meaning of every word you use and only use words that are unambiguous in the context in which you use them. A second part of that rule is perhaps the best reason for plain English: use only words that you're certain your reader will know and will understand without conscious thought.

There's another side to this issue that's worth considering. Critics of plain English call the style sterile and lacking in color. They argue that by removing long words from your vocabulary entirely, you make your writing bland and boring, and that by taking out some of the Latin and French from legalese, plain English diminishes the grandeur of the law, particularly in the eyes of clients who expect a little linguistic mystery when they deal with lawyers. It even, they say, makes writing less clear because readers have grown so used to seeing phrases like *lex loci delecti* that when they see the plain English equivalent "the place where the incident occurred," they might see a slight, but important, difference in meaning.

Critics of plain English, especially when it's used in the drafting of transactional documents like contracts, also argue that a lawyer who has a command of language, and can turn it to whatever meaning the lawyer intends, and can create opportunities for the lawyer's client by getting the other party to the contract to agree, unknowingly, to terms more favorable to the drafter's client than were intended, should do so and should write in an intentionally complicated, abstruse style that makes the document almost impossible for the non-drafter to understand.

This last point is probably the most easily dealt with. No sensible lawyer will allow a client to sign something the lawyer doesn't fully understand. So if a drafting lawyer tries to use language to gain an advantage for a client, the lawyer for the other side should either request language changes to make the document's meaning clear, or should decline to sign the contract. Playing games with the language to try and get an advantage for your client probably won't be worth the extra time you take to draft the contract.

As to the idea that clients expect legal language to be impenetrable and mysterious, that sounds like the old guild mentality talking. Lawyers might like it if clients wished they couldn't understand what the lawyers wrote, but some lawyers also wish their clients would just do what their lawyers tell them to do and pay up in full as soon as they get their bills. In real life, though, clients are paying their lawyers a lot of money and these days, most of them expect to know what the lawyer is doing and why. And that doesn't seem like an unreasonable demand. If you were being asked to pay thousands of dollars a month for legal services—either personally or as the representative of a company—no one would blame you for wanting to understand how your money was being spent.

The most accurate criticism of plain English is probably that it can lead to bland, uninteresting prose. It's certainly possible that a long document with nothing but short, simple words could be dull and boring to read, just as it's possible—even likely—that a document filled with long, difficult words could be almost incomprehensible to a reader. In truth, a little variety in legal language is probably ideal and once you've found your voice as a legal writer you'll be able to hold your reader's interest by mixing some more complex words into a generally plain vocabulary. Before you do that, though, it's best to learn how to express any thought—no matter how difficult and complicated—in the simplest terms possible.

Some states have enshrined a preference for plain English by enacting statutes that require its use in various documents—contracts being the most obvious and prevalent example. Often these statutes will require the use of a formula that analyzes text to produce a number, often expressed as a score that locates the writing on a scale of how easy the writing is to read, at least according to the test that's being used. These tests are highly controversial, and many maintain that they give very little, if any, information about how intelligible a text actually might be.

For one thing, people are different—even people who have reached the same educational grade level—so one question these tests can't answer is how readable a text might be to a specific reader. And even if a text is "readable," how much information does it convey from the writer to the reader? At best, many critics maintain, these "readability" tests give a very general sense of the simplicity of language used in a particular text and can say nothing about how well the text might achieve its purpose of conveying meaning. This isn't really a criticism of the concept of plain English, more a concern that we can't really say when something is "plain" or not, except in such general terms as to make the distinction almost meaningless.

One critique of plain English that is heard less often is that it's a continuation of England's culture wars being fought out on a distant battlefield. When the Romans, and later but more permanently, the Normans, came to England, their languages became the language of power. The language spoken by those whom the Romans and the Normans conquered—it's difficult to call them the native "English" because they were themselves invaders and occupiers from earlier—became subordinated to the language of those in control. As England's courts developed under the Normans, they used French as the language of the law, and because Latin was also spoken by the educated classes, it too worked its way into legal language.

The distinctions between Norman and Englishman eroded over time, but the distinctions between those in power and those not in power remained and language was one of the most powerful ways of distinguishing one from the other; those in power spoke a much different form of English than those not in power. We can see the faint echoes of class distinction in language in some of the strange grammar rules that have grown up around English: we don't end sentences with prepositions, for example, because Latin doesn't have sentences that end in prepositions, and because you can't split infinitives in Latin, we're told that we shouldn't split infinitives in English either.[2] In fact, as grammarians will be happy to tell you, there's no actual proper English rule against ending a sentence with a preposition or against splitting an infinitive, but for generations we've been told that to do these things is not "proper"—that it's low-class, not high-class.

---

2. I'll happily stay away from the argument over whether or not the preposition "to" is part of the infinitive, allowing for the insertion of an adverb before the verb to split the infinitive—"to boldly go," for example—or whether "to" is merely a prepositional marker of an infinitive verb, making it impossible to split the infinitive in English as well. I'm guessing you are happy that this is a book about legal writing, and not a book about grammar.

This is the same fight as that surrounding the use of long, foreign-derived words: the words of Norman and Latin origin tend to be viewed as more complex than the shorter, simpler, blunter Anglo-Saxon equivalent; those who can use the foreign-derived words are viewed as more educated, or genteel, or higher class, than those who tend to use the simpler, more plain, words. As time went on, those positions became entrenched: the law, as a closed field open only to those with money and education, became one of the most notorious users of complex, dense English that became almost a secret language for those who had been inducted into its mysteries.

The plain English movement can be seen as a reaction to this elitism, a reformation that seeks to liberalize the law by making it open and understandable to everyone, not just trained lawyers. From that perspective, those fighting to establish plain English are continuing the conflict first contested in 1066 at the Battle of Hastings, when the Norman King William defeated the Saxon King Harold, and that was later fought, in reality or myth, by the Saxon Robin Hood against the Norman King John.[3]

Does any of this matter? Do the origins of the plain English movement affect its pervasive influence in the way legal writing is taught today, or the expectation that contemporary American lawyers will be able to communicate their analysis, no matter how complex, in ways that reasonably intelligent non-lawyers would easily understand? Perhaps not. Perhaps it doesn't matter, for your practical purposes, that some plain English principles like the "rule" against ending sentences with prepositions, for example, or the "rule" against split infinitives—are still very much with us and are likely the result of age-old class conflicts.

But there is a value to thinking about why we do what we do, rather than just accepting blindly that we should do it. And for lawyers, who should be especially thoughtful about the language they use, there can be little harm in thinking about the political and cultural dimensions about our language choices and what our word choices say about us to others. You need not spend much time thinking about these things, but spending some time thinking about language as a cultural artifact as well as a simple tool to accomplish your professional goals will enrich and deepen your approach to language use and, ultimately, to writing. That can't be a bad thing.

Words are endlessly fascinating and you can spend a lifetime thinking about them. In practice, though, you likely will have very little time to think about what the perfect word to describe a particular thought might be and where that word might come from. Lawyers write under severe deadline pressure and their writing needs to be made up of carefully chosen words that meet the needs of the moment and communicate as effectively as possible the writer's thoughts to the reader and which can be written down and strung together as quickly as possible.

That means you'll have to spend a lot of time in law school developing an approach to words that will give you access to a vocabulary that will be effective and easy to un-

---

3. Does this notion of a continuing cultural conflict seem fanciful to you? When you go to a store and engage in a monetary transaction for an orange, you probably say you "bought" the orange, using the simple past form of "buy," an old English word. But if you go on a television show to talk about an eighteenth-century painting of an orange, you'll probably say you "purchased" or "acquired" it, two words that came into the language from the French of King William. In fact, evidence of the language war surrounds us and we can see it every day if we pay attention.

derstand and that won't confuse, intimidate, or alienate your readers, no matter how intelligent and literate they might be. The time you spend debating what word to use now will save you time when you're writing on behalf of a client, so take as much time as you can now to think carefully about every word you use. If you're sure that every word you write is the correct word for your needs, then you've already taken a huge step towards becoming an effective and fluent legal writer.

Exercises

Review the following sentences and decide if there is a simpler and more effective way of saying what the writer is saying.

1. Come now Defendant Prodigiocorp, by and through their counsel Smith and Jones, LLP and John Smith, Esq., and by motion, and memorandum in support thereof filed contemporaneously with this motion, hereby asks and requests this honorable court, after full consideration given to this and any additional memoranda, motions, and/or any other document however styled, submitted in connection with the above-referenced matter, to grant summary judgment in its favor and for that reason, hereby states:

2. The putative class plaintiffs, who offer an obdurate, erroneous, misconstrued, and inappropriately sanguine argument in support of their motion citing nary a case or statute in support of their position (and, indeed, ignoring several cases that stand in direct and—one would imagine—fatal contradiction to several of the theories they so energetically and optimistically propound), clinging firm to the outdated belief that a simple assertion or claim—unsubstantiated by the evidence or, indeed, any form of admissible evidence whatsoever; evidence that would, even were it possible for them to produce it, surely avail the plaintiffs hardly at all—of their counsel's lack of conflict, even though such conflict has been amply, even abundantly, demonstrated in defendant's moving papers, and by their blithe disregard of recent Supreme Court precedent—*Amchem Products, Inc. v. Windsor,* 117 S.Ct. 2231 (1997)—a case that sets aside any possible doubt whatsoever that subclasses contained within larger putative classes, as there are in this proposed class, have divergent interests and that counsel seeking to represent the interests of putative class members of both subclasses, especially where the interests of the putative members of both subclasses are clearly and without any possibility of contradiction misaligned and contradictory, have an irreconcilable and disqualifiable conflict of interest that must, in all cases, result in either the removal of class counsel from one or, ideally, both putative subclasses, are fatally, demonstrably, irredeemably, and profoundly wrong.

3. Plaintiff brought this *qui tam* action asserting that defendants were in violation of several federal statutes including, *inter alia*, the billing provisions of Title XVIII of the Social Security Act but after defendants moved, in limine, to prevent plaintiff from offering inadmissible evidence and the court ruled in defendants' favor, plaintiff's case was eviscerated and should now be dismissed.

Focus Questions

1. How much time do you spend thinking about the words you use in your writing assignments? Is this too much time? Not enough? About right?

2. Would you say you have a large, small, or medium-sized vocabulary? Do you think your vocabulary will be adequate for your purposes in law school and the practice of law or do you anticipate that your vocabulary will be expanding to cope with the rigors of law practice? Is your current active vocabulary about the same size as your inactive vocabulary or do you think one is larger than the other?

3. Have you given thought to the notion of words being symbols for the concepts they represent? Does that insight help you as a legal writer? If not, why not?

4. How does the idea of words changing meaning over time affect us as lawyers? Is this a significant issue or one that lawyers can easily overcome?

5. Have you considered the notion that when you read fiction you are encouraging writers to lie to you? When writers use historical figures as characters in fiction or dramas, do you find yourself believing the fictional representations of an actual person or are you able to maintain the distinction between history and fiction?

6. Do you agree that plain English is a better choice for contemporary lawyers than legalese? If not, why not?

7. Have you considered the size of the English language before? Do you see why the sheer volume of words in the language can cause lawyers problems?

8. Have you ever misused a word you thought you understood? How did you feel when the mistake was pointed out to you? If you haven't had this feeling, how do you think you would feel if you were told by a senior lawyer or a judge that you had misused a word? What if a client told you the same thing?

9. Do you think plain English is "sterile" or "lacking in color"? Will that be a problem in your legal writing?

10. Do you agree with the theory, expressed in the text, that the plain English movement is a continuation of England's long-standing cultural wars? Does that idea help you as a contemporary legal writer or is it irrelevant to you?

Chapter 10

Sentences

What You Should Learn from This Chapter

This chapter looks at sentences. After considering what a sentence is, and considering what the passive voice is and why it should only be used sparingly and after careful consideration, the chapter goes on to consider some good practices for sentence construction.

After reading this chapter, you should:

- understand what makes a sentence a sentence;
- be able to identify the passive voice when you encounter it;
- understand the concept that every word in your sentence should work hard for you;
- be able to identify throat-clearing phrases when you encounter them in your own writing or the writing of others;
- be able to "listen" to your sentences in order to gauge their effectiveness;
- be able to avoid starting successive sentences in the same way; and
- be able to write sentences that flow effectively into each other.

A well-chosen word will help make your legal analysis clear, vivid, intelligible, or persuasive. But unless that well-chosen word is placed in a carefully crafted sentence, it won't do you much good. Sentences are the under-appreciated engines of good writing; they organize and place a structure around individual words and propel the reader forward in the text. If words are like a tune's melody, the sentence is the rhythm, the beat that gets your foot tapping.

They also tend to be invisible. Words stand out; we notice them when they're particularly well-chosen or particularly badly chosen. We might have a list of words we like, and maybe even a list of words we don't like. But sentences are less prominent in a reader's consciousness. Properly constructed, a good sentence fades into the background of a text and supports the work the words are doing without drawing any attention to itself. It's possible that you might notice that a piece of writing has energy and drive, or that it's dull and pedestrian but you probably wouldn't identify the sentence structure as the cause of either reaction. And yet sentences have the power to make writing—even legal writing—entertaining and interesting or dull and sleep-inducing. So it's probably a good idea to spend some time contemplating sentences and deciding how to construct them so they're as helpful to you as possible to the reader.

So what makes a good sentence? Well, let's first consider what makes a sentence a sentence, and then let's consider why that's wrong. Confusing? You bet.

A sentence, as you probably remember from some distant time in your past, requires four things: an opening capital letter; ending punctuation of some form (usually a period, but exclamation points and question marks work as well); a subject (a noun or a pronoun); and a verb. Combine those four elements and you have a sentence. If any of those elements are missing, you don't have a sentence. Except that it's not necessarily so that a sentence needs all four of those things.

Take, for instance, the one-word sentence "Confusing?" in the previous-but-one paragraph. It has a capital "C" and a closing question mark, so two of the four elements are met. And "confusing" is a verb, so the sentence has that element checked off as well. But where's the subject? And if there's no subject, how can this one word be a sentence? Well, in this case, it's because the subject is implied (this is another sentence for you to make note of). The sentence might only have contained the word "confusing," but you had to assume there were other words in the sentence in order for it to make sense. In fact, you probably assumed that the sentence actually read something like, "Do you find this to be confusing?" The subject "you" was implied by the context of the sentence and you supplied it without thinking about it.

So when you read that a sentence needs an opening capital letter, closing punctuation, a subject and a verb, that's true, but while some parts of the sentence must be visible, other parts can be hidden as long as the reader can supply them.

Another way a sentence can imply its subject is by using the passive voice. If you take another look at the sentence I asked you to make note of, you'll see that there's no subject in it either, but you probably didn't object when you read the sentence because the passive voice is such a familiar trick. The passive voice works by hiding, or deemphasizing, the actor in a sentence.[1] So when I wrote, "Well, in this case, it's because the subject is implied" you understood that I was really saying " … the subject is implied by the reader." One way you can identify the passive voice, in fact, is by supplying an actor at the end of a sentence: if the sentence makes sense with the supplied actor, it's in the passive voice.[2] Take this sentence, for example: "The boring article was written badly." If you add an actor—say, "the legal writing professor"—the sentence still makes sense: "The boring article was written badly by the legal writing professor." If, on the other hand, the sentence already had an identified actor and was therefore in the active voice, supplying an actor would turn the sentence into nonsense: "The legal writing professor wrote the boring article badly" would turn into "The legal writing professor wrote the boring article badly by the legal writing professor."

You doubtless have been taught to avoid the passive voice at all costs in your writing, but that's only good advice most of the time. The passive voice is almost always wordier than the active voice, and that's a good reason to not use it often. Readers also tend to find prose written in the passive voice to be tiring, perhaps because they have to con-

1. Technically, when the subject of a sentence acts, then the sentence is in the active voice, but when the subject is acted upon, the sentence is in the passive voice.
2. My thanks to a former student, Jarret Perlow, who told me about this tip.

tinuously identify the person taking action. It's usually a good idea to not tire your reader unnecessarily. But sometimes you might want to hide the actor, and the passive voice is a helpful tool to do that. That is, perhaps, why politicians use the passive voice so often: it's one thing to say "mistakes were made" and something entirely different to say "I made mistakes."

So far, then, this chapter has contradicted two things you were probably taught in school; one word sentences are possible, and the passive voice is not always wrong. Since I'm on a roll, let me contradict another thing your English teacher might have told you. It's perfectly acceptable to begin a sentence with a conjunction. And while this might seem startling to you, the truth is that English has surprisingly few rules. Moreover, there's no law that says you can't break what few rules there are on occasion.

But just because you can do something, that doesn't mean you should do it. You can go skydiving without a parachute, for example, but it's not a good idea to actually do it, especially if you want to skydive more than once. Similarly, just because you can break almost every English rule you learned in school because it isn't, in fact, a rule, that doesn't mean you should do it. In part that's because the "rules" usually have some good advice about how to write hidden within them: if a writer uses the passive voice too much, for example, a reader might lose interest in the writing. And in part you should consider following the "rules" because many people don't realize they aren't, in fact, rules. Even though you know that the English language has no rule against using a one-word sentence, that won't help you if your reader believes there is such a rule and that by violating it, you are an unsophisticated writer. And you don't know who will fall into the category of strict "rules" believer and who won't, especially when it comes to readers like judges and senior lawyers reviewing writing samples submitted as part of job applications. So there are distinct personal and professional benefits associated with being relatively conservative in your approach to English "rule"-breaking: if you think of most of the English "rules" you know more as strongly recommended guidelines, you probably won't go far wrong.

All well and good, but just because a sentence is a valid sentence doesn't necessarily make it a good one, and that's the more interesting issue. Unfortunately, it's also much more difficult to move beyond the technical requirements of a sentence and talk about what a good sentence might be. Here are some of the elements of that discussion, and while some of what I say here might sound like a rule to you, please remember that it's just a guideline; other than the formal requirements of sentence construction, there are no hard-and-fast rules to follow.

1. Sentences Should Only Be As Long As They Need to Be

If there's one over-arching suggestion you should remember about sentences, it's this: they should be only as long as they need to be and no longer. That isn't a very helpful statement, is it? What does "need" mean? And how is this Goldilocks test applied? How do you tell if a sentence is too long, too short, or just right? Here are some suggestions.

A. Every Word in the Sentence Should Work Hard

One way to know if your sentence is too long is to look to see if all the words in it are working to convey your meaning. This sounds like a really difficult test to apply, but it isn't. Take that last sentence, for example, and especially the word "really." What work does that word do in the context of that sentence? If you take it out, does the meaning of the sentence change or is the sentence any less effective? Instead of "[t]his sounds like a really difficult test to apply …" the sentence would read "[t]his sounds like a difficult test to apply …" The meaning hasn't changed, and while the slight emphasis added to "difficult" supplied by the adverb "really" is gone, it's likely that only the writer would notice the loss. The reader, who hasn't seen both choices, likely won't feel that the sentence is missing anything at all. In this case, then, "really" hasn't added anything to the sentence; it isn't doing any work to convey meaning and it's just taking up space in the sentence. You can't afford to have any words in your writing that do nothing for you; most legal writers work under strict word or page limitations, so their writing needs to be as tight as possible, and even if there were no restrictions, your readers only have a finite amount of time and energy to devote to your writing and you don't want to waste that by making them read unnecessary words.

The discipline of finding and eliminating unnecessary words will help you immeasurably when you need to trim your writing. Understanding how to select only those words that work hard for you, and not padding your writing with unnecessary, and unhelpful, words will be a valuable skill for you throughout your law school and practice career.

B. Avoid Throat-Clearing Phrases

Throat-clearing phrases are the phrases—usually at the beginning of sentences—that don't tell readers anything but that tell readers that they're about to be told something. In other words, they function like those throat-clearing noises we sometimes make when we're about to start speaking; they don't communicate any information, but they alert the person to whom we're speaking that we're about to communicate something, and they get our voices ready to start speaking.

Maybe an example will make this more clear. Take this sentence: "When all the facts of this case are considered, the inevitable conclusion will be that Ms. Smith is not liable for Mr. Jones's injuries." Not especially objectionable, perhaps, but longer and wordier than it needs to be. If all the sentences in the document where this sentence is written are as long and wordy as this, a reader will quickly become frustrated and the writer might not have enough room to make all the points the writer wants to make. The key part of the sentence comes at the end—"Ms. Smith is not liable for Mr. Jones's injuries." Does it matter if we eliminate "When all the facts of this case are considered, the inevitable conclusion will be that?" What work do those words do that is crucial to the meaning of the sentence? They remind us that we need to consider all the facts of the case, but is that crucial advice? In order to reach a conclusion about a case (and "inevitable" conclusion is more padding, surely), we already know we have to consider all its facts. So that part of the sentence seems unnecessary. Does the meaning of the sentence change if we leave those words out? No, the core of the sentence is untouched—we're still saying that Ms. Smith is not liable. So the start of the sentence is throat-clearing—unnecessary words that don't convey any information except to tell our readers that we're about to convey information. Because we don't have the luxury to send messages that don't have significance in our writing, eliminating throat-clearing is a way to tighten up our prose without diminishing its value.

But what, you might ask, about throat-clearing's other purpose—lubricating the communication medium to make it easier for us to communicate? After all, that's what actual throat-clearing does when we speak, so why deprive our writing of the same function? Well, actually we don't need to do that, as long as we're disciplined in our writing process. If we're able to recognize that the first drafts of what we write will be seen by no one except us, and that we will edit our work carefully and ruthlessly in order to make it as tight as possible without losing meaning, then there's no problem at all with writing as many throat-clearing phrases as you like into your drafts. Just as with the noises you make before you speak, written throat-clearing can help you get to the real point of your sentence and write it in a clear and forceful way. Once you write the sentence in your first draft, you can eliminate the throat-clearing noises during the editing process, leaving the clear sentence that was being obscured by all the unnecessary words. In time you might find that you don't need the help in writing clear sentences, but there's nothing wrong with relying on help like this as you develop your writing technique. Just remember that some of the words you type at first will never make it into the final version of the document.

C. Once You've Written Your First Draft, Listen to Your Sentences

As we've seen, the answer to the question "how long should a sentence be" is easy: "as long as it needs to be and no longer." But like so many answers, this one just tells us that we asked the wrong question. The better and more helpful question is "how long should a sentence be to carry out its function of conveying a single thought within the text in which it's contained?" The answer to that question requires us to consider the context within which the sentence finds itself and that, in turn, requires us to listen to the sentences we've written.

By "listen," I don't mean that we should read our sentences aloud, although there are times when that isn't a bad idea. Rather, I mean that as we read a sentence in a paragraph we need to use both our eyes and our internal ears to place that sentence in the context of the sentences surrounding it. This might sound mystical and too intangible to be helpful, but work with me for a second and I'll try to show you that this is solid and practical advice that anyone can use.

First, let's consider that "internal ears" comment. Those of you who have studied anatomy will know that there is, in fact, no such thing; we just have the ears on the outside of our heads and don't have additional ones hidden away somewhere else in our bodies. But we also know that we "hear" writing as we read it, even if we don't consciously sound out the words in our minds. This phenomenon explains the use of metaphors like "voice" to describe a writer's style and "conversation" when we speak about the communication between a writer and a reader. We don't mean that we can actually hear the writer's voice as we read, but that the writing style allows us to generate those internal sounds as we read. And we don't mean that the writer and reader are engaged in a literal conversation, but that the questioning process that characterizes active reading, and the answering process that characterizes empathetic writing, are both embodied in the aural concept of a conversation. These metaphors remind us that no matter how highly evolved we have become, verbal communication is also, at some deep level, aural communication, just as it was for our early ancestors.

With that idea in mind, let's go back and consider the idea of "listening" to a sentence in context and how that can help our sentences to meet the Goldilocks length test. A good sentence, as I noted at the start of this chapter, propels the reader forward in the text. As writers, we control the speed of that propulsion in several ways: by the length of the words we use, by our use of active or passive voice (that word again), by our inclusion, or elimination, of non-essential words, by punctuation, and by sentence length. But it's important to remember that when we think of "propulsion" we don't mean that writing should move the reader as quickly as possible through the text. We could do that, of course, if we wanted to, but the result would be a (metaphorically) breathless reader who has had no time to contemplate the text's meanings and who has been hurried along from start to finish.

It's better to think of the process as a journey you and the reader take, with you as the guide. There are times when you might want to move the reader along—because this part of the journey is uninteresting but must be travelled in order to get to more interesting parts later, perhaps, or even because you don't want the reader to think or observe something too closely—and there are times when you want to slow the reader down to fully take in the view.

So it should be apparent that there's no way to judge the appropriateness of a sentence's length on its own. Sometimes sentences need to be short, and sometimes they need to be long. The context in which a sentence is placed, and the goal the writer has for that sentence in that place, determines how long or how short it should be with the idea that short sentences tend to move a reader along more quickly and long sentences— especially long, meandering sentences that can seem to have no end in sight, like this one—slow the reader down and give the reader time to contemplate everything the writer has been saying.

Variety is the key. A string of short sentences can be effective in moving the narrative along. And a string of long sentences can help to slow the reader down. But too many short sentences can leave a reader exhausted, and too many long sentences can send a reader to sleep. The important thing for the writer to do is to listen to the sound of the sentence in the context the writer has created for it in order to know if the sentence will have the desired effect.

So, how long should a sentence be? The same length as a piece of string: as long as it needs to be to do the job, whatever that job might be. If you want an actual number, then an average sentence of legal writing should probably be between 20 and 25 words long. That last sentence, by the way, was 22 words long, counting the numbers as words. And that sentence was 15 words; short in terms of the average but as you were reading it did you hear (or see) how its flow was interrupted several times by the commas that set aside the parenthetical clause "by the way" and the one that put an audible pause between "long" and "counting"? At 52 words, that last sentence was more than double the recommended average length. Did it seem too long? Did it have unnecessary words in it? Did it disrupt the flow of this paragraph or did it seem to fit in with the context I developed for it? Those are the questions you should ask of your writing when you "listen" to it during the editing phase of the writing process.

2. Nearby Sentences Shouldn't Begin the Same Way

This "rule" of writing is one that seems to be particularly difficult for lawyers and legal writers to follow, especially when they talk about the details of cases they're reviewing. The easiest way of introducing some detail from a case is to write "In *Smith*, the court held that ..." and to follow that with "In *Jones*, the court held that ...". Sometimes these two sentences follow each other consecutively and sometimes they're separated by other sentences — even an entire paragraph. But the sameness of the opening formula will always stand out and its repetition will be the thing on which the reader focuses.

In fact, the classic "In *Smith*" opening is a perfect candidate for elimination during editing because it is a textbook example of throat-clearing. Let's consider this opening more carefully to see what I mean. Here's a hypothetical example of this type of sentence. "In *Smith*, a federal district court in Maryland stated that Maryland law does not recognize the tort of negligent infliction of emotional distress. *Smith v. Jones*, 123 F.Supp. 2d 456 (D.Md. 2010)."[3]

This sentence has one of the hallmarks of throat-clearing; the action happens at the end. But, you might object, the fact that this holding comes from a specific case, and that the case was decided by a federal district court in Maryland, might both be important pieces of information. And I would agree, except that the formalities of legal writing require that both pieces of information be supplied by the citation, placed after the sentence in its own citation sentence. There's no getting around this requirement. It makes lawyers unique, in that we place our bibliographical information in the body of the text rather than in footnotes, but this is a feature of our writing style and until we're ordered to do it differently, that's how lawyers will write.

So in the case of our hypothetical sentence, the citation after the text is unavoidable. And that citation tells us the name of the case (*Smith v. Jones*), the fact that it was decided by a federal district court (only federal district court opinions are published in the Federal Supplement, second series, which is what "F.Supp. 2d" means), and that the federal district court was located in Maryland (that's what "D.Md." means).

With this in mind, let's reconsider what the words at the start of the sentence tell us that we won't learn from another part of the sentence. The name of the case? No. The type of court? No. The location of the court? No. So the start of this sentence is throat-clearing and can be removed without changing the meaning of the sentence or losing any information: "In *Smith*, a federal district court in Maryland stated that Maryland law does not recognize the tort of negligent infliction of emotional distress. *Smith v. Jones*, 123 F.Supp. 2d 456 (D.Md. 2010)" can become "Maryland law does not recognize the

---

3. The citation is invented.

tort of negligent infliction of emotional distress. *Smith v. Jones,* 123 F.Supp. 2d 456 (D.Md. 2010)" without any degradation of information.

This is the perfect solution to the "In *casename*" sentence formula that so often heralds the arrival of the discussion of cases. Once that phrase, and the words necessarily accompanying it to introduce the actual point of the sentence, are eliminated, the sentence becomes leaner and more powerful without losing meaning. And the byproduct of this editing, of course, is that no matter how long the string of cases under consideration might be, no two case analyses will begin the same way: your sentences convey the same meaning while being shorter and more effective and while following the "nearby sentences should not begin the same way" guideline.

3. Sentences Should Contain One Thought

Another guideline that can help organize your thinking and your writing is that sentences should only contain one thought. This should be a fairly straightforward guideline to follow, since there's no limit to the number of sentences you can have in a paragraph, or a document. The same general idea applies to all units of writing, and that acts as a natural limiter on the number of sentences you'll include in any larger unit, so there's no reason to let your sentences amble along, picking up new ideas as they go.

But what does "one thought" mean? In a sense, this entire book is about legal skills, so does that one thought mean that this entire book could be one sentence long? It worked for James Joyce, after all, so why not here? Well, for one reason, James Joyce was a better writer than I am, and for another, the "thought" required for the "one thought in a sentence" guideline is a little more specific than the broad theme of "legal skills." Rather, the thought required at the sentence level is the smallest part into which an idea can be divided.

An appellate brief, for example, is about all the issues raised on appeal. Each section in the "analysis" portion of that brief deals with one individual issue, and each subsection of that section deals with each separate part of that single issue. Within those subsections, each paragraph deals with one discrete portion of the sub issue—the rule that applies to it, for example, or an opinion that explains that rule, or how that opinion applies to the issue raised by the case for which the brief is being written. And each sentence in each paragraph deals with just one part of the portion of the brief covered by each paragraph. To use an architectural metaphor, sentences are the bricks in an argument's structure; each one is a separate unit and each one, taken alone, would be ineffective in accomplishing a building's purpose. But when bricks are combined skillfully, and in a careful and planned way, they can build almost anything. Just don't try to make the brick too large for its purpose.

4. Sentences Should Flow from One to the Next

Here we run into one of the hazards of using extended metaphors in writing: extend the metaphor too far, and it will likely get mixed. In the last section I said sentences were like bricks, and now I'm going to suggest that your sentences should flow together.

But bricks don't flow, and if they did they wouldn't be discrete entities. Each brick is its own unit, attached to other bricks by a smear of concrete. Even when the entire structure is complete, a close enough inspection will reveal each separate brick standing alone. There is no flow.

But maybe there's a way of saving this metaphor after all. Sentences are themselves discrete entities, after all, and you can identify where one ends by the closing punctuation and where the next one begins by the capital letter. Maybe what I mean by "flow" is really just the verbal equivalent of the concrete that holds the two sentences together, joining them seamlessly so they form part of the larger whole.

Maybe. Or maybe this is an example of a metaphor that's too extended to be of much use. Either way, the concept of "flow" requires more explanation, and more thought, than a simple metaphor can provide. Let's consider it in more detail.

Take a look at the beginnings of the two previous paragraphs. I don't hold them out as great writing, but they give a practical demonstration of flow, at least in a very simple way. The second paragraph demonstrates the way in which a conjunction like "but" can join two sentences together, even when separated by a paragraph break. It's important to remember that even though different paragraphs contain different ideas, those ideas can be related to each other—one can build on the previous paragraph, if you will. And conjunctions like "but" and "and" are simple ways of showing the relationship between sentences, and between paragraphs. The last sentence of a paragraph should be the culmination of the thought contained in that paragraph, and the first sentence of the next paragraph should show how that thought is being developed, continued, or contradicted. "But" suggests contradiction, "and" suggests continuation, and a word like "moreover" suggests development. Readers should have no difficulty understanding why they are reading the next sentence because they can see the relationship between the two.

The third paragraph of this section uses a different technique to demonstrate flow. In doing so, it violated two of the previous guidelines—it was a one-word sentence that began the same way as a previous sentence. Here the violation was even more extreme because the two sentences were consecutive. The last sentence in the second paragraph began, "Maybe what I mean by 'flow' is ..." and the next sentence, the one beginning the third paragraph, was a one-word sentence: "Maybe." By starting the same way as the last sentence of the previous paragraph, this opening sentence showed readers that the two sentences were related, and by its brevity it implied that the optimism of the previous sentence was not going to be maintained, a notion strengthened by the beginning of the next sentence: "Or maybe ..." No reader should have been in doubt that the two sentences—in fact the two paragraphs—were related and that the new paragraph was flowing directly from the previous one.

Flow is tricky. Sometimes you want it to be overt, as in the examples described in the last two paragraphs, and sometimes you want it to be more inherent, as in the start of this paragraph, which showed its relationship to the other paragraphs by restating the principal theme of this subsection: flow. However you establish it, though, flow—the unbroken movement of a reader's eyes from left to right across a page, from the top of the page to the bottom, and from one page to the next—is a crucial element of effective writing in any medium and especially for legal writers. The more a piece of writing flows, the more control you have over your reader. And control over the reader is what we're after in all forms of writing, and particularly, for our present purposes, in legal writing.

By "control," I don't mean anything sinister. This doesn't reflect my desire to brainwash my readers or to take over the world. All I mean by this is that legal writers want to move their readers through the documents they write as smoothly and painlessly as possible: if the document is a contract, they want their readers to understand as readily as possible what the obligations of the contracting parties are to each other and what other conditions might apply; if the document is a will, they want their readers to understand how their client's estate is to be divided up; and if the document is persuasive, like a brief filed with a court, they want their readers to believe that their client's position on the issues is the correct one. Lawyers achieve these ends by controlling their readers, by leading them gently but firmly through the document from beginning to end by (to use the metaphor I used earlier) showing them some sights along the way and hustling them past other spots that might be less interesting or less helpful to their client's position. And flow is one of the technical features they have at their disposal to help them in this goal.

When sentences flow from one to the next the reader is given little chance to become distracted and the writer has a chance to keep the reader firmly focused on what the writer wants the reader to see. The writer who can move a reader through a document with ease has at least a chance of accomplishing that document's goal.

Conclusion

Sentences might be under-appreciated and invisible most of the time, but with care and attention they can move your reader through your writing under your control. By carefully structuring your sentences and organizing them so they fit together and so the bond between them is tight and secure, you can construct a persuasive analysis, a clear contract, a will that leaves no uncertainty or ambiguity, or achieve any goal you want your writing to accomplish. Skillful, well-crafted sentences are an essential part of any piece of thoughtful writing. You should pay close attention to your sentences in both the drafting and editing stages of writing to make sure that your sentences are doing as much work for you as possible. If you do, your writing will almost certainly improve.

Exercises

1. For each of the following sentences, decide if the sentence is in passive voice and, if so, rewrite it in the active voice. In each case, assume the writer was the actor if necessary.

    a. Mistakes were made.

    b. The check's failure to clear was the result of my secretary's inadvertent failure to deposit sufficient funds into the account.

    c. The plaintiff's deposition was taken on June 14, 2013, in Washington, D.C., at the offices of Lewis, Fry, & Atwood, LLC.

    d. Civil liability and criminal penalties are both possible results of the inattention to basic business practices demonstrated in this case.

2. Rewrite each of the following sentences to eliminate any throat-clearing phrases or unnecessary words.

    a. When all the evidence is carefully considered, it will become clear to the Court that the defendant had no role in the alleged fraud.

    b. In *Bowling*, the federal district court held that the law of place of injury, rather than the law of the state of manufacture, should apply to class claims. *Bowling v. Pfizer*, 143 F.R.D. 141 (S.D.Ohio 1992).

    c. As Plaintiffs argued in their initial brief on this issue, to the extent that the County now asserts that the question of "ambient temperature" is not relevant to a discussion of whether heat has been discharged into the Ten Mile Creek in violation of the Clean Water Act, the County is wrong.

    d. It is clear to anyone paying any attention to this matter that Largecorp followed all applicable state and federal regulations.

3. Rewrite each of the following sentences to shorten them without changing their meaning. If it helps, you need not keep your rewritten version to one sentence.

    a. It is not the case, nor should the Plaintiff assume otherwise, that the Defendant will simply allow its pocket to be picked by someone making unsubstantiated claims against it concerning the acts of its employees, who acted in this matter in strict compliance to the Defendant's Manual of Conduct and who, in any case, caused no harm to the Plaintiff nor injured her in any way.

    b. Seller and Buyer agree that the item at issue, a violin with the label "Antonius Stradivarius: Brooklyn, 1926" is not, in fact, a violin made by the Seventeenth Century violin maker Stradivarius, but rather, is a twentieth century copy of a Stradivarius violin, made by Bert Greiser in his basement workshop in New York, even though the instrument conforms precisely to the measurements of the violin known as the "Messe" Stradivarius, and that its value should be calculated on the basis of its being an original Greiser rather than an original Stradivarius.

    c. You have asked me to consider the question of whether Ms. Stafford, who lives at 2486 North Avenue, is permitted, under City Ordinances, to share her house with 275 cats and, if the answer is "no," which of several possible candidates is the appropriate agency to enforce the relevant Ordinance against Ms. Stafford and, as a collateral, but important, matter, how that agency should manage the removal and care of the cats that now live in Ms. Stafford's home.

    d. Tax liability is, of course, an important consideration as we move forward and you can be assured that our highly trained staff of accountants, actuaries, and attorneys will be working with you and your staff to make sure that any liability is kept to a minimum and that, going forward, your relationship with the Internal Revenue Service is improved and that all taxes owing to the government are paid in full, always being mindful of your desire to minimize your tax burden and to maximize any and all deductions which reduce your overall tax load.

Focus Questions

1. How much time do you spend thinking about your sentence structure when you write?

2. Do you understand how to form (and avoid) the passive voice? Can you easily identify the passive voice in your own writing? In the writing of others? Have you been told to avoid the passive voice in your writing? Were you given a reason for this advice or were you just told to do it?

3. Are you surprised to learn that there's no rule against starting a sentence with a conjunction? Or that split infinitives are not against the rules of English grammar?

4. Had you considered the assertion, made here, that English has fewer rules than people think and that many of the "rules" of English are more properly thought of as guidelines? Does that change the way you think about writing?

5. Have you considered the idea that words should work hard for you and that a word that isn't doing work in a sentence should be deleted?

6. Have you caught any throat-clearing sentences in your own writing? The writing of others?

7. Does the idea of listening to your sentences seem to you to be a useful one? Have you considered the effect that varying sentence lengths can have on your reader?

8. Thinking back on writing you've done, do you think you've fallen into the trap of beginning successive sentences the same way in your previous work?

9. Are you surprised to learn that lawyers place their bibliographical information in the body of the texts they write? Do you care? Do you see how this practice could be used to your advantage as a writer?

10. Are you familiar with the idea that sentences should only contain one thought?

11. Do you think about ways to make your sentences flow when you're editing your work?

Chapter 11

Paragraphs

What You Should Learn from This Chapter

This chapter discusses paragraph structure and how to generate workable paragraphs that don't appear too formulaic to the reader. The chapter discusses familiar concepts like topic sentences, thesis paragraphs, and paragraph length and flow, and shows how these concepts are particularly important to legal writers.

After reading this chapter, you should:

- have re-familiarized yourself with the notion of topic sentences;
- be able to identify when one of your paragraphs is too long or too short;
- be able to control the flow of your paragraphs to make your writing easy to read; and
- be able to identify and draft a thesis paragraph when your writing requires one.

The writing process is like a fractal structure, in that much of the advice at one level repeats at other levels. This means that most of what we said about sentences can also be applied to paragraphs. Paragraphs, like sentences, should be limited to one thought or idea, should be long enough to fully express that idea but no longer, and should be constructed with care so that they flow from the previous paragraph and into the next one.

There might be less to say about paragraphs than any other important structural unit in writing. But I've already said some things that need to be discussed in a little more detail, so let's take a moment to do that now.

1. Topic Sentences

Probably the most commonly known piece of wisdom about paragraphs is that they should start with topic sentences. Topic sentences introduce the topic—the one thought or idea—of the paragraph and make sure that the reader is oriented and ready to consider the information the paragraph has to offer. Topic sentences, the common wisdom runs, are an essential element of well-organized writing.

Well, maybe. In general, topic sentences are a good idea. Good non-fiction writing, and good legal writing in particular, should be relatively unsurprising and should move in logical steps from idea to idea. Topic sentences are an excellent tool for organizing material and helping the reader to understand what information the coming paragraph will contain.

But there are times when we need to break the predictable pattern of paragraph structure in order to maintain interest and, especially, in aid of flow. The previous sentence, for example, came at the beginning of a paragraph but you could not tell from it what the rest of the paragraph would be about. It followed logically from the last sentence of the previous paragraph, and therefore maintained flow, and the use of the conjunction "but" might have been sufficiently intriguing to you that you wanted to read the rest of a sentence that seemed to contradict the common wisdom expressed in the previous paragraph. If so, the sentence did its job, even though that job wasn't to be a topic sentence.

This isn't to say that topic sentences are bad. Most of the time, in fact, topic sentences are the right choice for legal writers (and remember, this book is not an example of legal writing, so some of the choices it reflects wouldn't be appropriate for legal writing) and the common wisdom is called that because it's generally agreed to be wise. Legal writing is a conservative style and legal writers should rarely attempt to defy convention and seek for creative forms in which to place their analysis.

But rarely is not never, and in a theme I'll come back to often in this book, context determines form. In other words, the context you develop for a thought is the most important element in deciding how that thought should be presented. That context might be the standard non-fiction paragraph, with topic sentence used to introduce the subject of the paragraph and the remainder of the paragraph used to fully develop and contemplate that topic. Sometimes, though, there is value in surprising the reader just a little—in subverting the genre expectations of style, if you will. In those cases, sometimes a non-standard paragraph is the appropriate choice.

You shouldn't try to surprise your reader too often in a document. Constant surprise is no surprise, and you should try to avoid being too obviously seeking to startle your reader. Doing so will draw attention to your writing as writing, not to your writing as a vehicle for analysis, where the analysis itself is what the reader should focus on. But sometimes—probably more often in persuasive writing than in the more clinical style of objective legal writing—it can be helpful to jolt the reader from the standard paragraph structure in order to emphasize a point or to hold the reader's attention at a point where you think it otherwise might flag. And when that seems advisable, remember that context determines form. If the context you have established for the thoughts you are expressing suggests a non-standard form, try it. Just be ready to edit the structure into a more conventional approach if, after reviewing the result, it doesn't seem as effective in practice as you thought it would be in theory.

2. Paragraph Length

The advice about context determining form also applies to paragraph length. Just as with almost all writing advice, there is a standard answer when it comes to paragraph length but that standard answer only applies to most situations, not all. If there are legitimate reasons to consider an approach different from that suggested by the standard answer then you should at least consider them, always remembering that variations from the expected approach will have an effect on the reader. Your job as a writer is to anticipate and manage how your writing strikes the reader, and paragraph length is certainly a tool you should use in that endeavor.

The standard advice about paragraph length is that paragraphs should be relatively short: a topic sentence and maybe three or four additional sentences (the short sentence expected of non-fiction writers and legal writers in particular) to develop that topic. Then on to the next piece of the analysis and a new paragraph. The average page of text should be able to accommodate multiple paragraphs on it; two easily, sometimes three or more on each page.

This is good advice. It sends a strong message to the reader that you are taking care to organize your analysis and that you're working hard to make the information you're transmitting as easy to understand and digest as possible. Turning a page and seeing several paragraphs waiting for you to read can be a pleasurable experience. If you have already been drawn into a piece of writing, a well-organized page can, by its appearance alone, fill readers with the expectation that by the end of the page they will have been helped in their goal of becoming as well informed as possible about the subject of the document they're reading.

By contrast, there are few things more daunting, as a reader, than to turn a page and face an unbroken page filled with text; it is almost a physical assault, a hostile gesture from writer to reader with the clear message that the writer couldn't be bothered to organize the material carefully and is instead expecting the reader to do that work. Only a very generous reader, or one who has no choice, will willingly enter a single-paragraph page, and all readers confronted with such a page will get the clear message that the writer has no consideration or thought for them. If you're trying to persuade a reader of a position, there are few worse messages to send.

Does the opposite hold true, though?

One sentence paragraphs, like the previous paragraph, are generally disfavored in formal documents of the kind lawyers typically write. They seem flashy or gimmicky— designed to draw attention to themselves rather than to the analysis they should contain. They are an inescapable, and often desirable, feature of fiction writing; they can contain a line of dialog, or a crucial thought in a character's mind—something that requires its own paragraph in order specifically to draw attention to itself. That's rarely the case in legal writing, though, where everything typically proceeds in a more orderly and supported fashion, and where single ideas are rarely so important that they require the visual punctuation supplied by single-sentence paragraphs.

But as with all writing guidelines, this is a guideline, not a rule. It can happen that a legal writer might want to drive a point home by isolating it from all other words or distractions, and a single sentence paragraph—usually a short sentence of one, tersely worded, thought—can provide that effect more successfully than in any other way. Again, and as always, the context you develop for an idea determines the form used to express that idea.

In part, of course, writers are at the mercy of their material. If an idea requires a substantial amount of discussion before it is fully explored, the paragraph containing that discussion will be longer than if the idea under discussion is a relatively simple and non-complex one. But careful writers understand that they can break lengthy, complex paragraphs into multiple paragraphs, sometimes by adding a new topic sentence before the paragraph changes course slightly. That slight course change, together with the new topic sentence, can turn one too-long paragraph into two shorter ones, breaking up the uninterrupted flow of words facing the reader and clarifying the analysis at the same time. This attention to paragraph structure is a crucial element of flow, that difficult-to-define and yet crucial element of good writing.

3. Paragraph Flow

The idea of flow is particularly important to a well-constructed paragraph. And this can cause a conflict with the commonly offered advice that paragraphs should start with a topic sentence. Topic sentences, as we have seen, are important and valuable, but they can also be deadly to flow because they tend to announce something new and therefore different from the previous paragraph. But if a paragraph is to flow effectively, it needs to take up where the previous paragraph left off. The problem can be solved by careful attention during both the writing and editing stages, but making sure paragraphs flow on from each other while still being limited to one idea that isn't a repeat of what's been said before can take some editing skill and a willingness to move things around.

Moving paragraphs from one part of a document to another was possible in the typewriter era, but it was difficult to accomplish without retyping the entire document—something most writers (especially those under deadline pressure like lawyers) were usually unwilling to do, making it crucial that the structure of the document was finished before writing began. This is no longer true; the ability to cut and paste on a word processor means that a paragraph can be easily relocated to a different place in the document, and this leaves the editor with a much more challenging task than before.

These days, a writer must follow a careful two-step process: having written a document, the writer must step back from the writing process and pay close attention to the internal structure of what's been written and be willing to make drastic changes in that structure if the document's balance is improved as a result. And having made such significant changes, the writer must be willing to move paragraphs back to their original location if, after reflection, the changes didn't help. Paragraph structure, perhaps more than any other part of the editing process, requires a blend of intellectual rigor, to make sure the ideas are communicated in the best way possible, and an almost musical sense of balance and forward momentum, to make sure one paragraph moves irresistibly into the next.[1]

One thing that helps us with the structure and balance of paragraphs is that the written unit probably closely matches our thought process as we map out some analysis in our heads. We don't usually think in sentences, because each sentence is too small to register in our large-scale planning, and while we probably think of analysis in terms of sections, we break each of those sections down into the steps necessary to complete

---

1. Even then, the writer's task isn't finished. Once writing and editing are completed, proofreading begins. And finding mistakes in your own writing is perhaps the hardest task of all. We'll speak in detail about proofreading soon.

that section. Those steps are usually paragraph-level steps, and while we are in the throes of the writing process we might find we need more paragraphs than we had first anticipated. If so, that original step-by-step paragraph map will serve us well as a guide to what things should be in our analysis and the order in which they should probably appear.

4. Thesis Paragraphs

Sometimes, of course, an entire paragraph serves as introduction to a section, in much the way that a topic sentence introduces a paragraph. It's the same sense of fractal structure I mentioned earlier, where each part of the structure repeats at each different level. Thesis paragraphs are valuable organizing tools that explain what the next section of the analysis will be about and, most importantly, how it will end. Most legal writing should do away with suspense and should let the reader know very early on what the result will be. You can still move the reader through a piece of writing without trying to keep the reader in suspense; in any case, if you're writing a brief in support of the plaintiff, the reader will probably guess that you want the plaintiff to win, so suspense would be difficult to maintain.

As a writer, it's important to consider your reader's cultural or genre expectations when writing a document, and most legal readers will expect a thesis paragraph at the start of a section. For that reason alone, it's a good idea to think about starting each section you write—whether it is a large chunk of the analysis or just a small sub-section of that larger piece of the analysis—with a thesis paragraph. Using this structural device will help orient your reader to what's coming next, and it will also help you to organize your own thoughts as to what needs to come next in the document and the order in which you should present that information.

It is rarely the case that legal analysis is improved by the writer diving right into it, without first explaining to readers where this portion of the analysis will end up or how it will get there. This approach—often called the umbrella approach, because it covers every piece of the analysis coming up, or the roadmap approach, because it sets out the final destination of the analysis and also the route it will take to get there—is expected by readers trained by years of exposure to writing that developed analysis in the same way. Of course, where writers are confronted with such expectations, they have two choices: to meet them or to subvert them by going in a different direction. As always, the usually correct choice is to meet the readers' expectations and to use thesis paragraphs to outline the path a section will take. But "usually" is not "always," and you, as a writer, should make this decision each time after thinking about the structure you want and carefully weighing the desirability of following, or not following, the conventional wisdom.

Conclusion

As with most things to do with writing, effective paragraphing takes great skill and thought and, if done well, will be completely invisible to the reader. Few things are more important, though, in the communication of ideas from writer to reader than the careful attention to balance and flow necessary to make good paragraphs and to combine them to make a coherent, logical, and continuous section of analysis. Poorly considered paragraphs can make a text almost unreadable, while well-constructed paragraphs can make a text almost effortless to read. You would be well advised to pay close attention to the structure and flow of your paragraphs.

Exercise

Reorganize this text so its paragraph structure makes more sense.

You have asked me to give my opinion as to the advisability of the firm's accepting a case from Mr. Martin Nealon, a prospective client. For the reasons stated below, I recommend that the firm decline to proceed with this potential litigation. Martin Nealon wants his neighbor, William Hudson, to pay to cut back the trees and vines that have encroached onto his property. Mr. Nealon claims that the tree limbs are a nuisance and the leaves clog his gutters every fall. In addition, he claims that vines from Mr. Hudson's property are pernicious and quick-growing and that the only way to control them is to cut them back at the source. He wants us to sue Mr. Hudson for the damages he has incurred in keeping his property, located in Baltimore at 854 Lead Avenue, free from all encroaching vegetation coming from Mr. Hudson's property. The Maryland courts make clear, however, that the only remedy available to Mr. Nealon is self-help and that Mr. Hudson will not be found liable for any costs incurred by Mr. Nealon in the cleaning up of his property. The Court of Appeals considered the question of whether a landowner has a cause of action for damage caused by encroaching vegetation in *Melnick v. C.S.X. Corp.*, 312 Md. 511, 540 A.2d 1133 (1988). Writing for the Court, Judge Eldridge noted that courts across the country "uniformly hold that a landowner has a right to a self-help remedy." *Id.* at 514, 1136. This right is limited to the landowner's own property; there is no right to enter onto the adjoining landowner's property without consent and to cut back or in some other way prevent the encroaching vegetation from coming onto the landowner's property. *Id.* at 515, 1137. The rule commonly applied by courts when considering questions of this kind is known as the Massachusetts Rule after the case of *Michalson v. Nutting*, 275 Mass. 232, 175 N.E. 490 (1931), in which the Supreme Judicial Court of Massachusetts concluded that self-help was the most efficient and equitable way to resolve the problem of adjoining landowners with vegetation that encroached from one property to the other. *Melnick*, 312 Md. at 516, 540 A.2d at 1138. The Restatement (Second) of Torts has adopted a similar rule when the encroaching vegetation is natural, although it does impose a duty in certain circumstances when the encroachment is caused by a man-made, or "artificial," condition. Id. at 517, 1139. In the present case, however, Mr. Nealon's property is affected by the trees and vines that grow on Mr. Hudson's property and Maryland courts are unlikely to adopt the Restatement's exception in light of *Melnick*'s clear holding that limits a property owner's relief to self-help. An additional exception has been recognized by some courts where the encroachment is in some way unusually harmful to a landowner's property. Variously known as the "Virginia" or "Hawaiian" Rule, this exception imposes liability on the landowner's neighbor where the encroaching vegetation is noxious or causes harm "in ways other than by casting shade or dropping leaves, flowers, or fruit." *Whitesell v. Houlton*, 2 Hawaii App. 365, 632 P.2d 1077, 1079 (1981). The Court of Appeals, however, considered and rejected the Hawaiian and Virginia Rules in *Melnick*. Accordingly, even were Mr. Nealon able to assert that Mr. Hudson's trees and vines were causing him unusual or special harm, he would be unable to persuade a Maryland court to allow him to pursue Mr. Hudson for damages or other relief. Because it is unlikely, under Maryland law, that Mr. Nealon will be able to survive a Motion to Dismiss his claim for failure to state a claim, and because there is no principled justification for seeking to apply the Virginia or Hawaiian exceptions to the Massachusetts rule in the case of overgrowing vegetation encroaching on a landowner's property from the property of his neighbor, I recommend that the firm decline to represent Mr. Nealon in this matter.

Focus Questions

1. How much time do you spend thinking about your paragraph structure when you write or edit? Do you think this is enough time or should you spend more or less time on paragraphing?

2. Were you taught that good paragraphs begin with topic sentences? Do you follow that advice when you're writing and editing?

3. Were you taught about thesis paragraphs when you were learning composition in school? Do you think about the value of thesis paragraphs when writing?

4. Does the notion of context dictating form make sense to you? Is this advice helpful to you?

5. When editing, do you think about paragraph length? Have you ever noticed the lengths of paragraphs in writing you have read? Have you criticized paragraphs that were too long or too short? Have you ever felt that the length of a paragraph was a sign that the writer didn't care about the reader? How did that make you respond to the writer's work?

6. Do you concentrate on paragraph flow when you write or when you edit? Do you see why flow is important for a reader?

Chapter 12

Section Headings

What You Should Learn from This Chapter

This chapter discusses the often-ignored subject of section headings and their role in effective writing. The chapter explores the relationship between section headings and analysis outlines and discusses why narrative headings are better for legal writing than abstract headings, and includes technical suggestions for the length and structure of headings.

After reading this chapter, you should:

- have developed an appreciation for the importance of section headings in complex analytical writing;
- have understood why narrative headings are superior to placeholder, abstract, headings; and
- be able to construct headings that guide your reader through your documents.

We've all had the experience of sitting in a darkened movie theatre, waiting for the movie begin, and instead seeing a series of previews for movies that haven't yet been released—some of which won't be released for months.[1] Something about that preview grabs your attention; maybe it's the actors involved, maybe it's the plot or the story, maybe it's some lines of dialog, maybe it's even the costumes. But something about that short preview makes you think that you'd like to see the entire movie when it comes out.

You've just been primed. The preview has prepared you to see a movie you didn't know about until a few seconds ago and you'll likely remember that movie and wait for its release with eager anticipation. And when you go and see it, you'll sit in the darkened theater and, before the movie starts, watch additional previews, all carefully selected to appeal to the type of person who would see the principal movie, and the whole process starts again.

Sometimes the movie doesn't meet the expectations set up by the preview. It can happen, for example, that the blend of picture with movie score was the thing that first

---

1. Thanks to Professor Steve Johansen, who introduced me to the relationship between movie previews and priming in the law. Steven Johansen, *Coming Attractions: An Essay on Movie Trailers and Preliminary Statements*, 10 Leg. Comm. & Rhetoric: J ALWD 41 (2013).

interested you about the movie but the movie's ultimate score had not been completed by the time the preview was shown and so the film's producers used some music that was appropriate to the movie excerpts being shown but that was not ultimately going to be used in the movie. It's also possible that the movie's producers wanted to persuade you that a movie was, perhaps, comedic when in fact the comedy plays only a small part in the movie, most of which is gloomy or even tragic. This dissonance between preview and movie might have been intentional on the producers' part; they might assume that the actual movie would not sell as many tickets if the audience were fully aware of the movie's plot, and so they tried to persuade the audience to come and see a different type of movie, in hopes that the audience would not be too jarred by the difference between preview and final movie.

It can also happen that the preview can reveal too much of the movie. We've probably all had the experience of realizing, after leaving a movie, that all the interesting parts had been first revealed in the preview and that the movie itself was just a loose framework built to support its few gripping moments. Again, the producers might have realized that the final product was weak and tried to use the preview as a means of bringing audiences into the theater expecting that the entire movie would be filled with such moments. The audience might leave disappointed, but the preview would by then have done its job.

The role of section headings in legal writing is much like that of movie previews. Just as with previews, they are not the main event but they can prime their audience to expect something. And just as with previews and movies, headings can fail to do their jobs properly: they can fail to meet the expectations they set up, or they can set up expectations that are inconsistent with the analysis they precede. Handled correctly, though, headings can prime a reader to receive information and they can remind a reader of the thrust of the analysis when the reader browses the section headings after reading the document. Headings, it turns out, can be powerful tools.

1. Outlines and Section Headings

Before we start talking about section headings, though, do you outline your work before you start to write, or do you just start typing and see where things end up? It's almost always a good idea to map out what you plan to say before you start writing. This short detour will relate back to section headings. Really.

Outlines are flexible documents: they can be used for multiple purposes, they can take several forms, and they can be detailed or loose, depending on the writer and the purpose for which the outline is being prepared. For the moment, let's only consider the outlines you prepare once your research is completed and you're ready to begin writing a document, whether it's a memo, a brief, or something else. The best outline to meet that purpose is the linear outline—the type that starts with a series of major points with each containing subparts to indicate subordinate points under the principal point. Other outlines, like branching outlines, have other virtues like helping you to get your thoughts about an issue down on paper without worrying about the hierarchy of those thoughts or the order in which they should appear in your final analysis.

Let's assume you're writing a memo to a partner in your firm about class action certification in federal court, a process that's governed by Rule 23 of the Federal Rules of Civil Procedure. And for the purposes of this discussion you don't need to actually know anything about class certification. Once you take a look at the rule, your outline for the class certification portion of the analysis might look like this:

Class Certification

1. Requirements
   - Is There a Class?
   - Is the Class Representative a Member of the Class?
2. Rule 23(a) Prerequisites
   - Numerosity
   - Common Questions
   - Typicality
   - Representative Will Fairly and Adequately Represent Class
3. Rule 23(b)(1)
   - Risk of Inconsistent or Varying Adjudications
   - Risk of Individual Adjudications That Would Dispose of Class Claims
4. Rule 23(b)(2)
   - Injunctive or Declaratory Relief
5. Rule 23(b)(3)
   - Questions of Law or Fact Predominate
   - Class Is Superior to Other Forms of Resolution, and
     — Class Members' Interest in Controlling Litigation
     — Extent and Nature of Already Existing Litigation
     — Desirability of Concentrating Litigation in Forum
     — Difficulties in Managing Class[2]

In this example, then, the outline has one heading ("Class Certification"), five subheadings (designated by the numbers), four sub-subheadings (designated by the bullets), one of which is further subdivided by use of four dashes. You doubtless are familiar with the appearance of this type of outline.

This outline can form the basis of a memo on this topic, with the various headings and subheadings taking on the same role in the memo. And that's how outlining and section headings are related: when things go well, your reader can read your section headings and see the outline of your analysis. You can imagine how helpful it is when you, as a busy reader, can identify quickly and easily all the separate stages a writer took to reach a conclusion to the question posed at the outset of the document. If you're only interested in a specific part of that analysis—even a sub-sub-part—you can go directly to that portion of the analysis and read what the writer has said about it.

---

2. Those of you who might be familiar with the specifics of class certification will already know that this is a woefully inadequate outline that misses even some fundamental parts of the analysis. It's offered as an example of the type of outline we're discussing, not as something upon which you should rely if you're ever asked what it takes to certify a class action in federal court.

But if you look closely at the outline, you'll see that it isn't as helpful as it might be. It certainly tells you what topics will be discussed under each subheading, but it tells you nothing about what conclusions my analysis reaches about each topic. Section headings like these tell the reader something, but not as much as they could. That's why narrative headings are preferable by far to the bland signposts in the example.

2. Why Narrative Headings Are Superior to Abstract Headings

All legal writing is persuasive writing. In law school we sometimes speak of "objective" writing to distinguish it from the "subjective" writing lawyers engage in when they write briefs and other persuasive documents written to persuade a reader of the correctness of a position. In fact, though, even "objective" writing is persuasive; we just try to persuade the reader that we're being objective and even-handed. There's nothing untoward or deceitful about this because when we write as "objective" writers we genuinely are trying to analyze an issue without arguing in favor of one interpretation of the law over any other interpretation. But the reality of legal writing as a persuasive art means that legal writers should take every opportunity to inform their readers of what their analysis might say.

Law students sometimes mistake the meaning of that last sentence. They think that "every opportunity" means "most opportunities," perhaps, or that every word of the analysis should inform their readers. But while it's certainly true that every word of the analysis should be informative, that isn't enough; every mark in the document—every punctuation mark, every word regardless where it appears—literally everything in the document should be calculated to have an effect on the reader. This is a level of precision to which most law students have not been held before law school and it can take them some time to adjust their writing to these higher expectations. One way to make that transition is to realize that headings, while seemingly functional and utilitarian, also have a key function in informing or persuading the reader.

Let's consider the two subheadings under "Rule Requirements" in the sample outline above. "Is There a Class?" and "Is the Class Representative a Member of the Class?" are bland and not especially accurate paraphrases of the rule language that "[o]ne or more members of a class may sue or be sued as representative parties on behalf of all members...." Fed. R. Civ. P. 23(a). Those two sub-headings represent choices, one of which was to omit the language "may sue or be sued" that allows for defendant classes as well as the much more common plaintiff classes. That might be a significant omission or might not, depending on the facts in a particular case—a useful reminder that no legal analysis exists in a vacuum.

The two subheadings also reflect some analysis. The heading "Is There a Class?" attempts to encapsulate part of the essence of the quoted language from Rule 23(a): if a member of a class may sue on behalf of the class, a class must first exist and be definable. If a court cannot describe a class with sufficient clarity to be able to say whether someone coming before it is or is not a member of the class, then it would be difficult to say that a class exists, other than in the too-broad sense that a human being is in the class of human beings.[3]

If we assume that these are the facts of a case, how might they be reflected in the headings we select for the memo? Let's consider the answer to that question from the perspectives of both the "objective" writer—the one not trying to slant the analysis in one direction or the other—and also from that of the persuasive writer, who attempts to slant everything to support a particular position.

A. Narrative Headings Help Objective Analysis

The objective writer does not overtly seek to persuade the reader of anything and so need not worry about taking a position in the heading. Nonetheless, a heading like "Is There a Class?" conveys no information at all other than the vague sense that this part of the discussion will deal with the question of whether or not a class exists. Let's try to improve on that.

If you have no specific facts that caused the document to be written—if, for example, a partner at your firm asked you for a general survey of the law of class actions and specifically class certification—you might opt for a narrative but general heading, something like "A Class Must Be Identifiable Before It Can Be Certified" or "In Order to Seek Class Certification, a Class Representative Must Define the Class with Specificity." Both of these are wordy and could stand some additional editing to cut them down a little, but both convey much more information that the simple "Is There a Class?" heading in the original outline. Reading those headings, a reader would understand much more about the section's content and would be primed to take in the analysis that follows the heading. It's likely that the reader would also recall that analysis later when re-reading the heading; one of the remarkable things about carefully drafted headings is their ability—like movie previews—to help the reader recall much more information about a subject than one might expect, and certainly much more than would be possible without the heading.

B. Narrative Headings Improve Persuasive Analysis

Narrative headings are even more important when you get into persuasive writing. Here, the heading can prime your reader to understand your argument for this part of your document. Taken together, narrative headings form a complete outline of your argument and after reading the document (sometimes even before reading it), your reader should be able to construct, or re-construct, that argument in some detail.

From the perspective of someone seeking to certify a class, our subheading might be "The Class Can Be Identified with Specificity," or "The Class Definition Allows the Court

---

3. This possibility is not theoretical. It's possible to think of many situations where a group of people might have been affected by some action, yet don't have the ability to show that they belong to that group. If that happens, it might be difficult to show that a definable "class" exists for Rule 23 purposes.

to Identify Class Members." By contrast, a defendant might attempt "No Class Can Be Certified Because the Class Cannot Be Sufficiently Defined," or "Class Certification Fails Because Class Members Cannot Be Distinguished from the General Public." Again, these examples might be wordy and imperfect, but they show both the difference between persuasive and objective headings and they show how headings, like movie previews, can be used to prime the audience for what will follow.

3. Headings Can Show You When Not to Include Analysis

But it's important to remember that unlike movie previews, the legal writer shouldn't tinker with a reader's expectations, setting the reader up for an analysis that won't be delivered. In that sense, headings are much more restricted than movie previews; legal writers can't prime a reader for an analysis and then fail to deliver that analysis or deliver one that is in conflict with what the reader has been led to believe will be coming.

In part, that means the legal writer must evaluate whether or not an argument furthers the point being made by the document. And this points out yet another useful feature of narrative headings to a legal writer: they can show you when not to analyze something.

Again, let's consider the sub issue of class identification we've been discussing. In a complete review of class certification law, of course, this analysis is crucial; without it, the reader might simply assume that a class can always be formed by the simple act of calling it into being. The class might fail to meet some of the other certification requirements but the question of class identification might simply not be apparent to the reader without being pointed out. In the general, objective review of class certification procedure, then, this analysis is vital and should be included in the document.

The question is not so clear in the persuasive context, where an actual argument—supported by facts—is being constructed. In this situation, the facts might or might not justify inclusion of this subpart of the broader analysis. It's possible that the question of class identification is the crucial question and both plaintiff and defendant would have to address it. But it's possible that the facts make clear that a class can easily be defined and in that case there would be very little point making an argument about this prerequisite to class certification. Neither side would likely waste their precious pages (or words, if the court operates on a word count basis for its documents) or the judge's patience on an irrelevant argument.

An inexperienced attorney might include the analysis in a first draft of a document seeking or opposing class certification, but either that lawyer or a more experienced one should be able to see, from the failure of the analysis to live up to the claims of the heading, that the analysis should be cut from the final version of the document. In this way, a careful reader—sensitive to the balance between the expectations set up by the heading and the ability of the analysis to meet those expectations—can make intelligent decisions about what arguments to keep and which ones to cut.

4. Include Enough Headings to Make Your Analysis Digestible

Balance is a crucial element in deciding how to break up your work in order to make it easy for your reader to work through and appreciate it—"digest" it, in the metaphor used to describe how a reader consumes analysis. The balance here is between having so few headings that the reader is left without signposts to recognize significant parts of the analysis and so many that the reader becomes numb to the headings and fails to register them.

Writing that has too many headings is choppy, stilted, and ineffective. When you try to prime the reader for everything, you usually prime the reader for nothing because the reader likely will stop paying attention. The trick is to find the balance that allows you to inform your reader of important points in your analysis without overloading the reader with too much information. The law helps to a degree in this task: whenever a rule has several subparts, for example, you likely should address each subpart under its own heading. But deciding how to break up the analysis further, so that each important subpart of the larger picture gets its own heading, is a matter of judgment. As a general rule, if an issue requires its own rule statement and factual application, it needs its own subsection and heading. Another general rule that might help is that it's rare—although not unheard of—to have more than a full page of text without a heading of some sort; there are some legal sub issues that might take more than a couple of pages to analyze, but there are surprisingly few of them.

5. Headings Should Be Relatively Short

A heading that's too long will likely put off a reader who wants to get to the analysis and probably isn't too interested in spending time assimilating a long heading that is, after all, only a preview. Of course, how long "relatively short" might be is difficult to say with certainty: a few lines will usually be fine, more than four might be too long—as always, you as the writer will have to decide. Here a few things to consider as you look at the length of a heading.

A. Don't Include Too Much Detail

Some apprentice legal writers have the urge to make their headings into miniature versions of their analysis. They include case names, even case citations on occasion, and try to cram every crucial piece of information from their analysis into their heading. It's an understandable impulse, but one that should be strongly resisted. Remember that a heading is only a heading; the actual analysis follows under it and can be as extensive as necessary.

As always, it's easier to judge the appropriateness of a heading once you see it written down, so don't worry too much about trying to make each heading the perfect length in your first draft. You won't be showing that draft to anyone, so it doesn't matter how rough it is; the key is to be able to edit honestly and carefully once your first draft is completed. So try not to worry too much about details like the length of your headings as you write your first draft, but always go back and work on them ruthlessly after that first draft is finished.

As you edit your headings, ask yourself if they preview the analysis without actually analyzing the issue. If they do, and they're no more than four lines long, then the headings are probably not too long and don't have too much detail in them.

B. Try to Keep Your Headings in the Active Voice

As always, the advice to write something in the active voice comes with the reservation that there's nothing inherently wrong with the passive voice. But for most purposes, the active voice is a better choice and that is particularly true when it comes to section headings. The active voice places emphasis on the actor, is generally easier to read, and is almost always shorter than the passive voice.

Headings are actually a perfect place to start looking for, and eliminating, the passive voice during the editing phase. While the passive voice might be relatively elusive when buried in the middle of a lengthy piece of analysis, headings—by their nature—stand out and you should be able to identify the passive voice fairly easily. Once you've found and fixed (if desirable) the passive voice in your headings, you should find the passive voice in the rest of your document much more easily.

C. If You Have One Subheading, You Need at Least One More

Keeping your headings short doesn't mean you should skimp on them. And while this piece of advice probably looks strange, it's generally true that it you need to have at least two subdivisions at any given subordinate level in order for the analysis to be properly divided. It's easier to explain this in practice than it is in the abstract.

This chapter is divided into subdivisions by number—1, 2, 3, and so on—and into sub-subdivisions by letter—A, B, C, and so on. If a piece of writing has a "1" to indicate a subdivision, then it needs at least a second section, or a "2" in order to be properly divided. Similarly, if there's an "A," there must at least be a "B." If you can't find a second sub or sub-subdivision, you need to rethink the structure of your analysis.

Why this advice? Because if you divide an issue you should be able to divide it into at least two parts. If you can't do that, there was no need for the division and you could analyze the issue in one piece. And while the advice might seem odd when written down, it's almost always easy to follow it in practice; if you divided an issue once, you can usually see, at least during the editing phase, where a second division would help the analysis. If you can't see that, you can usually see that the initial division wasn't necessary and that addressing the issue as one thing will probably be more effective than attempting an artificial division.

Conclusion

This was probably more time than you expected to spend thinking about section headings in your work. But as priming tools, they actually are enormously important in making your analysis understandable and, in the case of persuasive documents, making that analysis persuasive as well. Headings also function as an outline of your document, and they can help you diagnose flaws in logic and in flow throughout your document. Word for word, headings are the most powerful and important portions of almost any document you will write. They're worth the time and effort you devote to them.

Exercises

1. Review any outlines you've started to help you organize the material in your other classes. Have you used narrative or placeholder section headings? If you've used placeholder headings, do you think narrative headings would help you find relevant materials faster and more efficiently? Will you change from placeholder to narrative headings? If you use narrative headings, are they sufficiently concise to alert you to what falls below the heading without trying to analyze the topic in the heading?

2. Review the section headings in this book. Could they be improved? Which headings would you change and why? Look at the table of contents. Do you get a sense of what a chapter contains by looking at the subheadings? If not, do the headings and subheadings need more information or should they be redrafted to read more easily?

Focus Questions

1. How much time have you devoted to thinking about your section headings in the past?
2. Does the "movie preview" metaphor make sense to you? Can you think of other ways in which headings are similar, or dissimilar, to movie previews?
3. Can you think of ways in which readers might be primed to accept analysis before reading it?
4. Do you outline your work before writing it down? Will you change your current practice now that you are in law school?
5. Have you considered the difference between abstract and narrative headings before? Do you see why the text makes the claim that narrative headings are better? Do you agree?
6. Does the idea that "legal writers should take every opportunity to inform their readers" seem extreme to you? Are you concerned about the level of scrutiny to which your writing will be subjected? Do you feel that your writing has been scrutinized to this level before you came to law school?
7. Do you understand the notion that headings can help you to decide when to omit analysis? Do you think that this insight is useful?

8. Is the advice to include not too few, not too many, but just enough headings useful or is it too vague?

9. Do you find your headings to be too short? Too long? Has anyone talked to you before about the headings in your written work? If so, what did they say?

10. Have you been given the advice that two is the minimum number of subheadings you can have in a piece of writing? Do you find yourself persuaded or unpersuaded by the reasons given for this suggestion?

Chapter 13

Case Quotations and Why to Avoid Them

What You Should Learn from This Chapter

This chapter is about quotations and why they are unhelpful to legal writers. It proposes, perhaps surprisingly, that quoted language tends not to persuade readers and suggests that the act of inserting quoted language into a document is passive, requiring no engagement by the writer in the concepts discussed in the quoted language. It also discusses why block quotations should be avoided if at all possible.

After reading this chapter, you should:

- be aware of some of the dangers associated with quotation;
- have considered whether you find quoted language persuasive;
- have considered the importance of engaging with ideas rather than quoting someone else's engagement with those ideas; and
- have considered why the text cautions against block quotes in particular.

Many things about legal writing are obvious. Advice like "make sure your work is technically perfect," and "make sure your readers have all the necessary information to understand the advice you're giving them" sounds so straightforward it almost doesn't need to be said.

But some of the advice you get about legal writing might be more surprising to you, and perhaps the most surprising piece of advice is this: try to never quote from a case. Instead, paraphrase the court's language by reformulating the court's language into your own statement of what the court said.

You should be attuned to the careful use of language by now, so note that you're not being advised to never quote. The qualifications in that piece of advice are actually very important, so let's go through each of them.

First, "try" suggests that you sometimes will have to quote, and that's correct. It would be foolish to say that you should never quote from a case; that's too high a standard. There will be times when it's almost impossible to say something in a way that's different from the way the court expressed the thought and when you encounter that situation you will find yourself with no alternative but to quote. The important thing is to try hard to find a better way to express the thought through your own paraphrase; if you do that, you'll find that you'll rarely have to use the court's language.

And second, the advice suggests that you never quote "from a case." That's important, because when you're extracting rules from statutes and regulations, the opposite advice applies: you should quote directly and carefully from those sources. The reasons for this should be obvious. Statutory and regulatory language should be precise and carefully chosen, and it's possible to change the nuances of meaning—sometimes significantly—by paraphrasing that language. By contrast, court language is rarely (not never, just rarely) so precise that a paraphrase will work too much of a change in meaning.

Having explained the qualifications, let's look more closely at why you should avoid quoting from cases. And in particular, let's consider a question which you might be asking: wouldn't courts find it more convincing to be given the precise language another court (or perhaps even the court to which you're writing) used to describe a fact, or articulate a rule? Shouldn't this advice, in fact, be exactly the opposite?

No. Courts typically don't find quoted language persuasive at all. And for that reason alone, you should avoid quotes as much as possible.

1. Quoted Language Is Unpersuasive

Contrary to what you might expect, quoted language is less persuasive than a paraphrase of that language. And since your goal is to be as persuasive as possible, in everything you write, you should avoid anything that makes your writing less persuasive.

Quotations, by their nature, break up the flow of writing. To the reader, quotations are imports from somewhere else; they weren't written by you, they contain language that wasn't written for your reader, and they concern a set of facts that aren't the same as those in your document. The effect isn't so pronounced when the reader is faced with one quotation, but the cumulative effect of a series of quotations can be strong, and negative.

Think about it. Writing a series of quotations into your work tells the reader several things: it tells the reader that you found authority to support your position that you believe is relevant, of course, but that's not anything that the citation—which you have to provide regardless of whether the language is taken directly from the case or is paraphrased by you—wouldn't tell the reader; it tells the reader that you couldn't be bothered to work with the concepts expressed in the case, and preferred instead to lift the language from one place and insert it into another, something a reader might think is lazy; and it tells the reader that you don't care very much about whether your writing is taken seriously or not, since you're not actually writing the quoted words—you're borrowing what someone else wrote for your own purposes. That suggests that you don't respect your own writing, and perhaps you don't respect the reader much either, since you're willing to subject the reader to a patchwork of different writing styles, none of which match yours.

Some novice writers don't realize that the style of the quoted case is substantially different from their own. In fact, sometimes law students take language from a case without putting it in quotation marks, thinking that a citation at the end of the "quoted" passage will be sufficient to prevent their actions being criticized as plagiarism. Perhaps so, but the important thing for our present purposes is that this approach is almost always obvious to the reader because the writing style of a mature judge, writing an opinion explaining a decision to lawyers, and often in an opinion written many years earlier, is dramatically different from a persuasive piece of lawyer writing, prepared to persuade a reader that some action is or is not appropriate. Judicial writing and lawyer writing are written for very different reasons so we shouldn't be surprised that the styles are different as well.

Quoted language wasn't written with your case in mind, so it almost never will be as effective in conveying what you want it to convey as language you've written especially for the document you're preparing. By paraphrasing, you can seamlessly incorporate the important concepts from the authority on which you rely into your document because your document will be the same throughout and the emphasis will be on the facts and the law, not on the words.

And that's perhaps the most important reason why quoted language is unpersuasive. When we use quoted language, there's no flexibility to mold the concept because we're hostages to the mode of expression used by someone else. Quotations put the emphasis on the way the thought is expressed—on the language used to articulate a concept—not on the concept itself. And that puts the emphasis in the wrong place, because we should never want our readers to think more about the language we use than about the ideas contained in the words.

2. Quoted Language Doesn't Force Us to Work with the Expressed Ideas

When we find a case that supports a position we want to take, or that explains how a court might rule when confronted with a question we're trying to answer, we're relieved because we have one of the pieces to the puzzle we're trying to solve. But upon reflection, the piece might not fit into our puzzle as snugly as we might at first have thought, and we might decide that another case is more helpful for our current needs.

We'll only reach that point, though, if we've worked with the opinion, thinking about its language and the ideas it expresses. And that won't happen if we just cut some language from the case and paste it into our document. If we do that, we likely won't think much more about the language but rather will move on to the next part of the puzzle we're trying to solve; our answer for this part might not be the best answer, but we'll persuade ourselves that it's good enough.

In the law, though, "good enough" is never good enough. We should always strive to generate the best analysis possible, and to do that we need to think carefully about how every word we put in our documents advances the analysis we're bringing to the reader. Quoted language is a barrier to that careful consideration, because no thought is required after the selection of the quotation. By contrast, paraphrasing the quoted passage requires us to think about the idea encapsulated in the words and as we consider the idea itself, we might realize that it's not as closely related to the situation as we might at first have thought.

That's true in both the writing and the editing phases of our work. During the writing stage, we don't grapple with finding a way to expressing a quoted thought because the writer of the quotation has already done that work for us. And when we're editing, we tend to be distracted by the fact that the language is quoted, and focus only on making sure that the quoted language is accurately reproduced, rather than thinking about whether or not the thought it contains is best suited for the purposes for which we're using it. By contrast, when we edit something we've written ourselves, we should be carefully attuned to every nuance of meaning contained in every word. If the thought being expressed doesn't capture exactly what we want it to capture, we should sense that problem during editing, even if it eluded us while we were writing the passage.

3. Quoted Language Can Lead to Block Quotes

As I've said before, just because you can do something doesn't mean you should do it. So just because citation manuals provide you with rules that govern when you must put quoted language into block quotations, and style manuals will give you technical advice about the use, or non-use, of quotation marks and the location of citations to the block quotations, that doesn't mean that you should actually use block quotations in your writing.

In fact, block quotations are a dreadful thing to encounter when you're reading a document. Many judges won't even read language that's presented in a block quotation, feeling that if the writer doesn't have enough respect for them to have taken the quoted language and paraphrased it, they don't need to show the writer any respect by reading the block quotation. As a reader, there are few more hostile acts you can encounter from a writer than being faced with a long block quotation. The spacing of the text is usually altered in such a way as to make the text even less readable than it was before, the words are compressed together because the margins of a block quote are brought in on both the left and right hand sides of the page, and all of this is done to ensure that there is no question the reader is reading language selected by, but not written by, the document's writer.

Am I exaggerating? Do you think I'm using the rhetorical technique of *hyperbole*— intentionally making the use of block quotations seem worse than they are in order to make my point? See for yourself. Take a paragraph from this chapter at random and time how long it takes to read it. Now time yourself reading this.

> This is a classic block quotation, except that I'm not actually quoting anyone. Instead, I've formatted my own writing and put it into block form. In the law, we form block quotations when the quotation is of fifty words or more, and we form blocks by moving in the indention markers by half an inch on both the left and right margins, and changing the spacing to single. Block quotations are notoriously more difficult to read than regularly spaced and formatted text, and they affect a reader's comprehension speed dramatically. If you read this block quotation more quickly than a standard paragraph, I suspect that you weren't timing yourself correctly—something like this should always take longer to

read than a comparable paragraph formatted in a normal way. Compressing the text reduces the space within which the eye gets the clues that allow it to process a word's meaning by the shape and organization of its letters, and as writers we should never want to impede our readers' ability to read and understand written information as easily as possible.

So was I exaggerating? Do you see how unpleasant it is to be confronted with a solid wall of text like that? Some briefs are filled with block quotations like that, giving readers the strong impression that the writer affirmatively dislikes them. That's not the impression you want the reader to have.

Sometimes, of course, quotations are necessary. So how should you quote language from a source if the situation is thrust upon you? Try to enter the quotation as late as possible and get out of it as quickly as you can. You'll often see an entire sentence quoted where the key portion was only a few words or a phrase long. What the writer should have done was quote only the key words and write around the quotation to set it up and place it in context. Readers will appreciate that you take the trouble to quote as little as possible and will forgive quotations prepared like this. It's only the long quotations taken wholesale from other documents and dropped, without seeming thought, into your document that will irritate legal readers.

Conclusion

Not all quotations are block quotations, of course. But all quotations suffer from the other problems we discussed, and any quotation of fifty words or more—a fairly low threshold—has to go into a block if you're following citation manual rules. The simplest and best way to avoid these problems is to discipline yourself to avoid quotations whenever possible. If you follow the suggestion that you quote directly from statutes and rules, you'll doubtless have enough direct quotations in your work in any case, without having to add more from cases.

Even though you might think judges and lawyers would be more readily persuaded by the direct quotation of a court's precise language used to describe a concept, rule, or factual situation, it isn't so. Almost all legal readers prefer writers to paraphrase court language for them, molding it more directly into the analysis it's being asked to support.

Exercises

Try to paraphrase these quotations in ways that you could use them in a legal memorandum. If no paraphrase is possible or advisable, indicate that as well.

1. "In addition, when the language of the contract is plain and unambiguous there is no room for construction, and a court must presume that the parties meant what they expressed. In these circumstances, the true test of what is meant is not what the parties to the contract intended it to mean, but what a reasonable person in

the position of the parties would have thought it meant." *Calomiris v. Woonds*, 353 Md. 425, 436, 727 A.2d 358 (1999).

2. "Pollution means any contamination or other alteration of the physical, chemical, or biological properties of any waters of this State, including a change in temperature, taste, color, turbidity, or odor of the waters or the discharge or deposit of any organic matter, harmful organism, or liquid, gaseous, solid, radioactive, or other substance into any waters of this State, that will render the waters harmful or detrimental to: (1) Public health, safety, or welfare; (2) Domestic, commercial, industrial, agricultural, recreational, or other legitimate beneficial uses; (3) Livestock, wild animals, or birds; or (4) Fish or other aquatic life." Md. Code Envir. Art. §9-101(h).

3. "We review the underpinning facts of a jury verdict of nonobviousness for substantial evidence, according due deference to the jury, as always, in its role as the fact finder.... Our review of the facts, regardless of whether they are explicit or implicit within the verdict, is bound by this high level of deference.... Thus, even when the jury is given an essentially black box verdict form—that is, a form that merely asks the jury to answer 'yes' or 'no' as to whether a claim is obvious, such as was done in this case—we presume all factual disputes were resolved in favor of the verdict." *Agricap, Inc. v. Woodstream Corp.*, 520 F.2d 1337, 1342–43 (Fed. Cir. 2008) (other citations omitted).

4. "[A plaintiff bringing a claim of tortious interference in Connecticut must establish:] (1) the existence of a contractual or beneficial relationship, (2) the defendant's knowledge of that relationship, (3) the defendants' intent to interfere with that relationship, (4) the interference was tortious, and (5) a loss suffered by the plaintiff that was caused by the defendants' tortious conduct. Unlike other torts, in which liability gives rise to nominal damages even in the absence of proof of actual loss, it is an essential element of the tort of unlawful interference with business relations that the plaintiff suffer actual loss." *Appelton v. Bd. of Educ. of Town of Stonington*, 254 Conn. 205, 757 A.2d 1059, 1063–64 (2000).

Focus Questions

1. Does the advice contained in this chapter surprise you?
2. Have you paid much attention to when a document you were reading quoted from other writers?
3. Did you identify the qualifications in the text's advice? If not, do you now see why they were inherent in the language selected for that advice?
4. Are you surprised to read that quoted language is not thought to be persuasive?
5. Had you considered that quotations might be taken as a sign of lazy writing? Do you agree with that perception?
6. Had you considered that a reader might interpret your use of quotation as a lack of respect?
7. Have you noticed a change in writing style between quoted and non-quoted passages within a text you were reading?

8. Had you considered the problems the text describes with quotations preventing a writer from working with the ideas encapsulated by the quoted words?

9. Do you share the text's dislike of block quotations? Do you think the text is exaggerating the problems associated with block quotations?

Chapter 14

Legal Citation: Why Do We Care?

What You Should Learn from This Chapter

This is the first of two chapters concerned with legal citation. This chapter discusses some of the more theoretical aspects of citation, such as why lawyers are so concerned that legal authority is correctly cited. In particular, this chapter discusses the idea that lawyers view citation as a proxy for a lawyer's attention to detail and it considers the implications of this for you as a junior lawyer and law student, including the reality that good citation skills can get you a job and that poor citation skills can keep you from even being considered for some jobs. The chapter also deals with the ways legal citation practices, as they have developed, can hide authority as well as reveal it.

After reading this chapter, you should:

- have formed an appreciation for the importance lawyers attach to citation;
- understand that good citation skills can have a significant effect on your job searches while in law school;
- have developed an understanding of the ways citation practices can influence your research practices; and
- have considered the effects citation practices can have on open sources of legal information.

Legal citation excites few people. You might get excited about what a court says in an opinion, especially if the court's opinions are mandatory authority in the jurisdiction where you're working and the court's language directly supports something you want to say, but the technical bibliographical requirements necessary for you to actually use that court language are likely not going to thrill you. At best, you'll recognize that you have to follow these requirements in order to properly present the court's language to your audience and will go about the task carefully and diligently, albeit unenthusiastically. At worst, you'll dislike the process so much that you won't pay proper attention to the finicky details and will present a citation that's incorrect. "What's the worst that can happen?" you might ask. "Will the court rule against me because my citation form is wrong?"

And, to be sure, the answer to that is "probably not." The "probably" should trouble you, because "probably not" could also be expressed as "possibly yes," and you never want to act, or not act, in a way that leaves it open to the court to rule against your client; that's not doing your job properly and lawyers should always do their jobs properly. But even though the court might not rule against you specifically because of your poor citation form, there are other possible consequences of not understanding how to cite to cases properly and these should get your attention. Let's consider them, and citation generally, in more detail.

1. Incorrect Citation Makes Your Authority Difficult to Find

The first, and most obvious, problem with poor or incorrect citation is that the judge, or the judge's law clerk, can't find the cases you cite to in your document. If you leave out or get incorrect the series number of the volume you're citing to, or if you transpose the volume or page numbers—both easily made mistakes—the opinion might be impossible to find except by independent research. And while judges or law clerks might do the research necessary to find the opinion you're citing to—and "might" is an important word here—they won't be happy with you for wasting their time. As you can imagine, that doesn't improve your chances of being taken seriously.

The idea that citation is the thing that makes a case findable or not findable is actually both a blindingly obvious and a very subtle point. It's obvious, because what else is citation for? Citation is a predictable method of recording all the bibliographical detail necessary to communicate the location of a document—in this case legal authority—from the writer to the reader.

The more subtle part of this proposition is what happens when the citation format for some authority is not available. Citation rules determine what is and is not a "proper" citation and to what sources you can and can't refer. If you find the authority you want to use in a source that isn't provided a citation form by the citation manual you're using, that source is, in a very real sense, invisible because the rules don't allow you to communicate its location to your reader. So citation has the power to reveal but it also has the very important power to hide. We'll come back to this quality of citation later.

2. Lawyers Believe That Citation Is a Proxy for Attention to Detail

A second consequence of incorrect citation is that other lawyers and judges—the people you want to take you seriously—might not do so. Most judges and lawyers view correct citation form as a sign that the writer is careful and pays attention to detail, and that, many believe, carries over to the quality of the writer's legal arguments. Conversely, they believe, a lawyer who is sloppy or careless about citation form is probably a less reliable legal analyst. They also believe that the ability to interpret and follow the specific directions of a citation manual like *The Bluebook* or the *ALWD Guide to Legal Citation* (which I'll call the *ALWD Manual* here because it's a shorter name) is sufficiently akin to the ability to interpret a complex code, statutory scheme, or regulation that signs of an inability to cite are taken as signs that a lawyer won't understand codes or regulations either.

This type of proxy thinking might not be reasonable or even logical—there are, after all, many possible reasons that a citation might be incorrect, and even the concept of "correct" is more difficult to pin down than many believe—but you have no control over what others think. It's probably best to expect that every senior lawyer you encounter believes that correct citation form, at least what they think of as correct citation form, is at least a sign of attention to detail, and that incorrect citation form is a sign of sloppy thinking.

And that notion carries with it some profound implications. If, in order to be thought of as a credible lawyer and legal analyst, you have to assume that your reader has prejudices and beliefs about writing style of which you are unaware, and if you have to assume that you might suffer a loss of credibility if you violate those beliefs, then you will have to understand those beliefs in order to protect yourself from losing credibility. And you will have to adopt a very conservative writing style in order to make sure you don't accidentally alienate your reader.

3. Good Citation Can Get You a Job

Setting aside all other considerations, this alone is reason enough to take correct citation seriously: it can get you a job. Conversely, poor citation can harm your short term and even your long term job prospects. In fact, there are at least three ways in which your citation skills can affect your ability to get a job.

First, and perhaps most obviously, citation ability is usually tested as part of legal writing assignments in law school so only if you understand how to generate correct citations will you score well on that part of the grading rubric. Admittedly, citation is probably only a small part of the overall grade, and the legal writing grade usually is only part of your overall GPA. But good citation might raise your grade by a grade division—from B+ to A-, for example—and poor citation might have a similar lowering effect. There aren't many law students who come to law school with the intention of getting anything less than the highest possible grades, and it's generally true that good grades impress potential employers more than poor ones, so the influence of citation on your grade, no matter how small, should be enough motivation—on its own—to persuade you to work as hard as possible on getting your citations right.

But while your legal writing grade might not occupy the largest numerical role in your overall GPA, it probably has a profound influence on prospective employers. If you hope to work, for example, in a civil litigation firm, the lawyers there might not be as interested in your contracts or property grade as you might imagine. They'll want to see that you did well, of course, because doing well in law school is viewed as a proxy (that concept again) for your ability to learn what it means to practice under the pressures of actual practice. To put it bluntly, a lot of lawyers—not all, by any means, but a lot—are less interested with the specific legal knowledge you might acquire in law school than they are with how well you coped with the demands of the law school environment. Grades are signs of that coping, and lawyers pay attention to them, but they might be forgiving of a slip-up in one class, as long as it's not too significant.

But almost all lawyers take legal writing seriously. They might not expect you to have many marketable skills right out of law school, but they almost certainly will expect you to be able to write well. Writing and researching often make up the bulk of what junior associates are asked to do in law firms, and you'll need to be able to persuade a potential employer that you have advanced skills in those areas to make them willing to hire you and invest the time and money it will take to make you a profitable attorney. So they'll want to see good legal writing grades from you, and they'll also want to see a writing sample so they can evaluate your writing for themselves. And part of that evaluation, of course, will involve your citations, so poor citation form can hurt you twice with prospective employers; once with a lower than necessary legal writing grade, and a second time when they look at your writing sample.

The third way in which citation can have an effect on your employment prospects, both in the short and long term, relates to membership on a law journal in your second and third year. Many legal employers want to see that a student is a member of law review or other journal before considering that student for a job. There are probably two reasons for this: first, because journal membership, and especially law review membership, is restricted to those students who either get very good grades or who can write particularly well on a legal subject, the students who are offered a place on those journals are, legal employers believe, pre-selected as being those with abilities that match their requirements for summer associates and junior attorneys; and second, because many hiring attorneys were themselves members of journals when they were in law schools, they might be more comfortable hiring someone who has a similar background to them. It's usually believed that people like to hire themselves, or people who have the same characteristics as them, and journal membership is something that tends to be self-perpetuating, at least in some law firms.

The link to citation here is direct and strong. Most journals expect their junior staff members—the second-year students—to check the citations of all articles the journal will publish to make sure that they're flawless. Authors are rarely scrupulous about their citations, perhaps because they know that if the article is accepted for publication the student editors will work very hard to make sure the citations are perfect before the piece is published,[1] so the students doing this type of work must be highly skilled at legal citation in order to preserve the journal's reputation. This, in turn, means that journals pay very close attention to a candidate's citation skills when determining who should be on the staff for the coming year, and many law reviews and journals hold citation tests as part of their evaluation process. Good citation likely won't guarantee a place on a journal, but poor citation will almost certainly disqualify many otherwise acceptable candidates each year.

You only have one shot to make it onto a journal—two, if the journal has a competition that allows prospective staff members to submit a long piece of writing, usu-

---

1. If there's truth to the idea that citation accuracy is a valid proxy for attention to detail, it would be fascinating—although probably impossible—to research how important it is for an article submission to have citations that are at least close to correct. One might imagine that journals could use an author's care to generate accurate citations as a sign of how perceptive that author is and how well-received in the scholarly and lawyering communities the author's article will be. If the horror stories some students tell about the appalling standard of some article footnotes is any measure, though, it seems that this is not one of the criteria law journal editors use to evaluate a submission for publication.

ally something of the length of the note or comment expected of journal staff members (and even then, citation is almost certain to be one of the criteria on which the article is judged). So if you want a firm that pays attention to journal membership to hire you, you need to have good citation skills.

4. The Hidden, and Hiding, Effects of Citation

As we've noted, one of the lesser appreciated aspects of citation form is its ability to hide a source from public view. That can make the law harder to find, and it has the effect of consolidating the position of one legal publisher—West[2]—over all others. Whether or not that's a good thing is a discussion for other people and another time, but we should at least consider this effect of citation in more detail in order to have a more fully rounded appreciation of how citation works in the law.

Let's suppose you're given a legal research task. As a law student, or as a junior lawyer in a firm, you have access to LexisNexis, Westlaw, Bloomberg, and a library full of books and indexing aids that will allow you swiftly to identify the relevant area of the law and then search for an issue within that area by jurisdiction and date. Using any of these tools, or using them in combination, you should be able to, if not answer the question, then outline the most relevant legal authority and to start the process of crafting an answer that meets the specific factual situation. And you should be able to do this quickly and efficiently, from your office desk or after a short trip to the library.

But you do none of these things. Instead, being the contemporary law student or lawyer you are, you go to Google. Now Google is a wonderful search engine, and it does indeed have access to a vast database of primary law through its Google Scholar service, but it might not be every lawyer's first choice as a legal research tool. Nonetheless, studies suggest that at least among the younger generation of lawyers, Google is the first stop for most legal researchers. It might not be a good idea, it might even present some problems of which the researchers are unaware, but the reality is what it is: you probably will go to Google.[3]

And because Google is a remarkable search engine, and because you put in it the right combination of search terms, you quickly find a case from your jurisdiction that is mandatory authority and that has facts so similar to the case you're working on that it answers your question. So you're done; all you have to do is write up your research and move on to the next assignment, right?

Sadly, no, because you can't cite to the case as you've found it on Google. When you go to *The Bluebook*, or the *ALWD Manual*, you'll see that Google is not a recognized source for which a citation form is provided. If the case you're looking at is federal, then only the self-published United States Reports, for Supreme Court cases, or the

---

2. I'm using the old name here. West was bought by Thomson some years ago and the corporate name has changed many times since then. At the time of writing, the official name was Thomson Reuters, but there's no guarantee that that name won't change again at any time. For consistency's sake, then, I'm going to keep referring to it as "West."

3. We'll talk later about legal research in more detail, and specifically about some of the advantages and disadvantages of Google.

West-published set of federal reporters—including the Federal Reporter (first, second, or third series) and the Federal Supplement (first or second series)—are recognized sources that have primary citation forms, the kind you're required to use by the citation manuals if they're available. If it's a state case, your state might self-publish the decisions of one or both of its appellate courts, and West will also publish that decision in one of its regional reporters and, if the state is large enough, in a variety of state-specific reporters. All of these publications will have citation formats, and an order of preference in which to use these sources in a formal legal document, but Google does not have a recognized citation format.

You might think this doesn't matter, because Google gives you the information you need in order to generate a basic citation—volume number, volume, and first page number of at least one of the reporters listed in your citation manual, the deciding court, and the year in which the decision was published. With the name of the case and this additional bibliographical information you can construct a citation for the case, so that should work, right?

Again, sadly, no. And for two reasons. First, you should never cite to a source you have not personally looked at. The Google version of the case might give you bibliographical information for a West-published version of the case, but without actually looking at the West-published source, can you be sure it is identical in all respects? It almost certainly is but again, in that "almost" lies enough uncertainty to make a lawyer nervous. Let's put it this way: are you confident enough that the two sources are identical to put your grade on the line? Your client's case? How about your job? If there's transmission error between the West and Google version of the case, and you rely on the incorrect version, bad things might happen to your client and to you. How happy are you about using the Google version now?[4]

The chances of a mistake are low, so you might be willing to take the chance. The second problem with using a Google version of a case, though, is crippling and insoluble. Google doesn't provide pinpoint page citations to its cases. These are the indicators that tell you when there was a page break in the original paper version of the source. Both Westlaw and LexisNexis will give you that information, allowing you to use them

---

4. It would be reasonable to ask how confident you are, or should be, that the Westlaw and LexisNexis versions of legal sources are error-free, or, if they are not, how much more error-free they are than Google. And the answers are, respectively, probably not and we don't know. What an "error" might be in this context becomes a somewhat metaphysical question. Because LexisNexis and West editors will look over a case, for example, before publishing it, and might identify potential mistakes in a court's slip opinion which the court might, upon reflection, correct before the opinion is published, the original slip opinion and the final published opinion might be different, but which one has the error? Of course, additional, and more traditional "errors" might be introduced into the process, making the published version different from the court's original slip version. But because these are the final versions of the opinion, even if they differ from what the court might have intended, are they in error? As to how often these differences might occur, and how that compares to Google's error rate, there just isn't enough information to say. What we can say, though, is that lawyers and judges rely so heavily on LexisNexis and Westlaw as definitive legal information sources that they are, in effect, definitive because we need them to be definitive. That need is not, at least not yet, a feature of the law's relationship with Google and other no- and low-cost legal information sites. So they are likely to be viewed as non-definitive because we don't need them to be definitive. All of this, of course, is subject to very rapid change.

as replacements for the print-versions of books because the citation rules, and common sense, require you to provide pinpoint citations whenever you draw information from a source. Cases can be very long documents, and just giving the reader a citation to the first page on which that document appears is not helpful; the reader might have to spend hours finding the specific language on which you rely. Without that pinpoint citation information to add to your citation, you'll have to go to either Westlaw or LexisNexis (or, heaven forfend, the books) and find the pinpoint page information from them. If you're going to have to access those sources eventually, why bother going to Google first?

There might, in fact, be a good reason to use Google as a first-line research tool: it's free. If cost is an issue—and when, these days, is cost not an issue?—then Google might give you a good place to start your primary source research.[5] But you almost certainly will need to move on from Google to a fee-based resource if you want to have accurate citation information for your source document, and that means that citation has made the Google source functionally invisible, at least to the reader of your work.[6]

This ability of citation to reveal or conceal a source of legal information simply by providing, or not providing, a citation format for that source has some troubling implications. By requiring citations to West-published sources, for instance, a citation manual can limit the usefulness, or even the viability, of alternative legal information sources.

That's particularly disturbing when it comes to free, or open, sources of legal information. Lawyers working for wealthy clients can afford to use Westlaw or LexisNexis for their research, but less well-to-do clients might be less willing to pay the high prices of database access. Even a relatively simple legal issue, appropriately researched, could cost a client $10,000 or more just for the cost of database access. Recognizing the problems such fees were causing law firms and their clients, both LexisNexis and Westlaw developed alternative fee structures, allowing firms to pay a flat rate each month for access to their services, rather than charging them a per-minute or per-database fee, but this often had the effect of raising a firm's hourly rate because the database fee now is factored into the firm's overhead costs.

Free, or open-source, legal databases are a way firms—and non-lawyers seeking to either learn about the law or litigate a case on their own (a practice known as appearing *pro se*—we really can't avoid all Latin terms in the law)—can access the law with-

---

5. I emphasize "primary source" research here because, as we'll discuss later, it might well be best to start the entire research process looking at secondary sources that allow you to gain a sense of what the law in a particular area is before starting to look at the primary sources. Although you'll need to get to the primary sources eventually, it's possible that starting there can give you a distorted and inaccurate view of the law in a particular area.

6. There's another significant reason that will compel you to move from Google, or any other free or low-cost research tool like it, to either LexisNexis or Westlaw before using a source. The last step any legal researcher must take before relying on a resource for any purpose is to update the law to make sure the source is still "good" law—that it's still a valid source to support the proposition for which you're using it. Cases are overturned, statutes are amended or repealed—the law is a dynamic and ever-changing process. There are simple ways to update the law, but they require that the researcher have access to either Westlaw or LexisNexis. One method of updating the law—Shepardizing—used to be available in book form also, but it's anachronistic to speak of this as a viable option these days, since most if not all law libraries have discontinued their purchases of this book-based service and it's almost only used in its online version.

out incurring the spectacular database access fees charged by the commercial providers or, in the case of non-lawyers, having to learn the arcane practices of book-based research that lawyers are, mostly, still taught in law school. But without the ability to cite directly to the sources they contain, lawyers should be hesitant to commit too much of their research efforts to using those resources, because they will have to duplicate much of their efforts in a commercial database.

Understanding this, some jurisdictions have enacted their own "public domain" citation formats, and require that any citations, in documents filed in that jurisdiction's courts, to materials generated by that jurisdiction must include the public domain format that allows for a litigant to rely on a source regardless of where that source was found. The effect, however, is somewhat spoiled by a citation manual like *The Bluebook*, which requires citation to both the public domain and commercially published version of the same source. A jurisdiction's courts, of course, might not adopt *The Bluebook*'s requirements; although *The Bluebook* gives itself the title of "[a] [u]niform [s]ystem [o]f [c]itation," it really has only been uniformly adopted by law reviews and other scholarly journals (and even here there are a few exceptions). But *The Bluebook*'s decision to circumvent the spirit of public domain citation format is nonetheless unfortunate.

There is, however, a reason for its decision that makes perfect sense. In order to be effective, a citation format should accurately identify not just the source of a document (the court that wrote an opinion, for example), but also the location in which that opinion can be found. Public domain citation formats do a fine job of the first part of this requirement but they generally are poor at the second part. A public citation format, for example, might rely on information that will tell the reader that a case was decided in a particular year and was the xth opinion handed down by the court during that year[7] but that citation will give the reader no sense of where to go—electronically or physically—to read a copy of that decision. With the increasing tendency of judges and lawyers to read materials on computers or tablets, the possibility that URLs linking a document to a source might become viable substitutes for *Bluebook*-type citations, which are, after all, a way to locate books on shelves, grows increasingly likely But we're not there yet.

Conclusion

At present, the public domain citation movement has somewhat run out of steam and citation manuals still require citation to commercially published versions of virtually all legal sources. How long that will last, though, is difficult to gauge. Information accumulates on the internet at a remarkable rate, and when lawyers become convinced

7. If the citation format relied on docketing information, an obvious source of public domain citation data, the reader would be substantially less well informed. A court's docket is established when the case first comes into the court's system, which can be years before the case is decided. Using docketing information, then, would give the reader a way of identifying the case but would tell nothing about the date of the decision and how that decision fits into other decisions handed down by the court. Since this is sufficiently valuable information for the reader to have, a docket-based public domain citation approach is probably not the best approach to take.

that the legal information found on the internet is sufficiently reliable to be used with confidence, it seems likely that a citation format that will allow for both identification and location will gain rapid acceptance. For now, though, citations still require information from commercially published sources.

And because lawyers still view citation skill as a proxy for other skills, and because law schools and journals require you to have high-functioning citation skills as well, you need to become familiar with the details of a legal citation and you need to be able to generate your own precise and accurate citations to legal sources. About that, at least, there is no doubt.

Focus Questions

1. Are you surprised to learn of the importance many attach to legal citation? Does this importance seem sensible to you? Does it seem in or out of proportion for the role citation should play in legal writing?

2. Have you given much consideration to proxy thinking, in which the way a person performs one task is thought to provide information about how the person will perform a different task? Does this type of thinking seem sensible to you? Can you see any possible connections between proxy thinking, metaphor, and analogy? Is proxy thinking a form of rhetorical device?

3. Have you considered the possibility that good citation skills could help you to get a job, whereas weak citation skills might make it more difficult for you to get a legal job? Does that affect the way you will approach learning about and performing legal citation?

4. Had you considered the importance of working on a law review or journal and how that experience might enhance your ability to get a legal job? Does your answer, and the fact that many journals and law reviews use citation skills as at least part of the process of selecting their members, change your thinking about the importance of legal citation skills?

5. Does the text's discussion of the potential hiding effect of legal citation surprise you? Had you considered the practical effects of mandatory citation formats before?

6. Does using Google as a legal information source seem like a good idea to you? Why? If not, why not?

7. Are the criticisms offered about public citation formats valid, in your opinion?

Chapter 15

Legal Citation: The Mechanics

What You Should Learn from This Chapter

This second chapter devoted to legal citation discusses the mechanics of generating correct long and short citations for federal and state courts, statutes, and regulations. After reading this chapter, you should:

- understand the process of writing accurate long and short form citations for the various sources with which you are likely working this year in your writing assignments;
- have an appreciation for some of the criticisms directed at legal citation practice; and
- understand that your citation manual is the best place to go for citation advice.

Having spent some time thinking about the theory of legal citations, we should consider the practice of them. The best guide to this, of course, is your citation manual—probably either *The Bluebook* or the *ALWD Manual*. Although there are a surprising number of citation manuals and formats, most law schools use either *The Bluebook* or the *ALWD Manual*, with *The Bluebook* leading the way. There are some very slight differences in the way these manuals expect citations to be generated, but none of any real substance.

This chapter is only intended as a quick guide to some of the more common citation forms. Importantly, if anything here seems to disagree with what you read in your citation manual or something your legal writing professor tells you, ignore this and pay attention to the citation manual or your professor. And as you read, please keep this warning in mind. Citation manuals are dynamic books with frequent new editions, meaning that some of the information in this chapter might be out-of-date when you read it. The manuals themselves are the best guide to their rules.

There's one threshold issue you should consider and keep in mind throughout this discussion. In law practice, we provide our bibliographical information—our source citations—directly in the body of the text we're writing. We don't put our citations in footnotes, leaving the reader to choose whether or not to interrupt reading the main text to find the source of information that came from somewhere else. Instead, our citations follow directly after the sentence in which the source is used or referred to, and in the body of the text itself.

This practice has been criticized, and some suggest that we should change it and place all bibliographical information in footnotes. This would, they argue, make the texts we write easier to read and more compelling as well. These critics are probably right: there's little as disruptive to the narrative flow than having to break it up after every sentence with citation information (and it really is after almost every sentence in a carefully written and researched piece of legal work). But the critics have not budged most lawyers or judges, and the traditional location of citations is still the location we're expected to use. So all source citations in non-academic legal writing go in the body of the text, not in footnotes. For those of you used to academic or scholarly writing, this will look very odd indeed and will take a lot of getting used to.

1. Introduction

We're going to walk through the basic mechanics of generating the most common forms of legal citation, in both their long and short versions, without specific reference to the rules in either *The Bluebook* or the *AWLD Manual*. My goal here is to provide you with a way to get started on citations without providing a comprehensive guide to either citation manual. To write something that detailed is far beyond the scope of this book and besides, such guides exist and, if you feel the need for them, they doubtless will help you. The best guides to generating citations, though, are the citation manuals themselves. They might be a little tricky to get through at first, but they have a wealth of information in them that will be revealed to you if you study them carefully.

2. Court Opinions

Court opinions are the most basic sources to which lawyers cite. In law school, you'll write many citations to court opinions. Once you leave law school, if you go into a litigation practice you'll cite to hundreds of court opinions every year. If you go into a transactional or other non-litigation practice, the number might be fewer, but every lawyer must be able to generate a case citation easily and fluently when the need arises.

Because there are some differences in the way we cite to cases depending on whether they come from the state or federal systems, let's consider both separately. And before we go, let's pause for a second to remember that these are entirely hypothetical examples with invented case names. If you go to the indicated reporters and look up the cases that fall at the volume and page locations indicated, you will not find a case that corresponds to the one indicated here.

But in concept, at least, if not in execution, one feature of these hypothetical citations is accurate. The number of pages in which each parallel reporter reports the opinion are different in each case. That's not because the number of words in the court opinion are different, or that one reporter includes more or less words than another. All reporters, regardless of publisher, report every word the court wrote and there should be no discrepancies at all in those words between reporters. The difference in page number comes about because of different formatting, and because some commercial publishers include additional information, usually in the form of indexed finding aids, that lawyers can use to help them locate the opinion during research into the legal issues covered by the case.

We'll discuss both full citations and a couple of short-form citations that are typical for most documents you'll be writing. Where a short-form citation can be supplied, it's correct to rely on that in preference to a full, long-form citation.

A. Federal Court Citations

There are three principal federal courts: the United States Supreme Court is the highest court in the federal system, the Circuit Courts of Appeals are the intermediate appellate courts in the federal system, and the federal district courts are the lowest, trial-level, courts in the federal system. Each court reports its opinions in a different reporter, and we'll cover all three here.

i. The Supreme Court

Let's assume that we're trying to cite to a 2001 Supreme Court decision stemming from litigation between John A. Smith and Jane Jones on one side and the Greenacre Corporation on the other. The opinion is reported in three different reporters: the United States Reports, volume 123, between pages 456 and 490, the Supreme Court Reporter, volume 987 between pages 654 and 712, and the Supreme Court Reports, Lawyers' Edition, volume 654, between pages 321 and 375.

a. Names

The first thing to do is ignore the first names of the parties. Legal citations only deal in last names of individuals. So it's "Smith and Jones," not "John A. Smith and Jane Jones." Next, only the first named person or entity on each side of the "v." is included. So it's "Smith," not "Smith and Jones."

Next, we need to add a "v." to show that the party to the left was the one seeking the court's jurisdiction and the one to the right was the opposing party. Note that a party's location to the left of the "v." does not mean that the party was the plaintiff in the case, because this is an appellate case. In a trial-level opinion, the party to the left of the "v." will be the plaintiff, but once the case makes its way to the appellate court, the original defendant and plaintiff can switch places if it's the defendant, not the plaintiff, seeking appellate jurisdiction to have the case heard and decided. This can cause untold problems for law students until they realize that the legal designations of "plaintiff" and "defendant" are really only helpful at the trial level. At the intermediate appellate level the legal designations are "appellant" and "appellee," and at the Supreme Court level the parties are "petitioner" and "respondent." Better by far to just call everyone by name. Those usually don't change.[1]

---

1. Usually, though, is not always. If a party dies before the case moves to an appellate court, or otherwise drops out of the continuing litigation, that party's name is removed from the case and the name of the person or entity continuing the case is substituted. As you would expect, there's a citation format for that situation. But we're not going to cover it here because it's not a common occurrence.

The other thing to note is that lawyers indicate the word "versus" by writing a "v" with a period after it. We never use "vs." That's for boxing matches. Litigation can sometimes feel like bare-knuckle brawling, but we never allow our citations to reflect that.

The party on the other side of the "v." is the Greenacre Corporation, but "Corporation" is one of those words that are always abbreviated in legal citations. You should read the abbreviation rule very carefully, and then make sure that you refer to it every time you write a citation until the words with standard abbreviations are so familiar that you find yourself abbreviating them by second nature. Even then, it's a good idea to check every time you generate a citation. And always remember that citations are binary: they're completely correct or they're completely wrong—there's no partially correct legal citation.

The word "Corporation" gets a standard abbreviation form of "Corp." So the name of the party on the right side of the "v." is, for citation purposes, Greenacre Corp. Since there are no other parties on this side of the "v.," our citation name is now complete.[2]

The name of the citation, then, is "Smith v. Greenacre Corp." but we still have two things to do before the name is correct. First, we have to underline or italicize the name. Underlining used to be the only option when typewriters were standard, but since italics have become so simple to produce with the advent of the personal computers, legal citation now allows italics as an alternative to underlining. Many lawyers—especially older ones—still prefer underlining (there are some practical reasons for legal writing professors to prefer underlining as well, so if your legal writing professor tells you to underline, it's no defense to say that your citation manual allows for italics as an alternative), but if the choice is up to you, then make the one that best suits your aesthetic sensibilities. There will be very few chances to do that in the law, so make the most of the ones you get. Once made, though, your choice should be consistent throughout your document; you shouldn't underline some case names and italicize others.

The other thing we need to do is add a comma after the name. Citations are properly thought of as sentences, and just like textual sentences, they have internal and ending punctuation. A comma after the name indicates that the finding information supplied after the name comes in a separate clause of the citation sentence. The comma is not part of the name, though, so it is not underlined. If it helps to think of citations as sentences, then the comma (like the comma in this sentence) should be easy to remember. If it doesn't help you to think of citations in this way, then the comma will have to become second nature to you. Either way, the citation needs a comma after the name so the correct citation, so far, is "*Smith v. Greenacre Corp.*," and now we get into the finding information portion of the citation sentence.

b. Finding Information

Finding information—that part of the citation that tells you where the case with this name can be located—is always organized the same way. First comes the volume number, then comes the volume name (abbreviation, actually), and then comes the

---

2. I hope you've been paying attention and recognized that our citation name would be complete even if there were other parties on the right side of the "v." because as with Mr. Smith and Ms. Jones, only the first-named party on either side of the "v." is listed.

first page on which the opinion can be found. There might be additional information, but these three things are always in a full citation to a court opinion and they are always, regardless of which court issued the opinion, placed in this order.

Before we deal with the specifics of the particular citation we're working with for this example, it's worth thinking about the nature of legal citation finding information for a second, because it makes clear that even though most lawyers have moved from paper to electronic research as a principal means of finding legal information, the books still exert a powerful influence over the law.

Even though most lawyers will not use books to find their information, and might no longer even have the books known as "reporters" in their libraries and can only access court opinions through the internet, we all—book based and computer-based legal researchers alike—use book-based information as a finding aid. This need not be the case. The principal legal information databases provide information that would allow a reader to find a case on those services and the book-based information is becoming increasingly anachronistic, although it does provide a convenient shorthand way of identifying court opinions.

But that shorthand almost always refers to reporters published by West (I say "almost" always because opinions from the Supreme Court, as we're about to discover, don't rely on a West reporter), thereby solidifying its place as the principal publisher of legal information. The discussion of whether citations should be acting as unofficial agents of West, which is, after all, a for-profit corporation, is an interesting one but not one we need to have at the moment. For now, it's enough to observe that while we might not actually use books that much anymore, their physical features of volumes and pages are still the dominant model for providing finding information within legal citations.

Although the Supreme Court's opinions are published in three different reporters, we cite to the United States Reports version if available, and we don't provide parallel citations to the other two reporters. So if you see a citation to a Supreme Court case with three separate citations, one each for the three different reporters that publish cases, that citation is not correct by formal citation standards. As you might expect, West—which doesn't publish the United States Reports but does publish the Supreme Court Reporter—supplies parallel citation information for the other reporters, one reason among many why you should disregard the suggestion to "cite as" found at the top of all West-published opinions. Although the citations West provides are accurate according to its own citation system, they are hardly ever correct citations for formal purposes.

Since we know the order in which the finding information should come, and we know that we only need to provide the information for the United States Reports version of the opinion, we just need to identify the correct abbreviation for the United States Reports before the finding information portion of the citation sentence is complete. When you look it up, you'll learn that the abbreviation is "U.S." and that means that our finding information portion of the citation should read "123 U.S. 456" and the citation—"*Smith v. Greenacre Corp.*, 123 U.S. 456"—is nearly complete.

c. Date Parentheticals

But there is a third component to each court opinion citation that new law students often omit, making otherwise correct citations wrong. It is the only portion of the citation that requires some judgment from the writer, making it the trickiest part of the citation to prepare. This section is known as the "date parenthetical," and that tells you two important things: first, that the information in this section is contained within parentheses, and second, that it includes a date.

The tricky part is that sometimes that's all the section includes and sometimes it isn't. The date parenthetical must also include enough information for the reader to identify which court issued the opinion unless—and this is where the interpretation comes in—that information has already been adequately disclosed by the reporter information previously provided. What does that mean? Well, in the citation we're working on, the fact that the opinion is published in "U.S.," a reporter any legal reader should know only publishes decisions from the United States Supreme Court, tells the reader that this opinion comes from the Supreme Court and that fact need not (in fact, should not) be repeated in the date parenthetical. We'll find a situation where that isn't the case in the next example we look at.

For now though, we have enough information to construct the date parenthetical. We know we need only include the year the case was decided within the parentheses—(2001) to be correct. Just remember that even though this section of the citation is called the date parenthetical, you need to check the preceding information to make sure that the issuing court is readily identifiable before limiting the date parenthetical just to the date.

There is only one more detail to add before the citation sentence is complete. Because this is a citation sentence, it requires some closing punctuation. If it is part of a string citation (other than the last citation in the string), the punctuation will be a semi-colon. But the much more typical situation is a lone citation, and then we need the traditional punctuation at the end of a sentence—a period. With this final detail in mind, the completed citation for this opinion looks like this: *Smith v. Greenacre Corp.*, 123 U.S. 456 (2001).

There are a few possible refinements to this citation, depending on the purpose for which it's being used. It might be preceded by a signal, like *See* or *See also* or *accord* or *Cf*, but these signals, while important, are a refinement we're not going to cover in this basic introduction to citation. The citation might also be followed by some subsequent history information, especially if that information might change the importance with which a reader views the opinion. If the case has been overruled, for example, you would have to indicate that in the subsequent history portion of the citation (and you should have a well-considered and persuasive explanation for why you're citing to an overruled or reversed opinion in your document); there are several other possibilities for subsequent history and all should be noted after the citation. Again, though, these are refinements which we're not going to discuss now.

The most important element of a citation we haven't talked about so far is added when you've referred to a specific page, or pages, in the opinion just before you cited to it. You usually won't be including just general citations, though, and will be citing to specific parts of sources. When you do so, you need to provide the specific page numbers for the pages you're referring to. This is called "pinpoint citation," and it's standard practice for most legal citations.

d. Pinpoint Citations

Pinpoint citations are preceded by a comma, and follow right after the first page of the court opinion. In our example, if we want to refer to language written by the court on page 462 of the opinion, the citation would look like this: *Smith v. Greenacre Corp.*, 123 U.S. 456, 462 (2001). Court opinions are dense and often very long, so it's vital that you give your reader a chance to find the relevant language quickly and easily. If court opinions were published on lined paper we'd give the line designation as well, but as it is, the page is the best we have.

e. Short-Form Citations

If only we were done. But what you've done is construct a full, long-form citation to this case and there are three types of short-form citations you also need to understand. Long-form citations happen the first time you refer to a case but after that you'll usually use one of these short forms. Your citation manual will have rules about re-using long form citations after a certain amount of text has gone by, and you should refer to those rules when you're writing long documents and are citing to some court opinions only infrequently.

The first short-form citation form is the most complete. It requires you to give the most distinctive name of the two in the full form citation, the volume number, volume, and pinpoint page information for your source. There's no need for a date, because that information was provided in the long-form citation, as was the deciding court information if that isn't clear from the citation. Let's talk about those in turn.

The most distinctive name is usually the first name—the one before the "v." That would certainly be true in our example: the short-form version of the case name is *Smith*. It wouldn't be true, though, in most criminal cases. In those cases the prosecution is the first-named party, and since every federal prosecution is conducted by the United States of America, the first name of those cases is always *United States*. That isn't sufficiently distinctive to be of any help, and so in those cases the second name—that of the defendant—is used to identify the case in a short-form citation.

The volume number and the volume information are exactly the same as in the long-form citation. The reader needs that information in order to be able to find the opinion, of course. But because this is a short-form citation we dispense with the first page of the case and give instead just the pinpoint page information. The assumption is that if we're referring to a case again, after the full long-form citation, we must have a specific reason for that citation and that therefore there will be a particular page to which we are citing.

So, in the case to which we've been citing, the short-form citation would look like this: *Smith*, 123 U.S. at 462.

The second and third short-form citation forms both assume that the opinion to which we are citing is the same as the one to which we just cited. If so, we can simplify the citation even more and simply use *Id.* Of course, in legal citation nothing is quite as simple as it looks, but this form is close.

One complication is that the period after *Id.* must be underlined or italicized. This didn't use to be the case, and you can sometimes date lawyers in much the same way as you can date trees, by looking to see if they emphasize the period after *Id.* or not. The second complication is that in law, as opposed to some other scholarly citation styles, we use *Id.*, not *Ibid.* It's not worth knowing why this is, if there even is a reason. All that's important is that it's *Id.* in the law. The citation form follows the rules of punctuation, meaning that it gets a lower case—"*id.*"—if the citation falls anywhere but at the beginning of a sentence, and a capital letter—"*Id.*"—if the citation comes at the beginning. You should try whenever possible to keep your citations to their own sentences, so the capitalized version should be more common in your work.

A citation of "*Id.*" means that everything in this citation is exactly the same as in the previous citation. If the pinpoint page to which you are now referring has changed from the last citation, you need to signal this with the third short-form citation format: "*Id.* at __," where the underline represents the new pinpoint page. If we assume that our discussion of the *Smith* case has moved on to the next page of the opinion, our short-form citation would now look like this: *Id.* at 463.

One last thing. Note in the previous paragraph that I emphasized the case name of *Smith* even though I was just referring to the name and wasn't citing to the case. We do this to distinguish those times when we speak of a person—Mr. Smith, for example—and when we speak of a case. Case names are always emphasized—through underlining or italicization—in order to show the reader that we are speaking of a case, not a person.

ii. *The Courts of Appeals*

The various Courts of Appeals publish their opinions in the Federal Reporter. At the time of writing, the Federal Reporter was in its third series, another sign that books are still the dominant model for legal citations, since there would be no need for series designations if opinions were only published online.

The Federal Appendix reporter series also publishes opinions from the Courts of Appeals, but the opinions in this reporter are non-precedential—what used to be called "unpublished" decisions until the existence of the Federal Appendix made that name manifestly inappropriate. The citation format for Federal Appendix opinions is fundamentally the same as that described here, although the reporter abbreviation will be different. For the correct abbreviation, you should refer to your citation manual. Finding that information, and using it correctly in a citation, will be a good test of your skills in getting around the manual.

The Federal Reporter is abbreviated as "F.," with the second series abbreviated as "F.2d" and the third series—predictably enough—as "F.3d." If the case name and other finding information we've been working with remains the same, then the citation would be mostly correct if we write it as *Smith v. Greenacre Corp.*, 123 F.3d 456 (2001).

The citation is only "mostly" correct, though, because unlike in the Supreme Court citation, we can't identify which Circuit Court issued this opinion just based on the finding information. We know that the issuing court must have been one of the Courts of Appeals, because only the Courts of Appeals publish their decisions in F.3d, but which of the several Courts of Appeals might have written the opinion we don't know and have no way of knowing, based solely on the information we have.

In fact, let's assume the decision comes from the Seventh Circuit. We add that information in the date parenthetical, and if we add the pinpoint information as well that makes the full and correct citation *Smith v. Greenacre Corp.*, 123 F.3d 456, 462 (7th Cir. 2001).

As you can see, citations actually give us a lot of information about the case in a relatively efficient form. From the citation alone we know the court that decided the case, the year in which it was decided, where the case can be found, and where the specific language on which the writer has relied can be found as well. Although legal citation is often criticized as an overly formalistic process that is irritatingly precise in its requirements and has the effect, if not the intention, of restricting more open access to legal information by its requirement that opinions receive their West-published citations whenever possible, it nonetheless provides a consistent and information-packed approach for us to use when we refer to legal sources.

iii. Federal District Courts

Opinions from the federal district courts carry no precedential value, since courts can only bind those directly below the deciding court in the order of hierarchy and no courts fall below the trial court. Even with other courts in the same district, a district court opinion is only at the same level rather than above, and is therefore not binding.

Nonetheless, federal district court opinions are often important because the federal district courts confront many complex federal issues and write careful and thoughtful opinions explaining the ways they resolved those issues. Because federal district courts consider state law issues when they sit in diversity, they can also be useful when seeking to argue a state law issue as well. The opinions might not be mandatory and binding on any other court, but they often can persuasively support an argument.

Federal district court opinions are published in the Federal Supplement reporter or in the subsequent series of those reporters—at the time of writing, the Federal Supplement has reached the third series. This is a West reporter, and has all the familiar West research and finding aids. In addition, some federal district court opinions interpreting the various Federal Rules are collected in the Federal Rules Decisions reporter, a treasure trove for those interested in rules interpretation that also includes some supplementary materials—speeches made during court ceremonies honoring federal judges, for example, and sometimes even articles related to rules interpretation—that makes this one of the more interesting and diverse publications in the West group of reporters.

Let's assume that the name and all the volume and page information for our test case has transferred down to a federal district court opinion that appears in the Federal Supplement, Third Series. Let's also assume that the opinion comes from the District of Maryland. You should be able to predict that the citation will look as follows: *Smith v. Greenacre Corp.*, 123 F.Supp. 3d 456, 462 (D.Md. 2001). One helpful thing about the formalistic approach to citation shown by citation manuals is that there are few surprises, at least at the basic citation level. Because the same rules apply regardless of the level of the court, citations should become increasingly easier to generate (although you should be careful not to get over-confident and should check your citations each time you generate them, at least for a while, to make sure that they are correct) and they begin to vanish when one reads them, at least until one needs to use them to find the information on which the writer relied. This effect is perhaps why legal citations continue to appear in the body of legal documents; they become functionally invisible to the reader until the reader has need of them.

B. State Court Citations

Things become a little more complicated, but only a little, when we have to generate citations for opinions decided by state courts. Some states—although fewer than earlier—publish their own reporters, and West publishes reporters that cover all state appellate courts. These West opinions are gathered together in what West calls "regional reporters" and that conform very generally to geographical designations (although how Kansas ended up in the "Pacific" region is a mystery). That means an opinion might be published in two different reporters[3] and the legal writer is left wondering whether to include citations to both or, if only one, which one.

i. Parallel Citation

The general rule is relatively straightforward, even if it doesn't answer all questions you might have. In essence, you only cite to the West regional reporter unless the court whose opinion you are citing to is from a state that publishes its own reporters, state citation rules require citation to the state reporter, and the document you are writing will be filed in that state's courts. If each of those conditions is met, you cite to the state reporter and then include a parallel citation to the regional reporter location for the same opinion. You will have to look up each state's practice in your citation manual before filing in state court.[4]

It's worth taking a second here to consider why we bother with parallel citation. The practical reason for this clunky process of citing to the same opinion in two separate places is courtesy and convenience. Some lawyers stock their libraries with both state and regional reporters when both are available for a particular state, but more often they will pick one or the other because books are expensive to buy and to store. And some states will provide state reporters for their judges but not regional reporters. So it was—and I use the past tense here carefully—possible, even likely, that the two attorneys on opposite sides of a case, and the judge deciding that case, would have access to a state's appellate decisions in two different places. In order to facilitate the process, and to make sure that everyone could gain speedy access to the opinions on which both sides relied to make their arguments, parallel citation was a sensible and efficient citation practice.

But does it still make sense in today's world where almost everyone has access to computer databases that have all the cases in one place and will likely use those databases in preference to the book-based version of those opinions? Is this not just another anachronism of the book-based era extended unnecessarily and inappropriately into contemporary law practice? Well, maybe. But the question assumes something that might or might not be true. Access to computer-assisted legal research is increasingly common today but it still not universal. In particular, lawyers in rural areas, lawyers who practice for low and no-income clients, and non-lawyers who seek to litigate cases on their own are unlikely to have access to Westlaw or LexisNexis, except, perhaps, on some public terminals where access is limited. And some of these potential users might be unfamiliar with the search protocols and other subtleties of use that can make those services difficult to learn, even for law students.

---

3. Actually more than two, depending on the state. West publishes some state-specific reporters for the larger states, meaning that an opinion can be found in multiple printed reporters as well, of course, as multiple online databases.

4. If a lawyer from one state is writing a document to be filed in the state court system in a different system, the lawyer will typically be working with local counsel whose role it will be to advise on technical details like this, as well as participating to some degree in the case. Some states require local counsel to sign pleadings, and even to speak on behalf of the client—even though they might not have actually prepared the argument.

For some subset of consumers of legal information, then, book-based information might be helpful or even vital, and a change to a citation system that relies entirely on computer access would be inappropriate, at least at the moment. How long this situation will continue is difficult to say, and it is likely that the law will miss the moment when it would be safe to move to a citation system based on the computers alone and will continue to require book-based citations when that truly is anachronistic. But that time is not yet.

Parallel citation raises another interesting question. If a lawyer has access to a library or service that allows the lawyer to look up an opinion in both places where it is published, then providing parallel citation information—including the page information necessary for pinpoint cites—is laborious but not difficult; one simply goes to both volumes and makes note of the relevant page information and then slots it into the citation form. But if the lawyer only has access to one published source—the state reporter or the West regional reporter—then how does the lawyer provide accurate parallel citation information?

If the lawyer only has access to the opinion in the state-published form, the lawyer can't provide this information without using a computer and finding the case using one of the commercial databases. If the lawyer can do that, the parallel information is easy to find. But if the lawyer only has access to a regional reporter, it is still possible to provide parallel information, at least in more recent opinions. One of the editorial features West includes in its regional reporters (and in its Supreme Court Reporter for United States Supreme Court cases), is a parallel paging indication. West editors review the state-published reporters in which the same case can be found and note where the page breaks are found in each opinion. That information is transferred to the regional reporter version of the case, explaining why you might see small superscripted numbers that crop up at seemingly random points in the text. These numbers are located at the exact place where a page break occurs in the state-published reporter, allowing lawyers who only have the regional reporter to give full and complete parallel citations where those are required.

So after all this, how is a parallel citation constructed? Using exactly the same process we've already learned, except that the name—for obvious reasons—is only given once. Assume that our case was decided by the South Carolina Court of Appeals (the intermediate appellate court in South Carolina), and published in volume 123 of the state reporter that publishes cases decided by that court, with the opinion starting at page 456, and the pinpoint page we are interested in being 478. Let's assume further that the opinion is published in the relevant regional reporter, at volume 987, starting at page 654, with the pinpoint page being 672. The year is still 2001. And let's assume that we're including this citation in a document filed with the South Carolina Court of Appeals, the same court that wrote this opinion.

The rules governing the name are the same as those we learned earlier, so the name of the case—*Smith v. Greenacre Corp.*,—is the same as always. The state reporter citation information should come first, so you need to look up South Carolina in your citation manual to learn the correct abbreviation for the reporter in which this opinion can be found. In this case, the reporter is the South Carolina Reports, and the abbreviation for that is S.C. You now have the South Carolina part of the citation complete: *Smith v. Greenacre Corp.*, 123 S.C. 456, 478. South Carolina opinions are published in West's South Eastern Reporter, and the abbreviation for that reporter is S.E.2d (opinions from 2001 fall within the second series of the South Eastern Reporter), so you now can complete the next part of the citation puzzle: *Smith v. Greenacre Corp.*, 123 S.C. 456, 478, 987 S.E.2d 654, 672. Note that the two different citation forms are separated by a comma.

All that now remains is the date parenthetical, and if you recall, you now need to decide if the deciding court is revealed in the citation. If it is, that court need not be included in the date parenthetical, but if it is not, you will have to add that information in before you give the date of the opinion. It would appear that the court is revealed because you have state information as part of the parallel citation form, but when you look at your citation manual you'll learn that the South Carolina Reports publishes opinions from both the South Carolina Court of Appeals and the South Carolina Supreme Court. This is not true of all state-published reporters: sometime the state will publish a separate reporter for intermediate and highest appellate courts. But that isn't what happens in South Carolina, so the mere fact that the opinion appears in the South Carolina Reports is insufficient to reveal what court decided the case and you must include that in the date parenthetical. The abbreviation for this court is S.C. Ct. App., so the full and correct parallel citation is *Smith v. Greenacre Corp.*, 123 S.C. 456, 478, 987 S.E.2d 654, 672 (S.C. Ct. App. 2001).

If you were including this citation in any other document but one filed in the South Carolina court system, though, the correct citation would be different: *Smith v. Greenacre Corp.*, 987 S.E.2d 654, 672 (S.C. Ct. App. 2001). The court information would still be necessary in the date parenthetical because the deciding court would still not be revealed elsewhere in the citation.

Citation might seem like a complicated process, but it really is just the relatively mechanical application of a series of rules set out in your citation manual. The legal writer must be careful to apply all the rules, and the easiest thing is to have a good idea of what a final citation should contain and then to fill in the information you know must be necessary. But no matter how experienced you are, you would still need to look up the specific citation information for South Carolina unless you were familiar with that specific state's publication process. Most lawyers are familiar with the state in which they practice, and perhaps one or two other jurisdictions as well. For all the others, a careful lawyer—even one in practice for years—will use a citation manual to check citation information for any citation that falls outside the ordinary.

ii. Short-Form Parallel Citations

Short-form parallel citations follow the rules for short-form citations, so in the longest of the short-form citation forms you need to provide pinpoint page information, where appropriate, for both sources: *Smith*, 123 S.C. at 478, 987 S.E.2d at 672. When the pinpoint information doesn't change from one citation to the next, it is acceptable to use *Id.*, but you need to be sure that both pages are still correct. It's possible for one page to change but not the other. Where that happens, this should be reflected in the longer *id.* form: *Id.*, at 478, 673. Note that as with the other *id.* forms, you don't have to restate the volume number or volume information, but you should separate the two pinpoint page citations with a comma.

3. Statutes

While case law has the most involved citation form most lawyers with United States practices will deal with, much, if not most, law these days is legislative, meaning that lawyers must become very familiar with the citation forms for federal and state statutes as well. These still require some knowledge and thought, but are simpler in form than court opinion citations.

A. Federal Statutes

Federal statutes in their final, codified form are published—like Supreme Court cases—in three different places, one official and two unofficial. The official location is the United States Code, and the two unofficial sources are the United States Code Annotated, published by West, and the United States Code Service, published by LexisNexis.

Even though many federal statutes have names—the "Clean Water Act" for example—many of these have lost those identities by the time they're codified. We'll talk more about the codification process later, but a short explanation now might be helpful. An act—let's take the Clean Water Act as an example—has many different components when it's introduced, debated, and voted on by Congress. It sets some goals in a specific area, like the environment, and it likely includes civil and criminal penalties for violation of its requirements. In fact, in as overarching a piece of legislation like the Clean Water Act, the act might touch almost every part of what the federal government does. Where the Act does preserve its name, though, and where you're citing to the codified version of the entire Act, you should include the name. The citation format for that is explained in your citation manual.

After the act is passed, it's usually broken up into its constituent parts, so they can be placed beside other legislation that controls similar issues; all the criminal penalties are taken and placed beside the other criminal penalties authorized by Congress, for example, and all the civil penalties are placed with the other civil penalties. Federal legislation is so vast and complex that it would be impossible for anyone to keep track of what's supposed to happen, and what's supposed to not happen, if the laws enacted by Congress were not organized this way. That process is called "codification," because the various parts of congressional enactments are placed in the United States Code.

This is relevant for our present purposes because you don't have to know the name of the various act you're citing to when you're citing to a Code section, and that's what you do typically (although by no means always) when you're writing a piece of legal analysis in a law firm memo or for submission to a court. By contrast, when you write law review articles, you might find yourself more frequently writing about the act and less about where a particular part of that act ended up. Context, as always, determines form.

Citations to the United States Code should be to the official code only; while citation manuals provide citation formats for the two unofficial versions of the Code, we should cite to the official version whenever possible.

This can make for an interesting decision by a lawyer, because the official United States Code is, for very good reason, one of the least-used books in a law library. In fact, the official United States Code is rarely found outside federal or academic law libraries because it is so rarely used. The unofficial services are both so useful that almost all lawyers use one or the other of them (and sometimes both, because their additional services are complementary rather than duplicative) and hardly anyone uses the official code. But, of course, lawyers should only cite to sources they have actually seen, meaning that they should cite to the unofficial source. And yet the citation manuals want citation to the official Code if the relevant provision can be found in it. It is up to the individual lawyer to solve this conundrum.

The United States Code is abbreviated — doubtless to the approval of all graduates and current students of the University of Southern California — as U.S.C. If you are citing to an unofficial reporter, the abbreviation form for the United States Code Annotated is U.S.C.A. and — predictably enough — the abbreviation for the United States Code Service is U.S.C.S. As with court opinion citations, the volume number — in this case the "title" of the Code section — comes before the abbreviation and the page number — in this case the section number — comes after the abbreviation. You'll need to know where to find the section symbol — § — on your word processor so you can precede the section number with it. A correct citation also requires a date parenthetical, because legislation can change from year-to-year and the reader should know when the particular language being referred to was enacted. Surprisingly, you're also required to add either West (for the United States Code Annotated) or LexisNexis (for the United States Code Service) to the date parenthetical, even though the publisher is clear from the abbreviation used for the version of the Code to which you're citing.

As you can see, it's not very difficult to construct an accurate Federal Code citation. Suppose you want to cite to section 1983 of title 42 of the United States Code — a famous section that allows an individual to sue a state actor for an alleged deprivation of Constitutional rights. This provision was originally passed in a piece of legislation — known by several names, one of which is the Ku Klux Klan Act — in the aftermath of the Civil War, in 1871. The current form of the language has changed little since then, but we are citing to it from the United States Code edition from 2012. The citation for this provision, then, would be 42 U.S.C. § 1983 (2012). No publisher information is necessary because this is the official Code version: if we were citing to the United States Code Annotated, the form citation would be 42 U.S.C.A. § 1983 (West 2012), and if to the United States Code Service, it would be 42 U.S.C.S. § 1983 (LexisNexis 2012).

B. State Codes

The citation rules for state Codes differ from state to state, and the only way to be sure you have the correct citation form is to refer to your citation manual for the specific state to which you're referring and get the citation format for that state.

If the state has divided its code into sections with names, it's likely that those will be included in the citation form. Let's look for example at California, a frequently cited state. When you refer to your citation manual, you'll see that California has multiple different codes, each for a different part of its governmental structure. If the provision to which you would like to cite, for purposes of a document to be filed in court, is section 987 of the California Penal Code, and you're citing to West's Annotated California Code published in 2012, then the citation format should be Cal. Penal Code § 987 (West 2012). If you're citing to the Deering's Code version of the same provision, then your format should be Cal. Penal Code § 987 (Deering 2012).

Note that this might not be precisely what you see in The Bluebook. If you were following what appears on the page, your citation to the West version of the Code might look like this: CAL PENAL CODE § 987 (West 2012). But the large and small capital letter form, is only correct for law review articles and we were preparing a citation for use in a court document. This underscores the importance of being cautious. If your citation manual gives examples for journal citation style, and you are writing a document for practitioners, you will have to convert the journal style into practitioner style. A correct citation in the wrong style is incorrect.

4. Regulations

You might think of regulations as the least important of the trinity of documents typically thought of as governing conduct: the common law has historical resonance, and much of what we deal with in law school comes from case law, and we generally acknowledge the growing importance of the legislature in every part of our lives. But regulations are sometimes dismissed as merely the workaday details of how legislation is actually enforced. In fact, though, for most people regulations are the form of legal rule with which they most often are in contact. Regulations actually control how things get done in large areas of society, and many lawyers spend their careers working in heavily regulated areas.

Federal regulations are published in the Code of Federal Regulation, or C.F.R., as it is abbreviated and mostly known. The citation format for federal regulations closely tracks that for code sections, with the title number first, then the abbreviation for the Code, a section symbol, the specific section to which you're citing, and the date of the edition to which you're citing. A citation to title 21 of the Code of Federal Regulations, section 184.13, from 2009 would look like this: 21 C.F.R. § 184.13 (2009).

The C.F.R. is revised in full every year, so you might wonder why you might want to cite to a version that is several years old. The reason is important. Regulations change with remarkable speed; federal regulatory agencies are constantly looking at their regulations to make sure that they function properly and meet the demands of the ever-evolving world. The regulations in force today, then, might not have been in force at the time a litigant, for example, acted or failed to act in a way reflected by litigation. If Greenacre Corporation manufactured a widget in 2009, and Mr. Smith and Ms. Jones were injured by that widget in 2011 and filed suit in 2012, the regulations under which the widget were manufactured were those in force in 2009.[5] Simply finding and citing to the C.F.R. language currently in force, or in force at the time suit was filed, will not help your client's case if the language has changed. This can be tricky, because many libraries discard the older versions of the C.F.R. when the newer versions come in (you

---

5. To be accurate, they're the regulations that were in force on the day the widget was manufactured. Careful lawyers will not just look up the relevant C.F.R. for that year, they'll work back through the Federal Register to make sure that the C.F.R.'s language was not changed prior to the widget's manufacture. This can be a time-consuming process, but if you don't do it, you can be sure that a lawyer on the other side will and if the language was changed to your client's detriment, the other lawyer will certainly let the court know about it.

can tell which is which quickly by the color of the binding on the book's spine; it's different every year), and if you're using Westlaw or LexisNexis, the language updates every time there is a change so the commercial legal database language is always current. If you need older language, you should look for a library that keeps historical versions of the C.F.R. or else look for computer services like Hein Online that allow you to access historical versions of the C.F.R.

We won't talk in detail about the citation format for state regulations. These are sufficiently different from state to state that there isn't enough uniformity to make a general discussion meaningful. And you should understand the rules of how to construct a citation well enough by now to know how to use your citation manual to make your own citations conform to that manual's requirements.

Conclusion

Citations are finicky, precise things that take practice and care to get right. It can seem that this is wasted time; the reader surely cares more about the quality of our analysis than about the form in which our sources are recorded, so why should we bother with whether or not a period is underlined, or whether we use initial capital and lower case letters or large and small capitals? Isn't this all form over substance, the very type of formalistic approach that Harvard's legal scholars, among many others, so earnestly condemn?

Yes. So what?

That answer was flippant on purpose, but it contains an important core message. Our personal opinions about much of what we write—citations or complex legal analysis—aren't especially important, at least not to most readers. Rather, what's important is the message our writing transmits.

All writing—every symbol we place on a page, whether it be an electronic page or a physical one—carries significance, and our citations carry several important messages to our reader. On the surface, of course, is the message that the analysis the reader just read is supported by a legal source and the citation provides not just the fact of support but also the information necessary to find that support.

Another crucial message carried by citation, though, is that a legal writer understands the conventions by which legal information is transmitted and has taken the care to conform the document the reader is reading to those conventions. Careful, accurate citation sends messages of professional competence and attention to detail that are invaluable to a writer, just as inaccurate or sloppy citation sends negative messages that are the last thing a writer would want a reader to see.

Everything we write carries significance. So regardless of how you personally feel about legal citation, if you write a document with perfect citations you are much more likely to be taken seriously as a lawyer than if your document is peppered with inaccurate citations. And as opposed to the facts and the law—neither of which are within your control—you have complete control over how accurate or inaccurate your citations are. It's up to you what messages you send with them. Just be certain that your citations will carry messages about you that you would like the reader to hear.

Exercises

For each of the following sources, create correct formal citations from the provided information as requested:

1. John W. Bradshaw, suing the Unity Marine Corporation and Phillips Petroleum Company, in a case decided by Judge Kent of the Southern District of Texas and announced on June 27, 2001. The opinion was published in the second series of the Federal Supplement, starting on page 668 of volume 147.
    a. A full citation
    b. A short-form citation to page 672 of the opinion

2. Wilbur Lee Evans, also known as ("a.k.a.") Wilbur Willie Lee Evans, a.k.a. Wilbur Jones, a.k.a. Wilbert Jones, Junior, a.k.a. Wilbert Jones, a.k.a. Grace, appellant, and the State of Mississippi, appellee, in a case decided on May 27, 2007, by Judge Chandler of the Court of Appeals of Mississippi, and reported in the second series of the Southern Reporter, starting on page 430 of volume 957.
    a. A full citation
    b. A short-form citation to page 458 of the opinion
    c. A short-form citation, appearing immediately after the previous citation to this case, to the same page of the opinion
    d. A short-form citation, appearing immediately after the previous citation to this case, to page 460 of the opinion.

3. The United States Code, title 21, section 848, in the version published in 2013.
    a. A full citation
    b. A short form citation

4. Rule 12, subsection b, sub subsection 6, of the Federal Rules of Civil Procedure.
    a. A full citation
    b. A short-form citation

5. Section 73.609 of the Code of Federal Regulations, title 7, in the version published in 2012.
    a. A full citation
    b. A short-form citation

6. A full citation for a portion of the Water Pollution Control Act Amendments of 1972, enacted by the first session of the ninety-second Congress in 1972, and found at section 316, House of Representatives number 11, 896.

Focus Questions

1. Have you spent much time considering citation issues in your academic career up until now? Are you surprised that lawyers seem to take citation so seriously? Do you think it makes sense to care so much about how legal authority is cited?

2. Look through your citation manual. If you've spent time with academic citation manuals in other disciplines, does this manual seem more, less, or similarly confusing when compared to those other manuals?

3. Are you comfortable using indexes? Do you see why your citation manual's index is so crucial?

4. Are you confident that your citations will always be 100% accurate? Do you see why the text says citations are either correct or wrong, and that there is no partially correct citation?

5. Does the concept of citation sentences help you to understand how citations work?

6. Are you surprised to learn that legal citations still use books as a basis for their format, even though most lawyers don't find legal information in books these days?

7. Why do you think there is a publication that publishes non-precedential opinions? Can you imagine any use for such a publication?

8. Are you confident you understand court hierarchy and structure well enough? Do you understand why the text says Federal District Court opinions are non-binding on any other court, but that such opinions can still be helpful to lawyers?

9. Do you understand the legislative process well enough to follow the discussion of codification?

10. Are you surprised by the claim that most people encounter the law in the form of regulations?

11. Do you understand why it might be important to be able to find out-of-date regulations?

Chapter 16

Writer's Block and Some Ways to Overcome It

What You Should Learn from This Chapter

This chapter discusses writer's block, one of the most feared aspects of the writing process. The chapter suggests that there might be some good news associated with the idea of writer's block and proposes some ways to stop writer's block before it starts. Because these techniques are not always successful, the chapter also proposes some ways to cure writer's block once it has taken hold.

After reading this chapter, you should:

- have considered why some writers are blocked while they work;
- have considered some strategies you can employ to protect yourself from being blocked while you are writing; and
- have considered some ways to dissolve a writer's block if you have developed one while writing.

For professional writers—and lawyers are professional writers—there can be few more feared two-word combinations than "writer's block." Some won't even speak of it, perhaps fearing that mentioning its name or giving it any acknowledgement will call it into being, like an evil incantation conjures up bad spirits.

Well, let's not get too wrapped up in magical thinking. Writer's block is a debilitating and unpleasant, but usually temporary, condition. Ideally we'd prefer never to experience it at all, and we'll talk about the causes of writer's block and some techniques you can use to keep it at bay, but since it's almost inevitable that you will experience writer's block at some point in your writing lives, we'll also talk about some things you can do to clear the block once it's firmly in place. None of these techniques involve counter-incantations.

1. The Good News about Writer's Block

Anyone who's ever experienced writer's block might laugh scornfully at the idea that there's any good news associated with it. The feeling of helplessness as you sit looking at a blank screen with an incessantly flashing insertion point, incapable of typing a word that you don't immediately delete, and feeling the pressure to write something—anything—building and building is not something you would expect to have any positive associations. But there is one good thing about writer's block, and it's very good news indeed: you only get writer's block if you care about what you write.

Think of it this way. Writer's block is the inertia you experience when you can't think of the right word to write (or type, these days) next. It can happen at the beginning of a document or it can happen at any point during the composition of a piece of writing but the root cause is always the same; you can't think of the best word to come next. You probably can think of many words that could come next, but you're stuck because you're evaluating all the choices and you can't pick the best of them.

If you didn't care what came next, though, writer's block wouldn't be a problem. You could sit at your word processor and just write whatever word you wanted to without caring if it was the best word or even if it was a good one. For someone like that, writer's block will never be a problem. When you're in the throes of writer's block, you likely will envy the person who writes like a typist, without any apparent thought for quality or introspection. If you do find yourself blocked, though, try to hold onto this positive thought: you care about your writing. The symptom might not be especially pleasant, but the cause is fundamentally a good thing.

2. Ways to Stop Writer's Block Before It Happens

It sounds obvious to say, but the best way to cure yourself of an illness is to prevent yourself from getting it in the first place, and what is true of medicine is true of writing as well: the best way to cure yourself of writer's block is to not get it. Easily said, but not so easy to do. Still, there are things you can, and should, do to minimize your chances of suffering through a miserable experience.

A. Stop Caring about Your Writing (At Least At First)

This will sound ludicrously contrary but stay with me. The first and best thing you can do to stop writer's block from happening is to stop caring about your writing. Okay, yes—I said that caring about your writing was a good thing just a paragraph or two ago, and now I seem to be saying the opposite. But there is, or should be, a dramatic difference between what you sit down and type into your word processor for the first time and the finished product that ends up in your reader's hands. You've written multiple drafts of your document before you've finished, and edited and proofread it many times since you started to write. Each part of the writing process is different, and your critical senses aren't important for all of them. In fact, as we've just seen, they can be very unhelpful when they intrude during the initial writing stage and cause you to become incapable of picking the "best" word to right next. During the writing stage, in fact, the concept of "best" should be as far away from your conscious mind as possible.

All you should care about during that initial writing stage—we sometimes call it the "drafting" stage to make it seem even more like blue collar labor and less like the art of "writing" or "composing"—is getting your ideas down on paper in some coherent form. Ideally your sentences will hang together grammatically, but even that isn't too much of a problem; it's certain that not all your words will be spelled correctly. But if you notice grammatical mistakes or spelling errors as you're looking at your screen, try to ignore them. There will be time to fix any mistakes later, when you go back over your work carefully. That's the time to fix obvious errors, to tweak the structure so paragraphs aren't too long or too short, to make sure the writing flows smoothly from one word, sentence, paragraph, and idea to another, and that's the time to start thinking about good, better, and "best" words to capture your thoughts.

This isn't easy to do, and many writers—even knowing that they shouldn't be editing themselves as they write their initial drafts—find themselves doing it anyway. I do it myself; the word "their" in that previous sentence was misspelled when I wrote it, so I went back and fixed the spelling of the word, even as I appreciated the irony of advising one thing and doing another. But it's important to try hard not to let the editing part of the process intrude into the writing part of the process as much as possible. If you can do that, and just concentrate on getting the next word typed, you'll reproduce that person you were envying a second ago who seems to be more like a typist than a writer. That, in fact, is precisely the state in which you want to find yourself during the first stage of the writing process. Don't care what your work looks like or reads like; you can fix it later. Just get things down on paper, because you can't fix what isn't there. And remember that no one, unless you want them to, will read your first draft, so it can be as bad as you like.

B. Schedule Your Writing Time

Perhaps the worst type of writer's block—although they're all bad—is the type that prevents you from even starting work on a document. You engage in all sorts of displacement activity—cleaning your apartment, baking brownies, watching television, doing work for other classes, or anything else that prevents you from sitting at your desk and typing words into your word processor—and you probably justify it by saying that you always write better under time pressure so you're really better off by not starting to write sooner, or some similar excuse that makes the fact that you're not writing sound more like a good idea than a bad one.

It isn't. It's a bad idea. No one writes better under time pressure. They write differently, certainly, but even those writers who write under time pressure all the time—journalists, usually but sometimes lawyers as well—will tell you that they would write better if they had a chance to polish and edit their work. What they turn in is competent, articulate, and technically correct, but these writers can make words leap off the pages if they're given the chance to revise and edit what they've written.

In fact, what you're doing is rationalizing, and even inviting, writer's block. By telling yourself that you write better under time pressure, you're really saying that you're concerned that if you tried to write sooner than you absolutely have to, you'd experience writer's block that would be so debilitating that you would never be able to get going. This way, you tell yourself, you'll get the writer's block out of the way without actually having to experience it, because you won't be sitting at your word processor. And once you think the block will have cleared, you'll be able to write more fluently because the time pressure under which you're now working will force you to get words down. Well, either you're telling yourself that or you're just trying to avoid the editing process; either way, it's not a strategy that's calculated to produce your best final work because you're limiting, or even eliminating, the amount of time you have to edit your first draft.

For those of us who don't have time pressure imposed on us from outside, it's almost always a bad idea to impose such pressures on ourselves voluntarily. And one way to avoid doing that is to block off some time in the day when we should be writing. This is easier to do in law school than it is in practice, but it's a good idea to do it when you're trying to instill good writing practices. It might seem odd to think of actually putting writing time into our calendar, but if you find yourself drawn by the lure of displacement activity, giving yourself a specific chunk of time each day when you should be sitting at your word processor can be a way of curing writer's block before it begins.

C. Write in a Place without Distractions

Distractions are death to concentration, and if there's one thing writing demands from a writer more than anything else, it's concentration. We need to be able to let the writing process absorb us completely, to the exclusion of anything else. Writing takes— or should take—as much or even more concentration than driving a car, and we know what can happen when you're distracted while you're driving. With writing, of course, the results aren't potentially fatal, except to the work you're trying to produce. Reading and answering texts, looking out the window instead of at your screen, answering the telephone, thinking about what you're having for dinner, or any one of an infinite number of other things can take your mind away from what you're writing and the result is hardly ever positive. At best, you'll be writing on automatic pilot and find that you've typed a lot of words of which you have no memory. Maybe they'll hang together as sentences and paragraphs—the subconscious mind can do amazing things—but more often than not they're a series of disconnected words and phrases that bear little if any relation to what you should have been writing. And at worst, you'll find that you're blocked, and you can't return to what you were writing after your concentration was broken.

This isn't to say that you should always write in a room with four walls, no window, and no telephone, internet access, or sound to bother you. Those might be the ideal writing conditions for some, but fewer and fewer people these days are comfortable in silence and without any connection to the outside world while they write, and for them, the absence of distractions might itself be a distraction. And in any case, there are very few people who can find somewhere to write that has no distractions; certainly while you're in law school or are working in a law firm you'll likely find it impossible to be completely free of distractions, so the key is to find ways to minimize them.

Substituting a distraction that doesn't bother you for one that does is one way to minimize negative distractions. Many athletes, for example, go through as much of their pre-competition process as possible listening to music on headphones. That allows them to concentrate on something familiar and comfortable—the music they've picked to listen to—rather than the random, and not always positive, sounds of the crowd and the arena in which they're going to perform. Similarly, if you find you have to write in a law school building where there are all sorts of random distractions to listen to, you might find that listening to music on headphones allows you to concentrate on your writing. If you do, though, be careful: you shouldn't have the music turned up so loudly that someone else is distracted by the sound that inevitably leaks out from the headphones, nor do you want the sound to be so loud that you can't concentrate on anything but it. If you must listen to music to help you to concentrate, it should ideally be loud enough to block out surrounding distractions without itself becoming a distraction.

You can do other things to stop you from being distracted by the outside world. Turning your cell phone off or putting it into airplane mode is a good way of blocking out those distractions. If you find yourself uncomfortable at being disconnected, you can schedule short breaks from your writing—every couple of hours, perhaps—to switch your phone back on and find out what you've missed. And if you're lucky enough to be able to write in a room—an office, perhaps, in a law firm—you might get a "do not disturb" sign for the door and hang it on the outside when you're working. That won't stop partners from disturbing you, or clients calling you, but it might deter some more casual visitors from dropping by and distracting you.

D. Stop Before You Have To

Of all the ways to stop writer's block before it happens, this might be the best, especially if you often find your writer's block to be worst when you sit down at your word processor to start a writing session. If you're writing a long document that will take multiple writing sessions, try to end each session a little before you have to. This might seem counter-intuitive; if you do this you would, in essence, be creating a mini-block by stopping yourself from writing when you know what the next paragraph or two should be. Surely the best thing to do is to write until you can't go on so that you get every last word wrung out of your system for the day? Stopping early doesn't seem like the best use of your time.

But you almost certainly won't forget what you were going to write from one session to the next, especially when you read what you had written as a prelude to starting to write the next day or whenever your next session is. And remembering what you were going to write should make it easier for you to start writing at that session, because you're already written it in your mind. Having been able to write a paragraph or two without much difficulty, you might find that your usual difficulty in starting a writing session doesn't prevent you from continuing and your writing session goes smoothly from start to finish.

Of course, one can take this advice too far and stop writing before one has properly even started, in order to give yourself as much as possible that's "pre-written" to start the next session, so it's best to stop writing only, at most, a couple of paragraphs from where you otherwise would have stopped for the session. But even that couple of paragraphs can be an enormous help to get you going again. Using this technique also can have the benefit of letting your subconscious chew on what you were going to write, and can lead you to write something that wasn't planned, but is better and at least as fluent as what you expected to write when you stopped.

3. Ways of Clearing Writer's Block Once You Find Yourself Blocked

Despite all the good things we do to encourage ourselves to write as effectively as possible and to keep ourselves block-free, writer's block can creep up on us. Suddenly we find our fingers hovering over the keys, incapable of dropping to the keyboard and actually pushing down letters. After a few minutes of this, the words "writer's block" form in our minds, and once you've given the phenomenon a name, you've created an adversary against whom you must fight with all the skills and techniques at your disposal. Let's consider what some of those techniques might be, starting with the easiest and shortest and working up from there.

A. Take a Short Break

The most obvious and simplest thing to do when you're experiencing writer's block is to stop trying to write for a minute or two. Get up, stretch your legs, go get yourself a cup of coffee, have a chat with someone at the water cooler—there are many things you can do to take a five-minute break. Try to limit yourself to five minutes or so, though; this shouldn't be a complete cessation of writing for the day.

While you're taking this short break, try to not think about what you're writing. If you talk to someone, try to talk about something completely unrelated to work, so you give yourself a genuine break. Sometimes this isn't possible, of course, and if you're working in a law firm where everyone around you is focusing on the same case, it might be impossible to get away. Going for a breath of fresh air outside is a way of getting away from work conversations, but often it's difficult simply to leave an office in the middle of the day. If you can, though, try to find somewhere in the office where you can get away from work for a minute or two.

B. Change Your Writing Medium

This might seem like an odd tip, but it can work. If you usually write by typing into a word processor—and these days, that's the way most people write—try picking up a pen and a notepad and continuing to write by hand instead of by computer. Once you've written a page or so that way, open your document back up on the word processor, type in what you've written by hand, and then keep going.

It's unclear why this tip works. It might have something to do with the relative slowness of writing by hand as opposed to typing; the pace of handwriting might be better suited to stopping our minds from straying too far ahead too quickly and to keeping us focused on what we're writing rather than trying to edit what we've already written. Or it might have to do with the physical change from typing with individual fingers to writing with the entire hand. Or it might just be as simple as forcing us to think differently because the mechanics of writing are different.

Whatever the reason, though, it's probably true that this advice is less helpful now than it used to be and that it will become increasingly less useful as time goes on as people become less and less used to writing down information. For those who started off in school with writing as the only option, typing can still seem like an exotic and uncomfortable way to write, and there's something familiar and comfortable about going back to writing with a pen. For those who grew up with computers, though, pen and paper is an alien medium and trying to compose using them likely feels as uncomfortable and strange as writing on computers does for those of older generations.

If you're not too disturbed by writing with a pen, though, this tip might be just the thing to knock you out of familiar patterns and get your writing past your block. You needn't spend too long writing by hand—half an hour or so will probably be enough for you to get things flowing again. And if you're concerned that that is time lost, you should think about the time you've saved by not sitting at your desk letting the block get more solid and damaging. Writing by hand might be slower than typing, but it's still faster than not writing at all.

C. Take a Longer Break

If the short break and the change to handwriting still hasn't worked, it's time for a longer break. Stop working on this project and move on to something else you have to do if you can. Of course, this advice won't help if you have a brief that's due tomorrow morning and you have pages still to write, but even in that situation you probably have other things you need to do; drafting the certificate of service, for example, or the transmission letter that accompanies the copies of the brief you will send to the other side, or maybe even drafting the actual motion for which the brief is merely the support. Whatever the other tasks associated with the document are, it's likely that there are some things you were putting off until the brief was finished but it doesn't matter when they're done because they have to be completed at some time before the brief goes out. So setting the brief aside for a while and getting those tasks accomplished might not be a bad idea.

If you're writing something that doesn't need your immediate attention, try to set it aside for the rest of the day. Work on whatever else you need to work on, make or return phone calls, prepare for tomorrow's classes if you're still in law school, or—if you're caught up with all your work—go to a movie or cook some dinner or do something to take your mind off the document you're trying to write. And whatever you do, try to get plenty of rest before you think about writing again; being tired can play a significant part in forming writer's block and sometimes all you need is a good night's sleep to shake off the block and get writing again.

D. Write an Outline of What Should Come Next

So you woke up calm and relaxed after a good night's sleep, you almost skipped to the keyboard you were so excited to get back to writing, you opened up your document, read through what you'd written before, clicked on the document to get the insertion point at the right place to type the next word, and … nothing. More writer's block. And now the pressure's worse, because you're a day closer to your deadline and the words won't come. You start cursing yourself, me, the project, the person who first suggested law as a career, pretty much everyone. What to do now?

First, relax. This rarely happens so it's unlikely you'll be facing this situation. But if you are, relax nonetheless; pressing doesn't help the writing process at all. If you've written an outline for this document, go back and review it. Are there other parts of the document that might come easier? If so, try writing those; sometimes it's easier to bridge a gap between two parts of a document than it is to write the whole thing in linear order and sometimes you might discover that what you thought was writer's gap was really just your instinct telling you that you didn't need to write that section at all and that the document is just fine without the part you couldn't write.

If you haven't written an outline for your document, though, this is a good time to write one. Don't feel constrained to write a particular type of outline. Yours can be a traditional hierarchical outline, with each issue given its own number or letter, and with each sub issue lined up under the other sub issues, or it can be a branching outline, with each issue getting its own limb and each sub issue branching off the main issue in no particular order, or it can be any other type of outline that works for you.

Instead of working out your outline on a computer, you might prefer to use a piece of paper and a pen, or maybe even a whiteboard and a marker if you have them available to you. The only important thing is that you let your mind think about all the things you need to write about and try to get some words describing those thoughts written down. If you're writing a piece of legal analysis, you might want to include a note of what authorities you'll use to support your analysis of a particular issue, and maybe make a note of what facts you'll use to illustrate the points for which you're using the case. In fact, this is a good time to think about the structure of your analysis: What rules will control this part of the analysis? What authorities will you use to articulate those rules? What facts from those authorities are necessary to illustrate and explain the rule? How does that rule apply to the facts of the case on which you're working? What conclusions will you ultimately draw from all of this?

If you can answer those questions, you'll discover that you've written your analysis. The end result might not look that pretty, but remember—this is a first draft. You have time to edit and fix this once you've got something on paper; hardly anyone ever suffers from editor's block. So sometimes outlining your work, and then moving on to a consideration of how the structural nature of legal writing can be applied to that outline, is all it takes to overcome writer's block and get you something on which you can work as an editor rather than as a writer.

E. Freewriting

When all else fails, it's time to think about freewriting. Freewriting is a last step because it isn't really intended to be a cure for writer's block. Rather, it's a very useful tool for starting the creative process and many writers use it as a way of getting going in the morning, much like a musician might play scales before starting to practice a piece. But because it can help you get words on a page, and because that's what we're struggling with when we have writer's block, it can serve as a way of freeing the clog and letting words flow more freely onto the page.

Freewriting is traditionally done with a pen and paper, although perhaps it's better to say that it's appropriate to use whatever medium you usually use to write. So if you usually write using a word processor, then try freewriting with that (but keep the pen and paper option available in case you find that it works better than typing). Get to a blank screen, or a fresh sheet of paper, and start writing. Anything. Whatever words come into your mind, write them down. They don't have to be related to the document you're trying to write—in fact they probably shouldn't be related to that—and they don't have to make grammatical sense. Just start writing and don't stop. Not stopping, in fact, is the key. Start typing and keep going; don't even look at the screen to see what you're typing.

Keep going with out any break for a defined period of time; try five minutes at first, and you can move up to ten minutes if you think that would be more helpful. You shouldn't stop your fingers moving even for a second (that's why it's better with pen and paper—it's easier to sustain momentum when you're writing a little more slowly than it is when you're typing quickly) and you shouldn't stop to read what you've written. Just keep writing until time is up and then stop. Take a quick look at what you wrote, just to see if you said anything interesting and then (assuming you didn't, in fact, write anything interesting, which is usually the case), delete the document or throw away the sheet of paper and go back to the document you were trying to write. You should find it easier to write now.

Why does this work? Psychologists might have an explanation, but this is one of those times when explanations don't really matter. When you have writer's block, you want something to help you unclog the block. If it works, the reasons why don't matter, and if it doesn't work, the reasons why it should work don't matter either. There likely is some beneficial result caused by writing any words that helps us get past whatever caused us to be blocked in the first place that is related in some way to the technique of freeing your inner ear from listening to the same tune over and over again by forcing yourself to imagine a competing song. There likely is something in the act of forcing your brain to undertake a different, but related, task that causes the first impediment to drop away, whether it be an irritating tune or something that prevents you from writing. But again—the "why" matters much less than the result. If you can unblock your writer's block, just be happy and keep writing.

Conclusion

Writer's block is one of those uncomfortable aspects of writing we try to talk about as little as possible. But denying its existence seems to give it more power than just confronting it head-on. The fact is, every writer suffers from writer's block now and then, and there are things you can do to minimize its frequency and to mitigate its effects once you're afflicted. Remember that it's a good thing to care about the quality of your writing, and remember that it's a bad thing to care at the wrong time. Try to get lots of rest, try to maintain a healthy diet with enough exercise to keep yourself alert and awake during normal working hours, and try to give yourself enough time to get a first draft completed sufficiently ahead of the submission date that you can edit thoroughly and frequently. Do all of these things and writer's block won't be the affliction you might have feared it would be.

Exercises

1. Consider some work you need to submit within the next few weeks and draft an outline of what you want to say in that project. If you do not have any work due for submission soon, take one of your doctrinal classes and draft an outline of the work you've covered so far in preparation for writing a more extensive outline of the course.

2. Try a freewriting exercise of the type described in this chapter. Start with a five-minute exercise and then reflect on what you've written and how you think this exercise might help you overcome writer's block. Try a second freewriting exercise, this time using a different medium, if possible, from your usual writing medium: so if you usually write with a pen, try to use a computer for this second exercise, and vice versa. Consider whether you found any differences in the experience this time. If so, what were they?

3. Think about any times you've experienced writer's block and consider why it was you think you experienced the block and what you did to overcome it.

Focus Questions

1. Have you ever experienced writer's block? For how long? If you have experienced writer's block, do you remember if you did anything specific to overcome it?
2. Have you considered the idea that writer's block might be caused, at least in part, by caring too much about what you write?
3. Do you experience the temptation to edit your work as you write it? Have you identified that as a problem? Do you think you will be able to resist that temptation?
4. Will you be able to schedule some time for writing? Do you usually write when you can or do you have a definite time each day set aside for writing projects? Do you maintain an active calendaring system for your time?
5. Do you have a location to write that is free from distractions? Do you have a way of creating a distraction-free environment for your writing?
6. Have you ever stopped writing before you had to? Do you think you will try this tip to prevent writer's block? If not, why not?
7. Have you tried writing in a different medium? Do you usually draft by hand or on the computer? Do you think you will try to write in a different medium the next time you experience writer's block?
8. Do you usually outline as part of your writing process? What type of outline do you use?
9. Have you tried freewriting as a writing tool or as a way of clearing writer's block? Was it effective for you? What did you like or dislike about the technique?

Chapter 17

Editing and Proofreading

What You Should Learn from This Chapter

This chapter discusses editing and proofreading, the two most important parts of the writing process. The chapter explores why legal writers should finish the drafting of their documents in sufficient time to allow for adequate editing and proofreading. The chapter proposes some strategies for successful editing, including the development of an editing sheet that is designed specifically for the challenges you have experienced in your writing. The chapter also discusses the separate, but equally important, role of proofreading before you submit your work and proposes some strategies for effective proofreading.

After reading this chapter, you should:

- have considered the importance of editing and proofreading to effective legal writing;
- have considered the most effective editing and proofreading strategies for the way you work; and
- have considered what elements will go into the editing sheets you prepare to help you edit your work effectively.

Editing is the most important stage of the writing process for legal writers. You might instinctively disagree with this contention: how could editing be more important than, for example, the actual writing of the document or the research that provided the doctrinal underpinning for the analysis? Most experienced writers would concede that these are both crucial stages in the process, but would argue that they both lead to a first draft that is probably shapeless, poorly worded, and unpersuasive. That draft will turn into a fine document, but at the time the first draft is finished it is in no condition to show anyone. Careful editing is what will turn the document from a collection of words into a powerful piece of legal analysis.

There's no magic involved, just a lot of hard work and a lot of honest, critical appreciation of your own work. It's almost always easier to edit someone else's work, because the flaws are much easier to spot and you have no investment in the document; someone else spent the time assembling the research and writing the words that comprise the document so you don't subconsciously make the same allowances for a less-than-well-chosen word, for example, as you would with work over which you've struggled.

And once you're done with editing, you have to start proofreading, another difficult but crucial part of the refining and finishing process that needs to happen before you submit your work for evaluation, whether in law school or in practice. These days, with spellchecking programs built into the word processors we use, it's easy to think of proofreading as an almost automated process, requiring little time and a few mouse clicks to accomplish. In fact, though, proofreading requires a combination of automated spellchecking and careful reading through the document to make sure that all words are correctly spelled in the context in which they're used, all formatting is correct, all citations are properly presented and that your work is free of technical errors. No matter how brilliant a piece of analysis is, or how well expressed it might be, technical mistakes will erode the reader's confidence and, in some extreme cases, might even make the reader stop reading your work. Writing can only achieve its purpose if it's read, and that's why good proofreading is so important.

1. The Editing Process

Editing is the process of reorganizing, reconsidering, and—where necessary—redrafting a less-than-final version of a document. Some people believe that editing is simply cutting out parts of a document, and others think that editing is adding in parts to a document that were unwritten the first time around. But editing really is thinking—and acting—critically about every mark you've put on paper; every word, punctuation mark, every sentence, paragraph, and section of your work.

This definition of editing tells you something very important about when to start editing. If it's the act of working on a less-than-final version of a document, you should wait until that version is finished before you edit it. It's impossible to stress this strongly enough: you should wait until you've finished a draft before you start editing it. There are few things more destructive to the creative process than trying to edit as you write; you'll neither write well nor edit well if you try to do both at the same time.

Think about it. Imagine you're sitting at your desk, writing a memo, with someone standing right behind you looking at the screen. After each word or two you write, the person standing behind makes a disgruntled noise or a critical comment: "That's not the right word to use there!" "Wouldn't it be better if you moved that to a new paragraph?" "Is that really what you want to say there?" A few comments like that and you wouldn't be able to focus on what you were doing, you would experience symptoms of stress, and you would spend the entire writing session doubting every writing decision you made and getting much less written than you should, something that would cause even more stress and would increase the pressure on your next writing session where, in all likelihood, the whole downward spiral would start again. You can get documents written this way, but they're rarely your best work and they take more time and effort to write than they should.

One of the writing strategies many people develop to cope with this self-destructive process is to leave the writing until the last possible second. By doing this, they hope to silence their internal critic by the powerful voice of impending disaster: you have no choice but to get the document written and so you can mute, if not completely silence, the editor standing by your ear. This is an effective strategy for producing a first draft, but it's a terrible way to produce polished, finished documents because by starting to write so late, you have little or no time to edit the document properly. You might be able to trick yourself into thinking that you "work best under pressure," or that you "write best when you start at the last second," but when you think that, you're admitting that you haven't developed an efficient and effective writing style yet.

Sometimes, of course, circumstances force you into writing something with very little time. If a partner walks into your office and tells you that another associate has dropped the ball and a memorandum in support of a motion has to be filed with the court tomorrow and you've been assigned to the task, you won't have time for a leisurely drafting, editing, and proofreading cycle. You'll likely be in your office all night, trying to learn what the motion is about, checking to make sure there are no gaps in the research, and getting the document on paper in as finished a form as possible—and never underestimate how much time it takes simply to type the number of words necessary for a typical legal memorandum. Court documents also have technical requirements—certificates of service, captions, and, for motions, the actual motion itself—it's remarkable how often the motion is forgotten in the heat of getting the memorandum in support drafted and ready for filing. With all of that going on, it's unlikely that you'll have much time for careful editing.

But that's an atypical situation, forced on you by circumstance, rather than the artificial crisis you create for yourself by delaying the start of a writing project until the last second. The more you avoid creating those artificially pressured writing situations for yourself, the better you will be able to cope with the infrequent speed writing assignment you're sometimes confronted with in practice.

Another reason for not editing while you draft is perhaps less obvious but is no less crucial. You can only edit writing when you have a clear idea of what it is you want to say and you almost certainly won't know what you're going to say until you've written it. That sounds wrong perhaps: you've been given an assignment and you've done the research necessary to start writing, so surely you know what you're going to say. Probably not. Hardly ever, in fact. You probably have the end goal of the document in mind, and that might not change during the drafting stage, but you almost certainly will discover things you didn't realize about your analysis as you're in the process of writing it, and you often will discover that the research you thought was complete has some significant holes once you write it. The additional research might suggest new and better ways to achieve the document's goals—new strategies or legal arguments that hadn't occurred to you before you started to write the document. If you're as open to these possibilities as you should be, you might discover that the document you ended up with - wasn't the one you had planned to write, and you shouldn't be editing that document until you know what you're doing with it.

This might seem like contradictory advice: on the one hand, I'm suggesting that you shouldn't be editing the document as you write, while on the other hand I'm saying you should be receptive to the possible changes of direction and emphasis you experience as you write the document. How can you do both? How can you simultaneously keep your critical faculties at bay for editing purposes while, at the same time, listening to the internal voice that suggests new approaches and tells you that your research isn't adequate to support a point you're making?

It's not easy to do this, perhaps, and it might seem like a semantic distinction without much substantive meaning to you, but editing is a technical process of improving the manner in which a document makes its point, and paying attention to the document as you're writing it is a crucial part of writing. Writing is not simply typing; you have to think about the significance of the words you're writing as you write them and you have to listen to the sense of those words to make sure that you're getting the outlines of the document drafted as carefully as possible. Once the first draft is in place, the editing process will help to make the document more effective—and that might involve refining or reconceiving the document's contents—but listening to the document as you write is very different from listening to your critical voice about the way you're writing.

So, how do you edit? Simple. Once you have a finished draft, compare it with what you want the document to say. If anything on the page interferes with what you want the document to do, delete or change it. Once you're done, start again. Keep going until you can't—no matter how hard you try—change anything. After that, go back and edit one more time. If you still can't change anything, then you're done with the editing process. Easy to say, not so easy to do. Let's talk about some ways you can go about editing your work.

2. Edit on Paper

It might seem old-fashioned, and even ecologically unfriendly, to say that you should edit on paper. But there are three sound reasons for printing your work out and editing on paper before you transfer those edits to the computer: ease on the eyes, freedom from distraction, and time for thought. Let's consider these reasons separately.

A. Ease on the Eyes

It's no secret that computer screens are hard on the eyes. The glare from reflected light causes eye strain, and screen resolution—while impressively high compared to computer screens from only a few years ago—is still relatively low. Your eyes get tired quickly when you read for too long on a screen. You'll be doing a lot of reading over the years, so it's a good idea to limit the harm that reading on a computer screen can do to your eyes.

Of course, reading on paper alone will not ease eye strain. You also need to read in a well-lit location where you're not having to strain to see what's on the paper. Ideally, you should be reading in a room with plenty of ambient lighting and also some lighting focused on your document by means of a desk lamp. If all this sounds overblown and unnecessary, remember that you will be reading thousands of pages a month for the rest of your legal career. If you have good vision, be glad for it and don't endanger it. And if your eyesight is already compromised in some way, try hard not to make it worse. Reading documents on paper gives you the best chance at protecting your eyesight, so wherever possible it's probably the best choice.

B. Freedom from Distraction

Another reason to stay away from the computer during the editing process is its ability to distract you. While you're editing, you shouldn't have access to any device or form of social media you use to communicate, or even—and this is very old-fashioned—make or receive phone calls. You shouldn't be able to play computer games or do anything else other than work on your editing. You should be completely isolated from all distractions for the time you block out in your day to edit your work.

That's why you should stay as far away as possible from the computer. Editing is hard work, and it would be much more pleasant to be doing almost anything else than sitting at your desk, pen in hand, marking up a document over which you already worked hard. But you need to put in hard work in order to improve something you wrote and you need to focus on your editing if your writing is to improve over the course of time. While editing gets easier the more you do it, it is never easy and the need for concentration is even greater than when you write. You stand more of a chance of getting that distraction-free time when you edit away from your computer, and with your phone switched off.

C. Time for Thought

The third reason for editing away from your computer seems odd, but it's actually the most important of all. Computer editing is very quick. You decide to make a change, place the cursor on the appropriate spot, and either delete or add text. Once you've done it, the change is made, without any time for reflection or reconsideration. You move on to whatever is next on your editing agenda and the change is left behind.

Editing on paper, by contrast, is a two-step process. You write in the change you want to make, but that change is only made on your paper copy of the document, not the electronic version. In order to change that document, you have to open up the file and go back over your paper changes, entering them, one by one, into the document. You should be doing this some time after you completed the change on paper, and maybe you've been thinking about that change since you made it, unsure that you made the correct decision. Or maybe you look again at the change you've made and decide, in retrospect, that it wasn't the best decision and that a different change, or none at all, will work better.

That time for thoughtful reflection is very important and you should make good use of it. Entering in the changes you made during the editing process is not a mechanical task; it should be carried out with the same degree of concentration and focus as the actual editing you did, and you should be thinking carefully about whether you still want to make the changes you decided on earlier. Almost all the time you'll decide that your earlier decision was correct, but sometimes you might decide that there's a better option and you should then take the time to weigh the alternatives carefully before going on. You don't have that time if you edit directly onto the computer, and it's a loss.

3. Things to Look For While You Edit

Describing the editing process is relatively simple. Actually editing a document, though, is very hard. There are some things you can do to make sure you're going through the process in as methodical a way as possible, but the decisions you have to make as you edit are difficult ones, involving a ruthlessly honest appraisal of work that's taken you a lot of effort to produce. Editing is tough on the ego. It gets easier in time, as you become more confident in your writing and editing skills, and as the lessons you learn each time you go through this process help you to generate better and better first drafts, making the editing process easier to go through. But "easier" doesn't ever mean "easy," and even the most experienced writers can dread having to face the prospect of editing their work. They all recognize, though, that it's a crucial step—maybe even "the" crucial step—in making their work the best they can produce.

A. Look at Your Point Headings

One way to start the editing process is to look closely at your point headings. You might have written the headings ahead of the actual analysis as part of the outline you later expanded, and when you write the content below the headings you might discover that it changed somewhat from what you thought you would be writing and that your point heading no longer accurately summarizes the section's content.

If that happens, you should ask yourself whether to rewrite the heading or the analysis so that it more closely matches the heading. Headings are, after all, an outline of your analysis and sometimes you had a stronger sense of what needed to be included in your analysis before you started to write. If your writing took you off on a tangent that doesn't help you make the points you need to make in your document, then a rewrite of the content might be in order. But if you learned more about what your document should be about as you were writing it, maybe it's the heading that needs to change.

Even though you thought you knew what a section would contain when you wrote the heading, you might have been wrong. That's fine: it happens to everyone. When the document is finished, though, the headings and what comes underneath them should be aligned and the heading should accurately summarize the section for the reader.

B. Look at Your Paragraphs

It's relatively easy to tell if your paragraphs are too long just by looking at them. In fact, before you even read the words contained in each paragraph, you should just look at how long the paragraph is on the page. If, for example, your paragraph takes up an entire page of text, you should know that it's too long without having to do any reading. If, on the other hand, the paragraph is only one line long, that's a good indication that you need to be thinking about either adding more text to the paragraph, incorporating that single-lined paragraph into an adjacent paragraph, or cutting it altogether.

You shouldn't actually make decisions about where to cut based on just a visual inspection, of course, but a quick glance at the length of a paragraph will tell you if it needs some immediate work or whether it can wait for the more detailed reading you're going to give it. If you're going through the whole document quickly, you might want to make a small mark next to the paragraphs that obviously need work as you go. Something like a paragraph symbol—"¶"—drawn in the margin can act as a shorthand that you need to work on this paragraph later.

When you come back to your paragraphs and read them in more detail, ask yourself if they only contain one principal thought or if they include two or more different ideas. If they have more than one thought—and it wouldn't be surprising if they did because you weren't worrying about things like paragraph divisions too much while you were drafting the document—then separate the text into different paragraphs at the most logical place. It can often happen that a simple paragraph break can turn one bad, rambling paragraph into two crisp, easy-to-read ones, but it can also happen that by creating the break you might need to add a topic sentence at the start of the second paragraph in order to orient your reader to what's coming.

You should also be thinking about transitions as you look at your paragraphs. Does one paragraph flow logically from the one before it, and into the one after it, or do they read as separate blocks of text that have no relationship? All good writing has flow in order to maintain the reader's interest and in order to move the reader through the document as easily as possible, allowing the reader to concentrate on the substance of the document without any undue distractions. Transitions between paragraphs can help with this flow, and they are often simple, one word or short phrase, additions that can help your writing beyond all proportion to their size. If a paragraph continues with a thought from the previous paragraph, for example, a simple "Moreover" or "In addition," will show your reader that you are still working with the same thought. But if the second paragraph contradicts the first, or goes in a different direction, the addition of "by contrast," "but," or "however" will show the reader that what is to come is not the same as what was in the previous paragraph.

Transitions are not things that necessarily come naturally during the drafting phase, but they are crucial to the ultimate success of the document, so during the editing phase you should look for every opportunity you can find to add them and to make sure the document flows smoothly and seamlessly from one section to the next.

C. Look at Your Sentences

What is true for paragraphs is also true for sentences. A quick visual inspection should tell you when a sentence is too long or too short, and sentences should also contain just one idea and should flow from one to the next so that the reader is carried easily along by your writing instead of having to ask what connection one sentence has to another.

Flow and connection are why the use of conjunctions at the start of sentences—something often frowned upon by high school English teachers—can be so effective and desirable. The danger of using a conjunction in a sentence is that its careless use can lead to sentence fragments, something that is hardly ever a good idea. But used carefully, a conjunction at the start of a sentence shows the reader whether this sentence enhances or contradicts the previous sentence. For example, the "but" that started the previous sentence told you, without any effort on your part, that the sentence would show why the danger of sentence fragments was something that should be faced, and that the use of a conjunction could still be a useful tool for legal writers.

Another aspect of sentences with which legal writers need to be particularly careful is the location of citation sentences within a text. Although citation manuals like *The Bluebook* allow for citations to come in the middle of textual sentences, that's only an acceptance of the practice, not an endorsement of it. In fact, few things disrupt the flow and connection of thoughts in a sentence more effectively than a citation in the middle of the sentence, and you should strive at all times to improve flow and connection, not impede them. Even though you can place a citation in the middle of a sentence, there's never a need to do this and your work will be better if you place your citations at the end of sentences.

This might require some rewriting on your part. A sentence that was written with the idea that the citation would fall in the middle of a sentence can almost always be rewritten to locate it after the textual sentence. When you do that, you give the reader the choice of paying attention to the citation reference or, as often happens, gliding over the citation during at least the first reading of the document. If the citation is important to the reader, it's always possible to go back and check out the source later, after going through the document to understand what it's saying. Readers use documents in different ways at different times, and by disrupting the flow of text to present the citation in the middle of a sentence, you give the reader more control over how to use the document. The reader will thank you for it, and a happy reader is always a better reader.

D. Look at Your Words

To say that writers make sure the words they're using actually mean what they think they mean seems like the most basic possible advice, but in legal writing it's by no means guaranteed that what you've written is what you intended to write. Let's consider some of the ways in which you can go wrong.

The most obvious potential trouble area is when you're using non-English words like Latin phrases. Unless you're one of the very few people who speaks Latin fluently, you need to be very careful if you need to use a Latin (or Old French) phrase in something you write. Since you don't speak those languages, it's almost certain that you got the phrase from a source, so go back to that source and make sure you transcribed it correctly. Better still, find a way of saying what you want to say in English, using words you actually know.

This isn't like college, where fancy words were probably considered desirable and the more twisted and convoluted your writing could be, the better it was. In legal writing, the simpler and plainer your language, the better it will be received. Always remember, it's not the complexity of language that's prized in the law, it's the complexity of thought that's important, and the simpler you can make a complex thought appear, the more your reader will appreciate your work.

Another obvious source of trouble is a person or corporation's name. It makes a great deal of difference if, for example, a person spells his name as "John" or "Jon," "Smith" or "Smythe," or "Thompson" or "Thomson." And the difference between "Blackacre, Corp." and "Blackacre Corp." can be the difference in having to defend against a motion to dismiss for failure to name a party in interest or not. You'll probably be able to defend such a motion and reform a pleading to make sure that the correct name is used, but "probably" is not "definitely." At the very least, you lose tempo in the litigation, and you lose face with the opposition and, perhaps, with the judge and attorneys in your firm. Careful spelling of names is crucial.

A less obvious, but nonetheless critical problem is when you think you know what a word means but you're wrong. This is tricky, of course, because you can't fix a mistake you don't know you're making. This is one excellent reason to use the simplest vocabulary you can in your writing. Bigger words are harder for the reader to read, and can make your writing flabby and long-winded, but they are also more likely to get you in trouble because you're more likely to misunderstand their meaning. If you have any—any—doubt about what a word means, find a simpler way to say what you want to say. The simpler way will almost certainly be more effective with your reader and will take you out of any danger of having your meaning misunderstood.

A related issue is the danger of using words that are too colloquial or too contemporary for your readers. A word that might seem perfectly appropriate to you might be too informal for the context of your document or for your reader. A perfect example of this is "cop," a word now apparently accepted as a shorter substitute for the more formal "police officer" (and never "policeman," since avoiding gender stereotyping through language is very important). Using "cop" appears to meet all the requirements of using simple, shorter words than their longer equivalents, but while "cop" might have been accepted into the general conversational vocabulary, it's an abbreviation for "copper," a derogatory and slang word for the police, and one that is not acceptable in a lawyer's formal language. It's a word you should never use in practice, unless someone else used it and it's important for you to quote directly. Even if you find yourself speaking to police officers and they use the term, it's not one you should use back to them; there's a long tradition of groups appropriating terms that were used towards them in a derogatory manner and turning them into badges of honor within the group, but it's as well for outsiders to avoid those terms.

This is one of those tricky places where the best advice is for you to use your best judgment, remembering that the formal language lawyers use in writing is not the same as the conversational language they use in day-to-day speech. Keep your language as simple, yet as formal as possible without, of course, sounding too pompous. If this sounds frustratingly arbitrary, it is. Over time, you develop a feel for what is and isn't appropriate as long as you keep your ears open.

If it helps to think of it this way, try to think of your words as your representatives—your advocates—who are going out on your behalf to speak with the reader. When you write, in fact, you're very much in the same position as the client who hired you to be the client's advocate in court: the client can't speak in court, so the client hired you to make the best possible argument on the client's behalf. Similarly, when you write a document, you're relying on the words you chose to make your arguments for you; you can't speak to the reader directly, you can only communicate through the words you send to the judge's chambers to speak on your behalf and on behalf of your client.

So if a word isn't doing its job as effectively as it could, or even worse, is actively getting in the way of getting your point across, then fire that word and hire another one that will be more effective. It's your reputation on the line, not the word's. The word can always get work in another document, but you don't get many chances to impress a reader with your writing skills. Don't let any misplaced affection for a particular word get in your way of changing it if doing so will make your writing better.

Remember that words are the lifeblood of our writing, and try to always use the best possible word for the context in which you're writing. That can mean that you spend a considerable amount of time pondering over the weight and balance of every word in your document, but if that's the cost of writing something that perfectly conveys the meaning you're looking for, it's time well spent. Editing takes a long time if it's done right.

E. Look at Your Punctuation

There can be few things as unappealing as checking punctuation to make sure it's accurate, but it's a crucial step in making sure your document actually says what you want it to say.

This isn't the place for a revision of the functions of the various punctuation marks in English. The good news for you is that some of them—the dash (like that), the parenthesis (like these), and the exclamation mark—you'll use very little if at all, and others—the question mark, the bracket (square parentheses, like these [ ]), the semi-colon, and the colon—you won't use much. The semi-colon and the colon are both extraordinarily useful forms of punctuation but they're misunderstood and misused so often that the best advice is to stay away from them until you're completely confident that you know how to use them.

Other punctuation marks, though—especially the comma and the apostrophe— are crucial to any piece of writing and are just as frequently misused as the semi-colon and the colon. It's very important that you examine each punctuation mark you have used and think carefully about whether it's the correct mark for your purposes and whether you've used it correctly.

4. Editing Should Involve Some Cutting

One of the important goals of editing is to make your work shorter. Stop and think about that for a second. One of the important goals of editing is to make your writing shorter. This likely goes against every instinct you've developed as a writer before law school, and against every strategy you developed to be a successful writer in high school and college. There, length was prized and your success was probably, at least in part, built on being able to stretch your work out as much as possible.

That's all changed for you now. Lawyers are prized for being able to write as concisely as possible to get their points across. Not only is there no benefit to writing 15 pages when 10 will do, there's a penalty associated with the extra length because your writing will be thought of as flabby and unnecessarily long. It's not that lawyers don't want to read much; they read all the time and successful lawyers are very good at reading text and extracting information from it. But lawyers get impatient when a document is longer than it needs to be because the extra length doesn't add to the value of the document and because they feel their time is being wasted. So get used to a new reality: you're no longer writing for college courses, you're writing as professional legal writers. And in the law, as short as possible is definitely better.[1]

---

1. And to be clear, "as short as possible" doesn't necessarily mean "short." Legal arguments can sometimes take up a lot of space and we can draft documents that are very long. But only as long as they need to be and no longer. A reader will be happy to read a 50-page brief if it's clear that the writer has done everything possible to make it as tight and concise as it can be. Conversely, a reader will be very unhappy reading a 20-page brief that could have done its work in 10 pages. So as you edit your work, don't eliminate points you need to make in order to make your analysis effective, or words that are necessary to convey your intended meaning, just to make your work shorter. Just eliminate the words that don't do any work for you.

When we draft documents we almost always use more words than we need. That's an understandable practice; when we write we're not editing ourselves, so using more words than are necessary is easy to do, and we're not going back over what we've written right away to cut those extra words out. Instead, we're moving on through the drafting process, confident in our ability to come back later and make the document shorter and tighter.

It's difficult to give more than a very general rule about how much to cut, but a broad target is to reduce your work by 10% each time you edit it. That seems like a lot of words to eliminate, but you'll be surprised by how much you can cut without changing meaning.

Adverbs can clutter up first drafts because writers use them almost automatically to convey emphasis. It's easy, in the first draft of a document, to write something like "the two documents were absolutely identical," but since "identical" is an absolute that requires no amplification, "absolutely" serves no meaningful purpose in the sentence. Another example would be the use of "meaningful" in the previous sentence; it doesn't convey any meaning and instead serves only to clutter up the sentence. If you cut it, the sentence reads " … serves no purpose in the sentence." That means the same as the first draft but is one word shorter. Those eliminated words here and there can add up: set your spell checker to find every word ending in "ly" (it's best to do this by searching for "ly" and a space) and look to see if eliminating those words would make a difference to the sentence's meaning. If it wouldn't, cut those words and your document will be shorter and tighter with little effort on your part.

Another easy way to shorten your work is to identify and eliminate the passive voice. A sentence in the passive voice is almost always longer than a sentence in the active voice, so turning all sentences into active voice—except where the passive voice is desirable because your goal is to hide the actor—will help you cut excess words from your document. The bonus is that your work will likely be easier to read, because active voice is less fatiguing than the passive voice.

One important tip to remember when editing your work is the famous advice to "murder your darlings," first offered by the English writer and professor Sir Arthur Quiller-Couch. The advice is phrased in strikingly violent language to make a point: it's hard to eliminate language over which you have worked long and hard, but if you find yourself unable to cut a phrase or even a section of your work because you're just too fond of the way you expressed the idea, or for any other reason, that's quite possibly the first thing that should go when you edit your work.

The point here is that if you have lost the capacity to view your work dispassionately and critically you will almost certainly miss any defects or lapses in logic in it. And only those issues, arguments, and discussions that are crucial to your analysis should remain in your document at the end of the editing phase. So when you find yourself wondering if you should cut something but feel unwilling to do it because you're just too fond of that passage, you're not thinking critically about your work and that's when mistakes can creep in. So if you're in doubt, cut the passage and set your work aside for a while before you re-read it. It's likely you'll find that the missing passage or section wasn't crucial after all, and that your work hangs together better without it.

Of course, "likely" is not definitely, and we have one advantage Sir Arthur's students didn't have: we can cut something from our documents without losing it permanently. The phrase "cut and paste" comes from the typewriter days, when you either had to retype a document in its entirety during the editing phase or else type out a new passage, cut it from the paper where it was typed, and paste it into the old document to replace the edited passage. These days, word processing software makes this a seamless process, and the cut portion of a document can be lost forever or can be pasted into a new document.

And that's probably the best thing to do with substantial passages that you cut from your document. Rather than consign them to electronic oblivion, open up a new document, call it something like "cut from X," and then paste all those passages of which you were so fond. If, in a few days, you re-read the edited version of your document and decide that it really needs one or more of those cut passages, you won't have to redraft or retype them, but can simply cut them from the cuttings document and paste them back into the main document.

5. Editing Is an Active Process

It seems almost unnecessary to say it at this point, but editing is an active, not a passive, process. You should constantly be questioning yourself as you sit with a document, asking yourself if the structure works; if the analysis is fully developed; if the words you have chosen are the best possible words to convey your meaning; if you understand the words you have used; if any counter-analysis would help to make your meaning clear; if your writing flows from sentence to sentence, paragraph to paragraph, and section to section; and any other questions that occur to you as you're going through the document.

It's vital that you not edit on auto-pilot and that you constantly question yourself and your document. This is the same active questioning you should use when reading; it's easier if you form actual questions in your head—aloud if you like and you're in a place where you can't be overheard—and require yourself to answer these questions. This is likely not the way you've edited documents before, and it will undoubtedly seem a little strange at first. If you stick with it, though, you'll soon find the practice of active editing becomes almost second nature and you'll be asking yourself questions almost subconsciously. Be careful that you're not letting yourself lapse into more passive editing and make sure that you're still closely examining every mark you've made on the paper and that, if asked, you could justify why that mark is there.

6. Editing Sheets

We've talked a lot about editing and you have a lot of information about the editing process that you might not have had before. It can seem overwhelming, and a natural human tendency when we feel overwhelmed is to try to avoid the thing that's overwhelming us. That's why so many people try to avoid editing by waiting until the last possible second to start writing. If there isn't any time to edit, then editing can't cause us any stress. We feel better because we haven't had to confront our writing "deficiencies," and we come to believe that we're better writers when we place ourselves under time pressure.

Two things. First, it's wrong to think of the mistakes we make while drafting as "deficiencies" or any other negative word. Almost every professional writer (with the possible exception of those who truly are deadline writers—journalists and screen writers who have to write new scenes as the need arises are two obvious examples) will tell you that the first draft is just that; it is a first draft that is dreadful as a final draft but is a useful first step to a finished product. So thinking of your writing as bad just because the first draft is bad is being horribly unfair to yourself and is, simply, a mistake.

Second, there's a way to automate the editing process—to an extent—that will make it much easier for you to get through it. The editing sheet is a simple idea that can help as you start out to learn an efficient editing process and there's no reason you can't hold onto this technique throughout your years in law practice.[2]

The editing sheet itself is a simple thing to create. Simply write down, on a separate line of the page for each item, a list of all the things you want to edit your work for. We've talked here about word choice, sentence length, paragraph structure, and so on. Those are probably all things you should itemize on your editing sheet. Also—and this is why the editing sheet idea is particularly helpful in practice, when you work for numerous other lawyers—note down any specific preferences your reader has. Some readers, for example, can't stand a sentence that begins with "however" or are particularly hostile to the singular use of "they." If your reader has told you about such things, make specific note of them on your editing sheet and look for them in your work. If you can eliminate 100% of the things your reader dislikes, you will have produced written work that your reader will probably like. And you can, and should, prepare different sheets for different readers so you can edit your work to meet the specific likes and dislikes of different attorneys in your firm.

This is so easy it almost seems like cheating. All you have to do is pay attention to the comments you get about your writing and make note of the things you didn't do well, add them to your editing sheet, and make sure those issues don't recur in future documents. Sometimes those issues are actual mistakes, sometimes they're simply reader preferences, but whatever they are, they're things your reader prefers not to see and by eliminating them you will make your writing better in your reader's eyes. And always remember, writing is the act of communicating with a reader. Anything that prevents that communication, or that makes it more difficult, is better avoided. The editing sheet makes that goal easier to achieve.

The editing sheet is also an effective way of improving your scores in your legal writing course. Every time you turn in work, your legal writing professor will give you comments about what went well and what went less well. If you take everything your professor didn't like and add that problem to your editing sheet, you have a good chance of not making that mistake again. You might, of course, make new mistakes—writing is a hard skill to master—but if you do, add those to your editing sheet and, in time, you'll be producing work that, if not perfect, at least conforms to your writing professor's expectations. And it's not cheating.

The underlying principle of the editing sheet is that you should edit your work for a specific purpose and only for that purpose at any one time. If, for example, you're going to edit your work for word choice, then only edit for word choice: if you find a sentence

---

2. A sample list of checklist items for an editing sheet is included as Appendix 1 to this book.

that seems overly long, leave it alone; if you find a paragraph that seems to ramble, leave it alone. You will come back to edit your work again for sentence length and paragraph structure later, and you'll fix those problems then. Don't even make a mark on your page to remind yourself that you had thought there was a problem with the sentence or the paragraph, because you don't want anything to distract you from the editing task you're working on at that moment. Editing requires concentration and focus, and editing for just one thing helps you to achieve that. Any distractions, including trying to edit for something else at the same time, will disrupt that focus and will dissipate the concentration you need to make your work better.

Once you've edited for word choice, go to the next item on the sheet, and work your way through the document multiple times until every item on the editing sheet has been crossed off. This might seem like a lot of time to take on editing, and it does take a lot of time. But remember, this stage in the writing process is at least as important as the initial drafting, so it should come as no surprise if it takes as long, or even longer, than it took you to get the first draft written. Every second you spend editing is time well spent because you are making your document stronger and better.

Once you're finished, take a break (ideally at least overnight) and then start again. Remember that your goal is to try to eliminate about 10% of the document each time you edit it, so be on the lookout for things you can cut this time around. This is often when you have to make hard decisions about eliminating passages you really like. The first time through the document, you might give yourself a break and decide that you really liked the passage too much to cut it. This time, though, those easily cut passages are gone and you still need to find 10% of the document to cut. Try cutting those favorite passages out and pasting them into your holding document; you can always add them back if you need them.

And once you've finished that second editing pass through your document, take a break (ideally, overnight again) and then start again. And again. And again. And each time, remember to focus anew on each element on the editing sheet. It's no use to say to yourself that you evaluated that word before and you decided it was fine in the sentence. You might have changed the sentence structure after you edited for word use, and now you need to evaluate the word in the context of the new sentence in which it sits. Or you might have changed some other aspect of your analysis and you need to decide if a paragraph still does the job it needs to do. Would the paragraph be better off somewhere else in the document? It's very common for a paragraph or even a section to be necessary to some analysis but to be incorrectly positioned after an editing pass. It's a simple task to cut the relevant passage from one part of the document and to paste it into another part, so take advantage of technology and be happy you're not working in the typewriter era.

Keep going until you can't cut anything from your document. Then take a break and edit one more time. If you still can't cut or change anything, you're probably finished with the editing process. Unfortunately, your document isn't ready to be submitted yet, because now you have to start proofreading.

7. Proofreading

No one will pretend that editing is much fun, and proofreading is even worse. There is at least some creativity involved in editing a document, molding it and shaping it into the best possible expression of your thought and the most direct form of communication you can achieve between you and the reader. By contrast, proofreading is a distressingly mundane and basic task. Proofreading is, simply, the identification and correction of technical mistakes in your work. Proofreading is finding the double commas that were placed into your work by mistake when you pasted a passage in from a different location in your document, and it's the identification of the missing comma that was inadvertently cut when you moved the passage. Proofreading is the finding and fixing of typos, it's making sure that all your headings align to the correct tab stop for the level of subordination appropriate for the subsection the heading identifies, it's making sure that there are no typographical inconsistencies in your work—that everything is in the same font and the same point size, and it's fixing every other similar problem. Cosmetic? Yes. Crucial? Absolutely.

You might wonder why this is so important. But consider this. When you were admitted to college, you probably got a letter in the mail confirming your acceptance. Was your name spelled correctly? If it had been spelled incorrectly, what impression would you have formed about the school or, at least, of the person who wrote the letter? Would you believe that this was someone to whom details were important? Would you feel a little insulted? Would you feel that your achievement in getting accepted into college was a little diminished by the sense that the school couldn't even get the spelling of your name correct? A typical, and not unwarranted, response would be to wonder if the college had so little respect for you that it couldn't even be bothered to get your name right. And if it made this mistake now, might it make the mistake again in the future? Will your school ID have your name incorrectly spelled? Your diploma?

You likely would not have been especially happy about that typo, and suppose the letter had a few more mistakes in it; would that affect the way you thought about the college and its approach to professional behavior? To put it mildly, you probably wouldn't be too impressed. And that's why proofreading is so important. It doesn't change the substance of a document, but a document filled with mistakes doesn't inspire much confidence in the reader. And fairly or unfairly, that can affect the way we respond to a document's substance as well. Never doubt for a second that proofreading is a vital stage in getting a document ready to be read by its intended reader.

There's no point in starting to proofread a document until you're sure you've completed its editing. Editing, like anything else, can introduce mistakes into a document— typos, artifacts from cutting and pasting, and so on. If you proofread too early, you might miss some of those mistakes and submit a document that looks as if you haven't proofread it when, of course, you have. Your reader won't be able to tell the difference between something that wasn't proofread and something that was proofread too early, though, so wait until you've made the last editing change in your document before you start proofreading.

The best way to approach proofreading is to use a similar methodology as the editing process; make a separate stage for each potential mistake you might have made with the document. You can even add the proofreading stages to your editing sheet so that you don't forget to check the document for some things.

The most obvious first step to take is to spellcheck the document using your word processor's spellchecker. But be very careful as you do this, because your spellchecker likely isn't set up for some of the words you might be using as a legal writer and if you have a Latin phrase for it to evaluate, it likely will flag each word as wrong and make incorrect guesses as to the correct spelling of the word. You should neither accept the spellchecker's incorrect assumptions as to the word you were trying to write nor should you simply assume that the spellchecker is wrong and hit "ignore"; just because the spellchecker doesn't know how to correctly spell a Latin word doesn't mean that you spelled it correctly. Rather, you should check the spelling of each such word in your source document or in a legal dictionary and make sure that it's spelled correctly before moving on.

You should use the same caution when evaluating the spellchecker's suggestions for misspelled English words. Spellcheckers are highly sophisticated pieces of software, and they do a remarkable job of suggesting the correct word for an incorrectly spelled one, but they are not perfect and sometimes the second, third, or even lower option is the correct one for the word you intended to use. If you blindly accept the computer's first suggestion without thinking about what you were trying to say, you can end up with a document that has some remarkable mistakes in it, all of them correctly spelled and effectively unfindable by the spellchecker ever after. You can be sure, though, that your reader will find the mistake and will be critical of you because of it.

Having checked your spelling automatically, though, you now need to check it again manually. And as with editing, this is a task best done, if possible, on paper rather than on the computer screen. You need to move slowly through your document to make sure that each word, even though correctly spelled, is correct in the context in which you used it. The words "to," "two," and "too" are all correctly spelled, but it's easy to see how they could be incorrectly used in context. These are mistakes that a computer cannot catch; if the word is spelled correctly, the computer will not be able to tell, from the context of the sentence, that you've made a mistake. Readers, though, will see this sort of mistake easily and again, will hold you accountable for sloppy proofreading.

So automatic spellchecking is not enough. Having checked your work by computer, you now need to check it again and this requires you to move very slowly through your document—another reason why paper is the better choice to the computer. It's very difficult to read documents slowly on a computer and it's very difficult to slow the pace of your reading down. And it's your instinct to read documents—especially documents you wrote—quickly. It's an understandable urge to be forgiving to yourself: you know what you intended to write in this sentence, after all, so your eyes don't actually have to focus on each word in order to know what you said. But you're not reading the document for its meaning at the moment, you're reading it to identify technical mistakes, and fast reading is the death of good proofreading.

There are numerous techniques to slow your reading down, but all of them will make you feel foolish. Don't worry. No one will see you employing these techniques or will know what you did. All the reader has is the finished document you submit. If there are mistakes in it, the reader will think you didn't proofread carefully. If there are no mistakes in it, the reader probably won't even register that you must have done a lot of work to proofread the work. Sadly, perfection is assumed in legal writing and only its absence is remarkable. So don't feel bad about trying one or more of these techniques for slowing down your reading. Only the result matters, not how you got there.

The simplest technique to slow your reading is to put a ruler or sheet of paper under the line you're reading so you can only read one line at a time. We have a tendency to read in larger chunks—to let our eyes scan an entire paragraph, say, and to derive meaning by focusing on a few key words we identify. That might be a good idea for speed reading, but speed reading is hardly ever a good way to get a detailed understanding of complex documents like legal documents, and it's definitely a bad idea when you're proofreading.

But that alone might not be enough to stop you from reading too quickly. If you find you're still making proofreading mistakes, try reading from right to left instead of from left to right. In other words, go to the end of a line and then read backwards to the beginning of the line. This disrupts the flow of your reading—you don't have as many contextual clues to go on so you can't just assume that you've read a word and glide over it because the context of the sentence tells you what that word should be. Rather, you have to work carefully to read the word on its own and doing that can help you decide if the word is correctly spelled or not. Of course, a technique like this makes it impossible for you to evaluate the flow of a sentence, but that shouldn't be a goal at the proofreading stage of your document preparation. Flow is a consideration for editing, and you should have finished editing before you started with your proofreading.

If starting at the end of the line doesn't slow you down enough, try starting at the bottom of the page and reading from right to left and from bottom to top. It's very difficult to read quickly this way and you should be able to weigh and evaluate each word to make sure that it's the correct word for the context of the sentence and that the word is correctly spelled for its present purpose.

But it's possible that even reading backwards won't slow you up enough. If that happens, the most drastic approach is to turn the paper upside down and read the document that way. This probably seems ridiculous, but the technique is based on our tendency to read based on word shape—a word like "two" looks unlike any other word and once we register what the word is and identify the sound of it, we might not bother to think about whether "two" should really be "too." But when the paper is turned upside down, we can't rely on the familiar shapes of words to stand as proxies for the words themselves, we have to take the time to think what that unusual shape might signify. That time is what's necessary to slow our brains down and not make automatic assumptions about the way a word is spelled.

Of course, you might not be an exceptional speller and might not have confidence in your ability to spot a misspelled word when you see it. That's one reason to always have a dictionary close at hand when you proofread your work; not only are dictionaries good for checking the meaning of a word, they can also give you the correct spelling when that's in doubt. And for the same reason, you should always edit and proofread your work with a citation manual with you. You might not remember all the arcane rules of citation (and really, there are better things with which to fill up your brain) but your citations still need to be accurate, so having the manual there to help you check them can be very helpful.

Once you've proofread your work and you're confident you caught every mistake, set it aside and proofread it again. This isn't a commentary on how skillful you are as a proofreader, just a caution that no matter how careful we are, we almost always make too many allowances for our mistakes and there's no harm in checking the work we did to make sure we're turning in a technically perfect document.

Once you're finished, it's a very good idea to run the computer's spellchecker one more time. If you haven't introduced any typos into the document since you last did this, it should let you know in less than a second that the document contains nothing but correctly spelled words. But even careful typists can make slips as they key in changes to a document and if this final check catches those mistakes it is well worth the minute or two it takes.

Conclusion

Once you've done the best job you can with editing and proofreading your document, there are only two things left to do: file it, and forget about it for a while. Once the document is out of your hands, it's no longer your document. Instead, it's the reader's document and the reader will make whatever use of it the reader choses to make of it. Nothing you do, and no additional edits you make in the document, will affect that in the slightest. So move on to the next task and try to forget, for a while, as much about the document as you can.

In law school, you'll be seeing the document again with marks, comments, and corrections all over it. Once you get a document back that's heavily marked-up, there's a natural tendency to take it personally, to feel that you're being personally criticized or challenged. You're not, of course; your legal writing professor is trying to help you become a better writer by pointing out the places where you might have gone wrong and showing you how you can do better the next time. It's okay to feel that sense of personal outrage for a minute or two, but then you need to set that aside, stop taking the criticism personally (no one thinks you're not a good person just because your writing might have some mistakes in it) and try to learn from the comments and corrections. If you can do that, apply the things you might have done wrong to your editing sheet so you don't make those mistakes again, and apply the suggestions to the next document you write, you'll improve rapidly as a legal writer and soon your documents won't have any marks on them at all.

Exercise

Construct your own editing and proofreading sheet, based on this book's recommendations about writing, your legal writing professor's classroom comments and suggestions based on a review of your writing thus far, and your own perceptions of writing problems you need to avoid. Share your editing sheet with the person sitting next to you in class. What similarities and differences do you find between the two sheets? In class, can you come up with a standard set of editing and proofreading suggestions that will ensure technically correct work if followed?

Focus Questions

1. Do you think of editing as the most important stage of the writing process? Do you agree with the claims the text makes for editing's importance?

2. The text outlines a detailed and time-consuming editing and proofreading process. Has your editing process taken up this much time in the past? Are you persuaded that you should spend more time editing now that you are a lawyer?

3. Do you find yourself editing your work as you write? Do you agree with the text that this is not a helpful process? Have you ever written something with someone standing looking over your shoulder? Was this an enjoyable or helpful experience?

4. Do you find yourself waiting until the last second before starting to write? Do you believe you turn in your best work when it's written under time pressure? Do you understand why the text suggests that this is not a good idea? Will you change your writing process to include more editing and proofreading time now that you are in law school?

5. Do you understand the text's position that you should not edit a document while you write it, but that you should listen to your text as you write in order to make sure that the document is doing its job correctly? Does this advice seem contradictory? The text suggests that there is a distinction between these two positions. Do you agree?

6. Do you usually edit on paper or on a computer? Given the text's preference for paper editing, do you think you will adopt that approach now that you are in law school?

7. Do you outline before you start to write? Do you use your outline's headings as a guide? Have you ever found that your headings and your analysis don't match up?

8. Have you ever written a paragraph longer than a page? Did you submit that paragraph unedited, or did you edit that paragraph into shorter parts during the editing stage?

9. Do you pay attention to flow and transitions in your written work? Do you see why the text pays so much attention to the value of transitions in legal writing?

10. Has it been your experience in college that "fancy" words were more desirable than plain ones? Are you frustrated now to learn that, in the law, plain English is considered to be superior to convoluted language?

11. Have you ever used a word in a piece of writing whose meaning you later discovered you didn't know? Did you suffer any consequences of which you know as a result of that? Do you see why such an act could pose problems for lawyers?

12. Are you concerned at the prospect of using language that is too colloquial for legal writing purposes?

13. Does the image of words being your hired advocates, going into a judge's chambers to speak on your behalf and on behalf of your client, help you to understand the importance of words to your analysis and the ruthlessness with which you must treat words that don't do their jobs as effectively as they might?

14. Are you comfortable with your level of skill at using punctuation?

15. Are you surprised to learn that length is not a desirable feature of legal writing? Was writing a document that came right to the end of the word or page limit one of your strategies as a college writer? Is it frustrating to learn that this is no longer a strategy for success? How will you adjust to this new reality? Will that adjustment be easy for you?

16. Do you edit your work for adverb use on a regular basis? Does this seem like a useful editing strategy?

17. Have you heard the advice to "murder your darlings" applied to writing? Do you think this advice will help you to develop your writing skills?

18. Do you find the description of editing as an active, as opposed to passive, process helpful to you?

19. Have you been introduced to the concept of editing sheets before? Have you used an editing sheet in your written work before now? Do you think this approach will help you as you edit your work from now on? Will you carry this approach into practice? If not, why not?

20. Do you have strong, average, or weak proofreading skills? What is your greatest proofreading strength? What is you greatest proofreading weakness?

21. Have you encountered poorly proofread work? What was your reaction to it? Do you imagine anyone has ever had that reaction to a piece of your writing?

22. Has your proofreading been criticized? Are you confident that your work will withstand careful scrutiny for technical mistakes now you're in law school?

23. Do the proofreading techniques suggested by the text seem extreme or do they seem helpful?

Chapter 18

The Legal Memorandum

What You Should Learn from This Chapter

This chapter discusses the legal memorandum, the most traditional form of recording and communicating legal analysis. The chapter considers whether the practice of asking law students to write memorandums of law is outmoded at a time when law practice appears to be moving inexorably to more informal means of communicating information, and suggests several reasons why law students can still learn from the process of drafting formal memos of law. The chapter then discusses the interoffice and trial memorandum forms in more detail.

After reading this chapter, you should:

- formed a conclusion as to whether memo writing in law school is a practice that retains vitality;
- have an understanding for how an interoffice memorandum is structured and why is retains that structure today;
- understand why all legally material facts should be included in a Statement of Facts; and
- appreciate the importance of the procedural posture in trial memorandums.

The title of this chapter is wrong. The word "memorandum" in the law means many things, so it's wrong to speak of "the" legal memorandum as if there's only one type of memorandum. But "memorandum" is an even trickier word, because its correct plural—"memoranda"—sounds old-fashioned, stuffy, and rigid, and the more commonly used plural—"memorandums"—looks wrong and grating to those who believe in upholding standards of precision and grammar in the English language generally and in legal writing in particular. And, in fact, "memorandum" is a word that hardly anyone uses these days, preferring the diminutive "memo." The plural of "memo," by the way, is well established as "memos"; you would get many strange looks if you went about speaking of "mema." In theory, it's a fascinating word that has multiple forms and meanings: a word that almost defies the writer to describe it.

The reality, sadly, is more prosaic. Although there are multiple meanings for the word, we encounter it most often in basic legal writing classes in two contexts: the interoffice memorandum and the memorandum in support of a motion.

Interoffice memoranda (-dums?) are the traditional method by which lawyers record anything related to a case (the word they tend to use is "memorialize," which sounds too much like something you would do to information that had died, even though that's not, in fact, what the word means) and by which they communicate in writing with each other. A memorandum is the way lawyers record their analysis of the facts and the law relevant to a particular issue, and case files can be filled with memorandums (-da? Can we agree on the more colloquial plural for the moment?) that can be read and re-read as the case progresses. You likely will be asked to draft at least one interoffice memorandum during your first year in law school.

Those of you who have worked in law offices recently might wonder why you're asked to write a legal memorandum. Your experience might have suggested that most lawyers record information these days electronically, and usually communicate by email instead of by memorandum. If the memorandum is an archaic form of communication, you might ask, why bother learning about it in law school? Wouldn't it be better to learn how to communicate effectively in the way lawyers actually write to each other than to write something that has changed little in its external form since the nineteenth century? Is this just another example of law schools being out-of-touch with the way the law is actually practiced today?

No. There are three valid reasons for continuing to teach you about the interoffice memorandum and how to write one. First, it's not necessarily true that law firms don't still use the memorandum to record information. Your experience might have been different, but it's important to remember that individual law firms, and even individual lawyers, vary widely in the way they practice law. You might have worked at a firm where the lawyers didn't write many memorandums, but your next job might be at a firm where that's the principle mechanism for recording analysis. It's better to learn how to write a memorandum and then not have to use that skill than it is to not know how to write one and then be expected to write them all the time.

The second reason is more pragmatic. Even at firms where lawyers don't write many memorandums by name, the form of the legal memorandum is so well-understood by lawyers that they often—usually, even—write in memorandum form even though the document they write doesn't have the name "memorandum" or some of the more formal trappings of the interoffice memorandum. You need to know how to write a memo so you can present your information or analysis in memo form, even if you don't head your document "memorandum."

The third reason to learn how to write an interoffice memorandum is suggested by the second one. Because the memorandum form is so pervasive in law practice, knowing how to write one is a cultural expectation in the law. Even lawyers who don't write memos themselves expect their associates to understand how to write them, and even though they might not use them in practice they expect to see them from job applicants who are seeking jobs after their first year of law school. The reason for this is simple: law schools typically teach their students how to write memos in the first semester and more argumentative documents like appellate briefs in the second semester, but job applications for first-year summer jobs usually go out at the beginning to middle of the second semester of a student's first year, meaning that the student has only completed the memo assignments at that point. Lawyers understand this and are happy to see memos as writing samples; well-constructed memos show them that the applicant understands how to present legal analysis in a coherent and culturally appropriate manner. A good writing sample might not get you a job, but a bad writing sample will almost certainly guarantee that you won't get one.

So while some law firms might not use the interoffice memorandum on a daily basis anymore, there are still very good reasons—both personal and professional—for you to learn how to write them. They have pedagogical value as well, providing a handy medium for you to practice the lessons about rule identification, structure, and technical perfection you're learning in your legal writing classes.

The second commonly encountered type of memorandum in the first year of law school is the memorandum written in support of a motion. These have some external similarities with interoffice memorandums—they both have a section identifying the issues to be analyzed (although the interoffice memo usually calls this the "issues presented" and the trial memo usually calls it the "questions presented"), they both have a section for a statement of facts, and they both present analysis that's divided and subdivided by discrete issue—but they are, in fact, very different documents. The purpose of the interoffice memo is to record information or analysis, and it usually does so in a neutral way. The trial memo, by contrast, is more akin to an appellate brief, and is a persuasive document through and through. Everything about the trial memo should be calculated to persuade the judge to rule in your client's favor. There is nothing about a trial memo that is in any way neutral.

And while there might be some question about how often lawyers still actually write interoffice memos these days, there is no question that trial memos accompany virtually every motion filed in court. In fact, when most lawyers speak of working on a motion all day, they actually are talking about the memorandum in support; the motion itself is usually a simple, one-page document that takes just a few minutes to write, whereas the memorandum in support can be a multi-page and complex document that takes days to write.

Let's look a little more closely at these two types of memorandum, recognizing, as we do, that lawyers might come in contact with many other types of memorandum, depending on the type of practice they do. We're going to limit ourselves to the basic forms now, but that's only to save space, not because the other types of memorandum are unimportant.

1. The Interoffice Memorandum

The basic memo has some standard information that identifies it immediately to anyone who has ever seen one. In order to properly be thought of as a memorandum a document must have this information.

The first thing common to memorandums is the word "memorandum," which comes at the center top of the first page of the document. It's not as if anyone could mistake this document for anything else, but calling it a memorandum is standard practice.

Next come the familiar "to," "from," "date," and "re" headings. These come on consecutive lines and are invariably written in that order. There's no real reason for that: the order could have developed as "re," "date," "from," and "to," but it didn't, and you're well-advised to follow tradition here. There are no points for originality in the memo form, save that for the originality of thought displayed in your analysis.

After those familiar introductory headings come the formal sections required of all analysis memos: the Question Presented, the Short Answer, the Statement of Facts, the Analysis section—the heart of the memo—and finally the Conclusion section. None of this is too complicated, but there are a few things you might not have thought about so let's take a closer look at what falls under each of these headings and why it's there. Sometimes understanding the "why" can ease your mind about whether all of this is mindless formalism or whether there is a practical reason for memos being laid out the way they are.

A. The "To" Line

"To" is simple enough. It's the person to whom you're writing the memo. Sometimes this is an inanimate entity, like "File," but more often than not it's the person who gave you the assignment to write the memo in the first place. Junior lawyers often want to show initiative, which is a fine thing but which can lead them to do work that ultimately can't be billed to a client or otherwise accounted for. That time is lost to the firm, and since firms need to make enough money to pay their staff, associates, and partners, the firm likely won't appreciate initiative that can't be accounted for. One way to prevent yourself from incurring this type of cost for your firm is to stick to doing only the work you're asked to do, at least at the start of your employment. Later, once you know how things work a little better, you might branch out and initiate work for yourself. For now, though, make sure that the person to whom you're addressing the memo actually asked you to write it.

B. The "From" Line

The "From" line is usually, but not always, you. Sometimes the memo might be a collective effort, reflecting work done by several associates. It's a good idea to make sure everyone who worked on the memo is credited with that work in the "from" line. If you get the reputation of someone who tries to get the credit for other people's work, you will not have a happy or long time at that particular law firm. Of course, sometimes you might be working for someone who wants you to put their name on a memo, indicating that it's "from" someone other than you. In what might seem to be contradictory advice, you should go ahead and do that without question, at least at the start of your time as a lawyer. You will quickly learn if a lawyer is trying to take credit for your work or if there are legitimate, institutional reasons to have someone else's name on the memo.

C. The "Date" Line

A "Date" is important because the law is dynamic, and might have changed between the time you write the memo and the time someone reads it. Of course, the law doesn't change on a daily basis, but memos are long-lived and can be referred to and used years after they were first drafted. Memos, in fact, form a large part of the intellectual capital of a firm and once they are indexed on a firm's database of documents they can be accessed and used by any member of the firm, even someone who isn't working on the same case as you and who you might never have met. That person needs to know when you wrote your analysis so as to be able to tell if it is still timely or whether subsequent events might have rendered it obsolete.

D. The "Re" Line

The "Re" line is the most important of the four memo headings, and is probably the last part of the memo you should write. It's fine to write a working heading here as you start, but you should always look carefully at the "Re" line once you've written the memo to make sure that what you've written does, in fact, match up with what you said you were going to write. Memos, like all other documents, can have a mind of their own and can become about something they weren't necessarily supposed to be about when the writer started work. In describing the subject of the memo you should try to be as informative as possible without overloading the reader with too much information. A heading like "Class Certification Requirements" might be adequate or might be too general, depending on what the memo is actually about, but a heading like "Rule 23(a)(4)'s Requirement That the Class Representative Be an 'Adequate' Representative of the Class Is a Problem in This Case Because Mr. Smith Has Numerous Inadequacies Which Will Likely Cause a Reviewing Court to Find Him Inadequate to Represent a Class" is certainly too long.

If the firm where you're working uses client matter numbers to identify specific files, your "Re" line should usually include both the client number and the specific matter number — usually something that looks like "603-32" and then enough text to let the reader know what specific issue relating to that case is being recorded. But remember that the line is to tell the reader what will be in the memo, and it's not a good idea to try to put the entire analysis in just one line.

E. The "Question Presented"

This is the section that provides the detail you might have been wanting to put in the "Re" line because this is the place to tell the reader why this memo was created; what the analysis is going to be about. If the "Re" line is the last thing you should write in a memo, this is the second-to-last ("penultimate" for those of you who want the $50 word for this concept) part of the memo you should write. You know the basic outline of what you've been asked to write, of course, before you start writing, but — and I can't stress this enough — the act of writing can change the nature of the analysis and the question presented should reflect the actual end product, not where you thought you would end up.

There's some mythology that has arisen about the Question Presented in a legal memo. Many lawyers were taught, and continue to believe, that the Question Presented must (a) start with the word "whether," (b) be one sentence long, (c) contain a conclusion immediately following the "whether," and (d) after the conclusion, there must be a comma, the word "where" and then a statement of the relevant facts or law, or both. To a great deal of practicing lawyers, a Question Presented should look something like this: "Whether the proposed class meets the 'numerosity' requirements of the federal class action rule, where Rule 23(a)(1) requires that the class be so numerous that joinder is impracticable and there are potentially as many as 100 class members in this case."

Two immediate thoughts might occur to you. First, this isn't a question. And second, this isn't even a sentence. For generations of practicing lawyers, technical details like that haven't stopped them; this is how a Question Presented should look so this is how it will look. And to be fair, it's not a dreadful way to start a piece of legal analysis, because at least it sets out the outline of what the memo will be dealing with. As long as the writer doesn't go beyond the 23(a)(1) discussion of "numerosity," this Question Presented has done an adequate job of informing the reader of what's coming up.

But it's wrong to think that this is the only way to write a Question Presented. It's probably better, for example, to actually ask a question if that's what the section is headed, and it's usually better to write in complete sentences when one is engaging in formal legal writing. And while the example Question Presented offered above is relatively short, and fits comfortably in one sentence, that's because the issue described is relatively discrete and compact. If the memo for which we were drafting a Question Presented was an omnibus memo covering all issues relating to class certification in this hypothetical case, the Question Presented could—if the writer let it get out of hand—be almost a page long. A page-long sentence is a bad idea at any time.

There is, in fact, no rule in some long-forgotten rule book that sets out the specific layout of a Question Presented, and appeals to "the way it's done" shouldn't hinder you from using a different approach if it seems more informative. Let's consider this as a possibility: "Will a federal court find this class to be sufficiently numerous where rule 23(a)(1) is silent on a number that is sufficiently 'numerous' to meet its requirement but courts in this jurisdiction have found that classes of more than 40 are presumptively 'numerous' and this proposed class has potentially as many as 100 members?" That comes in 54 words, so relatively short, and it's one sentence, but it's an actual sentence and it poses a real question.

In fact, there are many ways to write Question Presented sections and unless you are specifically told to write them in a particular way for a particular attorney, (and if you are, for goodness sake follow that advice) then pick the approach that works most effectively in the specific writing situation in which you find yourself. Remember always that context determines form, and that applies to every stage of the writing process.

F. The "Short Answer"

It's possible to be a little bit (but only a little bit) more definitive about the short answer, and in doing so we can have a discussion about another cultural expectation in the law that sets us apart—or should set us apart—from other disciplines. Here's the quick version of how to structure the short answer: answer the question first, and then explain your answer. Now let's talk about what that means.

There's an expectation—cultural, professional, call it what you will—that lawyers will answer questions, and that they'll do so directly after the question is asked. This isn't true in other fields: politicians, for example, are famous for answering the question they wish they'd been asked, and often you can hear an answer that seemingly has little, if any, relation to the question that was asked. You might notice the same tendency with some athletes and coaches, who have their own agenda for what they want recorded about their response to something.

This "sound bite" form of answer might work well for people in those areas, but it is a terrible idea for lawyers working in a legal context (lawyers speaking at press conferences are often engaged in a public relations exercise, and the rules for how to be-have in such a setting are those appropriate for public relations, not law). If you at-tempt to answer the question you wish you had been asked as a lawyer, or if you attempt to explain your answer before you give it, you will look evasive and untrustworthy. If you do this before a judge, the judge might well interrupt you and ask you the ques-tion again; few things make a lawyer look less believable than when the judge has to ask a question for a second, and sometimes even a third time.

What is true in an oral setting is even more true in writing, because there you get to frame the question yourself. If you can't even answer your own hand-crafted question, how reliable do you think you'll look? So you're strongly advised to answer the ques-tion you've just presented before you try to explain your answer.

In our hypothetical memo, you've asked yourself the question of whether a class will be sufficiently numerous to meet the 23(a)(1) "numerosity" requirement. As we dis-cussed, there are several possible ways for you to have framed the question, but they all lead to the same place. For your short answer, though, I'll recommend that you start in one of four very specific ways: "yes," "no," "probably," or "probably not."

Having answered the question directly, you can then expand on your answer—al-though only briefly—to explain to your reader in very compact form how the analy-sis in the memo will come out. Here's one possible short answer to the question we've been dealing with: "Yes. While a class opponent might be able to overcome the pre-sumptively sufficiently 'numerous' class if the class size was between 40 and 60, research has uncovered no proposed class of more than 60 people that was not sufficiently large as to make joinder impracticable."

As you can see, this short answer gives very little in the way of detail. There are no citations to authority to support the contentions in the short answer and very few specifics. That's because it's a precursor to the analysis, not the analysis itself. A reader will be primed by this answer to expect all of the detail to support this answer in the memo's "Analysis" section but for right now, a reassurance that this is the direction in which the memo is headed is all the reader needs.

In fact, the reader might only read the question presented and short answer sections of the memo and then stop if all the reader is interested in, at that time, is the answer to the question. The reader might go back and read the memo in more detail later, or the reader might already have read the memo and just wanted to be reminded of the answer now; remember that readers use memos for many different purposes and that you shouldn't write with only one of those purposes in mind. Your job is to write as ef-fective and complete a memo as you can and let the reader use the information for whatever purpose is appropriate at the time.

G. Statement of Facts

Law students are sometimes surprised by the emphasis we put on facts in law school. They came, after all, to "law" school, not "fact" school. And yet in doctrinal classes you doubtless have heard students recite the facts of a case many times (you might have had this experience yourself by now), and here in legal writing we again are talking about facts and why they're so important to legal analysis. Why is this?

The answer is simple, really. The common law process involves a synthesis of fact and law in order to predict a result. A court or a legislature announces a legal proposition and the courts then explore different factual situations to determine whether the requirements of that proposition have been met or not. In the hypothetical issue we've been considering in this chapter, for example, the rule we're seeking to analyze is very general: in order to be certifiable, a class must meet certain conditions, one of which is that "the class is so numerous that joinder of all parties is impracticable." Okay, but what does that mean? How numerous is "so" numerous? When does joinder become "impracticable"? The rule doesn't give us any additional information, and while there is a Note that accompanies the rule, we know enough about the way courts work to know that the Note won't be of any substantial help or support.

To understand the rule, then, we'll have to research the issues we've raised. We'll look in the particular federal (it has to be federal because we're dealing with a federal rule of civil procedure) jurisdiction in which we're thinking about bringing this class action, and we'll look for how the courts have interpreted these words.

We'll probably find lots of cases, but how do we chose between them to reach our conclusions? By looking at the facts. Cases with facts that are similar to ours are more helpful, cases with facts that are identical to ours are the most helpful. If you find cases with facts that are dissimilar to ours, those can be helpful as well, although you probably will only be relying on them if there are no cases that are more directly helpful.

This is why a statement of facts is so important in a memo. Without the facts relevant to the case you're working on, your legal analysis will only be helpful in the abstract. It might represent a lot of work, and it might be an accurate analysis of the law in a particular area, but it can't help you apply that law to a specific case because without those facts you can't choose between those cases that are more or less relevant.

This leads to an important question: what facts should be in the statement of facts? Each case has a large number of facts but not all of them are of the same importance, at least not all the time. And some things that you might think of as "facts" might not really be facts. It might be true, for example, that the class representative in the case we're considering here has been a class representative before, has a post-graduate education, including a law degree, and is energetic and committed to working on behalf of a resolution of the class litigation that favors all class members. Let's consider these "facts," remembering that the analysis we're working on in this memo has to do with the satisfaction of rule 23(a)(1)'s "numerosity" requirement.

Viewed through that light, the fact that our current class representative has been a class representative before, or has a good education, seems not to be very relevant. It might be, and probably will be, relevant to a consideration of rule 23(a)(4)'s requirement that the class representative be "adequate" to represent the interests of the class, but that is not the analysis in which we're engaged at the moment.

This demonstrates that facts can be legally material or immaterial, and that their materiality changes with the context of the legal analysis. These facts are presently legally immaterial, in that a change in them would not affect the result of our analysis here. But they would be material in an analysis of rule 23(a)(4), because were they to change, the outcome of that analysis would be very different.

How about that last "fact"—that the class representative is energetic and committed to getting a satisfactory outcome for all class members? That isn't really a "fact," is it? It's an opinion—something that you might believe, but that someone else might dispute. The class representative's level of education, or previous activities as a class representative, are objectively verifiable; but to say that someone is energetic is to offer an opinion about that person.

The distinction between fact and opinion is crucial, and one that many law students—and lawyers—find difficult to identify. We'll talk much more about what is and is not a fact in a separate chapter devoted to facts, but for now we can say that, by definition, only facts should be in a Statement of Facts and that only those facts that are legally material to the analysis should be included.

We'll also talk about the nature of the way facts are presented in all legal documents— predictive, like interoffice memorandums, and persuasive, like any memorandums filed in support of a motion. Facts in all legal documents should be written to appear as neutral as possible, meaning that you shouldn't characterize them in any way. This means that you should avoid words that characterize—especially adverbs—when writing a Statement of Facts.

The idea that facts should be written "to appear as neutral as possible" was carefully expressed. You never write in a neutral style; everything you write, even predictive memos, are persuasive documents in that you want to persuade the reader to accept your analysis as accurately predictive. And no mark that appears on the paper on which a persuasive document is printed should be placed there without careful thought as to how it will help to persuade the reader of the accuracy of your analysis. So never doubt that all legal writing is persuasive in some form or other, and that that should always be your goal.

But with a Statement of Facts, you are much more likely to persuade the reader if the reader believes that the facts are being presented in a neutral manner. Legal readers expect to understand the facts required for an analysis as facts, not as tools of persuasion. That means that you have to be more subtly persuasive when you draft, organize, and present those facts. You can't omit any important facts; if a fact is inconvenient, or destructive of a legal theory, you'll have to change your theory because lawyers don't get to run away from bad facts. And once you've worked out a theory that can accommodate all facts, good and bad, you have to include all those facts in your Statement of Facts.

So all the legally material facts should be included in the Statement of Facts. It's easy to forget this and to write a Statement of Facts that has many legally relevant facts, but to then include a fact later in the analysis because you'd forgotten at the time of drafting the Statement that a fact would be necessary for your analysis. If that happens, you need to be sure to go back to your Statement of Facts and include the fact on which you relied in your analysis. Actually, another way of thinking about what is and isn't a "legally material fact" is "every fact on which your analysis relies." If it's in your analysis, it should be in your Statement of Facts; you don't want your reader encountering facts for the first time in the analysis.

You might legitimately be wondering, though, if this requirement that only the legally material facts for this particular analysis be included is too restrictive. How can you inform your reader about the context for this analysis without a little scene-setting? And might that not require some facts that are included purely for that purpose, and not to further the analysis?

Yes. As always, the context determines the form, and in this context it's important that you keep the reader interested and informed during the Statement of Facts. That will likely require you to include some scene-setting facts that are not strictly necessary for the analysis.

There are no hard-and-fast rules about this. You need to use your own judgment about when a fact is necessary and when it's superfluous for the purpose of your analysis. Your best guide is to think of the Statement of Facts as a story you're telling the reader. Are you giving the reader enough information to understand the story of why an analysis of this issue is necessary, are you not giving the reader enough information, or are you giving the reader too much? No strict quantification or algorithm will help you in this process. Unfortunately, as with most things to do with writing, you're pretty much on your own. Use your judgment and try to keep the facts section as short as it can be while telling a story and including all the legally material facts for the analysis you're about to present to the reader.

H. Analysis

After all this discussion about the other parts of a memorandum, we now come to the heart of the document—the reason it was written. Everything else has been written in support of this section. Which is why it might seem strange that there's so little to say about it.

To be more correct, there's little to say about it here. In fact, of course, legal analysis—how it's written, structured, and presented—is the subject of most of this book. There's a tremendous amount to say about all of those things in various other parts of the book, but because of that there isn't that much to say about analysis that shouldn't already be apparent to you: your analysis in this section should cover the topic of the memo completely, but no more than completely, taking into account all legally material facts, and considering the topic from all sensible perspectives.

You shouldn't go beyond the boundaries of common sense when you analyze a legal subject. This country's laws would doubtless be different if America hadn't separated from Great Britain in the 1770s, for instance, but it wouldn't be sensible to engage in a full and complete historical analysis of the ways in which that political upheaval more than two centuries ago might have affected the law in the area you're currently analyzing.

A quick word on writing style is probably appropriate here. Remember that with the interoffice memorandum, you're not engaging in overt persuasion. In fact, the style in these documents is very even-handed, presenting the arguments for and against a particular result. Your theory should be able to accommodate all potential arguments offered against it, and it's better to test your conclusion by including those counter-arguments and showing why they're not as compelling as the conclusion you've reached. Counter-analysis is often an important feature of the analysis section of an interoffice memo.

There isn't much to say about the organization of the analysis section of a memo. Ideally, you'll give your reader a general sense of how the analysis works out, and why, before you get into the actual mechanics of the analysis. And it's usually best to break up the analysis into digestible, and logical, pieces, so the reader can be guided through the analysis by a sensible use of subheadings. But other than that, there isn't anything to add about legal analysis here.

I. Conclusion

Every properly constructed memo has a section headed "Conclusion," even though the memo will already likely have included multiple conclusions before the reader reaches this structural "conclusion" section. This section doesn't usually play a significant role in furthering the reader's understanding of the issues involved in the analysis, but it's there to give the reader security that the memo form has been followed. It's there, in other words, because it has to be, not because it does anything useful.

You shouldn't use the "conclusion" section to reanalyze the issues in the memo; one good sign that things are going astray in the conclusion, in fact, is the citation to any legal authority. Citation to the law is something that should be limited to the "analysis" section, just as citations to "facts" are more commonly found in the "statement of facts." The "conclusion" section should act as a structural wrapping-up, without itself containing anything substantive or new; it doesn't contribute to the analysis, it ends it.

In fact, if you've structured your analysis carefully, with an opening conclusion and with closing conclusions at the end of each section and sub-section of the analysis, any sort of structural "conclusion" section that attempts to restate what has already been written will run the risk of striking the reader as repetitive and a waste of time—two reactions you want to avoid when at all possible.

For that reason, many "conclusion" sections are extraordinarily bland, with something that looks a lot like a restatement of the short answer to the question presented, preceded by a neutral statement like "[f]or the foregoing reasons, …". That certainly prevents the writer from reanalyzing the issues in the memo, but it also seems like a wasted opportunity; the ending of a document can leave as strong an impression as the beginning and an ending like this won't impress anyone. At best, it will be ignored, and at worst it will suggest to your reader that you didn't care about part of your document.

The solution is to write something that restates your conclusions, but that does so in a way that doesn't restate the language you used to reach those conclusions. You should try to wrap up the memo in such a way that any loose ends are accounted for, and a reader who just flips to the back of the memo to see where you come out will have at least a general idea of how the analysis progressed. Any more than that would be too much, but any less than that would look careless and would suggest a lack of interest in the reader.

2. The Trial Memo

The trial memo has many of the same features as the interoffice memo. It has a section usually called "Issue Presented" instead of "Question Presented," but sometimes given the more generic title of "Introduction." Whatever name the section is given, it has the same function: to introduce the judge (and while these documents have many readers, they should always be written with just the judge's reading interests in mind) to the central issue, or issues, raised by the motion. The trial memo also has a "Statement of Facts," (often, but not always, called a "Statement of the Case") an "Analysis," and a "Conclusion" section as well.

But there is a crucial difference between interoffice memos and trial memos, and that involves the procedural posture in which you are arguing. An interoffice memo has no procedural posture: you're writing that document to inform the reader of some analysis, either because you were asked to answer a question or because, on your own initiative, you decided that the reader needed to know something. In a trial memo, though, there is always a procedural posture to consider. If you are filing a Motion to Dismiss, under Fed. R. Civ. P. 12(b)(6), for example, you have to show that the plaintiff has failed to state a claim upon which relief can be granted, whereas if you're filing a Motion for Summary Judgment under Fed. R. Civ. P. 56, you have to show that there is "no genuine issue as to any material fact and that [you are] entitled to judgment as a matter of law."

These procedural postures are crucial to the way in which you construct your analysis. If you're arguing in favor of a Motion to Dismiss, for example, you won't spend any time discussing whether a fact is legally material or not, because that just isn't part of the procedural posture of that type of motion. If, on the other hand, you're arguing in favor of a Summary Judgment Motion, the materiality of a particular fact might determine the fate of the entire motion, so it might be a crucial part of your analysis.

We won't spend much time talking about the civil procedural aspects of all this here; that's what your Civil Procedure classes are for. But it is important for us to consider the role these procedural issues play in our writing because they are directly relevant to how we persuade the judge in our case to rule in our client's favor. Judges are perhaps best thought of as rule-enforcers; they're not supposed to care which side in a dispute wins, they're supposed to care about which side has the better argument based on the rules. And that should tell you something very powerful about how you write your trial memo.

Let's consider a hypothetical situation in which Mark Blue is suing Joan Black in federal court in Illinois for negligence based on injuries he sustained in a car accident. Mr. Blue alleges that he was born and raised in Chicago and was driving his car in Carbondale, a city in the south of Illinois. He says that he was driving his Honda Civic through an intersection where the light had just turned green when Black, a life-long Carbondale resident who was driving a Ford truck, came through the intersection at a high rate of speed and hit him. Blue suffered serious internal injuries, a broken leg and arm, a broken pelvis, and a concussion as a result of the accident. He has been unable to work at his job as a corporate lawyer since the accident and he has experts willing to testify that he won't be able to work again as a lawyer. He's asking for damages of $25 million.

By contrast, Ms. Black contends that when she reached the intersection the light was still green, and that it changed to yellow when she was already in the intersection. She claims that Mr. Blue jumped the light because he was late for a meeting with a client and that he was in the intersection illegally. She, too, suffered injuries in the accident and wants to counter-sue Mr. Blue for her injuries. She has several eyewitnesses to support her contention that the accident was entirely Blue's fault, and she also has expert witnesses willing to testify that she will have difficulty working as a farmer, her job before the accident, and that her damages for present and future injury are around $2 million.

All very compelling, and an interesting case for the lawyers to try in front of a jury, requiring skillful questioning and cross-examination and well-considered arguments to the jury. Cases like these tend to settle before trial, but even negotiating settlements in cases like this can be tricky, and the terms of the settlement might well hang on how skillfully the lawyers are able to maneuver the case into the correct position for their clients, based on discovery and, particularly, the depositions taken by both attorneys.

At least, all that would be so if not for one glaring problem. Both parties are Illinois residents and Mr. Blue has sued in federal court under a negligence theory that is based on state law. Ms. Black's lawyers will certainly file a Motion to Dismiss under Fed. R. Civ. P. 12(b)(1) arguing that the federal court has no subject-matter jurisdiction to hear the case. They will likely concede that the case involves a dispute in excess of $75,000, as required by 28 U.S.C. § 1332, but will argue that the statute also provides that in order for a federal court to hear a case arising under state law the case must involve citizens of two different states. Because Black and Blue are both citizens of Illinois, they will argue, the case must be dismissed from federal court.

In the memorandum in support of their motion, Black's lawyers will not argue the facts that would support her contention that the accident was Blue's fault. In fact, they will concede, for the purposes of that memo only, that Blue's description of events is correct. That's because even if everything Blue said was exactly right, Blue still cannot win in federal court. There's no benefit to be gained by Black's lawyers by arguing that the facts are not as he described them in his complaint, or in arguing that Black's claim in much stronger than Blue's.

That's the importance of the procedural posture of the case. It tells the parties what to focus on and what to ignore or, at least, to downplay in their trial memorandums. The judge won't be in the least interested in reading arguments about whose fault this accident was, so there's no point in potentially antagonizing the judge by arguing that issue (although no matter how irritated the judge might be, there's very little chance— one always hesitates to say "no" chance—that the judge will not grant this motion if it is justified. No federal judge wants to spend time and energy on a case for which there is no jurisdiction).

And when the case is in a different procedural posture, the emphasis might change. Let's assume that the motion to dismiss was granted, and Mr. Blue's lawyers promptly re-filed in state court. Assuming there were no additional procedural impediments, such as the statute of limitations having run out on Mr. Blue's claim, the case would move forward to discovery where, let's assume, the basic facts didn't change from the ones outlined above. In particular, let's assume that Mr. Blue wasn't able to supply any eyewitnesses to support his version of events, but Ms. Black was able to provide five eyewitnesses, all of whom said that her light was green when she entered the intersection and that Mr. Blue started to enter the intersection when he still had a red light. After discovery, Ms. Black files a motion for summary judgment.

Although Ms. Black's lawyers conceded Mr. Blue's description of the facts when arguing the motion to dismiss, they will now argue strongly in favor of Ms. Black's version of the facts and Mr. Blue's lawyers will argue that there is a genuine issue of material fact in dispute—who had the green light to enter the intersection. And while likely conceding that the question of who had what color of light is a "material fact" that is in dispute, Ms. Black's lawyers will likely argue that the dispute isn't a "genuine" one because Blue has no support other than his own testimony for his position. The word "scintilla" will doubtless be discussed by both sides at great length and the court will rule one way or the other, depending on how skillfully the parties make their arguments and on the state of the law.

This is a simple example, but you can see that the procedural posture of the case has an important effect on the way lawyers will use the facts and structure their analysis. It's a good reminder that the law and the facts of a case interact in many different but important ways throughout the course of a case and that careful lawyers always consider the procedural context in which their arguments will be made.

Conclusion

Legal memorandums can take many forms, and the interoffice memo might even be thought of as obsolete by some lawyers today. But their formal requirements can still be useful to us as we look at ways to structure our analysis, knowing how to write them brings some practical benefits, and trial memos still form a vital part of a litigation lawyer's arsenal. So learning how to structure and write tight and coherent legal analysis in a legal memorandum form is still a useful skill for contemporary law students.

Focus Questions

1. Have you written any memorandums before? If so, were they legal memorandums or were they written in other disciplines? Are you surprised at the apparently strict requirements for legal memorandums?
2. Do you agree with the text that memorandums still retain some vitality or do you think that memorandums are obsolete? Do you expect to structure emails as carefully as the text suggests you need to structure a memo?
3. Had you considered the value of the memo form as a writing sample when applying for law jobs? Will the fact that you likely will be using a legal writing assignment as a writing sample for potential employment change the way you approach to these assignments?
4. Does the text's discussion of the various parts of a memo's structure strike you as rigid and formalistic or do you find the unchanging form of the memo comforting?
5. Which form of Question Presented do you find most useful? Do you think you will write different forms of Questions Presented based on the nature of the memo you're writing or will you find one form and stick with it?

6. Does the text's suggestion that you answer questions before explaining your answer make sense to you? Are you used to answering questions in this way or do you find yourself explaining your answer before you give it? If so, will you change your approach now?

7. Have you been surprised by the emphasis placed on facts in law school? Do you see why facts are so important to lawyers? Do you understand the distinction between legally material and immaterial facts?

Chapter 19

Legal Correspondence

What You Should Learn from This Chapter

This chapter considers some of the various forms legal correspondence can take and discusses some issues of medium and form in the letter. It also considers the "quick email" often now used for communicating legal analysis and suggests that this is really a memo in different clothing. The chapter looks particularly at cover letters, given their role in your job search process, and discusses some technical issues and what such letters can, and can't, do for you.

After reading this chapter, you should:

- have considered the differences and similarities between letters and emails;
- have considered the continuing importance of the letter form, in whatever medium it is used;
- have considered the role of the analysis email;
- have considered some of the functions of the cover letter; and
- have considered what a cover letter can and can't do for you during your job search.

It might seem anachronistic to you that lawyers still write letters to communicate with each other and with clients. In this era of email and other forms of electronic communication, why is the letter still hanging around? Is this just another sign—along with conservative clothing and a conservative approach to formal language—that suggests lawyers are just old-fashioned?

Does it matter? If letters are a standard medium of communication in the law, your need to understand the reasons for that fact might seem substantially less important than your need to understand how to write an acceptable letter. Do we really care about why some things are the way they are in the life of a lawyer?

Well, yes. It matters and we care. We should, at any rate. If there's a technical reason for the numbers of letters lawyers write—if the letter is a superior method of communicating and storing information—it would be helpful to understand why that is. And if there's another, more cultural reason (like inherent conservatism), it would be helpful for you to understand that as well; you're going to be working in the lawyering culture and the more details you can understand about it, the better you'll be able to decide how, or if, to conform your behavior to that culture. So let's spend a little while thinking about why lawyers communicate in the way they do before we discuss how to write those documents.

1. The Letter and the Email

Letters have few practical advantages over electronic communications like emails. They are slower to arrive (even a letter sent by messenger from one city office to another will take longer than the same information would take by email), they're less permanent (paper can burn or be dissolved by water, but emails will live on backup servers for ever), they take up more space and cost more to store, cost money to print and mail, and can only be filed in one place without having to make copies. And they're bad for the environment, with paper and ink both being especially pernicious substances to make.

To be sure, letters carry physical signatures, allowing their writers to be identified and that identity authenticated if that becomes an issue, but electronic signatures are readily available and authentication is possible for electronic communication as well. Letters can be signed by two or more parties, making letter agreements where both parties have signed the same document possible. But even if an electronic equivalent is not acceptable in this situation—and there are solutions to that problem as well—that need only accounts for a tiny percentage of the letters lawyers send each year.

It seems, then, that there's something else going on that makes letters still a viable method of communication. And without being able to point to any definitive support for this, lawyering culture seems to be the reason. We're all familiar with the idea that electronic communication is so common as to be entirely unremarkable, although generational reactions to email are fascinating. To the baby boomer generation, there is still something amazing about being able to communicate, in writing, almost instantly with anyone who is connected to the internet. Email is less formal than a letter, so less well-suited to business than paper letters, but it's still a useful, almost magical, method of communication. To your generation, though, email apparently is outdated, something that older people use instead of texting—appropriate for business communications, perhaps, but not a feature of your day-to-day lives.

These are generalizations, of course, and can't fully capture the way large groups of people think individually about these alternative modes of communication. But these generalizations point out the importance of cultural sensitivity when we speak about the appropriate roles of letters and emails, and that's something we'll encounter many times as we discuss different issues covered by this book. Just as there are differences in the way people from different countries think about things, and just as there are differences based on race, gender, and even geographical location within this country, so there are important differences between the ways people of different generations perceive many things.

There's a dangerous tendency to assume that we, and the various groups to which we belong, are "right" about the way we think about things and that other groups are "wrong." When it comes to generational differences, older people tend to think that younger people are inexperienced and don't yet fully appreciate all of the issues, while younger people tend to think that older people are conservative and set in their ways. And in most things, the concept of "right" and "wrong" really doesn't apply; there are just differences between the two perspectives. What's important is to remember that those not in your generation might think differently from you about things, and if we try to respect each other's opinions, we stand a chance of being able understand each other and to communicate effectively with each other. And that, after all, is the point of this entire book.

2.　Medium and Form

While the letter still holds an important role in legal communications, it seems likely that its time as a physical medium is drawing to a close. That doesn't mean, though, that the letter as a form will necessarily be any less of a presence in law practice in the future.

This separation of medium and form is something else we'll encounter over and over again when we consider the ways in which legal writing is changing. It's odd—especially for older lawyers—to have to think in these terms, because when they were growing up there was no meaningful way to distinguish between print media and their forms. One couldn't speak, for instance, about a letter form without speaking of a physical letter. For all practical purposes, the form and the medium were the same thing. Yet they are distinctly not the same now, and your generation has little difficulty understanding that.

The letter is a good way to consider these two concepts that used to be one. A letter as a "form" is readily understood. It's the piece or pieces of paper on which words are written or typed. It has certain common features, like a letterhead, a date, a salutation ("Dear …"), a body, a closing, and a signature. The letter is then placed in an envelope and conveyed from one place to another—usually by the mail, but sometimes by another common carrier like FedEx or UPS, and sometimes by a courier or a messenger.

The letter as a "medium" is a communication that retains all the non-physical characteristics of a letter—the common features I mentioned in the previous paragraph—but that is separate from the physical form of the letter. A letter that is typed on a word processor, for example, and then sent as an email attachment to someone else who reads it and stores it electronically is a "letter" in medium, because it has all the attributes of a letter except the physical form.

There's nothing complicated or difficult about these two concepts. Where things start to get interesting, though, is when we realize that a letter that is never intended to assume physical form need not, in fact, retain all of the attributes of a physical letter to remain a letter in medium. Email, for example, is a letter medium that is missing many of the letter's defining characteristics and yet it can, although need not, retain the essence of a letter—a document written by one person to convey a limited amount of information directly to a specific recipient: it is a unit of correspondence. The reality that an email can serve two different roles—as the informal communication it appears to be and also as a letter in medium if not form—is an important distinction that we should explore further.

3.　The Letter Medium

In order to do that, let's first consider the letter medium before tackling the email as its own medium. We'll consider briefly the letter form as well.

There are many different ways of defining the difference between the letter and email mediums (I'm using that plural to distinguish this discussion from a discussion of the "media," which usually evokes something different and specifically journalistic), but the simplest perhaps is that a letter is a document that signals the sender's intention to preserve the information being communicated while the email is intended to be more temporary and ephemeral. This definition isn't concerned with the reality of preservation since, as we know, anything transmitted electronically lives, for all practical purposes, forever, but rather it focuses on the writer's intent to preserve.

This definition carries some implications. For example, we tend, or should tend, to use language more carefully in documents we intend to be preserved. In fact, another way of defining the difference between letters and emails is that letters are more carefully written, and are written in more formal language, than emails. This care in language, though, is more the result of the communication's longevity than any substantive reason for using different language; put simply, we tend to take more care over documents we know will remain for people to read years from now than over documents we expect to be read and quickly deleted.

The fact of preservation need not, though, mean that the substance of the letter itself is intended to have special significance. Here's a typical letter from a lawyer to a client:

Dear Mr. Smith,

> *I have enclosed the transcript of your recent deposition. Please review the transcript carefully, as transcription errors can occur. It is important that the transcript be as accurate a record as possible of what you actually said at your deposition, so please make a note of any possible mistakes you find and I will ask for those changes to be reflected in the final transcript. Please note that this is not a chance to change an answer with which you are not now happy, only a chance to correct mistakes in the transcript itself.*
>
> *Please contact me with any questions or concerns you might have. Because we do not have too much time within which to request corrections, please contact me with any changes within the next two weeks from your receipt of this letter.*
> *Thank you for your attention to this matter,*

Very truly yours,
Lawyer Name

This isn't a document of tremendous substance, and it's not the content that the writer wants to preserve, it's the act that is memorialized in the letter that's important here. The lawyer needs to have a record in the lawyer's file that the client received a copy of the transcript. The lawyer will doubtless send the letter with a return receipt requested, and will be able to attach the returned, and signed, postcard to the letter, showing that the client was sent a copy of the transcript and received it. If the client ever alleges that the transcript was never sent, the attorney will have strong evidence that the transcript was both sent and received by the client. Lawyers send many of these simple, recordation, letters every year. They are often written in standard, boilerplate, language.

But lawyers also send out numerous letters each year that are very different from this simple letter. A lawyer might want to let a client know about the status of contract negotiations, for example, or to alert a client about a possible plea agreement in a criminal matter. These letters also have an important recordation function, of course, since the lawyers wants to have a record of sending important information to the client. But the main function of these letters is a substantive one: giving the client the information necessary to understand the progress being made on a case or to give the client the information necessary to make a decision, for example.

And, of course, there are many potential recipients. We have spoken in terms of client communication here, but lawyers also write to each other—either to opponents or co-counsel in a case—to judges, to witnesses, to any number of other people. Just as with the simpler letters lawyers write, these more substantive letters can be sent in paper form or electronically but all that will be different is the medium; the content will remain consistent, whether the communication is by letter or by email.

The important point here is that it's not the form a communication takes that's important, from a drafting perspective, it's the substance of the document that matters. Although you should take care to draft everything carefully—even the simplest handwritten note—simple recordation "letters" like the one earlier in this chapter take very little time to write and edit (although they should, of course, still be edited and proofread where necessary), whereas complex opinion letters can take days to write and edit until they perfectly express whatever substance the writer intends to convey to the reader. Whether those "letters" are in print or email makes no difference; it's the substance that's important, not the form. Once again, in fact, context determines form.

4. The "Quick Email" for Legal Analysis

Another factor comes into play when talking about the various ways in which lawyers prepare and send correspondence, and it can be a trap for the unwary. A reader, in the form of an assigning lawyer at your firm, for example, might ask you to do some work but rather than write it up in a formal memo, the lawyer wants you to just send an email with the essential points. You might be lulled into the temptation of thinking this is an assignment that requires less formality in expression, and even less careful thinking. In fact, though, it's only the external form that should be different, not the substance of your analysis.

The "quick email" form of transmitting legal analysis is really a misnomer, because what you're really preparing is a memo that's presented in a different form—the medium hasn't changed. And that's important because it should affect the way you research and write the document. Rather than being something you can dash off quickly before moving on to other tasks, this "quick" email requires you to go through the full memo writing process and then reduce that full memo into shorthand form for transmission.

This might seem wasteful of time and resources. The assigning lawyer doesn't want a memo, after all, and won't you be spending time on a task you weren't asked to do? At first, perhaps, but there's a crucial point here about the relationship between writing and analysis that is often overlooked and perhaps is misunderstood by the assigning lawyer as well. To put it simply, it's difficult to know what you think until you write it down. The act of reducing a series of thoughts to writing helps to clarify what it is you're thinking, and unless you research an issue and then test the quality and extent of your research by reducing your analysis to writing, you can't be confident that you've fully thought through and covered all the issues lurking in the task you were given. Only once you're sure you've thought through, and fully researched, all the potential issues in your analysis should you try to reduce them into email form, because only then will you be summarizing a full analysis, not a potentially incomplete one.

You'll get faster at this as time goes on, and you'll find that you're better able to think through all the issues as you're conducting your research. But if you're honest with yourself about the work you do, you'll probably never completely shake the need to write down your analysis before being certain of what it is you think. And for the moment, don't even try to skip the crucial step of writing and testing your analysis down in full. Better to take longer than expected to come up with a full and complete answer than to take not much time and make a significant mistake in your analysis.

5. Writing a Letter

Once you understand that the purpose of the document dictates its substance—a seemingly obvious concept that nonetheless seems to escape many lawyers—letter writing can become a relatively straightforward task. All letters have the same essential form— letterhead with the writer's contact information, the recipient's contact information, the date, a salutation, and, at the end, a conclusion with "very truly yours" (or some other formula, but this one works well for business and professional correspondence), a signature, and then a printed version of the sender's name.

If the body of the letter includes analysis of some legal issue, that will probably be taken almost directly from a memo you've already written on the subject. If you are including legal analysis, you need to think carefully who is getting the letter. If it's a client, the letter will probably be non-discoverable because of the attorney/client or work product privileges but if, for example, your letter is going to a potential expert witness, it will be probably sit in the expert's files and be discoverable if that witness is listed as a potential witness. You don't want to have a document that the opposition can read outlining your private analysis of the case, so think carefully about what information you send to whom.

On the other hand, it might happen that you send an opposing lawyer a detailed letter outlining your case. That can happen when you're deep in settlement discussions and you want to persuade the other side that you have a case that can't be beaten. It can be a very effective strategy. But for the first several years of practice, you should try and let someone else with more experience than you make the decision to send such a letter; you want to be sure that the letter will have the desired effect and not give the other side a blueprint of the case you're going to offer at trial unless the potential benefits of such a letter outweigh the risks.

Letters can also act as simple transmittal letters, as we've seen. Let's consider another example of that type of letter—one that you're either already familiar with or one you'll be sending soon: the cover letter.

6. Cover Letters

You send cover letters with your resume, transcript, and other supporting documents necessary for you to apply for a job. Law students across the country send thousands of these letters each year and many students take themselves out of the running for a job just by writing a poor cover letter. Looking at the mistakes these students make can help us better understand how to draft a letter that's appropriate for the context in which it's being sent and can have the side benefit of making you a more viable candidate for a legal job.

7. Technical Considerations

There are some technical considerations you should think about before you start writing. Plan on using normal paper for your letter, rather than colored or patterned paper or expensive resume paper. If you're writing a regular letter for a law firm, you'll likely be using the firm's letterhead paper and that will solve many of these technical issues for you. If you're writing a cover letter, though, you shouldn't use a law firm's letterhead—how would it look to a potential employer if it got a letter from you on your firm's letterhead?—and should instead create your own.

Your own letterhead should be the opposite of eye-catching. It can be stylish, but should be conservative, so that its presence is subconsciously recognized by the reader but not so much that you want the reader to actually read or even look at it. Letterheads contain vital information; if the law firm needs to contact you, the letterhead has all your contact information on it. And letterheads are crucial to making a letter a letter—without them, a letter just starts and would make it appear that you don't know how to construct a proper letter, which would mark you as an unappealing candidate for a job. But once the letterhead achieves its dual function of recording contact information and making a letter look formally correct, it should retreat into the background so the reader's attention isn't drawn to it.

There is also a crucial technical consideration for you to think about as you type and edit your letter. As in all documents, technical perfection is crucial. If anything, this is even more important in a short document like a letter—especially a cover letter, where the entire document will probably be less than a page. A typo in a letter like this—especially a misspelling of the recipient's name—can be fatal. Imagine the role of the lawyer who has to review these letters and supporting materials. The lawyer probably can't bill the firm for the time spent working as a recruitment coordinator, or whatever title the firm might confer on the lawyer doing that job. That means the lawyer will have to spend additional time working on billable matters in order to make up for the hours spent reviewing these materials, so any excuse to stop reading is likely to be accepted with appreciation. If you send that lawyer a letter and can't spell the lawyer's name correctly, the lawyer will likely—and understandably—take this as a proxy for your inability to pay attention to details; if you can't even get this detail correct, after all, why should anyone have confidence that you would spell a client's name correctly, or a judge's name, or get the correct spelling of a corporation's name onto a complaint?

A mistake like that, or a misspelling of your own name, or the firm's name, or, frankly, any misspelling in the letter, could spell the end of your candidacy for the open job. The reviewing lawyer might well take the rest of your materials and put them all onto the "reject" pile and move on without a second thought.

You'll likely never know why you didn't get an interview for the job, making it almost impossible for you to learn from your mistake, so you might continue to include typos in your documents. The only way to prevent this is to be certain that there are no mistakes in your letters, and remember that proper names are not candidates for spellcheckers so you'll have to check the spelling of your document by eye as well by computer.

8. Consider What the Letter Can Do and What It Can't Do

As you're writing a letter—a cover letter in this case, but the same process applies to any letter—consider what it can do. This might seem like a strange suggestion, but many letters are drafted and sent without a clear idea of their purpose and limitations. Like any other tool, a letter can do a limited number of things and can't do a range of other things that the writer might expect it to do. A realistic evaluation of a letter's limitations can help the writer draft an appropriate letter for the circumstance. This might become clearer as we think about what letters can and can't do, so let's do that now, in the context of a cover letter.

A. A Cover Letter Can Introduce You and Your Materials

The obvious function of a cover letter is to introduce you and your materials. In that sense, it works just like walking up to someone, putting out your hand to shake their hand, and saying "Hello, my name is ___." Once that sentence is uttered, the cover letter's work in introducing you is done. It can't persuade the person you're addressing to like you, to hire you, or even to talk with you; all it can do is introduce you.

If you understand the letter's limited role, you can tailor its content to meet that role. You will understand that there's not much point in putting a lot of information into the letter because that would be similar to saying "Hello, my name is ___ and here's my life story up until now. I was born …". You get the point. You wouldn't appreciate someone giving you all that information as they were introducing themselves to you in person, and your reader likely won't appreciate it much to get all that information in writing.

B. Your Cover Letter Can Explain Something Not in Your Materials

If it has to, your letter can give your reader an explanation of something not in the accompanying materials. In a cover letter, for example, you can explain a geographical association with the city where your law firm is located, for instance. If you're applying to a law firm in a city where you have no apparent connection, for example, your letter can let your reader know if there is a good, but non-apparent, reason for your application; your spouse is moving to the city to take up a medical residency, perhaps, or your family used to vacation there, so you know it well. Lawyers tend to be cautious about considering applications from people who are looking to move to a strange city just for a job, but are likely to look at the application of someone who has a connection to a place or is moving there anyway, regardless of whether they get a job at the firm or not, with more interest. So while that information likely won't be the reason you get a job, it might not be the reason you don't get the job.

Similarly, the letter about a deposition transcript included above had some information that wasn't contained in the transcript accompanying it; the reader can correct the transcript for errors, the reader can't change the language other than for error-correction, and so on. This is the sort of thing letters like this can do, as long as you don't try to give the reader too much information. A cover letter is not the place for a detailed analysis of the deposition process or your life history. You can, though, include a limited amount of specific information that clarifies the letter's purpose.

C. A Bad Cover Letter Can Prevent You from Getting a Job

Just as not all outcomes are positive, not all the things a cover letter can do are positive. And one of the things a bad cover letter can do is to prevent you from getting a job. A letter that contains mistakes, or shows that the writer doesn't understand how to write an appropriate business letter, will probably achieve the negative result—for the writer—of preventing the writer from getting a job. Similarly, a poorly drafted client letter—even something as simple as a transcript transmittal letter—can result in your being removed from a client's case if, for example, you misspell the client's name and the client takes offense. It's worth remembering that not all results are good, and that letters can have negative, neutral, and positive results. It's important to try as hard as possible to eliminate the negative effects, in order to increase the chances of a positive result. There's not much you can do about the neutral effects, so don't worry about them.

D. A Cover Letter Can't Make Anyone Read Your Materials

One of the neutral effects of a letter is that no one reads your materials, even though your letter was error free. There's nothing you can do about this; perhaps the law firm doesn't hire graduates of your law school, or perhaps the firm has a substantial number of applications from candidates with qualifications that it deems "better" than yours, or perhaps there's an entirely different reason. Whatever the reason might be, your cover letter won't be able to overcome it, no matter how perfectly drafted it is.

E. A Cover Letter Can't Substitute for Your Resume

Each document you write has its own purpose, and a cover letter has the limited purpose of introducing your supporting materials. Once it does that, it needs to stop its work and let your materials do their work. A cover letter can't substitute for your resume, because your resume has that job. A cover letter that tries to simultaneously introduce you and convince the reader that you're the perfect candidate for a job because you have this job experience and that job experience will detract from, rather than enhance, your chances of getting a job because it shows the reader that you don't understand the limitations of the documents you're writing. If you write a cover letter that tries to be a resume, will you write a transcript transmittal letter than contains inappropriate additional information? Perhaps, or perhaps not, but a lot of lawyers won't take the chance and will simply move on to the next application.

F. A Cover Letter Can't Get You a Job

Sadly, although a cover letter can prevent you from getting a job, it can't do the opposite and get you a job. The best effect it can have is to create the impression that you understand the purpose of a cover letter and then retreat into the shadows and let the rest of your materials do their work. The only exception to this is in a situation where there is relevant information that can't be found anywhere else on your materials that might explain why you should be considered as a viable candidate for the position. Anything more than this is too much work for a simple cover letter to do.

Conclusion

What is true of cover letters is true for other types of correspondence as well. Whether the document be a simple letter, a more complex letter, or an email, correspondence has a vital role to play in legal practice and each document can have an effect—positive or negative—far beyond its principal function. If you think carefully about what the correspondence is designed to do, and limit the document's content to accomplish that goal, you will likely be a successful correspondent. And success in this area, unlike most areas of legal practice, can usually be measured by how little you're noticed. If your letter or email does its job properly, it's the content that will be memorable, not the writer.

Focus Questions

1. How many letters have you received in the past year? How many did you send? Compare that to the number of emails you received and sent. Compare that to the number of texts you received and sent. Do you believe that the letter is still a viable or important means of communication?

2. Do you agree with the text when it says that it's important to understand the cultural issues involved in the ways in which lawyers communicate in writing?

3. Do the distinctions the text draws between medium and form make sense to you? Are these useful distinctions to you? Had you thought about these distinctions before?

4. Have you been asked to write a "quick" email carrying potentially complex analysis? If so, how did you treat the assignment? Would you be comfortable repeating the experience? Would you be comfortable about writing such an email to communicate important information to a partner in advance of a hearing or a meeting with a client? Do you see how this type of assignment can pose dangers to a junior lawyer?

5. Had you given thought to the idea that a cover letter has only a very limited role to play, and that its effects can be more negative than positive?

6. Do you see why complete perfection is crucial for cover letters? Had you considered the possibility that even one typo could spell the end of your candidacy for a legal job? Is this fair?

7. Had you considered the potential outcomes associated with a cover letter discussed in the text?

ANALYSIS

Chapter 20

Analytical Structure: Getting Started

What You Should Learn from This Chapter

This chapter begins the text's discussion of legal analysis and how to express that analysis in writing. It introduces the concept of a "standard unit of analysis," a building block of analysis that has several components within it. What these components are, and how they might best be organized in order to make up this "standard unit of analysis," is a subject that occupies much of the text's discussion of analytical structure.

After reading this chapter, you should:

- have considered why the order in which information is conveyed is at least as important as the information itself;
- have considered again how important it is for a writer to consider the reader's needs when writing a text and how frustrating it can be for a reader if the writer has ignored the reader's needs; and
- have considered several examples of possible analytical structure and have decided which is the best approach, and why.

Conversely, when handled poorly, all the reader will focus on is the lack of structure that makes the writing so difficult to understand. Just as sentences and paragraphs have their own internal structure that is necessary for them to function properly, so a larger piece of writing must have its own sense of structure that allows the reader to understand its meaning. Without that care, brilliant thoughts can be obscured by poor structure, and complex thoughts can become hopelessly muddled when not presented in a logical and helpful order. When done well, writing structure becomes almost invisible. In order for a reader to understand what a writer is saying, the writer must carefully structure the written text in such a way that the meaning is clear.

What? Well, in a very heavy-handed way, I tried to suggest why good structure is important to a reader. I wrote a paragraph and then reassembled the various sentences in it so as to make it as confusing as possible. Here's the paragraph as it was originally written:

> In order for a reader to understand what a writer is saying, the writer must carefully structure the written text in such a way that the meaning is clear. Without that care, brilliant thoughts can be obscured by poor structure, and complex thoughts can become hopelessly muddled when not presented in a logical and helpful order. Just as sentences and paragraphs have their own internal structure that is necessary for them to function properly, so a larger piece of writing must have its own sense of structure that allows the reader to understand its meaning. When done well, writing structure becomes almost invisible. Conversely, when handled poorly, all the reader will focus on is the lack of structure that makes the writing so difficult to understand.[1]

It might not be poetry, but it makes more sense in this form than it did when you first read it, doesn't it? And yet the words are the same, and they're even ordered within each sentence in the same way. The only thing that's changed is the structure of the paragraph—the order in which the sentences are presented. With each increasingly larger unit within a complete piece of writing, the role of structure becomes more subtle: a sentence that is structured incorrectly can seem like an incoherent jumble of words, and a paragraph that's structured incorrectly can have some seeming logic to it but, on closer inspection, can be every bit as confusing as the jumbled sentence. Legal analysis, often taking up several paragraphs, can seem, on first reading, to make more sense than the jumbled paragraphs that started this chapter, but without careful consideration of how best to present that information to the reader, it can end up being just as confused and confusing. The reader will have to work too hard to understand what the writer is saying and will either give up or be so frustrated that the writer's analysis will be unpersuasive. Neither result is the one you want.

In this chapter we're going to consider how to structure one single and discrete piece of analysis rather than how to structure an entire document. An analytical document, such as a memo or a brief, will likely have several of these discrete pieces of analysis in it and while many of the structural issues involved in presenting the entire document are similar to the ones we'll be considering here, it's best if we concentrate for now just on these single pieces of analysis—a standard unit of analysis, if you will.

There are two things for you to consider when thinking about the analytical structure of a standard unit of analysis, and they're related. First—and this should always be your primary concern—is how to give your reader information at exactly the right time. And second, you should think about how law readers have been trained to expect legal information; the cultural expectations of structure. Under normal circumstances, your reader will best receive a standard unit of analysis in the way the reader has been trained to expect that information, but there are times when circumstances might override the "normal" approach and might suggest a different structure.

We'll start by considering the "normal" approach, since that's what readers will expect most of the time. Once we've had that discussion, we'll move on to some possible exceptions to that approach and think about how a reader's expectations might

---

1. This paragraph is in a block because that's how long quotes appear in legal writing. Can we agree again, though, that blocks are ugly and are difficult to read?

change and how you, as the writer, can best adapt to those different expectations. Don't worry: this isn't as complicated in practice as it sounds in the abstract like this.

Let's take a look at some examples of analysis in order to decide what we want our standard unit of analysis to look like. Read these examples actively and critically, and decide how each piece is structured and why you do, or don't, like that approach. I'll give you my thoughts as well.

Before considering the analysis, though, you have to know what's going on, so here are the facts of the case we'll be working on.

Albert Smith is a journalist writing for the Baltimore Daily Times, *a newspaper in Baltimore, Maryland. He recently wrote a series of articles exposing what he contended was wide-spread corruption in the Baltimore City Mayor's office. But when he submitted the articles for publication, the newspaper's editor, Andrea McArthur, decided not to publish them. Ms. McArthur told Mr. Smith, both in person and in an email, that the claims he made in his articles were "insufficiently supported by credible evidence" and that Mr. Smith "had a long history of animosity directed towards the city's current mayor" and that his articles "read more like a personal vendetta than a piece of journalism."*

A week after Ms. McArthur declined to publish Mr. Smith's articles, the journalists and editorial staff held a regularly scheduled meeting to discuss editorial policy and to discuss what long-term journalistic projects were currently underway. At this meeting, Mr. Smith stood up on a chair and shouted that Ms. McArthur was a "gutless coward and a lousy editor because she didn't have the courage to run controversial stories" and that her actions were "criminal." After a private meeting with Ms. McArthur and representatives from the newspaper's Human Resources department, Mr. Smith was told that he was being dismissed from his position as a journalist with the newspaper, was escorted to his desk to allow him to remove his personal possessions, and was then escorted from the newspaper's offices.

Mr. Smith has sued the newspaper, and Ms. McArthur, for wrongful termination, and Ms. McArthur has counter-sued Mr. Smith for defamation. Our law firm has been asked to represent Mr. Smith and an associate at the firm has been assigned to analyze the likelihood that Ms. McArthur will succeed in her counter-claim. You have been asked to review that associate's work. The examples that follow are different versions of what that associate has sent you.

1. Example One

Smith will not be found liable for defamation because his statement was only an opinion.

Well, that's not very satisfactory, is it? We know that the writer doesn't think Smith will be found liable because his statement "was only an opinion," but we don't know if that's a valid conclusion to reach because we know nothing about the controlling law in the relevant jurisdiction, and we don't know what facts are and aren't relevant to the conclusion.

So Example One gives us an opinion, but no facts or law to allow us to evaluate that opinion. The writer might be right and might be wrong; we have no way of knowing. We don't have enough information to decide if this is anything more than a guess.

There's actually a name for the type of thinking demonstrated by this example. It's *ipse dixit* thinking; the term means "he, himself, said it" and *ipse dixit* thinking has been recognized as a logical fallacy since the time of Cicero, the Roman orator and lawyer who criticized the students of Pythagoras for falling back on the argument that if Pythagoras had said something, that alone made it true and unchallengeable.

As lawyers, we often find *ipse dixit*-type thinking in expert opinions. Experts often forget to connect up the dots in their opinions and merely state the opinions without support. It's important for you to recognize this kind of trap and make sure your expert doesn't fall into it during testimony because courts will likely be very critical of such testimony and might reject it completely if it isn't supported by anything more than the expert's say-so.

For our present purposes, though, you can see why this type of "analysis" isn't even worthy of the name "analysis." It's plain, unvarnished, and unsupported opinion — conclusion with no reasoning behind it. If you write something like this in a legal writing assignment, your legal writing professor will be highly critical of it, and you can see why. Without anything to support or explain the opinion, it fails to persuade you.

It's also worth pointing out that this type of "analysis" frequently crops up in law school exams. It's understandable, of course; you have a lot to do when you write an exam and you want to get to as much as possible to collect all the points a question has to offer. We give a lot of "issue spotter" exams in law school, so a student might be deceived into thinking that merely identifying the issue, and giving the conclusion that describes the ultimate outcome, would be sufficient. But it's not so. Just as in math, where you were always told to "show your work," legal analysis should provide the reasons and support for the conclusion along with the ultimate result. That's the reason for the famous IRAC acronym you hear all the time in connection with law school exams: Issue, Rule, Application (or Analysis), and Conclusion. If merely the issue and conclusion were required, the acronym would be IC, and that doesn't sound like a good thing.

If you're less concerned about these issues than I seem to be, and you think I'm making too much about the problems of *ipse dixit* thinking, consider this: you're being asked to speak to the firm's partners and to give your professional evaluation of the likelihood that Mr. Smith will be found liable. You will be the only person invited to give an opinion on this matter — the associate who wrote the analysis left the firm last week — so the firm's strategy in this matter will be completely your responsibility. You're being considered for partnership, and a wrong decision on this issue could cost you that and your job at the firm. Now, are you satisfied that you have enough information on which to base your opinion or would you like some support for the answer?

2. Example Two

Maryland law requires that a plaintiff satisfy four elements in order to make a prima facie case of defamation: "(1) that the defendant made a defamatory statement to a third person, (2) that the statement was false, (3) that the defendant was legally at fault in making the statement, and (4) that the plaintiff suffered harm." *Offen v. Brenner*, 402 Md. 191, 198, 935 A.2d 719, 723–24 (2007).

In this case, Mr. Smith told a gathering of newspaper journalists that, in his opinion, Ms. McArthur was a "lousy editor because she didn't have the courage to run controversial stories." Because Mr. Smith was airing an opinion rather than making a statement of fact, he is not liable to Ms. McArthur for defamation.

It's better, but not by much, right? We have a statement of law, which is helpful, but we still have no information that allows us to believe the writer's conclusion about whether or not Mr. Smith will be liable for defamation because the writer just tells us that Mr. Smith's statement was an opinion and that an opinion won't be enough for Ms. McArthur to prevail. We still don't have any support for that conclusion. So while this example has more words that the first one, we still need more useful information before we can trust this analysis.

3. Example Three

Maryland law requires that a plaintiff satisfy four elements in order to make a *prima facie* case of defamation: "(1) that the defendant made a defamatory statement to a third person, (2) that the statement was false, (3) that the defendant was legally at fault in making the statement, and (4) that the plaintiff suffered harm." *Offen v. Brenner*, 402 Md. 191, 198, 935 A.2d 719, 723–24 (2007).

A statement is defamatory when it "tends to expose a person to public scorn, hatred, contempt or ridicule, thereby discouraging others in the community from having a good opinion of, or associating with, that person." *Id.* at 198–99, 724, quoting, *Gohari v. Davish*, 363 Md. 42, 55, 767 A.2d 795, 805 (2007). Words that falsely repute criminal conduct to a plaintiff are defamatory. *Smith v. Danielczyk*, 400 Md. 98, 115, 928 A.2d 795, 805 (2007). And when a statement is made in the form of an opinion, it becomes actionable "only if it implie[s] the allegation of undisclosed facts as the basis of that opinion." *Thacker v. City of Hyattsville*, 135 Md. App. 268, 313, 762 A.2d 172, 196 (2000)(other citations omitted).

In this case, Mr. Smith told a gathering of newspaper journalists that, in his opinion, Ms. McArthur was a "lousy editor because she didn't have the courage to run controversial stories." Because Mr. Smith was airing an opinion rather than making a statement of fact, he is not liable to Ms. McArthur for defamation.

Well, this gives us more to go on and if we look up the cases we might find all the information we need. But as readers of legal analysis, we should expect that the writer has already done that work in order to reach the conclusions we've just read and it's reasonable for us to ask the writer to show us that work as part of the written analysis. Are these cases distinguishable from the present case? Do the facts in those cases support the conclusion our writer has reached or do they suggest a different result in Mr. Smith's case? We don't really know enough about the cases to know how closely they apply in this case. And why do we have to wait so long for the writer's conclusion? It comes only at the end of the analysis—wouldn't it be helpful for it to come at the beginning so we knew where the analysis was headed?

4. Example Four

Mr. Smith will not be found liable for defamation. He expressed an opinion rather than fact, and under Maryland law, unsupported opinions are not actionable.

Maryland law requires that a plaintiff satisfy four elements in order to make a *prima facie* case of defamation: "(1) that the defendant made a defamatory statement to a third person, (2) that the statement was false, (3) that the defendant was legally at fault in making the statement, and (4) that the plaintiff suffered harm." *Offen v. Brenner*, 402 Md. 191, 198, 935 A.2d 719, 723–24 (2007).

In looking at the first prong of this test, the courts have held that a statement is defamatory when it "tends to expose a person to public scorn, hatred, contempt or ridicule, thereby discouraging others in the community from having a good opinion of, or associating with, that person." *Id*. at 198–99, 724, quoting, *Gohari v. Davish*, 363 Md. 42, 55, 767 A.2d 795, 805 (2007). Words that falsely repute criminal conduct to a plaintiff are defamatory. *Smith v. Danielczyk*, 400 Md. 98, 115, 928 A.2d 795, 805 (2007).

When a statement is made in the form of an opinion, however, it becomes actionable "only if it implie[s] the allegation of undisclosed facts as the basis of that opinion." *Thacker v. City of Hyattsville*, 135 Md. App. 268, 313, 762 A.2d 172, 196 (2000)(other citations omitted). In *Thacker*, an apartment complex manager, Mr. Thacker, requested police assistance in removing a disgruntled tenant from the property management office. *Id*. at 278, 177. The tenant was unhappy because Mr. Thacker would not give him a temporary parking permit. *Id*.

An encounter between Mr. Thacker, the tenant, and the police officer, Officer Blake, ensued and Officer Blake accused Mr. Thacker of being racially prejudiced because he would not give the tenant the parking permit. *Id*. When Mr. Thacker responded to this comment, he was arrested. *Id*. He subsequently sued Officer Blake, and the city of Hyattsville, for defamation based on the officer's comment that Mr. Thacker was racially prejudiced.

In considering Mr. Thacker's defamation claim, the Court of Special Appeals held that Officer Blake's comment was derogatory but that it was based on an opinion rather than on fact. *Id*. at 313, 196. Citing the Supreme Court, the Maryland court noted that "if a statement is not provable as false or is not reasonably interpretable as stating facts, then it cannot form the basis of a defamation suit." *Id*., citing *Milkovich v. Lorain Journal Co.*, 497 U.S. 1, 18 ... (1990). The court held that "[t]he gravamen of Thacker's injury allegation is that Thacker was harmed by the arrest, and not by an accusation of racial prejudice.... Since there is no 'defamation by arrest' cause of action in Maryland, the circuit court properly granted summary judgment in favor of Blake and the City on the defamation claim." *Id*., at 314, 196.

Similarly, in this case, Mr. Smith told a gathering of newspaper journalists that, in his opinion, Ms. McArthur was a "lousy editor because she didn't have the courage to run controversial stories." Even assuming this statement to be derogatory, and it is unclear that the courts would consider it to be as serious as, for example, the accusation of racial prejudice in the *Thacker* case, it is at worst a statement of opinion.

Although Mr. Smith called Ms. McArthur's actions "criminal," there are no facts to support a contention that Mr. Smith was suggesting there were undisclosed facts to support his choice of words. The article Ms. McArthur declined to publish concerned alleged wide-spread corruption in the mayor's office, but while some might argue that Mr. Smith was implying that Ms. McArthur was involved in some form of criminal conspiracy by preventing the public from knowing of Mr. Smith's allegations, to do so would be mere speculation. The word "criminal" is used so often in the vernacular that it has acquired a robust secondary meaning as something undesirable but not necessarily descriptive of a violation of state or federal law. There is no credible suggestion that there are undisclosed facts that form the basis of Mr. Smith's opinion. Accordingly, what Mr. Smith said at the meeting, while it was critical of Ms. McArthur and her leadership of the newspaper, was not defamatory.

Mr. Smith was airing an opinion rather than making a statement of fact. Therefore, he is not liable to Ms. McArthur for defamation, and relying on *Thacker*, the circuit court should grant summary judgment in his favor.

What do you think? Better? It's certainly longer. It doesn't explain some of the earlier cases like *Offen*, but it gives a lot of information about *Thacker* and allows us to see not just the decision the court in that case reached but also why it reached it. We now have the relevant facts of *Thacker* to let us make up our own minds about whether a circuit court in our case will find *Thacker* to be a relevant case in the analysis of the *Smith* case and that allows the discussion of the facts in *Smith* to be more complete and persuasive. There's some brief counter-analysis, focused on the potentially ambiguous use of "criminal," and the analysis disposes of that potential argument. And we know where the analysis is headed right from the short opening paragraph because it serves as an introductory thesis paragraph — that favorite term of composition teachers everywhere — that tells us how everything will work out in the end.

Let's try one more example that's even fuller and more complete and then talk about which one we liked best.

5. Example Five

Mr. Smith will not be found liable for defamation. He expressed an opinion rather than fact, and under Maryland law, unsupported opinions are not actionable.

Maryland law requires that a plaintiff satisfy four elements in order to make a *prima facie* case of defamation: "(1) that the defendant made a defamatory statement to a third person, (2) that the statement was false, (3) that the defendant was legally at fault in making the statement, and (4) that the plaintiff suffered harm." *Offen v. Brenner*, 402 Md. 191, 198, 935 A.2d 719, 723–24 (2007).

The issue in *Offen* was the applicability of an absolute immunity defense to an allegation of defamation. *Id.* at 196, 722. Dr. Offen, a neurologist who reviewed claims filed against the Department of Health and Human Services ("DHHS"), and working in the Division of Vaccine Inquiry Compensation ("DVIC"), forwarded materials relating to a claim to Dr. Brenner, a rheumatologist who acted as an outside consultant for DVIC. *Id.* Dr. Brenner then sent a letter to Dr. Offen's supervisor accusing Dr. Offen of pursuing vendettas against "DVIC in general and several members of the office in particular. Indeed I believe that Dr. Offen has had something derogatory to say about each and every medical officer involved.... He positively gloated over Thom Balbier's transfer, telling me that he had been removed for incompetence and that you would be the next to go." *Id.* at 195–96, 722.

After being suspended for a period without pay and having his duties at DHHS reduced, Dr. Offen sued Dr. Brenner in federal district court, alleging defamation. The court granted Dr. Brenner's motion to dismiss on the grounds that Dr. Brenner enjoyed absolute immunity. *Id.* at 196, 722.

The Maryland Court of Appeals was asked to consider a certified question from the United States Court of Appeals for the Fourth Circuit. The Fourth Circuit asked whether "the duties and authority of the employee against whom [an allegedly defamatory] statement was made [should] be considered in determining 'the nature of the public function of the proceeding.'" *Id.* at 194, 721.

In looking at the first prong of the defamation test, the courts have held that a statement is defamatory when it "tends to expose a person to public scorn, hatred, contempt or ridicule, thereby discouraging others in the community from having a good opinion of, or associating with, that person." *Id.* at 198–99, 724, quoting, *Gohari v. Davish*, 363 Md. 42, 55, 767 A.2d 795, 805 (2007). Words that falsely repute criminal conduct to a plaintiff are defamatory. *Smith v. Danielczyk*, 400 Md. 98, 115, 928 A.2d 795, 805 (2007).

When a statement is made in the form of an opinion, however, it becomes actionable "only if it implie[s] the allegation of undisclosed facts as the basis of that opinion." *Thacker v. City of Hyattsville*, 135 Md. App. 268, 313, 762 A.2d 172, 196 (2000)(other citations omitted). In *Thacker*, an apartment complex manager, Mr. Thacker, requested police assistance in removing a disgruntled tenant from the property management office. *Id.* at 278, 177. The tenant was unhappy because Mr. Thacker would not give him a temporary parking permit. *Id.*

An encounter between Mr. Thacker, the tenant, and the police officer, Officer Blake, ensued and Officer Blake accused Mr. Thacker of being racially prejudiced because he would not give the tenant the parking permit. *Id.* When Mr. Thacker responded to this comment, he was arrested. *Id.* He subsequently sued Officer Blake, and the city of Hyattsville, for defamation based on the officer's comment that Mr. Thacker was racially prejudiced.

In considering Mr. Thacker's defamation claim, the Court of Special Appeals held that Officer Blake's comment was derogatory but that it was based on an opinion rather than on fact. *Id.* at 313, 196. Citing the Supreme Court, the Maryland court noted that "if a statement is not provable as false or is not reasonably interpretable as stating facts, then it cannot form the basis of a defamation suit." *Id.*, citing *Milkovich v. Lorain Journal Co.*, 497 U.S. 1, 18 ... (1990). The court held that "[t]he gravamen of Thacker's injury allegation is that Thacker was harmed by the arrest, and not by an accusation of racial prejudice.... Since there is no 'defamation by arrest' cause of action in Maryland, the circuit court properly granted summary judgment in favor of Blake and the City on the defamation claim." *Id.* at 314, 196.

Similarly, in this case, Mr. Smith told a gathering of newspaper journalists that, in his opinion, Ms. McArthur was a "lousy editor because she didn't have the courage to run controversial stories." Even assuming this statement to be derogatory, and it is unclear that the courts would consider it to be as serious as, for example, the accusation of racial prejudice in the *Thacker* case, it is at worst a statement of opinion.

Although Mr. Smith called Ms. McArthur's actions "criminal," there are no facts to support a contention that Mr. Smith was suggesting there were undisclosed facts to support his choice of words. The article Ms. McArthur declined to publish concerned alleged wide-spread corruption in the mayor's office, but while some might argue that Mr. Smith was implying that Ms. McArthur was involved in some form of criminal conspiracy by preventing the public from knowing of Mr. Smith's allegations, to do so would be mere speculation. The word "criminal" is used so often in the vernacular that it has acquired a robust secondary meaning as something undesirable but not necessarily descriptive of a violation of state or federal law. There is no credible suggestion that there are undisclosed facts that form the basis of Mr. Smith's opinion. Accordingly, what Mr. Smith said at the meeting, while it was critical of Ms. McArthur and her leadership of the newspaper, was not defamatory.

Mr. Smith was airing an opinion rather than making a statement of fact. Therefore, he is not liable to Ms. McArthur for defamation, and relying on *Thacker*, the circuit court should grant summary judgment in his favor.

We know from this version a great deal more about the *Offen* case, but does that knowledge add to our understanding of the *Smith* case? Not really. In fact, everything we learn about the *Offen* case tells us that it is a completely unrelated case to the one we're considering, and that the main issue in that case was one to do with "absolute immunity," a defense that doesn't appear to have any role to play in the *Smith* case. So while the *Offen* case is useful to us because it sets out Maryland's four-part defamation test very neatly, the details of the case aren't relevant to the details of the case we're analyzing. It might have been better if the lawyer who wrote this analysis had omitted *Offen* if one of the more relevant cases had given an equally succinct description of the defamation test, but in any case, limiting *Offen*'s role to just an articulation of that test, as did the writer in example four, was a better choice.

In fact, I would guess that the discussion of *Offen* did more than just take up space unnecessarily. It's likely that you were actively irritated by it because you read it carefully, and then at the end you found that there was no payoff—it wasn't relevant to the analysis after all. You might even have gone back over the *Offen* discussion to see if you'd missed anything, slowing you down even more after reading three unnecessary paragraphs.

There's an important lesson here. Analysis that's included just for its own sake is not only not helpful to the reader, it's actively unhelpful—not just neutral but actually of negative value. It's crucial that you keep this in mind as you draft your analysis assignments in law school and, later, in practice. Very often you won't know what's important and what isn't until you've finished the first draft of a piece of work and you finally have a clear idea of what you need to say in order for the reader to understand and, if it's the goal of the document, be persuaded by what you have to say. And when you understand what needs to be there you can also understand what needs to be taken out.

That can be hard to do. You might have worked hard on a description of the facts of a case like *Offen* and you don't want to think of that time just going to waste. Anyway, if high school and college taught us anything about writing strategy, it's that the more you can include the better. When you have a page limit, write so that your last word is the last word on the last possible page. More is better. Besides, showing a partner in your firm how you spent your time can't be a bad thing, can it?

Yes, it can. Very bad, in fact. You've just seen exactly how bad a thing it can be in a very small example. Example five might be longer than example four, but it's not nearly as effective or helpful and it's entirely possible that you felt irritated—cheated—by reading an analysis that didn't go anywhere. As lawyers, every word we write is important and should have meaning. If you write something, your reader will assume that it's important. If it turns out that a passage of your work isn't important, your readers will have difficulty trusting you again and will wonder why they should read anything you've written. You might be able to get them back, because it's human nature to forgive the first mistake, but if you waste their time again your readers might stop reading your work and never trust you again to not waste their time.

So excessive and unnecessary analysis can not only impede a readers' understanding of your actual analysis, it can lead to your reader no longer trusting you as a conveyor of information. Editing is truly an important skill.

Conclusion

We've seen how legal analysis can be described in terms of the Goldilocks effect: too little analysis is just as bad as too much. What we're looking for in a piece of analysis is the middle ground of "just right." We've seen that unsupported *ipse dixit* conclusions are irritating and unhelpful, and we've seen that discussion of tangential issues that have no relevance to the central topic under consideration are just as irritating and unhelpful. And we've seen that having an introductory summation of the direction in which the analysis is headed can be helpful in giving us an idea of where we're going to be going.

Next, we'll look more closely at the analytical structure and consider whether it really is the best approach for presenting information to a legal reader.

Focus Questions

1. In the writing you've done before law school, had you given much thought to the structure of your analysis? Thinking back on that work, would it have benefited from more careful structuring?
2. Do you see why the first example is inadequate as a piece of analysis? Have you ever experienced some *ipse dixit* thinking? When you were young, did your parents or teachers ever tell you to do something just because they said so? Having seen how inadequate and unpersuasive this approach is, do you think you will attempt to pass off *ipse dixit* thinking as analysis?
3. Example Two seems to be much better on first reading than Example One, but do you see why it is so inadequate? If the text hadn't pointed out Example Two's deficiencies, would you have been satisfied with it?
4. Again, Example Three seems more complete than Example Two. Would you have been satisfied with it without the text's commentary? Do you think that giving more information about the cases will be helpful? Do you think that an introductory summation of the conclusion will be helpful in your analysis?
5. Having now seen an introductory conclusion, do you agree that it helps to orient a reader in the analysis? If you were reading this analysis for the first time, do you think this introductory paragraph would make the analysis easier to understand as you went through it?
6. Did you find that the additional case information was helpful? Do you see why lawyers might want that level of detail to give their readers confidence that the case support for the analysis was sufficient, and that the cited cases actually supported the analysis?
7. Do you see why the text contends that Example Five is weaker than Example Four? Did you feel the irritation that the text predicts upon reading Example Five's unnecessary detail?

Chapter 21

Analytical Structure: Getting More Involved

What You Should Learn from This Chapter

This chapter continues the discussion of analytical structure begun in the last chapter. It considers why the various components of the "standard unit of analysis" are helpful to the reader and why a legal reader might expect to find these components in a piece of legal analysis. The chapter also includes a brief contemplation of the way in which metaphors can change over time and the problems we can experience when attempting intergenerational communication with ineffective metaphors. Although a seemingly esoteric subject, this concept will become increasingly relevant to young lawyers as technology continues to change our metaphorical vocabulary.

After reading this chapter, you should:

- have thought about the various elements of the "standard unit of analysis" in more detail;
- understand why legal analysis typically begins with a summation;
- understand why a rule statement needs to come before consideration of the rule's effects;
- understand the important role taken by rule expansion in legal analysis;
- understand why rule application—which might at casual glance appear to be the most important aspect of legal analysis—is appropriately located after the rule statement and expansion in this model of the "standard unit of legal analysis";
- understand the role of a conclusion in legal analysis;
- have contemplated the possibilities offered by diagramming legal analysis; and
- have considered the communication problems posed by the changes to our metaphoric vocabulary brought about by technological developments.

We started our investigation of analytical structure with several examples of a standard unit of analysis—some that were too short, one that was too long, and one that seemed about right. Let's look again at that example, this time in more detail. Here it is again:

Mr. Smith will not be found liable for defamation. He expressed an opinion rather than fact, and under Maryland law, unsupported opinions are not actionable.

Maryland law requires that a plaintiff satisfy four elements in order to make a *prima facie* case of defamation: "(1) that the defendant made a defamatory statement to a third person, (2) that the statement was false, (3) that the defendant was legally at fault in making the statement, and (4) that the plaintiff suffered harm." *Offen v. Brenner*, 402 Md. 191, 198, 935 A.2d 719, 723–24 (2007).

In looking at the first prong of this test, the courts have held that a statement is defamatory when it "tends to expose a person to public scorn, hatred, contempt or ridicule, thereby discouraging others in the community from having a good opinion of, or associating with, that person." *Id.* at 198–99, 724, quoting, *Gohari v. Davish*, 363 Md. 42, 55, 767 A.2d 795, 805 (2007). Words that falsely repute criminal conduct to a plaintiff are defamatory. *Smith v. Danielczyk*, 400 Md. 98, 115, 928 A.2d 795, 805 (2007).

When a statement is made in the form of an opinion, however, it becomes actionable "only if it implie[s] the allegation of undisclosed facts as the basis of that opinion." *Thacker v. City of Hyattsville*, 135 Md. App. 268, 313, 762 A.2d 172, 196 (2000)(other citations omitted). In *Thacker*, an apartment complex manager, Mr. Thacker, requested police assistance in removing a disgruntled tenant from the property management office. *Id.* at 278, 177. The tenant was unhappy because Mr. Thacker would not give him a temporary parking permit. *Id.*

An encounter between Mr. Thacker, the tenant, and the police officer, Officer Blake, ensued and Officer Blake accused Mr. Thacker of being racially prejudiced because he would not give the tenant the parking permit. *Id.* When Mr. Thacker responded to this comment, he was arrested. *Id.* He subsequently sued Officer Blake, and the city of Hyattsville, for defamation based on the officer's comment that Mr. Thacker was racially prejudiced.

In considering Mr. Thacker's defamation claim, the Court of Special Appeals held that Officer Blake's comment was derogatory but that it was based on an opinion rather than on fact. *Id.* at 313, 196. Citing the Supreme Court, the Maryland court noted that "if a statement is not provable as false or is not reasonably interpretable as stating facts, then it cannot form the basis of a defamation suit." *Id.*, citing *Milkovich v. Lorain Journal Co.*, 497 U.S. 1, 18 ... (1990). The court held that "[t]he gravamen of Thacker's injury allegation is that Thacker was harmed by the arrest, and not by an accusation of racial prejudice.... Since there is no 'defamation by arrest' cause of action in Maryland, the circuit court properly granted summary judgment in favor of Blake and the City on the defamation claim." *Id.*, at 314, 196.

Similarly, in this case, Mr. Smith told a gathering of newspaper journalists that, in his opinion, Ms. McArthur was a "lousy editor because she didn't have the courage to run controversial stories." Even assuming this statement to be derogatory, and it is unclear that the courts would consider it to be as serious as, for example, the accusation of racial prejudice in the *Thacker* case, it is at worst a statement of opinion.

Although Mr. Smith called Ms. McArthur's actions "criminal," there are no facts to support a contention that Mr. Smith was suggesting there were undisclosed facts to support his choice of words. The article Ms. McArthur declined to publish concerned alleged wide-spread corruption in the mayor's office, but while some might argue that Mr. Smith was implying that Ms. McArthur was involved in some form of criminal conspiracy by preventing the public from knowing of Mr. Smith's allegations, to do so would be mere speculation. The word "criminal" is used so often in the vernacular that it has acquired a robust secondary meaning as something undesirable but not necessarily descriptive of a violation of state or federal law. There is no credible suggestion that there are undisclosed facts that form the basis of Mr. Smith's opinion. Accordingly, what Mr. Smith said at the meeting, while it was critical of Ms. McArthur and her leadership of the newspaper, was not defamatory.

Mr. Smith was airing an opinion rather than making a statement of fact. Therefore, he is not liable to Ms. McArthur for defamation, and relying on *Thacker*, the circuit court should grant summary judgment in his favor.

This unit of analysis is made up of several readily identifiable and important parts, all of which combine to convey the writer's analysis.

1. Summations and Conclusions

It seems wrong to say that something begins with a conclusion, so let's instead say that this analysis begins with a summation and ends with a conclusion. The summation tells us where we're headed:

> Mr. Smith will not be found liable for defamation. He expressed an opinion rather than fact, and under Maryland law, unsupported opinions are not actionable.

And the conclusion tells us where we've been:

> Mr. Smith was airing an opinion rather than making a statement of fact. Therefore, he is not liable to Ms. McArthur for defamation, and relying on *Thacker*, the circuit court should grant summary judgment in his favor.

They aren't identical, because a legal reader doesn't have time to read exactly the same thing twice and besides, it's a bad idea to write exactly the same thing twice in any document, regardless of the purpose, unless there's a formal or rhetorical reason for repeating yourself. But while not identical, both passages perform a similar function; they orient the reader to the analysis, with the first passage telling the reader where we're going to go and the second passage telling the reader where we've been. This framing device—where you tell the reader what you're going to say, then say it, then tell the reader what you've said—is a common feature of analytical writing and is one of those cultural expectations legal readers have of legal writers. You can avoid writing something that uses this structural framing device, but you should have a good reason for doing so and you should realize that its omission will have an effect on your reader, who likely will be surprised not to see it.

2. A Brief Parenthetical Interlude

Before we move on to the next identifiable piece of the analytical structure, let's pause for a second to think about rhetoric and culture. It won't take long and it's actually very important for both our immediate and our larger purposes.

For years—probably for as long as legal writing has been taught—legal writing professors have described the "summation" portion of the analysis, and what might otherwise be called the "introductory conclusion" were that not a contradiction in terms, as a "roadmap" paragraph or section. It's also sometimes called an "umbrella" section, but let's focus on "roadmap" for the moment.

"Roadmap" is, obviously, a metaphor—a word or phrase that describes a completely different concept but that allows us to translate (some would say "map," but that's too close to the metaphor we're considering) the metaphorical concept into the text we're considering. The reason we might use it here is readily apparent: "summation" or "introductory conclusion" are relatively sterile terms whose meaning can be understood but which don't immediately grab the reader's attention or interest. By contrast, the notion of a "roadmap" immediately conveys the sense that this passage shows the reader the general path we're going to take to reach an ultimate conclusion. It conjures up associations of a trip or a journey—something that works well with legal analysis because the writer really is taking the reader on an intellectual journey, starting from a place where the reader doesn't know the answer to a legal question and ending, after taking several twists and turns along the way, in a place where the reader does know the answer. The writer is the guide on this journey, pointing out landmarks and points of interest along the way, and commenting on the significance of what the reader is seeing.

But it's a metaphor that is increasingly irrelevant today. Whereas drivers of a certain age are more comfortable with a map, allowing them to plan out their route before setting off and getting the overview of the journey, from beginning to destination, that a roadmap provides, other drivers—probably including most of you—are more used to, and comfortable with, the concept of a GPS unit providing you with directions to your destination.[1] And GPS doesn't work the same way as a map; you don't get an overview of the entire journey at the beginning, but rather you get turn-by-turn instructions that guide you eventually to your destination.

So the "roadmap" metaphor likely wouldn't carry as much power or meaning for you. That's the immediate purpose of which I spoke: there's no point in using a metaphor

---

1. Thanks to Professor Amy Sloan for pointing out the importance of journey metaphors in legal research and for her observation that some of these metaphors might not convey as much meaning today as they did in the past.

to translate a sterile concept into one that lives in your imagination if it doesn't actually do the job for which it was employed.

The larger purpose is much more important. Technology, and the gulf in technical understanding between many older and younger people, is making it harder for the generations to talk to each other. There have always been generational differences of course; one of the ways of defining a generation is to find words, phrases, and concepts that are instantly (and permanently) identifiable to the members of that generation but that are incomprehensible to most of the members of the older generations and are rejected as woefully out-of-date by the members of newer generations.

But technology is widening the gulf, and it's doing so very quickly. Web sites speak of their "pages," for example, but that's a metaphor that has increasingly less relevance. And when the identification with a bound volume of paper pages finally fades away, new metaphors will replace the outmoded print metaphors we use now and they will be comfortable and familiar for the younger generation and strange and alienating for the older.

It is, perhaps, easier for the older generations to recognize this problem because they are increasingly uncomfortable with technology. This can lead to a significant communication gap: for example, while the concept of metadata can easily be explained by reference to an example, the different generations will likely not understand each other's examples. For older generations, a library card catalog is a perfect example of metadata, while that concept makes very little sense to a generation that has grown up without having to learn how to use such catalogs.

The point is that metaphors are essential for us to communicate, but that in order to do its job the metaphor must be understandable by both writer and reader, and must translate a concept fully and completely from one person to the other. But if you don't speak the language into which the concept is translated, the translation will be meaningless to you. If you don't speak boomer, then metaphors that would work well for that generation might not work for you, and your millennial metaphors might not work for the boomers.

As you can imagine, this can be crucially important for lawyers. They rely on metaphors all the time to convey their complex messages to readers and if those metaphors don't translate into anything their readers understand, they're incomprehensible. The "roadmap" example is a fairly benign example of this danger, but it is illustrative of something that wouldn't have been true even ten years ago when maps were still common. Things are happening quickly these days, and metaphors are dying as a result. The dangers exposed by the "roadmap" example are significant and they're growing. You should be very careful to make sure that you know when you're writing metaphorically and, when you are, you should make sure that your metaphors adequately translate your thoughts to all readers, regardless of age.

3. Rules of Law

Well, let's get back to our consideration of analytical structure. Having set out a summation explaining where this analysis is headed, the writer next sets out the applicable legal test that's going to be used. As a reminder, here's the next paragraph:

> Maryland law requires that a plaintiff satisfy four elements in order to make a *prima facie* case of defamation: "(1) that the defendant made a defamatory statement to a third person, (2) that the statement was false, (3) that the defendant was legally at fault in making the statement, and (4) that the plaintiff suffered harm." *Offen v. Brenner*, 402 Md. 191, 198, 935 A.2d 719, 723–24 (2007).

The writer does this because of an assumption that the reader already knows the facts of the case as, in fact, you did when you first read this paragraph in a previous chapter. That's because the standard memo structure—the larger structure that contains this analysis section within it—would provide the reader with the question the memo seeks to answer, the short version of that question's answer (and thereby repeating, at a larger level, the structure we've just discussed, with the brief answer serving the same structural purpose as the summation or introductory conclusion paragraph of the analysis), and a summary of the facts of the case before moving into the analysis. Because the writer knows that the reader has just read the facts and can always return to them if the analysis gets difficult to understand, the writer need not remind the reader of the facts right away and can start with the law—the rules—that will be applicable to the analysis.

A simple statement of the four-part defamation test in Maryland, though, is not enough in this case. The reader needs additional information about the applicable law before the writer can launch into the applicability of the law to the facts in Mr. Smith's case, so the writer continues with an additional statement outlining the relevant law. Here's that passage:

> In looking at the first prong of this test, the courts have held that a statement is defamatory when it "tends to expose a person to public scorn, hatred, contempt or ridicule, thereby discouraging others in the community from having a good opinion of, or associating with, that person." *Id.* at 198–99, 724, quoting, *Gohari v. Davish*, 363 Md. 42, 55, 767 A.2d 795, 805 (2007). Words that falsely repute criminal conduct to a plaintiff are defamatory. *Smith v. Danielczyk*, 400 Md. 98, 115, 928 A.2d 795, 805 (2007).

We now have more specific information regarding the first of the four parts of the defamation test: the defendant must have made a defamatory statement to a third party. And while we might understand what "a third party" is, we need to understand what a "defamatory statement" is in Maryland. And that's what this paragraph does.

What do we make of the next paragraph, though? It seems to be a hybrid, starting off with another piece of information about what defamation means in Maryland and then going in a different direction to explore the facts of a specific case from Maryland's case law. Here's the paragraph:

> When a statement is made in the form of an opinion, however, if becomes actionable "only if it implie[s] the allegation of undisclosed facts as the basis of that opinion." *Thacker v. City of Hyattsville*, 135 Md. App. 268, 313, 762 A.2d 172, 196 (2000)(other citations omitted). In *Thacker*, an apartment complex manager, Mr. Thacker, requested police assistance in removing a disgruntled tenant from the property management office. *Id.* at 278, 177. The tenant was

unhappy because Mr. Thacker would not give him a temporary parking permit. *Id.*

The additional law information appears to be something more directly relating to the analysis of Mr. Smith's case, based on the understanding we have of that analysis given to us by the opening summation paragraph. We know from it that the issue of "opinion" is going to be important and here, for the first time, the word has come up in the analysis. And its importance seems to be highlighted by the writer giving us at least some of the facts of the case. We can call this "rule expansion" or some other term that allows us to understand that we're getting more information about a case. A hallmark of rule expansion—its signature, really,—is the phrase "in *casename*, …" Whenever you see a writer telling you that you're about to read some additional details about a case, that's a sure sign that the writer is expanding on the rule by going into more detail about what the court did and why. If the analysis is well-structured, you might not even notice that this is what's going on (although the "in *casename*" phrase is so often used that it can quickly become an irritating cliché that's better avoided more often than not), but if the rule expansion is out of position the analysis will be as jarring and difficult to read as was the opening paragraph of the previous chapter, when I jumbled the sentences up.

4. Rule Expansion

This rule expansion is very important. It allows us to understand why the court ruled in the way it did and by giving us the facts that led the court to rule, the rule expansion allows us to do what the writer is going to do and compare the analyzed case with the case we're being asked to consider—the *Smith* case in our example. It's this expansion that allows us to move smoothly from the rule itself to the way the rule applies in Mr. Smith's case, and it's so important that the writer gives us more detail from the case:

> An encounter between Mr. Thacker, the tenant, and the police officer, Officer Blake, ensued and Officer Blake accused Mr. Thacker of being racially prejudiced because he would not give the tenant the parking permit. *Id.* When Mr. Thacker responded to this comment, he was arrested. *Id.* He subsequently sued Officer Blake, and the city of Hyattsville, for defamation based on the officer's comment that Mr. Thacker was racially prejudiced.
>
> In considering Mr. Thacker's defamation claim, the Court of Special Appeals held that Officer Blake's comment was derogatory but that it was based on an opinion rather than on fact. *Id.* at 313, 196. Citing the Supreme Court, the Maryland court noted that "if a statement is not provable as false or is not reasonably interpretable as stating facts, then it cannot form the basis of a defamation suit." *Id.,* citing *Milkovich v. Lorain Journal Co.,* 497 U.S. 1, 18 … (1990). The court held that "[t]he gravamen of Thacker's injury allegation is that Thacker was harmed by the arrest, and not by an accusation of racial prejudice…. Since there is no 'defamation by arrest' cause of action in Maryland, the circuit court properly granted summary judgment in favor of Blake and the City on the defamation claim." *Id.,* at 314, 196.

Now we know the facts that led to the claim in the *Thacker* case and we know how, and why, the court in that case resolved the defamation claim. In fact, because we already know the facts of the *Smith* case, the relevant Maryland law, and how a Maryland court interpreted that law based on a set of facts that we also know, we're able to start reaching our own conclusions about how the *Smith* case should be resolved by the court and so that's the perfect time for the writer to give us that part of the analysis.

You see how information has been given to us in organized pieces, exactly at the point when we needed it? We first learned the facts of the case and then we learned—in summary form—how this case would be resolved. Then we expanded on that knowledge, learning more about the law that would apply to the case and, when we learned about the specific rule of law that we remembered from the summary would apply to this case, we were given more information about the case that explored that specific rule so we could compare the facts in that case with the facts in our case and start to see if the conclusions of the two cases would be similar.

5. Rule Application and Counter-Analysis

In order to reach that decision, we have to apply the applicable rule of law, and the conclusion the court reached in the case that explained the rule to us, and apply it to the facts of Mr. Smith's case. And that's exactly what the writer does for us now:

> Similarly, in this case, Mr. Smith told a gathering of newspaper journalists that, in his opinion, Ms. McArthur was a "lousy editor because she didn't have the courage to run controversial stories." Even assuming this statement to be derogatory, and it is unclear that the courts would consider it to be as serious as, for example, the accusation of racial prejudice in the *Thacker* case, it is at worst a statement of opinion.

First, you see that the writer is using a linking word to show you, as the reader, that this case is going to have the same outcome as the *Thacker* case. The simple "[s]imilarly" does a lot of work for the writer, because it moves the reader smoothly from one paragraph to the next, showing you that what you're about to read will be consistent with what you just read (if the outcome would be different, the writer might have used a word like "[c]onversely" or a phrase like "[u]nlike *Thacker*"—something to show you that what's coming is not the same as what came before) and therefore making the transition between two different parts of the analysis smooth and effortless for the reader.

After that linking, or transitional, word, the writer makes clear that we have indeed shifted between parts of the analysis by telling the reader that we're now considering "this case." That phrase is typically reserved for the situation the writer is analyzing, the case that caused the analysis to be written in the first place. So four words have easily moved the reader from the consideration of a case that was decided in 2000 to a case that hasn't been decided yet, and told the reader that the case is going to have the same outcome. Transition words and phrases can be very efficient.

Having made that transition, the writer now tells us why the outcome will be the same. The writer compares what was said in the *Thacker* case with what was said by

Mr. Smith and shows the similarity in form between the two statements. And, of course, it's the form that's important. If we searched for a case that had precisely the same words in it as those used by Mr. Smith, we'd never find it. But the law is able to strip out the details of a statement like this and look instead at the nature of that statement. Finding analogies between cases, and distinguishing one case from another based on the formal rather than specific differences between them, is a crucial lawyering skill.

The writer now offers some restrained counter-analysis, intended to inoculate against one possible claim that Ms. McArthur might offer in support of her defamation claim. Mr. Smith used the word "criminal," and that, in conjunction with the nature of the story Mr. Smith had written and Ms. McArthur had declined to publish, might suggest some undisclosed facts. That, in turn, could support a defamation claim. The counter-analysis introduces this possibility not by saying "Ms. McArthur will [or might] allege" or some other such formulation, but rather by using "[a]lthough" to introduce an acknowledgment that the word was used.

> Although Mr. Smith called Ms. McArthur's actions "criminal," there are no facts to support a contention that Mr. Smith was suggesting there were undisclosed facts to support his choice of words. The article Ms. McArthur declined to publish concerned alleged wide-spread corruption in the mayor's office, but while some might argue that Mr. Smith was implying that Ms. McArthur was involved in some form of criminal conspiracy by preventing the public from knowing of Mr. Smith's allegations, to do so would be mere speculation. The word "criminal" is used so often in the vernacular that it has acquired a robust secondary meaning as something undesirable but not necessarily descriptive of a violation of state or federal law. There is no credible suggestion that there are undisclosed facts that form the basis of Mr. Smith's opinion.

The use of "[a]lthough" tells us that whatever might follow in the sentence will be refuted shortly thereafter. It's a useful word to introduce counter-argument, and doesn't leave the reader with even a faint sense that the coming argument might be stronger, or more troubling, than the writer might like. In that sense, introductory words or phrases like "although" serve a more useful function than a phrase like "Ms. McArthur might allege" or something similar. That form tends to give the coming argument more credibility and strength than is desirable and, when used in a persuasive document, might actually give the other side an argument they hadn't considered.

After introducing the idea of counter-analysis, centered on Mr. Smith's use of "criminal," the writer attempts to dispose of that argument by relying on a quasi-linguistic, and unsupported, contention that "criminal" has acquired a common meaning that untethers it from its more technical meaning; the type of secondary meaning that might have a sports announcer decrying an umpire's "criminal" failure to call a third strike in a key moment of a baseball game or a gossip reporter's description of a celebrity's "criminal" lack of fashion sense. The lack of support for this counter-analysis would be unacceptable were this memo to be filed in opposition to an actual argument, but it might serve in the more informal context of an interoffice memo.

The key word in the counter-analysis, however, is "credible" in the conclusion that "[t]here is no credible suggestion that there are undisclosed facts that form the basis of Mr. Smith's opinion." The writer is saying here that while any number of possible arguments could be made in support of a contention that Mr. Smith was saying there was undisclosed information to support his critical comments directed at Ms. McArthur, none of these arguments will prevail because they are not credibly based on fact.

Having shown us how the two statements in *Thacker* and the *Smith* case were similar in form, and how any allegations that Mr. Smith was suggesting there were undisclosed facts to support his statements were incredible, the writer then suggests that the results of the two cases will also be the same.

> Accordingly, what Mr. Smith said at the meeting, while it was critical of Ms. McArthur and her leadership of the newspaper, was not defamatory.

And we're willing to trust that conclusion because it's the conclusion we had been set up to accept by the opening summation and, if it had been included, in the brief answer to the question presented at the start of the memo. But while those were conclusory statements that would, if left unsupported, have failed as *ipse dixit* logical errors, they are now supported by a combination of law, fact, and counter-analysis, and we can accept the conclusion much more comfortably.

6. Conclusion

All that's left is for the writer to round things off with a slightly more detailed (but only slightly) conclusion:

> Mr. Smith was airing an opinion rather than making a statement of fact. Therefore, he is not liable to Ms. McArthur for defamation, and relying on *Thacker*, the circuit court should grant summary judgment in his favor.

You might feel that there's no need for this final conclusion, and that the memo has sufficient conclusions already, with the brief answer and the summation at the start of the analysis also filling this role. But the conclusion here serves an important compositional function, signaling the reader that there's no more analysis to come and that things have wrapped up, at least for this issue. In typical memos, there is more than one standard unit of analysis, each with its own conclusion signaling the end of one unit and alerting the reader that the next thing to come will either be another unit of analysis or, if the total analysis is completed, then the structural conclusion—the section headed "Conclusion."

That too might seem unnecessary or duplicative, but remember that each of the summation and closing conclusions for the various units of analysis are only concerned with that particular unit. Once the analysis is over, the "Conclusion" section wraps up the entire memo, and it serves just as important a structural role as do the intermediate conclusions that end each unit of analysis.

Conclusion

We've looked at analytical structure in some depth now, but we haven't touched bottom yet. There are some additional considerations we haven't discussed yet and we also need to fit this discussion of standard units of analysis into the larger analytical model. That's for the next chapter.

Focus Questions

1. Some might use the metaphor of a news headline, then a full report, and finally a summary of the main points of the news, as a way of describing the process of giving a summation, then analysis, then a conclusion. Is that metaphor helpful to you? Can you think of other examples of this framing device?

2. Is the notion of a roadmap useful to you? Can you think of other examples of metaphors that appear to convey more information to those of an older generation than to your generation? Had the ideas of metaphors being generation-specific occurred to you? Do you have difficulty communicating with members of different generations? Does the idea that metaphors and other means of communicating might be dying as technology changes the way people think help to explain why members of different generations sometimes have difficulty communicating with each other?

3. Have you considered the effect of technology on your generation's ability to communicate with those of an older generation? Have you considered the speed with which technological innovation is changing the world with which members of older generations were familiar and comfortable?

4. Do you think the text is correct to identify communication problems between generations, or do you think the concerns expressed in the text are overblown? Have you ever used a card catalog?

5. Do you see why rule expansion is an important part of legal analysis? Would you be satisfied with analysis that simply set out the applicable rules and then moved directly to an application of those rules to the facts of the case under consideration?

6. The text speaks enthusiastically about linking words. Do you agree that they are helpful in moving a reader through text?

7. Is the formal requirement that a memo have a "Conclusion" section sufficient justification for including such a section in a document with many internal conclusions? Are the internal conclusions sufficient to render a structural "Conclusion" section vestigial in contemporary memos?

Chapter 22

Working with Facts

What You Should Learn from This Chapter

This chapter discusses the importance of facts to legal analysis. The chapter reinforces the importance of ethics when dealing with facts and discusses the dangers of characterization in fact presentation. The chapter also introduces the importance of narrative and "story telling" to legal fact presentation and suggests that getting our readers to see the action discussed in the facts is the most helpful way of getting the reader engaged with the facts. The chapter ends with a discussion of how best to organize facts within a facts presentation.

After reading this chapter, you should:

- be aware of the ethical problems inherent in characterizing facts;
- be aware of the importance of telling a story through your facts;
- have considered how to make your reader see the facts about which you're writing;
- understand the difference between material and immaterial facts; and
- understand how to use the legal standards that might apply to a case to guide your factual organization within a document.

Legal writing lives and dies with facts. That seems a contradiction; "legal" writing should be mostly concerned with the law, and the law is what lawyers go to school to study. But in a common law world, the facts are integral to the way the law works, and a lawyer's ability to organize and present facts is a key skill. Facts allow us to analogize and distinguish one case from another, facts draw readers into the documents they're reading, and facts allow us to construct the theories we use to persuade and inform our readers. Not to put too fine a point on it, facts are important.

This chapter will introduce you to some of the basic concepts we use when discussing factual presentation in legal writing. As with most things concerned with writing, though, this is not much more than an introduction to the way the pieces move on the chess board, not a detailed instruction manual on how to play chess. Each case presents its own challenges and opportunities, and as you write more and more sets of fact statements you'll become more comfortable with experimenting to find ways to put those facts forward in the best possible light for your client. That will come in time. For now, concentrate on presenting your facts in a clean, logical, careful way and you'll produce writing that will make your legal writing professor happy and—perhaps more importantly—make prospective employers happy with your work as well.

1. Remember Ethics

The first piece of advice concerning facts is probably the first thing you should always remember when embarking on any piece of legal writing: be ethical at all times. This has particular significance for the facts section of legal documents, though, so it's worth discussing it in a little more depth now.

It's obvious—or, at least, it should be obvious—that you can't make up facts to give your client an advantage and that you can't just ignore bad facts because they harm your client's position. This is easy: you can't do these things, you'll get caught if you do, and the best thing that will happen to you is that the other side will beat you like a drum while they point out your lapses to the court. The worst thing that will happen is that your client will lose the case, you'll be sued for malpractice, and you'll be disbarred for unethical conduct. So don't make things up and don't omit bad facts. There's no good reason to do these things and many good reasons to not do them.

The harder problem is the shading of facts. One of the most common ways this happens is by characterizing a fact, often by using an adverb. If a car was dented during the course of a car crash, for example, a lawyer who writes that the car received "enormous damage" has characterized that dent and has done so improperly. Why improper? Because there's no way to define the meaning of "enormous:" the dent is a fact, the characterization of it is not. If you can be specific, and if you have the facts to back you up, you could write that the car received a "5 cm wide and 15 cm deep dent on the driver's side front door" and that wouldn't be characterization or improper.

It's for this reason that lawyers are often cautioned to stay away from adverbs. They are imprecise words that are designed to characterize and create an impression in the reader that isn't supported by any evidence. In all legal writing, but especially in a facts section, you should be on the lookout for characterizations like this and you should edit them ruthlessly from your work. They persuade no one, leave an impression in the reader that the writer is unprofessional, and do nothing to help the client's case.

Another way to stray from the straight and narrow path of ethical fact presentation is to extrapolate from known facts into conjecture. You can always tell conjecture when a sentence begins with a phrase like "[i]t seems likely that ..." or "[b]ased on these facts, it is obvious that...." Words like "probably," "likely," "obviously," "apparently," and so on are signals that the writer has moved beyond facts into guesswork and that's not appropriate for factual presentation by lawyers. You might drift into some conjecture during your analysis—although even there it's almost always a bad idea—but you should never do it in your statement of facts.

The best way to protect yourself from any of these lapses is to have a citation after every sentence that lays out the source from which a fact was obtained. In some styles of writing citations like this are expected, but in other documents such detailed citation might not be required. Even if you take the citation out during the editing stage, though, it's a good practice to put it in as you're drafting the statement of facts for any document you write. That way, you'll know where you got the facts from and you'll know that each fact is verifiable as a fact.

2. Tell a Story with Your Facts

This might sound like odd advice, but you should try to tell the reader a story with the facts of your case. In fact, your entire document—facts and legal analysis—should be one coherent story that draws the reader in and carries the reader through the entire document, but that process starts with, and is most noticeable in, the facts section.

I've used "narrative" before but I'm going to use "story" here because I want to use the simplest, plainest word to convey my meaning. There's no functional difference between the two words, but this is an example of how one word can sometimes put too much of a distance between the writer and the reader. I want to avoid that distance here so I'll use the simpler word.

"Story," at least in the sense we're going to use it here, just means a collection of facts that are organized with care to show the reader how the entities involved in the case (they're usually people but sometimes they can be corporations) behaved and why. If you're telling a story with a person, there's often a goal at the end, but if you're telling a story on behalf of a corporation, that goal might be harder to define—the ultimate goal of every corporation has to be to make money for its shareholders, and that's not an especially helpful goal to describe because it's the same for all corporations and won't make your client look too sympathetic.

We're all human beings—even judges—and human beings are designed to respond to stories. There's a lot of research that shows compellingly that facts organized according to storytelling principles are more persuasive than facts that are organized less carefully. There's some debate about whether storytelling is a subset of rhetoric or whether the two are separate disciplines, but that debate needn't concern you; all that matters for your purposes is that you should try to tell your reader a story when you set out your statement of facts.

Scholars of storytelling use a lot of technical language to describe how to tell stories: words and phrases like "stock structures" or "schemas," "heroic archetypes," and the classical rhetorical triangle of "logos," "pathos," and "ethos" are all meaningful and relevant in describing the process, but explaining them would take more time and space than we have here.[1] The rest of this chapter will try to distill the essence of these storytelling concepts into the advice about factual presentation in this chapter so you understand the basics without having to worry too much about the vocabulary.

3. Try to Help Your Reader See the Action

We've spoken about writing a great deal, of course, and we've spoken about the aural metaphors like "spoken" we often use when talking, or writing, about writing. But writ-

---

1. If you're interested in reading further on all of this, there's an excellent book devoted to the subject: Ruth Anne Robbins, Steve Johansen, and Ken Chestek, *Your Client's Story: Persuasive Legal Writing* (Wolters Kluwer, 2013).

ing can also have a visual aspect as well, and it's particularly useful if you can write your facts in such a way that the reader can "see" what happened. If you can describe the facts in such a way that the reader "sees" what happened in the reader's mind's eye— to use the phrase often used to describe the location where result of this power of words and ideas to conjure images is perceived—then you've gained control of your reader's mind in a very powerful way. A reader who can "see" the facts unfolding while reading is a reader who is absorbed in your document, and is probably a reader who has willingly suspended disbelief, at least for a while.

The willing suspension of disbelief is crucial for anyone seeking to enjoy any form of fictional entertainment. When we buy a book of fiction, for example, we know we're going to be lied to by the writer because we understand that the nature of fiction is to tell us a story that isn't true. The story might be based on true facts, and might involve people who actually lived, but the nature of fiction means that the story itself is imagined and is retold primarily for our pleasure.

We're typically unwilling to be lied to, and we get angry when we believe that someone who's been telling us something has been lying to us, but we're perfectly happy to spend money to be lied to when we read a book or watch a drama or a comedy in a live or movie theater. We're only able to enjoy the experience, though, because we have become a willing participant in the process by volunteering to suspend our sense—knowledge, really—of disbelief. We know we're being lied to, but we chose to ignore that fact for the time we're reading or watching in order to gain the benefit of the experience.

What does this have to do with a legal reader? After all, we know that legal readers demand that we tell them the truth at all times, so any ethically written legal document they read is, by definition, not a work of fiction. What role does the willing suspension of disbelief have when the reader understands that the writer is only giving factual and legal information that is verifiably accurate and true?

Think about this from a judge's perspective. The judge expects you to be truthful, of course, but the judge also knows that you have a client who seeks a particular result and that it's your job to persuade the judge that the facts and the law compel the result your client seeks. And the judge also knows that there's a lawyer on the other side of the case who has a client who seeks precisely the opposite result and that the lawyer who represents that client will be doing his or her best to persuade the judge of the correctness of that position as well.

So any judge reading your work has some sense of disbelief, because that judge knows that while both sides are presenting objectively verifiable facts and law, they're both doing it in such a way as to persuade the judge that things are one way or another. Since both versions of the facts and the law can't be correct, the judge knows that you're both telling the truth but that one of you is telling a truth that the judge will accept more than the other. The judge, in short, is reading both documents with a sense of disbelief because the judge knows that if one document is "right," the other is "wrong," and until the judge has figured out which is which, both documents are suspect.

If that's the case, then the lawyer who can persuade the judge to willingly suspend disbelief, and to "see" the facts as that lawyer portrays them, has won an important battle. When the judge is reading your document and seeing the facts as you're telling them, the judge has been persuaded to enter the world you've created and the impressions you're able to create while the judge is in that world will be more persuasive than if the judge were receiving that same information presented in a more clinical and sterile way. You can persuade the judge to suspend disbelief and still not persuade the judge to rule in your favor, but you stand a better chance of prevailing if the judge is seeing the facts in the way you describe them.

4. All Material Facts, but Only Material Facts

We've talked about facts before enough that this will probably sound like a tired cliché, but let me say it again: your facts section should have all the relevant facts but only the relevant facts. Clichéd or not, it's important advice for all legal writers, especially ones who are just starting out. So important, in fact, that we should review the idea of material facts once more here.

Any case on which you work will be awash in facts. You'll learn a great deal about the behavior of the people involved in the case, the workings of any products involved, and so on. All the facts you learn will be facts, but they won't all be material facts all the time. An obvious example might demonstrate this distinction more clearly.

Ms. Smith drives a red Buick, which she bought on April 12, 2010. Mr. Jones drives a blue Chrysler, which he bought on July 16, 2008. On February 1, 2013, the two drivers, and their cars, were involved in an accident at an intersection; Ms. Smith claims that Mr. Jones drove through the intersection after his light had changed to red, and she also claims that her car accelerated without her putting her foot on the gas. Mr. Jones claims that Ms. Smith anticipated the turning of her light from red to green. A witness, Joe Student, saw the incident. Ms. Smith claims to have suffered soft tissue damage from whiplash as a result of the crash, while Mr. Jones claims he suffered a broken nose and bruises as a result of the airbag deploying during the accident.

Mr. Student doesn't know the names of the two drivers, but in his statement to the police and in his deposition and trial testimony, he said that the red car definitely had a red light when it entered the intersection.

If the lawyers in the case are writing about liability for the accident as between the two drivers, the facts that Ms. Smith's car was a Buick and Mr. Jones's car was a Chrysler are not material, but the colors of their cars are certainly material because that's how Mr. Student identified them. The date of the accident is material, but the dates on which both drivers bought their cars clearly are immaterial.

On the other hand, if Ms. Smith is suing Buick for the sudden acceleration she claims, then the fact that her car was red is immaterial but the fact that it was a Buick is highly relevant, and the date might be material as well, especially if there's evidence to suggest that other cars from that model year had acceleration problems. And if Ms. Smith is defending against Mr. Jones's claim that her soft tissue injury is a sham, then neither the make nor color of her car, nor the date on which she bought it, is material.

None of this is very complicated, but hopefully it illustrates that materiality changes given the legal context in which the facts are being presented. What doesn't change, though, is the importance a reader gives to every fact presented in a statement of facts. Legal readers understand the convention in legal writing that all material facts are presented in a statement of facts, so when the reader sees a fact there the reader will assume that that fact is material and will play a role in the analysis. If, in our example, a lawyer writes that Ms. Smith's car was a red Buick in a brief about her soft tissue damage, the reader will expect those facts to assume some importance in the analysis, and when that doesn't happen, the reader will be irritated and will lose confidence in the writer.

It also means that you must make some analytical decisions when writing your statement of facts, because you can't include all the facts you know about, since some of them—while facts—will be non-material to the issues being presented in your document. And that decision can be tricky; suppose you leave out a fact because it's not material to your argument but the other side includes it because they believe it will be material to the argument they're going to make. Have you committed an ethical lapse by omitting a material fact? Probably not, if you've done your job honestly and well. If you're convinced that you've included all the material facts that are relevant to the analysis of an issue in your statement of facts, you will probably be able to see how the fact the other side included is arguably not material to the case and you'll usually have an opportunity to point that out to the reader in a subsequent document if it's important enough of an issue to raise. But this danger points out again the importance of thinking carefully about your facts before you commit to them.

Can it happen that you include non-material facts that are necessary in order to tell the story of the case? Yes, but to do so carries the risk that you'll send the reader clues to a dead end, something that might be a good idea in detective stories but which will try the patience of a legal reader. If you need non-material facts to make the story of the case flow, try to keep them to a minimum and consider carefully if you really need a non-material fact before you finishing editing your work.

The flip-side to the advice about having only material facts in your statement of facts, of course, is that all material facts should appear in the statement of facts. If realizing that a fact contained in the statement of facts was not material is irritating to a reader, imagine how irritating it is for the reader to read a new fact buried in the middle of the analysis. Suddenly a case the reader understood has a different factual foundation from the one the reader anticipated, and the reader now has to adjust everything the reader knows about the case.

One way to avoid this problem is to write the facts section last, making sure that you know all the facts necessary for your analysis because they're already contained in the analysis you've just written. But this isn't the best approach, because often the materiality or non-materiality of a fact first presents itself when you're writing the facts section and understanding the factual framework of your case before you start the analysis can help bring the analysis itself into sharper focus for the writer. So a better approach is to write the statement of facts before the analysis, but to edit the facts last—after the analysis has taken its final shape and you can be sure what facts were necessary to make the analysis as effective as possible. Once you know that, you can go back over the facts and add and remove facts as necessary until your facts statement has all the material facts, but only the material ones.

One important aspect of fact writing flows from the advice that all relevant facts, but only relevant facts, should be in the facts section, and it's something that's often forgotten by legal writers. Because the facts statement presents all the material facts necessary for the analysis, the reader—who's an experienced legal reader and knows this convention well—will understand the importance of each fact contained in the section. Unwary writers, though, try to emphasize a fact by putting language before it that seeks to bolster the fact's importance. Words and phrases like "[i]t is important to note that," "[v]itally," and so on crop up all the time in facts sections written by novice lawyers and they can irritate the reader because they suggest that the writer is unaware that every fact—every word, really—in a facts section is important and vital.

If this is giving you the idea that the facts section is a difficult thing to draft, given the importance attached to every word in it, you'd be right. Facts form the foundation of everything that happens in a piece of legal analysis and sophisticated legal readers pay close attention to the way the facts are presented. Knowing this, you should recognize that the facts section provides you with time when you have a reader's full attention—something that can't be guaranteed when the reader is wading through the legal analysis portion of your document. In short, this is an opportunity. How can you best take advantage of this in order to enhance your client's chances of winning? Thinking carefully about organization, that's how.

5. Organize Your Facts the Way the Law or Facts Suggest

The standard, safe approach to factual organization is to work chronologically from beginning to end, giving the reader a sense of what happened first, what happened next, and so on. It's often the best choice as well, because cause and effect can often be a crucial part of the case. But not always, and it's a mistake to always default to chronology when thinking about facts. If you organize your facts in the way the law or the facts themselves suggest, you have the best chance of grabbing and maintaining your reader's attention.

Again, a simple example might best illustrate the point. The facts and law here are presented in no particular order, and in bullet point form.[2] Once you know what the case is about, let's think about how we might organize the facts depending on which side we're representing.

- Diabetics who suffer insulin shock can suffer slurring of speech, trembling hands, excessive sweating, irritability, and anxiety or nervousness;
- The Fourth Amendment protects against "unreasonable searches and seizures";
- The India Convenience Store had no orange juice available for purchase on March 29 of last year;
- Brian Jones suffers from diabetes;
- Officers Okamoto and Robbins were sitting in their patrol car outside the India Convenience Store at 8:25 pm on March 29 of last year;
- In determining a police officer's "reasonableness" under the Fourth Amendment, the court looks objectively at the facts and circumstances known to the officer on the scene at the time of the incident;
- Insulin shock symptoms can appear to be similar to the behavior of one who has taken certain types of illegal drugs, especially methamphetamines;
- Mr. Jones began to experience the symptoms of insulin shock at 8:20 pm and asked his friend, Sarah Smith, to drive him to the India Convenience Store where he could buy orange juice to alleviate his symptoms;

---

2. The facts here are very loosely drawn from *Graham v. Connor*, 490 U.S. 386 (1987).

- When Officers Okamoto and King witnessed Mr. Jones coming out of the store soon after he went in, and particularly when they noticed his behavior, they became suspicious and went over to him. When he became angry that they were detaining him, but without explaining why he was angry, the Officers attempted to handcuff him. He struggled with the officers and Officer King hit him with his flashlight to subdue him;
- Mr. Jones is an African-American man, Officer Okamoto is an Asian-American woman, Officer King is a white man, the India Convenience Store is located in a primarily white suburb of a large Midwestern city, and the police had received reports that the area around the store had been used for the sale of methamphetamines;
- Orange juice helps to alleviate the symptoms of insulin shock;
- Mr. Jones has sued Officers Okamoto and Robbins, pursuant to 42 U.S.C. § 1983 for using excessive force in detaining him. His suit will be analyzed based on the Fourth Amendment's standard for "reasonableness."

Those are the relevant facts in the case. There are many more facts, of course, but these are enough for our present purposes. Let's think how we would organize these facts if we represented Mr. Jones.

Because Mr. Jones is our client—the "hero" of our story—we probably want the reader to focus on him first. What characteristic of Mr. Jones do we want the court to think about most—his race or his medical condition? Perhaps both? Mr. Jones' race has nothing to do with the way he was behaving; we know that was because of his medical condition. But might his race have something to do with the way the police officers behaved towards him? Do we want to argue that his race was important to this story?

These are decisions we have to make now, because they affect the materiality of Mr. Jones' race to the case; if his race is material, we need to include it in the statement of facts, and if it isn't, then we should omit it because if we include it, but don't analyze the issue of race in the analysis section, the reader will feel misled by us because we provided a clue that didn't turn into anything.

We certainly want to emphasize the fact that Mr. Jones was hit with the flashlight while the police officers were detaining him. What word should we use to describe that? "Beaten"? Perhaps; it's a more powerful word than "hit" or "struck" and it carries some overtones of the way civil rights protestors were treated by the police in some Southern states in the 1960s, so it's a word that imports some concepts that we can't state explicitly but which we want the reader to think about nonetheless. In this sense, "beaten" is both a direct word to describe a fact and a metaphor (to rhetoricians) or stock schema (to storytellers) that carries into the discussion concepts from the reader's mind as well. It might be a little aggressive to use the word under the circumstances as we know them, but probably not so aggressive to be successfully challenged by the other side.

How should we organize the facts? Chronologically? That would mean that his race and his medical condition would come first—both happened before any of the events of March 29—and then would move through the events, viewed from his perspective. That might work. Let's see what happens if we take this approach. You'll see that I've added some detail that wasn't in the list of facts I gave you. You should assume, for our purposes, that everything in this proposed statement of facts is true and can be supported by a citation to the record.

Brian Jones is an African-American man with diabetes. His medical condition sometimes causes him to suffer the symptoms of insulin shock, a condition that can cause slurring of speech, trembling hands, excessive sweating, irritability, and anxiety or nervousness.

On the evening of March 29 last year, Mr. Jones felt the onset of insulin shock symptoms and asked a friend, Sarah Smith, to drive him to the India Convenience Store where he hoped to buy some orange juice, a product that helps to dispel insulin shock and its symptoms.

When Mr. Jones reached the store, he quickly learned that there was no orange juice on sale and was returning to Ms. Smith's car to look for another store when he was confronted by Officers Okamoto and King who asked him what he was doing. Mr. Jones, still suffering from the symptoms of insulin shock, was unable to answer the Officers' questions to their satisfaction, so they beat him with a flashlight and handcuffed him until they determined that he was suffering from a potentially fatal medical condition, not having a reaction to having taken methamphetamines. The Officers then released Mr. Jones and allowed him to leave in his attempt to find a bottle of orange juice.

What do you think? Does it tell a story? Is that story a compelling one? I decided to include Mr. Jones's race in the statement of facts, suggesting that I intend to make a feature of that in the analysis. How about that decision? How do you feel about the chronology? The use of "beat"—is that too aggressive? Would "hit" or "struck" or some other word be better? Can you do a better job?

Now, let's consider how to present the same facts from the perspective of the two police officers. What facts will become material in our telling of that story that weren't material to Mr. Jones's version? What facts, if any, will become immaterial? How will we handle the flashlight? And, perhaps most importantly, what structure will we employ?

When thinking about structure, look at the legal standard. The court is supposed to consider the facts objectively from the perspective (a good visual word that might help us construct the facts) of the officers, and based on what they knew at the time. That suggests a structure. Let's see what you think.

Officers Okamoto and King spent part of the evening on March 29 of last year sitting in their patrol car outside the India Convenience Store, an area known to them as a place where methamphetamines were sold.

At 8:25 pm, the Officers saw a car with a female driver and a male passenger pull up to the store's parking lot. The passenger got out, entered, and then returned from the store, behaving in a way consistent with methamphetamine use. Officers Okamoto and King approached the man and attempted to determine why he had been in the store and if, in fact, he had taken methamphetamines.

The passenger, Brian Jones, became belligerent upon being questioned. His speech was slurred, his hands were noticeably trembling, he was sweating profusely, and he appeared both angry and nervous about the officers' questions. Officers Okamoto and King decided to restrain Mr. Jones because of his behavior, and because of their concern that he had been taking methamphetamines, but he resisted being handcuffed and Officer King had to use his flash-light to control Mr. Jones sufficiently so that he could be restrained.

Upon discovering that Mr. Jones was a diabetic suffering from insulin shock, Officers Okamoto and King immediately removed the handcuffs and Mr. Jones was told he was free to leave.

It's a different story, but it's also the same one. Because the legal standard requires the court to view the facts from the perspective of what the officers knew at the time, I tried to present the facts in that way. The reader learns that Mr. Jones was a diabetic, but not until the officers learned it. Before that, the reader sees what they saw; a man displaying the symptoms of a methamphetamine user in an area known for its metham-phetamine use, who becomes belligerent (another word that imports meanings from the reader's consciousness into the facts) when questioned and who has to be "re-strained." His hands are "trembling," not shaking. "Trembling" is a synonym for shak-ing that is associated with nervousness, and the officers want Mr. Jones to appear nervous, as if he had something to hide from the police. The "beating" now becomes "use" for "control" purposes, and Mr. Jones is freed "immediately" upon the officers' learning of his condition. There's no mention of orange juice; Mr. Jones' reasons for going to the store aren't material to the story I'm telling here.

It's worth noting, in passing, that I haven't dealt here with the amount of time it takes for the onset of symptoms of methamphetamine use. I implied in this telling of the facts that one taking these drugs would display symptoms very quickly. Did you notice that? I talked about Mr. Jones going into the store and coming out again and I implied that not much time had passed. When he came out, I said he was displaying signs of methamphetamine use. I didn't say that the officers suspected him of taking drugs in the store, but by putting the idea of methamphetamine use into the reader's mind early (by saying, in the first paragraph, that the store was a place where metham-phetamines were sold) I prepared the reader for the assumption that the officers might think Mr. Jones had taken drugs while in the store.

That might not be a fair assumption. I don't know how long methamphetamine users take before they start displaying symptoms and nor, I suspect, do you. But I inten-tionally created that impression because I didn't think my reader (you, in this case) would know these details either and I wanted the officers' conduct to appear as rea-sonable as possible under the circumstances. I didn't lie, because I didn't actually say that they thought, or reasonably could have thought, that he had taken drugs, but I did let you form that impression for yourself. Did you? Is this going beyond what's ap-propriate?

Which side has the better chance of prevailing after you've read the statements of facts, based on the facts and your understanding of the law? You can find the real case on which these facts are very loosely based and see how the court organized the facts in its telling of the story, and how it reached the decision it reached.

This is all pretty obvious and unsubtle, but the principles demonstrated by this sim-ple example hold true no matter what the case: attention to organization, aggressive but justifiable word use, and an attempt to bring the reader as much into the facts as possible will always be important elements of a fact statement and a skillful lawyer will use all techniques ethically at the writer's disposal to start the process of persuading a legal reader of that writer's client's position.

Conclusion

It's impossible to overstate the importance of the facts to a legal argument. Although we go to law school, it's the facts that always help us to mold a persuasive case theory that helps to influence the reader to rule in our clients' favor. A successful theory—"story" if you will—always starts with the facts. And while you're stuck with the facts you have, and sometimes they can be less than helpful, when they're carefully phrased, thoughtfully selected, and appropriately structured, facts can win the day.

Exercise

Assume you have been asked to edit the work of a former associate in your law firm. The associate wrote a summary judgment motion on behalf of the defendant in a case involving a slip and fall in a local supermarket. You've been asked to reorganize the facts to tell a better story for the defendant, remove as many non-material facts as possible, and eliminate any improper characterization.

> Donna Goldman, an overweight woman in her mid-40s, was wearing inappropriately high heels when she came into "The Grocery Store," a well-known supermarket in Pittsburgh, on June 20 of this year. Ms. Goldman, who was wearing her shoes for the first time that day, was doing her shopping for the week and was using a large shopping cart as she moved from aisle to aisle.
>
> Apparently indecisive as to what she was shopping for, since she had come out without a shopping list that day, Ms. Goldman crossed and re-crossed the store several times as she remembered first one and then another item on her extensive list of purchases. As she went past one of the grocery aisles for the third or fourth time, she noticed that someone had dropped some produce on the floor, including a large cabbage that had split into many pieces when it hit the floor. Undeterred, Ms. Goldman continued to push her cart in search of a particular breakfast cereal she wanted to try.
>
> When Ms. Goldman found her cereal, and had also picked up a gallon of milk, she remembered that she needed some carrots for a dish she was planning later that week and so headed back to the grocery section of the store. As she went past the aisle with the dropped cabbage, she saw a sign saying "Caution: Floor Might Be Slippery" and noticed a store employee, Fred Pilikowski, trying to pick up the remaining parts of the cabbage, but she ignored the sign because she suddenly remembered that she needed to buy some bagels that were located back in the direction of the dairy section from where she had just come. Forgetting about her carrots in her sudden desire for bagels, and upon executing an abrupt and dangerous about-turn, Ms. Goldman's heels found

themselves in contact with a stray piece of cabbage that had eluded Mr. Pilikowski's best efforts to clean up and she slipped, turning her ankle as she fell.

In addition to her turned ankle, and what she describes as irreplaceable damage to her red heels, Ms. Goldman suffered some minor bumps and bruises—injuries for which she is now suing The Grocery Store for $500,000.

Focus Questions

1. Did you expect there to be such a focus on fact presentation in law school and in legal writing? Have you noticed your professors in other classes asking you to consider how a case would have been decided if the facts were different?
2. It should be obvious why you can't make up facts, but do you understand why ignoring bad facts is not a successful strategy? Do you see why characterizing facts is a bad idea?
3. Have you considered the idea of lawyers telling stories through the facts of a case? How does this idea of legal story telling strike you?
4. Have you considered the idea that helping a reader to "see" the facts is a useful writing technique for a lawyer to use when writing a statement of facts? Do you understand why this could be a useful technique to employ?
5. Are you familiar with the notion of the suspension of disbelief? Do you see why this concept is relevant to a discussion of legal writing?
6. Do you understand the difference between material and non-material facts? Do you see why adding non-material facts to the statement of facts, when they do not connect to any part of the analysis, could be irritating to a reader? Do you see why it would be equally disturbing to a reader to have a fact that was not disclosed in the statement of facts appear for the first time in the analysis section of a brief or memo?
7. Do you see why chronology might not always be the best approach to fact organization? Do you see why it is crucial that a legal writer understand the legal standard relevant to a judge's review of a case before preparing the facts of the case for a brief?
8. Do you think the use of the word "beat" in the example was too aggressive? Do the facts, as told from Mr. Jones' perspective, do a good job of persuading a judge that Mr. Jones was treated with excessive force?
9. Was the telling of the facts from the police officers' perspective too aggressive? Was the use of the word "use" to describe what Officer King did with his flashlight appropriate? Did you notice the way the facts created an impression of possible methamphetamine use without actually stating it? Was that appropriate or did that go too far?

Chapter 23

Identifying and Working with Legal Rules

What You Should Learn from This Chapter

This chapter discusses the nature of legal rules. In particular, it discusses the differences between mandatory, permissive, aspirational, and declaratory rules and the importance of identifying the type of rule with which you're working. The chapter also discusses the two main forms legal rules take—elements and factors—and suggests why the nature of the rule form is so important to a legal analyst.

After reading this chapter, you should:

- be able to identify the differences between mandatory and permissive rules;
- understand the differences between a rule that something "may" happen and a rule that says that something "may not" happen;
- be able to identify aspirational and declaratory rules; and
- understand how to distinguish between elements and factors rules and how the differences between these rules might affect the way a lawyer analyzes an issue.

"Rule" is a small word that carries a big weight on its shoulders. But what does it mean? It's an expressed requirement mandating behavior (you must do something) or non-behavior (you must not do something), certainly, and in legal terms a rule's requirements are backed up by the force of law. Those definitions, between them, capture most of what we think of as a "rule," perhaps, but they don't exactly make the meaning clear. Let's try this and see if it's more helpful: a rule is society's articulation of required behavior in a particular area. Well, yes, but that still doesn't quite capture it. We could go with something broader, like rules are law, but that really is just defining one word in terms of another difficult-to-define word; it's hard to say with precision exactly what "law" is, either.

But the essence of a "rule" is somewhere in those various definitions, as well as in our own common sense understanding of the word; we know what rules are. And we know that the concept of "rule" is embodied in a number of other words as well as the word itself: a "rule" is a rule, of course, but a regulation is a rule as well, as is a court "order," a statute, an ordinance, and any number of other synonyms. All of those other words might have specialized technical meanings that tell us how the rule came into being, but because they're all linguistic formulations that mandate or prohibit behavior in some way or other, they're all "rules" as we're coming to understand that word.

One of the important aspects of rules, at least in the common law world, is that very often the "rule" that we know is not, in fact, the rule. That was intentionally vague; let me try to explain.

One of the most famous rules learned by law students is the definition of common law burglary. You'll learn it in your criminal law class, no doubt, and again for the bar exam. Most lawyers you speak to—even if their practice has nothing to do with the criminal law—will be able to tell you that common law burglary is: the breaking and entering into the house of another during the hours of darkness with the intent of committing a felony therein. The last word is a little archaic; most people don't say "therein" anymore. But it's easily understood, and other than that there aren't any difficult words that complicate the rule. You might wonder about the motivation behind the "hours of darkness" requirement, until you realize that most people used to be at home and asleep when it was dark outside, making it more likely that someone would be home when the burglar entered into the home, therefore making it more likely that there would be violence. That made this a more serious crime than, for example, daytime housebreaking.

None of this makes the rule difficult to understand. And it's only when you start to plug in facts that the difficulties with the rule start to present themselves. Suppose your client broke a window in someone's house at 3:00 am and threw in a Molotov cocktail. Attempted arson perhaps, but was this burglary? You have breaking, the house of another, the hours of darkness, and the intent to commit a felony, but do you have entering? How about a client who broke into someone's house at 8:30 pm in the summer with the intent of stealing a painting? Is it sufficiently dark at 8:30 to constitute "the hours of darkness"?

Once facts present themselves, it quickly becomes clear that the burglary "rule" isn't complete. In fact, it's just a hook on which judicial interpretations of the "rule" can be hung until a full picture of the rule becomes clear. In fact, there are a wealth of cases that interpret the concept of "entering" to help courts and lawyers understand whether someone who stands outside a house can be said to have "entered" it through some object that they put into the house, and still other cases interpret the "hours of darkness" requirement to allow everyone to understand whether they include twilight.

The notion of a rule as a framework is important to our understanding of the concept, because the definitions we attempted back in the first paragraph are missing one crucial aspect of the concept of "rule." To understand it, let's go back to our arson example. And let's assume that someone can be said to have "entered" the house when standing outside and throwing something into it that would cause the house to burn down. But let's also assume that instead of a person standing outside, someone in a different part of the world hacked into the home owner's computer with the intent of stealing that person's identity. And let's suppose that there are no interpretations of the common law burglary rule that discuss this situation or anything like it; this rule was developed long before computers.

As lawyers, we can't just throw up our hands and say that since there's no interpretation of the rule, there's no way we can predict the result if someone is prosecuted for this behavior. Instead, we have to analyze the situation based on the principles that were expressed in the rule and its previous interpretations and then extend them into these new facts. We know, for instance, that physical entry into another's house isn't necessary in order to be considered "burglary," and that the use of a tool or other thing under the person's control—the word lawyers would use for this is "instrumentality," which certainly isn't the simplest or plainest word but does have the virtue of not using "thing" in describing the concept—is enough if that instrumentality does the entering. That suggests that sending the signals necessary to hack into the computer could also be seen as "entering," even though the hacker was thousands of miles away.

And while the hacker hasn't physically broken into the property, we know that the homeowner didn't invite the hacker in and that might be enough for a court to find that the hacker "broke" into the property; the hacker was "virtually" in the home, even if not physically. So we can predict that even though there isn't a rule interpretation that covers this specific situation, other rule interpretations have extended the range of the burglary "rule" sufficiently that it could be stretched to fit the computer hacker.

Of course, we could also make a policy argument that the rationale for the burglary rule—that people might be at home and asleep during the hours of darkness and that, therefore, this was a more serious crime—doesn't apply to a situation where the defendant's presence was "virtual," not actual. And if it were night where the computer was located, but day where the hacker was, did the hacker commit the alleged crime during the hours of darkness? Is it possible that this rule can't stretch far enough to cover this situation?

Perhaps. If you were actually confronted with this situation as a lawyer seeking to defend the hacker, you would have to assess the facts, plug them into the rule—including the interpretations of the rule that make up the complete, three-dimensional understanding of that rule—develop a theory that allowed your client's actions to fall outside of any reasonable interpretation of the rule, and then make that argument to the court. You would have to research the rule—in that word's broadest sense—then develop your theory, then conduct more research to test and refine your theory, then write the analysis down, and then refine your theory again once you saw how it looked when written out, and so on.

First, though, comes the rule. Understanding what rules are, and what rules apply to the facts of a case, is a crucial lawyering skill.

1. Rules, Regulations, and Statutes

Perhaps the easiest rules to recognize are the ones that are called "rules"; the federal rules of civil procedure, criminal procedure, and evidence, for example, and their state counterparts. Then there are "regulations," which are rules developed by agencies to define the limits of behavior in certain areas: the regulations put out by the Food and Drug Administration, for example, that govern the design, manufacture, marketing, and almost everything else to do with drugs and medical devices. And there are statutes, which are rules authorized by governments—either federal or state.

Rules, regulations, and statutes are usually presented in a logical and organized way that can deceive you into thinking they are complete. Here, for example, is Fed. R. Civ. P. 12 in its entirety. Take a moment to read it and then we'll discuss it:

Rule 12: Defenses and Objections: When and How Presented;
Motion for Judgment on the Pleadings;
Consolidating Motions;
Waiving Defenses;
Pretrial Hearing

(a)   Time to Serve a Responsive Pleading.

(1)   In General. Unless another time is specified by this rule or a federal statute, the time for serving a responsive pleading is as follows:

(A)   A defendant must serve an answer:

(i)   within 21 days after being served with the summons and complaint; or

(ii)   if it has timely waived service under Rule 4(d), within 60 days after the request for a waiver was sent, or within 90 days after it was sent to the defendant outside any judicial district of the United States.

(B)   A party must serve an answer to a counterclaim or crossclaim within 21 days after being served with the pleading that states the counterclaim or crossclaim.

(C)   A party must serve a reply to an answer within 21 days after being served with an order to reply, unless the order specifies a different time.

(2)   United States and Its Agencies, Officers, or Employees Sued in an Official Capacity. The United States, a United States agency, or a United States officer or employee sued only in an official capacity must serve an answer to a complaint, counterclaim, or crossclaim within 60 days after service on the United States attorney.

(3)   United States Officers or Employees Sued in an Individual Capacity. A United States officer or employee sued in an individual capacity for an act or omission occurring in connection with duties performed on the United States' behalf must serve an answer to a complaint, counterclaim, or crossclaim within 60 days after service on the officer or employee or service on the United States attorney, whichever is later.

(4)   Effect of a Motion. Unless the court sets a different time, serving a motion under this rule alters these periods as follows:

(A)   if the court denies the motion or postpones its disposition until trial, the responsive pleading must be served within 14 days after notice of the court's action; or

(B)   if the court grants a motion for a more definite statement, the responsive pleading must be served within 14 days after the more definite statement is served.

(b)   How to Present Defenses.

Every defense to a claim for relief in any pleading must be asserted in the responsive pleading if one is required. But a party may assert the following defenses by motion:

(1)   lack of subject-matter jurisdiction;

(2)   lack of personal jurisdiction;

(3)   improper venue;

(4)   insufficient process;

(5)   insufficient service of process;

(6)   failure to state a claim upon which relief can be granted; and

(7)   failure to join a party under Rule 19.

A motion asserting any of these defenses must be made before pleading if a responsive pleading is allowed. If a pleading sets out a claim for relief that does not require a responsive pleading, an opposing party may assert at trial any defense to that claim. No defense or objection is waived by joining it with one or more other defenses or objections in a responsive pleading or in a motion.

(c)   Motion for Judgment on the Pleadings.

After the pleadings are closed—but early enough not to delay trial—a party may move for judgment on the pleadings.

(d)   Result of Presenting Matters Outside the Pleadings.

If, on a motion under Rule 12(b)(6) or 12(c), matters outside the pleadings are presented to and not excluded by the court, the motion must be treated as one for summary judgment under Rule 56. All parties must be given a reasonable opportunity to present all the material that is pertinent to the motion.

(e)   Motion for a More Definite Statement.

A party may move for a more definite statement of a pleading to which a responsive pleading is allowed but which is so vague or ambiguous that the party cannot reasonably prepare a response. The motion must be made before filing a responsive pleading and must point out the defects complained of and the details desired. If the court orders a more definite statement and the order is not obeyed within 14 days after notice of the order or within the time the court sets, the court may strike the pleading or issue any other appropriate order.

(f)   Motion to Strike.

The court may strike from a pleading an insufficient defense or any redundant, immaterial, impertinent, or scandalous matter. The court may act:

(1)   on its own; or

(2)   on motion made by a party either before responding to the pleading or, if a response is not allowed, within 21 days after being served with the pleading.

(g)   Joining Motions.

(1) Right to Join. A motion under this rule may be joined with any other motion allowed by this rule.

(2) Limitation on Further Motions. Except as provided in Rule 12(h)(2) or (3), a party that makes a motion under this rule must not make another motion under this rule raising a defense or objection that was available to the party but omitted from its earlier motion.

(h)   Waiving and Preserving Certain Defenses.

(1) When Some Are Waived. A party waives any defense listed in Rule 12(b)(2)–(5) by:

(A)   omitting it from a motion in the circumstances described in Rule 12(g)(2); or

(B)   failing to either:

(i)   make it by motion under this rule; or

(ii)   include it in a responsive pleading or in an amendment allowed by Rule 15(a)(1) as a matter of course.

(2) When to Raise Others. Failure to state a claim upon which relief can be granted, to join a person required by Rule 19(b), or to state a legal defense to a claim may be raised:

(A)   in any pleading allowed or ordered under Rule 7(a);

(B)   by a motion under Rule 12(c); or

(C)   at trial.

(3) Lack of Subject-Matter Jurisdiction. If the court determines at any time that it lacks subject-matter jurisdiction, the court must dismiss the action.

(i)   Hearing Before Trial.

If a party so moves, any defense listed in Rule 12(b)(1)–(7) — whether made in a pleading or by motion — and a motion under Rule 12(c) must be heard and decided before trial unless the court orders a deferral until trial.

That's a lot of words, but then Rule 12 covers a lot of ground; when you consider how much ground, it's actually quite a concise rule. But the rule's drafters could only be this concise by leaving some things for others to decide. For example, all of the timing provisions have to read in conjunction with Rule 6 to see if that Rule's timing provisions modify the dates on which things are supposed to happen according to Rule 12, and Rule 6's recognition of the possibility of extensions of time also has to be considered. Then there's the timing of the "Motion for Judgment on the Pleadings." The rule says that it can be filed "after the pleadings are closed—but early enough not to delay trial…." How do you know if you're early enough or, perhaps even more important, not too late to file such a motion? You'll have to do some research to see how the courts have interpreted this part of the rule.

In fact, as perhaps you can imagine, there are a vast number of court decisions interpreting every part of this rule, and it is all those opinions, together with the language of Rule 12, that make up the "rule" for how and when to present defenses and objections and all the other things Rule 12 says it will do.

Let's look a little more closely at the language of this rule. In particular, let's assume that our firm has a client against whom someone has filed a complaint in federal court. Let's assume that the client is not the United States, nor is the client an Agency, Officer, or Employee of the United States. And let's say further that the complaint was served with the summons and complaint on April 1. We have to figure out, based on Rule 12's language (and avoiding, for the moment, any complications from Rule 6 or from court decisions), when the firm needs to file an answer to the complaint on the client's behalf.

A. Mandatory and Permissive Rules

Rule 12(a)(1)(A)(i) says that our client must file an answer within 21 days of the April 1 service of the summons and complaint, and Rule 12(a)(1)(A)(ii) says that if our client has timely waived service under Rule 4(d), the answer could be filed within 60 days after the request for a waiver was sent or within 90 days if it was sent to our client outside any judicial district of the United States.

Is there any wiggle room in this rule? Without trying to figure out what 21 days or 60 days or 90 days actually means, or what Rule 4(d) says, does the client have any other options? No, not according to the rule because it uses "must" and "must" is mandatory language. There's nothing left to choice in this part of the rule, and nothing optional about it. When a rule or regulation or statute (or court) says "must," or "shall"—another mandatory word often used in statutory and regulatory drafting—there's no ambiguity in the actions required to be taken. When a rule says something "must" or "shall" happen, then in order to comply with the language, you have to do what the rule says.

Although most statutory and regulatory drafters try to phrase language in the positive, it's also possible to have mandatory language that's negative. Rule 83(a)(2) of the federal rules of civil procedure, for example, states that "[a] local rule imposing a requirement must not be enforced in a way that causes a party to lose any right because of a nonwillful failure to comply." Just as with positive mandatory language, there's no ambiguity here, although the question of exactly what a "nonwillful failure to comply" with a local rule is one that would require further research.

Is there anything in Fed. R. Civ. P. 12 that is not mandatory? Sure. Look at the language of Rule 12(b), where the rule notes that a party "may" assert certain defenses by motion, including the famous 12(b)(6) motion alleging that the complaint fails to "state a claim upon which relief can be granted …". Language like "may" is permissive, acknowledging that a party or, sometimes, the court, has the capacity to take some action but has the discretion to take it or not take it.

But just when you thought things were simple, there's a little wrinkle in regulatory and statutory language. Even though "may" is a word of permission, and therefore signals a permissive rule, "may not" is language of prohibition, and if you see "may not" in a rule or statute, that's mandatory negative language; whomever is being addressed by the rule is forbidden from taking the described action. As with almost all things in the law, if you take things slowly and think through what the words actually mean, you won't get into too much trouble. The problem comes when the reader takes the understandably human course of looking for linguistic clues and then skimming over the rest of the text. If you did that, then a word like "may" might signal permissive rather than mandatory language and you would completely miss the point of the provision. It's a useful reminder to read everything slowly, carefully, and actively.

In fact, for the student of regulatory language, Rule 12 is a helpful laboratory because it has a combination of mandatory and permissive language, with mandatory and permissive provisions sometimes combined in the same sentence. In order to completely understand what a rule is saying, you need to be clear about whether action is required under the rule or is simply permitted. In order to better understand Rule 12, you might want to go back over its language, marking each piece of mandatory language in red and each discretionary, or permissive, provision in yellow. There's nothing wrong or childish in marking a copy of the rule in such a way as to make its meaning clearer to you, especially when the rule is as complicated as Rule 12.

B. Aspirational Rules

You can find two other types of "rule," although neither of them are very rule-like. Rule 1 of the Federal Rules of Civil Procedure states that "[t]hese rules govern the procedure in all civil actions and proceedings in the United States district courts, excepted as stated in Rule 81. They should be construed and administered to secure the just, speedy, and inexpensive determination of every action and proceeding." Should? That doesn't fit well into our definition of "rule" as a principle, regulation, or maxim, does it? At best, it's an aspiration—a hope that that's what the rules will do.

As a lawyer, you should always be thinking about the implications of language, and what the implications of this provision are if it's not followed. It doesn't seem as if there's a sanction or penalty if the rules are not construed or administered in such a way as to secure the just, speedy, and inexpensive determination of civil actions, does it? For that reason, it's unusual to find aspirational rules: they serve the general purpose of telling everyone what the drafters were hoping, but not much more.

C. Declarative Rules

The other type of "rule" is the declarative rule—one that makes a statement but that doesn't compel or permit action. Rule 2 of the Federal Rules of Civil Procedure gives us a good example of this: "[t]here is one form of action—the civil action." Actually, if one had read Rule 1 first, one would already know this because it says that the rules of civil procedure govern procedure "in all civil actions," and at the time these rules of civil procedure were drafted, there might have remained some question about whether one could bring an action in law or in equity, so the declaration served some purpose. But declaratory rules, like aspirational ones, don't require, prohibit, or permit conduct, so they aren't much help when trying to decide how to act or how a court might rule.

Such rules can be helpful when defining concepts, however. For example, here's part of 18 U.S.C. § 1111, the statute that defines federal murder:

(a)   Murder is the unlawful killing of a human being with malice aforethought. Every murder perpetrated by poison, lying in wait, or any other kind of willful, deliberate, malicious, and premeditated killing; or committed in the perpetration of, or attempt to perpetrate, any arson, escape, murder, kidnapping, treason, espionage, sabotage, aggravated sexual abuse or sexual abuse, child abuse, burglary, or robbery; or perpetrated as part of a pattern or practice of assault or torture against a child or children; or perpetrated from a premeditated design unlawfully and maliciously to effect the death of any human being other than him who is killed, is murder in the first degree.

Any other murder is murder in the second degree.

(b)   Within the special maritime and territorial jurisdiction of the United States,

Whoever is guilty of murder in the first degree shall be punished by death or by imprisonment for life;

Whoever is guilty of murder in the second degree, shall be imprisoned for any term of years or for life.

The declarative rule here—"murder is ..."—spells out what acts can be considered murder by the federal courts, although it's not the most helpful piece of language ever drafted. It tells us specifically what first degree murder is, but then unhelpfully adds that "[a]ny other murder" is second degree murder, leaving us to wonder what other types of "murder" there might be. Not every first degree murder, as defined here, or second degree murder is federal murder, of course; in order to decide if a particular murder could be considered federal murder, you would have to research what the "special maritime and territorial jurisdiction of the United States" might be. So just finding this rule—a statute in this case—will likely not answer all your questions, but the example shows the uses to which declaratory rules can be put.

2. Elements and Factors Test

In addition to the different types of rule—mandatory, permissive, aspirational, and declaratory—rules take different forms. The two main types of rule we deal with are elements tests and factors tests, so let's spend some time thinking about what those are and how they work.

Rule 23 of the Federal Rules of Civil Procedure is a helpful guide through these different rule forms since it contains both. Here's the first part of the rule:

Rule 23 Class Actions

(a)   Prerequisites. One or more members of a class may sue or be sued as representative parties on behalf of all members only if:
   (1)   the class is so numerous that joinder of all members is impracticable;
   (2)   there are questions of law or fact common to the class;
   (3)   the claims or defenses of the representative parties are typical of the claims or defenses of the class; and
   (4)   the representative parties will fairly and adequately protect the interests of the class.

(b) Types of Class Actions. A class action may be maintained if Rule 23(a) is satisfied and if:

(1) prosecuting separate actions by or against individual class members would create a risk of:

    (A) inconsistent or varying adjudications with respect to individual class members that would establish incompatible standards of conduct for the party opposing the class; or

    (B) adjudications with respect to individual class members that, as a practical matter, would be dispositive of the interests of the other members not parties to the individual adjudications or would substantially impair or impede their ability to protect their interests;

(2) the party opposing the class has acted or refused to act on grounds that apply generally to the class, so that final injunctive relief or corresponding declaratory relief is appropriate respecting the class as a whole; or

(3) the court finds that the questions of law or fact common to class members predominate over any questions affecting only individual members, and that a class action is superior to other available methods for fairly and efficiently adjudicating the controversy. The matters pertinent to these findings include:

    (A) the class members' interests in individually controlling the prosecution or defense of separate actions;

    (B) the extent and nature of any litigation concerning the controversy already begun by or against class members;

    (C) the desirability or undesirability of concentrating the litigation of the claims in the particular forum; and

    (D) the likely difficulties in managing a class action.

If you look at the first part of the rule, Rule 23 (a), you'll see an elements test. A class can only be certified if the four itemized elements are present. The rule states that "[o]ne or more members of a class may sue or be sued ... only if (1) ... (2) ... (3) ... and (4)." The "if ... and" construction is what tells you that this is an elements test.

By contrast, Rule 23 (b)(3) contains a factors test. The rule says that a court may certify a class where it finds that the common questions of law or fact (which the court had to find existed as part of elements test in Rule 23(a)(2)), predominate over any individual issues and that a class action is superior to other methods of adjudication. And then the rule gives a list of four matters that are pertinent to the court's findings, but notes that the pertinent matters "include" these four factors.

What's the difference between these two types of test? Simple: an "elements" test requires that all the different parts of the test be met before an action can be taken, while a "factors" test gives a list of things a court might consider but implicitly acknowledges that not all elements need be weighted the same, and that not all of them need be met. In the Rule 23 example, a court that found that the representative parties would not fairly and adequately protect the interests of the class could not certify a class because not all four of the 23(a) elements was satisfied. By contrast, a court that found that there would be extraordinary difficulties in managing the class could still certify the class if the court believed that, in this case, that rule 23(b)(3)(D) factor was less important that the other rule 23(b)(3) factors.

This can be confusing at first, especially when—as in the case of Rule 23—the rule mixes up the different forms of rules within the language of one rule. Nonetheless, the distinctions between the two forms of rule are important: the party seeking class certification doesn't have to win every part of the analysis under Rule 23(b)(3), for example, but must win every part of the Rule 23(a) analysis or else will lose the entire argument.

Conclusion

Rules are crucial to lawyers because the law is, viewed one way, a large assembly of rules. Understanding how to read them and understand what they require us or our clients to do, or not do, is therefore of paramount importance to us. And rules can be tricky to understand; their language is not always as clear as it might be and it's easy to get lost when trying to understand what's mandatory and what's permissive, what must be done and what must not be done, and whether a test has a list of required elements or a list of suggested factors.

As always in the law, the best approach is to take things slowly, read everything carefully, and if necessary, diagram the rule so that you can understand exactly what the rule requires. Once you understand that, your analysis will become much more straightforward.

Exercises

1. Take a look at a few of the Federal Rules of Civil Procedure you've been studying, or have studied, in your Civil Procedure class. Analyze them for structure. Are they elements tests or factors tests, or are they a combination of both? Can you find a declarative rule among the rules you've studied? A mandatory rule? A permissive rule? An aspirational rule? Compare your results with the person sitting next to you in class. Do you agree about the structure of the rule?

2. Look at some of the cases you've studied for one of your doctrinal courses, and identify the rules used by the court to reach its decision. Did the court derive that rule from one source or did the court need several sources to come up with the rule it applied to the facts of that case? Can you identify the nature of the rule you've selected? Again, compare the rule you've been looking at with the one chosen by the person sitting next to you in class and see if you both agree with your analysis of the rule.

Focus Questions

1. What is your definition for "rule"? What does your definition add that was missing from the definitions given by the text?

2. Although you might have had an instinctive reaction to the question of whether the attempted arsonist had committed burglary, do you see why you don't have enough information to reach a definitive conclusion on the issue?

3. The text proposes a policy argument in favor of the position that computer hacking is not as serious a crime as traditional burglary because the justification for the greater severity of burglary—the possibility of the burglar encountering am occupant of the house during the commission of the crime—is lacking in the case of a hacker. Are you persuaded by this argument? What counter-argument would you raise in opposition to this policy argument?

4. Have you studied rule language before? Had you marked the difference between the mandatory and persuasive portions of Rule 12 when you studied the rule in Civil Procedure? If you haven't studied the rule yet, did you notice those different parts of the rule as you read through it here?

5. Would you be confused if confronted with the mandatory (may not) and permissive (may) uses of "may"? Would it be less confusing if statutory drafters used a different term for mandatory negative rules?

6. Have you encountered aspirational and declarative rules in other contexts?

7. Are the differences between elements and factors tests clear to you? How will your analysis differ when confronted with an elements, as opposed to a factors, test? Which do you think is easier to argue in favor of, and which is easier to oppose? Why?

Chapter 24

Working with Statutes

What You Should Learn from This Chapter

This chapter discusses the challenges posed for legal analysts by statutes. It suggests a framework of three approaches used by courts to interpret statutes—the "textualist," "intentionalist," and "contextualist" strategies—and discusses what these judicial strategies might mean for us as lawyers. The chapter also discusses the role that the various canons of statutory construction still play in the analytical process, and concludes with a discussion of how lawyers interpret statutes in the work they write.

After reading this chapter, you should:

- have a clear understanding of the three principal interpretative strategies employed by judges when examining statutory language;
- understand the role played by the canons of construction; and
- have begun to consider how to use these various approaches to statutory interpretation when writing your legal analysis.

Statutes are laws enacted by legislatures. Some definitions would suggest that the legislatures wrote the laws as well, but that's not necessarily true these days so it's best to stick to what we know the legislature did, and that was to pass the legislation. It didn't become law when the legislature enacted it, of course; it still had to be signed into law by the head of the executive branch—the president, in the case of the federal government—or else the executive's veto had to be overridden. But a statute is a legislatively enacted law.

Not all statutes are well-drafted. But even the best of them leave many questions open once attorneys get hold of them and start to test what they mean. And it would be an unreasonable expectation for us to assume that a legislature could ever enact a statute that accurately predicted and answered every question that could be posed of it in advance of its being passed.

So statutes go before courts for interpretation, and it's up to the courts to decide what the statute means when considered in light of the facts of a case. How the court goes about that process, and how attorneys frame their arguments to persuade a court that it should reach a particular outcome, is the subject of this chapter.

1. The Three Modes of Judicial Statutory Interpretation

Courts usually take one of three approaches when it comes to deciding what a statute means. I'll call these approaches the textual, the intentional, and the contextual here, just for convenience. Not everyone will be familiar with these titles though, so you might not want to use them in your other classes. As long as you understand how these approaches work, you can call them what you like and other lawyers will understand what you mean.

One term that doesn't really help the discussion, even though it's a term that is often used in this context, is "strict construction." All three of the approaches we're discussing involve the "construction" of statutes, because "construing" statutes is just another word for interpreting them. In that sense, then, a judge employing any of these approaches is a "constructionist," even though that's not often what's meant by those using this term.

Viewed in this light, the "strict" qualification is meaningless because it just means that the interpreter is interpreting the statute strictly, but concepts of "strict" and "loose" don't attach meaning to the word "construction." All interpretation is interpretation, whether or not it's strict or loose. The term "strict construction" is often used to designate a judge who adopts a textualist approach to interpretation, and that term is more descriptive of the interpretative philosophy employed by that judge so it's best to stick to that and leave "strict construction" to others.

Before we start this discussion, it's important to note one thing. The act of statutory interpretation is often invoked as part of the political process, with "conservative" judges thought to be more likely to be textualists and "liberal" judges thought to be more likely to be contextualists. An intentionalist judge could be liberal or conservative, depending on the legislation.

These political concepts have no place in this discussion, though, and you should do your best to set them aside. As people, of course, we're entitled to—and should—hold our own political beliefs. But as lawyers we are only tangentially interested in politics, and then only to the extent of an awareness of how a judge's political philosophy might help us to predict how that judge might rule. A much more accurate gauge to that result, though, and a much more useful persuasion technique, is to understand how a judge approaches statutory interpretation. Once you understand that, you can ignore the judge's political beliefs, and your own, and focus instead on constructing an argument that will persuade readers to view the law the way your client wants them to. That's a more lawyerly process than relying on some fuzzy mapping of interpretative strategy to political belief.

2. The Textualist Approach

A textualist judge believes that the text of a statute is the only thing necessary to interpret it. All other considerations are irrelevant to such a judge; the last thing a textualist judge wants to hear is what the legislature "intended" to do, because a textualist judge believes that the language the legislature chose to express itself is the only legitimate tool to use when seeking to interpret statutory language.

Moreover, the textualist believes that to the extent language has progressed, and the meaning of words might have altered—significantly or subtly—such changes have no place in the interpretation of the statute; statutory language should mean what it meant at the time the statute was enacted, because the legislature could not have anticipated that, or how, language might change its meaning. The textualist will argue that the legislature intended for its language to carry the meaning the language had at the time the statute was enacted, and only that meaning. Any changes in linguistic meaning require changes in the legislation itself, and that is a task that can only be undertaken by the legislature.

A textualist judge might be persuaded to look at the legislative history of a statute in a clear case of ambiguity—where the language allows for two equally valid possible interpretations—or if there's a drafting error that is manifest from the statutory language. But even then, most textualist judges would argue that if the result of the statute is not ridiculous on its face—if, in other words, the "mistake" is not so bad that the statute makes no sense—then statutory language should be interpreted to mean what it says. If there is a mistake in statutory language, a textualist judge would likely say, and if the statute does not embody what the legislature intended to do, then it's up to the legislature to recognize and fix its own mistake. A textualist judge would say that the courts are not supposed to substitute their judgment for that of the legislature, and that their only role is to resolve disputes that might arise as the result of legislative action.

Almost all judges start from a textualist position, and hardly any judge would argue that the text of a statute is not the most important tool to use when interpreting that statute. Not all judges, though, would end their interpretative approach with textualism and some might move on to one of the other two principal interpretative philosophies.

3. The Intentionalist Approach

Intentionalist judges believe that their role is to interpret legislation in light of the legislature's intent. Although they would acknowledge that this intent is usually evident in the language the legislature chose when the statute was enacted, they might also argue that sometimes (often, these days) the language was not drafted by members of the legislature and that it is the principles behind the legislatures' decision to vote in favor of the legislation, not the specific language choices displayed in the final version of the legislation, that is important.

In order to glean the intent of the legislature, an intentionalist judge will almost certainly start with the language of the legislation but might not stop there. Documents reflecting the process by which the legislation was enacted—committee reports, testimony to the legislature (and the questions asked by legislators of those testifying before them), floor debates, speeches, and so on—all of these documents could be reviewed to determine what the legislature's intention was in enacting the legislation exactly as written.

The intention of the legislature can help judges fill interpretative gaps left by statutory language, and can help courts decide when the language of a statute might suggest a result that no one anticipated and that appears to be against the intention of those who drafted and spoke in favor of the legislation. A textualist would counter, though, that the "intention" of anyone cannot be determined after the fact, especially in documents so flawed as those that carry the legislative history of a piece of legislation. A legislator might insert comments into the transcript of a floor debate that were not made at the time of the debate and which might, if made at the time, have influenced some of those in attendance to vote differently from the way they did. The "intention" of a legislator, the textualist might say, is impossible for anyone—even the legislator—to recreate, and so the goal of interpreting language according to intention is irrational and illusory.

4. The Contextualist Approach

The contextualist judge acknowledges that both the textualist and intentionalist approaches have some merit, but argues that legislation can only be interpreted and understood in light of the circumstances of the times in which the legislation is being interpreted. The interpretation of a statute that was enacted over a hundred years ago, the contextualist would say, might have been appropriate for its time but times have changed and the language chosen by long-dead legislators should not be interpreted according to the meanings words carried at the time of enactment, but rather according to what words mean now.

Those who practice this approach—often called the "living language" approach to legislative interpretation—argue that legislation cannot be expected to anticipate the changes in society, any more than it can predict the possible questions that might be raised about the legislative language in the future, and that the intention of the legislature is equally irrelevant, since once legislation is passed into law it leaves the legislator's hands and moves in the judicial realm for interpretation. A contextualist would argue that the legislature should not be allowed to continue to exert control over its actions, either with legislation that was passed last week or last century. Accordingly, the contextualist would say, while the text and the legislative intention in passing that text are important starting places, they should begin the interpretative process, not end it.

5. What These Approaches Mean for Lawyers

The one thing that all three of these very different interpretative approaches agree on is the importance of the text: for the textualist, the text is all there is, for the intentionalist, the text is the best sign of the legislature's intent, and for the contextualist, the text is an important starting point in the search for the statute's current meaning. Although judges might end up in very different places for very different reasons, the text is of primary importance to all of them, so the text should be where all lawyers seeking to persuade a court of a statute's meaning should begin. If the result you're seeking falls squarely within the text's language, however that language is interpreted, or is barred by the statute's unambiguous language, giving the words of the statute their ordinary meaning (or their defined meaning; sometimes statutes will define certain terms and if they do, then those terms mean what they're defined to mean for the purposes of that statute), then your theory can depend on the statutory language without worrying about the legislature's intent or the contemporary context in which the language is being interpreted. It's highly unlikely that a judge would completely set aside the plain, unambiguous language of a statute in favor of a philosophically based interpretation that contradicts that language, and that judge's action would almost certainly be reversed on appeal.

If the result you seek is not readily discernible from the statute's language, though, your task is more complicated. And at some point in the process, you almost certainly will come into contact with the canons of statutory construction.

6. The Canons of Construction

Some might argue that by giving a collection of principles developed over time to aid in the interpretation of statutory language a name, judges and legal scholars are elevating these principles into something more cohesive and formalized. And it's certainly true that the word "canon" has overtones of religion and accepted authenticity that might make these canons of construction more law-like than they are.

The canons of construction have come in for a good deal of criticism over the years, especially from legal scholars who have pointed out that there are so many of them that one can pick and choose among them until one finds the particular canon that supports the decision you wanted to take in the first place; that they are, in effect, rationalizations for previously taken decisions rather than principles that guide a court to reach a particular result.[1] This might be going too far. Many of the canons are helpful principles that are commonly accepted and provide a level playing field for everyone when approaching the difficult question of deciding what a statute means. For example, the principle expressed earlier—that when interpreting a statute one should give the words used by the legislature their plain and ordinary meaning—is one of the generally accepted canons of construction.

Perhaps one of the reasons some canons of construction are viewed with some suspicion today is the Latin names by which they are known. For instance, the principle that when a statute lists an inclusive group of things, anything not listed should be omitted from the statute's scope seems like a reasonable way to interpret the statute, but that principle is a little harder to understand, and perhaps to accept, when given its Latin name *Expressio unius est exclusio alterius* ("the express mention of one thing excludes all others").

Another of the canons—*Ejusdem generis* ("of the same kind")—is a little more difficult to accept. It says, in essence, that if a statute lists a series of specific things and then makes a more general reference, that general reference is limited to other things which are related to the more specific thing. The example frequently given to explain this explanation is that if a statute lists motorbikes, cars, vans, trucks, and other motor vehicles, the "other motor vehicles" reference would not include helicopters, because even though they are vehicles, and they are driven by motors, they fly rather than travelling

---

1. This position was most famously expressed by Professor Karl Llewellyn in a law review article from 1950. Karl Llewellyn, *Remarks on the Theory of Appellate Decisions and the Rules or Canons About How Statutes Are to Be Construed*, 3 Vand. L. Rev. 395 (1950).

on the land, and that is a specific quality shared by the motor driven vehicles in the itemized list. On the other hand, since a helicopter is patently a "motor driven vehicle," a court applying the plain meaning canon of construction could reasonably conclude that a helicopter should be included within the scope of the statute. You can see how the canons of construction can be manipulated to suit a particular result.

You'll likely encounter another few canons of construction as you seek to interpret various documents. For instance, in a relatively new member of the canon, the Supreme Court has held that where an administrative agency administers a statute, the federal courts should defer to that agency's reasonable interpretation of a term the court finds to be ambiguous.[2] Courts also have held that they should resolve ambiguities in criminal statutes in favor of defendants, that they should seek to avoid statutory interpretations that lead to Constitutional problems for the statute, and that they should avoid interpretations that might lead to absurd or unjust results. But this is only a very incomplete list; it would take a lot of space and time to construct a list of all the canons of statutory construction, and such a list would show all sorts of contradictions and exceptions.

7. How to Interpret Statutes in Your Work

The general rule of legal writing—that it's better to paraphrase source language than quote directly from the source—should probably be avoided when it comes to statutes (and regulations as well). Experienced lawyers can avoid the problems that paraphrasing can cause, but starting lawyers are much better advised to quote the relevant language, although only the relevant language, directly from the statute. This is because the precise language used in the statute is so important, and any language changes might subtly affect the meaning a court would give to the statute. You certainly could construct statutory language that was better suited to your client's interests, but that isn't a helpful technique because your work could, and would, be criticized as inventing language that wasn't written by the legislature.

This isn't to say, though, that your own language isn't going to be important when expressing the rule you've identified as coming from the statute. Once you give your reader the exact language from the statute, you'll likely have to explain what that language means in the context of your analysis.

Once you've identified the relevant language for your analysis, and the rule you've drawn from that language, you should check to see that its meaning is plain and unambiguous. If it is, and especially if there are court opinions that agree with you, then you can apply that language directly to your analysis. And it's worth noting here that most statutory language is clear and unambiguous. You need to know what to do in case the language you seek to interpret is unclear or has potential ambiguities in it, but most legislation—especially legislation written recently—is clear on its face.

If there are ambiguities, though, you'll need to resolve them. Court opinions are probably the most helpful sources for assistance in the interpretation of ambiguous language,

---

2. *Chevron v. Natural Resources Def. Council*, 467 U.S. 837 (1984).

so research those first. If you can't find a decision to help you, then the canons of construction—because they are court-based principles of interpretation, and because they are so wide-ranging that one or more will almost certainly help you to resolve the perceived statutory ambiguity in your client's favor, are probably your next stop.

The legislative history of the statute is perhaps the last place you should look for help in interpreting the statute. That's not because you won't find help there; you certainly might find something that explains why the legislature used the language it did in seeking to express itself on a particular issue. But courts these days are increasingly hostile to legislative history as a source of help when interpreting statutes, so you might find that the information you derive from the legislative history, even though helpful to your position, might not be that persuasive to a judge.

Nonetheless, if that's the only place where you can find support for the interpretation you're proposing, or if the legislative history provides strong corroboration of an interpretation you've been able to draw using other techniques like the canons, you should certainly know about it and should weigh the advantages and disadvantages of using it. Even if a court doesn't rely on the legislative history in reaching its decision, the fact that it's consistent with your interpretation might exert some subtle influence on the deciding judge.

Conclusion

Statutes are vitally important to practicing lawyers today, so it's good to become as familiar as possible with the way they work, how to interpret them, and how to use them to support your arguments while you're in law school. And while judges can have very different approaches to their interpretation, the key for lawyers is to figure out what the words in the statute mean, what other courts have said about the language relevant to your analysis, and to remember the canons of construction that might apply to your situation. Understanding why the legislature acted in the way it did, to the extent the legislative history can tell you that, is also a useful tool to have; the legislative history might not be the most persuasive piece of evidence you can offer to the court to support your position, but it helps to know if it supports, or contradicts, the position you're planning to take.

Focus Questions

1. Had you read a statute before coming to law school? Have you read a complete statute since you have been in law school or have you only read the edited versions of statutes often found in law school textbooks? Have you found statutes to be easy to understand? Easier or more difficult than cases?

2. Have you heard the term "strict construction" before when applied to a judge's or Supreme Court Justice's interpretative philosophy? Are you persuaded by the text's description of the term as "unhelpful"?

3. Are the concepts of "textual," "intentional," and "contextual" helpful to your consideration of statutory interpretation? Recognizing that it is a judge's philosophy that concerns lawyers when working in their professional capacity, do you have a personal approach to statutory interpretation? What about that approach persuades you that it is correct? Do you think that your personal approach to statutory interpretation will make it easier or more difficult for you to persuade judges of a position or do you think it will make no difference?

4. Have you heard of the Canons of Construction in your other classes? What Canons have you studied? If a legislature assumes that a court will apply the Canons of Construction when interpreting statutory language, how should a textualist judge apply an extra-textual Canon? Suppose the legislature shows no awareness of the Canons of Construction. How would that affect your answer? Of what value are the Canons of Construction to an intentionalist judge? A contextualist judge?

5. Do you understand why the text suggests that you quote directly from statutes rather than paraphrasing them?

6. How helpful do you think legislative history will be in your use of statutes? Should it be more or less helpful, or do you think courts use legislative history appropriately?

PERSUASION

Chapter 25

How to Persuade

What You Should Learn from This Chapter

This chapter discusses how lawyers try to persuade others to take a position favorable to their clients. In particular, it proposes that telling people what to think is rarely, if ever, an effective persuasive technique, something many law students and junior lawyers forget. The chapter proposes that most law students already know the most important persuasive techniques, because they are little different from the various strategies they have already been using to persuade others to do something. The chapter offers various persuasive techniques that can be deployed effectively by lawyers in the interests of their clients, although it acknowledges that these are just some in a long list of persuasive techniques available to lawyers.

After reading this chapter, you should:

- understand that telling someone is not an effective way of persuading them;
- understand that many of the strategies you employed before law school to persuade people are likely going to be the strategies you continue to employ as lawyers;
- understand that as opposed to your life before law school, your audience as a lawyer frequently wants to be persuaded; and
- have considered a variety of possible persuasive techniques and decided which might be helpful to you.

There's a trick to persuading people to think the way you want them to think. It's been developed over years of careful study and thought about persuasive techniques and is being revealed in this book for the first time. This persuasive trick is guaranteed not to fail and it is beyond question that it will work in any context and with any audience. Once you learn this trick, and can use it smoothly and efficiently, you'll be invincible as a lawyer; you'll win every argument, you'll be successful in your career, and you'll be a client magnet. This trick will change your life forever.

There's no trick. Of course there isn't. You didn't believe a word of that last paragraph, even though maybe you wanted to. We would all like there to be a secret that, once learned, would make our jobs easy and would be ours to deploy at will. But common sense and experience in the way the world works should tell you that there are precious few tricks in anything, and that something as nebulous and complex as persuasion can't be distilled and bottled like a magical elixir.

But let's think a little more about that first paragraph because there's a powerful truth hidden away in it. In it, I told you there was a trick to persuading people, and yet you didn't believe me. This is crucially important, because it tells you that just *telling* people something isn't enough to persuade them that it's true. In fact, it's hardly ever the case that people will believe something just because you tell them it's so. And that, in turn, is a vital lesson for the legal advocate. As lawyers, we do a lot of telling, but the telling alone isn't going to persuade anyone of anything. And that, as it turns out, is—if not the trick to persuasion—at least a critical aspect of persuasive writing that every legal writer should remember.

Should you doubt this advice, consider something you believe in that others in this country feel passionately opposed to. It doesn't matter what it is; there are many so-called "hot button" social and political issues today that divide many of us, and you don't have to reveal to anyone which of these issues you've picked or what your position is. But think about the times you've heard the issue debated—on television, in person, or in print. The people opposed to your position have argued passionately and as-sertively in support of what they believed, and they have made many strong claims to try to persuade the audience that their position, not yours, is the correct one. Were you swayed? Did you change your position as a result of those arguments? Probably not. You likely heard what those opponents to your position had to say, listened to the other side as well, and then continued to believe what you believed before.

That's a perfectly reasonable response and this isn't a criticism of your position or your unwillingness to change it. But it is intended to suggest that it's very difficult to persuade someone based solely on telling them why a position is correct, especially if that person is predisposed to not agree with you. No matter how much you believe in your position, and no matter how passionately you argue in favor of it, you will have to do more to prevail, especially when asserting a position in writing, where things are more clinical and less impassioned.

This chapter will deal with some of the techniques—not tricks—we use to help to persuade others of the positions we take, discussed in no particular order. Persuasive writing is difficult, because someone will doubtless be trying just as hard as you to persuade the reader of a position that's the opposite of the one you're taking. But persuasive writing is also not as difficult as you might think for two good reasons: first, you already know how to do it, and second, the person to whom you're writing wants to be persuaded.

1. You Already Know How to Persuade Someone

You must have learned, by this point in your lives, how to persuade people to do things. We persuade people every day; sometimes to do things they want to do anyway and sometimes to do things they really don't want to do. The techniques are the same in both cases, and they're the same as the techniques you'll be using as persuasive writers. The vocabulary might change, and the ways in which you seek to persuade legal readers might have some superficial differences to them, but these are cosmetic differences only; the techniques themselves are easily identified as being the same.

So how do you persuade people? Almost certainly, you identify all the facts in a situation—both good and bad—and look for ways to stress the good while minimizing the bad. You're probably very sensitive to your audience and try to make arguments that will appeal to that person, and if you're sensible, you've tested your arguments beforehand to make sure that they're consistent both with the known facts (and any inferences that can reasonably be drawn from them) and with common sense, so you're not making outlandish claims that no one will accept. You've probably identified the ways in which the person you're seeking to persuade will benefit if they go along with your position, or conversely, what bad things will happen if they don't go along with it. Most importantly, though, you probably understand that the best way to persuade anyone of anything is to make them think that it's their idea to begin with. If it's already their idea, they can't very well disagree with it, can they?

So whether it's asking a parent for the car keys, getting someone to see a movie that you really want to see, try some food they haven't eaten before, or any one of the countless other things we try to persuade other people to do, you've spent your life refining your persuasive skills until you become a master of persuasion. In fact, you might even have been told that you were a natural lawyer because you were so skilled at persuading others to do things. If someone has told you that, believe them: the traits that person identified in you are exactly the traits you'll need as a lawyer. And if someone hasn't seen that skill in you yet, that just means you've been so good at persuading them that they haven't even realized you were doing it.

2. Your Audience Wants to Be Persuaded

And things are easier—in some ways—for you as a lawyer, because your audience typically is predisposed to being persuaded. It's true that you will probably have an opponent who will be trying hard to persuade your reader of something else, but in the law the reader very often has to choose between one of the two options being presented by the lawyers: choosing to do nothing, or coming up with a completely different plan, is usually not an option.

You might instinctively disbelieve this, but if you think a little more closely about the situation most judges, for example, find themselves in, you'll understand what I mean. A judge is a professional decision-maker. That's what judges are there for, in fact: to make decisions about a case after carefully considering the relevant facts and law. The parties present the judge with those facts and the law each side believes to be relevant, and lawyers—of course—put their own interpretations on the facts and law. But a judge is usually required to choose between one position or the other and to rule in favor of one side or the other. The judge can take the facts and law and come up with a different rationale for the decision, but almost always one side wins and one side loses.

Viewed in this light, judges need to make decisions—lots of them—every day, and the more readily you can persuade a judge that your position is the correct one, the easier you'll be making the judge's job. So while judges know that both sides will be trying to persuade them to do one thing or another, they also know that they have to choose one side or the other as a winner in each of the contests that come before them. This means that half your job as a persuader is already done for you just by virtue of the context in which you're seeking to persuade your reader of something; someone is going to win and someone is going to lose. A no-decision isn't an option and neither is a draw.

3. The Best Way to Win Is to Be Right

The most obvious advice anyone can give you about persuasion is this: the best way to persuade anyone of anything is to be right. If the facts and the law (if you're a lawyer) point objectively and inevitably to only one conclusion, and if that's the conclusion for which you're arguing, then your chances of winning are very good. You might still lose, of course: no sensible person in the legal business gives out guarantees of anything. But if the result you're seeking is the only logical one under the circumstances, then you have to like your odds of persuading the reader of your position.

Fine as far as it goes, of course, but that isn't very far. What does "being right" mean, anyway, especially when there are at least two possible, and divergently opposed, interpretations of the same facts and law? Well, if law school has taught you anything by now, it's that there hardly ever is one answer to anything. Almost everything can be argued, debated, or interpreted, so in that sense there is no "right" answer to any question that requires the intervention of the legal system. If there were only one "right" answer to everything, lawyers and even judges wouldn't be necessary; clients could go directly to justice machines with access to "the law," whatever that might be, and once they'd entered their positions into the machine, the answer would present itself.

That isn't the way things are, so that suggests this isn't what's meant by an attorney needing the "right" answer. The mistake was in maintaining that there's only one "right" answer. In fact, both sides in a case can have the "right" answer, and the judge's job is to pick between them. In order to prevail, attorneys have to start from the position that that their client's position is a "right" one, given the facts and the law.

What this means, in practical terms, is that the position you're arguing in favor of has to be consistent with all the facts and all the law that's relevant to the position. If there's an inconvenient fact, you have to have a convincing reason why that fact should not prevent your client from winning, and if there's a case that goes the wrong way— from your perspective—you have to be able to distinguish it from your case. If you can't do these things, you need to come up with a different theory because your position will easily be seen as the "wrong" one by the judge. And even if the judge is having difficulty seeing why you're wrong, you can be assured that the other side will be delighted to point out the problems in your position in graphic detail.

It's important to understand that legal argument differs from many other disciplines, in that we are presented with the position we need to assert at the beginning (the client wins or, to be more negative about it, the other side loses), and then we assemble the facts and the law to support that ultimate position. We call the argument we construct to support the ultimate position the "theory of the case" but this type of "theory" differs greatly from a scientific one where a "theory" is a prediction of a possible outcome and you reach an ultimate conclusion only after a careful consideration of the evidence. In the law, the "theory" follows, and supports, the conclusion rather than coming first and being subject to change based on experimental results.

But a legal "theory of the case" is very similar to the types of persuasive arguments you have made in your life, where the end goal was the starting point (you wanted to borrow your parents' car, or you wanted to go and see a particular movie) and you gathered up the facts and the precedent to support your pre-determined position.

4. The Truth Is Crucial

It's impossible to over-state this: no one wins a legal argument by being untruthful. Where facts are concerned, you cannot be anything less than completely honest. Facts can be contested, of course; it's entirely reasonable for you to argue that something isn't a fact, so long as you have evidence to back up your position. So if your client claims that a traffic light was green, and the other side maintains that the traffic light was red, you have a legitimate factual dispute and, if that dispute is material to the ultimate issue, neither party will win in writing and the case will go to a fact-finder for resolution. But if you have no support for your position, you can't merely argue that the light was green because that would be more convenient for your client.

Scrupulous truthfulness also means that you can't ignore, or hide from, bad facts just because they are bad. Not only would doing so be counter-productive, because the other side will quickly point out your omission, but it would also be dishonest, because you have a professional obligation as an officer of the court to not deceive the court. So telling the truth—the whole truth and nothing but the truth—is not just good argumentation technique, it's your professional obligation.

5. Don't Oversell

Remember the opening paragraph of this chapter, and its assurance that the persuasive writing "trick" I was going to reveal would work? I promised that "it was beyond question" that the trick would work in any context. Did you believe me? Of course not. That's a good sign that aggressive language won't help you if the position you're seeking to advance doesn't have any substance to it. Just saying something won't necessarily make it so.

In fact, most professional decision-makers—and judges are certainly that—are very careful to note language like this because it often points out a particular weakness in the advocate's position that the advocate is trying to cover up with language rather than logic. Some might think that an approach like this is akin to the understandably human, but ultimately unhelpful, strategy of making noise to reassure ourselves when something scares us: the phrase sometimes used to describe this tendency is "whistling past the graveyard," the tendency to make noise to scare away ghosts when you're afraid they might appear. It might make you feel better, but you've probably realized by now that such a strategy also draws attention to yourself, at precisely the time when you might not want anyone—especially ghosts—to notice you.

The same danger accompanies the strategy of overly aggressive claims on behalf of your analysis. If a lawyer writes that "it is clear that" something is the way the lawyer claims, many judges will pounce on that assertion as a sign that the position is not clear at all and that the lawyer has no real support for the claim being made. And a phrase like "it is undisputed that ..." is just asking for the other side to point out that there is, indeed, a dispute over that issue. If there truly is no dispute, you can highlight it by noting that your opponent does not dispute a point, but unless you are certain that that's the case, you're well-advised to stay away from language like this because it walks you unnecessarily into trouble.

This is not to say that your analysis should not be zealous or committed. On the contrary, you're writing to try to persuade someone that your position, and not that of the other party, should prevail and everything you do should be directed towards that goal. That will require you to think and argue zealously on behalf of your client. But it's your thinking and analysis that should reflect this zeal, not the language you use to express that thinking.

6. Don't Be Critical of the Other Side's Lawyer

This recommendation that you avoid aggressive language also applies to the way you refer to your opponents. It's the rare written argument, in fact, that should refer to the other side's lawyer at all, and if you have to refer to that lawyer you should avoid any personal attacks. There are few things that are more likely to irritate a judge than such attacks being leveled at another member of the bar and to engage in this kind of behavior is unpersuasive and illogical: personal attacks like this are known as *ad hominem* and this strategy, in which an advocate argues that the other side's position is wrong because the person making the argument is in some way a bad person, is widely recognized as a logical fallacy.

It can happen, of course, that you have to challenge another attorney's behavior. But if you find yourself in this situation, you should avoid making such a challenge in the context of a legal argument you're making; it should ideally be in a separate pleading or, at the very least, in a separate section where it can be quarantined from the rest of your argument. And even when criticizing an attorney's behavior, you should do so in professional language that presents the facts and, as much as possible, avoids characterizing the attorney's actions.

7. Let the Reader Characterize

In fact, avoiding characterization is a good idea for any lawyer seeking to persuade a reader of something. Characterization fails to persuade for the same reason as the first paragraph of this chapter failed to persuade you of anything; it's telling the reader that something is the way it is rather than allowing the reader to come to that conclusion. The reader might, in the end, agree with you, but you likely won't have persuaded the reader to come to that conclusion.

Let's consider an obvious example. If I say "Mr. Smith was driving in a reckless manner when he hit Ms. Jones as she crossed the road," then that, alone, won't persuade you that Mr. Smith was, in fact, driving in a reckless manner. But if I tell you that "Mr. Smith was driving at 70 mph in a 35 mph zone, and had driven through two stop signs without slowing down before hitting Ms. Jones as she crossed the road while she had a green light and traffic travelling in Mr. Smith's direction had a red light," your first reaction is likely that Mr. Smith was being reckless.

The point here is that by supplying the reader with the facts, you allow the reader to reach a conclusion without characterizing the facts for the reader, and the most effective way of persuading anyone of anything is to make them believe that the idea is their own. By staying away from supplying your own characterization of Mr. Smith's actions, you have allowed the reader to supply the characterization, and the reader is much more likely to accept that one as correct when allowed to reach it without being told.

Of course, sometimes the legal standard with which you're working requires some element of characterization. If the law requires that a plaintiff prove that a defendant acted willfully or recklessly, for example, then if you're the plaintiff's lawyer you can't completely avoid using those words when describing the defendant's actions. But you can wait until the reader has been allowed to reach that conclusion first before you confirm it by reference to the legal test.

8. Be As Concise As Possible

Just for a second, imagine that you're a judge. How do you picture yourself? Sitting in black robes on a bench in a courtroom, grilling attorneys with insightful questions that go to the heart of the weaknesses in their arguments? Well, that's certainly how you would be some of the time. But how about first thing in the morning? Judges don't sleep in their robes (well—very few of them) and when they look in the mirror while brushing their teeth in the morning, they don't see "the judge," they see the person they've always been. Similarly, when they sit down at their desk at work, at home, or—perhaps—on the sofa in front of the television, and open up a brief in a case over which they're presiding, they're both "the judge" and a real person who reacts with predictable human responses to what they see.[1]

What does this have to do with persuasion and conciseness? Everything. Because judges don't lose the capacity to be bored and frustrated with unnecessarily long legal arguments just because they're appointed to be judges. In fact, judges are more likely to react badly to overly long written arguments than are most people because they have so much reading to do: the idea of a judge reading a brief on the sofa in front of a football or basketball game is not as far-fetched as you might think because they have so much reading to do, and if your brief fails to engage them because it's so long and poorly written, the judge might prefer to watch the game and allow a law clerk to summarize your arguments. The law clerk might even do a good job, but do you really want to give up the chance to speaking directly to the judge and are you happy about the idea that someone else might speak on your behalf?

I hope not. You should want to engage in a vigorous and spirited intellectual conversation with the judge through the medium of your writing and if you're happy at the

---

1. My thanks to Professor Mary-Beth Beasley, who sharpened my thinking about these issues.

thought of the judge giving up on your work, you should consider a different profession. But when you think about how much a judge has to read every day, you have to realize that any conversation you have with the judge needs to be as short and focused as possible.

In practical terms, this means you'll need to edit your first draft many times to make it as concise and tight as possible, cutting words—and sometimes even arguments—in order to keep your document as short as possible without losing anything crucial. You should shoot for a document that is much shorter than the maximum allowed for, whether the limits are set by number of pages or number of words. When you're editing—and you really can't do this when you're drafting a document, only when you're editing it—you need to think about every word, clause, sentence, paragraph, and section in your document: if another word would better convey meaning, and save you a couple of words in the process, you should use it; if a sentence or two could be cut without altering the meaning of a paragraph, they should go; if a paragraph doesn't do the work it should be doing in moving your argument forward, you should remove it; and if a section doesn't make your argument stronger, it isn't necessary and should be eliminated.

This can be a painful process. But only by being ruthless about your work can you make it as short as it can be and only by doing that will you have a chance to persuade the judge about anything. Judges will say that they can tell if a brief contains a winning argument or not just by looking at how thick it is, with thin winning over thick every time. Even if that's an exaggeration, it probably isn't far from the truth. And besides, if the judge believes that, then it might become a self-fulfilling prophecy. So keep your documents as concise as possible, and remember that "brief" should also describe the substance, not just the form, of many court documents.

9. Only Fight the Fights You Need to Win

Part of the process of cutting your work down can involve eliminating unnecessary arguments. This is tricky, of course, because no lawyer wants to abandon any argument that might stand a chance of persuading a judge to rule in the lawyer's client's favor. And how does one know which argument is likely to attract a judge's attention and persuade the judge of the correctness of your client's position? Many lawyers lack the confidence to make that decision, and so leave their briefs cluttered with arguments that are, at best, collateral to the principal argument they want to make. And by doing so, they drown out the voice of that principal argument with the chorus of less important arguments, making it difficult or impossible for the judge to hear it.

There are times, of course, when you have to make many arguments. And if you do, then you have no choice but to make all of them. But more often than not, you can do away with several of the arguments you have worked on without doing any violence to your client's position and that almost certainly will help make your principal argument clearer and easier to appreciate.

How do you know which argument is your principal one and which arguments are ancillary to it? It differs, of course, with every set of facts and law, but try this: after you've written your entire brief, with all the arguments in (and this might seem like a wasteful process but you have to write it down before you can really see how strong or weak an argument is) review each part of the argument and ask yourself if it's necessary in order for your client to win. If it is, keep it in for now, but if it isn't, try cutting that part of the argument (and pasting it into a holding document; you might change your mind and it would be better to not have to rewrite that section) and then review the document again. If you don't miss the cut argument, it probably wasn't essential to your client's position and you can do without it.

10. Put Your Best Argument First

While you're evaluating the relative strength of your various arguments, consider taking the strongest one and putting it first in your brief or whatever document you're putting together. You might have been taught that it's best to end with a strong argument, and there are some types of writing in which that might be good advice. But to do that you would have to put your weaker arguments ahead of your strongest argument and, frankly, your reader might not stay with you long enough to get to the strongest argument. Better to get the best argument in front of the reader as soon as possible and give yourself your best chance of persuading the reader that your client's position is the correct one.

Some legal tests are organized in a particular order and your best argument might have to do with, say, the third prong of a four-pronged test. In a case like this, should you continue to place that argument first or should you follow the order in which the test is laid out because it would seem strange to the reader to see the test argued out of order? Unless there's a compelling reason, and the flow of the argument really doesn't work in any other way, it's almost certainly best to continue with the principle of placing the strongest argument first. It's possible that you might even concede some of the prongs of the test; if you argue that your client's actions were not the proximate cause of a plaintiff's injuries, for example, you might concede that your client owed the plaintiff a duty. If your proximate cause argument is stronger than an argument that the duty your client owed was not breached, though, it should come first, even though the familiar order of the negligence tort would have breach coming before proximate causation.

If you find you need to argue in a different order than that suggested by the legal test you're using, it's usually a good idea to explain this to the reader in the explanatory paragraph you've written to set out what your analysis will cover. It's always good to give your reader as few surprises as possible.

11. Try to Be Positive Rather Than Negative

We're lawyers, not psychologists, but when we're seeking to persuade people we have to think about what motivates our readers. And it's a general belief among lawyers that people are more motivated to be positive rather than to be negative. This suggests that as lawyers, we should try—as much as possible—to frame our theories in positive, as opposed to negative, terms.

What does this mean? A couple of simple examples might help. When articulating your question presented, try to frame it in such a way that the answer to your question is "yes," rather than "no." And when you're asking a judge for something, try to frame it in such a way that you're asking for the judge to grant relief rather than deny it. Obviously, circumstances can make this difficult to achieve in all situations; when you're opposing a motion, for example, instead of moving to seek relief you're inevitably going to be asking the judge to deny the other side's motion. But if you keep in mind the idea that you're trying to get the judge to rule in favor of your client, rather than arguing against the other side's position, you'll find opportunities to be positive even when you might not expect them.

This also means that you should focus on your own arguments as much as possible, and on your opponent's arguments as little as possible. If you think about it, it's very difficult to focus on the other side's arguments and remain positive, and that's as good a reason as any to concentrate on your side's position. The other principal reason, of course, is that the more time you spend talking about the other side's argument, the more you validate it. You don't want the judge to give the other side's argument any credence at all, so best not to focus your attention on it.

None of this is substantive, of course, nor will it substitute for a substantive argument: if you have the facts and the law on your side, you should win even if you're relentlessly negative in your approach, and no amount of positivity will rescue you if the facts and the law are implacably against you. But being positive sets a tone that can help to persuade a judge to consider ruling in your favor in the more close calls that form the majority of cases lawyers argue. And there's no harm in trying to take every advantage legitimately offered to you in your quest to prevail on behalf of your client. So try to be as positive as possible.

12. Write in Clear, Simple Language

Picture your judge again. Look around to see where the judge is reading your brief. Do you see the piles of other documents the judge has to read? The judge has to read other briefs in this case and briefs from numerous other cases as well, and there are memos from law clerks about cases, court opinions that are the result of research into the cases the judge is already working on, new court decisions the judge needs to read in order to stay current with developments, correspondence from any number of different people, emails from colleagues, committee documents from the numerous committees on which the judge serves, newspapers to stay informed about the world—the list is seemingly endless. If lawyers are professional writers, judges are professional readers, consuming hundreds of thousands of words each month.

Now picture your judge reading your brief. It's filled with Latin words and phrases, long sentences filled with multisyllabic words and complex internal grammatical structures that are correct but take a lot of time and care to understand; it's a brilliant piece of legal analysis, and there's nothing incorrect about its use of the English language, but it's very difficult to read. And just to complete your picture, consider this. Judges might be professional readers, but they're not compelled to read everything that comes before them. They read so much, in fact, that they hire other people—in the form of law clerks—to do a lot of reading for them.

Now. How much time do you think the judge is going to spend reading your brief? Do you think the judge will set everything aside, get out a pen and a notepad—and probably a legal dictionary and a regular dictionary as well—and start methodically working through your brief, making notes to make sure that anything that's potentially unclear is checked and clarified? Why do you think the judge will be willing to devote hours more than usual to reading this particular brief? Is it because you wrote it? Why should you receive preferential treatment from this judge? Or is it because a judge's job is to read everything filed in all cases the judge is considering? But isn't the judge's job really to make decisions in those cases? Reading every word might or might not be a part of that process.

Or might the judge stop after the first page or so of a difficult-to-read document, call in a law clerk, and ask the law clerk to summarize the principal arguments in a short memo that the judge can read on the sofa some evening? Suppose your answer is that you expect the judge to persevere and continue reading your brief. How happy do you think the judge will be in having to take so long to decipher the meaning of your analysis? Be honest in your answers.

It's not difficult to see what answers I'm expecting you to give, but it's difficult to believe that given what I've described, you would expect the judge to do anything but give up on the brief and call in the law clerk. In the rare case of a judge who keeps going, it's difficult to imagine the judge being happy about it or with you as the writer of the brief, or, more importantly, with your client.

What does this exercise tell us? Actually, a lot. It tells us that just because a piece of writing is "correct," that doesn't mean that it's readable or that it will be read. It tells us that your legal writing professor doesn't just talk about plain English because it's a pet idea of the discipline; plain English is the better choice for legal documents because it's a style that makes it more likely a document will be read by the person it's written for. And it tells us that you don't need to be persuaded of this because you already know it to be true.

This exercise also tells us that the best way to persuade someone of something is to construct an argument that they will listen to or, in the case of writing, will read. If you write something that's so dense and difficult to get through that the judge gives it to a law clerk to translate, you've lost the attention of a person who can make the decision to rule in favor of your client's position. Put simply, if the judge won't read your brief, you've made it substantially less likely that your client will win. That's not what lawyering is supposed to be about.

13. Dress Your Writing Appropriately for Court

Just as you should try to write your document in language that makes it likely your judge will read it, you should make your document look as appealing to read as possible. That means spending some time thinking about the cosmetic appearance of your document.

Some courts severely restrict your ability to make your documents appear more user-friendly and if the court to which you're writing has specific form or style requirements—use of Courier font, for example—then you have no choice but to follow those requirements; the first rule of persuasive advocacy is to do what you're told to do, because if you don't there's a good chance that your brief won't even make it into the court clerk's office.[2] No one ever said this but they should have done: the unfiled brief persuades no one.

But if your court doesn't have any specific requirements that restrict your ability to use different fonts, you should think carefully about how to dress your writing so that it looks appealing to the reader. Here are some basic principles:

- the chances are that your judge's eyes have been affected by all the reading they've done since they were young, so the font you choose should be as easy on the eyes as possible, and the size should be big enough to make the words easily legible;
- if you're working with a word count instead of a page count (and most courts frame their requirements in terms of word counts these days), then make sensible use of line spacing and margins to give your document an open, inviting look;
- block quotes are hostile and often go unread, so while there are no rules banning their use, you should think very carefully before using a block quite in anything you write;
- what works on a computer screen might not work on paper and your documents should be designed to be appealing in both print and on the screen. Many judges now read briefs on iPads or other electronic reading devices. So before you finish your document design review, be sure to make the last look at a printed version of your document to make sure that it looks right; and
- be careful to make sure your headings are aligned correctly, and that they are readable—meaning that they shouldn't be in all capitals—and all the lines are of a similar length, ideally with the last (underlined) line being slightly longer than the rest.

None of this will change your argument in any way, of course, and it won't turn a losing position into a winning one. But paying attention to the appearance of your document will convey the impression that you're an attorney who cares about every aspect of the document and that you care enough about the reader to make sure that you've produced a readable and clear piece of legal analysis. As an advocate, you want to take every possible chance to persuade your reader of your credibility and a well-designed and dressed document will help you to create that impression.

14. If Possible, Sandwich a Bad Fact between Two Good Ones

Inevitably, there will be some bad facts in your case—facts that you might wish weren't there. Your case theory should account for these facts, of course, or else you need to reconsider your theory. Nonetheless, you're concerned—and probably correctly—

---

2. The court clerk is a very different person from a law clerk. The court clerk's office is the front door through which all court-filed documents must pass, and it's the administrative hub of the court, but the court clerks don't do any legal analysis and they usually aren't even lawyers. A law clerk, on the other hand, is employed by the court specifically to help a judge or judges to do legal work and usually has no administrative function at all. This is another example of one word having multiple different meanings in the legal context. Legal language can be very confusing.

that the other side will use these facts to support its position. So how should you deal with these "bad" facts when presenting your statement of the facts of the case?

The natural human reaction would be to ignore them, but adopting this ostrich-like "head-in-the-sand" approach won't help you; the other side will certainly highlight these facts and will likely point out to the court that you failed to mention them in your brief. Rather than ignore these facts, then, you're going to have to make some mention of them in your statement of the facts, but you don't want to highlight them.

The best approach, if you can, is to sandwich a bad fact between two good ones for your client's position. If you can do this, the bad fact becomes irrelevant in your telling of the facts; it's there, but it doesn't matter because it's surrounded by so many other facts that are "good" facts for your client.

Research suggests that you shouldn't do this when offering criticism of others, because people tend only to remember the "good" news and ignore the "bad." But while a legal reader will not have the same emotional investment in the facts as someone whose work is being reviewed, you can achieve the same "halo" effect of making the "bad" facts seem less bad because of their proximity to "good" facts.

This technique isn't very complicated, as a simple example can demonstrate. Suppose you have a client who manufactured a drug that has been linked to a person's death. Criminal prosecution has already established that some quantity of the drug—let's call it Exdrug here—was diluted by one of your client's employees so that it wouldn't have the necessary potency to do what it was supposed to do when someone took a pill from the affected batch. The decedent Mr. Smith (and sometimes you really can't avoid words like "decedent") was found with only traces of the drug in his system, and his wife has sued your client for manufacturing and distributing diluted drugs.

The good facts are that the drug does its job when it's at its proper strength, and that there's no proof that the decedent's drugs were from a diluted batch or, in fact, that Mr. Smith took any drugs at all on the day he died. The bad facts, obviously, are that your client has admitted to selling diluted drugs in at least some batches, that Mr. Smith had taken the drug for three years and it had controlled his symptoms, and that Mr. Smith had only traces of your client's drug in his system, consistent with taking a diluted pill. Here's one way to present these bad facts:

> Mr. Smith's condition was well-controlled when he took Exdrug, and Exdrug had helped to keep Mr. Smith healthy for three years prior to his death. While he was found to have only trace amounts of Exdrug in his system, there is no evidence that he did, in fact, take any quantity of Exdrug on the day he died or that the bottle of Exdrugs found next to Mr. Smith were from a diluted batch of the drug.

Does this persuade you? Perhaps not. But all of the facts presented are true and you only need to put some doubt in your reader's mind at this point; the hard work will come when you make your argument that the plaintiff can't establish causation for Mr. Smith's drug based only on the amount of drugs in his system at the time of his death. All you need to do when presenting the facts is make sure that the reader doesn't foreclose the possibility that your client might not be liable. By not ignoring the bad facts, but putting them within a context that allows for a possibly benign interpretation of those bad facts, you are likely to at least not lose the reader during the facts statement of your document. Sometimes, that's the best you can hope for.

15. Consider Using Counter-Analysis

Counter-analysis is a helpful technique to use when seeking to persuade someone. As we saw in chapters 20 and 21, a writer can introduce counter-analysis to predict an anticipated argument. In persuasive analysis, a writer can also use counter-analysis to respond to an argument already made by the other side. This technique has to be used carefully, but it can be very effective when handled correctly.

It's crucially important to choose carefully which of your opponent's arguments you're going to counter. Counter-analysis is an effective technique, but only when used sparingly. If your opponents have offered five reasons why they should win and your client should lose, you should only select the main argument your opponents make for counter-analysis. More than that and you will have no space for your own arguments, and a brief spent explaining why the other sides' arguments don't work is not a persuasive document. At most, then, take your opponents' principal argument and counter it.

You should also think carefully about placing the counter-analysis. There are no hard-and-fast rules about this, but the standard advice would be to place the counter-analysis after your principal arguments. The thinking here, obviously, is that you don't want to give the other side's arguments too much prominence. To do so gives those arguments credibility and suggests that you might be concerned about them. Placing the counter-analysis after your own arguments allows the reader to become familiar with your position and still shows why the other side is wrong.

But don't make this a reflexive decision. Sometimes your opponent might have a compelling, and seemingly unassailable, position. To ignore that position—especially if you have a strong counter-analysis to show why your opponent is wrong—would likely strike a judge as odd and perverse, and might dilute the force of your counter-analysis. Other times, the document just might seem more effective with the counter-analysis placed first. As with all things, try not to fall back on standard formulas in your writing but rather try to draft the best document for the circumstances as they present themselves. In a case like this, a strong counter-analysis, showing why your opponent's argument is unsuccessful, followed by the arguments showing why your client should prevail, might be the best approach. Try always to be guided by your sense of what the reader will expect of your document and you likely will structure your document effectively.

A. The Dangers of Counter-Analysis

It's probably fair to say that even though counter-analysis is an effective tool that can be devastating in the hands of a skilled legal writer, it's the technique that causes the most concern to lawyers. This shouldn't be surprising: to offer effective counter-analysis, you have to first make the analysis you're going to counter. In essence, then, you're making the other side's argument. And because you're a good writer, you might be making the other side's argument better than the opposing lawyer. What if the judge reads your counter-analysis and decides that you've written the other side's argument so well that it actually has some merit, and that your counter to that argument isn't successful? Have you just handed the other side a winning argument that they couldn't make as effectively as you? Wouldn't the best approach be to just make your client's arguments and leave the opponent's arguments to the other side?

It's probable that questions like these run through a lawyer's mind each time the lawyer drafts a piece of counter-analysis and there's no easy answer to them because some of these dangers are very real. Of course, if you're countering an argument that's already been made, you need have no fear that you're handing an argument to the other side. And if you're a skillful writer, you need have no concern that you'll make the other side's argument better than they will; your writing technique will allow you to frame the other side's argument in a way that makes it look weak and ineffective.

But if you're writing first in a briefing contest, you might want to wait until the other side has filed its brief before offering some counter-analysis to an argument you assume they'll make unless you're confident of the arguments that will be offered against your client. You might be wrong, and the other side doesn't make the argument that had you most concerned. If you have to file first, you almost certainly will have the chance to reply to the brief your opponent files, and if you're going second, you'll see your opponent's brief before you have to file; no lawyer should hold a potentially winning argument back until filing a reply brief. And whenever you're filing your counter-analysis, make sure that it actually counters the other side's argument. If it doesn't, you might want to think carefully about your case theory.

B. Why Counter-Analysis Works

Perhaps the best way to think of counter-analysis is as an inoculation against the other side's principal argument.[3] In medical inoculation, one injects a patient with a weakened strain of a disease in order to encourage the body to resist the more active version of the disease when it's encountered. In legal inoculation, the legal analyst exposes the reader to a version of an opponent's argument and then shows the reader why that argument is ineffective, thereby creating a resistance to that argument in the reader.

Of course, inoculation in medicine only works before you're exposed to the disease; that's why you get a flu shot at the beginning of the flu season, not the end of it. Similarly, inoculation in legal analysis is only effective if it's offered before the other side makes its argument, meaning that in order to gain this benefit you have to preempt the other side and make its argument, albeit in a weakened and characterized form, before the other side makes it. As I noted above, that means you should be confident that the

---

3. I'm hardly alone in my use of "inoculation" as a metaphor for counter-analysis. For a very helpful discussion of the concept, within a broader (and also very helpful) discussion of counter-analysis, *see, e.g.*, Kathryn M. Stanchi, *Playing with Fire: The Science of Confronting Adverse Material in Legal Advocacy*, 60 Rutgers L. Rev. 381, (2008).

other side will, in fact, make that argument and that your counter-analysis is suffi- ciently robust that it will cause the reader to disregard your opponent's argument when it's encountered in its full-strength version.

But counter-analysis also has an important benefit that accompanies it no matter when it's offered. Put simply, counter-analysis shows that you're a grown-up who un- derstands that there are two sides to any dispute. If you're writing to a judge, you know that the judge understands that both sides in a dispute will make their own arguments and that the judge will have to choose between the two. By making your own argu- ments, and acknowledging and countering the other side's argument as well, you're showing that you're not afraid of what the other side has to say and that no matter how strong that argument might appear to be, there's an answer to it. The credibility you gain by offering effective counter-analysis is an important part of its benefit.

16. The Pros and Cons of Policy Arguments

Law school professors love policy arguments. By now, you might have been asked about the policy implications of a particular rule, and you might have been asked to invoke policy in support of an argument for which there is little or no case or statutory authority. Thinking about what the law should be in a particular area is an important part of a legal education, and every law student should have policy arguments available to sup- port answers to thorny doctrinal problems.

But what is effective in law school might be less effective in practice, and most legal decision makers are less impressed with policy arguments than law school experience might have suggested to you. When there is no law to support a position you're taking, and you have a viable policy argument—ideally at least supported by a law review ar- ticle or some other document—then you might have to make that argument as a last resort. And there is a noble tradition in the law, made famous by Louis Brandeis, of of- fering policy arguments to support positions; briefs that are principally or even exclu- sively supported by policy arguments are still known as "Brandeis Briefs."

What worked for Mr., and later Justice, Brandeis, though, might not work as well for you. Judges like to have authority on which they can rely to support their decisions, and if there is no authority to support a position you're arguing for, you should think carefully about whether there's another approach you can take that might rest on a more secure doctrinal foundation. If you can find an alternative path to reach your client's goal, you'd probably be better off making that argument and omitting the pol- icy portion of the argument from your brief; policy arguments might weaken, rather than strengthen, other arguments based on precedent.

If you must use a policy argument because there's no alternative, you should test it thoroughly to make sure that it's in line with the policies of the jurisdiction where you're arguing your case. There can be few arguments more certain to lose than pol- icy arguments that advocate a complete change in a state's well-established policy on a particular issue: you might be completely right that the state's policy is wrong and not in keeping with contemporary trends, but that likely will not help you in that state's courts.

17. Tell the Court What You Want To Happen

This seems like obvious advice but you'd be surprised by how many advocates forget to follow it. So you should be sure to tell the judge—assuming you're writing for a judge—exactly what you want to happen in the best of all possible worlds. Ideally you should do this twice, the first time at the beginning of the brief and the second at the end.

In addition to making it easy for the judge to understand what relief you're seeking, following this advice makes you think yourself of what it is you're asking the court to do and whether that relief is available or realistic. If, for example, you would like to not only have a civil judgment reversed but would also like judgment entered in your client's favor and perhaps an award of costs for the trouble and expense of appealing a verdict that, your client feels, should never have been allowed to stand at the trial level, you might have to review whether that relief really is available, or is likely to be granted. Instead of the absolute best case, which well might not be available under the law, asking the court to reverse the judgment and remand the case to the trial court for further proceedings in light of the appellate court's order shows that you understand the limits of the appellate court's reach and reminds the court of what relief you properly are seeking.

Telling the court what result you would like also might help you to frame your argument more appropriately. If, having drafted your brief, you realize that you were seeking relief the court could not grant, you might find that some hints of that unavailable relief have crept into your language. Going back and editing the document with your new appreciation of what relief you can legitimately hope for will make your entire document more persuasive.

Conclusion

There is no end of the list of things you can do to make your writing persuasive to a reader, and this chapter only touches on a very few of those techniques. Once you sit down to write a persuasive document, every word and mark you put in the document should be calculated to achieve the goal you're seeking, and it's crucial that having finished your first draft, you go back and edit the document with at least some time spent specifically with a mind to making the document as persuasive as you can. That will require you to put yourself in the mind of your prospective reader, whether you know who that person will be or not, and imagining what effect every word, sentence, paragraph, and section will have on that reader.

If you can empathize with your reader and consider the effect of your writing from the reader's perspective, you're well on your way to being a persuasive writer. You need to consider what a person in the reader's position would need to know in order to rule in your client's favor, when the reader would want that information, and what arguments will, and will not, seem persuasive to someone in the reader's position. Once you've made sure that your document's arguments as are carefully thought-through as possible, and that there are no logical gaps or factual problems that will cause your reader to wonder if your analysis is correct, and made sure that your document is written in as straightforward and direct language as possible, and is sensibly and thoughtfully designed, then you've written the most persuasive document you could under the circumstances. Sign it, file it, and move on to the next project.

Focus Questions

1.   Do you consider yourself as someone who's good at persuading others to do what you want them to do? Is this a skill that's prized in non-legal walks of life?

2.   What techniques do you use to persuade people to do things? Do you use any of the techniques described here? If not, what's different about what you do? Will you try to incorporate parts of the techniques you've used as a non-lawyer into your work as a lawyer?

3.   Are you surprised by the idea that you can't persuade someone just by telling them that something is as you claim?

4.   Have you considered the possibility that a judge is someone who wants to be persuaded? Do you find this to be a useful insight?

5.   Do you understand how important it is for a lawyer to be truthful? Are you surprised that lawyers have an affirmative obligation to disclose mandatory authority that's contradictory to a position they're trying to assert?

6.   Have you ever been faced with being oversold by someone who was trying to persuade you to adopt a position or to take an action? How did that make you feel? Did you feel more or less inclined to do adopt the position or to take the action?

7.   Do you see the danger of *ad hominem* arguments and the logical fallacy that lies at their core?

8.   Do you see why being concise is included as a persuasive technique? Are you surprised by the image of a judge reading your work while sitting on a sofa, watching a football game? Did you imagine that all legal work was read in an office, under ideal work conditions? Does this image change your approach to how you'll write from now on?

9.   Do you see the benefits of only arguing the issues you need to win? Do you see how difficult it might be to follow this advice?

10.   Are you surprised by the advice to put your best argument first? Had you thought that it might be best to hold your strongest argument for last? Does the text persuade you that this is not the best approach?

11.   Does the metaphor of properly dressed writing help to convey the importance of document design to persuasive writing?

12.   Have you used the technique of sandwiching a bad fact between two good facts in your non-legal attempts at persuasion? Was this technique effective?

13.   Have you used counter-analysis in previous arguments? How effective was it? Are you encouraged to try it in legal argument?

Chapter 26

Oral Argument and Oral Presentation

What You Should Learn from This Chapter

This chapter addresses the process and practice of oral argument, something that is becoming rarer in law practice but which continues to play an important role in most law students' lives. The chapter discusses the question of whether the emphasis placed on oral argument by law schools in anachronistic and concludes that it is not, and suggests reasons for that conclusion. It then discusses what happens during oral argument and suggests several techniques to help you get ready for an oral argument in which you might be participating.

After reading this chapter, you should:

- have formed an opinion on whether law school oral arguments continue to serve a useful purpose;
- have considered how to prepare for an oral argument;
- have understood the importance of listening carefully during oral argument;
- have considered how you react when placed in a stressful situation and how that self-knowledge can help you perform in an oral argument; and
- have considered the techniques proposed in this chapter to help you prepare for oral argument and have decided which of them might be helpful to you.

Oral argument is usually the culmination of litigation. It is most often the last public act in a process that can have taken years, and it is usually the last chance a lawyer has to influence directly the outcome of a case.

I've hedged my bets a little here, with "usually" and "most often" instead of more absolute words and phrases. That's because appellate courts do have the power to remand cases back to the trial court for further action, so not all appeals actually end cases and sometimes oral argument is just a stage through which a case must pass before its ultimate resolution. In fact, sometimes a case can reach appellate oral argument several times before it is finally over. There are very few absolutes in the law.

Oral arguments in practice are becoming rarer and rarer. Although cases continue to be appealed, appellate courts are granting oral arguments in fewer cases these days, preferring to resolve cases, where possible, on the strength of the briefs alone. That suggests why writing skills are becoming if anything even more important to lawyers than they used to be, and why law is more and more being thought of as a written, rather than oral, profession. Very few lawyers today will have the chance to go to an oral argument, let alone argue in one.

But oral arguments are still very much part of the law school experience. Most legal writing programs end their years with a form of appellate oral argument and moot court competitions form an important upper-level activity for many law students. Is this another anachronism of law school life, in which something persists in law school long after its practical value has vanished?

No, not really. It's true that very few lawyers currently in law school will have a chance to make an oral argument before a court, but almost all lawyers today will have to present information orally, whether in court, before an administrative body, in an office, or in some other setting. Regardless of a lawyer's practice area, oral presentations — to clients, to partners, to lawyers from other law firms — are common. So lawyers still need and use the skills to be found in oral advocacy, even if they don't use them in the courthouse so much anymore. It's a good idea for all lawyers to practice those oral skills as much as possible, and law schools give their students the chance to do that.

1. Oral Arguments in Court

When a lawyer walks into court to argue an appeal, the issues in that case have been set out and analyzed in great detail in the briefs that were filed with the court, usually months before the day of oral argument. The lawyers on both sides will have spent many hours preparing for the argument, usually involving a series of moot presentations with lawyers from the firm, or sometimes lawyers or retired judges brought in especially to provide a more realistic experience. The preparation process will have attempted to predict all possible questions, and to the extent it's possible, the individual preferences of the judges set to hear the case will have been researched and considered carefully.

The lawyers are not the only ones to prepare. The judges will read all the briefs filed in a case carefully, usually several times: just because a case might only have two parties doesn't mean that the appeal will only have two briefs. Anyone who has an interest in the outcome — an environmental group, for example, in a case that involves environmental issues — can petition the court to submit a brief as a "friend of the court," or *amicus curiae* and that can mean that a judge has a stack of long, complex briefs to read for a case. The judges' law clerks — usually recent law graduates who are hired to research and write for the judge — will also have read the briefs and might have written memos to the judge summarizing the arguments and perhaps even suggesting questions that the judge might want to ask.

With an oral argument, then, only a tiny fraction of the effort necessary to reach the actual argument is visible to the general public. Everyone involved in the process — lawyers, their associate staffs, and judges, their law clerks, and staffs — has worked long and hard to prepare for the thirty minutes, on average, of a typical appellate argument.

If you only remember one thing about oral arguments, it should be this: they exist exclusively to help the court reach a decision. Oral arguments aren't about giving the parties their day in court, and they aren't about giving lawyers a chance to practice their oratorical skills in front of a captive audience. They're working sessions at which the judges get to ask questions in order to help them reach a decision. Usually the judges will have reached at least a preliminary decision about the case before coming into the oral argument, and most judges will say that oral argument rarely, if ever, changes their minds about the outcome. But oral argument gives the judges a chance to test their impressions of a case: perhaps the answers to the questions they ask will confirm what they thought, perhaps they will help the judges to reach a different path to the same resolution, and perhaps they will introduce doubts that change their minds about the case.

The important thing to remember is that oral argument never changes an attorney's opinion of the case, nor is that its purpose. During oral argument, the only purpose an attorney should have is serving the interests of the attorney's client by making it as easy as possible for the court to rule in the client's favor. But the oral argument itself is designed to help the court, not the attorneys.

2. What Happens during Oral Argument

The name "oral argument" is misleading. Put simply, oral arguments aren't arguments. Non-lawyers sometimes get excited at the prospect of two lawyers standing up and shouting at each other, each trying to get their client's position across as forcefully and directly as possible. Entertaining though that idea might be, that isn't at all what happens.

Nor are oral arguments like speeches, in which first one and then the other advocate stands up and orates in carefully prepared rhetoric. That might be an interesting demonstration of oratorical skill, but oral arguments are supposed to be useful tools that help the judges on the court reach a decision about important issues in a case. The judges almost always have questions about a case or a lawyer's position, and the oral argument is where they get a chance to ask them.

In fact, oral "argument" is much more like a conversation, albeit a very high-level legal conversation conducted by very smart people. An attorney usually gets a few minutes to make a few points without interruption, but there are no rules to require this; questions can start even before attorneys have had a chance to give their names for the record and the questions can come fast and furious during the duration of an attorney's time in front of the court. And while it might seem like a daunting prospect to face a barrage of questions coming from a group of well-informed judges, most people who have undergone it are invigorated by the experience. Judges who have questions are engaged judges who have read the briefs and who have thought about the issues. An attorney can ask for no better audience than that.

If the court is hearing multiple cases in one session, the presiding judge will call out the name and docket number of the case and the attorneys who are arguing will move to the counsel tables, if they're not already there. Then the attorney who is to argue first—the attorney for the side that has invoked the court's jurisdiction in order to get the case heard—stands and approaches the lectern that is usually placed in the center of the courtroom, between the two counsel tables.

In courtrooms with a light system for signaling time, the moment the attorney reaches the lectern a green light usually goes on to signify that the attorney has time left to argue. Towards the conclusion of the attorney's time—ten minutes in, for example, if the attorney has a total of fifteen minutes to argue—a yellow light will usually go on to let the attorney know that it's time to start wrapping-up. Once the attorney's time is up, a red light will go on. Some courts will allow the attorney to finish a sentence or, if a judge is asking a question, might allow the attorney a limited amount of time to answer the question. Other courts, though, expect attorneys to stop talking as soon as the red light goes on. It's always a good idea to ask the court's permission to speak after the red light goes on; no lawyer should assume that it'll be acceptable to continue to argue once the red light is on.

The attorney who speaks first usually has the chance to reserve some time for rebuttal, meaning that the attorney can take some portion of the allotted 15 minutes— usually two or three minutes—and reserve it to reply to anything the attorney's opponent has said. That means the attorney now gets 12 minutes, if three minutes was reserved, and the yellow warning light will go on after 8 minutes, or three quarters of the attorney's time, is up.

The responding attorney doesn't get to reserve any rebuttal time. Rather, that attorney has the full 15 minutes to argue the attorney's client's position, after which the first attorney can—but need not—return to the lectern to give the final three minutes as rebuttal. Once both attorneys (in a case where only two attorneys speak—the usual number) have spoken, the presiding judge declares that the case has been submitted and the court will either move on to the next oral argument or will go into recess.

3. How to Prepare for and Argue in an Oral Argument

It is, of course, impossible to say that there is only one way to prepare for and argue in an oral argument. Every person needs to prepare in his or her own way, and the best advice anyone can give is that however you prepare, you should do lots of it; the only shield you have when you're standing in front of a group of judges asking you question after question is your confidence that you know every detail of your case and your argument, and that no one can shake you from the position you need to take on behalf of your client.

The process helps you in this regard. Usually—although by no means always—the person who argues the appeal is also the person who wrote the appellate brief,[1] and if that is the case with you, then you already know a great deal about the case, the law concerning it, and the arguments your client needs you to make. Although months can have passed between the time the brief was written and the oral argument, you might be surprised by how quickly the arguments come back to you.

---

1. It is less often true that the person who wrote the brief and who argues the appeal is the same person who tried the case. Although often those are the same person, trials and appeals require different skills and some firms will reserve appeals for lawyers who specialize in that work. Indeed, it is not at all uncommon for a client to retain an entirely different law firm to argue an appeal, sometimes in conjunction with the lawyers who tried the case and sometimes not. And for cases that go to the Supreme Court, it is possible that the client might change lawyers again and retain one of the few firms who do little but argue cases before the Supreme Court.

The baseline of preparation, then, requires the attorney to review the briefs in the case. The review should be comprehensive, meaning that not only should the arguments made in the briefs be fully assimilated and understood, but the attorney should also think carefully about what holes there are in both briefs, what cracks might have been papered over by skillful drafting but which the attorney, the attorney's opponent, or the court might now identify and seek to explore. In practice, this is a good time to bring in an attorney unfamiliar with the case to test and probe the strengths and weaknesses of both arguments. In law school, though, that might fall foul of the school's prohibition against collaboration, so you might have to do this work alone.

However it's accomplished, though, this is important work. By examining and considering your own arguments and those of your opponent, you really start to get inside the issues presented by the case. By exercising an active, and empathetic, imagining not only of what the other side might argue but also what the court might ask both parties, you are really getting to the core of your preparation for your argument.

It is at this point that some attorneys write out the argument they would like to be able to give, but it's important to note that they will not plan to read that presentation during oral argument. In fact, even though the drafting can be extensive—going through numerous drafts until the language is as polished and articulate as possible—this is a document that will never be used and might actually be destroyed prior to the oral argument. Drafting an ideal argument can be a good way to test how well your theories of the case work when they're spoken out loud (and always remember that there's a significant difference between written and spoken language; rhetoric that is clear and effective in writing can sound ponderous and labored when spoken), it can help you identify any gaps or holes in your argument that remain after your initial preparation, and—perhaps most helpfully—it can allow you to prepare some stock language and phrases that you can store away for the actual oral argument. But no effective oral advocate tries to read any part of a presentation during an actual oral argument. Some courts, in fact, have rules against reading and even those that do not actively disfavor the act of reading anything except direct quotations of documents.

One approach that can be effective is to write out a draft of an ideal presentation as you would give it—word-for-word—and refine it until it says exactly what you want it to say in the way you would best like to say it. You should plan for this presentation to take about half the time your actual oral argument will take, because questions, and your answers, should take up the remaining time. At a stretch, the written presentation could take up three quarters of your time, but no more than that; if you get no questions at the actual argument, you can say your piece and sit down early. Then read it aloud a couple of times, and then make an outline of that presentation. Destroy the original, and give the presentation again a couple of times using the outline. Then make an outline of the outline, and so on, until you have a single page, ideally, of point headings and principal points. You can use that page as the outline you take up to the lectern with you when you deliver your actual oral argument.

In fact, some lawyers won't even take notes with them to the lectern to protect them from the temptation of reading from them, but that might be going a little far. Most attorneys will make notes of both the principal points in their argument and the principal authorities on which they rely. There are many possible ways of doing this but a traditional—and cheap—way of doing this is to type, in large type (never underestimate the value of easily readable notes when you're in a stressful situation) a set of point headings on one or two pages and a list of citations on another page or two. Then take a plain manila file folder and staple the point headings on one side—say the left side of the folder as it lies open in front of you while speaking—and the citations to authorities on the other side. If necessary, you can staple multiple pages on one side and multiple pages on the other, but anything more than one page for headings and one page for citations risks your inability to find the crucial information when nervously standing at the podium. In this way, you'll have your most important arguments on one side of the folder and the authorities that support those arguments directly opposite them on the other side.

And it's important to remember what your principal arguments are because once the questions start to come from the bench, you can easily become distracted. Then suddenly the questions stop and you're expected to return to your argument. But to which part? What have you already argued and what do you need to get to next? Your notes and headings can remind you of where you were before the questioning started— some attorneys even keep a finger pointing at the heading where they were when a question interrupted their flow so that they can quickly find their place and return to their prepared argument.

4. Listening during Oral Argument

For an activity with a name suggesting that it's all about talking, oral argument is also very much about listening carefully to everything else that's said. Listening isn't a lawyering skill that gets all that much attention but it's very important at all times and it's absolutely crucial during oral argument.

If you speak first at an oral argument, you must first of all listen to what the judges say in their questions. That doesn't just mean that you should listen to the substance of the judges' questions, although you should, of course, do that very carefully indeed. But you should also listen to how they ask their questions. Do they use words that suggest they're looking for a particular answer? Do you want to give that answer? If you answer the question the judge seems to want you to answer, will that question lead you into a position you don't want to take in a few questions from now? Or is the judge actually asking you a question that helps your position? Is the judge friendly or hostile to the position you're advocating? What does the judge's body language tell you about what the judge is thinking? (Yes, you have to "listen" to all types of messages you can receive during oral argument.) Is the judge reading a prepared question or is this question coming from something you just said? (A judge who's reading a prepared question might be less engaged in the argument than a judge who's actively questioning your spoken position, but the prepared question might suggest a judge who's carefully considered the briefs beforehand.)

As you're thinking of all these questions, and trying to answer them, you're also formulating a substantive answer to the judge's question. And that can be a very dangerous moment for you, because when the judge started asking the question you probably formed a very quick sense of what the question was going to be and if you start to concentrate on the answer, and not the rest of the question, you might discover that the judge has gone in a different direction than you anticipated and that you're now trying to answer the question you thought the judge was going to ask rather than the question the judge actually did ask. Judges aren't often patient with attorneys who don't answer their questions, so remember to keep listening to the question all the way through to the end. You'll find that you can process all the information you're getting.

Once you're done with your argument, you aren't done with your listening, especially if you reserved time for rebuttal. If you did, you're now in the same position as was your opponent while you were speaking; you need to listen carefully to what the opposing attorney is saying, and what (and how) the judges are asking that attorney so you can decide if you want to use your rebuttal time and, if you do, what you'll say. You might be surprised at the notion that you might not want to use your rebuttal time, but if the other side doesn't say anything that requires clarification or that hurts your position, it can be a very strong sign to the court that you're confident in your position if you waive your rebuttal time. You shouldn't do this, of course, unless you are very confident in your position (or, I suppose, if you feel that your position is so hopeless that another three minutes won't help it, but that's a rather pessimistic way of thinking); it's all very well to send signs of confidence but it's much more important to take all available opportunities to make your client's case.

The lawyer going second in an oral argument can't reserve time for rebuttal, but that lawyer has an entire argument's worth of time to rebut the other side's position if that's the best way to use the time. Usually you'll have your own affirmative argument to make; in other words, you don't just win because the other side is wrong, you win because you're right. So you'll have your own prepared presentation and will be ready to launch into that once your green light goes on.

But it's almost always true that something that came up in the other side's presentation needs correction; it might be something your opponent said or it might be something a judge said that needs correction or clarification from your perspective. It's usually best to get to that point—usually, in fact, two or three points—right at the beginning of your argument. In that way you engage what are probably the most contentious and difficult issues in the case right at the beginning of your argument and, if necessary, you have the full duration of your allotted time to deal with them. You also keep the court engaged in the issues by delving back into issues that were already discussed in the argument and you show that you've been paying attention and aren't just ignoring everything that has gone before in order to give your prepared presentation. Judges appreciate and respect engaged lawyers.

5. Tips for Delivering an Oral Argument

There's a famous military maxim to the effect that all battle plans are useless five minutes after a battle starts, and while oral argument isn't a battle in any sense of the word, the principle holds true for this form of intellectual conflict. If you have a carefully prepared five-minute opening and a judge asks you a question about the weakest part of your case as you're approaching the lectern, your entire strategy for the oral argument has gone out of the window.

The tips in this section won't help you with that. The only thing that can help you in that situation is your preparation and familiarity with the facts, law, and issues in your case. What these tips will do, though, is give you confidence that you will not appear flustered or overcome by nervousness as you deal with the court's questions.

A. Understand How You React to Being Nervous

I said that you will not "appear" flustered or overcome by nervousness when you're speaking. That doesn't mean you won't, in fact, be extraordinarily nervous. Some people are comfortable in this type of arena and flourish in it, but most people are at least moderately nervous when they face a group of skeptical judges and some are very nervous indeed. The trick is to remain capable of functioning, even though you feel as if you're about to faint.

Experience helps, of course, but only to a point. Many seasoned oral advocates are very nervous before they begin to speak, although they usually calm down as soon as they get the first question—something that will probably happen to you as well. When the judges begin to engage you in the issues, you're thinking too much about the case and what you can interpret from the way the judge asks the question to be nervous. The next time you're likely to think about how you're feeling is on the walk back to the podium after the argument is over.

But understanding how your body reacts to being nervous is very important when you know that you're going to be nervous. Everyone reacts differently: some blush uncontrollably, some tremble, some have legs that shake, some laugh at inappropriate moments—there's a whole laundry list of possible physical responses to nervousness and, of course, they can exist in combination as well as individually. Think about previous situations in which you've been nervous; if you haven't ever participated in a public speaking exercise like oral argument, think back on when you were asked to speak in class. And if you even avoided that experience, seek out opportunities to make yourself nervous prior to your oral argument so you can evaluate how you react.

You might discover that you're one of those people who doesn't have any physical response to nervousness. If so, congratulate yourself on being extraordinarily lucky and continue with your preparations for the oral argument. If you're like most people, though, you'll discover something that happens to you when you're nervous. This is helpful information, because now you know what to expect. You probably won't be any less nervous the next time you speak, but because you know your own response to nervousness, you won't be taken by surprise by those responses and they won't, in turn, make you even more nervous. If, for example, you blush when someone asks you a question, you won't be surprised when that happens and you can move on to answer the question even while you feel yourself blushing. If you weren't prepared for this reaction, you might—and probably would—be distracted by the physiological response to nervousness and that would impede your ability to think straight, making you more nervous, making your physiological response even more pronounced, and so on. Nervousness can be a pernicious problem, resulting in a vicious downward spiral that ends in incoherence.

What you can't know until you're on the other side of the process is that most of the things that are so apparent to us while we struggle with nervousness are invisible to those watching us. And even when a judge notices that an attorney is nervous, the judge forgets that fact when listening to the attorney's presentation and responses to questions. Remember—this is a working session for the court to get information to help them and most judges have no interest in trying to make you nervous; they want you functioning at peak performance so they can make the most of their oral argument.

B. Keep Your Knees Bent at All Times When Standing

This doubtless looks like very odd advice, but you should really keep your knees bent at all times when you're standing and giving your oral argument. Let's take a second to consider why odd-sounding advice is also good advice.

You know, from home, from school, and from any number of other experiences in your life, that you shouldn't slouch. And that's particularly good advice when giving your oral argument. You shouldn't lean on the lectern, you shouldn't balance like a flamingo on one leg, you should stand up straight with your shoulders down and back. A person who stands chest-on and open to a listener looks credible and honest, while people who hunch over and look physically unbalanced look like they're hiding something and look untrustworthy. So stand up straight but keep your knees slightly—slightly—bent.

This doesn't mean that you should stand as if you're crouching down, but your knees should not be locked and should have a little play in them. Why? Because if you lock your knees, you might cut off the circulation to your brain and you might faint. If you don't think it happens, you haven't watched many military parades. Soldiers or other service people who stand rigidly at attention for long periods of time are well-aware of the tendency to pass out when the knees are locked in place and are taught to stand upright but not so rigidly that there's no give in their knees.

You don't need to understand why this happens. Just imagine how bad you would feel if you fainted in the middle of your oral argument. It happens. Don't let it happen to you.

C. Maintain Eye Contact as Much as Possible

If your body position can make you look trustworthy or untrustworthy, so can your ability to maintain eye contact. It might not be a rational response, but we tend to believe that people who look at us when we're speaking and when they're speaking to us are trustworthy, and people who can't maintain eye contact with us are untrustworthy. These responses are subconscious; it's unlikely that a judge would form the conscious impression that you're not to be trusted if you refuse to look at the judge during oral argument. But the judge is likely nonetheless to think less of your argument if you can't maintain some regular eye contact, and will likely think you're not paying as much attention as you should if you won't look at the judge while the judge asks a question.

This doesn't mean that you should stare unblinkingly at the judges at all times; "eye contact" is not "staring." But just as in driving you should keep your eyes on the road as much as possible, remembering to look into your mirrors and at your instruments as well, so you should try to keep your principal focus on the judges with occasional glances down at your notes.

In fact, the tendency of notes to draw our eyes to them is the reason some attorneys won't use them during oral argument. They fear that if they have notes with them, they won't be able to maintain eye contact with the judges because their notes will have an irresistible draw to them. If you find that this is your tendency then maybe you should avoid taking notes with you. Most people, though, can keep their eyes away from their notes most of the time as long as they're aware that that's what they should do. There's nothing wrong with looking away from judges occasionally and looking at your notes, just remember not to look only at your notes and rarely, if ever, at the judges.

D. Don't Keep a Pen in Your Hand While You Speak

If you've ever gone to an orchestra concert, you might have wondered why the conductor waves a baton in the air. It doesn't make a sound, other than a disconcerting whistling noise when the conductor makes large gestures, and it's too flimsy to use as defense if the audience or orchestra starts to rebel against the conductor's authority. The answer is simple: the distances between orchestra member and conductor can be quite large and the baton helps to provide a focal point on which orchestral players can concentrate—in the fleeting moments they can look up from their music—to see what the conductor wants them to do.

The reason why a baton is so useful to a conductor is the reason you should not hold a pen—or anything else, for that matter—in your hand during oral argument. If you hold a pen, the judges might start to focus on it rather than on what you're saying. Just like a baton, your pen will exaggerate any hand gestures you make and that can quickly become distracting and annoying to anyone watching you. The last thing you want to do is to distract or annoy the judges at your oral argument. So if you need a pen to write notes as the judges ask you questions, by all means take one to the lectern with you. But once you've written your note, put the pen down again. And remember to take it with you when you're done, especially if it's a good one; if you don't, you might never see it again.

E. Use Your Hands, but Not Too Much

One thing that happens when we're feeling self-conscious is that everything we do is subject to immediate and scathing internal criticism. Actors learn that one of the hardest things they have to do when they first act is to walk; a simple, normal human activity that they've done millions of times in the past suddenly becomes the focus of intense internal scrutiny and criticism and therefore becomes difficult to do. For lawyers, it's not walking but hand use that becomes unnatural and difficult the first time they stand up to give an oral argument.

Some lawyers react to this internal criticism by not using their hands at all, letting them hang by their sides. But that isn't an especially natural position for their hands and often their brains start telling them that they look ridiculous because they're not using their hands at all. That impulse can lead, in turn, to frenzied hand-waving, in which the attorney's hands attempt to mirror and explain every word the attorney uses. This can lead to the attorney looking like some form of strange human semaphore signaler, with hands and arms that are never still.

In an attempt to reach a halfway point between these two extremes, attorneys can grab hold of the lectern with what appears like a death grip, clutching with both hands until the muscles in their arms begin to give out from fatigue. Or worst of all, putting one or both hands in a trouser pocket. Few things are better calculated to make judges furious than the perceived insult of speaking to them with your hands in your pockets. This might be a generational issue, and judges of your age might not worry about such things. But how many judges are there of your age?

It's strange but often true: we practice the intellectual rigor of our oral arguments, and we practice the words and phrases we intend to use to express our analysis, but it's not uncommon for attorneys to never practice, or even consider, the gestures they make to accompany that analysis. That omission can lead to problems during argument when your brain finally recognizes that what you're doing with your body might not seem natural or normal to an observer.

Relax. Things are not as bad as you might think they are and there are ways to prepare to make sure that your hands never become an issue in your oral argument.

You should understand that while judges are looking at you while you speak, they are rarely as aware of you as you are of yourself. Unless you do something to draw attention to yourself, the judges are more likely looking at your face to see what clues they can learn from it than they are looking at what your hands are doing. If your hands don't appear to be gesturing in a way that's odd, or contradictory to your words, they will likely be visible but unnoticed by the judges.

Letting your arms hang by your side is not a good idea. It's an unnatural position and you'll start to realize that you're doing something that's not normal quite quickly. The goal here is to avoid anything that will cause you to become conscious of yourself at a time when all your attention should be focused on what you're saying and how the judges are reacting to it. But similarly, grasping the lectern like an overboard swimmer clutching onto a life preserver is also not the answer. It can look unnatural and will certainly feel odd to you, and having your arms up on the lectern can lead you to move them into a leaning position. Even if the lectern is sturdy enough to support your weight, few gestures are physically as much at odds with a formal oral presentation than casually leaning on something while you address the court.

The most natural position for your hands is resting together at about waist height and your elbows bent. Don't clasp your hands together, but rest one lightly on top of the other. It's a natural and neutral position that allows one hand or the other to gesture when appropriate, to turn a page on your notes if that's necessary, and then to return to the neutral resting position. Sometimes a gesture requires both hands, but try to keep your gestures as much as possible within the frame of your body; don't raise your hand above your head or spread your arms wide to the sides or make other broad gestures with your arms. And as much as possible, try to keep your hands open with your fingers slightly curved (think of holding a ball about the size of a soccer or basketball); don't make fists (something that looks aggressive and sends a negative message to the viewer); and don't point your finger (something that looks accusatory to someone watching). And don't pound or slap the lectern; it can hurt and your argument shouldn't need such audio enhancement.

Some gesture, though, is normal and appropriate. Don't rehearse your gestures; nothing will look less natural and more affected than a gesture that has been practiced and rehearsed. But looking at yourself in a mirror as you practice your presentation is a good idea, as is having someone watch specifically for your gestures as you speak.

Since we're talking about the way your body is presented to the court, let's spend a moment considering posture as well. Sadly, your mother was right about this. Stand up straight and keep your shoulders down and back. As much as possible, stand face on to the front of the bench and in as "open" a position as possible. Someone who stands this way looks welcoming, confident, and trustworthy, as opposed to someone who looks closed, hostile, and defensive. Ridiculous? Not really; we send all sorts of messages in different ways and body position is one of the most powerful ways of sending subconscious messages about ourselves to others.

F. Speak to the Back of the Courtroom

While you're standing up straight, with your hands in a neutral position, try to speak in a voice that will carry past the judges to the back of the room where you're standing. You don't want to shout at the judges, nor do you want to make them strain to hear you. Even with amplification, the sound in some courtrooms can be poor, with the room either too resonant or too dead. If you try to speak in a voice that's just loud enough to carry to the judges, you likely will be speaking too softly, so try to project so that your voice fills the room. This isn't easy; most of us aren't professional actors or singers and we don't have the training in vocal production necessary for us to be able to modulate our voices easily. And our normal speaking voices are often badly produced, making it seem that when we project adequately we're speaking too loudly.

We also have to rely on an inaccurate idea of what our voice sounds like to someone else. For reasons that are too technical to go into here, what we hear when we speak is not what everyone else hears, and what seems loud enough to us often isn't close to being loud enough for someone else to hear us, especially when we're talking in a large room. The only way to be sure that we're speaking loudly enough is to practice in a room that's the approximate size of the room in which you'll be giving your oral argument, with someone listening and telling you to speak more loudly or more softly. Once you have your dynamic range calibrated, try to learn what that sounds like to you, and what it feels like in your body to speak at that volume. It might seem like an imprecise way to regulate your volume, but it's all we have.

Finally, don't speak too quickly when you give your argument. Nerves, and the adrenaline that's produced when we're nervous, can cause you to speak more rapidly than you would normally, and most people speak more quickly in conversation than is desirable for intelligibility. That usually isn't a problem, with all sorts of contextual clues helping our listener to understand what we're saying and to bridge whatever gaps might have been introduced by not understanding a word or two.

But those contextual clues are harder to spot, and are less helpful, in formal presentations. The judges are further away from you than most people with whom you converse, and the artificiality of the situation robs you of some of the gestures and other contextual clues you would normally provide. So as you practice your presentation, ask your listener to also consider how quickly you're talking, and how clearly you're enunciating, and work to make your delivery as well-paced and clear as possible, remembering that you will speed up when you're nervous.

If you can't practice with someone else because of your school's honor code and its prohibition of collaborative work, consider recording a video of your oral argument and listen for the speed of your delivery as you review it. It's not as helpful as having someone watching you, but it might be all you're allowed to do and it's better than nothing.

All of this might seem overdone and unnecessary. Surely it's your words and thoughts that matter, not how you deliver them. Well, your words and thoughts are vital, of course, but if your listeners can't understand them, or if what you say is contradicted by a gesture or your listener is distracted by something you do while you're speaking, you will be less effective than you could have been without the distraction. A brilliant presentation can only be persuasive if it's understood. So devote at least a little time to the gestural, postural, and auditory parts of your presentation. Doing so will reap you benefits in the end.

G. Don't Speak When a Judge Is Speaking

Few things will irritate a judge as much as when an attorney speaks when the judge is speaking. There's a hierarchy in courtrooms and judges are at the top. That's why everyone stands up when they enter and exit the courtroom, that's why you stand up to speak to a judge (always—always—stand up when you speak to a judge. Even if you just have a word or two to say, and even if you don't get to full standing height, always raise yourself at least a little out of your chair every time you speak in court), and that's why you never speak when a judge is speaking.

This can feel unnatural. We're conditioned, in polite society, for someone to allow us to finish what we're saying before they start speaking. If you're saying something—particularly if you're saying something you believe to be important—you have a right to expect that you'll be allowed to finish your point without interruption. But not in court.

In court, when a judge speaks, attorneys stop speaking and listen carefully. It doesn't matter if you're in the middle of a sentence and are just about to make your most important point; if a judge starts speaking, you must stop. And yes, the judges' questions take up your time for oral argument. The time you're given—usually 15 minutes—is a total allocation of time, not the amount of time you get to speak. If the judges ask questions for 10 minutes, then you'll only have 5 minutes to speak. There's nothing you can do about this. You can't interrupt the judges to remind them that you only have a few minutes left and you really would like to get to some points that haven't been made yet. When judges talk, all you can do is stop talking and listen.

Unfortunately, this rule only applies to attorneys. Judges can speak over each other, although that happens rarely. When it does, though, it's up to you to figure out who's saying what; you can ask a judge to repeat a question and if you've had multiple questions it can help to explain how you're going to structure your answer and which question you're going to answer first.

Something less disruptive, but still tricky, can happen when the judges start to speak to each other through you. It's a tricky concept to describe, but once you've seen it happen you'll never forget it. According to the unwritten rules of decorum in court, the judges can't speak directly to each other while they're on the bench. But they can speak to the attorneys, and if one judge disagrees with something a fellow judge has said, rather than aim a comment directly at that judge, the second judge can accomplish the same effect by asking a second question to the attorney. That, in turn, can provoke a response from the first judge, and so on. There are times when an attorney can resemble a spectator at a tennis match, watching passively as question after question, without interruption, is knocked back and forth between the judges.

If this happens, there's nothing you can do except listen carefully. It's possible, although not necessary, that if one judge is disagreeing with you, the other judge might be agreeing with your position so take particular notice of how the third judge—if it's a three-judge panel—is reacting. Remember, you only need two out of the three judges on your side to win with such a panel. If the questioning pauses for a second, so you wouldn't be speaking over one of the questioning judges, try to reinsert yourself into the discussion by starting to answer one or more of the "questions" you've been asked and try, carefully, to steer the oral argument back to the positions you need to get across to the court.

H. Be Careful What You Drink

Aggressive questioning from the bench can make an already nervous attorney even more nervous, and an almost universal physical reaction to nervousness is dry mouth. To counter that, we tend to drink fluids to keep our mouths moist, but the type of fluid is very important because while some can help, some can actually make the problem worse.

No attorney should drink alcohol before an oral argument, of course. That should go without saying, but to be on the safe side I'll say it again: no attorney should drink alcohol before an oral argument.

But even non-alcoholic fluids can cause problems. In particular, caffeinated drinks like coffee and soda can make things worse rather than better. They deliver caffeine to the system, which can help to stimulate you. But it's likely that you'll be very stimulated in anticipation of the oral argument to begin with, and caffeine can make some physical symptoms of nervousness, like trembling, even worse. The real danger of caffeinated drinks, though, is that they can dry out your mouth rather than keeping it moist. That's probably not the effect you were hoping for when you drank something before your oral argument. So even if you typically prefer caffeinated drinks, you should try to stay away from them in the hour before your oral argument and during the argument itself.

The best choice of drink is also the simplest: water. Water will keep your mouth moist, is found readily in most public buildings like courthouses (there will probably even be a water pitcher on counsel table in your courtroom but unless you've seen someone bring it into the room, don't trust it; sometimes the water in those pitchers can go for days without being changed), and it can be carried—in a cup, not a plastic bottle, up to the lectern when you speak to the court. And as an important side benefit, water probably won't stain your clothes as badly as would, say, coffee if you spill it in your nervousness.

I. Dress Appropriately

Things get difficult when we get onto the subject of clothes. Clothing is an important part of personal style and dictating one mode of dress over another can be seen as inappropriate and meddlesome. And what does "appropriate" mean anyway? How long is a piece of string? How high is "high"? Rather than trying to set hard-and-fast rules that would be easily shown to be inapplicable in a variety of different settings, let's consider some fundamental issues and you can interpret those in a way that works in context and doesn't do violence to the self-image you want to project to the world.

Let's start with an obvious proposition. You need to wear clothes at an oral argument. A less obvious, but none the less important, observation is that your clothes will not help you win your argument; if they have any effect at all, it will be harmful rather than helpful. If, for instance, you attempt to give an oral argument in jeans and a t-shirt, the court will probably not allow you to speak. But the best-dressed (however "best-dressed" is defined) attorney will not win a case just because of the attorney's clothes, and nor would we want that result. If the law were so superficial it could be overborne by fashion, we would be in a very bad state in this country.

From these simple propositions we can derive a more concrete rule: your clothing should be appropriate to the situation and should not distract the court from your argument. In other words, you need to wear clothes but they should be functionally, if not practically, invisible. You should dress as the court expects you to dress, just as you should construct your brief to look and read like the document the court expects to get. Anything else and the court will focus on what you look like, and not what you're saying. That won't help your client, and remember—everything you do as a lawyer should be with the intention of helping your client.

In practical terms, what does this mean? It's easier to say for men that it is for women. For men, a dark business suit, with a white or blue shirt, tie that matches, and black shoes and socks: drab, perhaps; unimaginative, probably; and conservative, certainly. But also unremarkable, predictable, and neutral. In this context, those are desirable characteristics.

For women, the equivalent. Some courts will now accept pantsuits, but most prefer business clothing that is either in the form of a dress or a skirt and blouse and jacket in neutral, but usually dark, colors, with plain and relatively low-heeled shoes (some heel is fine, but be practical; anything that looks as if it might impede your ability to stand or walk—even if it won't—is too much). As with men, unremarkable, predictable, and neutral is the goal.

For both men and women, don't forget to make sure your hair is well cut and groomed for the oral argument. It can happen that a lawyer walks into court with expensive and well-chosen clothes and ruins the effect they would otherwise create by having hairstyles that are inappropriate to the situation. It's even more difficult to speak with any precision about hair than it is with clothes, and the best advice is general rather than specific: your hair style should be conservative, neat, and appropriate for the situation. More than anything else, it should be a conscious hairstyle for the situation, not just the hairstyle you happen to wear. If your regular hairstyle meets the situation, all the better, but try to make sure it's a conscious, rather than an accidental, result, and if you decide that your hair doesn't look like it should, try to schedule a visit to a hairstylist you trust before the oral argument.

Try to avoid jewelry that has the capacity to be distracting. This includes bracelets or anything else that might make a noise while you're speaking, as well as jewelry that might draw attention to itself and might therefore distract the court from listening to what you have to say. This doesn't mean you need to divest yourself of all jewelry before going into court, of course, but you should think carefully about every detail of what you're wearing and ask what it does to enhance or detract from your client's message.

One thing of which to be particularly cautious is jewelry that makes a personal, religious, or political statement. This isn't to suggest that you should be censored or forever prevented from expressing things in which you believe, but it is to say that oral argument—a time at which you literally are speaking on behalf of someone else—is not the time to make the court listen also to your personal beliefs.

If you're ever in any doubt as to whether something will be distracting or not, err on the side of caution: other than a small lapel pin in the shape of the flag (something which is patriotic but politically neutral), almost anything else that makes a statement might be something you could do without during oral argument.

You might resist this advice. You can dress yourself and you know what you look good wearing. You've prepared your argument carefully and effectively and you have strong points to make about the facts and the law. You're confident in your skills as an oral advocate and you're not intimidated by the prospect of speaking with the court. And your client has retained you—in all senses of what "you" is—to argue the case on the client's behalf. It's not fair that you have to restrict yourself to an outmoded dress code that has no contemporary relevance and that can have no effect on the substance of your arguments.

Of course it isn't fair. It just is what it is. Courts or individual judges might be more liberal in their approach to personal style than I suggest, but probably not. And the only way you would know is to take a chance on what you wear or how you look and see how the court reacts. If the court reacts badly, you won't have a chance to change. And since a bad reaction wouldn't help your client, that's not a good idea.

J. Always Be Respectful of Everyone Involved in the Oral Argument

Being anything other than completely respectful to everyone involved in the oral argument is a bad idea. It's good advice to be polite to everyone at all times, of course, but it's particularly important to remember on the day of oral argument. Stress can make people irritable and snappy and if you're one of those people you need to be particularly careful that you don't allow the way you feel dictate the way you behave toward others.

It might seem obvious to say that you should be respectful to the judges hearing your case but, to be fair, they can make it difficult. Judges can ask questions that seem foolish or misguided to you. It might seem that the judge understands nothing about the case or your position. That might or might not be the case; the judge might be asking a basic foundational question in order to get you to state a position that the judge plans to explore in much greater depth, or it might indeed be that the judge is ill-prepared. Whatever the reason for the question, the only appropriate response is to answer the judge's questions as carefully and fully as possible, keeping your client's position firmly in mind. If the judge is ill-prepared, this is your chance to inform the judge about what your client wants to say about the issue under consideration, and if the judge has another reason for asking the question, that will become clear. All you can do at the moment is answer the question as well as possible.

Judges can also appear dismissive, grumpy, or even downright angry about a position you're taking. The rule of being courteous to everyone involved in oral argument doesn't apply to judges, who can behave in any way they want. But you can't rise to the bait, because to do so wouldn't help your client and—to sound like a broken record—it's your client's needs you're serving while you act as a lawyer, not your own. So if a judge is rude or discourteous to you, you just have to accept the judge's behavior and remain calm and polite. It's entirely possible that the judge's bad behavior, and your calm and respectful response to it, will be noticed by the other judges and they might even take more note of your substantive positions as a result. You'll certainly gain their respect, and that's a good thing for any attorney to have.

Just as it's important to be respectful of the judges, so it's important to be respectful of opposing counsel. No matter how irritating you find the person, and no matter how much you disagree with that attorney's argument, you can't let that show in the way you behave in court. Just because a person is annoying, rude, or foolish doesn't make that person's legal argument any less effective and by being disrespectful or dismissive of the attorney, you might lead a judge to believe that you have no substantive response to that argument and are instead trying to deflect attention away from the substance and onto the person. Even if that isn't what you're trying to do, that's the way your behavior might be interpreted and that won't be effective.

So no matter how rude or disrespectful your opponent is being or has been before the oral argument began—and I'm sorry to say that some attorneys will behave badly on purpose, to try to rattle an opponent—during the argument you should remain polite and courteous at all times. In fact, if you feel your opponent is behaving badly towards you, consider that a good sign; it might mean that the attorney is nervous, or believes that your argument is strong and is hoping to knock you off your stride. The worse someone behaves towards you, the better a sign it is for your argument, so take it as a compliment and don't respond in kind.

But judges and attorneys aren't the only people who are involved in the oral argument. The court personnel—the court clerks, court reporters, and security officers—and the judges' staff, including secretaries and law clerks, might all be in and around the courtroom before the oral argument begins. And while some judges hold themselves aloof from everyone, most judges treat the court personnel and their personal staff as family: it's a small community that gets to go behind the bench and most judges are very close to the people with whom they work every day. And you know how you would feel towards someone who was rude to your sibling or your parent. One of the surest things one can say about oral argument is that any bad behavior on your part towards any of the court staff will make it back to the judges and they will think the less of you for it.

The safest thing to do, of course, is to always behave with politeness, respect, and friendliness to everyone. Courtesy and good behavior are most effective when they're natural and not put on for strategic purposes. But however you come to it, you should assume that from the first step you take into the courthouse on the morning of oral argument, everyone you meet will report to the judges in your bench on any act of rudeness or discourtesy. So whatever the reason, and whatever the provocation, make sure you are unfailingly polite and respectful at all times.

Even when you think you're alone, or talking to other lawyers or staff on your team, you should be careful about what you say. Most courthouses have doors that allow someone from a public area to get back to the judges' chambers, which are secure areas. These doors are usually locked and can be opened electronically by someone in chambers, but usually only after identifying the person and finding out his or her business. That usually involves a camera for visual identification and a microphone so the people seeking access can explain their business. What most don't know, though, is that these microphones are often left open at all times, meaning that any conversation that happens close enough to the microphone can be heard by anyone listening in a judge's chambers. Being polite and courteous to people in public will do you no good if you stand within microphone range and are rude and disparaging about the judges while in conversation with someone.

It might seem unfair to tell you that you should be guarded and polite every second of your time in a courthouse, but it is the only way you can be sure that you're not making a bad impression. Even when you think no one can hear you, you should remember that in a public building, no comment, no conversation, and no gesture is private.

K. Try to Visit the Courtroom before Your Argument

The lack of privacy in a public building might be a disadvantage to you, but the openness of public buildings is something you should take advantage of. In particular, you should visit the courthouse in which you're going to argue before your argument is scheduled, if possible, and familiarize yourself with the room, the process that's followed during oral argument, and even, if you can, what it feels like to stand at the advocates' lectern. Ideally, you would do this at least a day before your argument is scheduled so that you can take some time to imagine yourself in that setting without your thoughts being cluttered with your immediate pre-argument preparation.

Almost all court proceedings are open to the public, so you should be able to sit in the courtroom and watch other arguments — if there are any — a day or so before your argument is scheduled. Try to get a sense of the choreography of this particular court — how the judges come in to the courtroom, how counsel approach the counsel table and move to the lectern, all the little things that happen in every courtroom but happen slightly differently in each one — so that nothing that happens while you're arguing will distract or surprise you. Until you become an experienced oral advocate, you might be surprised at how the least unexpected movement can pull your focus away from your argument, even slightly, and how disturbing such distractions can be. Any chance to minimize or eliminate them is a chance you should take.

Viewing the courtroom before you argue also lets you get used to the lighting — some courtrooms can be surprisingly poorly lit and that might affect your decision about how much to rely on notes or, if you decide you really need the notes, affect the size of type you use to print them out. If you get permission, and the court is not in session (obviously), you might even have a chance to stand at the lectern and hear how your voice sounds in the room. Almost all courtrooms have amplification now, but the courtrooms were not built with acoustic design in mind and sometimes the amplification is not especially sophisticated. Knowing what your voice sounds like in the space you'll be in can be useful information.

Standing at the lectern, or the podium, can also tell you what you'll see when the court is in session and you're making your argument. Will you be able to see all the judges clearly without having to move your head or will you have to swing from left to right in order to maintain eye contact with all the judges? How far back can you stand from the lectern and still see your notes? Is the judge's bench raised so high that it will be difficult to see much of them or will you be able to see their hands as they listen to you?

This is all useful information to know. If you can maintain eye contact with all the judges without having to turn your head, you know that you can concentrate on simply moving your head up to look at the judges and down to look at your notes. If you have to move from side to side, you might have to practice that movement as you do your final preparations for the argument, because maintaining eye contact with all the judges is an important part of making sure that they all feel included in, and engaged in, your argument. If you can stand back a little from the podium and still see your notes and be heard through the microphone, you might find it easier to maintain eye contact, but in most courtrooms you will have to stand right up against the lectern in order to be heard and to see your notes.

And if you can see the judge's hands as you argue, you'll be able to see them writing notes, either to themselves or—as frequently happens—to each other. There are few things more distracting than making a seemingly benign comment in your argument and watching a judge look down and start to write a note. You might start wondering what it was you said that was so good, or so bad, that it merited a note from a judge, and then you're concentrating not on what you're saying but on what you said. Knowing that you'll have to avoid thinking about such distractions can be helpful as you get ready for your argument.

L. Don't Try to Be Funny During Oral Argument

Some people use humor as part of their way of dealing with stress. Perhaps they feel that if they can make someone laugh, they can turn that person into a friend who won't want to hurt their feelings by ruling against them, or perhaps they are naturally funny people (or believe they are) and humor is part of their way of speaking in any situation— the reason doesn't really matter. In a formal setting like oral argument, humor is— most of the time—inappropriate and should be avoided.

That's particularly true when discussing the facts of a case. There is nothing more inappropriate than laughing at, or trying to get others to laugh at, the people involved in a case under consideration. Never forget that the facts you're discussing are things that happened to real people and, if those facts caused their cases to be considered by any court, let alone an appellate court, those facts likely aren't funny to them. If you forget that, you can be assured that others—especially judges—will not, and they will find any attempt to use humor as distasteful and inappropriate.

As with all things we've been talking about, though, there are exceptions to this rule. Sometimes things happen during the course of an oral argument that can cause someone to say something that is—intentionally or not—funny. If that person is you, don't dwell on the moment but don't try to ignore it either. If the judges on your panel smile or laugh at something you said because it was funny, don't turn into a stand-up comedian and try to leave them laughing in the aisles, but don't deny the moment either. Take a breath, find a way of leading gracefully back into your argument, and move on.

Human moments are never out of place, even in an undertaking so serious as a court hearing, but they have to be limited because the court has serious work to do and an attorney's job is to help the court reach the position the attorney's client wants it to reach, not to entertain them.

M. Never Object

Humor is perhaps the best way to end this discussion of oral argument, and especially the unintentionally humorous effect that saying "objection" in an appellate court proceeding can produce in everyone involved.

Television has conditioned us to expect lawyers to stand up and say "objection" whenever an opponent says something with which they disagree. The image is false, even in trial proceedings: attorneys do object, all the time, but there is a way to object and a way to not object, and if real-life attorneys behaved in trial the way their fictional television counterparts behaved, many more attorneys would be jailed for contempt than actually are each year.

But what might—possibly—work in trial will not work on appeal. There simply is no provision for an objection in an appellate hearing, and an attorney who jumps up and says "objection" during an opponent's argument will provoke everyone to laughter. There are fewer things more destructive of you credibility than making someone laugh at—not with—you.

So never object during an appellate argument. Nothing good, for you or your client, will come of it.

Conclusion

Almost everything said here about oral argument could be said with equal force about any formal oral presentation. The preparation necessary; the ability to listen to, and respond to, questions; the role of gesture; drinking water instead of caffeine—all of these things are just as relevant to oral presentations as they are to oral arguments. Even informal oral presentations, like giving an oral explanation of some research you've done for a partner, will require many of the same skills and techniques, although the setting might be somewhat less formal (and only "might be." Some partner's offices, and some partners, can be formidable and can require a high degree of formality).

You might find that you don't enjoy being an oral advocate, or you might find that you're born to do it. But you almost certainly will have to present information orally to someone during your career as a lawyer, and likely you'll find that you have to do it over and over again. The oral arguments you engage in during law school can be tremendous help in familiarizing you with what it feels like to present a position and to be questioned about the details of that position. It will be to your benefit if you take as many opportunities as possible to gain experience in speaking in public and practice those skills as much as possible.

Focus Questions

1. How much public speaking have you done? Have you enjoyed it? Does the prospect of speaking to a group of people excite or concern you?

2. Are you surprised to learn that most lawyers—even litigators—don't speak in court?

3. Does the text's assertion that oral arguments are exercises designed to help a court reach a decision surprise you? Did you think that oral arguments would more attorney-focused than they appear to be?

4. Why are oral arguments called "arguments" if, as the text suggests, they are more like conversations between lawyers and the judge?

5. How do you plan to prepare for oral argument if you are required to participate in one?

6. Does the idea of writing out an oral argument that you will then discard strike you as strange? Helpful? A waste of time?

7. Are you looking forward to the prospect of answering questions during oral argument or does the prospect of questioning cause you concern?

8. How skillful are you at listening to questions and forming answers to those questions at the same time? Do you see why this is an important skill for lawyers in oral argument?

9. How do you react to being nervous? Which of the physiological responses mentioned by the text do you show? Do you have different responses from those mentioned in the text? Will being aware of them help you to function well under stress?

10. Do you have difficulty maintaining eye contact when you speak with someone? If so, do you plan to practice this before your oral argument?

11. Are you aware of your hand gestures when you speak? Will you video a practice oral argument session so you can be aware of your hand gestures and any other physical mannerisms you might display?

12. Do you have a loud voice, a soft voice, or one that's about right, regardless of the room or the context in which you're speaking? Do you understand the importance of being audible to the judge(s)?

13. Did you expect to read advice on what to drink and what to wear during oral argument? Do you think this advice is necessary? Helpful?

14. Will you take the text's advice and visit the courtroom before oral argument?

LEGAL RESEARCH

Chapter 27

Why Bother to Study Legal Research?

What You Should Learn from This Chapter

This chapter introduces some of the challenges associated with legal research. In particular, it discusses why legal research is an important skill for law students and junior lawyers. The chapter outlines some concepts important to research in general and legal research in particular and concludes, unsurprisingly, that research will be an important skill for you to develop, at least for the foreseeable future.

After reading this chapter, you should:

- have a more nuanced appreciation for why legal research is a crucial lawyering skill;
- have considered why the text says that "we are better researchers when we already know most of the answer"; and
- have considered how that insight applies particularly in the legal research context.

The answer to the question of why lawyers bother to study legal research should be simple: all impressions to the contrary, law school only teaches you a sliver of what you'll need to know as a practitioner and no lawyer who doesn't have at least minimal research skills can hope to survive long in practice. There are other reasons as well, and we'll discuss those later, but let me repeat that basic point because it's so important: you study legal research because you need those skills in order to survive as a practicing lawyer. No other motivation should be necessary for you to study this subject as effectively and carefully as you can.

The issue is more complex than that, of course. You're in law school so you should instinctively mistrust any answers that are as simple and straightforward as that one. Some of you, for example, might be thinking that it's easy for someone who teaches legal research to argue in favor of its importance to you, and that there might be some self-interest in my making the argument. After all, unlike legal writing, legal research does not seem to help you much in your other subjects; your textbooks have all been thoroughly researched and your doctrinal teachers do not, for the most part, ask you to do any additional legal research. And if you had access to many of the studies exploring the skills that are important for lawyers to make partner in their firms, you would see that legal research does not rank highly, if at all, in the responses lawyers give. In fact, you might know some solo practitioners who spend their time working in one discrete area of the law and who disclaim any need to do formal legal research. Perhaps, after all, legal research isn't all that important.

Let's start with practice first: legal research is a vital skill for most practicing lawyers if not, perhaps, all of them. It's certainly true that there are some practitioners—solo practitioners mostly, but some who work in multi-person firms as well—whose practice area is so limited and defined that they have no need to conduct much—or even any—legal research.

But that ignores the question of how they got to the point where they don't need to be researching the law. Hardly anyone starts off in such a practice right out of law school, and hardly anyone learned everything they needed to know about law practice from the three years they spent in law school. Almost all practitioners—even the ones who don't need to do research anymore—needed to research at the start of their careers, in order to learn what to do and what the law was in their area. Some areas of the law are sufficiently static that once practitioners know the basic law, they can stay updated through loose-leaf services or, increasingly more common these days, internet updates. You won't be starting with that level of knowledge, though—even if you go into those more static areas of practice—and until you've developed an understanding of the law, you'll have to research it effectively in order to learn.

The same answer applies to those studies that suggest legal research isn't an important skill to make partner. The studies are probably correct: most prospective partners have lower-level associates doing their research for them so they don't view their personal research skills as an important part of their quest to make partner. But when you go into a law firm, you'll be one of those low-level associates; the partner track for most firms is somewhere between five and ten years, and during at least the first few years of that track, you'll likely be researching almost every issue that comes up in the cases on which you're working. Your continued association with the firm will be, in part, dependent on how well and how efficiently you conduct that research. Put simply, research won't make you a partner, but if you can't research, you won't stay at the firm long enough to be even thought of as partner material.[1]

The answer to the question of how legal research skills can help you in law school, even though most classes don't require you to do research, is more complicated but it draws us closer to the heart of why legal research is so important. Once again, the answer can be expressed in simple terms—legal research helps you to think better—but

---

1. As with most things in the legal research world, we can't be certain if what was true today will be true tomorrow. For the past few years, there's been a lot of discussion about the outsourcing of legal research—the idea of sending legal research issues to firms in other countries with lawyers who are fluent in English and who often have training or degrees from American law schools. These lawyers can work more cheaply than American associates and don't cause American law firms to incur overhead expenses like health insurance. And because of time differences, these lawyers can often do their work during our nighttime, getting law firms answers to their questions by our morning. This means that their work can be, functionally, faster than the work done by an American lawyer. This isn't the time to discuss the ethical quandaries outsourcing can cause, or the problems of accuracy and interpretation that can arise, or even if outsourcing is a trend that is here to stay or is simply a cost-saving fad of the current economic climate. For now, at least, the ability to conduct legal research is a core skill for American lawyers. That's all that should concern us here.

once again, the simple answer requires explanation. To explore this answer more closely, we have to think about the research process itself.

1. The Research Process in General

Let's imagine you're planning to go and see a movie this weekend. Let's further imagine that the number one movie in the country this week is called *Mister Ed's Revenge*, a horror movie about a horse that talks to its victims as it tortures them to death in a variety of unpleasant ways. For some reason beyond explanation, this is the movie you want to see. In order to find times and locations for the movie, you likely will open your internet browser, enter a search along the lines of "Mister Ed My Town Times" or some other combination of words you think would constitute the relevant hooks for an internet search to latch onto a movie theater's listings, and you would likely find the times and locations for the movie within a fraction of a second. You might even buy the tickets online, but you'd certainly be able to make plans with your friends to meet at the movie theater and time of your choice.

Now let's imagine that you have better taste in movies and have decided instead to see the Bogart and Bergman classic *Casablanca*. Obviously it's not a movie that's in its first run, but you've heard a rumor that a local cinema might have a showing of the movie sometime this month. You go through a similar internet search, and sure enough, *Casablanca* is listed. Can you go ahead and make plans to attend?

Probably not, at least not without learning more. The internet result might not be for this weekend, for example; instead, it might be a listing for next weekend or last weekend. Or it might be a residue of a Bogart Film Festival three years ago. The Festival was popular and resulted in a substantial number of hits for the movie theater's website, many more than it has received for any other listing before or since. Because your browser returns results based on the number of hits the site receives, it might be that a relevant search result from several years ago is still ranked first. The listing for the performances of *Casablanca* you want to see are still part of your search results, but they might be the second or third (or lower) result rather than the first. Before you can make your plans, you'll need to read and evaluate the results of your search more closely than you did for the "Mister Ed" search.

There's a reason for this hypothetical discussion that goes beyond a recommendation to see a classic film from the 1940s. In fact, this simple example reveals a very important truth about all research: we are better researchers when we already know most of the answer. This sounds simplistic, or even naïve, but think about it for a second; when looking to find the "Mister Ed" listing, you knew the name of the film, the fact that it was currently in release, that your town is somewhere that shows major films when they're released (as opposed to some smaller markets, where it might take a week or so for a film to make it to the movie theater), and that your town's movie theaters put current movie times on their website. You knew, in fact, almost everything you needed to know except for a very specific detail. When your search revealed that detail, you had no need to test your search or to conduct further research into the issue; you had your answer, and you knew enough about the subject of your research that the results were instantly believable to you.

By contrast, you knew less about the *Casablanca* search, and you knew what you didn't know. In particular, you knew that *Casablanca* is a film that has only rare showings in your town these days, and you knew that the results of your search couldn't be guaranteed to be accurate. So rather than rely on them without further consideration, you opened up the link, discovered that it was to an earlier showing of the film, and returned to your main search and checked the other results until you found the one you wanted.

What applies in the very simple example of movie listings applies equally to legal research; we are better researchers when we know almost everything about the subject we're researching, and we need to know both what we know and what we don't know in order to be able to analyze the results of our research intelligently and efficiently. That requires us to think carefully about the state of our knowledge before we begin our research, and the better we are at thinking about our subject for research purposes, the more clearly we'll think about that topic for all purposes. Here's another example, this time more closely related to the lawyering process.

2. Research Process for Lawyers

Suppose you're given a simple set of facts. Wilbur Post went to see *Casablanca* when it was showing at the Bogart Film Festival in Manhattan. He slipped in a puddle of soda that the movie theater's staff failed to mop up. Wilbur suffered a concussion, broken ribs, and multiple bruises, and his clothes were ruined. He came to your law firm today and announced that he wants to sue the movie theater for $4,000 in actual damages and $10 million in punitive damages. Wilbur is the son of a very important firm client. You've been asked to evaluate the strength of his case.

What do you know? Probably not too much, at least at this stage of your legal career. You could leap onto Westlaw or Lexis and do some research, and you would surely find a lot of information without much difficulty. You might find, for example, a North Carolina case that discusses this exact situation in which the jury returned a verdict of $8.6 million, and a federal district court case from California that's also factually on point where the judge granted summary judgment in the amount of $3 million.[2] Let's say the research took you an hour of computer time, and another hour to write up the memo suggesting that Wilbur has a strong case; at current rates, that memo probably cost someone around $1,000.

And it was wasted money, because your research hasn't revealed anything relevant. If you'd thought about this, you would realize (a) that Wilbur's case arose in New York State, so the North Carolina case likely won't help much, if at all, and (b) that since this is likely a matter of state law, the federal case won't be much help either, unless by chance the California federal court was using New York law. Moreover, there's probably something a little odd about that federal court case, because decisions like that usually aren't made by the court during summary judgment.

You've missed some other things as well. The Bogart Film Festival was three years ago, meaning that Wilbur's case might have some statute of limitations problems; that is

---

2. In case you actually do some research on this, all of this is made up, including the cases.

something else you'll have to research. You'll likely need to know additional facts, like how long the puddle of soda was on the floor before Wilbur stepped in it, how observant Wilbur was while at the concession stand—you can probably think of more things you might want to know if you put your mind to it.

You should do all this thinking before you start to research, in order to decide where that research will be conducted (New York State law), how relevant results from other states will be (not very) and how relevant results from federal courts will be (not much, unless they're analyzing New York law, and even then perhaps not so much), what legal issues might be involved in the facts as they're described to you, and how other facts might change the analysis. In fact, what you're doing before you begin your research is almost exactly the process your professors will want you to adopt while you prepare your reading for their classes. They, too, will want you to think about what you're about to read before you read it, to think about how what you're reading fits into what you've read before, and how different facts might change the outcome.

So the better you are at the research process, the better you'll be at learning the law for your other classes. All of law school is, to a greater or lesser extent, about teaching yourself. Legal research models that process and helps you think about what you already know and what you don't know. It also helps you to learn the things you don't know, and that's the process we'll talk about next.

Focus Questions

1. Are you convinced by the discussion of why legal research is a core lawyering skill for American lawyers? Do you believe legal research will be as important to your career as a practicing lawyer as the text maintains it will be?

2. Have you had experience where information you found on the internet was wrong or out of date? If so, how did that affect your research habits? If not, do you think this concern is overblown?

3. The text says that we are better researchers when we already know most of the answer. Is this a useful insight to you? Can you think of examples other than the movie listing example the text uses where knowing most of the answer to your research before you conducted it was useful to you? Can you think of times when it would have been useful to know more about the topic before you began your research?

4. Did you predict the problems in the Wilbur Post research example? If not, do you now see why questioning the jurisdiction in which research is conducted, and questioning the nature of the results generated by a search, is so important?

5. Do you agree with the text that thinking about research before conducting it is an important part of the research process? Do you usually map out a research plan before you begin to research?

Chapter 28

How Do We Find Information?

What You Should Learn from This Chapter

This chapter introduces you to some of the important secondary-source tools lawyers have at their disposal when conducting legal research. The text explains the importance of secondary-source materials and discusses the importance of self-education to lawyers who must research many questions in areas of law with which they are unfamiliar. The chapter is more concerned with the materials discussed than the medium—analog or digital, paper or computer—in which the materials can be found, and that introduces an important theme that runs through this section: it is the information and how it is used that's important, not where it's found.

After reading this chapter, you should:

- have a basic understanding of the principal secondary sources of legal information;
- have a basic understanding of what information you might expect in each of these secondary sources;
- understand that sometimes secondary source information can be biased and how you can still use that information once you learn to identify, and adjust for, that bias; and
- understand that materials like Restatements and Model Laws are secondary sources of law, even though we sometimes mistakenly think of them as primary sources.

If the previous chapter showed anything, it should have been that the best way to research something is to know the answer—or most of the answer—before you start researching. That's fine in theory, but understanding how to apply that theory to practice, especially in the context of legal research, seems like an almost impossible challenge. Law is a vast area and it's impossible for one person to know anything more than a smattering about most of it. Even lawyers who have practiced for years might only know the law of one or two areas in detail, and might have, at best, a general sense of what the law should be in other areas.

In fact, though, finding out about areas of the law we know nothing about is easy, thanks to some very important research tools we'll discuss in this chapter. The hardest part about this process is making an honest evaluation of the state of our self-knowledge. If we allow ourselves to be ruled by ego, and tell ourselves that we're intelligent lawyers or law students, and that of course we must know enough about the legal question we've been asked in order to begin researching it, we stand the chance of missing important information or—even worse—finding the information but being unable to evaluate it properly. If you're willing to admit that you probably don't know enough about almost everything in the law, you'll be much better off and you'll be in the vast majority of lawyers. Once you accept that, the act of informing yourself is relatively easy.

The good news is that we're not alone in our ignorance of such a vast field as the law, meaning that others have long ago seen value in helping us to educate ourselves. Where there's a market for information, many people will seek to trade in it, and such is the case in legal information. There's an impressive array of secondary sources of legal information that we can use to educate ourselves about almost all areas of the law.

It's important to remember that these are secondary sources. That means we shouldn't use them to support legal arguments, because they're not the law, they're just commentaries and analyses of the law. Only primary law—constitutions, cases, statutes, and regulations—can persuasively support a legal argument. These secondary sources can help us find that primary law, and they might even quote directly from primary sources in order to accomplish that—but it's the primary law that supports our arguments, not these secondary sources. Be very careful about citing to any of the sources we'll discuss here in any assignment you submit in law school or in a legal job.[1]

1. Encyclopedias

Before Wikipedia, there were book-based compendiums of information known as "encyclopedias." And just as in other areas of knowledge, there are legal encyclopedias that break down legal information into digestible and easy-to-find pieces. There are two primary legal encyclopedias—*Corpus Juris Secundum* (or CJS, as it's universally known) and *American Jurisprudence, Second Edition* (or Am.Jur., as it's universally known). There are differences between these two encyclopedias, but their similarities are much more important, so we'll focus on those. You can find both CJS and Am.Jur. in print—located in large law libraries—and online.

A quick note about the coverage of these encyclopedias. As you'd expect, both Am.Jur. and CJS are, well, encyclopedic in their coverage; they try to cover every area of the law and provide at least some information on every jurisdiction's treatment of that area. As you would expect, the information is general, and a lot of specific information doesn't make its way into these encyclopedias. That's why they're a good place to start research, but they're hardly ever a good place to finish.

If you're not interested in how all states and jurisdictions have covered a particular topic, and are more interested with how the law stands in a particular state, you might

---

1. As with almost everything in the law, there are no absolutes so it would be inaccurate to say that you should never cite to secondary sources. There are some secondary sources—law review articles, for example—that are citable under certain circumstances. But this is the equivalent of surgery and requires the experience of a seasoned professional. By contrast, you have the equivalent of a basic knowledge of first aid and are standing over a patient with a knife. If you cite to a secondary source, you might get lucky and operate successfully on the patient. But what are the odds? And do you want to assume the responsibility of something going wrong? Far better to stick to primary sources for now.

look for state-specific encyclopedias. These give a more focused view of the law in a particular state, and the information can be more relevant, and easier to find, if your research is geographically limited. These resources are no more authoritative than the general encyclopedias, though, and so shouldn't be used by you as your only source of information. You'll have to research further, and look at the primary sources of law, before your research is complete.

Information in encyclopedias is stored by topic, so the table of contents and the index are both crucial finding tools. Think about the subject you've been asked to analyze and think what words or phrases might best be used to describe the question. Now look for those words and phrases in the table of contents or in the index. If you're doing this online, look for the table of contents or the outline of what's covered in the encyclopedia; in print or online, you'll quickly be able to refine your search to something that comes close to your topic of interest. Read the section that corresponds to your research topic, and you'll learn at least some general information about that topic.

You'll also see the references to primary authority that support what the writers say about that topic, but there are a couple of words of warning here. First, if you're using the print version of the encyclopedia, you should realize that the large, hardbound, volume you're holding isn't reprinted very often. That means that the information in the main volume is likely quite old. Encyclopedias use the same updating strategy as most multi-volume legal sources; they update using pocket parts. These are usually thin documents, updated regularly, that come with a hard piece of backing that fits into a pocket at the back of the large volume. These pocket parts are keyed to the text and/or sections of the main volume and, where text has been changed or a new source has been added to the footnotes, those changes are readily discernible. It's essential that you refer to the pocket part before closing out your reading of a section in an encyclopedia; you can't be done with this resource without checking both the main volume and the pocket part.

The second warning about encyclopedias is that no matter how much they've been updated, a lot of the sources they reveal are old. The sources are probably still good law— we'll discuss how you can, and must, check on that in a later chapter. But the primary sources revealed in encyclopedias tend not to be the most up-to-date cases, and that should reinforce the message of this sub-section: encyclopedias are valuable sources of information, but they're not the end of the research process. You can't simply read a section about your area of interest, note down the cases in your jurisdiction that discuss that area, go to those sources and check that what's been said about them and their holdings is accurate, and then write your results and submit them. The encyclopedia will get you going on your research, but you shouldn't think of it as the only source of information you'll need.

2. American Law Reports

The annotations in the American Law Reports Series (universally referred to as A.L.R.) are a holdover from a time when there were competing philosophies about how the law should be researched and presented. The West Company argued that all cases issued by the court in a particular jurisdiction were, essentially, equal in importance, and that all should be stored and retrieved using the same method. By contrast, the editors of the American Law Reports argued that some cases were more important than others, in that they articulated new ideas and new statements of the law. So the A.L.R. presented these leading cases, with an annotation written by an editor that gathered together all the other cases that were relevant to the leading opinion. A lawyer could read these annotations and stay current with developments in the law, referring to the cited cases for additional information if necessary.

The West philosophy won in the end, and we now think of the A.L.R. purely as a secondary research tool rather than as the primary source of legal information it was intended to be. But A.L.R. annotations can be valuable secondary research tools and wise attorneys use them when possible to gain information about their research topics.

There are a couple of warnings about using A.L.R.s. First, and most important, you shouldn't use the A.L.R. First or Second series[2] of annotations; those are no longer updated and are no longer accurate representations of the law. They are helpful to legal historians, who might want to reconstruct the development of legal thought in a particular area, but to no one else. They will not help you, and will only cause you problems. Don't use them!

Second, be careful to check the pocket parts in the A.L.R. volumes you use if you use them in book form. As with legal encyclopedias, the main volumes are reprinted rarely, and the pocket parts update both the annotations and the primary materials supporting them. Your research work in the A.L.R.s isn't complete until you've used the pocket part.

Third, think carefully about what jurisdiction you're researching before you start to use the A.L.R.s. If you're researching a federal issue, you should look at the A.L.R. Fed. and Fed. 2d, because they were created specifically for federal issues. The other A.L.R. volumes might be of help, since they will bring in some federal information when it's relevant to the topic, but the first place to start is in the series dedicated to federal topics. If, on the other hand, you're looking at state law issues, the A.L.R. Fed. and Fed. 2d are not the places you want to look, for the same reason; they were created specifically for federal issues.

As you would expect, there is an index to the A.L.R. annotations, itself a multi-volume set located next to the A.L.R. volumes. Look through the index and see if there's an annotation that seems relevant to your topic. If there is—and while A.L.R.s aren't encyclopedic in their coverage, they've been around for a while and their coverage is extensive—then take a look at the annotation and at the supporting material, not forgetting the pocket part. The level of detail often is superior to the encyclopedias and the updated supporting materials are often more extensive and more up-to-date as well.

3. Treatises

Treatises are encyclopedic treatments of one specific area of the law. If you are confident that your research topic can best be encompassed by a specific doctrinal con-

2. Legal publishers tend to publish only up to a certain number of volumes of a publication before they start the numbering back at "one." In order to do this, they publish things in "series," so you'll often see sets, like the A.L.R., published in multiple series. As you'll discover, West publishes its case reporters—books containing court opinions—in multiple series as well.

cept—torts, contracts, or property, for example—then a treatise will often be a good place for you to do extensive secondary source research.

Because they are specialist volumes, treatises might not be the best place to begin your research. You might benefit from the general introduction to the subject you can find in regular encyclopedias or A.L.R. annotations before diving into a treatise, because they will give you some context and vocabulary you might be lacking and which might help you navigate through the treatise. But there is little question that if there is a treatise that encompasses the topic you are researching, it will be a great help to you in your work.

The titles of treatises often include the names of the people who first compiled them: Wright and Miller on Civil Procedure, for example, or Prosser and Keaton on Torts. And because of the importance these editors have in their respective areas, many law students and lawyers think of their treatises as being more authoritative than other secondary sources; if Professor Miller wrote something about civil procedure, it must be virtually definitive, they think, and it can be trusted more than a simple encyclopedia entry.

Well, yes and no. There's no question that treatise authors are subject specialists with an extraordinary command of their area of the law. Often they literally helped to write the law in a particular area, playing significant roles in the development of model laws, like the Uniform Commercial Code, or in regulatory schemes like the Federal Rules of Civil Procedure, or else they have taught or practiced in an area for so long, and at such a high level, that they can speak with tremendous authority. But just because a treatise author knows a lot about an area of the law, or because the author might even have written some of the primary law itself, does not mean that courts continue to follow that author's interpretation of the law once it has been adopted into primary law. And you should always remember that it is the state of the law you are researching, not what one author thinks the state of the law should be, that's important.

This is not to say that treatises are not valuable research tools. In fact, they are often the most useful tools you will have to research for primary law in a particular area. But always remember that they are tools for research, not the law themselves. And while their authors' comments on the law might give invaluable insights into the law, how it has developed, and how it will—or should—continue to develop, it is the primary law itself, not commentary on it, that will form the support you will need to answer research questions. In the end, treatises are still secondary sources, not primary ones.

As with most reference works, treatises have tables of contents and extensive indices, and those are the best way to get into their information. You can find treatises in print form in the library, and you can also find them online. If you research them online, you should resist the temptation to search them using word or term searches; rather, you should find the online table of contents or index and use that to refine your search so you can quickly find the topic you're looking for. The reason for this should be obvious; until you've done the research in this secondary source, your knowledge of this area of law is as limited as it would be if you were searching for concepts in a primary law database, so you might use the wrong words or terms to conduct your search in this secondary source. Rather than replicate the problems that have caused you to search a secondary resource in the first place, you'll be far better off using the finding tools provided for you to help you find the relevant portion of the treatise, read that section or sections in order to inform yourself about the law, and then begin searching primary law using the vocabulary you've learned. Any other approach risks missing information or finding the wrong information.

4. Law Review Articles

Law review articles are a perfect example of the cliché that a little bit of information can be harmful. These secondary sources can be very helpful to a legal researcher, but only if they are handled correctly and if the researcher gives a lot of thought to their use. As we go through this discussion of law review articles, please remember this caution: only use a law review article when you're confident that you know what you're doing. Misuse of them can be harmful to your professional health.

First things first. We need to know what we mean when we say "law reviews," and we need to know who wrote the article you want to use. As you can see, when we talk about law review articles, nothing is simple.

There are many legal journals that generally group themselves under the title of "law review," but the journals we typically think of when we use that term are the student-edited and student-published journals housed in law schools. Most law schools have more than one journal, but only one law review. They are often thought of as being the most prestigious journals in law school, and membership on them is much sought by students about to move from their first to second years. The other journals housed in law schools address specialty topics, like international law, entertainment law, and so on.

Most law school journals, including most law reviews, are not peer reviewed; rather, their articles are selected by an editorial board of third-year law students. The articles are written by two groups: the main articles are usually written by faculty members, although not necessarily faculty members at the school where the journal is located. In order to gain tenure, faculty members have to publish a number of journal articles, and most try to publish their work in law reviews. In addition, each journal usually publishes a number of student-written notes and comments each year. These pieces are usually shorter than the principal articles, and are written around a much narrower topic—often a leading case that was recently decided, or a discrete area of the law.

There are journals that are not affiliated with law schools, and they are sometimes thought of as "law reviews," even though most of them do not have "review" in their titles. Journals like the Journal of the Association of Legal Writing Directors and the International Journal of Legal Information are published and edited by academic organizations, but have no direct affiliation with a particular law school. More often than not, these journals are peer-reviewed and are edited by faculty members who belong to the organization sponsoring the journal.

In addition, there are some journals that are not housed in the academy at all, but rather are published by various practitioner groups. The International Association of Defense and Insurance Counsel, for example, publishes a journal called "For the Defense;" it is, as you would expect from the title, a journal that caters to the interests of attorneys engaged in litigation defense, usually on behalf of large corporations. The articles are written, selected, and edited by practitioners, and are usually shorter and less doctrinal than articles published in student-edited journals and law reviews. They almost always deal with areas of practice that are particularly volatile at the time they were written.

As you can imagine, the place where an article is published, and the identity of the author, can affect the utility of the article for the legal researcher. A piece published in a journal dedicated to corporate defense, for example, will likely not carry an article that extols the benefits of a particular cause of action or that discusses why it is important that corporations be sued for a particular type of practice in which they might have engaged. Rather, such a journal will likely carry articles opposing the expansion of causes of action and proposing strategies for defeating a particular cause of action when it is brought. That might be valuable information for a researcher, both one who agrees with the position of the article and one who disagrees with it, but it is important to be able to identify the author's particular bias before one reads and uses the article as a research tool.

Similarly, a student-written piece will likely carry less weight and authority than a piece written by a distinguished academic on the same topic. That might not be fair; the student might have identified a unique perspective on a particular area of the law and the academic might be reprising stale views that have been expressed many times before on the same topic. But just because something is unfair doesn't mean it doesn't happen, and we are all aware that people tend to listen to someone who is readily identifiable as an expert on a topic much more willingly than a new voice.

But all of this assumes that the opinions expressed in the article are the reason you, as a researcher, will be reading it, and that is usually not the case. In fact, not many people pay attention to the opinions expressed in law journal articles, even when the articles are published in a law review, and even when the opinions come from distinguished experts in the law. Law review articles are most often read for the information that falls below the footnote line, not the opinions expressed in the main body of the text.

There is a general rule about law review articles that is often expressed, even though its origin is likely some form of urban myth: the ratio of text to footnote should be one third to two thirds. In other words, for every page of text a law review author writes, the article should contain two pages of footnotes. In practice, this means that most law review article pages have five or six lines of text and somewhere around fifteen to twenty lines of footnote (the ratio discrepancy is caused by footnotes being published with tighter line spacing and in a smaller font than the main body of text). This is an ugly style of prose to read, and is relatively unpleasant to write as well. But for researchers, it can mean a goldmine of information.

In an attempt to be as definitive and authoritative as possible, law review authors try to find as many sources as possible to support their opinions, and once the article is accepted for publication, the law review's editors continue the search and seek to add even more sources to bolster the article. In most law review articles, virtually every sentence is extensively footnoted, with most important secondary and primary sources that relate to the topic listed and analyzed. So while the opinions expressed in the article might, or might not, help you in your understanding of a particular legal issue, the footnotes almost certainly will be useful to you if the article is related to the topic you're researching.

This seems counter-intuitive, but it's very important for you to remember: while some articles might give you analysis or opinions that is helpful to you, they are secondary sources and their authors almost always are writing with an agenda in mind. For that reason, most seasoned legal readers handle law journal articles with care; if they are interested in the topic itself, they might read the article with interest to see what the author has to say. For your purposes, however, you should assume that your readers likely will be uninterested in the academic discussion that takes place in the main body of the article. The real interest in these articles, for you, lies in the rich vein of information in the footnotes. That information is lying close to the surface, readily available, and is waiting to be mined by you as raw fuel for your research.

How you mine that information is another question. Unlike other forms of secondary legal information, journals tend not to have their own, individual, indices. Even if they did, the indices would be next to useless because you would have to search each one individually to be sure that you have covered all possible sources of information. In the days before computer-assisted legal research, the *Index to Legal Periodicals and Books* and the *Current Law Index* were the standard tools to find article titles, but few people use these today. Instead, almost all law journal research is conducted online. And as you might expect, there are some dangers involved in this type of research.

As with all online searching, selecting the correct word, words, or phrases is crucial in order to find relevant information. And as with treatises, if you're researching journals in order to find the appropriate vocabulary for a particular issue, you might be in difficulty. So again, as with treatises, often the best way to begin is by going to the encyclopedias first, learning at least something about your topic, and then formulating searches that are calculated to recover the most relevant information and leave out information that is less relevant.

Another problem associated with journal searching online, though, is the depth of coverage for the database you're searching. When we search online for primary legal information—cases, statutes, and regulations primarily—we expect coverage in the main legal information databases to be complete; Westlaw and Lexis, in particular, will return results that span opinions written today, in some cases, to opinions written in the eighteenth century, when this country's courts were new. After habitual use of these databases, many researchers grow used to this extensive coverage and give little thought to the possibility that some materials might fall outside of our searches because the database itself doesn't carry all relevant materials.

When searching for law review and journal articles, however, it's good to remember that neither Westlaw nor Lexis is necessarily complete. There are practical reasons for this; law journal and law review articles tend to be about current topics, and after, say, twenty years, perhaps, an article's topicality might be so limited that no one would want to read it and, in fact, it might create a misleading impression of currency. So most of the time, these coverage restrictions might not cause a problem.

But sometimes, a researcher might want an older article in order to gain some historical perspective, and some older articles remain as vibrant and important today as they were on the day they were written. If they are not contained in the database you are searching, however, there is no chance that you will find those articles.

There is an alternative database source for law journal and review articles, however, and it is usually more historically complete than other potential sources. This is Hein Online, an online service that is free for most law students while they are in school. Hein's search interface won't win many prizes, but the site comes into its own both with its coverage—which usually lags a year or so behind the current date, but which usually goes back to a journal's first issue—and with its presentation of the articles. These are available in PDF format, making them substantially more readable than printouts from the better known commercial databases. In fact, many legal researchers will search for current articles on Lexis or Westlaw, but will locate and print those articles from Hein, because of the superiority of the print copies.

5. Loose-Leaf Services

Life used to be simpler than it is today, or at least so it seems to us old folk. Back in the eighteenth and early nineteenth centuries, there weren't as many courts as we have today and those courts that did exist weren't issuing opinions with the same speed as our courts today. In order to stay informed, a lawyer could simply read the opinions of the court in the lawyer's local jurisdiction, perhaps annotating those opinions a little to remember the salient points. If the lawyer was in a particular practice, it might be necessary to read the opinions from the Supreme Court of the United States as well, and if the lawyer was in a border area between two states, the lawyer might want to read the opinions from both states. But other than that, the job of staying informed was relatively simple.

Not so today. We are bombarded by primary legal information coming from the federal courts, legislature, and regulatory bodies and their state equivalents. And lawyers are charged with knowledge of all of this legal information; failure to find a relevant case or statute can cause lawyers to lose cases, be sued for malpractice, and—in extreme cases—perhaps even lose their licenses. It seems like a dire prospect.

In fact, though, for many lawyers, things aren't much different from the way they were in the eighteenth century. They can't read all the cases anymore of course—that would take forever. But they can pay someone else to read them and to report back to them when something particularly interesting happens in their chosen area of practice. That's the principle on which loose-leaf services are founded.

Loose-leaf services are so called because of their print origins. In the days before the internet, publishers would hire editors to read opinions, statutes, and regulations when they were issued and to write short, succinct distillations of the important points from those primary sources. The publisher would then gather together the relevant news from a particular area, publish it on flimsy paper that was pre-punched with the holes necessary for the leaflet to be inserted into a loose-leaf notebook, and then send the report on to subscribers. Law firms would get these updates—usually once a week, but sometimes twice a month or once a month—and the lawyers in the practice areas covered by the service would read the leaflet, make notes when necessary, and then insert the leaflet into the relevant notebook. In that way, lawyers would stay relatively current and well-informed on their area of practice. They would still conduct legal research when unique or complex issues arose, of course, but they were covered for the day-to-day developments in specific areas of the law.

Such print services still exist, but they have been augmented (and, perhaps, supplanted) by internet services. Nonetheless, they can be valuable sources of information for legal researchers, although like newspapers, they tend to be ephemeral in nature—yesterday's hot topic might be old news by tomorrow. For a sense of what is happening right now in a particular area of the law, though, these services can be invaluable, and careful legal researchers at least know of their existence and can find them if they have a research topic that is covered by one of these services.

As you might expect, services like this are particularly helpful if you working at a law firm that subscribes to one or more of them. They can give you a close-up view of current topics in practice areas that you might not have studied in law school—specific areas within products liability, for example—and you can usually research them without incurring additional costs for your firm, because the firm already has purchased a subscription to the service. You will have to confirm anything you find in these services using more conventional legal research techniques, of course, but these services can be a helpful and productive first research stop for a less-experienced lawyer.

6. Restatements and Model Laws

One of the most common mistakes made by first-year law students is the assumption that Restatements and Model Laws like the Uniform Commercial Code are primary sources of legal information. It's a mistake that is made by many experienced lawyers as well, so don't feel bad if you were under this misapprehension.

In fact, though, Restatements and Model Laws have no force of law at all until they, or portions of them, are enacted or adopted by courts or legislatures. When that happens, it is the enactment, not the Restatement or the Model Law, that becomes primary law. That sounds unnecessarily complicated; here's a more concrete example.

Suppose the American Law Institute (the body that promulgates and publishes Restatements) comes out with a Restatement of Legal Research. And suppose that Section 400(a) of that Restatement requires that all lawyers perform secondary source research before conducting primary source research. That might be an admirable statement of how things should be, but it's just that: a suggestion of an ideal state. Now suppose that the state legislature in East Carolina introduces a bill that adopts, word-for-word, the Restatement of Legal Research, that the bill is enacted into law, and Section 400(a) of the Restatement is codified at title 5, section 159(a), of the East Carolina Statutes. The language of this statute is identical to the Restatement language. But it is the statutory language, not the Restatement language; that is the law of East Carolina.

That's the situation with real Restatement provisions, like the well-known Section 402(a) of the Restatement (Second) of Torts. This is the provision that first articulated the now-familiar concept of strict liability in tort, but 402(a) itself is not the law anywhere. Instead, virtually all states have recognized the concept of strict liability and have introduced it into their laws, but it is the state action, not the ALI's language, that is state law.

Once the true nature of Restatements and Model Laws is understood, they become valuable secondary sources of legal information. The bodies that promulgate these Model Laws collect a large amount of information to support their views of what the law "should" be, and they publish that information in order that all who read their model laws understand the basis for their opinions. All of that information is grist for a legal researcher's mill, especially one trying to understand why a model law provision was drafted in the way it was. If your job is to support (or oppose) the enactment of a particular provision taken from a Model Law, you will want to know every step that was taken to reach the final version of the language, including all previous drafts, so you can tell how the thinking about the provision developed. And you will want to know what has happened to that language since it was enacted—how many legislatures and courts have adopted it, rejected it, or adopted it in modified form. Often, model provisions have alternative versions and courts and legislatures adopt one version but not another; again, this is relevant information for the legal researcher in this area.

As with all sources, you must be careful to think through what information you might reasonably expect Restatements and Model Laws to contain, and how that information might be revealed to you, before you start using them. If you begin researching without thinking through what you are likely to find and how you are likely to find it, you will end up with a lot of information but very little idea of what you have found and what you have not found. As always, thinking and planning before you start to look is the most important step in legal research and the part perhaps most often overlooked by legal researchers. If you can avoid making this mistake, and can resist the impulse to search before you think, you will be many steps ahead of most lawyers.

Exercises

1. For each of the resources discussed in this chapter, locate their physical location in the library and their location in Westlaw and LexisNexis.

2. Timing yourself, find an encyclopedia entry that will help you answer the question of what possible criminal penalties one might face for the wrongful disposal of a body in both the physical copy of Am.Jur. and the online version. Which search took longer?

3. Find a treatise dealing with one of the doctrinal subjects you're studying this semester and find an entry in the physical copy of the treatise on the topic you've been studying this week. Is there a difference in the level of detail in which the topic is covered in the treatise, as compared to your casebook, or are the levels of detail about the same? Find the same entry in the online version of the treatise. Are there any differences between the physical and online versions?

4. Find your law school's law review and look at the most recent print version you can find in your library. How many articles are there in the volume you're looking at and how many Notes or Comments written by students are there? Using Hein Online, if your school gives you a subscription to that service, find a law review article written by one of your professors. Can you find a physical version of that article in the library collection?

Focus Questions

1. Do you understand the difference between secondary and primary sources and why this is a crucial distinction in legal research?

2. Is the concept of an "encyclopedia" useful to you? Have you used a print encyclo-pedia? A web encyclopedia? Did you find them to be useful research tools? If so, do you think that the legal encyclopedias described here will be helpful to you? What features of legal encyclopedias described here appeal to you, or bother you?

3. Do you understand the importance of the pocket part in updating your research when using print volumes? Will you ever use books when performing legal research?

4. Are there any features of the A.L.R. series that particularly appeal to you or make you think you would not use this resource?

5. Have you ever used a treatise before? Does the discussion of treatises here suggest to you ways in which you might use legal treatises in your research?

6. Do you think that just because a treatise is named for someone famous, the book must be definitive? Or that if someone's name is on a treatise, they must be famous?

7. Does the discussion of law review articles make clear the potential dangers of au-thorial bias in secondary source legal research? Are you surprised by the thought that law review footnotes might be more valuable to a legal researcher than the text of the article?

8. Are you surprised to learn that Westlaw and LexisNexis might not have complete coverage of law review and journal articles? Do you foresee this being a problem for you when you conduct research?

9. Have you ever used a loose-leaf service? Are you surprised to learn that some lawyers use these services as their primary source of information about specific areas of the law?

10. Are you surprised to learn that Restatements are thought of as secondary sources of law? Other than the Restatement (Second) of Torts, are you familiar with any other legal restatements?

Chapter 29

Where Legal Information Is Stored

What You Should Learn from This Chapter

This chapter introduces you to several of the most important repositories of legal information, including the online services of Westlaw, LexisNexis, Bloomberg, and Google. It also introduces you to the opportunities, and some of the problems, associated with some of the free sources of online legal information. It then introduces some of the most important paper-based stores of legal information that you can still find, and use, in most law school libraries.

After reading this chapter, you should:

- have a basic understanding of what you can expect to find in the Westlaw, Lexis-Nexis, Bloomberg, and Google Scholar legal databases;
- have an appreciation of some of the possibilities and dangers associated with free and low-cost legal internet sites; and
- understand that paper sources of legal information retain vitality as important research resources.

Before we talk about how to find legal information, you need to know where to look and what you might reasonably expect to find when you look there. There's nothing complicated about this, and it's something that will become second nature to you in time, but it's important that you start thinking about this now because you can waste a lot of time and effort looking for information in the wrong places.

1. Online Sources of Legal Information

It used to be that legal information was only available in paper form. Then came Lexis—soon to become LexisNexis—and then came Westlaw. And there things remained for a long while, until very recently. With the advent of the world wide web, and in particular with the availability of cheap storage for massive amounts of online data, things have changed and continue to change at a remarkable speed. This overview of online sources of legal information won't try to be definitive, for the simple reason that new databases are being added too quickly for any static document like this to keep pace.

A. LexisNexis and Westlaw

The two most important sources of online legal information are LexisNexis and Westlaw. These services are available to you during your time in law school at no additional charge to you (some of your tuition money goes towards paying the law school's LexisNexis and Westlaw bill). You can, and should, collect your identification cards for each of these databases as soon as possible and should start acquainting yourself with them and how they work. Both services also offer a lot of material that can help you in other classes, and while this is an unsubtle way of trying to get you to become familiar with their services so you will default to that service when researching in law school and, later, in practice, there's no point in turning down support for your other classes if you find it useful, especially when it is, for your purposes, free. Just remember why it's being offered and make your research medium decisions based on what source of information will best be suited to the research task at hand.

LexisNexis and Westlaw might be functionally free to you, at least while you're doing school-based work, but they are extraordinarily expensive for lawyers to use, something that's covered in more detail in a subsequent chapter. For now, it's important to understand why these services are so expensive. The primary legal materials that we're concerned about for the moment are all in the public domain. How can it be, then, that LexisNexis and Westlaw charge so much for us to read them on their services?

They don't. In theory, at least. Instead, they charge money for us to view and use the information they've added to the cases, and very important information it is. We pay to use the search tools—including the ones that are also available in West's print versions of the law—that allow us to research issues when they're raised, we pay to be able to update the law using the Shepard's service (on LexisNexis) or KeyCite (on Westlaw), and we pay for the depth of coverage available to us on these services. Most of all, perhaps, we pay for what we believe is the security of knowing that the information we find on these services is correct—that there are no typos, missing words, added words, or other mistakes that might affect our ability to rely on the cases, statutes, and other forms of law we find on them. That perception might not, in fact, be accurate, but it's one that virtually all lawyers and judges have.

Although the coverage on LexisNexis and Westlaw is not identical, both are comprehensive databases, meaning that they have equal access to complete databases of most primary legal information—all cases published by the courts in all state and federal jurisdictions, statutes and regulations (both federal and state), and many secondary sources of information as well.[1] In addition, both services offer a variety of additional databases—newspapers, public records, SEC documents, and so on—that can be very helpful. As always, though, you should remember that what appears to be free to you during law school is definitely not free once you are out in practice.

---

1. Their coverage of some of these secondary sources—law review articles, for example—might not be as complete as researchers might expect. As with all online databases, it is sensible to check the scope of coverage of the sub database being searched before one begins to research in them.

As I mentioned, you can also find statutes and regulations on both LexisNexis and Westlaw for the federal system and the states as well. In general, it's easier to research these materials in print form than it is online. This sounds like an old person trying to persuade you that the books still have some vitality, but almost everyone—from second-year law students to the designers of the sophisticated search engines used by the commercial legal databases—agrees with me. It irritates some of the computer scientists no end, but they haven't yet come up with a way to improve on the books, at least in this area.

If you insist on reading and researching statutes and regulations online, please remember to start off by using the table of contents for the appropriate jurisdiction or type of law you're researching, and then drill down in the table until you find the specific provision or regulation you're looking for. If you open up the database and attempt to do either a Boolean or natural language search, you'll be swamped by answers that have little to do with what you're researching and the chances of your finding the correct language are low. It really will be easier for you if you use the books here.

B. Bloomberg

The most recent major player in the legal information market is Bloomberg, the well-known publisher of business information. Bloomberg is targeting the corporate market, hoping, perhaps, to draw some business away from LexisNexis and Westlaw from those firms that do mainly high-end corporate work and who use other Bloomberg products already. For those lawyers and law firms, having a suite of information—including legal information—all in one place might well be useful and might make the high cost of full-service databases like LexisNexis and Westlaw (which duplicate a lot of the information already available on Bloomberg) unnecessary.

Such firms likely have no need for the research tools built into LexisNexis and Westlaw, which were designed with litigation in mind. A lawyer who has no need for such sophisticated tools doubtless feels unhappy about having to pay for them, and will, perhaps, embrace a service that offers just the information the lawyer needs, particularly when bundled into a service the lawyer already uses.

But Bloomberg has three features that will likely appeal to more general-practice lawyers as well as those doing corporate work.

First, Bloomberg recently bought BNA, a publisher of loose-leaf services. This was an expensive move (the costs of these things are always unclear to the public, but news reports put the purchase price at $990 million), but it gave Bloomberg two things: immediate access to a deep store of secondary material it could put on its website to make that site more useful to lawyers, and, perhaps more importantly, instant credibility. The BNA brand was trusted by many lawyers and they will now trust Bloomberg as well, and those who thought about it realized that with a move like this, Bloomberg had shown itself to be serious about competing with LexisNexis and Westlaw. There are many other legal information sites seeking to compete in this market but few, if any, can marshal the resources necessary to make a move like this.

Second, Bloomberg has rationalized its pricing policy. It's still not a cheap service (although it has, like LexisNexis and Westlaw, made itself available to law students at a reduced price and is, for your purposes, essentially free for you while you're in law school), but it's very easy for a law firm to know what its costs will be when it uses Bloomberg, something the firm can't necessarily say when it uses LexisNexis or Westlaw. Managing (and predicting) cost is very important to any business, and Bloomberg's approach to pricing will doubtless be attractive to law firm managers. And those managers make important decisions regarding the way legal research is conducted in many law practices.

Third, Bloomberg has revolutionized the way lawyers can access federal docket information stored on PACER ("Public Access to Court Electronic Records"). Don't worry: we won't go into the details of this because it's probably not something you need to worry about in your first year of law school, so what follows is a very brief introduction to PACER and its importance.

PACER is the way every lawyer gets access to federal court records these days. Docket information, briefs—anything related to a case—is filed on PACER. The interface is a mess and the service is costly, but every lawyer engaged in federal litigation needs to have some way to gain access to PACER. And Bloomberg now provides one way to gain that access. Lawyers still pay for a PACER document if it hasn't already been retrieved (if it has, and the document is now on the Bloomberg servers, subsequent retrieval of that document is free to Bloomberg subscribers), but the prospect of having that access combined with the other services Bloomberg offers is likely a very attractive prospect for many practitioners.

And that's what makes Bloomberg's decision to offer access to PACER so interesting. It's not the most attractive or fascinating feature to the casual observer but it shows attorneys who know what they're doing that Bloomberg looked closely and carefully at the legal market and made some shrewd and strategic decisions about what would appeal to practicing lawyers. Maybe Bloomberg can't compete with LexisNexis or Westlaw on the sophistication of its primary law databases and search engines, but by being good enough with those, and by providing useful services as well, Bloomberg has established itself as an important seller of legal information for the long term.

C. Google Scholar and the Internet

It might surprise you to find the internet listed as one of the principal stores of legal information, but reality is reality. An overwhelming number of lawyers at least start their research on the internet, probably using Google Scholar (actually, they probably just use Google, but Google itself sends you to Google Scholar when it flags the results of law-based research). Legal research experts are divided on whether this is a good development or not, but while we debate the issue, more and more lawyers are going ahead and using the service. It seems foolish to continue a debate like this if no one is going to pay attention to the conclusions we reach, and it's much better to just talk about the pros and cons of conducting legal research on the internet.

We'll talk here about Google Scholar. It's almost certainly the most commonly used of all case law-based legal information sites on the internet and the issues users face when they research with it stand as a proxy for all the other free legal information sites on the internet as well.

And there is no better sign of the volatility of the legal information world than the existence of Google Scholar's legal collection. This service was unveiled late in 2009 and there is no doubt that it has changed the face of online legal information. While Google Scholar has had a dramatic effect on legal information, it is much less certain that it will be a useful service for you as lawyers.

The coverage provided by Google is more limited than that offered by LexisNexis and Westlaw. Google has cases from state and federal courts, but not necessarily all cases, and users should be careful to check the scope of coverage before relying on the results as a complete and accurate reflection of the law in a particular jurisdiction for the researched topic. You will also find some secondary sources, like journal articles, on Google Scholar, but again, it's necessary to understand the scope of coverage before being confident that your search has generated all relevant results. Google itself is very careful to make no broad claims about the quality of its coverage, and you should be very cautious before relying too heavily on this tool for your legal research. In fact, no one warrants that the information found on LexisNexis or Westlaw is complete or accurate either, but Google is wise to disclaim any such warranty because there are some differences between the opinions found on Google Scholar and those found elsewhere.

For one thing, of course, the opinions on Google Scholar have none of the editorial and research-based enhancements found on LexisNexis and Westlaw. That means there are no editor-written headnotes[2] or other pre-indexing tools that make the cases easy to search by issue: those are proprietorial to LexisNexis and Westlaw and Google couldn't reproduce them without facing a large lawsuit. Some Google opinions do appear to have parallel citations added to them, although others do not. That likely means that at least some of the opinions Google has uploaded were obtained from a source that had, in turn, obtained them from one of the larger commercial legal information publishers, but that Google is likely updating its database from public domain websites.

To the extent that Google's coverage has chronological limitations, that might or might not be significant depending on the issue you're researching. If you research a state law issue and don't find a case decided before 1950, is that because there are no such cases or is it because Google's coverage starts at 1950 and any cases directly related to the topic decided before then are not included in the database? Are there relevant pre-1950 cases you need to read before reaching a definitive answer to the question you've been posed? Most of the time, probably not: sixty years of state court decisions is probably enough to get binding authority on a substantial majority of legal issues, and many (if not most) of the cases decided before 1950 have either been overruled, superseded, or are simply not recent enough to carry much persuasive power.

But most of the time is not all of the time, and that difference is, for lawyers, everything. Put it this way: assume that every time you base your answer to a question on a less-than-complete source of information, your client's case and your job are on the line (as, in practice, they probably are). If the information you've used is adequate, your answer will be fine and no one will know the difference. You'll save the firm and the client money and everyone will be satisfied with your work. If the in-

---

2. A "headnote" is a short paragraph that appears at the beginning of a case that tells you what part of the case is about. Most cases published by West, or that you find on LexisNexis, have multiple headnotes, one each for the various issues the court deals with in the opinion. The headnotes published by West are written by West's editors, while the headnotes that appear in LexisNexis versions of the same case are extracted from the case using the court's language.

formation you've used is inadequate, your client might lose, you'll probably be fired, and you'll have great difficulty finding another job as a lawyer. And this is true for every legal research assignment you get. Now, how confident are you about using an incomplete database?

It's not a fair question, of course, because few things in life are as straightforward as this comparison makes it appear. In fact, Google is a useful tool for several purposes. For example: if you already know the citation of a case you need and just need to find the text of the case (and the case falls within Google's chronological restrictions); if you know that a legal proposition is relatively well established, and you're just looking for a recent case that says what you already know the law is; or if you're looking for a cheap place to start doing some primary source research,[3] then Google might be for you.

Remember, though, that Google comes with no bells and whistles. There is no service to update a case to make sure that it's still good law, there's very limited ability to use secondary sources to inform yourself about a legal issue before you begin primary source research and—significantly—there's no ability to change the way your search results are presented. That might not seem like an important detail—Google works very well for most things so why should the search engine be less-than-ideal for legal research?

Well, much of the time, we don't really know how well it does work; we're looking for some relatively straightforward information and when we find it in the first or second window, we don't continue to look to see what else Google might have uncovered. Legal information isn't simple, though, and we're rarely looking for just one case in order to answer a question; we want to find all the cases that address the issue so we can make sure that we've looked at both the legal and factual issues in those cases in order to be sure that the courts will rule the same way as we predict when confronted with facts like the ones in the case we're working on. That means that we can't just stop when we find the first case that gives us the "answer" to our question, even if such a concept means much in the law, but rather we need to keep reading until we're satisfied that we've read enough to be sure that we have enough information to be able to give a satisfactory answer. We might be able to get enough information from Google to allow us to feel that confident, but unless you're sure, you're gambling with your client's case and your professional future if you use it.

The bottom line on Google and, indeed, on internet research in general, is that it might be useful for lawyers, but we don't know enough about it to be sure. What we do know about most of the internet-based legal databases, including Google, is that they really aren't intended for us. Rather, they're intended for non-lawyers who are interested in the law to be able to look up some cases for whatever reasons they have. For this limited function, they perform admirably: they provide an important service in making the law more open and accessible than it has ever been before. For lawyers, though, Google Scholar is still too experimental a tool to be reliable. That won't stop lawyers—or law students—from using it, but my best advice to you is to be very careful. Relying on Google research—at least today or tomorrow—could be dangerous because Google might not give you all, or even enough, of the information you need

---

3. As you'll discover, however, it's inadvisable to begin your research with primary sources, so this is almost always a poor choice for a wise legal researcher.

to properly support your analysis. At the speed with which the legal information world is moving, though, it's impossible to say that this will remain true for long.

D. Other Online Sources of Court Opinions

One can find legal information in a number of other places, both for a fee and at no cost. Services such as Fastcase, Loislaw, and Casefinder offer extensive, although not exhaustive, libraries of legal information for a much lower cost than LexisNexis or Westlaw.

Some of these services are not marketed at individual lawyers, but are geared instead for bar associations. These organizations subscribe to the service and then make it available for a minimal fee, or for no cost at all, to their members. That makes these information providers particularly important to solo practitioners and to lawyers who work in small firms and in rural areas, who often have no easy access to full-service legal libraries.

These services differ in their search interface and in the services they offer, but none of them have the comprehensive finding tools offered by the high-cost legal information providers, and the researcher's ability to update the law using these services is limited as well.

Even with their limitations, though, many lawyers use these services because their legal research needs differ from time to time and from assignment to assignment. While you might be better served (as long as money is no object) using LexisNexis or Westlaw for most research tasks, many experienced lawyers feel they don't need the bells and whistles offered by those services, and they certainly don't want to pay the high prices those services charge. So they might use a lower cost service, like Fastcase, to meet their day-to-day needs—finding a recent case that sets out a state's summary judgment standard, for example—and reserve their LexisNexis or Westlaw use for those times when they have a more complex legal issue to research. That's a perfectly valid strategy to employ when you know what you're doing; it's much like using Google to check on the movie times for a movie you know is playing in your town. It might be a less effective strategy for you at present, although knowing that such services exist and having a general sense of their uses and limitations is a good idea. It's certainly possible that services like these will form an important part of the legal research landscape for many lawyers in the foreseeable future.

There are also many free services that offer court opinions: we've discussed Google Scholar, and Findlaw is another such service, although you should know that Findlaw is actually owned by Westlaw, so you can imagine that it doesn't really offer a viable alternative to that service—no for-profit corporation would offer a free product that competes effectively with its flagship product. LexisNexis also offers a stripped-down version of its product, although the same reservations apply to its use; helpful for non-lawyers, but perhaps not sufficiently rich in information to be a viable alternative to the full fee-based version of LexisNexis. Many courts also offer their opinions free on their websites, and it might seem to make sense to use those to perform research, especially of recent developments in a jurisdiction. But there are some important considerations that make this an unproductive path for most legal research.

The first of these is a simple one: the opinions are often not located in a website that's full-text searchable. In other words, in order to find a case, you must either know the case's name or its docket number; there isn't any capacity to search the entire database for, say, a case using the words "products liability" anywhere in the text. That limitation alone severely restricts the usefulness of court websites as a research tool. They're very handy for getting the text of a case that was decided today, and they're useful repositories for recent cases when you know the name of the case, (again, both situations where you already know most of the answer before you begin researching), but not for much more. This isn't true of all court sites, but those that are not full-text searchable have very limited usefulness to you.

Slip opinions[4] from court websites are also lacking some basic information that would allow you to cite to the case. Although there are citation formats for slip opinions, these are usually a last-ditch option when the case can't be found anywhere else. When it can—and these days, opinions often pop up on LexisNexis and Westlaw within minutes of being handed down by the court—citations to those services are preferred.

Another practical limitation of these sites is the lack of any finding tools to aid in your research. Even if you can search the text of all opinions together, you're limited to just the language the court wrote, without any pre-indexed analysis or treatment of the legal issues that helps you to figure out what a case is all about. Sometimes the court's unvarnished language is all you need, but often it helps to have more information to help guide you through what can be long and complex pieces of writing.

And, of course, there are no secondary materials on the court's website to help you understand the broader legal context in which an opinion might have been written. Unlike LexisNexis or Westlaw, for example, where you can bounce between a legal encyclopedia, law review articles, and other secondary materials before launching into primary source research, court websites only have primary materials.[5] Again, that's fine if all you need is to look at the court's language, but not so good if you need some help before starting your research.

And actually, these sites might not be so good if what you need is the court's final language either. That sounds wrong, doesn't it? What could be more definitive than

---

4. "Slip opinions" are the first form in which a court's opinion is distributed, and they're usually the last version the court itself has anything to do with. When the court finishes its opinion, it sends it out to the parties involved and, if the opinion is going to be published, it sends it to the publishers as well. This version is called the "slip" opinion; it's a publishing term which indicates that later versions are to follow. To the parties in the litigation, though, this version is the final word.

5. There are exceptions to this general rule. Some court websites have very handy guides to litigation for pro se litigants or for criminal defendants who are seeking some form of post-conviction remedy on their own. These guides might be written for non-lawyers, but they're also extraordinarily helpful to lawyers who are just starting out; they're often written in plain, easy-to-understand language, they have cites to the leading cases in a particular area, and they're often updated to keep pace with new opinions and current trends in the court. As with all secondary source materials, though, be cautious when you use these materials. A non-lawyer might be able to persuade a court to overlook a mistake that was made based on reliance on information in a guide that is wrong or outdated, but a lawyer will have much more difficulty making this argument. So if you find a guide that's helpful to you, by all means look at it but be sure to verify the information by conducting separate research and, at a minimum, be sure to update all cases it mentions before using them to support any argument you might be making.

the court's own website for finding the court's final language in an opinion? Several things, as it turns out.

Courts post their slip opinions on their websites. Those are the same form of opinions they send to the parties in the cases to alert them of their decisions. Slip opinions are usually posted to the website on the day the decisions are made public, and Lexis-Nexis, Westlaw, and other publishers get the text of the court's decisions from these slip opinions. Once they have them though, LexisNexis and Westlaw have a battery of editors who go through a court's decision, analyzing the issues for their headnotes, adding parallel citations for citations the court has made to other opinions,[6] and—and this is crucial—identifying potential mistakes in the court's language. The editors might catch straight typos—juxtaposed numbers in a citation, for example, or misspelled or misused words (even courts are not immune from misspelling "statute" as "statue," for example)—but they will also flag apparent mistakes as well—an omitted "not," for example, so a sentence reads, "The court will countenance such behavior," instead of the apparent contextual meaning of the sentence, which might be "the court will not countenance such behavior."

While fixing typos might not seem like such a big thing, fixing potential mistakes like this is a very big thing indeed. Of course, changes like these are not made without reference to the court, and it's the court that makes the final decision on whether something is a mistake or is, in fact, what the court meant to say. But any mistakes that are caught, flagged, and fixed in this manner will not be fixed on the slip opinions; those have been public for weeks or months before these mistakes are identified, and it's unlikely that the court will go back, withdraw the slip opinion from circulation, fix the mistake, and then file the amended slip opinion. Rather, there will be two versions of the case—one as the court originally wrote it and one as amended—perhaps by the court, and perhaps only by the publisher. And the court's version will not be the definitive or final version.

This might not seem to be a terribly important issue, and we have no idea how often such changes might occur to slip opinions; LexisNexis and Westlaw are not particularly forthcoming about their editorial process and it's only occasionally that we get a glimpse into what they do. But the possibility exists that the slip opinion you read from a court website might not be the final, definitive word from the court on that subject, and relying on the court's language from such an opinion might get you into trouble.

This issue really becomes significant when the researcher reads a court's opinion from a service that obtained the unedited version of the court's language rather than the edited version. Google Scholar, for example, appears to have most of its older opin-

---

6. Neither LexisNexis nor Westlaw use *Bluebook* form for their citations, whereas courts frequently write their decisions adhering strictly to the requirements of *The Bluebook*. As noted previously, *The AWLD Manual* generates citations that are, for practical purposes, virtually indistinguishable from *Bluebook* citations, so I use *The Bluebook* here as a shorthand way of referring to citations conforming to both books. One well-known issue that can arise from this is that United States Supreme Court cases might appear in slip opinions with citations only to the official reporter, United States Reports. Both LexisNexis and Westlaw will add parallel citations to the United States Reports citation, meaning that the researcher can now find the text in any of the three reporters that publish Supreme Court cases— United States Reports, the Supreme Court Reporter, and United States Supreme Court Reports, Lawyer's Edition. When you see parallel cites to a Supreme Court decision in a case, it's a very good bet that those were added by private publishers after the Court issued its slip opinion.

ions from a source that had been edited, because the cases have added parallel citations, when the court slip opinions for the same decisions don't have these parallel citations. But the newer court decisions Google Scholar posts seem to be taken directly from court slip opinions. It's possible, then, that a researcher relying on a case found using Google Scholar's search engine might be relying on the slip opinion language instead of the final, edited language. That might not be a problem, and there might be no difference at all between the slip and final versions of an opinion. But we can't say for certain that there isn't a difference, and any uncertainty should cause a legal researcher concern.

E. Online Sources of Statutory Information

You can find federal and state statutes in a variety of open access websites, but you should be very careful about using them. Without going into this topic at length, there's a concern that few, if any, of these sites have statutory texts that are verified as "official," and without that assurance, it's difficult to be certain that the text you're using is sufficiently accurate to be reliable. Surprisingly, this is true of most state's websites; the site itself might be "official," but there's no assurance that the text is.

This doesn't mean that there's any suspicion that a state, or anyone, is intentionally providing inaccurate information or that there is anything wrong with the text you find online. But it's by no means impossible for outsiders to hack into a state's database and change a statute's language (even though we have no indication that such a thing has happened yet) and statutory language is so precise, and the interpretation of that language is so demanding of perfection, that even the slightest deviation from the official text—a misplaced comma, for example, or a missing word—could have serious consequences. This is one area where it really is safer to go with the text found in more generally accepted locations, such as the paper forms of statutes or, at least, the Westlaw or LexisNexis versions. These are no more "official" than any other version of the text, but if for some reason the language on which you rely is challenged, it's easier to justify your decision to use statutory language obtained from Westlaw or LexisNexis.

One useful free online site is the Legal Information Institute ("LII"), hosted by Cornell University Law School. It has the full text of the United States Code, and while it's not completely up-to-date, and doesn't have any of the additions that make West's unofficial United States Reports Annotated or the LexisNexis-published United States Code Service so helpful to researchers, it's a handy place to go if you just need the wording of a particular statutory provision. As an added bonus, the LII site also has the text of the commonly used federal rules, such as the Federal Rules of Civil Procedure and the Federal Rules of Evidence and some state statutes as well—very handy if you're away from your desk and you need to remember the precise language of Rule 11 or the state equivalent.

2. Paper-Based Sources of Legal Information

Compared with the ever-changing world of legal information online, things are much more straightforward when it comes to legal information stored in books. There are a few wrinkles to keep in mind, but things have changed little in a long time, and as long as books remain viable, they're unlikely to change much more.

You need to keep a few things straight when it comes to books. The first, and perhaps most important, thing to remember is that the books where court opinions are stored are called "reporters." It doesn't matter if the court is federal or state, Supreme or District, the generic term for the types of books in which its opinions are stored is the same. There are many different reporters, of course, but the important distinction to bear in mind is that of "official" and "unofficial" reporters. Let's talk about that next.

West publishes reporters that contain the opinions of each state's highest court and many intermediate appellate courts as well. It used to be the case that many states would also publish the decisions of their own courts. The cost of doing this has driven many states out of the decision-publishing business, although some states—Maryland, for example—still publish their own decisions (in Maryland's case, these are the Maryland Reports ("Md.") for the Court of Appeals, the highest court in the state, and the "Maryland Appellate Reports" ("Md. App.") for the Court of Special Appeals, the intermediate appellate court). When the state publishes its own decisions, that version is generally thought of as the "official" version and the West version is the "unofficial" version. Most states, though, have decided that since West is going to publish the decisions anyway, it might as well let the West version be the official version.

This can be an important distinction. You might be required—by your citation manual, by local custom, or by the attorney for whom you're working—to "parallel cite" the cases on which you rely. That means you might have to provide citations to all the different reporters in which a case might be found. And since you likely will have to provide pinpoint citations that require citations to the specific page of the case as well as the first page of the case, you will have to provide a lot of information for each citation you use. Often, but not always, the West versions of cases will show you both the West page number and the page number of the official reporter.[7] If that's not the situation, you'll have to look up the case in both the official and unofficial reporters or, as is more and more the case these days, look up the case online, where both page numbers can be identified with relative ease.

How will you know which states publish their own reporters and which don't? Simple. Your citation manual lists each jurisdiction, state and federal, and the reporters in which its decisions can be found. Often you'll see that a state used to publish its own decisions and then stopped; your citation manual will give you the dates of publication so you can tell whether you'll need to parallel cite or not.

For federal court, the situation is simpler. Only the Supreme Court publishes its own decisions. All other federal courts—from the Court of Appeals down to the Bankruptcy Courts—rely on West to publish the print versions of their decisions. And West

---

7. The West versions of cases almost always take up more pages than the official versions of cases because West publishes every word that is contained in the official version of the case, and adds Key Numbers and headnotes for every case as well. The headnotes can frequently take up several pages. Differences in typography and printing style also mean that the pagination on the official and unofficial versions of a case will often have little to do with one another.

publishes an unofficial reporter of Supreme Court opinions as well, so all published[8] federal cases are covered by West's Key Number research system.[9]

The federal reporters are as follows:

Supreme Court:	United States Reports (official), Supreme Court Reporter (unofficial), and United States Supreme Court Reports, Lawyer's Edition (universally known just as the "Lawyer's Edition") (unofficial)
Courts of Appeals:	Federal Reporter (first, second, and third series), Federal Appendix
District Court:	Federal Supplement (first and second series), Federal Rules Decisions
Bankruptcy Court:	Bankruptcy Reporter

West groups the states into regions and publishes the decisions of each region's courts in a regional reporter. Here's a list of states, organized by reporter:

Atlantic:	Connecticut, Delaware, District of Columbia, Maine, Maryland, New Hampshire, New Jersey, Pennsylvania, Rhode Island, Vermont
Northeastern:	Illinois, Indiana, Massachusetts, New York, Ohio
Southeastern:	Georgia, North Carolina, South Carolina, Virginia, West Virginia
Southern:	Alabama, Florida, Louisiana, Mississippi
Southwestern:	Arkansas, Kentucky, Missouri, Tennessee, Texas
Northwestern:	Iowa, Michigan, Minnesota, Nebraska, North Dakota, South Dakota, Wisconsin

---

8. The questions of what is and isn't a "published" opinion, and what percentage of a court's opinions are "published" each year, aren't as straightforward as they might appear. It's probably more accurate to speak of "precedential" and "non-precedential" opinions although we often revert to speaking of cases in terms of publication, since this is the way they were referred to in the days before the internet. Many courts issue a high percentage of non-precedential opinions, and almost all courts (except the United States Supreme Court) issue more non-precedential opinions than they do precedential ones (all Supreme Court opinions are precedential). The non-precedential opinions were called unpublished because that's what they were—you couldn't find them because they weren't published anywhere. But once computer-assisted legal research came into being, LexisNexis and Westlaw sought to make available as many court opinions as possible, even those that weren't "published." So a strange, anomalous situation arose where opinions could simultaneously be considered "unpublished" and were still published and immediately available on LexisNexis and Westlaw. In fact, things got even stranger when West started publishing the Federal Appendix, a reporter that published unpublished decisions. Finally, the semantic lunacy of this became so disturbing that the "precedential" and "non-precedential" labels came into currency. It might still be troubling to you that a majority of a court's decisions are considered non-precedential, but at least we can have the discussion without engaging in the existential debate about whether an opinion can be both unpublished and published at the same time.

9. We'll discuss Key Numbers in more detail later.

| Pacific: | Alaska, Arizona, California, Colorado, Hawaii, Idaho, Kansas, Montana, Nevada, New Mexico, Oklahoma, Oregon, Utah, Washington, Wyoming |

Whether or not the opinions in these reporters are "official" or "unofficial" depends on whether the state continues to publish its own opinions. As a practical matter, though, almost all paper-based legal research is done in the regional reporters because of the ubiquitous nature of West's Key Number system. How that system works, and why it is a helpful means of conducting legal research, is described in a later chapter.

The situation is also pretty stable when it comes to statutes and regulations in print form. Each state has its own statutory and regulatory publications; the best way to find out the names of these is to go to your citation manual and get the information there. Most law libraries—even the very large ones—don't have full sets of every state's statutes and regulations, so if you need to research the law of a jurisdiction other than the one where you are at present, you might need to use Westlaw or LexisNexis. Again, remember to use tables of contents and other relevant tables when at all possible: try to avoid, at all costs, doing word searches in statutory or regulatory databases.

For federal statutes, we have an official code, the United States Code, published by the federal government, and two unofficial versions, the United States Code Annotated ("USCA"), published by West, and the United States Code Service ("USCS"), published by LexisNexis. As a practical matter, you should only use one of the unofficial codes; they're so much better as research tools than the official code that there's really no comparison. The reason is simple: the USCA has all the information the official Code has, and in addition, it gathers up every case that has cited to a Code section or subsection, and organizes them by topic. It's an extraordinarily useful idea, because you rarely just want to know the language of a provision, you also want to know how courts have interpreted and used that provision, and here—all in one place—you have that information, presented in a clear, easy-to-use, indexed format. The USCS follows a similar approach, but is stronger when you're doing regulatory research; it does a very good job of gathering up references to the regulations used to implement various statutes and providing cross-references to those after every section of the Code.

The unofficial codes are updated using pocket parts and, as always, no research is complete without having used the pocket parts as well as the main volume. It's the only way you can be sure you've done a comprehensive job of updating your research using those materials.

Focus Questions

1. Have you picked up and registered passwords for all the online services available to you, including Westlaw and LexisNexis? If not, you should do that as soon as those passwords are made available to you.
2. Are you surprised to see Google listed as one of the principal sources of primary legal information? Have you ever used Google for this purpose? Does the fact that the text cautions you about the reliability of legal information found on Google

surprise you? In your opinion, does the text adequately describe the potential dangers of using a less-than-complete source of legal information?

3. How often do you think you will use sources of legal information other than Lexis or Westlaw? Will you consider Bloomberg as a possible legal research source? Do you think you will conduct legal research in books? How often did you use books as sources for research during your previous academic career?

4. Are you surprised to read that court-issued slip opinions might not be the most definitive source for a court's opinions? Do you understand the text's discussion of why that might be so?

5. Have you considered the possibility that statutory information might be more difficult to find online than it is in the books? Does this affect your answer as to how often you will use books for legal research?

6. Are you disturbed by the possibility that a state's laws could be hacked and altered? What if Westlaw and LexisNexis were to be hacked and either changed or made unavailable? What effect would this have on the American legal system? Should states, and the federal government, take steps to ensure the integrity of their official statutory and regulatory presences on the internet? Why might they not do this?

7. Are you surprised to learn that the unofficial versions of the United States Code might be more useful to legal researchers than the official version?

Chapter 30

The Cost of Legal Research

What You Should Learn from This Chapter

This chapter introduces you to a tangential, yet crucial, aspect of legal research: its cost. Although the cost of legal research materials is included in your law school tuition, and is therefore not something about which you need worry during law school, the cost of legal research is a vitally important part of law practice. The text discusses the way in which cost can be counted and gives you a sense of how much legal research costs law firms and their clients. It also discusses briefly the important reality that not all clients can afford computer-assisted legal research and the implications of this for their lawyers.

After reading this chapter, you should:

- have at least a sense of how much the research you conduct might have cost were you working at a law firm;
- understand why both computer-assisted and paper-based research materials are expensive tools for lawyers to use;
- understand the basics of how law firms account for the cost of research materials; and
- realize that the cost of legal research materials can make computer-assisted legal research unavailable for some clients.

First things first. The legal research you do as part of your work as a law student will cost you nothing in addition to what you already pay to go to law school. Part of your tuition money goes to paying for the research tools you'll use while in law school—the books in the library, Hein Online, Bloomberg, LexisNexis, and Westlaw—and you won't get an additional bill for their use as a law student.

The situation is less clear if you use your student ID to do work for an employer during the summer. It used to be true that such use of a student ID was prohibited and was a violation of your agreement with these services. In fact, LexisNexis and Westlaw would switch off your access to their services and you would have to petition to have access, usually because you needed it for journal work or for work you were doing for a professor. Then Bloomberg permitted students to use their student IDs without restriction during the summer, and both Westlaw and LexisNexis changed their policies, loosening up the restrictions on student ID use somewhat. But like most things to do with legal research, these decisions can change quickly and what was true in one year might not be true the next. The best advice is to check with the legal information services to find out what restrictions might apply to your student password in the summer if you want to have access.

Things are both more simple and more complicated once you leave law school. You, or someone, will have to pay in order for you to have access to LexisNexis, Westlaw, and Bloomberg. How much it costs to use LexisNexis and Westlaw as lawyers, though, is one of the more mysterious questions we can pose about our universe, and there is no definitive answer. Why that is, and what it means for you as lawyers, is something we'll discuss in this chapter.

While the question of how much legal research costs is virtually impossible to answer specifically, the general answer is easy: it costs a lot. As a benchmark for you, a 2013 article put the cost of an hour's research on a 50-state survey of an area of the law in WestlawNext at around $3,400.[1] That number will only be going up as time moves on. And while there are cheap (or no-cost) alternatives to LexisNexis and Westlaw, you should be very cautious about their use.

In particular, you should never use them without checking first with a more senior lawyer in your firm, ideally the person who gave you the research assignment in the first place. That lawyer might be happy for you to use a no-cost research service, but the lawyer might also have reasons why you should not use such a service. This is one time where you should get advice and follow it; this isn't the time to be showing initiative.

Law firms face costs to acquire and store the materials necessary to perform legal research, and the time it takes attorneys to conduct legal research. While these costs are often defrayed by clients, it is becoming increasingly difficult for firms to recover these costs and it is important for you, as future junior associates in law firms, to understand a little of the economics behind legal research in order to understand why efficient and effective legal research techniques are so important for you.

1. The Cost of Print-Based Research Materials

Many law firms still maintain extensive print libraries, although the number is dwindling each year. The cost of these libraries is very high, and none of it can be recovered directly from clients.

---

1. Emily Marcum, *The Quest for Client Savings in Legal Research: WestlawNext v. Westlaw Classic*, 32 Leg. Ref. Services Q. 142, 144 (2013). The same article concluded that use of WestlawNext was twice as expensive, to law firms, as the use of Westlaw Classic, the original version of Westlaw (with, of course, many updates) that was discontinued in 2014. *Id.* at 157. West would doubtless object to the methodology used to generate these conclusions, and would argue that each firm's experience would differ. It would also point out that the article speaks specifically of the costs of "billing back" or "cost recovery," not the raw cost of using the databases. At the time of writing, the name "Westlaw Classic" was still being used, although it seems at least possible that by the time you read this the name will have reverted to simply "Westlaw." As an interesting sidelight on the cost of these services, the article notes that WestlawNext cost "more than $1 billion to develop during five years...." *Id.* at 157, Any service that cost that much might reasonably be expected to charge a lot in order to attempt to recoup its costs.

The cost of print-based legal research materials comes from a number of different sources, primarily:

- the cost of the materials themselves;
- the cost of housing the materials; and
- the cost of maintaining the materials.

We'll consider each of these costs in turn.

A. The Cost of the Materials Themselves

Books cost money to buy, and legal research books cost a lot of money. Much like buying school textbooks or any other kind of books, law books can be bought second-hand, but the quality of the materials might not be comparable with the quality of new materials.

How much the books cost depends in part on the jurisdiction under consideration. Several years ago, materials for a smaller state, like Rhode Island, would cost less than for a larger state like, for example, California. Here are some examples:[2]

- the cost of a core set of new materials[3] for Rhode Island in 2002 was approximately $7,300, with an annual supplementation cost of $2,400. The cost of a set of used materials was approximately $3,400, annual supplementation costs of $2,400;
- the cost of a core set of new materials for California was approximately $10,800, with an annual supplementation cost of $4,100. The cost of a set of used materials was approximately $4,500, with an annual supplementation cost of $4,100.

But even a barely adequate library would need more materials than just these and that could drive up the cost substantially. A set of federal materials in 2005, for example, cost $41,173 new, $10,021 used, and $12,098 in annual supplementation costs. The cost of secondary materials necessary to search these federal materials was around $14,000 new, $5,800 used, and $13,000 in supplementation costs.

Supplementation costs—vital if the print library is to remain viable as a research tool—have increased at an alarming rate recently. The supplementation costs for Am.Jur. 2d were $1,300 in 1993, $3,058.75 in 2001, and $4,560.75 in 2005. Costs have only continued to increase since then.

---

2. Most of the information in this chapter is taken from an article I wrote in 2006: Ian Gallacher, *Forty-Two: The Hitchhiker's Guide to Teaching Legal Research to the Google Generation* 39 Akron L. Rev. 151 (2006). The other main source is Kendall Svengalis, *Legal Information Buyer's Guide and Reference Manual* (2002). This is old information, and every year that passes makes the specific dollar amounts quoted here more out-of-date. But even information that was completely up-to-date on the day that is was written would be hopelessly out-of-date when you read it. This information is included to give you at least a sense of how much all of this costs. You can assume that, as a general rule, the cost of materials is not going down, so everything is likely much more expensive today than the numbers here might indicate.

3. "Core materials" includes a set of state statutes, reporters covering the state's appellate courts, a digest allowing a researcher to research the reporters, a Shepard's citator, and a set of rules governing practice in the state's courts.

The cost of print materials alone for even a modest collection of legal materials is probably around $200,000 annually, and that number goes up quickly when the collection increases in size.

B. The Cost of Housing Print Materials

The least obvious, but often most significant, cost of a print-based legal research collection is the cost of housing it—literally the cost to the firm of the space the collection occupies.

Library space is nonproductive space to a law firm. To understand this concept, consider what happens in an associate's office in a firm. The associate sits at a desk, doing the firm's work—making phone calls, writing memos, letters, and briefs, and so on. All of this work can be billed to a client on whose behalf the work is being done, and the office is therefore productive space—the work done there generates income. By contrast, the library is nonproductive, because it just stores the print collection. It's possible that an associate might take up a chair in the library in order to perform some legal research, but for the vast majority of time, the library is passive—or nonproductive—storage space. And yet the space must be lit and heated in the same way as the associate's office and—crucially—the firm must pay rent or mortgage to cover the space taken up by the library, even though no, or very little, work is being done in that space to generate income in order to pay for its cost to the firm.

C. The Cost of Maintaining the Materials

Some firms delegate the task of maintaining small print collections to an office worker or (rarely) to a junior attorney. When that happens, the library is usually just one of a number of duties that person performs, and the cost of maintaining the library can be spread across all that person's jobs.

When a library is more extensive, however, the firm will likely have to hire a part- or full-time librarian to maintain the collection. That librarian's salary, benefits, office furniture, and other expenses, like other non-billing employees of the firm and, indeed, the cost of the print materials and their storage, are accounted for as an overhead expense of the firm. Sometimes the librarian's time can be billed to a file—when the librarian is asked to do specialized research on behalf of a client, for example. But most of the time, the librarian is engaged in important, but non-billable, work.

D. Expenses and Income

A law firm has many overhead expenses: salaries, office furniture, electricity, heat, rent, and so on. By contrast, a firm has only one way (usually) of making money: fees paid by clients for the firm's services. For each dollar of fee paid into the firm, some of it (the large part of it) goes to paying for the firm's expenses, and the remainder goes into profit which, in most law firms, is divided among the partners or shareholders of the firm. For a law firm, the trick is to set an hourly billing rate that is high enough to pay for the firm's expenses and still leave enough for a lot of partner income, yet not so high as to discourage clients from retaining the firm to do its legal work.

2. The Cost of Computer-Assisted Research

Based on the above, it would be reasonable to assume that the cost of computer-assisted legal research would be relatively low. The information all exists in an analog form, and the cost of storing and making information available digitally is substantially lower than is the cost of printing, binding, and shipping books. Yet that is not the case.

As I said earlier, though, we can't say with any great certainty how much LexisNexis and Westlaw charge law firms. That's because the pricing changes almost firm-by-firm, depending on the type of plan the firm buys. There used to be only two types of plan; the hourly plan, where a user paid for each minute of time on the database, and the transactional plan, where the user paid for every search run, regardless of how much time it took. Yet even that is misleading, because each database was priced differently: in general, the larger the database, the more it cost to use, regardless of whether the user was paying on an hourly or transactional basis.

The beauty of this approach, though, was its transparency for the client. For each search conducted, an attorney enters a client code that is attributable to both the client and the specific matter for which the firm is doing work. A code of 865-15, for example, might mean that research is being conducted for the firm's 865th client (say, Megacorp.) and the fifteenth matter for which the firm has opened a file on behalf of Megacorp. (say, the *Smith v. Megacorp.* litigation). Every time an attorney researches an issue related to the *Smith* litigation on Westlaw or LexisNexis, the attorney types in 865-15 before beginning the research and the cost of that research, down to the penny, is automatically broken out on a bill the firm receives at the end of the month. It's a simple matter to transfer that cost to the client on the bill the firm prepares and sends out to Megacorp, together with the bill for the attorney's time for researching the issue.

The problem is, some time ago clients decided that they didn't want to pay for legal research. For one thing, they said, it costs a lot of money. And for another, they said, didn't your lawyers go to law school? Didn't they learn the law there? Why should we have to fund their research into something (the law) they should already know? Maybe they'd pay for the lawyer's time, but they certainly weren't going to pay for these expensive database charges. How expensive? Hundreds of dollars per search, often tens of hundreds each month, sometimes hundreds of thousands. If this surprises you, remember the 2013 article that concluded that a full 50-state search on WestlawNext could cost around $3,400 per hour. It's not at all a stretch to imagine one client engaged in large, complex litigation paying well over $1,000,000 in legal database costs over the course of a year.

These are substantial costs, and firms were forced to pay them from their own pockets because, as you can imagine, their contracts with West and LexisNexis had no provision in them about not paying the database providers if the firms weren't paid by their clients for the research performed on those services. Perhaps as a response to this billing issue, both LexisNexis and Westlaw came up with a creative new approach to billing: now they would offer a firm a flat, monthly fee. Attorneys at the firm could do as much research as they liked on the databases (with some restrictions; not all sub-databases were contained within the flat rate, for example) for the same cost. And because this was a flat cost, it could be accounted for in much the same way as the library—as an overhead cost spread out over all the hours billed by attorneys at the firm over the course of the month.

The crucial thing to remember about flat fees, though, is that they can change over time. A firm will typically negotiate a flat fee arrangement for a year or two—the length of the contract probably reflects the firm's bargaining power, with the stronger firms being able to negotiate longer contracts. When the end of that flat fee arrangement comes around, the parties will typically renegotiate, and one measure the parties can use in this renegotiation is the average usage during the prior contract term. In other words, suppose a firm negotiates a flat fee for legal database access for $Y per month for two years. During the term of the contract, the firm uses the database at a rate that amounts to $Y x 2. The fee for the next contract will likely be closer to $Y x 2 than it will be to $Y.

This means that even if a firm where you work has a flat fee arrangement with Westlaw or LexisNexis, the amount of time you spend using that database will still be recorded and is still important to the firm, because it will serve a part of the calculations for the next contract. So if you use, say, LexisNexis as a home page, and log on to it for ten hours a day, every day, you probably won't cost your firm much this year, because of the flat fee arrangement, but you could cost your firm a substantial amount in subsequent years. And firms pay attention to that sort of thing.

Flat fees are not, in any case, cheap, and some clients continued to complain—clients, for example, for whom no legal research was being performed but who still had to pay hourly rates that were not adjusted downwards to account for the absence of research—but, by and large, the flat fee billing approach quieted concerns about the cost of computer-assisted legal research for those firms who could afford such services to begin with.

3. Not Everyone Can Afford Computer-Assisted Legal Research

And, of course, that's a crucial caveat, because not all firms—and certainly not all clients—can afford computer-assisted legal research. As you can imagine, costs for research mount rapidly and the monthly LexisNexis and Westlaw bills can be jaw-droppingly large, especially if you're paying the bill yourself. Most individual clients simply can't afford to pay costs like this, and more and more corporate clients are unwilling to pay those costs either.

There are alternatives available to lawyers with clients who can't pay such costs, most of them requiring the lawyer to perform print-based legal research.[4] For firms that don't have their own libraries of materials, there are law school law libraries—most of which are open to the public and to the bar—and bar association and courthouse libraries, usually located in county seats, where lawyers can gain access to at least basic print materials and research legal issues, usually for a minimal annual membership fee.

All of this works as long as the books are still available for use. But what if print-based legal research materials are no longer printed? This hasn't happened yet, and West—

---

4. This is one of the reasons legal research programs keep teaching print-based legal research techniques, even though most of you believe (privately, if not publically) that computer-assisted legal research must be a superior approach. Some firms have clients that won't let you do computer-assisted research, and some government legal employers take the same position. So no matter how outmoded print-based materials might be, you still have to know how to use them.

the largest publisher of print-based legal materials—has offered numerous assurances that it won't happen in the foreseeable future either. The ever-increasing cost of print materials, however, has made some observers suspicious that legal publishers might be trying to get as much as they can for the print materials now and, when enough subscribers discontinue their subscriptions because the costs are just too high, they might find that it's unprofitable to continue to print legal information. If that happens, how will those who can't afford the expensive, full-service databases be able to compete with those clients who can pay for LexisNexis and Westlaw?

The answer to this question lies, inevitably, with online services. The costs—both financial and ecological—associated with print make it virtually impossible that a publisher willing to develop and print an alternative to West's print-based legal materials will appear. The internet, by contrast, offers a low-cost medium by which to disseminate legal information. We've seen a lot of low and no-cost legal information providers popping up recently, and many of them are very helpful, but no alternative to West's well-established pre-indexed research system known as Key Numbering has yet appeared. Because pre-indexed research is so important, that means that Key Numbers, and the digests in which they are indexed for research purposes, get their own chapter. That comes next.

Exercise

When you next research an assignment, time yourself to find out how much net time it took you to conduct the research from start to finish. If you conducted research in several different sessions, time each of them and add up the total amount of research time. Give yourself a billing rate of $500 per hour. How much did your research cost your hypothetical client? If you used Westlaw or LexisNexis, how much time did you use those services? Assume, for our purposes, an hourly cost of $1,500 for online research and add that to the cost of your time. Now how much did your research cost your client? If you were writing the bill to send to your client, would you bill the client for every minute of your research time, assuming that client will pay for legal research? If not, how much time would you deduct? Why?

Focus Questions

1. Have you considered how much a print library would cost a law firm to maintain? Do you have a sense of how much of that cost is attributable to housing and maintaining the materials?
2. Had you considered the issue of productive and non-productive space in a law firm? Do you see why this is an important consideration for law firms that are trying to keep costs down?
3. Are you surprised to learn how much Westlaw and Lexis cost law firms? Do you have any thoughts about why the charges are so high?

4. How do you respond to the idea that some clients won't pay for legal research? What is an appropriate response for a law firm to make to a client that takes such a position? How might that response affect a law firm's bottom line? If your results of your answer would compel the firm to lay off some associates, would your answer remain the same?

5. Have you heard of the flat-rate approach to legal database billing? Are you surprised to learn that the amount of time an attorney spends on using such a database might be used to calculate a renegotiated fee in subsequent years?

6. Had you considered the extent to which the cost of legal research might restrict a low-income client's access to the legal system? Are there fundamental fairness questions raised by the potential disparity in access to the courts caused by the expense of legal research?

Chapter 31

Key Numbers and Digests

What You Should Learn from This Chapter

This chapter introduces you to a specific legal indexing tool developed by, and available only from, the West Company. The chapter doesn't endorse the use of this particular tool, but acknowledges that it is so ubiquitous that an understanding of how it works is crucial for all lawyers, regardless of whether they use this tool or not. The Key Number system is also a useful way to introduce the concept of pre-indexed legal research, a concept that will become important as we continue our discussion of research technique. The chapter emphasizes that Key Number searching is something that can, and should, be done in both paper and digital media.

After reading this chapter, you should:

- have at least a basic understanding of the Key Number system;
- understand how a Key Number is associated with a particular sub-topic of the law;
- understand how using Key Numbers can help legal researchers to uncover cases that include a discussion of the issue as they are researching; and
- understand that even though Key Number researching was designed for paper-based research, it is still a valid strategy when conducting computer-assisted legal research.

These subjects properly belong in the chapter devoted to secondary legal information, but they're so important that they merit their own special treatment. Digests are books—there's no real equivalent to them in the computer-assisted research world—but they're one of two types of book you should really learn about (the other is the annotated statute—we'll talk about that later). Let's talk first about what Key Numbers and digests are, and then discuss why digests are so important.

1. Key Numbers in General

The Key Number system is owned by West. That company invented the system and it owns the copyright. That's very important to understand: there's no copyright in the language of cases themselves—they're public documents and there's old and well-established Supreme Court precedent that makes clear that the text of court opinions lies in the public domain. Other aspects of cases—the citation, for instance, and the page numbers—probably aren't in copyright either, although the issue is a little less certain. There are cases that hold that such details aren't copyrightable, but they're not from the Supreme Court and it's certainly possible that West might think about challenging those cases someday.

But there's no question that Key Numbers (and the information overlay LexisNexis puts on its cases; we'll only talk about West here because, frankly, it's been around longer, is better known to most lawyers, and is relevant to both print-based and computer-assisted legal research) are very much copyrightable and are in copyright. Key Numbers are the reason West can charge so much money for a service that, in many other ways, simply takes public domain documents and presents them for a large fee.

And there was no question that the charge was justified, at least until the advent of computer-assisted legal research. Without Key Numbers, lawyers would have been almost unable to find relevant cases to aid them in their work. By contrast, with Key Numbers, legal research was made easy.

Key Numbers are, in essence, an index to the law. Think about that for a second. Every case, decided and published by every state and federal court since they were established has been indexed using this system. That's a massive undertaking. And it's even more complicated than it might at first seem, because unlike the decisions typically found in your casebooks, actual court decisions often rule on multiple legal issues that arise in a case, and all of them are indexed using the Key Number system.[1] It seems obvious, even on the face of the problem, that a conventional index like the one you read in the back of a normal reference book, just won't suffice in a situation as complicated as the law.

In fact, while it doesn't necessarily look much like a regular index, the Key Number system bears a lot of striking similarities to what we might think of as a normal index. Let's dive in to a discussion about the system and maybe some of those similarities will become apparent.

2. The Key Number System in Theory

Any index requires the segmentation of a large subject into smaller, more manageable, components. The law is no different. And because the process is much like the one you've already experienced in law school, it shouldn't be too difficult for you to understand.

When you came to law school, you likely told friends and family that you were going to study "the law." When you came here, though, you discovered you were going to study things called "torts," "contracts," "civil procedure," and so on. These are just di-

---

1. The opinions you read in your casebook likely resolved multiple issues as well, but your casebook editors have edited out everything that doesn't relate to the issue they're using the case to illustrate. That's why opinions that can be very long when written by courts can show up in a page or two in your casebooks.

visions of some larger concept known as "law," and while they're somewhat artificial,[2] they're very helpful to us when we study law and when we research it.

Carving an area like "torts" away from the broader "law" gives us a more manageable chunk of information to work with. And it allows us to subdivide even further: we can call one part of the "tort" division "negligence," for example, and other part "strict liability." And we can go on and on, subdividing within those areas, until we can group together all the cases that talk about one discrete area of the law. That's what you did when you discussed, for example, the notion of "duty" within the larger division of "negligence," within the larger subdivision of "torts." And that's exactly what the Key Number system does as well.

In essence, the Key Number system allocates a number to each division and subdivision within the law, and then assigns that number to every case (or part of a case) that analyzes that issue. As long as you know the correct number, then, you can find all the cases organized according to that number and have confidence that you've read every case that discusses that issue. Substitute an alphabetical listing for number, and substitute page numbers for cases, and you've just described a regular book index. But these differences are important, and so is the sheer size of the undertaking. You might see why if we look in more detail at how this process works.

3. The Key Number System in Practice

Let's use as an example the first issue discussed in the case of *Abram v. San Joaquin Cotton Oil Co.*, 46 F. Supp. 969 (S.D. Cal. 1942). There's nothing at all important or significant about this case in particular. We're using it here because I used this case to discuss the Key Number system in an article I wrote a while ago.[3]

Before it got to the heart of the issue being raised by the parties, the court first made the general statement that "[f]or the purpose of a motion to dismiss the complaint, all facts well pleaded in the complaint must be accepted as true and correct."[4] Even though this is a very commonplace assertion of familiar law, the West indexer had to make a note of because it's a point of law in the opinion. In its most general sense, this is an issue of federal civil procedure, so the indexer gave the issue the appropriate key number for federal civil procedural issues—170A.[5] Because this is an issue relating to dismissing a complaint, the indexer got more specific and gave the issue the designation

---

2. In real-life law practice, cases typically involve any number of doctrinal areas—there's no such thing as a "torts" case that doesn't involve "civil procedure" too, for example, and very often other concepts get dragged in as well. To lawyers, these doctrinal divisions don't matter and are often invisible.

3. Ian Gallacher, *Mapping the Social Life of the Law: An Alternative Approach to Legal Research* 36 Int. J. Legal Inf. 1 (2008).

4. *Id.* at 972.

5. *Id.* at 969. Actually, things were a little more complicated than this. Back when the opinion was decided, West used a different numbering system to designate civil procedure issues. The designations I've used here are the contemporary ones, but the periodic updating and revising of this system adds a layer of complexity to research in older cases.

170AXI and because the issue is even more specifically about the involuntary dismissal of a complaint the designation became 170AXI(B).[6] Things get even more specific, though, because the opinion depended on the resolution of a proceeding called to decide whether an involuntary dismissal of the complaint was justified. With each layer of specificity, a new part of the designation was added so the issue was now indexed as 170 AXI(B)5.[7] And so on, until the final designation—the one that precisely captures what happened to this issue in this case—is achieved.

But that's just the first step. Motions to dismiss are civil procedure issues, so they have to be analyzed under a civil procedure designation, but they're also questions of pretrial procedure, and those issues have their own set of designations. That meant that the indexer had to go back and reanalyze this issue under a whole new set of index criteria: 307A for pretrial procedure, 307AIII for dismissal, 307AIII(B) for involuntary dismissal, 307AIII(B)6 for proceedings and effect, 307Ak686 for matters deemed admitted, and 307Ak 687 for well-pleaded facts.[8] And there are nineteen other legal issues[9] that require analysis in this case. Indexers do a lot of work to help lawyers find issues in cases quickly and efficiently.

In addition to coding issues discussed in opinions according to the master list of issues and sub-issues prepared by West, the editors also write a brief textual description of the issue as presented in the specific case being analyzed and include that description, along with the specific sub-issue designation, at the top of the case. This text is usually called the "headnote" text, even though that's an imprecise term that can mean several different things as well.[10] In the *Abram* case, there were twenty total sub-issues identified by the West editors, and each of those sub-issues, together with the brief headnotes, appear at the beginning of the decision, before the court's language begins.

It's important to understand that this textual description of the issue is written by the West editors, and not by the court. Because it doesn't form part of the court's decision, and because it wasn't written by the court, it can't be used to support your analysis of an issue. This is a crucial point and one that many lawyers forget. But they do so at their own peril because lawyers can be, and have been, sanctioned for forgetting this, so let's restate it: the headnote text falling under the Key Number information is not part of the court's opinion and cannot be cited or be used to support your analysis of an issue. Really. Please don't forget this.

Well, not the most elegant description in the world, perhaps, but you get the idea. If you've ever peeled an onion, or seen a Russian nesting doll you know that each slice, or doll segment, takes you closer to the irreducible core, and with the legal issue, each successive number gets you closer to the precise definition of the specific legal issue the

---

6. *Id.*

7. *Id.*

8. *Id.*

9. *Id.* at 969–970.

10. Sometimes the court will write its own summary of its opinion, or sometimes someone associated with the court will write such a summary. Those summaries are also sometimes called "headnotes." Don't get confused by this; the important thing to remember is that all headnotes are for reference only, not for citation or to be used to support analysis.

court was analyzing. If you search for 170Ak1835, you'll find all the cases West has identified that deal with the issue of admitted facts pursuant to a motion to dismiss.

4. Digests

But where will you search using that number? What resource will you use? We know now how cases are segmented to reveal the specific doctrinal issues the courts have analyzed, but where do we go to look up the Key Numbers relevant to our search? The answer—obviously enough—is "digests," if we're researching using books. We can also do this research online, using Westlaw, and we'll talk about that process in a second.

First, though, we need to talk about digests. Even though books are not the research medium of choice among many law students these days, digests are still a helpful and important research tool. Many law firms still want junior attorneys to use books as their primary research medium, in part because older lawyers are more comfortable with print research and are therefore more comfortable in the results of print research when conducted by others, in part because many experienced lawyers are, frankly, mistrustful of junior attorneys' research skills, and in part because those firms that continue to invest in print-based research materials continue to expect a return on that investment. Whatever the reasons, if you work at a firm that expects you to conduct research in books, digests will be extraordinarily important to you.

For such an important research tool, digests are remarkably straightforward to understand. They are, in essence, compilations of Key Numbers and the textual explanations written by West's editors. They're organized alphabetically by Key Number topic name ("pretrial procedure," "involuntary dismissal," and so on), and then—within each Key Number subdivision—by court. Within each court, the entries are organized chronologically.

The Digests themselves are grouped in various different ways: the Federal Digest, for example, only includes cases from the various federal courts, the regional digests cover both the federal and state courts in the region, the state digest covers state court opinions and federal court opinions from federal courts located in the state, and the combined digests are more inclusive. Of the combined digests, the Decennial Digest is probably the most useful, although it is a truly massive compilation of every court decision in the ten years covered by that particular digest.

Coverage for all digests is an important consideration. Because of the sheer volume of cases decided by each of the federal and state courts, digests fill up quickly, and when they become too large, West starts on another "series." So be sure that when you're conducting research on a particular topic, you've looked up all the relevant Key Numbers for your research in all the relevant digests and, within digests, that you've looked at all the various series so you can be sure that you've covered all possible avenues offered by digests to research your issue. It's a good idea to start with the most recent series and work backwards from there.

You should remember also to make sure you've looked at all relevant parts of the digest volumes. Digests are, like so many other legal reference books, updated by pocket part. So your research in a digest is only complete when you have looked at both the main volume and the pocket part for all entries for all Key Numbers you're interested in and using any updating volumes at the end of the set as well. Forget this step and you won't find the most recent relevant cases—a serious error.

Having decided to use a digest, you have a couple of different ways to begin your research. If you know the relevant Key Number or Numbers for your research topic, you can look directly for the digest volumes that contain those numbers. It's not as far-fetched as it might seem that you would have those numbers. If you have, for instance, done some research in secondary sources like Am.Jur. or C.J.S., you might well have found some Key Number information along with a general description of the state of the law in your particular topic. If you've done this—and if you've made a note of the relevant Key Numbers—then you can look for the digest volume relevant to your en-quiry and dive into reading the headnotes. When you find a case that looks as if it might be helpful, pull that case from the shelf and read what the court actually wrote; some-times you'll read a headnote and then read the actual court language and wonder what the editor was thinking to summarize the issue in the way it's summarized in the head-note. Remember—it's the court's language, not the headnote, that's important, so if the court's language is less helpful to you than the headnote language, move on and find another case that's better for you.

If you don't already have a Key Number to help you with your research, consider looking in the "Descriptive Word Index" that's found with each digest, usually shelved at the end of the set. As you'd expect, the Descriptive Word Index is an index to words and concepts that are covered by the Key Number system. You should be able to come up with at least some words that are relevant to the research you want to conduct (and if you can't, it's definitely not time for you to be at this stage yet; go to the secondary sources and do some preliminary reading), and the Descriptive Word Index can help you to refine your vocabulary and can guide you to relevant Key Number designations that will give you an entry point to the digest.

Alternatively, since the digests are organized according to broad topic, you can look up the general area you're researching and look at the front of the entry. There will be an outline-style listing of all the subdivisions covered by that entry, along with the rel-evant Key Numbers. Once you find a subdivision that looks as if it might be relevant to you, you can open up the digest to that entry and start reading the headnotes.

However you find your way to a digest topic, though, don't be surprised if, once you start reading, the cases don't seem to be very helpful or—even more likely—they seem to be almost, but not quite, on point for the topic you're researching. We often will read the same information and have a slightly different way of describing it to others, and the same is true for the case editors. You and they will probably agree most of the time on how to describe a court's analysis of an issue, and in any case, re-member that it's always the court's language that counts. If that happens, though, take a second to browse and look at the headnote for the Key Numbers on either side of the one you've been researching; often you won't hit exactly the correct number during your research and you'll find that reading the headnotes of surrounding Key Numbers will help you to focus in on the Key Number most directly relevant to your research.

5. Key Number Searching Online

It might seem perverse to conduct pre-indexed searching, like Key Number searching, in an environment designed to permit the freedom of self-indexing. The first computer-assisted legal research database (Lexis, before "Nexis" was added to its name) was set up specifically to allow lawyers to escape the confines of pre-indexed searching and its creators were vocal about the benefits of this escape from pre-indexed research and its constraints.

But users quickly learned that self-indexed research has its own limitations and that pre-indexed research has some advantages that can't be found in a self-indexing environment. So computer-assisted legal research now offers users the best of both worlds: researchers using Westlaw can now index the relevant database themselves, using their own Boolean-based search terms or using a natural language option, or they can search the databases using Key Number designations, in essence creating their own digest for that particular term from among the cases stored in a particular database. Users using LexisNexis can do the same thing using LexisNexis's proprietorial pre-indexed system. I'll stick to discussing Key Numbers here, because they're available in both print and computer forms. That's not to endorse one company's product over another's, just a recognition that West prints books while LexisNexis doesn't—at least not research books like digests.

Westlaw and LexisNexis are constantly changing, so we won't consider specifically how to search using Key Numbers, in case West changes the approach in later versions of WestlawNext.[11] In general though, you should look for indexes or outlines that are available as menu options and use those to navigate through the database until you find cases that are helpful to you. Remember that you have to read the text written by the court before you can reach the conclusion as to whether or not a case is helpful to you—nothing but the court's own language will do.

If you know the Key Numbers you want to search, you can usually enter those directly into a search box and review the results. Because Westlaw will search the full text of cases as printed by West, and as the Key Numbers are part of that text, a search for, say, 170Ak1835, will return all the cases in the database you've selected that have that number in them.[12] This is the easiest way to see that you are, in fact, developing a self-digest, or index, of the cases in the database that are relevant to that particular Key Number.

Note the provision "in the database you've selected" in the previous paragraph. Database selection has been a crucial part of computer-assisted legal research, because—just as with the books—if you are looking for a particular Key Number in state court

---

11. As a general note on legal research, you will never be able to relax and stop learning how online legal information can be found. This is different from the old days, where book research stayed essentially the same for almost a century. Now, changes happen almost daily and these are changes to which you should pay attention and understand (unless someone else in your firm has this assignment) if you plan to be the most effective lawyer as you can be.

12. Note that you likely will have to type in something more specific than just this combination of numbers and letters. The most current version of Westlaw will doubtless have a "help" feature that will show you how to search for a specific Key Number.

cases only, but if you search in a federal database or digest, you will find no relevant results. This might no longer be true, or might not be true for much longer. The new form of Westlaw is much less concerned with database distinction than were previous versions of this service. Whether that remains true in the long term or not—and firms will likely be very concerned about this because the broader the database coverage, usually the more money it costs to search the database, meaning that this could be a hidden, but very significant, increase in the cost of using Westlaw—it's still very important for you to think in terms of database coverage during your research. This is important because the only thing worse than finding no cases that are responsive to your research is finding cases that are exactly on point but which you can't use because they are from jurisdictions that don't help you—a case from Arizona, for instance, when you're looking for cases from Massachusetts. True, you can use the Key Numbers in the Arizona case to conduct a search in a digest or database that will return results from Massachusetts state courts, but many students might forget to take that step and might try to use the Arizona case. That would be an unsuccessful strategy.

Conclusion

Key Numbers and digests are extraordinarily helpful sources of information. But just like any other tool, they are only helpful when wielded correctly—a hammer is very good at pounding in nails, for example, but is not much help if you're trying to cut wood. As with all legal research devices, then, you have to understand how to use these tools in both theory and practice. That's what the next couple of chapters will cover.

Exercise

Take one of the cases you have been reading this week for one of your doctrinal courses. Find that case in its original published form, either in its physical form in the library or online, using Westlaw. Compare the actual case to the casebook version. Are they identical? If not, what are the differences? Find the issue, or issues, for which you have been reading the case and locate the Key Number or Numbers relevant to that issue. Using one of those Key Numbers, find other cases that discuss the same issue. Are there many cases? Are they recent? Are there any cases that appear to contradict the holding of the case you've been reading?

Focus Questions

1. Have you noticed Key Numbers on any of the materials you've read in law school so far?
2. Do you find the insight that Key Numbers are an index to the law to be useful? How often do you use a book's index? How often do you think of indexing and the value of indexes as a way of organizing large amounts of information for easy retrieval?

3. Are you surprised by the text's assertion that doctrinal divisions like "tort" and "contract" are artificial distinctions that don't have any substantive meaning? Do you agree?

4. Do you understand how the constant division and sub-division of legal concepts can be a useful way of indexing issues so they can readily be found?

5. Do you understand the Key Number process as it's discussed here? Do you see how you might use Key Numbers in the research you're conducting this semester?

6. Do you understand why the text is so concerned that you not quote from a headnote? Is this advice you will remember when under pressure to get a document written?

7. Are digests still useful research tools for you, or do you think they've been superseded by online research tools?

8. The text talks about pre-indexing and self-indexing. Are you comfortable with those terms and what they mean? Do you understand that all internet searching is, in essence, the self-indexing of the internet for specific terms you have selected? Does this notion cause you concern? If these concepts are unfamiliar to you, the text will discuss them in much greater depth in the next chapter.

9. The text emphasizes the importance of database selection. Do you see why properly selecting a jurisdiction to search online before beginning your research is so important?

Chapter 32

The Research Process in Theory

What You Should Learn from This Chapter

This chapter introduces some of the theory underpinning legal research and is an important step along your path to becoming an effective legal researcher. In particular, this chapter explores in more detail the core concepts of pre-indexed and self-indexed information and discuses the benefits and drawbacks of both approaches as they are applied in the legal research context. Although computer-assisted research is often assumed to be the default research medium these days, the chapter discusses some specific problems associated with this medium, particularly in regard to legal research, and suggests that you keep these problems in mind when conducting your research.

After reading this chapter, you should:

- understand, at a deeper level than you did before, the differences between pre- and self-indexed research techniques;
- understand the benefits and drawbacks associated with both pre- and self-indexed research;
- have considered the ways in which ranked searching can mitigate some of the disadvantages of self-indexed research, but can introduce some different problems for legal researchers;
- understand why the Google model of internet searching poses challenges for legal researchers; and
- understand the problems posed by coverage, accuracy, specificity, and language when conducting online legal research.

You are likely prepared to be bored by the next few pages. You doubtless feel that you came to law school to learn how to be legal researchers, not to learn about the theory of legal research, and certainly not to learn about the theory of research in general.

Please bear with me. This isn't difficult to understand, and it will help you to be significantly better legal researchers. It won't take long, and if you concentrate on this material, everything about legal research should be easier. It might not be interesting—although some of you might find this fascinating—but it will be helpful.

1. Organizing Information

You should be generally mistrustful of statements that begin "the world of (some complex concept) can be divided into two: ..." We all know that almost every complex idea has a myriad of subdivisions and anything so simplistic as a binary division almost can't, by definition, express the nuances necessary to capture the idea. I'll hope you'll suspend your disbelief here, though, and agree with me that the world of information organization can be divided into two parts: pre-indexed and self-indexed information.

Perhaps that's even too broad a statement. Perhaps the reality is that information is either pre-indexed or is not organized at all—a jumble of random concepts until we impose some order on it by the type of search we conduct. But since chaos doesn't lend itself too well to the imagination, let's stick with my pre-indexed and self-indexed approach for now. At least that gives us two terms we can understand and work with.

A. Indexing

It's probably important to note at this point that "indexing" is one of those terms that has more power for the older generations and less power—maybe less relevance—for your generation. When computers were unavailable for research (or for any purpose), and all research was conducted using books, the use of indexes was learned and indexes were used by students as second-nature; you couldn't conduct research without them. Nor was it possible, except under unusual circumstances, to self-index material: everything was pre-indexed.

Computers, and especially the internet, have changed this. But almost as profound as the change to search capability is the change in the way we think about research. Whereas self-indexing was impossible until a decade ago, it's now the dominant model of research in the non-scientific world; every time you search on Google or some other internet search engine you're self-indexing the internet for a term or terms you've selected. Pre-indexes have fallen largely, if not completely—and very swiftly—out of favor.

We could debate the merits of these changes for a long time and not reach a resolution. But that's not the purpose of this discussion. Rather, the point here is a simple but important one: as lawyers, you're going to have to come to terms with both types of research—pre-indexed and self-indexed—and you'll need to understand the benefits and detriments of both. This is new, and it will be more difficult for you than it was for lawyers of earlier generations to learn about self-indexing because the concept of "indexing" itself was familiar to them. In order for you to understand legal research, though, you will first have to become secure with the concept of indexing. Only then should you be confident in your research skills. Because older lawyers can't imagine a research world without familiarity with indexing, many will have difficulty understanding any problems you might have in wrestling with the concept of indexing in the law.

Sadly, this is one of those generational problems you will experience from time to time, brought about by the rapid and permanent changes in the way we do things in this digital age. Rather than the generations getting frustrated with each other, it's better to understand the cause of the issue, and it's probably going to fall to your generation to understand and forgive the older generations for their confusion.

B. Pre-Indexed Information

Pre-indexed information is simply information that someone has indexed before the information reached you. If you go to any large reference work—one of your textbooks, for example—and look in the back, you'll see an index that lists the major concepts discussed in the book and the corresponding pages on which those concepts are discussed. Some large reference works, like paper encyclopedias, might not have indexes, but the information in them is organized in relation to a specific organizational principle—usually the alphabet—that allows the reader to find specific information quickly and easily. Those works are pre-indexed also, just in a slightly less obvious manner.[1]

In the legal context, as in almost all other fields, pre-indexing was the only meaningful way of conducting research in the twentieth century before the advent of computer-stored information. Imagine the alternative: you're asked to research an issue—let's say the statute of limitations for personal injury cases in New York; you go to the library and stand in front of the reporters containing cases from New York state; you pick a reporter (probably the most recent one, since you're researching current law), and start reading; and if you don't find the answer to your question in that reporter, you move on to the next one, then the next, and then the next, and so on until you find a case that discusses your issue.

That's analog self-indexing, and just describing this approach explains why it's impossible to put into practice. As with all sets of complex information, you need an index to help you cut quickly to the information you need. Thankfully, such an index exists. More than one, actually, but let's stick with the most commonly known and used one: the West Key Number system.

Some quick history here. Long before the corporate behemoth now known as West, or Thomson Reuters, or whatever its name is when you read this, came into being, and before its most famous product—Westlaw—was invented, there really was a Mr. West. His name was John B. West, and he was from Massachusetts, although he settled in St. Paul, Minnesota, in the late nineteenth century. This was a time at which more courts were writing more opinions than ever before, making it difficult for lawyers to keep up with the flow of information. West was a businessman who sensed an opportunity when it presented itself, and in 1879 he compiled together opinions from courts in Iowa, Minnesota, Michigan, Nebraska, Wisconsin, and the Dakota Territory. Within ten years, West was publishing opinions from all state and federal jurisdictions, and publishing them in volumes he called "reporters." But, of course, the information organizational problem remained; the opinions were gathered together in one place, certainly, but the amount of information in each reporter was still daunting and couldn't reasonably be self-indexed by anyone.

The answer came in 1897 with a series of volumes called "digesting sets." These contained brief synopses of each case, organized under West's Key Number system. This

---

1. This differs, of course, from Wikipedia, the encyclopedia with which you might best be familiar. The way in which you search Wikipedia—entering search terms—is a perfect example of self-indexing; you identify the term or terms you're interested in and the search engine pulls up the articles in Wikipedia that correspond to those terms. There is no physical form of Wikipedia (unless someone has undertaken the monumental and incomprehensible task of printing the whole thing out on paper), and so no need for alphabetical or pre-indexed organization.

is the indexing tool that has become familiar to every lawyer since the turn of the last century and which is still the dominant model for book-based legal research today.

We discussed the Key Number process in the previous chapter, but it's worth reminding ourselves how simple and powerful an idea it is. The "unlocking" metaphor implicit in the use of "Key" in the name is accurate; once the reduction of cases to a collection of doctrinal slices was complete, every case—from the most recently published one back to the earliest decision—could be used to support a legal argument. Instead of facing an opaque shelf full of reporters, the researcher now had a transparent index to opinions that allowed for complex, accurate, and speedy research. West's innovation was powerful, and it remains so today; the matrix that defines the nature of each subdivision has been refined over time, and new subdivisions are added as the law becomes more nuanced and concepts are refined by the courts, but the fundamental idea of Key Numbers and digests remains today and is the preferred mode of research by many lawyers.

There are many things to be said in favor of this approach. Most importantly, it reduces the possibility of making a mistake based on linguistic incompatibility. If you conduct an online search for cases involving "wife beating," for instance, your search will not include cases that employ alternative phrases like "spousal abuse." The concepts are the same (or closely related), but the words themselves are different. That happens all the time in the law. But West editors have read the cases, and they have likely made the adjustment necessary to slot cases that discuss similar legal concepts, but use different words to discuss and describe those concepts, into the same box, making them readily retrievable by the researcher.

That advantage to the system, though, is also the basis for one of the main criticisms of it. In order for the process to work, the researcher must make the same set of analytical assumptions as the editor. These often involve narrow distinctions between different subdivisions of the law in a particular area. If the editor decides a case should go in one box, and you search for cases in a different box, you won't find some cases that might be relevant to you. And sometimes, despite all the safeguards and protections, editors make mistakes. Careful researchers can adjust for this problem, of course, by conducting searches in multiple boxes that appear to be related. Nonetheless, some cases likely remain undiscovered by researchers who aren't sufficiently able to imagine the same path for allocating Key Numbers as are the West editors.

The larger criticism of the Key Number approach, though, is more conceptual. Imagine you have a large, multi-volume history of the Civil War, and you are interested in a comparison of how the Union and Confederate armies were able to supply their troops with food. You go to the index at the back of the final volume, only to discover that the history has not been indexed with the concept of food supply in mind. You read the entire history, and you discover that it does, indeed, contain numerous mentions of food supply issues, complete with detailed statistics. But these references are scattered throughout the multiple volumes, and the only way to gain meaningful information about your topic is to read every word in all volumes and to take careful notes of where and what you find, in essence, self-indexing the work for a specific concept. As you can imagine, this would be a time-consuming and frustrating experience.

So it is with cases indexed using the Key Number system. If the concept for which you are searching is not one for which the cases were coded during the editing process, that information will be virtually invisible to you: it can be found in plain sight when you read a case that contains the information, of course, but the only way for you to know that is for you to read all volumes that might possibly contain that information and that, as we already know, is a practical impossibility. So while pre-indexing renders transparent the information that is indexed, it renders opaque the information that is not indexed.

One of the most significant pieces of information that is not contained within the West Key Number system is the name of the judge. Were you, for instance, to be working on a federal case that had been specifically assigned to a particular judge, you would have no way of researching how that judge had ruled previously on issues that might come up as part of the case you are working on, were you limited to using the Key Number system. From a doctrinal perspective, this might not be a significant omission: the law is the law, after all, and even if a judge's opinions suggest that the judge might be opposed to ruling in a particular way, the judge will have little choice but to rule in that way if the law compels the result, and the law can still be searched using the Key Number system. As any practicing litigator knows, however, knowing the judge allows the lawyer to frame arguments in a way that might make it easier for a judge to rule the way you want the judge to rule. It hardly ever hurts to know what your judge thinks about an issue.

More subtly, and yet perhaps even more importantly, the Key Number system— any pre-indexed system, in fact—sets boundaries for our thinking. It is easy to fall into a way of thinking about the law that is bounded by the divisions and subdivisions of the Key Number system and to forget that there are ways of thinking about law that have little to do with those divisions. It is impossible, for example, to use the Key Number system to examine the relationship between two concepts—the way in which courts consider the idea of "numerosity" in class action cases and the way in which the federal Multi-District Litigation Panel thinks about numerosity when deciding on which cases to refer for treatment as multi-district cases, for example. Pre-index systems like the Key Number approach are inherently singular, not relational.

Over time, lawyers grew more and more frustrated with the practical and theoretical limitations of pre-indexed searching in the law, and sought alternatives that would allow them more flexibility and freedom to search in ways that made sense to them at the time they were conducting the research, not to the editors at West. The computer finally allowed for the flexibility lawyers were looking for.

C. Self-Indexed Information

Commercial computer-assisted legal research came to the law in the 1960s, first with Lexis—developed initially by a group of Ohio lawyers who had grown frustrated with the limitations of pre-indexed research—and then, a few years later, with Westlaw. After Westlaw caught up with Lexis, the two services have offered essentially complete databases of primary law, although they differ in secondary source coverage and in the types of finding aids they offer. Before we consider the specifics of these services, let's consider their approach to searching.

But even before we do that, we should remember that both services—at the time of writing, at least—offer the ability to conduct pre-indexed searching as well. In fact, although lawyers and law professors often use the concept of "computer-assisted legal research" as a way of distinguishing computers from "book-based legal research," the dichotomy is a false one. The true distinction is between pre- and self-indexed research approaches, because both LexisNexis and Westlaw offer the researcher the opportunity to conduct pre-indexed research.

Westlaw does this by incorporating the Key Number system, allowing researchers to interrogate the various primary law databases with queries that use the same doctrinal segmentation as they would use in the books. There are no digest volumes online, but a researcher can create a unique "digest" for each research topic, simply by entering in the Key Number information and the relevant sub-database or databases within the complete Westlaw database for the search under consideration. Westlaw will return the results, allowing the researcher to analyze the synopses of cases just as would be possible using the books.

LexisNexis can't use the Key Number system, because that's copyrighted by West. Instead, it uses a feature currently known as[2] LexisNexis Headnotes, which also provides a synopsis of various parts of a court's opinion, although unlike West's Key Number headnotes, LexisNexis' headnotes are taken directly from the language of the case, rather than being specially written by a team of editors. In practice, though, you can search both LexisNexis and Westlaw by use of topic indexes. There may be differences in operation, result, language, and appearance, but both services allow for this pre-indexed type of search, meaning that the more useful distinction is between pre- and self-indexed research, not between books and computers.

Any time you run a computer search using any form of search engine—the ones that power the old or new forms of Westlaw or LexisNexis, the ones that power Google, Yahoo, Bing, or any other search engine you can name—you are, in effect, indexing the contents of the database you're searching for the terms you enter. If, for instance, you enter the terms "Casablanca," "My Town," and "times" into Google, you are asking the Google search engine to look for all examples of those terms and to return the ones that rank most highly (using Google's complex ranking algorithm) first, and the ones that rank less highly further down. The results appear very quickly, so it's difficult to appreciate how much information has been sifted in order to generate the results, but an indexer would generate similar results in time, given the search and ranking parameters under which Google was operating.

Speed is not the only difference, of course. For one thing, a self-indexed computer search allows for one concept to be searched in relation to another concept. So, in my previous example, you're not just searching for "Casablanca," you're searching for a movie in relation to a place and in relation to the times the movie is being shown. That's more than most pre-indexes will allow, although you will see some books in which the

---

2. If this book sounds cagey about what these services contain, or the names for these various features, it's with good reason. At the time of writing, the legal information world is experiencing a period of volatility that is almost unprecedented. The only comparable time might be the period when Lexis and Westlaw were first introduced, and even then, there were many fewer users or services. Part of the changes we're seeing at the moment have to do with the way both LexisNexis and Westlaw (or WestlawNext, as West is currently calling its new incarnation and LexisAdvance, as the newer Lexis product is known) present information. With rapid change comes insecurity, hence an unwillingness to be definitive about what features these services offer or what they're called.

primary search term is segmented by subdivisions that allow some semblance of relational searching: in the multi-volume Civil War history we hypothesized earlier, for example, you might find an entry for "Lincoln, Abraham" and a series of page references, or you might find something like "Lincoln, Abraham, … assassination of, … Booth, John Wilkes," and so on. Each of these segmentations allows you to search for one concept and its relation to the principal entry. You might find later entries in which "Booth" is the principal entry, and segmentations like "escape," "medical treatment of," and "death of" allow for similar relational searches.

West's Key Number system doesn't allow for this sort of relational searching, as we discussed earlier. But self-indexed research, available on Westlaw and LexisNexis, allows the researcher to create highly sophisticated relational searches that allow the researcher to search for multiple concepts and to define the closeness of the relationship between those concepts. Until now, that type of searching was undertaken using Boolean logic, a term honoring the mathematician George Boole.

2. Boolean Searching

Even if it were easy to explain to you how Boolean logic works, I wouldn't try, because the attempt would likely finish any chance I might have that you would continue to read this chapter. Suffice it to say that Boolean logic allows the researcher to construct a search that allows the computer to search a given database or databases for a term or concept, including variants of the words used to describe the term or concept, and, if the researcher chooses, to search for additional terms or concepts and—and this is the crucial part—to define the nature of the relationship between the various search components.

So, for example, you could search LexisNexis or Westlaw for the term "statute of limitations," and limit your search to the New York state law database, or you could search for that term in two or more different state databases—New York and California, say, or all state court databases, or all court databases, including the federal courts as well. And you could look for a relationship between "statute of limitations" and your judge, or you could look for a relationship between "statute of limitations" and the concept "slip and fall." Or "personal injury." Or anything else you chose. If you're concerned that the court might have said something like "this court will limit all actions based on a theory of personal injury to those filed within three years of the date of injury"—a wordy way of saying something very similar to "statute of limitations" but not an inconceivable way for a court to write—you can search for variations of "limit" that would include the word itself, but also forms like "limitations" within a certain number of words of the term "personal injury," or you could define the relationship as the same sentence. Or the same paragraph. Or the same case.

You get the idea. Self-indexed research opens up a huge world of possibilities that pre-indexed research foreclosed. Once meaningful self-indexed research was possible (and it took a while for that to happen, but it's certainly here now), the researcher had almost complete control over every aspect of what was to be indexed, and how those results would be presented. It was a remarkable leap forward in legal research, and it allowed lawyers to research in ways that were almost literally inconceivable before computer-assisted legal research came along.

3. Problems with Self-Indexing

But along with these possibilities came some problems that hadn't existed before, and we need to consider those as well. These problems are true for all computer-assisted searches and they're particularly relevant to lawyers who conduct searches on the large, commercial databases like Westlaw and LexisNexis.

The first, and biggest, problem is easy to describe and perhaps harder to grasp. Put simply, when we find a lot of information, we lose precision over what it is we're finding. And when we increase the precision of our search, we don't find a lot of documents that might have been relevant to our searches. If we use Boolean-based search engines, it seems that there's nothing we can do to change this effect; it happens regardless of how experienced the researcher might be, even those who are relatively familiar with the database they're searching.

An example might make this problem easier to understand. Suppose you're asked to search a database consisting of millions of documents. The broader your search, the more documents you'll recover, but many of those documents will only have tangential relevance to your search. You read through your results but quickly realize that a lot of what you're reading doesn't help your research. You probably have all the relevant documents to assist you, but you won't find them because they're buried in a sea of irrelevant information.

Frustrated, you enter a much more precise search request into the search engine, and you end up with very few documents, all of them highly relevant. As it turns out, though, you will have excluded from your search result a number of relevant documents as well, and you won't know what you haven't seen. And because you won't know what you haven't seen, you have no way of knowing if your search was too precise or whether it was about right.

A lot of lawyers didn't understand this problem at first. But this relevance/precision dilemma can cause real issues for lawyers if they forget it. If you're asked to do a discrete search with a readily identifiable answer—what the statute of limitations for slip and fall cases in New York state might be, for example—the relevance/precision problem might not show itself; you might only recover five percent of the relevant cases that give you the answer, but for this query, that might be enough. You answer the question quickly and correctly and believe that computer-assisted research is infinitely superior to the older, book-based approach.

If you're asked a complex question that requires analysis, interpretation, and the ability to analogize and distinguish cases from each other, the absence of relevant cases that are not recovered in an overly precise search, or the mass of information recovered in an overly broad search, could have serious ramifications. You might fail to identify relevant cases, or even relevant lines of analysis, that might help or hurt your case. And there's nothing that can be done to improve your results.

4. Ranked Searching

Or is there? The large legal database providers never fully accepted the implications of the relevance/precision problem. They argued that their programs had made refinements that lessened the effects of the problem, and many lawyers believed that their particular knowledge of the subjects they were searching meant that they could tell if a large chunk of information was missing, so the problem wasn't as serious as information scientists were telling us.

The commercial database providers went further when they introduced "Natural Language" searching. Using this technique, a legal researcher could enter a query written in English—"statute of limitations for personal injury," for example—and the computer would produce a set of results. How it did that is very important for us to consider.

For those being introduced to Natural Language searching when it was first available on Westlaw and LexisNexis, it looked like magic. The computer looked like it was able to read the researcher's mind and come up with answers to their questions, rather than making them contort their search into a mathematical equation. But that, of course, was exactly what was happening; it was just that the computer was making the decisions about the form that equation would take, not the researcher. In fact, our Natural Language search was being reduced to a Boolean search by operation of an algorithm written into the search engine, the search was being run, and the results presented were being ranked and then displayed. That meant that control was being taken away from the researcher and placed in the hands of the programmers who wrote the algorithm at a couple of crucial points along the way; first, when the search was stripped of external words and possible extensions and root expanders were added—removing the "of" and "for," for example, in the "statute of limitations for personal injury" search—and second, when the results were ranked.

All computer searches are ranked, but not all are ranked the same. In the commercial databases, Boolean search results are typically ranked by order of court importance—highest court first—and then by date. So if you search a database containing all federal cases, your results will be ranked as follows: Supreme Court (most recent case first, least recent last), Courts of Appeals (most recent case first, least recent case last), District Court (most recent case first, least recent case last). You can see a listing of all results, so you can opt to start reviewing your results with, say, some Circuit Court cases rather than looking through all the Supreme Court cases. But all cases that match your search will be listed.

Searches using Natural Language protocols, though, are usually ranked according to how closely the results match your search. So a District Court case might come first and a Supreme Court case might come last if the District Court case uses language more closely related to your search than does the Supreme Court case. And the number of returned results is limited; not all results that match your search are available for review.

These rankings, and the limitations placed on the number of results generated by a Natural Language search, arguably went some way to addressing the relevance/precision problem—one could tell fairly quickly how successful the search had been and if it was not returning the type of cases the researcher expected to see, a new search was readily available. And by ranking the results in terms of how closely they matched the inputted search, the program was attempting to return precise results, without drowning the researcher in information.

But many researchers were unhappy with Natural Language searching. They felt that it limited their ability to recover relevant documents, and they felt the loss of control inherent in allowing an algorithmic disambiguation of a complex legal search. Then Google showed up, changing everything.

5. The Google Generation

There are many ways to describe your generation. The most accepted way is to refer to you as "millennials," as opposed to the older "generation X," or "baby boomer" cohorts. This isn't the place to discuss the merits of grouping individuals together and ascribing generational traits to you all, regardless of your individual backgrounds. Suffice it to say that for some, at least, you are all more properly thought of as the "Google generation."[3]

Google is, without question, a remarkable phenomenon. As a search engine, it appears to capture more quickly and more accurately the thought behind our searches and it returns results that are better suited to our search, often, than could fairly have been expected based on the search we entered. For those who had grown used to less effective search engines, it once again seemed like magic.[4]

It isn't magic, of course, just very skillful programming combined with a new way of looking for information. This isn't the time for a detailed description of the Google search engine. For our present purposes, the general knowledge idea of a web crawler, combined with a ranking process that ranks the results in the context of what other people searching for similar information have done with it, is more than sufficient. For one thing, it should tell us that while the Google approach works extraordinarily well when looking for general information, it presents some challenges for legal researchers.

Ranking, in general, is something that should cause legal researchers concern, because it means that the information we receive in response to our query is being organized according to how someone else thinks we should receive it and, since the process is automated, that decision is not conscious, but is rather the result of some general decisions about how information should be organized made by a programmer whose interest and knowledge about legal information is unknown to us. That doesn't mean that the decisions are necessarily bad ones, or that we'll disagree with them. But it does mean that information is being presented to us in an order not of our choosing. And with legal information in particular, the decisions other people have made about the materials responsive to our searches might be helpful, but they also might not.

It's this uncertainty that is problematic to legal researchers: the results might be definitive, and they might be missing crucial information; we might have uncovered all we need to know, and there might be a lot we still need to learn. We can risk it and finish our research quickly, but that likely isn't the best strategy in the long term. This

---

3. If the way to describe generational differences is through the technology that defines a cohort's era, then my baby boomer generation might be better thought of as the "television" generation and generation X might be thought of as the "personal computer" generation. Or not.

4. In fact, one useful definition of who makes up the "Google generation" is "anyone who hasn't found Google magical when using it." If you're so used to Google's results that there's no surprise when it does what it does, then you're probably a member of that generation.

problem is inherent in forced-ranking research; we've learned to so trust Google's speed and accuracy in day-to-day research that we might believe that the first few result panels we review contain most of the relevant information, and believe that most of the other panels will contain duplicative or less relevant information. It's not necessarily true, though, as you will have learned if you've drilled deeply through the search results for something you've looked for on Google; often highly relevant information will be revealed well down in the search results. The information is down there because not many people have looked at it or because of some other artifact of Google's ranking process, forcing it deeper into the substratum.

But just because other people haven't looked at it doesn't mean that it's not helpful to our analysis. In fact, in legal analysis, sometimes it's the thought that others haven't had that helps us to overcome a conceptual block and craft a persuasive argument. We'll come back to the danger of forced-ranking searching when we talk about specific databases; for now, though, please remember that there are issues relating to this type of research of which we should be aware before engaging in it.

6. Other Problems Associated with Computer-Assisted Research

There are four other problems associated with computer-assisted research we should touch on briefly here. These problems are obvious, and will come as no surprise to anyone who's used a database to conduct research. They are, nonetheless, problems, and we should bear them in mind when we conduct computer-assisted legal research.

A. Coverage

The first problem is coverage. Obviously, we can't find something in a database if it's not there to be found. Most of the time, this isn't really a problem for the large commercial databases, especially LexisNexis and Westlaw. They both have deep coverage for all primary databases—cases, statutes, regulations, and so on. They might have slightly less profound coverage for some of their secondary and tertiary databases— law reviews, for example, and newspapers and other reference materials. But these are small concerns; for most of the research you'll be doing in law school and as junior lawyers, these databases are more than deep enough.

That's not necessarily true of other legal information sources. Some have complete coverage for some databases but only partial coverage for others, some have partial coverage for all databases—the only thing that's consistent is the inconsistency between various databases and services. And this isn't necessarily a problem; sometimes partial coverage is good enough and will get you the results you need. But sometimes you will need to do some historical research; when a statute or regulation has been changed since the event precipitating litigation, for example, you likely will need the relevant language at the time of the incident, not the present day. It's important to know what data set you're working with, in order to be sure that the results you're generating are sufficiently deep for the specific research you're doing.

It would be a simple task to decide upon your favorite source for legal information and note down the coverage for that source. Then you would always have that information ready to hand and could check it if a coverage question came up. Unfortunately, as we all know, the information stored in databases is dynamic and ever-changing. It's not likely that a legal information database would take away coverage, and much more likely that it would add coverage to its already-existing information. But it's not impossible that once-available data might no longer be available, especially on sites that are affected by changes in political administrations (information on federal administration agency websites, for example, often changes when a new president is elected), and even if a site adds coverage, that changes the nature of the results you might generate. The safest practice, then, is to check the coverage for every database you use, at the time you use it. You probably don't have to do this for LexisNexis or Westlaw, but it's advisable to do it for every other site you use.

B. Accuracy

The second problem associated with computer-assisted research is obvious to anyone who has typed a word, only to see a different result on the screen. Put simply, the computer will search for exactly what you asked, even if you misspelled a word or a name. That's something we all understand, and we've all had experience of typing the wrong thing into a search engine and having it come back with results we didn't understand. But for lawyers, typos can have important consequences when researching.

Imagine, for instance, you're a junior lawyer working for a law firm, and you type "statue of limitations" instead of "statute." It's a mistake that happens all the time. But if you do that when you search, you might get no results, or, at least, no meaningful ones.[5] Most likely, you will realize your mistake quickly and retype the search. But depending on the pricing structure your firm uses, that search might have incurred some costs for your client. If the client doesn't want to pay for it, your firm will have to pay for that research itself. The firm won't be too happy with you if you force it to pay for too many mistakes you've made.

C. Specificity

The third problem is more subtle. If you search for my name—Ian Gallacher—on Google, for instance, you'll find that I'm either a law professor, a pastry chef, a jeweler, an actor in a movie, or a designer of scenic backgrounds for computer games. But if you search for the more common spelling of my name—Ian Gallagher—you'll find that I sing for an Irish show band based in New Jersey, I'm a member of the Northern Ireland Policing Board, I'm a fictional character in a British soap opera (that one feels

---

5. The large legal databases now have context-sensitive spell-checkers that are designed to fix this type of mistake and to search instead for what the database assumes you wanted to type. You've doubtless seen the same sort of thing on Google. These spell-checkers can minimize the accuracy problem if you make a mistake the system recognizes, but nothing can eliminate it completely. And, of course, if you want to search for a term the computer wants to change, you'd have to wrestle with the computer so that it actually runs the search you want it to run.

oddly accurate sometimes), or that I am, or have been, the strength and conditioning coach for the Vancouver Giants (certainly not true).

The obvious point here is that spelling matters, and in a matter like a name search, one wrong letter can mean the difference between a correct result and an incorrect one. Even with the correct spelling you'd have to do some work to decide which of the various "Ian Gallacher" possibilities best fits me, but if you spelled my name incorrectly you might never know you were looking at the wrong series of people.

There's nothing surprising about this, and almost nothing to be done about it either. Both LexisNexis and Westlaw have some checks in place to look for words that might have been misspelled, but even they can't make allowances for less-than-common misspellings. We just have to be as careful as possible when using computers that we don't set ourselves on the wrong path, dooming our research to failure.

D. Language

The final issue that often comes up with computer-assisted research is, in a way, related to the typo problem. Because computers can only search for those things you ask them to search for, you must correctly predict how a court, or a legislature, or a rule-making body has discussed a topic if you're using a word-based search to find information. If you search for a statute or regulation using a table of contents, this problem is eliminated, which is one reason that's such a good strategy to use when searching those databases. But if you're looking for a case, you have to predict what words or terms the court will use, or you will not find all relevant information.

If you look for "spousal abuse," for example, you won't find "domestic violence." The two concepts might be related, and the two terms might be used interchangeably, but the words themselves are completely different and computers can only search for the words you ask them to search for. This puts a tremendous burden on the legal researcher to predict the language courts use when describing legal issues and to search for all possible variations. It's possible to do, but it's still an important limitation to remember.

It's also worth remembering that this is a limitation that doesn't apply to pre-indexed legal research. The indexer has read the case before indexing it, and has made the adjustment that is easy for us as humans to make and impossible for computers to make. A case that discusses spousal abuse and a case that discusses domestic violence will likely receive the same coding, allowing the researcher to find both with equal ease.

This is why one of the safest approaches to legal research is to combine pre-indexed and self-indexed techniques. Searching for the same information in two different ways might seem redundant but this is one area where redundancy makes sense. Why that is, and how you might do it, is a topic for the next chapter.

Focus Questions

1. Have you ever thought of information as being divided into pre-indexed and self-indexed groupings before? Do you find this insight helpful? Do you use paper indexes often?

2. Do you see how the Key Number system makes an index of the law?

3. Do you see the advantages and limitations of a pre-indexed approach to legal research? Had you considered these advantages and limitations when conducting research previously? Do you think you will use pre-indexed research techniques now that you've been introduced to them?

4. Do you see the advantages and limitations of a self-indexed approach to legal research? Had you considered these advantages and limitations when conducting research previously? Will you keep the limitations of self-indexed research in mind when you conduct research from now on?

5. Have you used Boolean logic in computer-assisted research before? Did you find it easy or difficult to use? Were you satisfied or frustrated with the results this approach yielded? Although the newer forms of Westlaw and LexisNexis make it more difficult to find, Boolean searching is still possible on these databases. Do you think you will attempt to use Boolean search techniques in your legal research? If so, why? If not, why not?

6. Were you aware of the problems associated with self-indexed searching? In particular, were you aware of the relevance/precision dilemma, and will knowing about these issues change the way you conduct self-indexed legal research?

7. Do you think that natural language searching is an improvement over a Boolean-based approach to computer-assisted research? If so, why do you think this, and if not, why not? Do you see why legal researchers are concerned about the perceived loss of control inherent in natural language searching?

8. Do you think of yourself as a member of the "Google generation"? What do you think of an attempt to categorize generations in terms of technology? How would you describe the baby boom generation in terms of technology (or would you not make such an attempt?)? Do you consider computers "technology"? The internet? Google? Books?

9. Have you thought of coverage, accuracy, specificity, and language as problems associated with other computer-assisted research you have undertaken? In retrospect, do you think these problems might have affected research you have conducted in the past?

Chapter 33

The Research Process in Practice

What You Should Learn from This Chapter

This chapter introduces techniques that should help you in your legal research. In particular, the chapter advocates the benefits of thinking carefully about a research task before beginning to research. That preparation should include an honest evaluation of how much you know, or don't know, about the subject of your research. The chapter proposes that in most cases, researchers should first go to the secondary sources to educate themselves in the general area of the research topic before engaging in primary source research. The chapter discusses ways to evaluate your research results, how to gauge when to stop researching, and—crucially—it introduces the vital role that citators like Shepards and KeyCite play in the research process.

After reading this chapter, you should:

- understand the importance of thinking about your research approach before beginning your research;
- understand the value of secondary sources in the research process;
- understand how to move from secondary to primary research;
- understand how to evaluate your research results and decide whether to continue researching or whether to stop; and
- understand the crucial role played by legal citators.

So much for theory. How does legal research work in practice? After all this talk, can't we get down to talking about how to research legal issues? Yes, we can. This chapter has a series of suggestions for how a legal researcher might best conduct research. As a threshold matter, though, we should acknowledge that everyone is different and that you should mistrust any one suggested standardized approach to research. There's no one approach to research that will work for everyone or for every research situation. The important thing is for you to understand how the various research tools available to you work—what their strengths and weaknesses are—and how to use them in combination with each other. You also need to understand your own approach to research and how you work most efficiently. If you know all that, you will be able to develop your own research strategies that will work best for you in a variety of situations. So consider what you're about to read as a set of first principles: they won't all work for you all the time, but if you understand them all, you'll be able to fall back on them when other approaches aren't working for you.

1. First, Stop What You're Doing

The first thing you should do as a legal researcher is to stop researching. This is very important; if you've been given a research task and you've started to research immediately, you need to stop what you're doing. Put any writing implements down, take your fingers away from your computer keyboard, and sit on them if you have to in order to prevent yourself from doing anything.

Action should never be your first instinct as a researcher. Rather, you should stop and think about the assignment you've been given. Doing this will spare you countless problems down the road. Just five minutes of careful, concentrated thought will allow you to develop a research plan that's well suited to your assignment; it will save you time because you won't be going down blind alleys, and it will save you from proudly presenting an obviously incorrect answer to your professor or law firm partner.

Imagine the following situation. After a few years of being the person who was always given research assignments to do, you are now the person who gets to ask junior associates to do some research for you. Your work is mainly in federal class actions, so your research tasks often require you to ask junior associates to come up with some law that interprets some version of the federal class action rule, Federal Rule 23; what recent case law had written about the meaning of the "adequacy" requirement of Fed. R. Civ. P. 23(a)(4), for example. You ask a junior associate to do this work and the associate sets to the task enthusiastically, spending a full day researching and writing a detailed memo describing the research. And every cited case comes from a state court.

Junior lawyers should know what you perhaps don't know, but what I'm guessing you now understand: state court decisions have no relevance to the interpretation of a federal rule of civil procedure.[1] Federal courts will rarely (lawyers should rarely say never) be interested in what a state court has said about a federal rule, or its state equivalent. And the junior associate you asked to research the issue should have known that.

The associate probably did, in fact, know, at some level, that state cases were not relevant to this task. As soon as you point out the problem, the associate understands it immediately. But the associate has wasted a day of time (you can't bill failed research like this to a client) doing excellent, but completely irrelevant, work. If the associate had taken five minutes at the start of the assignment to think through what had been asked, the problem wouldn't have arisen. And the associate would have completed the as-

---

1. The reverse isn't necessarily true. It can be the case that federal interpretations of a federal rule of civil procedure are relevant to state courts seeking to interpret their own rules. State rules that are derived—sometimes word-for-word—from federal rules often have little or no case law interpreting them immediately after they've been adopted, and state courts will issue opinions saying, in effect, that they'll consider what the federal courts have said about that rule until they've developed their own body of jurisprudence.

signment much more quickly, because there is an excellent research tool that would quickly have given access to all the cases needed to answer your question.[2]

What would that process have looked like? Let's try to imagine it. First, the associate (let's call him Jeff, because calling someone "the associate" all the time is a little sterile) would ask what he knew about class actions, and would likely conclude that he knew nothing at all; we don't spend all that much time on them in law school—there's too much law to spend time on everything. So the first thing on Jeff's research plan would be to learn more about class actions, and particularly this odd "adequacy" requirement of Rule 23(a)(4).

Then Jeff would look again at the assignment and realize that you were looking for information on a federal rule. That would tell him that only federal materials would be relevant to the research; state cases, rules, and statutes—as well as any secondary materials that covered state law—wouldn't be helpful and spending time with those wouldn't be productive. That decision alone would save Jeff hours of wasted time.

Finally, Jeff would at least consider what materials might be relevant for his research. Thinking back to the wonderful legal research instruction he had in law school, he would know that the Annotated Code would be an excellent place to begin, but he would also list some other materials: federal reporters, for example (in either print or digital form); federal digests (but not regional digests, because they're devoted to state court cases); and a copy of the Federal Rules of Civil Procedure, so Jeff could look up the language of Rule 23 and see exactly what it says. Then Jeff would consider possible secondary sources to help him start his work—treatises on the Federal Rules, for example, and perhaps a treatise on Class Actions, as well as encyclopedia entries and perhaps an ALR annotation if one appeared to be on point—and would start reading those secondary sources, making notes as he went, before launching into primary source research.

This isn't an idealized description of the research process. Rather, it's a fairly standard approach to analyzing a typical day-to-day problem that comes up in law firms. An average law firm associate should only spend two or three minutes coming up with a plan like this, and if Jeff followed this plan carefully, he would have finished the research and written the short memo you needed in a couple of hours; although it sounds incomprehensible if you don't know what's going on, the question of "adequacy" in the class action context is well understood and easily researched by those who take a few minutes to orient themselves in the law.

Actually, "orientation" is a good metaphor for what you should do before you begin to research. If you're taken blindfolded to a strange town and then the blindfold is removed, you're told where you are and given a map (no GPS in the car), and you're told to get from your present location to a different part of town, you wouldn't just start driving right away. Rather, you'd spend a minute or two locating your present location on the map, then you'd find the new location, you'd plan a route to get you from one place to the other, and only then would you start to drive. In effect, that's all you should do when you begin your legal research. Take a minute or two to orient yourself.

---

2. That tool is the United States Code Annotated, by the way. It's perhaps not the most intuitive tool to use for researching a Federal Rule, but once you understand how it works, you'll also understand why I recommend it so highly for this purpose. We'll talk about it later.

2. Be Honest about What You Do and Don't Know

It would be good to say that ego plays no role in legal research, but no one is that naïve. We all know that our ability to perform well in a professional task like this will be very important to our self-esteem, and we all believe that we will be more than just capable legal researchers. And it's fine to believe that, as long as that belief doesn't get in our way. This is not the time to be hindered by our ego forcing us to ignore our lack of understanding about a particular legal issue. Rather, we need to set those notions of self-worth and knowledge aside for a second and make a realistic assessment of our knowledge of the legal issue under consideration, recognizing that it's okay to know nothing. We have the capacity to learn.

If we're being honest, you don't know much about the law yet. No one in your position could. You've been in law school much less than a year, and you've only had some core courses. You probably know quite a bit about those subjects, but there are still large swaths of issues related to each of those subjects. And there are entire areas of the law that you haven't studied yet, and even more areas that you won't study at all.

This isn't a commentary on you or your professors: it's simply the way things are. The important thing is to know what to do if you're asked to research an issue in an area of the law with which you're unfamiliar. But just as most self-help programs recognize that you can't start solving a problem until you admit you have one, so you can't start learning about an area of the law until you admit that you don't know anything about it; if your ego gets in the way and tells you that you know enough about this topic to start delving into the primary resources, you probably won't do yourself much good.

So admit to yourself that you don't know enough about a legal issue to start researching it. You'll be surprised at how liberating that admission can be! Now you're ready to begin educating yourself about the subject, and that's a crucial step to being ready to research it.

What do you need to learn? Vocabulary, certainly. It's difficult to research the law using pre- or self-indexed techniques without knowing the vocabulary courts and legislatures use to discuss an issue. Law is, at its core, all about words, and if you don't know what words lawyers, law-makers, and judges use to describe an issue, you won't make much headway in researching the topic.

A more subtle sense, but one that's just as important to learn, is one of the context around the issue you're researching. And that you can often obtain by looking at secondary sources.

3. Go to the Secondary Sources First

Perhaps the reason lawyers sometimes forget to use secondary sources first is simply a semantic one: we think that something called a "secondary" source should be used second, while something called a "primary" source should come first. That would be a terrible mistake, of course, because the labels we give these sources have nothing to do with the order in which we use them, but rather have to do with the priority we give to the information they contain; we can rely on primary information but we can't rely on secondary information when making an argument. As research tools, though, secondary sources almost always should be used before primary sources.

Perhaps the reason so many lawyers start their research by using primary sources, though, is a combination of arrogance and impatience: "arrogance" because the lawyer believes that he or she already knows enough about the area of the law to dispense with the secondary sources, and "impatience" because the lawyer believes that time spent researching secondary sources is time wasted. Both of these reactions are mistakes. As we've discussed, you shouldn't let ego play a role in the research process, and beginning your research with primary sources will likely cause you to spend more time going down wrong alleys and then backtracking once you realize your mistake.

Of course, you have to use the right secondary source for the topic you're researching. If you're in doubt, start with one of the two principal legal encyclopedias: CJS and Am.Jur. Neither of these sources has a deep analysis of any topic, but they cover almost everything and they'll get you started. They'll give you some vocabulary and they'll give you a sense of how some courts, at least, have treated the issue you're researching. Don't worry if it looks as if the cited opinions come out on the "wrong" side of the issue, at least as far as your client is concerned; this is just the first research step, not the last.

Having gained at least a basic understanding of the issue, consider another secondary source with more detailed information—perhaps an ALR annotation, a treatise on the broad topic you're researching, or perhaps a law review article. All of these sources will give you a deeper understanding of the issue and they'll also refer you to some cases that probably get you closer to the heart of the specific issue you're researching than did the encyclopedias.

Remember that there's no limit to the secondary sources you can review. If you've picked, for example, an ALR annotation and it hasn't given you as much information as you had hoped, look for a treatise, or a law review article, or some other secondary source that might be more productive. Don't limit your reading at this stage, and remember to take good notes; there's nothing worse than finding useful information but failing to take note of what it was and where you found it.

4. Moving from Secondary to Primary Source Research

Once you feel you have a good background sense for what's going on, and you think you've found at least one case that looks as if it might be relevant to your analysis (even if the result goes against you, and even if the case isn't in a jurisdiction that will help you), this might be the time to move from secondary to primary source research. Take a look at the case you've found. Does the issue it analyzes seem to be on point, even if the court gets the answer "wrong," for your purposes? If so, what are the Key Numbers (plural because there will likely be more than one) for the issue you're researching? Now take the Key Number information you have, and plug that into a source that will take you to cases in the jurisdiction or jurisdictions that are relevant to you.

What is that source? If you're using books, it will be a digest that encompasses your jurisdiction: if you're searching for a state court issue, it will likely be a state or regional digest, and if you're searching for a federal issue, it will likely be the Federal Digest. Remember to look at the coverage for the digest you're using, and make sure to research all series of the relevant digest, not just the most recent one. And remember—always, always remember—to search the pocket parts and update volumes at the end of the set to make sure you have the most up-to-date information possible.

If you're doing your research using a computer, then select the appropriate database for your research and use the Key Number (if you're using Westlaw—Key Numbers don't work in LexisNexis) to generate a list of results. If you're using LexisNexis, once you've found a case that's on point for your research, instead of looking for the relevant Key Numbers, look at the list of topics the Lexis editors have identified for that case and then search for more results like that.

5. Refining Your Research

You have probably noticed that you haven't performed a Boolean-based or Natural Language search in either Westlaw or LexisNexis. These options are available to you, but you're better to avoid them as much as possible during the first stages of your research project, even as you become more experienced legal researchers. Those tools are better used once you've already generated some initial results using the pre-indexed approach described above. Once you know you're on the right track, and only then, you can feel comfortable about expanding your research using techniques designed to gather in cases that might have fallen outside the indexers' nets.

If you follow this approach, you might find that you're finding most of, if not all of, the same cases you found using the pre-indexed approach. That's good news. It means that your initial research was thorough and that you didn't miss much, if anything. There's another stage to go, and we'll discuss that in a second, but you should feel relatively secure that you know most of what you need to know if you aren't finding much new information at this stage.

On the other hand, if you find a whole galaxy of new cases, don't panic! First, evaluate the new cases you've found. Are they relevant to your topic? If so, what does their existence tell you about your initial, pre-indexed research? Did you miss something when you were looking at the secondary sources? Did you, perhaps, make a note of the wrong Key Number (it happens all the time) or did you misread what the headnotes were actually saying? Whatever the reason, try very hard to figure it out, and then—armed with the knowledge of where your pre-indexed research went wrong—go back and do it again, this time using the correct information. You need to do this to be sure that you've covered all ways of obtaining information: your pre-indexed research is being checked by your self-indexed research, and vice versa. Using one technique alone isn't advisable; you're safer if you use both.

You're in the heart of the research process at the moment, and it's important to remember that it's a dynamic process that requires a tremendous amount of concentration and analysis. There's nothing mechanical about any of this: you can't just follow a set of pre-determined steps, making note of the results as you go, and then stop, assuming that you've learned everything you need to learn. Rather, you need to be thinking constantly about how what you're reading matches what you expected to read, based on your secondary sources research. Are the results consistent with what the secondary source led you to expect? If not, what's different? And are these results helping you to answer the question you've been asked to answer? If not, and based on the increasing knowledge you have about this area of the law, can you recontextualize the question you've been asked in order to reach a more satisfactory answer? Can you distinguish what appears to be negative law based on the facts of the reported cases and your case? (It can often happen that a negative result can turn into a positive result when the facts are considered. The court might, in essence, be saying that it's ruling the way it is because of the facts before it, but if the facts were different—the same as they are in the case you've been asked to research, for example—it would rule differently and in a way that would favor your client. That can be a very helpful case to find.)

So remember that there's a lot of to and fro going on at this point in the research process, reading cases, considering carefully what they mean and how they affect your analysis, and then going back to find additional cases—perhaps cases referred to by the case you're reading that look as if they might be relevant, perhaps cases that share Key Numbers or similar headnote language. And you should be actively thinking about everything you read; there's nothing passive about legal research!

6. What If You Don't Generate Good Results?

What happens if you've done everything right and you can't find anything relevant to the topic you've been asked to research?[3] Well, there's one of three possible causes for this: the first is that you've found a unique issue, one that no court has ever considered before in a reported opinion. If you think about the massive number of court opinions—from all jurisdictions since the beginning of recorded legal decisions in this country—you can probably guess how unlikely it is to find an issue that's never been decided before. But if this is truly what's happened, you need to drop back and consider how courts have analyzed similar issues to the one you're researching, thinking about policy considerations and principles that courts have articulated in analogous situations to the one in your case. It might take some time, but you will almost always be able to come up with a well-reasoned and supported answer to the question you've been asked.

The second, and more likely, possibility is that no court in your specific jurisdiction has analyzed the issue but that courts in other jurisdictions have. If that happens, you need to expand your research until you find courts that have ruled on your issue, and combine that research with the "similar issue" research described in the previous para-

---

3. Notice that this is a very different question to the one that asks what happens if you've done everything right and can't find any authority that helps you answer the question the way your client would like it to be answered. Sometimes you just can't give your client—or the attorney who asked you to perform the research—the answer they want to hear. But if you're confident that you've done your research correctly, then you can at least be comfortable that you're giving them the correct answer. Part of being a lawyer is learning to deliver bad news as well as good.

graph. You'll need to be able to answer the question of how other courts have dealt with this issue and you'll need to able to show that those decisions are consistent, or inconsistent, with the way courts in your jurisdiction have resolved similar issues.

The third, and most likely, possibility is that you haven't done everything right at all. Rather, you've made a mistake somewhere in the research process that has taken you down a blind alley. If you suspect this is what's happened, then you need to retrace your steps and figure out where that mistake might have occurred. If you've disregarded my advice and started your research in a primary source database, plugging words and terms into a Boolean or natural language search, now's the time to stop that process and go back to the secondary sources: you'll have lost some time, but all is not lost, and the secondary sources will probably help to put you on the right path. If you started by looking at secondary sources, go back and decide if you used the right ones; you might well find that you made some initial misassumptions about the issue you were asked to research and those have affected everything you've done since then.

The important thing to remember is that for virtually all legal issues that can be researched, there is an answer available to you if you look for it in the right way. It might not be the answer you or your client wants to hear, and it might not reveal itself easily, but if you keep looking and thinking about the question you've been asked, you almost certainly will be able to work your way to an answer. Don't give up, and don't stop looking.

7. How Do You Know When to Stop?

The hardest part of legal research is knowing when to stop doing it. There's always the concern that one more secondary source, one more search in one more database, one more Key Number search, one more something, will net us the elusive perfect case that wraps everything up in a bow and makes the answer to our question certain, leaving no room for doubt.

In fact, though, that one search will turn into ten, and then twenty, and then fifty, and you'll be no closer to finding that "perfect" case than you were before you started your research, largely because it's rare that we find a "perfect" answer to the questions we're asked. We almost always find enough information to answer those questions, but the answer is usually cobbled-together from a variety of different sources and from our own analysis that connects all the information we've found.

So how do you know when to stop researching and not perform that one more search? The usual answer is that you should stop when you keep finding the same cases, or learning the same information; if you aren't finding anything new, then one more search likely won't add to your fund of knowledge either. This is good advice, but it's also a little dangerous. If you've started looking down the wrong road, for example, you might end up in a place where you're not finding out anything new, but you might be in completely the wrong place. Stopping your research at this point would be very unwise!

The answer, as is usually the case, is that before you do anything, you need to think about it. So once you start finding that you're getting the same results over and over again, and that you're not learning anything new about the way courts are handling the issue under review, stop researching and start thinking about what you've done and what you've learned:

- Have you looked at an appropriate array of secondary sources?
- Have you identified the jurisdiction or jurisdictions that are most appropriate to answer the questions you've been asked?
- Have you performed both pre-indexed and self-indexed searches in primary source databases that are appropriate to those jurisdictions?
- Are the results you've been generating consistent with what you expected to find, based on your understanding of the issue?
- Can you answer the question you were asked, even if the answer is one your client might not want to hear?
- Are you sufficiently confident in your answer that you feel comfortable about staking your professional reputation on it?

If you can answer "yes" to all these questions, then you've almost finished your research. There's one more crucial step ahead of you, and then you're done.

8. Shepard's and KeyCite

To call this step "crucial" is no exaggeration. Failure to follow this step could ruin all your hard work, could get you fired, and—in an extreme case—could lead to your being sanctioned by your state bar association. Seriously: it's a crucial step!

Everything you've found up until now leads you to believe that you know the answer to the question you've been asked. But what if the law has changed? What if the cases you've read have been overruled? If that has happened, then everything you think you know is wrong, and everything on which you're planning to base your answer is no longer valid. Imagine getting a call from an attorney on the other side of a case you're working on. The attorney tells you that an opinion on which you relied in a recently filed brief was overruled several years before. You're getting the call as a courtesy to tell you that a brief to this effect has just been filed in court, seeking, among other things, sanctions against you for misleading the court. Now imagine how you'll break this news to your supervisor and your client.

Relax. There's a simple step that will solve this problem and—as an added bonus—give you one final way to check that you've covered the possible sources of information about the issue on which you're working. You have to take this step every time you do case-based research, but once you've taken it, you'll never have to worry about getting a call like that from an opposing attorney.

This step is updating your research, and it's given the generic name of "Shepardizing," although the "Shepard's" citator service is just one of two principal forms of updating now available to lawyers. The Shepard's service is owned by LexisNexis; West has its own citator service called "KeyCite." They both work in basically the same fashion, and while some insist that a careful lawyer should use both Shepard's and KeyCite before relying on authority, the cost of using either one of these services is sufficiently high that it's unlikely many practitioners actually do this.

It's easy to understand the need for a service like Shepard's or KeyCite if you think about the way the common law works. A court articulates an opinion, published in a case, about a particular issue. Subsequent courts rely on this opinion to reach their own opinions, or, perhaps, decide to move in a different direction and distinguish the original opinion from their decisions. In time, perhaps, another court decides that the original opinion was wrong and, if it has the authority to do so, overrules that original opinion, meaning that it's no longer good law. But none of this would be reflected in the original published version of the case you found. That was published in a reporter many years before, and because print publication is static, nothing about the subsequent history of the case changes the print version of the case. That might not necessarily be true in the digital world, where subsequent treatment of a case could be incorporated into the original document, but it's certainly true of print.

In order to make sure that lawyers stayed current with the development of a case after it was published, publishers developed citator services, of which the Shepard's system was the most successful. Here's the essence of how it works. Each published case is given an entry in a large table of all cases. A team of editors scours each new opinion and, when that opinion refers to an earlier case (as they almost all do), that fact is recorded in the table under the original case's entry. Even more helpfully, the types of reference the new case makes to the original case are given as well, so the researching lawyer can see at a glance if the newer case overruled the original case, or if it adopted its holding on a particular issue, or if there's a different treatment. In this way, a lawyer can see quickly how an older case has fared, and—crucially—whether it is still good law or not.

It used to be the case that all of this was done on paper. Large, hardbound Shepard's tables were published each year, and updates—each in different colored bindings—came out at various times during the year. In order to be complete, lawyers had to check not just the hardbound volumes, but also all of the different colored bindings and look up the original case in all of them. With practice, one could become quite proficient at looking up cases quickly and getting a lot of information about them, but one was always limited by how up-to-date the Shepard's tables were; if the most recent update was a month old, one couldn't see if any cases within the last month had added anything to the subsequent treatment of the original case.

This is one place where computer-assisted research is a vast improvement over paper. Shepard's (on LexisNexis) and KeyCite (on Westlaw) are updated almost instantly, and lawyers can, and should, check on their relied-on sources to make sure they have the most current information before filing a brief or conducting oral argument. In fact, online Shepard's and KeyCite are so much better than their paper versions that very few libraries now carry the print version of Shepard's: it's expensive to buy and shelve and hardly anyone would use it even if it were available.

As opposed to the codes that used to be attached to the print form of Shepard's, both online Shepard's and KeyCite now use a flagging system to alert researchers to subsequent history. These should be used with care; just because a case has a red flag attached to it doesn't mean that the case as a whole has been overruled. The part of the case you need might still be good law and available for your use. One can do this, although there is a special citation form necessary to show the reader that another part of the case is no longer good law. The moral here is that just as with everything else, the careful researcher reads and makes decisions for him or herself. The flagging system is a helpful guide, but it shouldn't be used as a substitute for the researcher's own analysis.

Using Shepard's or KeyCite is obviously a crucial last step that one must take before relying on a case; a case that's been overruled doesn't support anything and would be very harmful to your position if you relied on it. But equally as obvious, not all cases are overruled or even have their holdings called into question. In fact, many cases are relied on by subsequent courts in order to reach their decisions, and because Shepard's and KeyCite record all instances in which subsequent courts cite to cases, these services have an obvious appeal as research tools as well: if you find a case that helps you, and through using Shepard's or KeyCite, you find another ten cases that relied on the case that helps you, you've now discovered eleven cases, not just one, that might be helpful to you.

The only way to know if these new cases will be helpful, of course, is to read them. Sometimes the reference to the original case is more tangential than substantive, and sometimes the facts of the subsequent case are so different that it's of no help at all. But sometimes the facts of the original case weren't too close to the issue you've been researching, and the later cases might have facts that are much closer to the facts of the case on which you're working, making them even more helpful than the original case— the only way to know is to locate and read them. And, of course, if you decide to use the subsequent cases, you need to Shepardize or KeyCite those cases as well, to make sure that they haven't themselves been overruled, and to see if they've been cited by other helpful, or unhelpful, cases.

Conclusion

This might all seem like an arduous and time-consuming process, and it can take up a fair amount of time, even for experienced researchers. That shouldn't be a shock, though; law is complicated, and it should be no surprise that it can take a long time to unravel all the various strands in order to reach a careful and considered answer to a legal question. Part of that answer is, inevitably, the law that supports the opinion you're offering, and in order to find that law you need to conduct thoughtful research.

Like anything else, you'll get better and faster at legal research the more you do it. What seems complicated and unwieldy at the moment will become more natural and more seamless over time. But only to a point. Legal research, when done correctly, will always take time and thought and it's a process that can't be rushed. No matter how experienced a researcher you become, you likely will always have to think about what secondary sources you want to look at in order to learn more about a topic, and what jurisdiction or jurisdictions will yield the most useful results for you. In order to be sure you're getting the most out of your research, you'll have to consider conducting both pre- and self-indexed searches of the relevant databases (even print digests can be thought of as databases, so the term applies to print and computer-assisted research), and you'll certainly have to update your research by using Shepard's or KeyCite in order to complete your research. All of this will take time.

But it's time well spent. Nothing will impress your employers more than thoughtful answers to their questions. If you can write your answers in a clear, easy-to-understand style, supported by careful research that shows intelligent analysis and attention to detail, and if you can do this every time you're given an assignment, you'll have a lot of work ahead of you and that, as every associate will tell you, is a very good thing for young lawyers.

Focus Questions

1. Do you understand why thinking about the research process before you actually begin research is a useful approach? Is this something you have done as a matter of course in your previous research tasks? Is this an approach you will adopt when conducting legal research? Is the text's use of "orientation" a helpful one for you? How familiar are you with map-reading as a process for identifying routes?

2. Do you think your ego might get in your way as a legal researcher?

3. Have you experienced a situation where a court has used non-standard language to discuss a legal issue? Do you see why having a general sense of a topic, and the vocabulary used to discuss a topic, is so important for a legal researcher?

4. Are you surprised by the text's advice to go to the secondary sources before researching in primary sources? Is this a strategy you think you will adopt? Is this a strategy you have used before in your research tasks?

5. Have you experienced a situation where you have been researching but not found good results to answer the question you were asking? Have you developed strategies to help you in such situations? Does the text suggest strategies that are similar to the ones you have used in the past? Do you think your prior strategies will be useful to you in a legal research context?

6. Have you found research to be a dynamic process in your pre-law scholarly life? Do you see why the text makes this claim for legal research?

7. Have you experienced the problem of not knowing when to stop researching? If so, did you develop strategies to help you with that problem? Are the strategies the text discusses here similar to the ones you had developed? Have you ever thought your research was complete only to discover later that you had missed some important information that would have had a bearing on your answer?

8. Does the text sufficiently emphasize the importance of using Shepard's or KeyCite to update your research results? Do you think the text over-emphasizes the potential dangers of not updating your research? Do you see the value in a citator service like Shepard's or KeyCite?

Chapter 34

Legislative History

What You Should Learn from This Chapter

This chapter introduces the topic of legislative history. While it suggests that the best way to conduct legislative history is to use the fruits of previously complied legislative histories, the chapter also outlines ways in which lawyers conduct their own legislative history research. It discusses the types of information typically to be found in a legislative history and it describes ways to maneuver through legislative materials, both in paper and online.

After reading this chapter, you should:

- understand why previously compiled legislative histories are so valuable to legal researchers;
- understand what types of information can be found in legislative histories;
- know how to identify legislative materials at various stages of the legislative process; and
- understand where at least some legislative history information can be found.

Legislative history is one of those things you don't need to know how to do until you have a desperate need to do it. Most lawyers don't spend much time on legislative history, and some judges even deny that it has any value at all. But there are times when knowing what people said about legislation before it passed can be very helpful. Sometimes you have to base arguments on the legislative history because there's little else to support a position you want to take. And knowing what witnesses said during testimony before various committees can give you an insight into them and their positions, which can be helpful when you're looking to retain experts or looking for information against experts the other side has retained.

We're only going to talk about federal legislative history here. The states maintain legislative history information as well, but the differences in format and method of information retrieval are so varied that it would be impossible to summarize them all. The best I can say here is that if you need to do state legislative history, find someone who can walk you through the process for the state you need to research. This is one place where local expertise is crucial.

1. Compiled Legislative Histories

The easiest way to get a legislative history together is to get someone else to do the work. And you might be in luck; compiled and published legislative histories for many important pieces of federal legislation already exist. Before you begin the lengthy process of getting your own legislative history together, remember that someone might already have done everything you need, so take a look to see if there's a compiled legislative history for your legislation.

There are several ways to look for compiled legislative histories, but the easiest is to look at one of the bibliographies that list the various compiled legislative histories. You can find those by looking in your law school's library catalog. You can also find the compiled legislative histories the library has by searching in this catalog. If you're no longer in school and need to do this type of research, and your firm doesn't have a librarian who can help you, the best approach is to go to a local courthouse or bar association library and use its resources.

2. Doing It Yourself

If you're unlucky and there's no compiled legislative history for your particular legislation of interest, or if you don't have access to an already-existing legislative history, then you'll need to compile your own. This might seem like a massive and complicated task, but as with all such tasks, the thing to do is to cut it down to manageable steps. And as with all research, the first step would be to stop and reflect about what actually might be in a legislative history and then where you might find information about that particular piece of the history.

A. What Information Is in a Legislative History?

You're too far along as lawyers to spend much time here on the legislative process.[1] In very broad outline, pre-enactment legislation is known as a bill, and once a bill is introduced (to either the Senate or the House—most can be introduced in either place first), and assuming it doesn't die along the way, as most legislation does, it typically makes its way through various committees and floor debates, first in the chamber in which it was introduced and then—after passage there—in the other chamber, until final passage and presidential signing. There are many variants on this process, and there isn't room enough to cover them all. But the rough outlines of the process are enough because they show us the several principal sources of legislative history:

- the bill, and all the amendments that are typically made to it;
- the transcripts of hearings before the various committees, together with any accompanying documents;
- the committee reports that typically accompany the bill on its passage;

---

1. There's a more detailed description of the process in Appendix 4, in case you need a refresher.

- the transcripts of floor debates about the bill; and
- any presidential statements about the bill at signing or veto.

This last item on the list might seem a little surprising. Presidents are, after all, part of the executive branch, not the legislative branch of government, and therefore would not technically fall within the orbit of "legislative" history. But presidential action might be important, particularly if the president imposed a veto which was later overturned; in such a situation, the statements accompanying the veto would form a crucial part of understanding how and why the bill came to be law in its present form, and would therefore form part of the bill's legislative history, regardless of the formal Constitutional labeling of the participants in the process.

Each step in the process generates documentation, and each document is important to the development of a legislative history. But not all documents are necessarily equally important. You need to understand why it is that you're compiling the legislative history before you start gathering up every available document—there can be a lot of them. If, for instance, you're looking at some potential experts, for you or against you, then you might be more interested in the committee hearings, because that's likely where they testified, and you might be less interested in the floor debates, since only representatives and senators speak during those. If, on the other hand, you're interested in what motivated the legislators to act in a particular way—to determine congressional "intent" for a piece of legislation or for a concept within that legislation—then everything related to the legislation or to the concept within the legislation that is relevant to your work might be equally important to you.

B. Process and Numbering

In order to find anything in the class of documents related to legislation, you need to know a little bit about the pre- and post-enactment process that you might not have learned in civics class, and you need to know how everything is numbered during the process. This is a very (very) cursory discussion that should help to put the rest of this chapter in context.

When a bill is introduced, it's given a number—an H. R. number if it's introduced in the House of Representatives and an S. number if it's introduced in the Senate. Once legislation is enacted, though, it gets a new number that locates it, in order, within the session of Congress in which it was passed. This is known as the Public Law number, and a bill with the number 100-58, for example, would be the fifty-eighth piece of legislation enacted by the 100th Congress. As with court opinions—which are published in slip opinion fashion before being permanently bound into reporters—so Public Laws are published in slip law form.

After a while, the slip laws are gather together and are published in a bound, chronological, publication known as Statutes at Large. This publishes all the laws enacted in a particular session of Congress, and in this form they're known as "Session Laws," although that's not a particularly helpful or meaningful designation—there's no difference in the language of the legislation in its slip law or Session Law form.

What is important is that the numbering system changes; Session Laws are not organized by Public Law numbers, but rather by Statutes at Large citations. As with reporters, these are organized with the first number representing the volume number and the second number representing the page number on which the first page of the legislation can be found within the volume: so a citation of 100 Stat. 500 would guide you to page 500 of Statutes at Large, volume 100.

The next step in the process, though, is what usually throws everyone out. You likely won't remember the specifics of this within an hour of reading this section, but try hard to remember that something odd happens to the organization of legislation, and that you can find out what it is by referring back to this. There will likely come a time once you're out in practice when you're completely confused by all of this numbering and remembering that you know where to look to figure it out will be a big help to you.

The law is now codified, meaning that the legislation we've tracked through its H. R. or S. number, then its Public Law number, and then through its Statutes at Large citation, now gets broken up and sent to potentially numerous different locations within the United States Code. The Code is organized topically, with each topic getting its own "Title," and every piece of legislation is broken up so that each part that relates to a particular topic is placed under the appropriate Code Title.

Just like court opinions, legislation usually doesn't deal with just one subject. So just as a court case might, for example, deal with issues related to summary judgment, evidence, and products liability, so legislation might deal with the treatment of animals for medical research, the civil and criminal penalties for abuse of animals, how such animals are to be transported, and so on. That means that the piece of the legislation that deals with criminal penalties will be broken out and placed in the Title relating to federal crimes, the piece that deals with civil penalties will be placed in the Title relating to civil litigation, and so on. What was once a unified piece of legislation can now be scattered across multiple pieces of the Code and if you tried to gather all the pieces together again using the Code as your only source of information, you would likely be at the task for a very long time.

It's important that the Code be organized in the way it is, of course, because in the normal run of things, we're much more likely to be interested in the particular topics than we are in the way a piece of legislation was originally organized. And besides, if that is what we're interested in, we can always retrieve the original form of the legislation if we have the Public Law or Statutes at Large information for the legislation, and each part of the United States Code Annotated (the West-published unofficial version of the Code that is much more helpful than the official Code when working on legislative histories) gives you those numbers so you can see where each part of the Code came from.

The confusion comes when you're dealing with government agencies who only deal with particular pieces of legislation, not the Code as a whole. When you speak to lawyers from the Food and Drug Administration, for example, they'll likely refer you to sections of "the Act," meaning the Food, Drug, and Cosmetics Act and its various amendments. They might even refer you to sections of the Act, like Section 510k. If you look for the language of Section 510k in the Code, though, you'll be horribly confused because this citation refers to the enacted legislation, not the codified version of it. If you look up the Food, Drug, and Cosmetics Act, and find the Public Law or Statutes at Large citation, and then look up Section 510k, you'll find the language the agency is referring to there. It's in the Code as well, of course, but you'll have to look through the conversion tables that come with the Code, to look up the Public Law or Statutes at Large citation and then use the table to find the equivalent Code citation.

It sounds more complicated than it is, and once you've experienced the uneasy feeling of realizing that the citation you have doesn't mean what you think it means, you'll remember that you have to convert one citation into another and you'll remember how to do it. For now, though, just keep in mind that whenever you hear or read about someone referring to "the Act," they're not referring to "the Code."

C. United States Code Congressional and Administrative News

Now that you're thoroughly confused, back to legislative history. If you're looking for committee reports, the United States Code Congressional and Administrative News, known universally as "U.S.C.C.A.N.," is a place to start. It doesn't publish everything, but it publishes a lot, which means that it can be large and a little unwieldy to use. Legislation in U.S.C.C.A.N. is organized by its Statutes at Large number, and it also publishes committee reports in volumes called "Legislative History." So if you look up the legislation you're interested in, and you see a reference to a committee report published in U.S.C.C.A.N., it's a fairly simple matter to follow the citation and find the report. The only trick to remember is that U.S.C.C.A.N. volumes are numbered by year, so 2001 U.S.C.C.A.N. refers to legislation enacted in the year 2001.

D. Congressional Information Service

The Congressional Information Service, or CIS, used to be the best way to retrieve large amounts of information about legislative history, because it published its material on microfiche, making it possible to store a lot of data in a small space. The internet has made microfiche outdated, though, and while LexisNexis has put CIS online, it's harder to negotiate through legislative history information online than it is in print form.

Although CIS is more of a specialized librarian's tool than it once was, it's still a handy place to find information that might be difficult to track down elsewhere, particularly if you're looking at older legislation. If you need to use it, though, I'd strongly recommend that you find a librarian trained in its ways to help you.

E. Congressional Record

Perhaps the best way to think of the Congressional Record is as a newspaper that covers the day-to-day activities of Congress. In it, you'll find a record of everything that happened—or that the Congress people want you to think happened—on the floor of Congress. The qualification in the last sentence is there because information can be added to the record after a floor session has taken place, meaning that a carefully edited version of a Congressperson's remark can be substituted for the potentially less articulate comments the Congressperson actually made. This makes the Congressional Record a little suspect as a source of legislative intent, but it's what we have if the floor debates are important to you.

As you can imagine, in the Congressional Record, legislation is referred to using its H. R. or S. numbers; the legislation hasn't been enacted when it's under debate, and therefore has no Public Law or Statutes at Large citation. What's less easy is the way information in the Congressional Record is cited, because it appears in two separate, and yet identical, versions—the daily version (with House and Senate coverage numbered separately), and a permanent edition which is compiled at the end of each congressional session with all pages numbered consecutively. If you're looking at a Congressional Record citation, there's a simple way to know whether you're looking at a reference to the daily or permanent editions: because the daily version numbers House and Senate coverage differently, it needs an "H" or "S" before the number, so if the citation you're looking at has a letter, it's the daily version, and if it doesn't, then it refers to the permanent edition. There are citations to the relevant parts of the Congressional Record in U.S.C.C.A.N., and the Congressional Record itself has an index that lets you look up pieces of legislation.

Although the Congressional Record is relatively simple to use, it's still a good idea to consult with a librarian if you're going to be using it extensively to compile a legislative history for a particular piece of legislation. Most lawyers don't spend enough time with these materials to be sufficiently comfortable with their use to be sure that they're getting everything out of them and it's better to speak with experts if you can than to blunder your way through the process.

F. Commercial Database Sources of Legislative History Information

There's simple advice for anyone contemplating doing legislative history research online: don't. You can, of course—all the materials are available to you (although some might fall outside even the broad coverage offered by your academic password)—but it's a time-consuming, and therefore expensive, endeavor for a practicing lawyer.

Shepardizing and KeyCiting is possible for statutes, and that will give you some, but not necessarily all, legislative history materials. And the Annotated Code is available on Westlaw, with hyperlinks to the materials related to your legislation of interest Westlaw has elsewhere on its databases. But if you're using these services in practice, you should be very careful that clicking on these links doesn't take you outside any flat-rate agreements your firm has with Westlaw (or LexisNexis, if you're using their equivalent service). This is a trap for the unwary, and can cause you to unintentionally run up large charges for computer-assisted research that might not be covered under the standard billing arrangement.

As with all things to do with legislative history, the safe approach is to speak with a librarian before beginning your work. And the safest approach of all is to not use Westlaw or LexisNexis when undertaking this type of research.

G. Congress.gov

The good news for those of you who are uncomfortable conducting research in any form other than computers is that a superb, free service is available for relatively recent legislative history work. That source is Congress.gov (formerly called "Thomas," after the Library of Congress' founder, Thomas Jefferson), a government website published by the Library of Congress. Congress.gov links to the Government Printing Office ("GPO") website, which makes online versions of the Congressional Record available to you as well.

The site's most significant limitation is that it will not give you access to testimony offered in front of congressional committees. So while you can track legislation though its various amendments, and you can read what the Congressional Record reports about floor debates concerning the legislation, you can't rely on Congress.gov for a full legislative history for a piece of legislation and, if the testimony before congressional committees is your primary interest, Congress.gov will be of no help at all.

H. Hein Online

Hein Online is another online service that is helpful when working on legislative histories. Although you might have a subscription to Hein as a law school student, not all law firms subscribe to this service so you should check before relying on it if you are compiling a legislative history for work.

Hein is often thought of as a source of law review articles online, and it is a superb provider of this information. But it also carries a lot of legislative history information, including compiled legislative histories for significant pieces of legislation. If you have access to a subscription to Hein, you might want to search its resources first, before embarking on compiling your own legislative history for a piece of legislation.

Conclusion

You might sense a general reluctance to give too much information about the legislative history research process, and you'd be right. It's important to know about some of the principal sources of this information, but it's also important to recognize that this is a specialized area and you can get in too deep, and run up too much expense, if you dive in without knowing what you're doing. And since most lawyers engage in this type of research rarely, if at all, during their careers, spending more time than this on the process of researching legislative history seems counter-productive.

So the best tips on offer here are simple: try to find a librarian who has received special training in legislative history research if you need to delve into this area, and if you have to do this work yourself, try to do it using paper rather than for-cost computer databases. Congress.gov is a valuable source of free online information and Hein Online can be very helpful if you have access to it. But Westlaw and LexisNexis can be very expensive if you use them for legislative history work, not just because such research can take a lot of time and is, in any case, more difficult to do online than it is in print form, but also because some of the databases on which legislative history information might be stored might fall outside your firm's flat-rate fee agreement, and using them could significantly increase the cost of research.

If you're concerned that you'll need to be doing legislative history research at work—because you want to work in politics or lobbying, for example—then the best advice is to take an advanced research course while in law school. You'll be able to spend more time working on this material and you'll become more fluent with all the sources necessary to become an efficient legislative history researcher.

Focus Questions

1. Are you as familiar with the legislative process as the text assumes you to be? Are you sure? If you have doubts, will you review the longer discussion at Appendix 4 or other discussions of the legislative process?

2. Had you considered that the history of legislation might have value to lawyers? Have you spoken in your doctrinal classes about the ways some judges and Supreme Court justices feel about legislative history? Do you see the difference between the way a judge or justice might think about legislative history and the way a practicing lawyer might think about it?

3. Will you remember the different numbering systems used to identify a piece of legislation at different points in the process? If not, will you retain this text, or another like it, that will allow you to look up that information when you need it?

4. Do you think you will remember the relevance of the codification process to the problem of communicating with government agencies?

5. Were you aware that text can be inserted into the Congressional Record? In your opinion, does this make the Congressional Record more or less useful as a source of legislative history or is its value unaffected?

Chapter 35

Statutory Research

What You Should Learn from This Chapter

This chapter introduces you to some of the particular issues related to statutory research. And while this text generally supports the idea that research is possible in both print and online mediums, this chapter notes that statutory research is easier in print than it is online. The chapter discusses the differences between the official and two unofficial versions of the United States Code and, understanding that you likely will want to conduct statutory research online even though the print medium is easier for this kind of work, it suggests some approaches for making online statutory research a little easier.

After reading this chapter, you should:

- be able to differentiate between the various versions of the United States Code;
- be able to select the unofficial code best suited to your research needs;
- understand why and how to update your statutory research using Shepard's or KeyCite; and
- understand the advantages and disadvantages of open access services for statutory research.

There's an important truth about statutory research: it's easier to do it in print than it is online. Perhaps it's because the limited scope of each statutory provision makes it difficult for drafters to use sufficiently different language, so that Boolean searches tend to return a high percentage of false positive results, or perhaps there's some other reason that makes statutory provisions more impervious to full-text searches than cases; whatever the reason, it's true that the print versions of statutes—the unofficial versions of them, at any rate—are far easier to search than their online equivalents. This isn't to say that Westlaw and LexisNexis aren't getting better at presenting statutory information, or that one can't use those services to search through statutes (indeed, for state statutes, they're often the only choice since even large law libraries tend not to have complete sets of all state statutes). But it is to say that where you have the choice, you'll usually find your answer faster and more accurately when you use print than when you use the computer.

1. The United States Code

As a threshold matter, we're only going to talk about federal statutes here. If you need to research state statutes, the same general techniques will apply, but there are so many variations in the way states present their materials that it would take a much larger work than this to encompass everything. If you understand how to research the federal materials, and you need to conduct state statutory research later, you should be able to adapt quickly to the way those materials are presented.

Speaking practically, there are two things you should know about the United States Code, the official version of the Code printed by the United States Government: (1) it exists, and (2) you should never look at it. It is the official version of the Code, but it's so basic, and the unofficial versions of the Code are so superior to it for research purposes, that it really has no utility for you whatsoever. Only large law libraries carry it, in any case, compared to the unofficial codes, which are commonly available. Really. Stay away from the official version of the Code.

2. United States Code Annotated

The United States Code Annotated ("USCA") is published by West, and its most useful feature—of many useful features—is the annotation that accompanies each code provision. There, listed right underneath the code provision you're interested in, is a list of every case that has interpreted or cited to the language of that provision, broken out by topic, court, and then chronologically within each court system. You'll also find other useful information, including the history of the provision (amendments and revisions to the statutory language, including Public Law and Statutes at Large citations), citations to some secondary sources that discuss or analyze the provision (if there are any), references to relevant sections of the Code of Federal Regulations ("CFR") that relate to the provision you're looking at, and Key Numbers in some instances.

You won't find all of this information after each statutory provision, but you'll usually find enough that it makes researching the statutory language much simpler than having to assemble all of this material yourself. This is why if you're researching the meaning of statutory language, the USCA should be your first stop. It gives you the language itself, but it also gives you a lot more.

The USCA is updated by pocket part or, as is usually the case with heavily quoted statutes, slip volumes that sit next to the hard-bound main volumes. As with all materials updated by pocket parts, your research isn't complete until you've looked through both the main volume and the pocket part or slip volume.

You can find statutory provisions in a number of different ways. Remember that the Code is broken down into various Titles and that while the original act was a unitary document, its various provisions might have been scattered across multiple Titles of the Code when the act was codified. That means you might need to look in a variety of places in order to find out everything you need to know about a particular provision. If, for example, some action related to a medical device is prohibited, and carries potential civil and criminal penalties, you'll likely need to look in the part of the Code

that deals with the action itself, then at the part of the Code that deals with civil penalties, and then at the part of the Code that deals with criminal penalties. The USCA contains cross-references to other relevant portions of the Code to help you find these related, but far-flung, provisions.

Finding the initial provision requires an understanding of a couple of different finding tools. First, and most obviously, if you know a provision has to do with prescription drugs, you might scan the various Code titles and see that Title 21 is called "Food and Drugs." It might be reasonable to assume that the provision you're interested would be in that Title, and if you look at the beginning of the volume, you'll see that each of the various sections and subsections are listed, and that each have names that allow you to form at least a general impression of what they contain.

A more reliable way to start your research might be to look at the USCA's General Index, a multi-volume document that is usually shelved right next to the USCA. Making sure that you have the most recent index, you can look through it like any other index until you find what you're looking for. You might find several references that sound like the topic you're looking to research; make note of all of them and be sure to look at them all so you can be certain you've seen everything that might be relevant to you.

Sometimes, though, the index won't be as helpful as you would like. That's particularly true if someone asks you for a provision in a particular act—the Clean Water Act, for example. Perhaps you've even been given a section number from the Act to research. As you now know or could deduce, the Clean Water Act was the name of the legislation as it passed through Congress, when it had an "H. R." or "S." number. After it was enacted it had a Public Law and then a Statutes at Large citation. But now that it's been codified, the various provisions of the Clean Water Act have been dispersed throughout the Code, and the act's section numbers have all been changed, so how are you supposed to find them in the Code?

Mercifully, the USCA has Popular Name and Conversion tables, usually physically shelved next to the USCA and the index. If you know the name of a statute (like the Clean Water Act) but not its code citation, you can look it up in the Popular Name table. That will give you the Public Law, Statutes at Large, and Code citations for the statute's locations within the Code. And if you have the specific section of the act, you can look it up in the Conversion table by Public Law number or Statutes at Large citation (which you can get from the Popular Name table if you don't already have them) and then by section number; the Conversion table will give you the Code titles and sections where the language you're looking for has been codified.

You should remember the USCA's index, Popular Name, and Conversion tables, and should make a point of looking through them and trying to find information using them. They're not complicated to use, and once you know how to use them they can save you hours of wasted time. They'll make you look good to the attorneys with whom you work and with your clients as well. They're really very helpful tools.

3. United States Code Service

The United States Code Service ("USCS") is the other unofficial code, this time published by LexisNexis. It is particularly strong on CFR cross-references, and is a tool to consider if you're researching a statutory issue along with its regulatory implementation. Like the USCA, the USCS is a helpful and well-organized resource in its paper form.

If you're researching online, and you're using LexisNexis, the USCS is the annotated code you'll be using, and it's in its online version that most lawyers encounter it.

4. Statutory Research Online

As you can imagine from the opening of this chapter, the best advice for conducting online statutory research is to avoid it. Statutes really are simpler to research in paper form and will probably remain so for the foreseeable future.

Nonetheless, sometimes you're stuck with no choice but to use online resources, and if that's the case, you need to choose between the commercial providers—LexisNexis and Westlaw in all likelihood—and the free sites that offer the Code. We'll talk about both options briefly here.

A. LexisNexis and Westlaw

Both LexisNexis and Westlaw offer their respective annotated codes online. They both offer the same finding tools as they do in print, as well as full-text searching—something you should avoid doing at all costs, at least as the first step in research.

The process of searching for statutory materials online should follow the print process laid out above. Look for tables or indexes and then drill down in the tables until you find a heading that looks like a provision you might be interested in. If you have the popular name of an act, but not the relevant Code citations, you can use a Popular Name table, and there are Conversion tables available online as well.

The key with online searching is to make it simulate the print research process as much as possible. The closer you can get your research to approximate the print approach, the faster and more efficient you will be. This might seem counter-intuitive and might sound suspiciously agenda-driven, but really, the only agenda here is to make you the most effective legal researcher you can be.

In one area, though, online resources are crucial. As with case research, you can update your statutory research with citators—Shepard's on LexisNexis and KeyCite on Westlaw. Even though the statutory language is updated regularly in the online versions, it's still a good idea to finish off your research by using a citator to make sure everything is up-to-date, and these days, that's almost impossible to do in print. So while you might well be doing the bulk of your statutory research in print form, you're likely to end up using an online citator to make sure your research is current before you finish.

B. Open-Access Services

There are several ways to search the Code online for no charge. The most popular (more popular even than the various sites offered by the federal government) is Cornell University Law School's Legal Information Institute.

The two things to remember about all free sites that offer the Code is that they might well be out-of-date, and that there are no annotations or research aids to help you find anything. These are two important issues, and drastically limit the usefulness of these sites for the serious legal researcher. Nonetheless, a free online site can be helpful if you are stuck without access to a library and you need some statutory language, and it's a good idea to have links to at least one free online site bookmarked on your computer.

The easiest way to get to language on these open-access sites is to drill down from the Title heading level until you find the statutory language you need. Again, though, be very cautious that you're not using an out-of-date version of statutory language that might have been recently amended.

Focus Questions

1. Had you considered that statutory research might be easier in book form than in computer-assisted legal research databases? If not, do you now see why it might be easier to do such research using books?
2. Are you surprised that the text suggests you ignore the United States Code as printed by the government?
3. Have you looked at print volumes of the USCA and USCS? Do you see the differences between the two services? Which do you think will be more valuable for you as you conduct statutory research in law school? In practice? Might your answer depend on the type of research task you've been set? Might it be important to understand the strengths of both services so you could align your research strategy carefully with the desired research outcome?
4. Do you appreciate the dangers of open-access services when conducting online statutory research?

Chapter 36

Regulatory Research

What You Should Learn from This Chapter

This chapter introduces you to the various resources available to you for conducting regulatory research. The chapter begins with a brief review of the federal rulemaking process and then moves on to a discussion of the Code of Federal Regulations and the Federal Register, the two principal locations of federal regulatory information. As with statutory research, the text suggests that paper resources are more helpful than online for this type of research, but includes some suggestions for using online resources.

After reading this chapter, you should:

- understand the federal rulemaking process, at least a little better than before;
- understand what you can find in the Code of Federal Regulations and the Federal Register;
- understand how to update your regulatory research and why updating is so important; and
- be able to recognize some of the dangers associated with online federal regulatory research.

Administrative law is extremely important to lawyers and to the general public. While a great deal of attention is devoted to the Supreme Court and its activities, and to Congress and its wranglings, there's little doubt that the actions of administrative agencies like the Food and Drug Administration ("FDA") or the Federal Communications Commission ("FCC") affect our day-to-day lives at least as much as the rulings of the Court or the legislative enactments of Congress.

The work of the agencies is so important because they're the entities that actually put into effect the pronouncements of Congress. It's one thing for Congress to say that there are different types of medical device, for example, but it's up to the FDA to promulgate regulations that say what devices belong in each category, the process they will need to go through before they are approved for use, and so on. That understanding alone should tell you two things: regulations are very important, and there are lots of them.

What should be obvious for our present purposes is that if there are a lot of regulations, the research challenge is increased; the more information there is to sift through, the more difficult the process. Fortunately, there aren't too many places for us to look for regulations, so that part of the puzzle, at least, isn't too complicated. A quick discussion of the rule-making process will help to orient us before we start thinking about researching federal rules; as with statutes, we're not going to tackle each state's approach to regulations here.

1. Federal Rulemaking

The rulemaking process usually starts with an announcement in a publication called the Federal Register that an agency is going to issue regulations concerning a particular area and soliciting comments or proposals from interested individuals or bodies. That can often involve lawyers in a lot of work, preparing draft regulations that are drafted to meet the interests of their clients. The agency has its own ideas of how its regulations should look and what they should do, of course, but this comment period allows everyone interested in the area to have a voice in the process.

Often the agency will publish draft regulations in the Federal Register and invite the public to comment on them. Again, that will often involve lawyers, who develop extensive comments in support of, or in opposition to, the proposed regulations. Although a cynical mind might assume that this is just an exercise in due process, allowing everyone to say what they think before the agency goes ahead and does what it would like, it will often happen that an agency withdraws its proposed regulations in light of the comments it receives and will rework them to remove some concerns that came to light as a result of this comment process.

Once a regulation is final, it's published in the Federal Register and then—like statutes—is codified, this time in a publication called the Code of Federal Regulations ("CFR"). Just as with the U.S. Code, the CFR is divided into "titles," which are subdivided into "chapters," further subdivided into "parts," and finally subdivided into "sections." For citation purposes, you're given the title number (which acts like a volume number with a case), the publication (always the CFR), and then the part and section numbers (taking the role of the page numbers in case citations). So 21 CFR 500.15 tells you that a regulation can be found in title 21 of the CFR at part 500, section 15.

2. The Code of Federal Regulations and the Federal Register

If you ever have to maintain a small law library, the CFR might become the bane of your existence. Because the entire CFR is updated each year—with roughly a quarter of the titles updated each three months—it seems that you are perpetually taking old volumes off the shelves and putting new ones up. There are some features of the CFR that mitigate the irritation of constant shelving though: each new year's CFR has a different colored binder, so you know easily, just by look, if the volume you're looking at is from last year or is the new, updated version; and because the entire Code is reprinted each year, there are no updates and no pocket parts to worry about.

Instead of CFR updates, new regulations are published in the Federal Register and are not integrated into the CFR until the volume into which they will be placed is published. And as you can imagine, there are many new regulations each year, and many revisions to already-existing regulations, meaning that simply looking at the CFR to find the most up-to-date information about a particular regulated area is insufficient.

You can find CFR citations in several ways. If you're looking at a statute and are wondering what regulations have been promulgated to implement it, you can find that information from an annotated code; the United States Code Service ("USCS") is more helpful for this task than the United States Code Annotated ("USCA"). The CFR also has a subject index, which should be located on the same set of shelves as the paper CFR. Researching the CFR online is covered below.

The Federal Register is a massive publication. It's published every day, and it contains all manner of information. The thought of researching it can be daunting. Mercifully, there's an extraordinarily useful publication that makes your life much simpler: it's called the List of CFR Sections Affected ("LSA") and it does exactly what its title suggests. The LSA is published monthly, and it's cumulative, meaning that it updates regulations from the last time the CFR volume containing them was published up through the end of the month before the LSA was published.

As you've probably noticed, though, there's still a little gap between the LSA's coverage and the day you're doing your research, and because the regulatory world can change rapidly, you have to plug that gap as well. The Federal Register helps you to do this by publishing a list of CFR sections affected as part of its daily publication. In order to be complete in your research, therefore, you have to find the CFR section you're interested in, update it using the most recent LSA, and then update that by reading through each daily Federal Register from the days between the publication date of the LSA and the day you're conducting the research.

The Federal Register will also tell you if an agency has announced that it is contemplating action in a particular area, and if that action will affect a regulation you're interested in. Even though a regulation hasn't been formally updated, anyone interested in asking you to research a particular regulation will likely be interested in the possibility of revisions to that regulation, so it behooves you to keep an eye open for such notices as well.

3. Online Resources for Federal Regulatory Research

As with almost all legal information these days, the CFR and the Federal Register are available online, and you will almost certainly need to use either Westlaw or LexisNexis at some point during your regulatory research because few, if any, libraries carry Shepard's volumes for the CFR and the use of a citator—Shepard's on LexisNexis or KeyCite on Westlaw—is vital.

Both LexisNexis and Westlaw have the CFR available online, and both services keep their versions as updated as possible by incorporating changes from the Federal Register when they appear, so the online versions of the CFR available from the commercial databases are much more up-to-date than the print versions. This is important to remember if you do your work on paper and are sloppy about updating it, and someone else—perhaps an opponent in a case—does research online. You might end up with two different versions of the same rule because the online version is more up-to-date than the now-outdated paper version. Remember, though, that this is one time when being up-to-date might not be helpful. In litigation, the relevant language might be that in operation at the time of the event under consideration, not the most current language. If the CFR has changed since the date relevant to the litigation, you might have to do some research to find the operative regulatory language for that date. This is one place where Hein Online, which is very strong in archived versions of old documents, can be very helpful to you.

When using the online version of the CFR, it's much simpler to use the table of contents, and to drill down through the various subheadings until you reach a subject heading that looks like it's related to your research interest, than it is to use a word search. It's very easy to flounder around for a long time, and to run through a lot of searches, if you're trying to locate a specific set of words in relation to one another, because it's even harder to predict regulatory language than it is to predict court language and, as you'll recall from reading about Boolean searching earlier, predicting the document drafter's language is a crucial aspect to this research strategy.

The CFR and the Federal Register are also available free on several sites, with the Government Printing Office's site probably being the best. But—and this is a crucial but—be very careful about the currency of the CFR on the GPO's site. Although this might seem strange to you, the GPO's CFR site is the equivalent of the published CFR, and the volumes are only as current as the printed volumes. That means that none of the changes from the Federal Register have been incorporated into the GPO online version of the CFR. So if you use this online version of the CFR, you'll have to go through the same updating process as you would if you were using the print version, something that's not true if you're using the Westlaw or LexisNexis versions of the CFR. This is a trap that can catch even experienced legal researchers, but it's one into which you shouldn't now fall.

To make things even more complicated, the GPO also offers something called the Electronic CFR that's unofficial,[1] and that does update the CFR with daily changes from the Federal Register. All of this will doubtless change many times over the next few years, as the government improves the sophistication of its online resources, so the important thing for any researcher is to think each time before using a resource—even if you last used it only a month or two ago—and check to see whether the resource is official and whether it is current. Once you know that, and how to update information that isn't fully current, you'll be able to conduct competent, efficient research no matter what resource you're using.

---

1. Why does it matter that this resource is designated "unofficial"? Since it comes from the GPO, isn't it as "official" as one can get? Well ... yes and no. On the one hand, it's unlikely that the GPO is going to tinker with the wording of an unofficial CFR and alter it from the official version without approval of the appropriate agency. On the other hand, "official" versions of web-based information are usually protected by security measures that come close to guaranteeing (one can rarely say that anything is guaranteed in the world of the internet, as hackers are constantly improving their technique) that their text is precisely the same as that enacted by the administrative or legislative body. Very few government websites—federal or state—contain "official" versions of documents, something of continuing concern to all of us.

The GPO's online version of the Federal Register, however, is updated daily, just like the print version. And if you use the GPO's official CFR site, you'll have to follow the same steps to update the text as you would if you were using the print version. The LSA is available online, and you should use that, and the Federal Register, to update the CFR in the same way described above.

Focus Questions

1. Are you surprised to see the text stress the importance of administrative agencies in our daily lives? Can you think of a way in which the rulings of an administrative agency might have affected your life today?
2. Are you secure in your understanding of the regulatory process?
3. Have you ever read a federal or state regulation?
4. Did the discussion of online resources for federal regulatory research confuse you? Do you understand the importance of LexisNexis and Westlaw providing up-to-date versions of the CFR, while the GPO version of the CFR might be out-of-date?
5. Do you understand why you might need an out-of-date version of regulatory language instead of the most current version of the language? Do you see how this could pose problems for the unwary legal researcher?
6. Do you feel confident in your ability to update regulatory language with the LSA and the Federal Register? Do you understand why the text is so emphatic about the importance of updating regulatory research to the day, or do you think this concern is overblown?
7. Do you think you will remember how to perform regulatory research once you enter practice? If not, do you plan to keep your copy of this book, or buy another book that covers regulatory research, as a reminder of how to conduct this type of research once you are in practice?

Chapter 37

What to Do When Things Go Wrong

What You Should Learn from This Chapter

This chapter suggests some trouble-shooting ideas for your research process when it doesn't appear to be working as well as it could. The principal theme of this chapter is that you shouldn't be concerned if you're not getting the results you expected: after some thought and reflection, you'll either change your research plan to a more effective one or you'll modify your expectations in light of your better understanding of the topic under research. The chapter suggests approaches to take in the unlikely event that you don't find enough information, the much more likely event that you find too much information, and—crucially—what you might want to do if the information you find makes no sense, something that happens to every legal researcher now and then.

After reading this chapter, you should:

- feel secure that you have some trouble-shooting strategies to fix the research problems you might encounter;
- understand that no legal research problem is insoluble;
- recognize that all legal researchers encounter problems from time to time; and
- appreciate the importance of setting aside enough time in the research process to fix problems when they come up.

No matter how carefully you think about what you're going to do before beginning a research project, and no matter how carefully you've mapped out your strategy and the appropriate tools for conducting that research, sometimes things go wrong: you don't find anything useful, you find too much that's useful, or you just don't know what you've found.

When this happens, there are a couple of things to know. First, and most importantly, don't worry. This happens to everyone. The second thing to know is that when the initial results of research aren't fruitful, in whatever way and for whatever reason, we have to stop, re-think what we're doing, and start again. It's not complicated and it's not worrying. In fact, it's better when things go wrong early; at least you've had a chance to spot the problems in your research plan before you spent too much time and money going down the wrong path. And remember that it's always better to learn you're on the wrong path yourself than to have it pointed out for you by a more senior lawyer at your firm or a lawyer on the other side of a case, or, worst of all, the judge.

1. What to Do When You Don't Find Enough Information

Actually, not finding enough law on the topic you're researching is probably the simplest problem of all to fix. That's usually a sign that you just didn't understand the question being asked of you, and that you need to re-think the question you think you're researching.

The first thing to do in this situation (after you've thought through the question again, of course), is to go back through the appropriate secondary sources of information. If you looked at just one before launching into your unproductive research, perhaps it would be advisable to look at a few different secondary sources now. If you're looking at a federal statutory question, and you haven't looked at the Annotated Code yet, now is certainly the time to do that.

If you've taken all these steps and you still can't find anything helpful, then maybe you have found the rare question that hasn't been addressed yet; perhaps you have a new statute that hasn't been interpreted by the courts yet, or perhaps you have a question in an emerging area of the law. Let's tackle those two problems in order.

If you have a new statute, then think about where it comes from and what it's intended to accomplish. If it's a new state statute, for example, is it modeled after a federal statute or statute from a different state? If so, you might find federal or state cases that interpret the source statute that will be helpful to you.[1] If not, can you think of statutes that provide analogous relief—if a state statute involving foster children talks about "the best interests of the child," for example, and no court has explained how that language is interpreted, is there an adoption statute using the same language that has been interpreted? If so, you might be able to make the argument that the language is analogous and therefore the interpretation should be analogous as well.

That's probably the best technique to use if the issue truly is one of first impression in your jurisdiction. If that's the case, and you're comfortable with a partner from your firm walking into court and telling a judge—based only on your advice—that no court in your jurisdiction has considered the question before, then you might look for other jurisdictions that have looked at the issue and try to use them in support of your analysis. If not, are there similar issues that your home jurisdiction has analyzed that might

---

1. If you're in this situation, you should also research your state's case law for a case that says, in essence, when the state takes language from somewhere else—a federal statute, for example, or a statutory provision from another state—then the state courts will look to the law from the places from which the language originally came to help them in interpreting the language. Many states have cases like this; it doesn't matter if they're not talking specifically about the statute you're researching, it's the general principal that's important. Language like this helps you to use cases from a foreign jurisdiction in the state you're being asked to research; courts typically aren't interested in opinions of courts from other places but there are times when they will look at such language and this is one of them.

be used to argue for similar (or different) results? Learning how to analogize and distinguish authority is one of the hallmarks of a good lawyer and this is probably the most challenging of situations in which that skill comes into play. You have to think carefully about each step in the chain that gets you from your (unanalyzed) issue to the other (interpreted) issue and make sure that there are no logical gaps or assumptions in that chain that can be attacked. Once you're comfortable that you have a solid, unassailable, connection between the two issues, then you're in good shape and can go ahead and use the research you've undertaken of the related issue in support of the question you've been asked.

If none of this works, there's another approach that feels a little like cheating but can actually be very helpful. Both LexisNexis and Westlaw have research attorneys available for either online chats or phone calls. They'll ask for your ID number, to make sure that you're someone who's entitled to use the service, but they are available to speak with law students. You should confirm whether this service is available to you if you're working on a graded assignment: you don't want to commit an unwitting honor code violation by calling for some research assistance.

Assuming you're allowed to speak with these research attorneys, you can work through the research question you've been asked with them, and they'll help you to construct searches that might generate positive results. They won't share the results of those searches with you—their job is, after all, to help the companies for which they work to generate income, and that will only happen if lawyers who are paying for their services run searches—but they'll give you the searches themselves, which allows you to run them in whatever database you think would be appropriate. The research attorneys can be very helpful

2. What to Do When You Find Too Much Information

Although finding no information can happen to every researcher, it's much more common to find too much. This usually happens when you've started your research online, in a full-text search mode, and you plugged in two or more words in relation to one another ("product w/10 liability") for instance. Try this search and LexisNexis or Westlaw will almost certainly stop immediately and say something to the effect of "this search will generate too many results. Try again."

Finding too much information is almost always the result of not thinking through the research process carefully enough, and the solution is almost always to stop for a second and to think again about what you've been asked and how to encapsulate that concept in a search that will generate a good number of results, but not so many that you can't read and analyze them all. That often means you need to go back to the secondary result stage and read around the topic more closely, because perhaps you don't understand the topic as well as you thought you did.

It can happen that even though you understood the question perfectly, there's still too much information to process easily: perhaps you're looking at a statute that's been widely interpreted and commented-upon, or perhaps you're looking at a case that's been the subject of a lot of law review article interest. If that's your situation, try break-

ing the topic down into smaller, more manageable pieces. Perhaps the topic you're researching has been analyzed by many cases, but they are mostly coming down one way
or the other. Try reading the cases to see why the courts have reached their decisions
and see if you can analogize the facts of the case you're working on to those of the previously decided opinions. If you can, then you can probably predict how the court will
rule in your case.

And if you're finding a lot of secondary source commentary on the case or the topic,
try selecting a few of the many articles and notes and read only them; don't worry about
all the other information that's available because, after all, the secondary sources are only
helping to inform you about the topic, they're not there to answer your question. Once
you know enough about the general topic, leave the secondary source information to
one side and start your primary source research. You can always come back to the secondary sources later if you need them.

The research attorneys at Westlaw and LexisNexis can be helpful if you're finding
too much information as well. Sometimes the chance to speak to an informed outsider
about your research topic helps to clarify things for you and your own thinking about
the subject becomes better and more focused. And sometimes, of course, they're able
to lend a perspective on the subject that you didn't have; they are attorneys and they
have a lot of research experience under their belts.

3. What to Do If What You Find Doesn't Make Any Sense

One of the more dispiriting experiences a lawyer can have is to research topic A and
realize that the results are all about topic B; it's as if you were looking for the height of
Mount Everest and you found out how to prepare vegetable korma. The good news is
that this problem is usually easy to fix.[2]

If you're researching the topic online, the first thing to consider is a simple typo or
other mechanical mistake. If you've mistyped a case name, for example, or left out a
word in your Boolean search, your results will likely be difficult, if not impossible, to
interpret. Fix the cause and you should fix the symptom.

Of course, the truly dangerous situation is where you make a mechanical mistake and
the results make sense, even though they're wrong. If you make that sort of mistake,
you might not catch it until it's too late, when the mistake's pointed out for you by
someone you'd prefer had not noticed. The only safe solution for this is to check and
recheck your typing to make sure that what you're searching for is what you want to be
searching for.

The other likely cause for this problem is a simple misunderstanding of what question you were asking. If you don't understand the question you ask, you likely won't understand the answers you get. In that case, the best thing to do is to go back to the
secondary sources (or, if you didn't start with them, go to them now) and try to make

---

2. Another piece of good news might be that vegetable korma is a very tasty dish and now you know
how to make it. Never underestimate the benefits of serendipity.

sense of what you're being asked and what you, in turn, are asking your research source. A quick refresher on the topic should clear up any lingering confusion.

4. What to Do If You Find the Right Case in the Wrong Place

Suppose you work at a firm in Virginia and you're asked to answer a question about Virginia law. You do your research and you find a great case that's directly on point. Elated, you type up a memo with your answer, supported by your case, and only then do you realize that case comes from West Virginia, not Virginia. The situation is not uncommon; the case is perfect but from the wrong place. Can you use it? Well … yes and no or, to be more exact, no and yes.

No, you can't use a case from a foreign jurisdiction directly to support your analysis. It's not binding on a court from a different jurisdiction and often—as in the Virginia/West Virginia situation—trying to use a foreign case will do much more harm than good.[3] But yes, you can use the case indirectly, if there's no case from your jurisdiction that deals with the topic. You have to set up your use of the case carefully by showing: no case from the home jurisdiction exists on point; ideally, some other cases from your jurisdiction that have used foreign cases to answer related questions; similarity of jurisprudential philosophy in similar cases between the courts of the two states; and, if possible, facts that are directly on point in the foreign case.

Most helpfully, though, you can use the out-of-jurisdiction case as a research tool. If it really is factually and legally on point, then the Key Numbers or other analytical headnotes accompanying the case will be directly relevant to your research, so take them and apply them to cases in your home jurisdiction—either in paper or online—and see if you can find any home cases that analyze the same issue. If you can, then the foreign case has made your research much simpler.

Conclusion

These are only four of the most common problems that can arise when you conduct research; the actual number of things that can go wrong is limited only by the number of different searches you undertake. In general, though, the advice to solve any problem is the same: stop what you're doing, because it isn't working; think through carefully what you think you've been asked and what you think you've been asking; go back (or go now) to the secondary sources and either find new ones or re-read what you've found so you can think again through your research; try using different research tools the second time around—go online if you've had no success with the books or (and this

---

3. That's particularly true if you try to use a West Virginia case in Virginia. The circumstances that led to the creation of West Virginia as a separate state should suggest why the decisions of its courts aren't always welcomed in Virginia courts.

is much more likely) try the books if you're not having success online; and, when all else fails, try speaking with a LexisNexis or West research attorney.

One or a combination of these steps should help you to fight through whatever problems you're having. If they don't, stop for the day and do something else. It's amazing how just a few hours away from a seemingly intractable problem can help make things much less difficult.

Focus Questions

1. Do you anticipate a situation where your research doesn't generate enough results on a particular topic?
2. Do you recall the advice to leave your ego out of the research process? Will you be able to do this when you encounter problems of the type discussed here?
3. How do the recovery strategies discussed in this chapter compare to the strategies you have employed during the research you conducted in your previous academic career?
4. Have you considered calling a research attorney to help you with your research? Do you see why this might be a particularly helpful strategy for an attorney who has to bill a client for a research task? How about for an attorney who isn't allowed to bill for legal research?
5. Have you considered the finding of too much information as a potential problem?
6. Are you surprised to learn that finding search results that don't make sense is a possible outcome of legal research?
7. Had you considered the possibility of using cases from a jurisdiction other than the one that is involved in your research project to help you make an argument? Are you surprised to learn that you must take several steps before you can be confident about using such a case and that it's inadvisable to simply cite to out-of-jurisdiction authority without any preliminary work to justify such a citation?
8. Do you think any of the recovery strategies discussed in this chapter will be useful to you as a legal researcher? If not, what recovery strategies do you plan to use when you run into research problems?

Chapter 38

Conclusion

That's it. There's lots more to say about writing and research, of course, but all books have to pick a place to start and a place to stop, and this book stops here.

That isn't to say that your work on writing or research has ended. If you're lucky, your law school will offer advanced writing and advanced research classes and I hope you take full advantage of them. I'm biased, of course; I teach legal writing and so I suppose it's only natural that I would suggest you should continue to take classes in my subject. And I certainly recognize that law schools are crammed full of interesting and valuable classes, and that you almost certainly can't go wrong no matter what courses you chose to study. There's also the bar to consider; you could be the most skilled researcher and writer in the law and it wouldn't matter a bit if you don't pass the bar. But don't forget the advanced writing and research classes while you're filling out your dance card for the next two years.

My suggestion that you continue to study legal research and writing while in law school is grounded not just in my own biases (I hope), but also comes from the reality that writing and research are skills that law firms look to when they're hiring new associates. And once you're hired, your employers will want to see good work from you soon, and the best way to show them that is to be a skilled writer and researcher. Moreover, you'll soon realize that you're still working on improving your skills once you're in practice; in fact, if you're conscientious you'll find that you're working on improving your writing skills for the rest of your life. So making the decision to start that continuing skills study while in law school shouldn't be too controversial a decision.

Of course, you don't need a formal course to continue your skills improvement. Every time you write anything—an email, a letter, a moot court brief, an academic paper—you should concentrate on choosing the right words to express your point, you should consider what voice you want to use and make sure that your content matches that voice, you should edit and proofread your work carefully to make sure that it's technically perfect, and so on. You should do, in fact all the things we've been talking about here. If you're careful about following a well-thought-out writing and research process, you'll find that legal writing becomes easier the more practice you have (never easy, just easier).

More than anything else, though, try to keep two people firmly in mind at all times when you write. The first is your reader: all writing should serve the needs of the reader and if you're constantly aware of the questions an active reader will be asking of your text, you'll be finding ways to answer those questions and your readers will greatly appreciate your efforts. The second, and most important, person you should remember is your client. Unless there are some strange circumstances involved, all lawyers work on behalf of clients and we're honor-bound to serve our clients' needs to our best abilities within the bounds of ethical representation.

If you keep those two people in mind as you write, you'll constantly be looking for ways to get your clients' positions in front of your readers in the best way possible, however "best" can be interpreted in the context in which you're writing. And if you do that, no one will be able to fault your writing for lack of effort, and no one can ask more than that you give your best work.

Inevitably, and as I predicted at the beginning, there will have been parts of this book with which you agreed and parts with which you disagreed. Thank you for sticking with me through the parts that weren't to your liking, and for forgiving me any lapses in my ideal of answering your questions as they formed; I tried to follow my own advice and think of my readers as I wrote, but to the extent I wasn't able to meet your expectations, I hope you still found useful answers to many of your questions.

As I said in the introduction, one thing that often gets overlooked when thinking about legal writing and research is how much fun they can be. There is, or should be, a tremendous amount of enjoyment and satisfaction to be derived from thinking through a complicated piece of legal analysis, finding the right support for your theory, and explaining it clearly and effectively to someone who knows nothing about what you're talking about. So while a lot of the writing and research you'll be doing in law school and in law practice might seem technical and dry to non-lawyers, try to find pleasure in expressing yourself in the doing of it. No matter the subject, that enjoyment will also communicate itself to the reader and that can be almost as powerfully persuasive as a well-analyzed case theory.

With all the changes that technology is bringing in the writing and research areas, it's possible to forget how persuasive a well-constructed piece of writing can be, and how difficult it can be to write something that is well-constructed. If I've been able to help you forget the difficulties—just a little—and if that helps you persuade your readers, then this book has been a success. Thank you for reading it.

APPENDICES

Appendix 1

Checklist for Editing Sheets

Every writer's editing sheet will be different because each writer faces different writing challenges. The purpose of this checklist is to give you a sample of some of the items you might want to include in your own editing sheet, but you shouldn't use this as a template. Rather, you should pick and choose the items from this list that are most relevant to your writing, and add in any items not on this list that you have identified as things you should look for and improve in your writing. Remember to include problems or issues your legal writing professor identified in your writing. And remember that your editing sheet will change as your writing changes: when an item on your editing sheet no longer is a problem for you, or is a step you take automatically, you should remove it from your sheet and replace it with any issues you've noticed in your writing recently.

What voice did you intend to use? _____

Does your writing effectively use the voice you intended? _____

Is your writing primarily in Plain English? _____

Do you know the meaning of every word you use? _____

Are non-English words or phrases used correctly? _____

Is your writing primarily in active voice? _____

Can you justify any use of passive voice? _____

Have you eliminated adverbs from your work? _____

Do you have any split infinitives in your work? _____

Does every word you use do its job effectively? _____

Have you eliminated all throat-clearing phrases?   _____

Are your sentence lengths sufficiently varied?   _____

Do subsequent sentences begin differently?   _____

Do your sentences flow?   _____

Do you have transitions between paragraphs?   _____

Do you have enough section headings?   _____

Are your headings narrative in style?   _____

Are your headings of an appropriate length?   _____

If you have one subheading, do you have more than one?   _____

Have you avoided quoting where possible?   _____

Have you avoided block quotations?   _____

Are all your authorities cited correctly?   _____

Have you avoided referring to yourself?   _____

Have you avoided factual characterization?   _____

Are you allowing the reader to characterize the facts?   _____

Is your case theory sufficiently developed?   _____

Is your case theory persuasive?   _____

Have you allowed yourself enough time to edit?   _____

Are you editing on paper?   _____

Are you editing in a place that allows you to concentrate?   _____

Have you checked your spelling manually?   _____

Have you checked your spelling with a spell checker?   _____

Have you cut everything that can be omitted?   _____

Appendix 2

Judicial Structure

Courts are the most visible manifestation of the law and a lawyer's role in it. The most common image of lawyers at work shows us in a court setting, questioning witnesses, making arguments to juries, speaking with judges, and sparring with other attorneys. The fact that this is a gross distortion of what lawyers do, even for the most active trial lawyer, won't change the way we're portrayed; there is nothing especially photogenic about a lawyer sitting at a word processor typing the thousands of pages each lawyer writes each year or conducting the painstaking research necessary to formulate and support case theories, doing the paperwork necessary to accomplish the client's goals, or doing the myriad number of other things lawyers actually do on a daily basis.

In fact, the image also distorts the true nature of court, because a substantial amount of court time is spent with judges speaking directly to litigants with no lawyer present; if we include all the small-claims and local courts into the mix, most cases in this country are litigated *pro se* by the people directly involved.

But courts are crucial to the legal system and the written decisions those courts hand down will be the basis for almost all the work you do as you study the law. So it's important that you understand how the courts are organized, how they function, and what importance attaches to the court decisions — often called "opinions" — you're reading.

1. The Different Court Systems

We generally speak of two separate types of court system in this country: the federal and state court systems. There is one federal system, and while each state has its own separate system, they all tend to follow the same basic pattern. But to speak of only two systems ignores the many different court systems that exist in this country, most importantly the tribal courts of the American Indian nations and the military court system.

Most lawyers will have no contact with tribal courts, and that means we will not take much time talking about them here, but that does not mean we should not acknowledge their existence. To do so would be disrespectful of a culture that predates the Anglo-European culture that now dominates in this country and if there is one fundamental truth about the law, it is that it should respect all people, not just the majority. Indian courts might exist on the margin of the American legal system, but they do exist, operating under their own rules, hearing cases in the way their cultures prescribe, and deciding disputes between parties in their own ways. We do no honor to our own system by ignoring them.

Many more lawyers will encounter the military justice system than will set foot in tribal court, but it too is often ignored when we consider the different courts in this country. While most of the lawyers who appear in those courts are military lawyers who have received special training from the law offices of the various branches of the military, civilian lawyers also appear, from time to time, at the trials of military personnel. And while the organization and influence of those courts is, like the organization and influence of tribal courts, so specialized as to be beyond the scope of this book, it would be a mistake to ignore their existence. While the rest of this appendix, the rest of this book, and the rest of your legal education might suggest that there are only two different types of court system in this country, please try to remember that the real picture of court justice here is much more populated than law school might lead you to expect.

2. Where Court Decisions Can Be Found

Courts can issue oral orders, but most courts will write their decisions down so there can be no ambiguity as to why they ruled in the way they did. That act is crucial to the common law system of law because it's through those written decisions that we're able to build up a body of precedent that allows us to predict how a court will rule in future cases. By writing down the facts of a case, the rules of law applicable to those facts, and the reasons why the court applied the rules to the facts to produce a result, courts allow us to take a different set of facts and compare them to the facts of previous cases, and analogize or distinguish one case from another.

Court opinions are found in books called "reporters." The term comes from the historical reality that courts used to deliver their opinions orally but those oral opinions were written down by someone who would then publish the opinions. That person, just like today, was called a court reporter: today's court reporters transcribe court proceedings and provide those transcripts, at a price, to the litigants. Early Supreme Court opinions are still today referred to, in part, by the court reporter who wrote down the Court's decisions: Mr. Dallas, who was the court reporter from 1790–1800, Mr. Cranch, who was the court reporter from 1801–1815, and so on, up to Mr. Wallace, who reported the Court's opinions from 1863–1874. After that the Court dropped the convention of using the actual reporter's name and began publishing opinions under its own name. But the books in which those opinions were published were also called reporters and the name stuck.

It might seem anachronistic, in today's world, to speak of cases being published in books. And it is true that while most lawyers today find cases online, in databases, rather than locating them physically in printed books, those books are (for the moment, at least) still printed. We are, in fact, in a rapidly changing transitional time for the law. Many lawyers in practice today can remember when books were the only viable medium in which to find court opinions and the speed with which computers have taken over from books has been startling to many. As is typical in such transitional moments, the names we use to describe things remain the same, even though the medium we use has changed. So we still speak of cases as being in reporters, even though we might rarely, if ever, now go to an actual book to find the case. If it helps, think of the reporters as file names; a form of uniform resource locator, or URL, which can be used to find a defined subset of court opinions. It's a convention that almost certainly will change when the books have vanished, but for the moment the convention of referring to reporters is still the standard practice in American legal citation.

Similarly, we use page numbers as a way of identifying the more direct location of specific text within the opinion, even if a case found online has no need for page designations. Because screen size affects the number of screens necessary to display information, though, "pages" are still a useful way of thinking about displayed information in order to provide citations that are medium-neutral. As with reporter information, this convention will likely change once books are no longer relevant to legal citation, but that hasn't happened yet.

3. The Hierarchy of Authority

Before we talk about how the various courts are organized, it's crucial that you understand how those courts wield their influence. If there's one thing most law students (and many lawyers) are fuzzy on, it's the effect that language from one court will have on another court. Many times, law students believe that if one court writes something that supports an argument they want to make they can use that language with impunity and consider their argument supported. Perhaps this is a by-product of the way in which you learn about the law in law school. In the pedagogical process of legal education, court opinions are mined for the rules they disclose and the legal principles they discuss without much regard to court hierarchy; we're more interested in general legal concepts in law school, and less interested in what a particular jurisdiction's approach to a legal issue might be.

But that's not the way things work outside of law school. In fact, a court's authority is part of a binary system: either a court has the authority to bind another court or it doesn't. If the court's authority is binding, we call it mandatory precedent. If the court's authority isn't binding, we call it persuasive precedent. The same court language can be mandatory or persuasive, depending on which court is considering it. And that's why understanding the hierarchy of authority is so important.

This all might seem complicated and difficult to understand, but in fact it's fairly simple. There's one overarching principle you need to understand: the power to bind another court flows directly downward. In other words, a court can bind those courts directly below it in the hierarchy of authority. A court can't bind those courts that are either at the same level as it or which don't fall directly below it. Once you have that principle clearly in mind, everything else becomes a question of where courts are located in relation to the court that issued the opinion. Most lawyers are able to identify the relationship between two courts without conscious thought but that's only because they've had years of practice. You can get that practice by actively thinking about which courts might be bound by every opinion you read. This doesn't take much time and will strengthen your understanding of the court system immeasurably. It will also prevent you from making the mistake of assuming court language will be significant to any other court that reads it.

The only way to fully understand the principle that court power flows directly downward is to understand something about the federal and state court systems and the way they relate to each other. Let's do that next.

4. The Federal Court System

We'll start by talking about the federal court system. That isn't because it's more important than the state court system—the notion of "more" or "less" important doesn't apply to courts, despite what you might believe from news reporting of various court decisions—but because the federal system is unified, meaning that its structure is the same across the country. That isn't true of the state system, so the federal courts are an easier place to start.

There are three levels to the federal court system: the Supreme Court of the United States, the various Courts of Appeals, and the various District Courts. We'll consider them from the top down.

A. The Supreme Court

Proper names matter, so it's as well to point out that the Supreme Court of the United States is properly called exactly that, not the "Supreme Court" or the "United States Supreme Court," even though those are the names you most often hear for that court. The informal "the Supremes" is best left to discussions of Motown groups fronted by Diana Ross. Nonetheless, for purposes of our present discussion, I'll call that court "the Supreme Court" because the proper name is too bulky for common use.

The Supreme Court is the only federal court that publishes its own reporter with its opinions in it. That reporter—the "United States Reports," or "U.S." as it's abbreviated, is the official reporter of Supreme Court opinions and under strict citation rules it's the only reporter you should use to cite to a Supreme Court opinion. There are also, however, two commercial (and unofficial) reporters that also publish Supreme Court decisions, and it's highly likely that when you do your own research to find cases, you'll use one of these unofficial reporters to locate Supreme Court decisions. These unofficial reporters—the "Supreme Court Reporter," or "S. Ct." as it's abbreviated, and the "United States Supreme Court Reports, Lawyers' Edition," or "L. Ed." (or "L. Ed. 2d") as it's abbreviated—have indexing tools and supplementary materials that make them more useful, in a practical sense, than the Supreme Court's own reporter.

You can also find Supreme Court decisions in a loose-leaf service known as United States Law Week ("U.S.L.W."). Law Week used to be the fastest way to get the actual text of Supreme Court decisions for most lawyers; the reporters are months behind the court, even when they are published in advance of the hardbound and permanent book form. These days, of course, the fastest way to get a Supreme Court opinion is either from the commercial database services of Westlaw, LexisNexis, or Bloomberg, or simply to go to the Court's website—www.supremecourtus.gov—and find the "bench" or "slip" opinion version of the Court's decision.

The bench decision comes first, and is usually posted at the same time as the opinion is being announced in the court. The slip opinion follows closely after, and is usually identical to the bench opinion, although obvious mistakes in the opinion are corrected before it is published in slip opinion form. Relying on either the bench or slip opinion of a Supreme Court decision can be dangerous, though, because the final versions of the opinions are thoroughly checked for any mistakes—typographical or editorial—that might have been missed as the earlier forms of the opinion were prepared. Rarely, but occasionally, the fixing of those mistakes can change meaning and it is only the final, printed, form of the opinion that is deemed to be official.

Although the name of the court declares it to be "Supreme," and the Court is often referred to as the "the highest court in the land" (that term is also used to refer to the basketball court located on the top floor of the Court's building in Washington, D.C.), names can be misleading when we're talking about court hierarchy. The trial court, or lowest court, in New York's three-court system, for example, is also known as the Supreme Court. When you encounter a jurisdiction with which you're unfamiliar, you should always check the name to see where that court lies in its particular chain of authority. Never assume that the name gives you that information.

The Supreme Court really does lie at the top of the federal court system, though. The nine justices on the Court (the Chief Justice of the United States and eight Associate Justices) don't hear that many cases a year, compared to the workload of the other two courts in the federal system, but the cases they do hear are often of crucial importance to the country. The Court has jurisdiction to hear many different types of case, including direct disputes between two states (did you ever wonder where Maryland goes to sue Virginia? The answer is the Supreme Court), but it's best known for resolving federal Constitutional questions and questions of federal law. The Constitution is a relatively short and clear document, but determining whether a governmental action is or isn't Constitutional can be an enormously complicated business and it occupies a substantial amount of the Court's time.

Note that I specified "federal" Constitutional questions. The states all have their own constitutions, and while they're subordinate to the federal Constitution in matters where they overlap, if a state has granted rights in its constitution that go beyond the rights protected by the federal Constitution, the Supreme Court isn't the place to resolve disputes about those rights. Some states, for example, passed their own Equal Rights Amendments to state constitutions, even though the federal Equal Rights Amendment didn't secure enough states to amend the federal Constitution. If citizens of a state that has such an Equal Rights Amendment believe that their rights under that amendment have been infringed, it's the state's highest court that should ultimately resolve that issue, not the Supreme Court. That's why it's misleading to think of the Supreme Court as the highest court in the land. It is, but only for those questions it has the authority to answer.

Unless a case falls within its original jurisdiction (like a dispute between two states), the Supreme Court has the discretion to hear or not hear cases. And it hears only a fraction of the cases it's asked to hear every year. One asks the Supreme Court to hear a case by filing a petition for a writ of *certiorari*. Writs are a holdover from ancient English practice and while their history is fascinating, it isn't necessary that you understand it for our present purposes. Only a few writs remain in the American system, the writ of *habeas corpus* being the most famous.[1]

---

1. In addition to the writs of *habeas corpus* and *certiorari*, most lawyers learn about the writ of *mandamus* when they study the case of *Marbury v. Madison* in their Constitutional law course. They might

Like most, but not all, of the federal courts, the Supreme Court is authorized by Article III of the Constitution. An Article III judge, or Justice in the case of the Supreme Court, is nominated by the president but must be confirmed by the Senate. The Senate Judiciary Committee usually holds a hearing for each nominated Article III judge, before which there is an extensive review of the nominated judge's record. If the Committee votes in favor of the nomination, the full Senate considers and votes on the nomination. The nominee needs a simple majority vote of the Senate in order to be confirmed.

After being sworn in, an Article III judge has several important Constitutional protections: the judge's salary can't be cut, for example, and the judge can only be impeached by Congress, not simply dismissed. Those steps help to keep the federal judiciary insulated from political influence, and politicians frequently are irritated by their inability to control federal judges or bend them to their will. Although politicians often talk about finding ways to diminish the federal judiciary's power, no actual steps along this path have been taken yet.

One final thing to note about the Supreme Court. The Court often refers to the decisions "we" took in the past—"in [x v. y,] we decided that …"—in a way that might make the non-lawyer reader think that the same people had been on the bench for over two hundred years. That is, of course, a mistaken impression: federal judges often remain on the bench for a long time, but Article III status can't confer immortality. What the Justices are doing when they write of decisions "we" took in the past is emphasizing the unbroken chain of authority that stretches back to the Court's founding. The Justices can (and do) change their minds about what the law should be, but they do so in such a way that makes it appear as if the Court itself is a continuous, plural entity.

That's fine for the Court: the Justices can write in any way they want, and no criticisms of their writing style will affect them. But we, as lawyers, are not so immune from criticism and we need to follow the conventional rules of grammar when we write about the Court. And that, in turn, means we have to refer to the Court as a singular and neuter entity. That can cause confusion for lawyers as well as law students, so it's a convention you should learn now and practice often.

The practical effect of treating the Supreme Court—and all courts—as singular and neuter forms is that lawyers should write about a court using "it" not "they." Although there are nine Justices on the Supreme Court, there is only one Supreme Court, just as AT&T might employ more than a quarter of a million people but there is only one AT&T. And while the Supreme Court Justices might write about "we" in a way that suggests that the Court is human and plural, the Court is, in fact, an inanimate singular corporate entity for which "it" is the correct pronoun.

This rule applies to corporations as well; you might hear or read something like "When AT&T makes a decision, they …" but that's wrong because there is only one AT&T and it's not a living person (it might be considered to be a person for legal purposes, but that's a legal fiction, not a grammatical one).

It might seem as if this is a stuffy, conservative, and overly restrictive way of referring to a court. Modern convention is more accepting of using "they" to refer to sin-

---

also encounter the writs of *coram nobis*, prohibition, and attachment, as well as several of the other remaining writ forms, but the most common writs of all—subpoenas—have become so detached from their origin as to not be thought of as writs at all today.

gular entities; in particular, we often will use "they" as a means of avoiding sexist language: instead of assuming a gender for a person within a group—assuming all lawyers are male, for example, and writing "a lawyer ... he," some will write "a lawyer ... they." And this more modern way of writing is inoffensive to many. English is an extraordinarily flexible language with remarkably few absolute rules, so it allows innovations like this to quickly become accepted and acceptable.

But not to everyone. Or, at least, not right away. For now, the singular use of "they" is not accepted by everyone. To some, in fact, it is a sign of illiteracy—a red mark against the user. And some of those for whom the singular use of "they" is offensive are the very lawyers and judges you, as a junior lawyer, are seeking to impress with your legal writing skills. You might never meet your reader, but if your writing sample contains what that person believes to be a mistake, your writing—and you—might be discounted.

So the question is not whether you, the others of your generation, or even grammarians, believe the use of "they" to describe a singular neuter corporate entity like a court is acceptable, it's whether the person reading your writing will consider that usage to be acceptable. If so, then there is no problem with the usage. But if not—and the reality is that by no means all lawyers and judges believe that this usage is acceptable—then you are better advised to be stuffy, conservative, and overly restrictive in your writing style. Better to be thought of as old-fashioned and right than contemporary and wrong, because only "wrong" matters.

B. The Courts of Appeals

The first thing to note about the various Courts of Appeals is that the plural of "Court of Appeals" really is "Courts of Appeals." Some lawyers use "Courts of Appeal," but that's wrong. Because the various Courts of Appeals hear cases from various Circuits, and are properly called "the United States Court of Appeals for the X Circuit" they are usually known informally as the Circuit Courts, but that can be confusing because there actually was a court system known as the "Circuit Court." Those courts were eliminated early in the Twentieth Century, but you'll still see references to them in older cases, and that can be confusing because the Circuit Courts were trial-level courts, whereas the Courts of Appeals are the intermediate appellate courts in the federal system.

For purposes of this court system, the country has been divided into twelve circuits, with each circuit but one incorporating multiple states. The exception is the D.C. Circuit, which only hears cases from the District of Columbia. In addition to the twelve circuits based on geographical distinctions, there is a thirteenth circuit—the Federal Circuit—which hears appeals from some specialized federal trial courts and also hears intellectual property appeals. Each Circuit Court has a home city, where the Court has courtrooms and where its administrative offices are located.

Not every Circuit Court judge must live in that city, or even the state in which that city is located, and the Circuit Courts can hear appeals in any of the states covered by their geographical territory. Circuit Courts sometimes will come to a law school and hear some appeals in the school's formal courtroom. Those are extraordinary learning opportunities and any law student lucky enough to have the chance to attend a Circuit Court argument should take every opportunity to sit and watch judges and lawyers grapple with the complex issues presented by all appeals.

The states covered by each Circuit are determined by Congress and appear at 28 U.S.C. §41. The number of active judges allocated to each Circuit is also determined by Congress, and that appears at 28 U.S.C. §44(a). A judge who reaches 65, or who is disabled in some way, can take senior status. Senior judges can continue to hear cases, and many judges continue working full-time for years after achieving senior status, but only active judges are counted on a Court's roster of judges. So even though a judge continues to work as a senior judge, the act of taking senior status opens a vacancy on the Court that must be filled by presidential nomination and Senate ratification.

In addition to the active judges on each Circuit Court of Appeals, each Court has a Supreme Court Justice assigned as its Circuit Justice. These Justices can—but usually don't—sit on the courts for which they're assigned, but they are the Justice to whom some matters are assigned after an issue has been resolved by the Circuit Court. These matters are usually emergencies, and you'll usually hear of this procedure when a Circuit Court has turned down a request for a stay of execution and the lawyers for a death row inmate are seeking a stay from the Supreme Court. Those issues will, at least at first, go to the Circuit's designated Justice.

Here's a list of the states included within each Circuit, together with the city where each Circuit Court has its principal seat, the number of active judges authorized for each Circuit Court, and the current Circuit Justice for each Circuit.

Federal Circuit

Principal Seat	Active Judges	Circuit Justice
Washington, D.C. All States	12 Judges	Roberts

D.C. Circuit

Washington, D.C. Washington, D.C.	11 Judges	Roberts

First Circuit

Boston Maine Massachusetts New Hampshire Puerto Rico	6 Judges	Breyer

Second Circuit

New York Connecticut New York Vermont	13 Judges	Ginsburg

Third Circuit

Philadelphia	14 Judges	Alito

Delaware
New Jersey
Pennsylvania
United States Virgin Islands

Fourth Circuit

Richmond	15 Judges	Roberts

Maryland
North Carolina
South Carolina
Virginia
West Virginia

Fifth Circuit

New Orleans	17 Judges	Scalia

Louisiana
Mississippi
Texas

Sixth Circuit

Cincinnati	16 Judges	Kagan

Kentucky
Michigan
Ohio
Tennessee

Seventh Circuit

Chicago	11 Judges	Kagan

Illinois
Indiana
Wisconsin

Eighth Circuit

St. Louis	11 Judges	Alito

Arkansas
Iowa
Minnesota
Missouri
Nebraska
North Dakota
South Dakota

Ninth Circuit

San Francisco	29 Judges	Kennedy

Alaska
Arizona
California
Idaho
Montana
Nevada
Oregon
Washington
Guam
Hawaii

Tenth Circuit

Denver	12 Judges	Sotomayor

Colorado
Kansas
New Mexico
Oklahoma
Utah
Wyoming

Eleventh Circuit

Atlanta	12 Judges	Thomas

Alabama
Florida
Georgia

Circuit Court opinions are found in two different reporters, depending on the kind of opinion. For precedential opinions, Circuit Court decisions are found in the Federal Reporter, cited to as "F." This is a commercial publication, not something published by the courts themselves. The Federal Reporter was first published in 1891 and, as you can imagine, there have been many Circuit Court decisions since then. Once a book is sufficiently bulky, West—the publisher of these reporters—starts on a new volume, and once the volumes reach 999, West starts numbering the next book as 1 again, but it's number one of a new series. The series is designated by a number after the "F," so "F." with no number is the Federal Reporter, first series, "F.2d" is the Federal Reporter, second series, and "F.3d" is the Federal Reporter, third series (the current series). It makes a big difference if the opinion you're looking for is in 250 F., 250 F.2d, or 250 F.3d, so be careful with this, both when you look for cases and when you cite to them.

So far, so good. But what is a "precedential" opinion? Put simply, a precedential opinion is one that sets precedent. As we've seen, precedential opinions bind all courts directly below the deciding court. So a precedential opinion from the Fourth Circuit Court of Appeals, for example, binds all federal district courts in Maryland, North Carolina, South Carolina, Virginia, and West Virginia; the states in which federal district courts fall under the jurisdiction of the Fourth Circuit. It wouldn't bind district courts in other states or state courts—even the state courts in the states covered by the federal Fourth Circuit's jurisdiction, because those courts are in the state, not federal, system and therefore don't fall directly under the Fourth Circuit's jurisdiction.

C. The District Courts

The United States District Courts are the trial-level courts in the federal system. Each state has at least one federal district, and the larger states are divided into geographical subdivisions; the Northern, Southern, Eastern, and Western Districts. In particularly large states, these geographical districts might themselves be subdivided into divisions. The United States territories also have District Judges, although they sit in Territorial Courts.

District Court opinions are sometimes published, even though they are never precedential, because no court falls below the district court in the judicial hierarchy. Even though they have no precedential value, though, federal district court opinions can often be very helpful to lawyers who are trying future cases and can give them a good sense of how the district court might rule if a similar question is brought before it.

Contemporary district court opinions are published in different reporters, both published by West. The first, for most opinions, is called the Federal Supplement ("F. Supp."), which is now in its second series ("F. Supp. 2d"). Opinions specifically interpreting the Federal Rules of Civil or Criminal Procedure are published principally in the Federal Rules Decisions reporter ("F.R.D."), although—confusingly—an opinion dealing primarily with rules issues might be published instead in the Federal Supplement. Rules decisions can also be published in the Federal Rules Service ("Fed. R. Serv."), which is now in its third series ("Fed. R. Serv. 3d").

The District Courts were not specified in the Constitution, but were instead authorized by Congress. Federal District Judges in the 50 states are Article III judges and enjoy full Article III protections. Federal District Judges in the various territorial courts, however, are not Article III judges and serve limited terms.

As with all Article III judges, District Judges can take senior status when the right combination of age and years in service has been reached or in the case of some disability that prevents them from being fully active judges. And as with other Article III judges, District Judges can sit on other courts "by designation," when invited to by the chief judge of that court. In this way, you might find a District Judge sitting on a Circuit Court panel, or a District Judge from one district trying a case in a different district. You might also find a judge from the Court of International Trade—another Article III court, although one with a specialized jurisdiction that is obvious from its name—sitting on a criminal trial in a federal district court. Even more rare, but by no means unheard of, you might find a former or even current Supreme Court Justice sitting in a circuit court hearing or even at a trial.

District judges, like all Article III judges, have a budget for staff. All judges usually have a secretary and a law clerk. Active district judges have a budget for two law clerks, usually recently graduated law students for whom this is a first legal job. Law clerks usually serve for one or two years, although some judges hire what are called permanent clerks—people for whom being a law clerk becomes their principal, and sometimes only, job after law school.

Law clerks perform a variety of functions for the judge; sometimes, in smaller courts, they will even cry the judge onto the bench at the start of a court day, but more often law clerks research and write draft opinions for the judge, help in the day-to-day management of the judge's chambers (as a judge's suite of offices is called), and prepare jury instructions, preliminary instructions, and *voir dire* questions—the questions a judge (in federal court) will ask prospective jurors to see if they are biased for or against a particular party. The lawyers in the trial will submit proposed questions and instructions, but it's the court's job to actually ask the questions and deliver the instructions, so the law clerk usually has the job of preparing them according to the judge's preferences.

In federal courts, cases are assigned to a specific judge as soon as they're filed, and that judge will follow the case throughout its time at the trial level. Federal District Judges hear both civil and criminal cases, and because criminal defendants are entitled to a speedy trial, their cases take priority on the court's calendar. This can cause problems when a criminal case that was expected to plead out suddenly moves forward to trial. Federal judges will usually have multiple trials scheduled for the same day with the assumption that one or the other will be resolved without going to trial, but if both cases move forward, the civil case will find itself being bumped, often at the last minute. This can be a frustrating experience for the lawyers who spent months getting their cases ready for trial, only to be told at the last minute—often only a couple of days before trial is scheduled to start—that their trial is being postponed, often for months or, in the case of the very busy trial courts in large urban areas, for a year or more.

D. Other Federal Courts

Although the Supreme Court, Courts of Appeals, and District Courts are the ones you'll encounter most often while studying the law, there are several other federal courts and they're all important. For example, there's the Court of International Trade, the Court of Federal Claims, and the Court of Appeals for the Federal Circuit, which handles intellectual property and patent issues for the federal system. There's also the Court of Appeals for Veterans Claims and the Court of Appeals for the Armed Forces, the jurisdiction for which is clearly spelled out in their names.

There are also two very important lower-level courts: magistrate courts and bankruptcy courts. The judges in both these courts are Article I judges as opposed to Article III, meaning that they don't have life-tenure and serve for specific terms of years, although they can be, and frequently are, reappointed. This doesn't mean they are any less able than the Article III judges, though, and as specialists in their areas they are highly knowledgeable judges who expect a lot of the attorneys appearing before them.

Magistrate judges handle a great variety of matters that could also be handled by the trial courts, and their work frees the district courts to hear more trials than they otherwise would be able to. They can even hear full civil trials if both parties agree to have their case handled by a federal magistrate judge, and because they can't hear criminal trials their calendars are a little more predictable than district judges. Magistrate judges also often handle discovery disputes related to federal civil cases, and that means their law clerks often get a fascinating post-law-school education in the intricacies of federal discovery practice—invaluable knowledge for anyone planning to practice in litigation.

5. The State Court Systems

Each state has a court system that resembles, if not exactly mirrors, the federal system. Every state has a trial court and appellate court, usually with two levels, and states usually have a variety of small claims and other lower-level courts that handle cases that, while they are vitally important to the litigants involved in the cases, might not justify the time and resources of the overstretched trial-level courts.

Most of the time the state and federal courts exist in parallel, aware of each other but not paying too much attention to each other. State courts are courts of general jurisdiction, meaning that they can hear almost all cases brought before them, but they are bound by the federal Supreme Court's decisions on questions of Constitutional interpretation. By contrast, the federal courts are courts of limited jurisdiction, meaning that they can only hear those cases that the Constitution and Congress have determined that they should hear. That can mean, though, that they can hear some cases for which they need to rely on state law (the federal courts have, under certain circumstances, "diversity jurisdiction" in civil cases) and, in those cases, the federal district courts behave like state trial courts and align themselves directly under the state courts for matters of state substantive law (they still apply their own procedural rules).

But—and this can be very confusing—the federal district court doesn't necessarily apply the state law of the state where it's sitting; each state has choice of law provisions that tell the state courts which laws they should apply in cases where two or more states might expect to be able to apply their own different laws to a case. The federal district court will act as would a state trial court in that situation, and apply the choice of law rules to decide which state's law it should use.

Sometimes the state and federal courts might both have jurisdiction over a particular civil case. The plaintiff then has a choice of filing the case in state or federal court. If the plaintiff chooses state court, the defendant can, under the appropriate circumstances, "remove" the case to federal court. It's important for lawyers to understand that "removal" is a technical term and the removal process involves a complicated series of steps, all of which must be correctly taken in order for a state case to become a federal case. It is not enough for a party who is unhappy with the way things are going in state court to simply take the court file and walk out of the state court with it, bringing it to a geographically close federal court building and declaring that the case has been "removed" from state to federal court. That sort of action will almost certainly get the lawyer sanctioned severely for improper behavior.

It can also happen that a state might not have resolved a substantive question of law. Although federal courts are very skilled in predicting how a state court would act if presented with most questions of law, it can happen that the federal court is unsure about what to do if a new question is raised. In that case, the federal court is permitted to ask the state's highest court a question about how it should respond; the process is called "certifying a question." The state's highest court can answer the certified question, giving the federal court guidance, but it need not if it feels the answer is sufficiently obvious.

It's impossible to summarize each separate state court system, because they are all different from each other. The two principal citation manuals—*The Bluebook* and the *ALWD Manual*—have extensive tables that will, at least, give you the names of the various courts in each state and will tell you where the opinions of those courts are published. That information is vital to law students trying to understand where a particular court falls in the judicial hierarchy but is often overlooked by students who think citation manuals are just for helping them to understand how to construct accurate citations. In fact, though, both citation manuals have a lot of valuable information that can be helpful when you find a case and are wondering how best to use it to support a position you are trying to take. A quick look in the tables can tell you if the opinion comes from a state's highest court, its intermediate appellate court, or its trial court (and you really can't tell based on the court's name), and that information will allow you to decide how much weight a reader might give the opinion.

Conclusion

A lot of the information in this chapter might seem irrelevant to you at present. You're probably much more concerned with understanding what a court said at the moment, and don't care much about what court said it and where that court is located in the large picture of court hierarchy and structure.

But while what a court said, and what that means, is very important, it's no less important to understand what court said it and what attention other courts must pay to those words. It's a very different matter if the opinion you're reading binds all courts in the state, or the trial courts in a particular circuit, or if the opinion binds no one at all. You'll learn that the Circuit Courts of Appeals and the Supreme Court will only pay attention to a district court's opinion if there's a specific standard of review that requires the higher court to take notice of a lower court's decision. If the trial court was writing in a different case from the one currently under review, though, the federal appellate courts will likely pay very little heed to what it said, even though the facts and law in that case are very similar to the facts and law in the case the higher court is now considering. Similarly, state courts tend not to be very interested in what the federal courts have said about matters.

That's not to say that you can't use a court's language to support your arguments, even if that court isn't directly to the court to whom you're writing. But it means that you'll have to construct your argument differently than you would if the court's language was mandatory authority. In law, there are very few absolutes when it comes to using support for arguments, but there are many cautions about using support carefully and effectively. The first step in understanding how best to use helpful language is to understand where it came from and how authoritative it will be to your reader.

Appendix 3

Litigation Process

Litigation is a much-misunderstood area of the law. For most people, it conjures the image of lawyers in a courtroom, questioning witnesses and making impassioned pleas to a jury in favor of their client. For lawyers, though, litigation is better thought of as the legal process of dispute resolution. There might be a courtroom involved, but more often than not—in the vast majority of cases—there is a settlement or plea bargain rather than a trial. But at every step along the way, lawyers will write documents, so understanding the litigation process is essential for lawyers who are learning to write.

This is a very broad overview of some of the steps involved in the civil litigation process. Your Civil Procedure classes will give you a more detailed understanding of the steps involved in civil litigation, and later you will probably study criminal procedure as well. For your purposes as a first-year law student, though, it's the civil process that is most important, so that's why I'll spend time talking about that here. And this description shows just one possible path down which litigation might go. The only typical thing about litigation is that every case is unique.

Do you need to know all of this in order to learn about legal writing? No. But while a lot of this information is second nature to practicing lawyers, at least some of it can be confusing to law students and sometimes your professors might forget that you don't know these things. So this is intended to be a guide through at least some of the litigation maze. There's a lot of information not covered here, and almost everything is just touched on rather than discussed in detail. Litigation—even simple, straightforward litigation—is a complicated process.

1. The Dispute

Litigation starts when the involved parties stop talking to each other about a dispute they have. That dispute can involve almost anything that isn't specifically criminal in nature, and often civil disputes can have an element of criminal law as well; that part of the dispute will be handled by the criminal law process, but it would be misleading not to acknowledge that it's there. Almost always, if there is a criminal aspect to the dispute, that will be handled first. That's in part because the Constitution guarantees the right to a speedy trial to all those accused of crimes, meaning that the courts give those cases scheduling priority over civil cases; criminal cases are often tried relatively quickly after the incident at issue, whereas civil cases can take years before a trial is scheduled. But civil lawyers representing the plaintiff are often happy to let the criminal part of a dispute go first because of some benefits that can accrue to their clients as a result of going second.

First, the criminal case will doubtless produce a lot of documentation and even sworn statements to which the civil lawyers can gain access. The statements and testimony given in the criminal case might not be directly useable at the civil trial, but they are still extraordinarily useful to the civil lawyers, and can help to lock a person's testimony in place.

Second, the civil case will proceed under a much lower standard of proof than will the criminal case. Criminal cases are always conducted under the "beyond a reasonable doubt" standard, whereas most civil cases operate under the "preponderance of evidence" standard, with only a few cases being conducted under the heightened "clear and convincing" evidence standard. That can bring some procedural advantages to the civil case making it much easier to try when its time finally comes.

2. The Parties

In standard civil litigation, there are at least two parties involved—one claiming that the other is at fault over the subject of the dispute. The person or entity invoking the court's jurisdiction—the person claiming to be injured, usually—is, at the start of the litigation, called the "plaintiff," and, predictably enough, the person on the other side is called the "defendant." I say "at the start of the litigation" because these legal designations can change as the case moves forward. If the case goes to appeal, for instance, the party who seeks the appellate court's jurisdiction is called the "appellant" and the party who opposes the appellant is known as the "appellee." And if the case goes even higher—up to the highest court in the jurisdiction—the party seeking relief from that court is often called the "petitioner" (because that party will have to petition the Court to hear the case—the appeal usually isn't one of right) and the other side will be called the "respondent."

And if this isn't confusing enough, the positions of the parties can change with respect to the "v." at various stages in the ligation. Suppose Ms. Smith sues Mr. Jones. At the initial stages of the litigation, the case is called *Smith v. Jones*; Ms. Smith is seeking the court's jurisdiction in a dispute against Mr. Jones. And let's assume that Ms. Smith wins at trial and Mr. Jones appeals. The case might now be called *Jones v. Smith*, because it's Mr. Jones who is seeking the appellate court's jurisdiction in order to overturn the adverse trial verdict he received. It's the same case, and it's the same parties, but their legal roles have changed and sometimes (and just for fun, this doesn't always happen) the case name changes to reflect that.

Of course, if Mr. Jones prevails at the appeal, Ms. Smith can petition the jurisdiction's highest court to take the case. If it does, the case name might well go back to being *Smith v. Jones*, again reflecting the legal status of the parties. And just to be completely confusing, if Mr. Jones has died during the course of the litigation, but his claim didn't die with him and is being maintained by his daughter, who has the married name of Desprez, the case will now be called *Smith v. Desprez*. It's the same case, with the same legal and factual issues as before, and if this happens, the citation will probably have the designation "sub nom" added to it to show that it's the same case proceeding now under this new name.

All of this should tell you one simple truth: nothing about litigation—even the name of the case—is as simple as you might have thought it would be.

Separating the names of the two sides in the case name is a "v.," which stands for "versus." It's rare that law employs the boxing poster convention of using "vs." as an abbreviation for versus; the v with a period is one of the signs that the dispute between the parties ought to be settled without violence.

But that's only the most straightforward possible way of looking at things. There can be cases when only one party is involved; cases involving the custody of a child, for example, or cases involving attorney discipline. These types of cases—in which the state plays an important but non-adversarial role—are usually recognizable by their name, which will either use the Latin phrase *In re [name]* and a name, or the English equivalent—*In the matter of [name]*. If it's a case involving children, the name often won't be given and a placeholder name will be substituted; *In re Baby M*, for example.

Sometimes disputes involve hundreds, thousands, or even millions of people on one side. These are usually class actions, and the people are usually making a claim against a person or—more commonly—a corporation. These types of case are identifiable by their name as well: if you ever see a case captioned *[name], et al v. [name]*, the *et al* is a strong clue that you're looking at a class action.

More commonly, though, disputes involve just a few people or entities as plaintiffs or defendants. One of the conventions of legal names, though, is that only the first name on either side of the v. will appear in the case citation; so just because there's only one name on either side of the v. in the citation does not mean that the case only involves two people or entities.

Sometimes disputes involve things, not people. This type of litigation, in which the state seeks control over a thing, is conducted under a special kind of jurisdiction—*in rem* jurisdiction—that you'll study in Civil Procedure. Those cases are identifiable because the thing in dispute is identified in the name of the case: *In Re The Yacht "Drug Proceeds,"* for example, or *In Re $1,500,000 of United States Currency*. As the examples suggest, this type of case is often (although not always) initiated as part of a forfeiture related to criminal activity.

3. Pre-Litigation

Let's assume that Ms. Smith wants to sue Mr. Jones for injuries she claims to have suffered in a car crash. What happens right after the crash? Well, any number of things. Ms. Smith and Mr. Jones might speak at the crash site and Mr. Jones might agree that the crash was his fault and that he'll pay for Ms. Smith's injuries. While private deals like this do sometimes happen, lawyers generally disfavor them, and not just because we don't get a fee. There's always a concern when something like this happens that one side or the other had unequal bargaining power and got a bad deal; either Mr. Jones was able to limit his potential liability by cutting a quick deal that didn't take into account the extent of Ms. Smith's injuries, or else Ms. Smith got Mr. Jones to admit to liability when it might not be that clear who was at fault for the accident. Although people often fear the legal system and would prefer to stay away from it when at all possible, the system can help the parties reach a more appropriate result than they might be able to achieve on their own.

In fact, people will usually contact their insurance companies, especially if there's the possibility that someone in the crash sustained any injuries, and the insurance companies will do what insurance companies do in these situations. But if Ms. Smith doesn't like the resolution the insurance companies come to, she might want to sue Mr. Jones for the injuries she claims to have suffered. To make this as simple an example as possible, let's assume that she's already been to see a doctor and the doctor has given her an opinion that indeed she was injured as a result of the accident.

Ms. Smith can do a number of things at this point, but since you're law students, let's assume she visits Mr. Green, a local lawyer who typically takes cases on behalf of plaintiffs. It's likely that Ms. Smith will sign a retention agreement, often in the form of something known as a contingency agreement with Mr. Green, in which Mr. Green agrees to represent Ms. Smith without a fee, and that Ms. Smith will pay Mr. Green a percentage—often one third—of any recovery in the case, whether it comes by way of settlement or from a jury verdict after trial. The agreement usually stipulates that Ms. Smith will be accountable for all expenses and fees that Mr. Green incurs while representing her, and these can often be considerable; expert witness fees alone can run into the many thousands of dollars.

Mr. Green has a number of options open to him, but the most likely is to contact Mr. Jones' insurance company to find out which attorney is representing him. He can't contact Mr. Jones directly because an attorney can't speak with someone who is represented by counsel, and Mr. Jones will be represented by an attorney if Ms. Smith is because his insurance company will require it; all communications from this point forward must go through the attorneys.

The attorneys might now negotiate a settlement. It's unlikely, but it does happen that both sides agree on all the significant facts in the case and are able to come up with a dollar amount that works for them both. This period—after the accident but before any formal legal proceedings have been initiated—is also a phase in the litigation process, sometimes called the pre-filing phase. It can last from the date of the accident until the relevant jurisdiction's statute of limitations operates to end the possibility of litigation. The length of this pre-filing stage can vary wildly between jurisdictions, and it is crucial that Mr. Green identifies in which jurisdiction the case will be filed, if it is to be filed, and what the relevant statute of limitations is. It's highly unlikely that he'll be able to negotiate a settlement from Mr. Jones's attorney—let's call her Ms. Orange—after the statute of limitations has expired.

Accident cases like this are usually classified as torts cases, although that distinction is really only meaningful in law school; in the real world, cases often involve multiple different doctrinal areas. Even in this simple case we've been discussing, we've already identified torts and civil procedure issues. Often the interpretation of an insurance contract will be at issue as well, meaning that contracts and insurance issues come into play, and other doctrinal issues—property, Constitutional law, evidence, and so on—

are also considerations. A skillful plaintiff's attorney will analyze a case to determine what legal theories will likely be involved, and will then decide which jurisdiction is most favorable to the attorney's client on these issues. Typically, a case like this would be filed in state court if both Ms. Smith and Mr. Jones are citizens of the same state in which the accident occurred. But if a different state is involved, Mr. Green might want to consider whether the case would be better brought in federal court, or whether Ms. Orange will try to take it into federal court after he files suit.

4. Pre-Filing Investigation

Mr. Green will typically be doing more than just conducting legal research on the various jurisdictional issues though. For example, he'll need to learn everything he can about the accident. If he is conscientious, he will also check to see if there any incidents in Ms. Smith's past medical history that Ms. Orange will discover later and that might cause problems in the litigation. If Ms. Smith sustained similar injuries in a separate car accident last year, for instance, it might be difficult for a doctor to decide how much of her present injury is attributable to her accident with Mr. Jones and how much is attributable to her pervious accident. He'll want to speak with Ms. Smith about other issues that might call her credibility into question, and generally learn everything he can to strengthen her case and prepare him to anticipate and deflect any defenses Ms. Orange will present on behalf of Mr. Jones.

Ms. Orange will doubtless be doing the same thing, speaking with Mr. Jones and learning as much as she can about her client and the accident, and trying to anticipate any legal issues that might arise from the jurisdiction where Mr. Green decides to file suit. Both attorneys will be trying hard to bolster their cases and trying to anticipate what the other side will claim.

And very often they'll be sharing the results of these conversations with each other. Law students are sometimes surprised by the notion that lawyers might exchange long letters setting out in great detail the strengths of their cases during this pre-filing stage of litigation. In fact, though, the attorneys know that the other side will learn all this information during the discovery phase and if they can use it now to convince the other attorney that it is not worth pursuing the case and that a settlement is in everyone's best interests, then there is no reason to keep the information secret.

5. The Pleadings

Although pre-filing settlements are possible, the more likely result is that negotiations will break down and Mr. Green will file a complaint, starting the litigation. Complaints are formal documents that invoke the jurisdiction of a court and ask the court to do something on behalf of someone. The complaint usually must specify, in detail, what facts justify the request, how much money is being requested (or what other action the plaintiff is requesting), and what separate theories—called "counts"—the plaintiff is pursuing. The specific content of a complaint varies from jurisdiction to jurisdiction: many jurisdictions require the plaintiff to provide the address of the defendant, to aid in the service of process, some jurisdictions require the plaintiff to declare if a jury trial is sought, and so on. Most complaints are laid out in numbered paragraphs, so everyone involved in the case can focus on very specific allegations if they need to. This is particularly important when the defendant is answering the complaint, as we'll see in a second.

The specifics of what each jurisdiction requires in a complaint can be found in the relevant rules of civil procedure, and most jurisdictions also have form books that an attorney can buy and that provide sample complaints for almost every cause of action. As an attorney, it's important not to place too much reliance on these forms though; they can be out-of-date, they might not be particularly well written, and they certainly don't reflect the specific circumstances of your client's case. So while they can be helpful hints for what a complaint should look like, no conscientious attorney should rely on them without question.

Once the complaint is filed, it still has to be served. An unserved complaint has the potential to harm the defendant, but until the formal rules of service have been followed, and a copy of the complaint has been placed into the defendant's possession, that potential is only theoretical. If the plaintiff files a complaint but then doesn't follow it up with service of process, the court will—eventually—dismiss the complaint for failure to prosecute it.

Once served, though, the responsibility shifts to the defendant to do something about it. The jurisdiction in which the complaint is filed will set a timeline within which the defendant must take an affirmative step, either answering the complaint or moving to dismiss it.

If Mr. Green filed suit in state court, and if the circumstances warrant it, Ms. Orange might also consider removing the case to federal court. The decision on whether to remove or not is one made typically on instinct and a belief about the way state and federal courts operate, rather than on any empirical or legal analysis. Defense lawyers often believe that they are more likely to prevail in federal court, and they also often believe that an out-of-state defendant will be treated more fairly by a federal judge and jury than by a judge and jury who are citizens of the same state as the plaintiff. They might be right, they might be wrong, but there usually is little in the way of hard data that will help them in the decision.

For purposes of our case, let's assume that Mr. Green filed suit in state court and Ms. Orange can't remove the case to federal court even if she wanted to. So her decisions now are limited to answering the complaint or moving to dismiss it.

Although a non-lawyer might not understand the significance of the term, a motion to dismiss is a very specific legal maneuver. It will only be successful if the plaintiff has asked for relief that is simply unavailable under the relevant jurisdiction's law. It is unusual for an experienced plaintiff's lawyer to ask for relief that the jurisdiction doesn't permit but it can happen, and it saves everyone's time and efforts if that issue can be resolved before the case goes any further. If the defendant believes that a motion to dismiss is justified, it can file to dismiss as much of the complaint as it believes isn't supported by the jurisdiction's law. That can result in a complaint being dismissed in whole or in part.

Again, for purposes of our example, let's assume that Ms. Orange decides, after careful study of the complaint, that a motion to dismiss isn't justified. Her only option now is to answer the complaint. She does this in—no surprise here—a document called an "Answer." The answer mirrors the complaint's numbered paragraphs: if paragraph 3 of the complaint alleges something, paragraph 3 of the answer should address exactly that allegation. Typically, there are three answers possible for each allegation a plaintiff makes: the defendant admits something, the defendant denies something, or the defendant claims to be without sufficient knowledge to admit or deny something— that response has the same effect as a denial. If the complaint was drafted tightly, with each numbered paragraph containing only one allegation, then the answer will typically be similarly tight. If the complaint was drafted more loosely, with each numbered paragraph containing multiple sentences, each with several allegations, the answer will have to go through each allegation, admitting some, denying others, and indicating where the defendant is without sufficient knowledge to do either.

There are exceptions to this: if the state where the suit is filed permits something called a "general answer," Ms. Orange can file a very simple document that says, in effect, that her client denies everything Mr. Green alleged in the complaint. That can be a time-saving (and cost-saving) approach, but it leaves the litigation wide open, and everything will have to be argued over later. In those jurisdictions where specific allegations must be met by specific responses, it is often in the defendant's best interests to admit everything about which there is no dispute, leaving only the key issues still in contention. Similarly, it can be in the plaintiff's best interests to draft a complaint very tightly, only alleging the key issues necessary to win and leaving out any superfluous information.

How one drafts one's complaints and answers is almost completely up to the individual attorney. State and federal rules allow for a lot of variation and individual preference, and even at such an early stage in the litigation process, one can learn a lot about one's opponent from the way in which the pleadings are drafted. Skillful lawyers look closely at every clue they can to learn as much about the other side as possible, and rhetoric—even in such a formal document as a pleading—can provide much valuable information. Knowing this, one can send messages about who you are, or want to be perceived to be, through the language you choose to use in drafting the pleadings. No word a lawyer writes should ever be less than carefully chosen for both its simple and its rhetorical meaning.

After the answer has responded to all the allegations in the complaint, there is still one important part of the pleading process that remains. If the defendant wants to assert any affirmative defenses, those should be pled in the answer. These defenses are often very important to the case, and defendants who have any such defenses available to them should avail themselves of them.

Asserting such defenses will likely involve pleading the facts necessary to reveal that the defense is a plausible one, and that will pave the way for discovery by the plaintiff into seeking more detail about the defense or defenses. Once the pleadings stage of litigation is concluded, the discovery stage begins.

6. Discovery

There was a time when litigation proceeded without discovery. Lawyers filed their pleadings, prepared their own cases, and then went to trial, confident that their skills as oral advocates would allow them to deal with any surprises the other side pulled on them. Those who practiced in those times believed that the better lawyer would usually win, and derided discovery as an expensive process that caused traditional lawyering skills to become unimportant.

Another way of looking at discovery, of course, is that by making all relevant information about a case available to both sides, it allows for a fairer dispute resolution process, since the person with the stronger claim, or the stronger defense, should prevail most of the time.

There's probably merit in both positions. Discovery is certainly an expensive process, and since fewer and fewer cases are going to trial, fewer lawyers need to have the courtroom skills of their predecessors. But by taking the surprises out of a case—or, more accurately, having the potential to take the surprises out of a case—discovery allows for the possibility of faster, and fairer, resolution of a case than did the trial-by-ambush approach.

Whichever side is right, though, discovery is what we have now and there's little likelihood that it will go away soon. And discovery has become a crucial—perhaps the crucial—stage in the litigation process. Whereas discovery used to be a free-for-all process, in which parties tried to reveal as little as possible, the federal rules, at least, now require some initial disclosure that forces the parties to give each other much of the information on which they plan to rely and which previously would have been hidden until specifically requested by the other side.

There are four principal discovery tools: the interrogatory, the document request, the deposition, and the request for admissions. There are several other types of discovery, and you'll learn about all of them in your civil procedure class, but these are the four we'll look at a little more closely here.

Interrogatories are written questions you get to pose to your opponent. You can ask anything you like as long as it's calculated to lead to the discovery of admissible evidence, so the scope of these questions can be pretty broad. And naturally, you want to get as much information as you can, because you might not know too much about the facts the other side will be relying on in order to prove their case and you don't want to ask a question that's so narrow that you miss crucial information. But you have to be careful not to make your question too broad; if you do, the other side will likely challenge your question as being overbroad, and they might either refuse to answer or—and this can be even worse—they might select what information they're willing to give you.

For example, Ms. Orange likely will want to know what doctors Ms. Smith saw after the car crash, but she will also want to know if Ms. Smith had any previous injuries that might be related to the ones she suffered in the crash with Mr. Jones. In an interrogatory, she could ask Ms. Smith to provide the names of all the doctors she saw as a result of the accident and, if she forms the question in a non-objectionable way, she likely will get that information. But that might not give her much information about previous injuries, so she might be missing some crucial facts that would help her defense. To prevent that, she might ask Ms. Smith for the names of all the doctors she has ever seen, but that would certainly trigger an objection from Mr. Green; Ms. Orange is asking for the names of every doctor Ms. Smith has seen since she was born, and if the question is interpreted literally, she's even asking for the name of the doctor who delivered Ms. Smith. The court will almost certainly rule that providing that much information places an unfair burden on any litigant and that the question is overbroad.

Mr. Green might file an objection to the question and then provide the names of the doctors Ms. Smith has seen as the result of the accident anyway. That way, he's selecting the information Ms. Orange gets as the result of her question and Ms. Orange now has the difficult task of trying to get more information from him, even after she asked a bad question. Precision in the use of language, and a careful evaluation of all the objections the other side might reasonably make to a question you're planning to ask, is a crucial skill for any lawyer engaged in litigation.

The same issues come up in regard to document requests. These are often filed at the same time as interrogatories, and they are, as you would imagine, requests for one side to produce documents. As with interrogatories, they have to be drafted carefully so as not to allow the other side the opportunity to object to the request and either keep crucial documents hidden or, at least, drag out the process and make it difficult and time-consuming for everyone.

Depositions are face-to-face encounters between the attorneys and the prospective witnesses in the case, at which the attorneys get to ask questions and the witnesses, under oath, have to respond. There's no defined order by which discovery has to proceed, but it's usual for both sides to send out interrogatories and document requests first and, once those replies have been received and processed, to send out deposition notices.

There are different kinds of deposition—the usual type is a pure discovery deposition in which the attorneys are seeking as much information as possible in order to prepare their cases, but there are also depositions which are taken in order to preserve the witness's testimony if both sides know the witness will be unavailable for trial. That can happen, for example, when a witness is dying. If a preservation deposition is sought, there's usually a discovery deposition taken as well; sometimes the discovery deposition and the preservation deposition are taken on the same day, which can mean that the attorneys must process information quickly.

Requests for admission usually come much later in the process and are usually used to narrow the issues that will be litigated in a trial. Some lawyers try to use requests for admissions to get the other side to admit to damaging facts which would hamper their case. That rarely works and is not really what requests for admissions are intended to do. The more common use of a request for admission asks the other side to admit that a document that will be used at trial is genuine. If both sides agree the document is genuine, that fact doesn't have to be established at trial, and that can shorten the amount of testimony necessary at trial to just those things about which there is a genuine dispute.

7. Motions

After discovery is closed, one or the other sides—or both—might ask the court for summary judgment. You can ask for partial summary judgment, meaning that you win on some of the counts of the Complaint, or you can ask for summary judgment over the entire case. If the court grants the motion, that issue is deemed to have been decided, so the stakes are very high for this motion.

If the court grants one of the parties summary judgment on the entire case, then that decision can be appealed by the losing party. If that happens, the process follows that described in the "appeals" section of this chapter. In some cases, though, the court can make a decision that is so significant to the progress of the case that the losing party can seek what is known as an "interlocutory" appeal—an appeal that puts the progress of the case in the trial court on hold while the appellate court resolves the issue.

If one of the parties feels that an issue should be reviewed by an appellate court at some pre-verdict stage but the other party or the court does not agree, the aggrieved party can ask the appellate court to issue what's known as a writ of *mandamus*. This is truly extraordinary relief and is very rarely granted. The party seeking the writ is, in essence, moving against the trial judge personally—the judge's name is listed on the petition and the judge usually has to hire a lawyer (or, more accurately, have a lawyer hired—the court should pay for this) to defend the judge's actions. Only a small fraction of *mandamus* petitions result in a hearing and of those, only a small fraction result in the appellate court issuing a writ. If the court does issue a writ, though, it's an order for the trial court to do something or to stop doing something and the trial court has no alternative but to obey.

Although summary judgments are the most typical motions to be filed at this stage in the litigation, they are not the only motions a party might file. If Ms. Orange doesn't answer Mr. Green's recovery requests on time, for example, or files what Mr. Green believes to be inadequate or incomplete responses, Mr. Green can file a motion to compel discovery responses. And both sides might file motions to prevent the other side from raising something at trial—the confusingly named motion *in limine*. In fact, the parties can file motions with the court about any number of things; there's no rigid formula for the types of motion that can be filed and their motions can be called anything they want to call them. There are a few standard types of motion—to dismiss, for summary judgment, *in limine*, and so on—but if a party wants the court to do something, it can style the motion in any way that best reflects the action it wants the court to take.

Law students and younger lawyers are sometimes surprised by how free litigation can appear, with the parties filing motions that no one taught them about in law school. In fact, though, the civil procedure rules are designed to give the courts and the parties a lot of freedom to try cases, and that means that there can't be too many restrictions on the types of motion that can be filed. The motion, after all, is just a formal way of asking the court to take some action, and the courts very rarely will do something without being asked. When they do, it's often said that they're acting "on their own motion."

8. Settlement

Right from the start of the process—from the first conversation between Mr. Green and Ms. Orange—the parties can settle their dispute. They can settle the dispute before the Complaint is filed, before the Answer is filed, during discovery, after discovery, before the trial, during the trial, before the jury returns a verdict, after the jury returns a verdict, before, during, or even after an appeal is decided. Some times are more likely than others for settlements, of course, but the chance of a settlement is always there if the parties decide to agree.

One of the more likely times to settle the case is after discovery is over and the summary judgment motions, if any, have been resolved. Now both sides know as much as they're likely to know about the other side's case, they know what issues will be tried before the court, and they've had a chance to assess the strength and weakness of their own witnesses and those for the other side. Both sides can make their strongest case about why they should win, and it's possible that one or both of the parties is ready to settle rather than face the prospect of the case dragging on indefinitely.

Courts sometimes require that the parties engage in serious settlement negotiations at this point, and will often facilitate those negotiations. The parties can also hire their own mediator who can help them come to a settlement, or the attorneys can try to sort things out on their own.

9. Pre-Trial

Assuming the case doesn't settle, the parties will enter the pre-trial stage of litigation after discovery is over and all dispositive motions (motions that would dispose of some or all the case) have been resolved. The court will usually hold a pre-trial hearing, at which a trial date is usually set and other administrative details are hashed out. The court will often require the parties to submit their proposed jury instructions and *voir dire* questions (the questions the parties want the judge to ask prospective jury members to identify possible bias, if the parties themselves aren't allowed to ask the questions), and any motions *in limine* they have in advance of this hearing.

The court might also require the parties to submit any portions of deposition transcripts on which they intend to rely at trial, along with the page and line designations that identify specifically what testimony will be used. Depositions can be used, under certain circumstances, at trial, but most courts will want the parties to let the other side know in advance specifically what parts of the deposition will be read to the jury. Testimony—whether from depositions or at trial—is usually transcribed onto paper that has both page and line numbers, so it's easy to say that you want to use a portion of testimony from page 3, line 6 to page 4, line 8. That way, everyone knows exactly what will be read to the jury.

Although the pre-trial hearing serves the administrative purpose of making sure the case is ready for trial, the prospect of having to do a lot of preparatory work well before the trial is scheduled can often provide an incentive for the parties to settle; there's no point doing all that work and incurring a lot of money in fees if the case will settle anyway, so the run-up to pre-trial hearings often sees a case settle.

Once the pre-trial hearing (or conference; some courts have these meetings in chambers rather than in the courtroom) is concluded, the case is usually ready to be tried. There's still some paperwork to be done, though. Most importantly, the attorneys need to let the witnesses know when they'll be expected to testify, and they will often need to issue subpoenas to those witnesses to compel them to attend. Many junior lawyers are surprised to learn that the lawyers get to send out those subpoenas, but while they're court orders, it's standard practice for lawyers to fill them out and send them to the witnesses they want to testify. And while there's sometimes some social stigma attached to the notion of a subpoena, they're actually neutral documents that just say someone is supposed to be at a particular place at a particular time. Very often, an employer requires an employee to have a subpoena on hand before excusing that person from work, so issuing a subpoena is not necessarily a sign that the attorney believes the witness is unreliable and won't show up unless ordered to do so.

10. Trial

As you can see, a lot has happened to get the parties to trial, and not many cases survive to this point: they either settle or the court issues an order resolving the case. And trial dates—especially civil trial dates—can be very difficult to get. The speedy trial requirements of the Constitution mean that criminal cases take priority in the court schedule, and there are only so many hours in a court's day.

But civil trials do happen, and they usually unfold in the same way. If a jury trial has been requested and is appropriate for the type of relief being sought (the availability of equitable relief, for example, is decided by a judge, not a jury, and some other cases are required by statute to be heard by a judge), the jury has to be selected. A pool of potential jurors is examined for possible bias and knowledge of the facts of the case— sometimes by the attorneys for the parties and sometimes by the judge, who might use questions presented by the parties. This process is known as *voir dire*.

After the jury is picked and sworn in, the judge might make some introductory remarks and then the parties get to make an opening statement. This isn't opening argument, and inexperienced attorneys can get into trouble if they start to argue the merits of the case at this point. Rather, the opening statement lets the jurors know what the case is about, who the parties are, and how the trial will unfold. The attorneys can lay out what they think the evidence will establish, but they have to be careful not to veer into actually trying to argue the case. The plaintiff gives the first opening statement and the defense has the choice of giving its opening statement right away or waiting until the start of its case.

After the opening statements, the plaintiff's case begins. The plaintiff's attorney calls witnesses and, after the witness takes an oath to tell the truth, asks them open-ended questions designed to get them to tell what they know about the case. A witness can be a fact or expert witness, with fact witnesses—as the name suggests—telling what they know about the facts of the case and expert witnesses testifying to their opinions about some aspect of the case. Sometimes the judge will ask the witness a question. This should only happen when there's an issue that's unclear and the judge's question will serve to clarify things simply and quickly, but it can sometimes happen that judges—who often were trial attorneys before going onto the bench—can get carried away and start asking a lot of questions. This places attorneys in a difficult position, because they often have a very specific plan for what information they want to get, and—sometime more importantly they don't want to get—from a particular witness. They can object to the judge's question, of course, but since the judge is also the person who will rule on the objection, attorneys often feel that objecting to a judge's question is a waste of time.

Attorneys can object to any question they feel is improper, either in form (leading when it should be open-ended) or because it asks for evidence that this witness is not able to, or should not be asked to, supply. Attorneys usually try not to object too much because they don't want to give the jury members the sense that they're using legal ploys to keep relevant information from them, but some objections are necessary if the questions are improper. Sometimes the attorney only has to stand (attorneys should stand at all times when they speak to a judge unless the judge has specifically instructed them that they need not) and say "objection" for the judge to rule, but sometimes the judge will ask for the basis of the objection. That usually requires the lawyer making the objection to give the specific rule of evidence that supports the objection—the lawyer might say "802," for example, if the case is in federal court and the lawyer believes that the question calls for the witness to offer hearsay testimony. Some judges will allow the attorney to simply say "hearsay" as the basis for this objection, but many judges are concerned that the jury might get a clue to the nature of the objection from the word or words used to support it, and therefore ask lawyers to limit themselves to the rule's number.

If the objection is more complicated and requires a more substantial explanation, or if the other side has something to say in opposition to the objection, the court might ask the attorneys to approach the bench. Objections are, in fact, mini-motions and in order to preserve the record for possible appeal, most lawyers will ask to be heard in support of, or in opposition to, the objection. If there is a bench conference, as these brief meetings are sometimes called, the judge might switch on an system that generates a static buzzing noise that obscures the voices speaking at the bench so that the jury can't hear what's being said, although in any case the lawyers and the judge will usually keep their voices down during the bench conference.

If the issue is more complicated than can be handled in a few seconds, the judge might call for a recess and allow the jury to go back into the jury room and then continue the hearing in the courtroom, or might call the parties back into chambers—which usually has a small conference room for meetings like this—where the arguments for and against the objection can be discussed. Wherever that meeting is held—at the bench, in the courtroom, or in the judge's chambers—the court reporter will be present, recording everything that is said by both parties so there is a full, verbatim record of every word. That record is the basis for any appeal that might result from the trial. Once the objection has been resolved, the attorneys might need the court reporter to read back the last portion of the trial before the objection to remind everyone where things stood before the objection was lodged.

After the direct examination, the defense has the chance to cross-examine the witness, and here leading questions are acceptable. Cross-examinations are usually limited to the testimony the witness gave on direct examination, but there are some exceptions; where the defense attorney seeks to impeach the witness, for example. Contrary to what you might expect from watching television dramas, not all cross-examinations are dramatic confrontations between shifty witnesses and attorneys trying to force the truth from them. Most cross-examinations are calm, polite affairs where the attorney seeks to identify inconsistencies in the witness' direct testimony or else to get some additional information from the witness that is more favorable to the attorney's client. But most is not all, and sometimes cross-examinations can be at least as fiery and dramatic as anything you've seen on television.

The plaintiff's attorney has the chance to go back over the testimony given on cross-examination, trying to correct any misunderstandings or misimpressions the attorney believes might have been left after the cross-examination. This is, predictably enough, called re-direct examination, after which there might be a re-cross examination. It is possible—but unlikely—that the judge will allow a re-re-direct, and a re-re-cross examination as well, but the party that didn't call the witness almost always gets the last chance to question the witness.

And so things proceed. In our case, Mr. Green calls the witnesses on behalf of Ms. Smith and, after all questions have been asked by both sides, he rests his case. Ms. Orange will likely then move the court to dismiss the case because Mr. Green has failed to make out a *prima facie* case. This means that even if all the evidence—testimony, documents offered into testimony, and any other forms of evidence—is taken as true, the plaintiff still hasn't done enough to win the case. The judge will usually deny this motion, but this isn't the only opportunity Ms. Orange will have to have the court resolve the case without letting it go to the jury.

If the judge denies the motion, Ms. Orange starts to present a defense on behalf of Mr. Jones. If she reserved her opening statement at the beginning of the trial, she gets to give it now, before calling witnesses. If not, she calls her first witness right away unless the judge decides that the jury has spent enough time listening to the case that day and dismisses everyone for the day. Non-participants in the process sometimes are critical of courts for having short trial days, but this misses two essential points. First, the days often aren't that short. The type of listening the jury is being asked to do is much more concentrated than the type of attention we typically pay to anything, and even if the jury is allowed to take notes (and there are still judges who won't allow the jury to take any notes at all, requiring them to remember every crucial piece of testimony in trials that often can take days or even weeks), the act of listening intently to everything that's happening at trial is something with which most people aren't familiar. The court can only expect a jury to listen with that much attention for a few hours in a session without taking a break, and only for a limited number of hours each day. Any more and the jury's attention would start to wander and that's not something anyone wants.

The other crucial thing to remember is that just because the court stops proceedings in a trial for several breaks during the day, that doesn't mean the court stops working. In fact, the judge might have had a hearing in another case before the trial started in the morning, might hear motions in other cases during the mid-morning break, might work on a decision in still another case over the lunch hour, and might have a pre-trial conference in still another case scheduled during the afternoon break. Judges and court staff will typically continue working on other matters, or hearing motions in the trial, after the jury is released for the day as well. Judges are, in fact, extremely busy people and presiding over actual trials is only one part of what they have to do in a day.

After both sides have called all their witnesses, both attorneys can ask the judge to rule in their clients' favor without letting the case go to the jury. At this point, though, it's unlikely that the judge will agree; the same motions can, and should, be made after the jury verdict is recorded and the judge might be more willing to grant one party's motion then. That way, if the case is appealed and the other side wins, the jury's verdict might be reinstated without having to retry the entire case, thereby saving time and money for everyone.

Assuming the motions are denied, the attorneys both get to give closing arguments. These are very different from the opening statements the attorneys gave at the start of the trial. Then, the jury hadn't heard the evidence and the attorneys couldn't say what the jury would hear, except in very general terms. Now, though, the jury members have heard all the evidence and the attorneys are allowed to remind the jury of what the evidence was and to draw their attention to whatever parts of it they think are important. They can even suggest possible interpretations of that evidence that might lead the jury to rule in their clients' favor.

Although closing arguments aren't as important as the examining and cross-examining of witnesses, they are very important parts of the trial and attorneys often spend a great deal of time preparing for them, working late into the night during the trial to make sure that their closing arguments are as effective and well-prepared as possible. The party with the burden of persuading the jury gets to go first in closing arguments, and also gets to speak again after the other side has spoken, meaning that the plaintiff in civil cases gets both the first and last word during closing arguments.

After the parties are done, the judge has to instruct the jury about the law in the case. This often seems like a dry reading of arcane legal principles, but it is, in fact, one of the most crucial times of the case and both the attorneys and the jurors should pay close attention to what the judge is saying: these legal principles will dictate how the jury evaluates the evidence it has heard, and the attorneys need to listen closely (even though they've probably been given a written copy of the instructions the judge intends to give) because if an attorney believes the judge has made a mistake in instructing the jury, the attorney needs to object to the instruction in order to be able to appeal if the jury result is unfavorable. Attorneys can only appeal on mistakes they've given the court a chance to fix before the jury comes back with a verdict and their objections need to be made at specific times—often more than once—in order that their record be preserved. Judges are sometimes unhappy with attorneys for making objections throughout the trial but will usually allow the attorney to speak if the attorney notes that the objection is being made to "make a record;" a judge who doesn't allow an attorney to preserve an issue for appeal is likely to be found to have made a mistake by the appellate court.

Once the jury instructions are completed, the jury is sent back to the jury room to consider its verdict. In civil cases, the parties have usually been asked to draft proposed verdict sheets, usually in the form of questions the jury will be asked to answer. These sheets will almost always ask if the defendant is liable to the plaintiff, if the plaintiff was partially responsible for the plaintiff's injury (and, if so, the percentage of the plaintiff's harm that is attributable to the plaintiff's actions), the amount of liability, if any, as well as any other questions that the facts or law of the case suggest. The court will usually take the competing jury forms and use them to create its own form, which can often be a very long document. Juries often have a lot of hard work to do during the deliberation phases of a trial.

The jury can take a long time to reach its result or it can decide very quickly. As long as the jury's discussions are not deadlocked, the judge will usually give the jury members as long as they need to reach a verdict, and the judge will usually work on other cases while the jury is deliberating. If it appears that the jury is going to be some time, the attorneys will usually go back to their offices and do other work while they wait for the verdict; the bailiff or judge's secretary will usually have the attorneys' contact information and will call them back to court before the jury returns its verdict.

The attorneys will also be called back if the jury has a question for the judge. These questions are always in writing and are sent from the jury, through the court bailiff who is guarding the door to the jury room, to the judge. Sometimes these questions can be procedural, asking if the jurors can go home for the day, for example, sometimes they're asking for questions of law to be clarified—the judge will usually read back the portion of the jury instructions that answers the question in that case—and sometimes the questions ask that portions of the transcript be read back to the jury so it can consider again what a witness said about an issue. The judge always gets the question before the jury comes back in to hear the answer and will usually tell the attorneys what the answer will be. Sometimes the attorneys will disagree that the answer the judge proposes is the correct one, and if that happens the judge will usually allow argument on the issue and will allow any dissenting attorneys to place their objections on the record before going forward with the answer.

Sometimes, though, the jury will tell the judge that it's deadlocked and can't reach a verdict on some or all of the questions being asked of it. If that happens, the judge has two choices: either the judge can tell the jury to go back and continue deliberating (and if you've ever heard that a judge was giving a jury an *Allen* charge, that's what was happening) or the judge can decide that the deadlock is hopeless. If that happens, all the judge can do is declare a mistrial, excuse the jury, and set a date for the whole case to be tried again, right from the beginning. Understandably, judges try hard to avoid declaring a mistrial because that means everyone's time and hard work has gone for nothing and the entire case will have to be retried. In fact, when a jury deadlocks, many cases will settle because at least the parties have a sense of what caused the problem and the attorneys can use that information (plus the probable cost of retrying the case) to more precisely reach a valuation of the case.

If the jury is able to reach a verdict, that verdict will be announced—usually by the jury foreperson—in court. The party that loses might ask the jury to be polled, a process where the judge asks each juror in turn if they agree with the verdict that's just been announced. It happens seldom, but occasionally jurors who were wavering during deliberations might have a final change of heart when actually hearing the verdict read out loud and might indicate that they now disagree with the verdict.

11. Post-Trial

Assuming that doesn't happen, though, the judge will dismiss the jury and will ask for post-trial motions. These will usually include a motion to set aside the jury's verdict and a motion for judgment notwithstanding the jury's verdict by the side that lost, but there are many post-trial motions that parties can, and do, file. If the plaintiff won, for example, the defendant will almost certainly ask the judge to lower the amount of the jury's award. Such motions might be based on a jury's award of punitive damages, if any, against the defendant, or if a jurisdiction has a cap on damages, the defendant will move for a reduction of the jury's award to fit underneath the statutory cap. The jury will likely not have been told about such caps, and might have no idea that a multi-million dollar award might be reduced substantially, often to a few hundred thousand dollars.

The judge can grant or deny these motions immediately or, if the judge wants to consider the issue more carefully, the judge can ask the parties to file briefs on the issues with the court. The judge will usually set a hearing date often a month or two in the future to allow the parties to prepare and make whatever arguments they need to make in support of their motions.

This is often a fruitful time for settlement discussions. The parties now know exactly how the case was valued by the jury and there are no longer any ambiguities about the case. The lawyers can judge the likelihood of a successful appeal, the cost of an appeal, and can come up with a very precise evaluation of the case. If settlement makes sense to both sides, they might now decide to end hostilities and come to an agreement. If not, and after the court has ruled on all post-trial motions, the losing side might file a notice of appeal.

12. Appeal

It's important to note that it's the losing side that has the right to appeal. Sometimes a client who won at trial doesn't like some aspect of the result and wants to appeal to get that aspect reversed. That client's attorney must explain, one hopes tactfully, that in the law you can only appeal when you lose.

The appellate process is dictated by the jurisdiction in which the appeal will be held, but usually the first act—the filing of a Notice of Appeal—is taken in the trial court. Given the complexity of what will follow, that initial document is a very simple one, often only a page long, and merely says that the filing party intends to appeal the result in the specified case. If the defendant lost at trial, the court's rules usually require the filing of a bond that secures the value of the jury verdict if the appeal is lost. That means that the defendant will often have to tie up a substantial amount of money in order to go forward with the appeal.

If the plaintiff lost at trial, the cost of the appeal might act as a deterrent to going forward. Appeals are often not covered by the contingency fee agreement the plaintiff might have entered into with a trial lawyer and appeals can be very expensive undertakings, with substantial costs and attorneys' fees associated with them. The principal costs associated with appeals are the preparation of the record extract and the attorneys' fees associated with writing the appellate briefs and making an oral argument in front of the appellate court.

Not all cases are given oral arguments these days. Sometimes the appellate court might decide that the issues in the case are so easily resolved that no oral argument is necessary, saving the parties' money and the court's time. But for a case to be considered by the appellate court, the parties will have to prepare a record extract for the court's use.

The "record" in the case is literally everything that was written, said, or introduced into evidence at trial. Not all of that is relevant to the issues on appeal, though; appeals are limited to legal questions and appellate courts won't listen to the witnesses again or try to resolve questions of fact. So although the entire record of a trial can be massive, the record on appeal need not be so lengthy. Even so, the record extract—the part of the record the parties believe the appellate court should pay attention to—can often run into several volumes of printed and bound material. Selecting that material and getting it printed up can be an expensive undertaking, but usually that cost is less than the cost of preparing an appellate brief.

To reduce a lengthy trial into a few appellate points, and then to draft a brief that argues why the trial court was right or wrong in the way those points were resolved, can take up many attorney hours. Appellate briefs are the most complex documents litigation lawyers have to prepare and they have to be edited and refined very carefully so they are as well-written and technically perfect as they can be before being filed with the court.

In an attempt to resolve as many cases as possible as early as possible, the appellate court might order the parties to engage in post-trial mediation to see if there's a way the case can be resolved. Some cases do settle at this point, but usually the parties are committed to following the appeal to its conclusion, having once decided to spend the money necessary to move the appeal forward. One factor that might make the parties change their minds, though, is the time an appeal can take. From the end of trial to the oral argument in an appeal can take well over a year, and from argument to decision can take at least as long again. Hardly anything in the appellate process moves quickly. And because jurisdictions impose post-trial interest on a jury award, the cost of an appeal to a losing defendant will continue to mount until the appellate court's decision is handed down.

Oral argument is the pinnacle of a litigator's job. And while most law students have a chance to engage in a mock oral argument during their first year of law school, and many upper-class students can take part in local, regional, national or—in some cases—international moot court competitions that give them the chance to make additional oral arguments while in law school, very few practicing lawyers get to make actual oral arguments in front of an appellate court.

The issues to be discussed at oral argument have been comprehensively analyzed in the briefs filed before the courts and many judges maintain that very few oral arguments have changed their minds about the way they were planning to rule after reading the briefs. But the arguments still give the judges a chance to test their conclusions, and it is still possible, although unlikely, that an attorney will come up with a way of framing the analysis in such a way that a judge might reconsider the result. In fact, although we use the term "argument" to describe what happens, "conversation" would probably be a more accurate term because that's what oral arguments most closely resemble; a highly stylized conversation between a group of intelligent participants at which complex legal issues are discussed. Most attorneys come out of oral arguments feeling exhausted but also feeling intellectually stimulated.

Even though an appellate court has many judges, usually only the highest court in a jurisdiction sits with all the judges listening to the same cases. The Supreme Court of the United States, for example, has nine justices and they all listen to the same oral arguments. The federal courts of appeals, though, have many more judges—the Ninth Circuit has 29 active judges—but they only rarely hear the same oral argument at the same time, in a special type of hearing known as an *en banc* review. For the rest of the time, the court divides into three judge panels and hears oral argument in those panels. In that way, the court can hear many cases at one time (even though not every judge sits on a panel every day; that would be an impossible workload, given the requirement that judges also write opinions).

During oral argument, each party is given a specific time—fifteen minutes each is a standard time these days although the court can increase the time devoted to oral argument if a case presents particularly difficult issues. The parties speak in order; first the party who brought the appeal (the appellant, although law students, lawyers, and even, on occasion, judges, get these formal legal designations confused) and then the opposing party (the appellee). The appellant can reserve time for rebuttal—giving that party the first and last word—but that has to be done beforehand. If the appellant doesn't reserve time, the court often won't allow the attorney to speak again. Timing is usually handled through a light system; a green light meaning you can speak, a yellow light to indicate that there's a defined period of time still to go (often five minutes), and a red light meaning "stop talking." If a court is concerned about time, it might cut an attorney off in mid-sentence once the red light goes on.

Although the attorney has fifteen minutes to explain why an appeal should be granted or denied, the attorney usually doesn't get fifteen uninterrupted minutes. The court, remember, can ask questions of the attorney, and if there are lots of questions it's possible that the attorney won't get through the planned presentation. In fact, many times the court will start asking questions before the attorney has even started to speak, although at other times the court might have no questions at all. When a court is active, and is asking many questions, attorneys refer to it as a "hot bench." Predictably, a court that asks few or no questions is known as a "cold bench." Judges can't talk directly to each other during an oral argument, but they often will talk to each other through the questions they ask the attorney. Watching that happen can be fascinating for a bystander, because we rarely get the chance to see judges discuss an issue as they are coming to a decision about it, but it must be a very difficult experience for the attorney, who can seem like a passive participant in someone else's conversation.

What happens after oral argument depends on the court, and courts don't often talk about their processes, but the commonly accepted view is that courts tend to have the conferences at which they decide—at least tentatively—the result of a case almost immediately after the oral argument is concluded. A court might hear a group of cases in a morning session, break for lunch and a conference to decide those cases heard in the morning, and then hear a group of cases in the afternoon, with a conference following right after those arguments are over to decide the results of those cases as well. These discussions are, of necessity, fairly short—although one imagines that the court will have a more protracted discussion if a case warrants it—and end in a vote. If other courts follow the Supreme Court's example, then the most senior judge in the majority assigns one of the panel to write the opinion in the case, and then the discussion moves on or the conference ends.

Courts are not under a formal timetable, and each judge has different work habits, so it is impossible to generalize about the opinion drafting process; sometimes the judge might draft the opinion alone, sometimes the judge might assign a law clerk to write a first draft, sometimes the result might be a communal effort of the judge and a group of law clerks—it's up to the judge to decide how the first draft of the opinion is written. Once it is written, though, it usually is circulated, although whether only to the judges on the panel or to every judge on the court is unclear and might depend on the practices of the specific court where the appeal was filed. If there is a minority position on the case, and if the judge in that minority feels strongly enough about the issue, that judge might draft and circulate a dissent to the majority opinion.

These draft opinions can sometimes change minds; a judge who was in favor of the majority position might change votes and might now vote for what was the minority opinion during the conference. If that happens, of course, it's possible that a 2–1 split in favor of one party now becomes a 2–1 split in favor of the other party. If there was a dissent, that now becomes the new majority opinion and what was a majority opinion might end up as a dissent. It's also possible that a judge might agree with the majority position but believe that a different rationale supports it. If that happens, the judge might draft a concurrence—an opinion that notes agreement with the result but outlines a different way of getting there.

Once all the back and forth with different drafts is over, the court issues the final form of the opinion, the dissent, if any, and the concurrence, if any. The court opinion is sent to the parties in the form of a bench opinion, and is placed on the court's website in what's called a slip opinion. There usually is no difference, except possibly the correction of obvious typographical errors, between the bench and slip opinions, and lawyers often refer to the two forms of opinion collectively as slip opinions.

If the opinion is to be published, though, the slip opinion is taken by West, which publishes the opinions in book as well as electronic form, and LexisNexis, which publishes the opinions in electronic form only, and is reviewed by their editorial staffs. These editors add indexing information that helps attorneys to find the cases when they're looking for court opinions to support arguments they're making, but they might also find what appear to be mistakes in the court's opinion as well; it's not impossible, for instance, for someone to have missed a "not" in a sentence while typing the court's opinion, and that type of omission could cause a significant change of meaning. The publishers won't change the substantive language of court opinions without checking with the court, of course (they will, however, make changes like adding parallel citations to cases where the court might only have provided a citation to one reporter), but changes can occur between the slip and final published versions of a case—one reason why lawyers should use the slip versions of cases found on court websites with care, since they might not represent the final word in what the court wanted to say about an issue.

13. Post-Appeal

What happens after an appeal depends, in part, on what the appellate court decided. If the court affirmed the result in the trial court, or completely overturned the result, thereby ending the case, the losing party has three possible avenues of additional review: it might ask for the panel to reconsider its decision because it's made an obvious mistake, it might ask the entire court to sit together and hear the appeal again—something known as *en banc* review, or it might seek permission to have the jurisdiction's highest court—the Supreme Court in the federal system or the state's highest court (which might be called the Supreme Court but equally well might be called something else)—review the issues presented by the case. While the first appeal was likely an appeal of right, this second review is almost always discretionary and the process of asking for it is usually lengthy and complicated; it's not inconceivable to imagine the process taking an additional year from the time the appellate decision was announced.

The appellate court, though, might have reversed the trial court result and sent the case back to the trial court for further proceedings. In that case, the losing party still has the same three options—panel reconsideration, *en banc* review, or second appellate review—but the losing party can also do nothing and let the case go back to the trial court. If that happens, the trial court once again gains jurisdiction over the case and the case moves forward as the appellate court ordered. It's not unheard of for a case to bounce back and forth between the trial and appellate court more than once before the case is finally resolved.

14. Enforcement

Once all appellate avenues have been exhausted, and once the case is resolved by the trial court, there is finally a winner and a loser in the litigation. If the original defendant is the winner, the case is over; the plaintiff might get a bill for attorney's costs and for the cost of an appeal, and the defendant will doubtless have been billed for attorney's fees throughout the litigation, but there are no more steps to take in court.

If the original plaintiff is the winner, though, the defendant is now liable for the judgment, as well as any pre-trial and post-trial interest and any costs levied by the various courts. It rarely happens, though, that the defendant sits down and writes the plaintiff a check at this point. Instead, the plaintiff will likely have to begin enforcement proceedings against the defendant, including getting a court order to enforce the judgment. And even with the order in hand, it might not be simple for the plaintiff to actually get money from the defendant, especially if the defendant doesn't have enough money to pay. Legal maneuvers like wage garnishment might be necessary in order for the plaintiff to begin to see some money, and the defendant might also declare bankruptcy if the situation warrants it; that can make it difficult or impossible for the plaintiff to get the full amount of damages and can often make it difficult for the plaintiff to recover anything.

It does not always happen that things are this complicated at the end of litigation, but it is worth remembering that just because a plaintiff wins does not mean that the plaintiff necessarily recovers anything, or recovers the amount announced as the judgment.

Conclusion

A trial like the one vaguely outlined in this chapter is a fairly straightforward one. Things can get more complicated when there are more parties—more plaintiffs or more defendants or, in some case, both—and especially when there are so many parties that the case becomes a class action. And no case is the same as any other case—the facts might be different, the law might be different, the parties, attorneys, and the judge will be different, and the issues raised during the course of the litigation process will certainly be different in each case.

The general outline of the process, though, will be the same from case to case. Understanding how a case moves forward from inception to final resolution is helpful because once you understand the various stages it becomes easier to place court decisions in their proper context and to understand what effect they might have had on the litigation and on the parties involved in the case. Once you understand how the various pieces of litigation fit together, it's easier to understand the meaning of the pieces themselves.

Appendix 4

The Three Branches of Government: A Quick Refresher

There can't be too much about the three branches of this country's government you don't know. This is the basic material for every civics class that's ever been taught in the United States and since you've made it to law school it's a safe bet that you know all the basics about the legislative, the executive, and the judicial branches of government.

Still, it can't do any harm to be reminded of these things briefly, and to have somewhere you can come back to remind yourself if one of these details slips your mind. Understanding how each branch works, and the way in which the three branches interact, is vital information for all lawyers to have at their fingertips and if one of these details slips your mind, you can feel at a disadvantage.

We'll just be talking about the federal government here. As always, this isn't a value judgment about the importance of the states or the federal systems, just a reflection of the reality that state governmental forms can differ in name, if not significantly in structure, from state to state but the federal government is the same for everyone.

The good thing about this discussion is that the material isn't difficult to understand. The drafters of the Constitution were smart people, and they realized that while the details of how a country as large and complicated as this was, even back in the eighteenth century, might be tricky to nail down, the big picture was relatively simple. For a country of laws, you need three things: people to make the laws, people to put those laws into effect, and people to answer any questions about those laws that might crop up. Each group gets its own section, or article, of the Constitution, so the governmental structure in this country really is as easy as 1-2-3.

1. Article I: The Legislature

In the United States, we have a bicameral legislature, which is just a fancy way of saying that Congress has two chambers; the House of Representatives (commonly shortened to the "House") and the Senate. Article I of the Constitution sets out different methods of organization for these two chambers, and the Senate has some unique functions, but each chamber has equal responsibility for enacting laws, which is the principal function of the legislature.

A "Congress" lasts for two years, and each Congress has two sessions, each one lasting a year. Each Congress begins and ends on January 3 of the odd years, so on the January 3 of each odd-numbered year, a new Congress is called into session. This has some important procedural ramifications, none of which need concern us here, but it's also important when researching legislative history, because once enacted, legislation is given a number that indicates the Congress in which the legislation was passed, as well as the order, in that Congress, in which it was passed. This is known as the Public Law, or PL, number; a bill numbered PL 100-58, for example, would be the 58th piece of legislation enacted by the 100th Congress.

A. The House of Representatives

Members of the House or Representatives (confusingly also called congressmen or congresswomen, even though the Senate is also part of Congress) are elected to two-year terms, must be at least twenty-five years old, must live in the state (but not necessarily the district) they represent, and have been United States citizens for at least seven years before election. House elections are held in even-numbered years, so there is one so-called "mid-term" election that occurs in the middle of the president's four-year term.

There are currently 435 representatives, each representing districts within states. The number of districts in each state is a function of population size. The states draw the lines of these districts, and the redrawing of congressional districts—usually each ten years after the census provides the most recent information about population distribution within a state—frequently results in allegations of gerrymandering, the practice of drawing political divisions to favor one or other political party. Litigation in the federal courts is often necessary to resolve these disputes.

The presiding officer of the House is the Speaker of the House of Representatives. This person is elected by the members of the House of Representatives and, as a practical matter, is the candidate proposed by the party in the majority after the most recent popular election because the vote for Speaker almost always breaks down on strict party lines. In practice, the Speaker frequently delegates the role of presiding over the floor proceedings in the House to another representative.

The Speaker has a number of important administrative functions within the government, but the most important role of the office is that of being second in line to the presidency after the vice president. Although no Speaker has ever risen to the presidency because of that position alone, it is an important consideration when vice presidents resign, as Spiro Agnew did in 1973, or when the vice president ascends to the presidency, as also happened in 1973 when President Nixon resigned and Vice President Ford became president, creating a gap that would, in the event of his resignation or death, have been filled by the Speaker until a new vice president was appointed.

B. The Senate

Senators are elected to terms of six years, with the process of electing them staggered so that roughly one third of the Senate is up for election in each two-year election period. The Constitution requires that each senator must be at least thirty years old, must live in the state they represent, and have been United States citizens for at least nine years before election. The Senate is thought of as being the more senior of the two chambers of government, and has historically been a more congenial and bipartisan place than the relatively contentious and partisan House. Whether those distinctions have much meaning today, however, is at least open to debate.

There are 100 senators, two for each state regardless of that state's size. Rather than representing specific districts or divisions within the state, both of the state's senators are elected by, and represent, the entire state. Because of the staggered process of scheduling elections, one senator in each state has always served longer than the other, and by tradition the longer-serving senator is known as the "senior" senator of a particular state; the term only has to do with length of service, though, and doesn't mark any distinction in the type of work each senator can or can't do.

The vice president is the *ex officio* president of the Senate and can vote in the Senate to break any vote ties. These days, the vice president rarely presides over the Senate except for noteworthy occasions like joint sessions of the House and Senate; probably the most noteworthy each year is the president's State of the Union address. Rather than the vice president, the Senate usually elects a senator to act as president *pro tempore* or *pro tem*, meaning "for a while." That person often delegates authority to another senator, meaning that you can't tell who is actually acting as president of the Senate on any given day without checking.

The senators you usually hear speaking on behalf of the Senate are the majority and minority leaders, which are political functions rather than Constitutional ones, and fall on those elected by the senators in, respectively, the party that enjoys a majority in the Senate and the party in the minority. Just as with the Speaker of the House, a senator can retain his or her seat but can lose the position of majority or minority leader by internal vote of the senators in his or her party or by a change in the political composition of the Senate.

The Constitution gives some vital functions to the Senate alone, thereby emphasizing the idea that the Senate is the more senior of the two chambers. Among these powers is that of advice and consent to various presidential nominations, the approval of treaties, and the power to sit in judgment during impeachment trials (the House has the responsibility of prosecuting impeachments, but it's the Senate that makes the decision whether or not to impeach).

C. Making Laws

Congress does many things, but its principal activity is making laws. Both chambers have a crucial role in this process, a very simplified version of which follows. As you go through this, remember that Congress can play almost infinite variations on this very simple theme and that every piece of legislation that has moved through the process has done so at a different pace and in different ways. There is no one way in which this works, and most legislation fails to make its way from beginning to end of the process.

i. Starting Out

Most legislation can start in either chamber. Although there seems to be a popular belief that legislation must start in the House and make its way through the process there before moving to the Senate, it's just not true. With some exceptions that needn't concern us here, legislation can begin in either chamber; all that matters is that it goes through both eventually.

In fact, though, these days legislation often begins somewhere else entirely. You can draft legislation—anyone can, and many people do. Many groups that have particular interest in a particular area draft legislation and then try to persuade members of Congress to sponsor that legislation. These are often referred to as "special interest groups," although the "special" is unnecessary—if a group has an interest in something, that interest is going to be "special" because the group's interest is focused on that area, not on the general state of the country.

Interest groups are often criticized for their role in the legislative process, but it's also true that we all want people to speak up for the things that are important to us. So while "interest group" or, more typically "special interest group" is used as a term of criticism, we might speak of "advocacy group" when we agree with the group's position on things. Politics and government are wonderful areas for seeing the power of issue framing as an important tool in shaping the debate, and giving a name to something you like, and a name to something you dislike, is a good way to start framing an issue.

Regardless of how the legislation gets drafted, though, we can agree that it has to be introduced in the House or the Senate before anything can happen with it. And at this stage in the process, a piece of legislation is called a "bill." If the bill is introduced in the House, it gets an H. R. (House of Representatives) number, and if it's introduced in the Senate it gets an S. number. We'll go forward by assuming that the legislation is introduced in the House, which any representative can do by placing it in a box called the "hopper" or by giving it to the clerk. If the legislation is introduced in the Senate, a senator simply announces its introduction after being recognized by the presiding president of the Senate.

ii. Committee Referral

Once it's introduced in the House, the bill is referred to one of the standing House committees for consideration. Almost immediately, the bill is likely to be referred by the committee to a subcommittee, and it's there where the work on the bill starts in earnest.

The subcommittee can do any number of things with the bill including kill it, but the most familiar action is scheduling hearings about it. Those interested in the bill—either because they want to see it passed or because they want it to be defeated—can testify before the subcommittee, and the subcommittee can also call experts and others to testify before it. This process provides a wealth of information for the researching lawyer who has an interest in the bill's subject matter.

Once the subcommittee is finished considering the bill, it can vote to table it—effectively killing it, at least in its present form—or can vote to send it for consideration by the full committee. The full committee can also vote to table, or can vote to move the bill on in a process called "reporting out." As the name suggests, this involves a report—more useful information for the researching lawyer.

iii. Floor Consideration

Once the bill is reported out of committee, it goes on the House calendar for action. Eventually—and remember that there are a lot of bills moving through this process at any given time—a successful bill will make it to the floor of the House for consideration. That involves a reading, debate and the addition of amendments, and—assuming everything goes well—a final reading followed by a vote. If the bill accomplishes a simple majority of House members, it moves on to the Senate.

iv. Moving to the Other Chamber

Once the bill has been introduced in the other chamber—the Senate, in our example—it starts the whole process all over again, moving to another committee where it can be the subject of hearings, can be tabled, or can be released back to the full Senate for consideration.

The Senate has some processes that differ from the House, including the filibuster and cloture. In essence—and there are few things as difficult to reduce to their essence as the procedural rules of the Senate—a senator may speak about a bill, saying whatever he or she chooses, for as long as the senator chooses until a vote of three-fifths of senators (60 votes in the current 50-state United States) cuts off the time for debate. This vote is called cloture.

Assuming that no ills befall our bill, the Senate can, and usually does, amend it and will eventually vote on it. Assuming it achieves a simple majority of votes, it now exists in two accepted, but likely different, forms—the one voted on by the House and the one voted on by the Senate.

v. Conference Committee

In order to resolve the differences between the two versions of the bill, it is now referred to a conference committee made up of representatives and senators. And if the differences between the two versions can be resolved, the final version of the bill goes back for a vote to the House and the Senate. And assuming that it doesn't fall at this almost-final hurdle, the bill is signed by the Speaker and the vice president and goes to the president for the president's signature, the last step the bill needs to take before becoming law.[1]

vi. Vetoes, Pocket Vetoes, and Overridden Vetoes

Maybe. It doesn't happen often, but sometimes the president decides not to sign the bill into law. And the timing of when the bill comes to the president is very important in determining what happens next because the president has ten days to sign the bill or it becomes law automatically. But if Congress adjourns for a significant time within that ten-day period, the president can refuse to sign the bill—in metaphorical terms, put the bill in a pocket—and the bill will die.

The more formal veto requires the president to reject the bill and to send it back to Congress. At this point, Congress has two options: it can accept the president's veto, in

---

1. The two versions must be identical before they can move on, and the version that goes to the president must be identical to the version agreed to by the House and the Senate. When a bill was passed to remove air traffic controllers from the budget-cutting effect measure known as the "sequester," the version of the bill sent to President Obama contained a typo that prevented the president from signing the bill into law until Congress could send a corrected version of the legislation to the White House. Typos can happen to anyone.

which case the bill dies, or it can attempt to override the veto. An override requires a two-thirds vote in both House and Senate, and if the veto is overridden, the bill becomes law.

vii. Legislation and Sausages

There's an old joke that the two things you should never see made are laws and sausages, and maybe that's true for sausages but it's not really a fair way of thinking about the legislative process. It's easy to be cynical about the state of politics in this country, but that's always been true; we tend not to have members of Congress engaging in physical brawls on the House or Senate floor anymore, and they don't fight duels with pistols or swords either. And while political rhetoric can sound robust to our modern ears, it's tame when compared to some of the things representatives and senators said to each other in previous centuries.

What's remarkable about this country's government is not how poorly it works, but rather how well it does the job of governing such a large and complicated place. And while the legislative process can seem overly complicated and slow, it's difficult to imagine how it could be improved without impoverishing the democratic ideals that inspired those who created the process in the first place. And for lawyers, the process produces an endlessly fascinating stream of documents that can be useful to us for any number of purposes. Whatever one might think of Congress, one can't deny that it gives us lots of information while it does what it does. And information is what lawyers need in order to do their jobs.

2. Article II: The Executive Branch

When we think of the executive branch of the government, we typically think of the president, the head of that branch and easily the most prominent member of the governmental structure. And the president has a crucial role to play in much of what goes on in government, of course, so it's appropriate that the person occupying that role gets a great deal of attention.

Often overlooked, though, is the executive branch's other role as—literally—the branch that executes the laws passed by Congress. It's in this role that the executive branch has the most direct effect on people's lives, because it's the executive agencies that make and enforce the regulations that directly affect how things are made, how food is grown, how products and people are transported—almost all the details that make up contemporary life. If you think the executive branch of government is only relevant once every four years at election time, think again.

A. The President

In keeping with the Constitution's underlying assumption that greater age brings greater wisdom, and that the greater the responsibility, the greater the age necessary to undertake that responsibility, the president must be at least thirty-five years old. Unlike other governmental positions, the president must be a "natural-born" citizen of the United States, a concept which seems clear but which has provoked some intense debate. The Constitution recognizes that presidents might have lived outside the country for a while, but requires that the president have been a permanent resident of the United States for at least fourteen years before taking office.

The president is elected to a four-year term, and under the Twenty-second Amendment, each person is limited to two terms as president. Each term runs from noon on the January 20 of the year following election, which occurs on the first Monday after the second Wednesday in November. That is not, of course, the date of the popular vote, but rather is the day on which the members of the Electoral College meet to cast their votes, the votes that actually elect the president. Their result is sent to Congress, where it's announced to a joint session of the newly elected Congress by the vice president in his role as president of the Senate.

B. Presidential Powers

The president has some crucial powers, perhaps the most significant of which is the role of commander-in-chief of the country's armed forces. The president also nominates a large number of people to positions within the federal government, including federal judges, but these nominations must be confirmed by the Senate in its role of providing advice and consent to presidential action. The president also negotiates treaties on behalf of the country, although the ratification of these is again dependent on the Senate, this time with a two-thirds majority vote.

The president enjoys two significant legal privileges which can shield many presidential actions from public view: the state secrets privilege allows a president to decline to participate in discovery related to litigation if to do so would harm national security, and the executive privilege doctrine extends the same protection to any actions taken directly in the president's executive role.

And it's that executive role that, as noted earlier, probably has the most direct effect on most people. The president sits at the top of a vast network of departments and agencies that make and enforce the regulations that put the laws enacted by Congress into effect; in a very direct sense, they "execute" the laws.

Given that Congress passes, and has passed, many laws in its time, there's a lot to execute. And in order to give the manufacturers of medical devices—to take one very simple example—an understanding of what is required of them, the regulations developed by the Food and Drug Administration, an executive branch agency within the Department of Health and Human Services, are extensive and detailed. While the president does not, and could not, know and read all the regulations and other actions taken by all executive branch departments and agencies, all those actions are taken by people who report up a chain of command that ends with the president. When viewed that way, the presidency really is an extraordinarily powerful position.

3. Article III: The Judiciary

As powerful as the presidency is in the American constitutional system, though, it is arguably less powerful than the federal judiciary. On the one hand, of course, the judiciary has almost no power at all; it commands no police force or other military service that could be used to enforce its judgments. On the other hand—at least until now—presidents, Congress, and everyone else has obeyed the Supreme Court, the highest of the three federal courts, when it issues a ruling. Politicians might detest a court ruling, and might seek to overrule it through legislation, but everyone obeys the Court's decisions until an alternative is passed through the legislative process. It's one of the most remarkable facts of a remarkable governmental system that the court power is exercised by common consensus, not through coercion.

The Constitution provides for the establishment of the Supreme Court, and leaves the creation of any lower federal courts to Congress. Congress established the Circuit Courts of Appeals, and the federal District Courts. Although things have worked differently at different times in the country's history, the District Courts today hear and resolve cases at the trial level. Appeals from the District Courts go to the Circuit Court of Appeals which has jurisdiction over the district court that heard the case. At its discretion, the Supreme Court can consider decisions of the various Circuit Courts. It also has very limited authority to hear certain types of cases directly, most typically (although even these are not common) disputes between two states, as well as constitutional issues that arose in state courts.

There are no age or residency requirements in the Constitution for federal judges, but Article III judges (to distinguish them from Article I judges—magistrate judges, bankruptcy judges, and the judges of other courts established under Congress's Article I powers) have some significant protections, designed to shield them from political influences: they cannot be removed from their positions except by impeachment, and their salaries cannot be cut. Appointment to an Article III judge position is often thought of as a lifetime appointment, although some federal judges do resign or retire. Once a federal judge achieves senior status, though, the judge can effectively "retire" without giving up Article III protection and will continue to be paid, even if not hearing cases.

Federal courts are courts of limited jurisdiction, meaning that they can only hear and consider cases and controversies in areas defined by Congress. Federal courts most typically hear cases that arise either under federal law or under the Constitution, or are between parties from two different states, if the case exceeds the value of the congressionally mandated amount in controversy. Because federal courts are courts of limited jurisdiction, it is vital for any lawyer practicing before those courts to understand the rules governing jurisdiction and to analyze each case carefully to be sure it meets federal jurisdictional requirements before bringing it.

Index